# CAPE COD, NANTUCKET
# & MARTHA'S VINEYARD

28th Edition

Where to Stay and Eat
for All Budgets

Must-See Sights
and Local Secrets

Ratings You Can Trust

Fodor's Travel Publications   New York, Toronto, London, Sydney, Auckland
www.fodors.com

**FODOR'S CAPE COD, NANTUCKET & MARTHA'S VINEYARD**
**Editor:** Michael Nalepa

**Editorial Contributors:** Andrew Collins, Susan MacCallum-Whitcomb, Sandy MacDonald, Laura V. Scheel

**Production Editor:** Astrid deRidder
**Maps & Illustrations:** David Lindroth *cartographer*; Bob Blake, Rebecca Baer, *map editors;* William Wu, *information graphics*
**Design:** Fabrizio La Rocca, *creative director*; Guido Caroti, Siobhan O'Hare, *art directors*; Tina Malaney, Chie Ushio, Ann McBride, Jessica Walsh, *designers*; Melanie Marin, *senior picture editor*
**Cover Photo:** (Lobster restaurant, Wellfleet): age fotostock/SuperStock
**Production Manager:** Amanda Bullock

28th Edition

ISBN 978–1–4000–0802–5

ISSN 1934–5569

## SPECIAL SALES
This book is available at special discounts for bulk purchases for sales promotions or premiums. Special editions, including personalized covers, excerpts of existing books, and corporate imprints, can be created in large quantities for special needs. For more information, write to Special Markets/Premium Sales, 1745 Broadway, MD 6-2, New York, New York 10019, or e-mail specialmarkets@randomhouse.com.

## AN IMPORTANT TIP & AN INVITATION
Although all prices, opening times, and other details in this book are based on information supplied to us at press time, changes occur all the time in the travel world, and Fodor's cannot accept responsibility for facts that become outdated or for inadvertent errors or omissions. So **always confirm information when it matters,** especially if you're making a detour to visit a specific place. Your experiences—positive and negative— matter to us. If we have missed or misstated something, **please write to us.** We follow up on all suggestions. Contact the Cape Cod, Nantucket & Martha's Vineyard editor at editors@fodors.com or c/o Fodor's at 1745 Broadway, New York, NY 10019.

PRINTED IN THE UNITED STATES OF AMERICA

10 9 8 7 6 5 4 3 2 1

# Be a Fodor's Correspondent

Your opinion matters. It matters to us. It matters to your fellow Fodor's travelers, too. And we'd like to hear it. In fact, we need to hear it.

When you share your experiences and opinions, you become an active member of the Fodor's community. That means we'll not only use your feedback to make our books better, but we'll publish your names and comments whenever possible. Throughout our guides, look for "Word of Mouth," excerpts of your unvarnished feedback.

Here's how you can help improve Fodor's for all of us.

**Tell us when we're right.** We rely on local writers to give you an insider's perspective. But our writers and staff editors—who are the best in the business—depend on you. Your positive feedback is a vote to renew our recommendations for the next edition.

**Tell us when we're wrong.** We're proud that we update most of our guides every year. But we're not perfect. Things change. Hotels cut services. Museums change hours. Charming cafés lose charm. If our writer didn't quite capture the essence of a place, tell us how you'd do it differently. If any of our descriptions are inaccurate or inadequate, we'll incorporate your changes in the next edition and will correct factual errors at fodors.com immediately.

**Tell us what to include.** You probably have had fantastic travel experiences that aren't yet in Fodor's. Why not share them with a community of like-minded travelers? Maybe you chanced upon a beach or bistro or B&B that you don't want to keep to yourself. Tell us why we should include it. And share your discoveries and experiences with everyone directly at fodors.com. Your input may lead us to add a new listing or highlight a place we cover with a "Highly Recommended" star or with our highest rating, "Fodor's Choice."

Give us your opinion instantly at our feedback center at www.fodors.com/feedback. You may also e-mail editors@fodors.com with the subject line "Cape Cod, Nantucket & Martha's Vineyard Editor." Or send your nominations, comments, and complaints by mail to Cape Cod, Nantucket & Martha's Vineyard Editor, Fodor's, 1745 Broadway, New York, NY 10019.

You and travelers like you are the heart of the Fodor's community. Make our community richer by sharing your experiences. Be a Fodor's correspondent.

Happy Traveling!

Tim Jarrell, Publisher

# CONTENTS

## MAPS

# ABOUT THIS BOOK

## Our Ratings

Sometimes you find terrific travel experiences and sometimes they just find you. But usually the burden is on you to select the right combination of experiences. That's where our ratings come in.

As travelers we've all discovered a place so wonderful that its worthiness is obvious. And sometimes that place is so unique that superlatives don't do it justice: you just have to be there to know. These sights, properties, and experiences get our highest rating, **Fodor's Choice**, indicated by orange stars throughout this book.

Black stars highlight sights and properties we deem **Highly Recommended**, places that our writers, editors, and readers praise again and again for consistency and excellence.

By default, there's another category: any place we include in this book is by definition worth your time, unless we say otherwise. And we will.

Disagree with any of our choices? Care to nominate a place or suggest that we rate one more highly? Visit our feedback center at www.fodors.com/feedback.

## Budget Well

Hotel- and restaurant-price categories from ¢ to $$$$ are defined in the opening pages of each chapter. For attractions, we always give standard adult admission fees; reductions are usually available for children, students, and senior citizens. Want to pay with plastic? **AE, D, DC, MC, V** after restaurant and hotel listings indicate whether American Express, Discover, Diners Club, MasterCard, and Visa are accepted.

## Restaurants

Unless we state otherwise, restaurants are open for lunch and dinner daily. We mention dress only when there's a specific requirement and reservations only when they're essential or not accepted—it's always best to book ahead.

## Hotels

Hotels have private bath, phone, TV, and air-conditioning and operate on the European Plan (aka EP, meaning without meals), unless we specify that they use the Continental Plan (CP, with a continental breakfast), Breakfast Plan (BP, with a full breakfast), or Modified American Plan (MAP, with breakfast and dinner), or are all-inclusive (including all meals and most activities). We always list facilities but not whether you'll be charged an extra fee to use them, so when pricing accommodations, find out what's included.

### Many Listings

| | |
|---|---|
| ★ | Fodor's Choice |
| ★ | Highly recommended |
| ⊠ | Physical address |
| ✛ | Directions |
| ⬚ | Mailing address |
| ☎ | Telephone |
| 🖶 | Fax |
| ⊕ | On the Web |
| ✎ | E-mail |
| ✦ | Admission fee |
| ☺ | Open/closed times |
| Ⓜ | Metro stations |
| ▭ | Credit cards |

### Hotels & Restaurants

| | |
|---|---|
| ⌂ | Hotel |
| ↵ | Number of rooms |
| ⛁ | Facilities |
| ¶◎¶ | Meal plans |
| ✗ | Restaurant |
| ⌂ | Reservations |
| ↘ | Smoking |
| ♧ | BYOB |
| ✗⌂ | Hotel with restaurant that warrants a visit |

### Outdoors

| | |
|---|---|
| ⚐ | Golf |
| ⚠ | Camping |

### Other

| | |
|---|---|
| ☾ | Family-friendly |
| ⇨ | See also |
| ⊠ | Branch address |
| ☞ | Take note |

# 1

# Experience Cape Cod

**WORD OF MOUTH**

"Cape Cod, for most people, is not something to 'see,' as there are few 'attractions' and most east/west roads are not really along the ocean. Instead, people go to spend a few days or weeks, relax, go to the beach, do some casual shopping, visit antique shops, dine—that sort of thing."

—gail

# CAPE COD TODAY

## The People

Although the Cape swells with visitors in summer, this world-famous vacationland has nearly 250,000 permanent residents, plus another 16,000 on Martha's Vineyard and 10,000 on Nantucket. (That's nearly half as many people as there are in Boston.) And though the Northeast's population has not gained significantly in recent years, the Cape has boomed, having more than tripled since 1960—it's the fastest-growing region in Massachusetts. Retirees and empty nesters (the region is home to 11 of the state's oldest median-age communities), artists, telecommuters, and small-business owners have contributed to the region's growth. Additionally, the Upper Cape is increasingly home to commuters who work in Boston or just south of the city.

Cape Cod is less racially diverse than other parts of Massachusetts, its population is about 95% Caucasian, 2% African American, and less than 1% each Native American and Asian. That being said, Native Americans have always been a dynamic force on the Cape—Mashpee has a sizeable population of members of the Wampanoag nation, as does Martha's Vineyard.

## The Economy

Tourism is the Cape's leading industry in terms of both revenue and employment, but business leaders and local chambers of commerce are always searching for new ways to diversify the local economy. Compared with the rest of the state, the Cape has a very high cost of living—yet average wages are significantly lower than elsewhere in Massachusetts. And although the prices of homes on the Cape have dropped dramatically since 2005, it's still a remarkably pricey place to buy a home (with the median price around $350,000).

The region's economic challenges have led to an increased number of older residents (who can better afford to live here) and a steady outflow of younger adults who are unable to find sufficiently high-paying jobs. With these obstacles in mind, the Cape has aggressively encouraged the development of viable and less seasonal industries such as marine science, technology, education, the arts, and alternative energy. One somewhat controversial development has been a large-scale "wind farm" in Nantucket Sound, comprising some 130 turbines, each about 260 feet tall and located several miles offshore. Construction is slated to commence in 2010.

## The Environment and The Outdoors

Cape Codders are fiercely protective of the environment—despite some occasionally rampant development in a few communities, planners have been careful to preserve nature here and encourage responsible, eco-conscious building. Nearly 30% of the Cape's 412 square miles are protected from development, and another 35% have not yet been developed—on Nantucket and Martha's Vineyard, the percentages of protected land are far higher. It's not surprising, then, that opportunities for sports and recreation abound here, as the Cape is rife with biking and hiking trails, serene beaches, and waterways for boating and fishing.

## The Politics

Cape Cod is one of the most liberal Democrat-leaning regions of one of America's most liberal Democrat-leaning states (only 12% of Massachusetts registered voters are Republicans). Although popular with tourists of all political stripes, the Cape has a year-round population that falls heavily to the left on political issues. There are some slight exceptions—blue-blooded Chatham, preppy Nantucket, and the swanky Martha's Vineyard community of Edgartown are stereotypically, if somewhat teasingly, referred to by some as Republican strongholds.

But the facts don't quite bear this out: during the 2004 presidential election, Chatham narrowly voted Democrat, and both Nantucket and Edgartown did by two-to-one margins. Make no mistake about it: the Kennedy legacy still looms large here. Cape Cod and the Islands general revel in their progressive labels, with the Outer Cape towns of Wellfleet, Truro, and Provincetown (with its highly visible gay community) cultivating an especially artsy, bohemian vibe.

## The Cuisine

Cape Cod kitchens have long been closely associated with seafood—the waters off the Cape and the Islands yield a bounty of lobsters, clams, scallops, and myriad other fish that make their way into everything from chowders and stews to pasta bowls and leafy salads. Culturally, the region's strong Italian and Portuguese influences have long accounted for the large number of pizza and pasta restaurants; you'll also find quite a few spots serving Portuguese specialties like bacalau (salt cod), kale soup, and various Portuguese breads and sweets.

But while culinary traditions remain strong in these parts, the Cape has—like other up-market parts of the country—experienced a huge influx of restaurants serving globally influenced, contemporary cooking. Menus at the Cape's top eateries now routinely feature such far-flung ingredients as Thai lemongrass, Moroccan harissa sauce, and Japanese eggplant. And chefs now routinely source from around the Cape and elsewhere in Southern New England for locally (and often organically) raised produce and meat.

## The Architecture

Virtually every period style of residential American architecture is well represented on Cape Cod, including—of course—that seminal form named for the very region, the Cape-style house. These low, one-and-a-half-story domiciles with clapboard or shingle (more traditionally the latter in these parts) siding and gable roofs have been a fixture throughout Cape Cod since the late 17th century.

But along the main streets of Wellfleet, Barnstable, Sandwich, Falmouth, Provincetown, Nantucket, and Edgartown, you'll also find grand Georgian and Federal mansions from the colonial era, as well as handsome Greek Revival, Italianate, and Second Empire houses that date to Victorian times. Many of the most prominent residences were built for ship captains and sea merchants. In recent decades, the region has seen an influx of angular, glassy, contemporary homes, many with soaring windows and skylights and massive wraparound porches that take advantage of their enviable sea views.

# WHAT'S WHERE

*The following numbers refer to chapters:*

**2 The Upper Cape.** This area has much to recommend it, starting with its proximity to the Massachusetts mainland. Cape Cod's oldest towns are here (Sandwich, for one, was settled in 1637), plus there are fine beaches and fascinating little museums. A growing full-time population makes it feel more residential than resort-y.

**3 The Mid Cape.** The Mid Cape has a bit of a Jekyll-and-Hyde complex. Route 6A is home to sophisticated colonial-era hamlets lined with antiques shops, smart taverns, and romantic bed-and-breakfasts, whereas Route 28 is crammed with motels and miniature golf courses. In the midst of it all sits Hyannis, the Cape's unofficial capital.

**4 The Lower Cape.** Casual clam shacks, lovely light-houses, funky art galleries… the things we typically associate with the Cape are found in abundance here. Its most stellar attractions, though, may be the natural ones: namely Monomoy National Wildlife Refuge, Nickerson State Park, and the start of the Cape Cod National Seashore.

**5 The Outer Cape.** The narrow "forearm" of the Cape—less than 2 mi wide in some places—is famous for sand dunes, crashing surf, and scrubby pines. There's a sense of wild abandon here. The same can be said for Provincetown (the peninsula's "fist"). Frenetic and fun-loving, it's a leading gay getaway.

**6 Martha's Vineyard.** The Vineyard lies 5 mi off the Cape's southwest tip. The Down-Island towns are the most popular and most populated. But much of what makes this island special is found in its rural Up-Island reaches where dirt roads lead past crystalline ponds, cranberry bogs, and conservation lands.

**7 Nantucket.** Nantucket, or "Far Away Island" in the Wampanoag tongue, is some 25 mi south of Hyannis. Ferries dock in pretty Nantucket Town, where tourism services are concentrated. The rest of the island is mostly residential (trophy houses abound), and nearly all roads terminate in tiny beach communities.

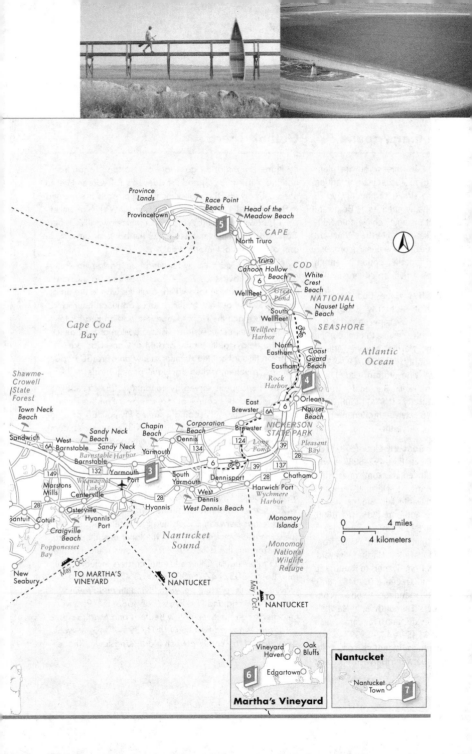

Province
Lands
Race Point
Beach
Provincetown
Head of the
Meadow Beach
**5**
CAPE
North Truro

Truro
Cahoon Hollow
Beach
White
Crest
Beach
Wellfleet
Great
Pond
NATIONAL
Nauset Light
Beach
South
Wellfleet
Cape Cod
Bay
Wellfleet
Harbor
SEASHORE
North
Eastham
Coast
Guard
Beach
Atlantic
Ocean
Shawme-
Crowell
State
Forest
Eastham
Rock
Harbor
Town Neck
Beach
East
Brewster
Orleans
Nauset
Beach
6A
Sandy Neck
Beach
Chapin
Beach
Corporation
Beach
Brewster
NICKERSON
STATE PARK
Sandwich
West
Barnstable
Sandy Neck
Dennis
124
Long
Pond
Pleasant
Bay
6A
Barnstable
Barnstable Harbor
134
Yarmouth
39
149
132
Yarmouth
Port
**3**
South
Yarmouth
6
39
137
28
Marstons
Mills
Wequaquet
Lake
Centerville
Dennisport
Chatham
28
West
Dennis
Harwich Port
Wychmere
Harbor
Santuit
Cotuit
Osterville
Hyannis
Port
Hyannis
28
West Dennis Beach
Craigville
Beach
Monomoy
Islands
Popponesset
Bay
Nantucket
Sound
Monomoy
National
Wildlife
Refuge
0       4 miles
New
Seabury
May-Oct.
TO MARTHA'S
VINEYARD
TO
NANTUCKET
May-Oct.
0       4 kilometers
TO
NANTUCKET

Vineyard
Haven
Oak
Bluffs
**Nantucket**
**6**
Edgartown
Nantucket
Town
**7**
**Martha's Vineyard**

# CAPE COD PLANNER

## Getting Around

**By Car** Unless you are planning to focus your attention on a single community, you'll probably need a car. Be aware that taking a vehicle onto Nantucket and Martha's Vineyard ferries is an expensive proposition (another option is renting upon arrival on either island).

**By Bus** Cape Cod Regional Transit Authority (800/352–7155, www.capecodtransit.org) provides service throughout the Cape. Martha's Vineyard Transit Authority (VTA) (508/693–9940, www.vineyardtransit.com) and Nantucket Regional Transit Authority (NRTA) (508/228–7025 www.shuttlenantucket.com) serve the islands.

**By Boat** Hy-Line (508/778–2600 or 800/492–8082, www.hy-linecruises.com) goes from Hyannis to Martha's Vineyard and Nantucket, and the Steamship Authority (508/477–8600; 508/693–9130, www.steamshipauthority.com) sails from Woods Hole to Martha's Vineyard, and from Hyannis to Nantucket. Island Queen (508/548–4800, www.islandqueen.com) connects Falmouth and Martha's Vineyard; and Freedom Cruise Line (508/432–8999, www.nantucketislandferry.com) travels between Harwich Port and Nantucket.

## Getting There

**By Plane** The major air gateways are Boston's Logan International Airport (BOS) and Providence's T. F. Green International Airport (PVD). Smaller municipal airports are located in Barnstable (HYA), Martha's Vineyard (MVY), Nantucket (ACK), New Bedford (EWB), and Provincetown (PVC). See Cape Cod Essentials in the back of the book for airport and airline contact information.

**By Car** Cape Cod is easily reached from Boston via Route 3 and from Providence via I–195. Once you cross Cape Cod Canal, you can follow U.S. 6 all the way to the tip of the Cape. Without any traffic, it takes about an hour to 90 minutes to reach the Upper Cape (the portion nearest to mainland Massachusetts) from either Boston or Providence. Because delays getting onto and off of Cape Cod are common throughout the summer, allow an extra 30 to 60 minutes' travel time when driving in peak periods.

**By Bus** The Cape is served by Bonanza (888/751–8800, www.peterpanbus.com)—part of the Peter Pan Bus Line—and by the rather misleadingly named Plymouth & Brockton Street Railway Company (508/746–0378, www.p-b.com). Both offer convenient connections from Logan International Airport and other mainland locales.

**By Boat** Bay State Cruise Company (617/748–1428 or 877/783–3779, www.baystatecruisecompany.com) and Boston Harbor Cruises (617/227–4321 or 877/733–9425, www.bostonharborcruises.com) both operate high-speed ferries between Boston and Provincetown from late spring to mid-October. In 2008, the latter also introduced a ferry serving the Gloucester-Provincetown route from late June to late August. Other seasonal carriers include Capt. John Boats (508/747–2400 or 800/242–2469, www.provincetownferry.com) between Plymouth and Provincetown; New England Fast Ferry (866/683–3779, www.nefastferry.com) between New Bedford and Martha's Vineyard; and Vineyard Fast Ferry (401/295–4040, www.vineyardfastferry.com) between North Kingstown, Rhode Island, and Martha's Vineyard.

# WHEN TO GO

The Cape and islands teem with activity during high season: roughly Memorial Day to Labor Day or, in some cases, Columbus Day. If you're dreaming of a classic shore vacation with lazy days at the beach, clambakes, and band concerts on the village green, this is prime time.

Needless to say, everyone knows it—which translates into daunting crowds and high costs. The good news is that the region is increasingly becoming a year-round destination. In fact, fall has begun to rival summer in popularity, at least on weekends through late October, when the weather is temperate and the scenery remarkable. A growing number of restaurants, shops, and hotels are remaining open in winter, too, making the area desirable even during the coldest months. On the islands and more far-flung sections of the Cape, though, many continue to close down January through March.

## Climate

Thanks to the warming effects of the Gulf Stream, the region enjoys fairly moderate weather most of the year, with highs typically in the upper 70s and 80s in summer, and in the upper 30s and lower 40s in winter. Snow and rain are not uncommon during the cooler months, and it can be windy any time. The following are average daily maximum and minimum temperatures for Hyannis. Average temperatures on the islands are similar.

For current local weather, coastal marine forecasts, and tide times, call WQRC's recorded information line in Hyannis (508/771–5522).

# TOP CAPE COD ATTRACTIONS

Even if you haven't already visited Cape Cod and the outer islands, you can likely conjure up a mental picture of "sand dunes and salty air, quaint little villages here and there." But that's just the beginning. On the ground, be sure to check out these superlative sites.

This region is rife with history. So it helps to bone up on the back story, en route to the Cape, in Plymouth. The famed rock doesn't live up its hype. However, **Plimoth Plantation**—an open-air museum that meticulously re-creates life among the Pilgrims and Wampanoag Indians in the 1620s—deserves to be on any traveler's itinerary. *Mayflower II,* a replica of the Pilgrims' iconic ship, is also well worth a look.

John F. Kennedy certainly knew a good thing when he saw it. During his presidency, Kennedy marked off a magnificent 40-mi swath of the coast, protecting it for future generations. Today **Cape Cod National Seashore**—comprising marshlands, uplands, cranberry bogs, and, of course, blissful beaches—remains the Cape's signature site. The preserve and exhibit-filled Salt Pond Visitor Center are open year-round.

Scenic trails and a broad selection of naturalist-led programs make the **Massachusetts Audubon Wellfleet Bay Wildlife Sanctuary** a favorite all-season migration stop for Cape vacationers. (It's pretty popular with birds, too.) The 1,100-acre haven is on the North Atlantic flyway, and more than 250 different species have been identified within its borders. Don't forget to bring your binoculars!

No question about it: the **Cape Cod Museum of Natural History** has engaging displays, including a working beehive, a live osprey cam, and tanks filled with an assortment of Cape critters. Yet these account for only part of the facility's appeal. The museum, which sits on an 80-acre property, also boasts its own nature trails, hosts outdoor ecological activities for all ages, and organizes a series of off-site excursions.

You don't have to be a marine biologist, a history buff, or a fan of *Moby-Dick* to appreciate the **Whaling Museum** in Nantucket. Devoted to the industry on which this island's reputation (and much of its wealth) originally depended, it contains everything from deadly harpoons and delicate scrimshaw carvings to a fully rigged whaleboat. The undisputed star attraction, though, is a 46-foot sperm whale skeleton.

**Distinctive lodgings** scattered around the Cape and islands are a definite draw for those who think that where you stay is just as important as where you go. Dozens of heritage buildings now welcome overnight guests. So you can bed down in a former sea captain's home, a converted church, or even a keeper's cottage at the Race Point Lighthouse. The very best of the bunch are designated as Fodor's Choices.

# CAPE COD'S TOP EXPERIENCES

It is said that "seeing is believing." But "doing" is better still! If you want to get a genuine sense of local culture, start by sampling these tried-and-true Cape activities.

## Follow the Light

In addition to traditional Cape-style houses, Cape Cod is known for another type of building—the lighthouses that rise along its coast like architectural exclamation marks. Some are active, others decommissioned; a few even offer tours. And a trek to any one of them is truly illuminating. Although each has its own personality, the literal highlight is Truro's Highland Light (the Cape's tallest). Eastham's Nauset Light ranks among the most beautiful, and the Chatham and Nobska Lights afford stellar views. The bluff-top Aquinnah Light on Martha's Vineyard and Nantucket's boldly striped Sankaty Head Light are island options.

## Explore on Two Wheels

Well-developed trails and relatively flat terrain make the Cape a magnet for avid and occasional cyclists alike. The Cape Cod Rail Trail is the definitive route. However, the Cape Cod National Seashore also maintains impressive trails (including an arduous one through undulating dunes), and Falmouth's Shining Sea Trail offers an easy 3½-mi coastal route with sublime views of Vineyard Sound. Truth be told, there are good places to ride and, if need be, rent bikes in just about any town on Cape Cod. Martha's Vineyard and Nantucket—each of which has dedicated bike paths and reliable cycle services—are equally enticing.

## Say "Anchors Aweigh"

Considering there is "water, water everywhere," it's no wonder that one of the optimal ways to appreciate the Cape and islands is from a boat. Area tour operators and outfitters offer everything from sunset schooner cruises to charter fishing expeditions. Mid-April through October, whale-watching adventures are particularly popular. (On a good day, Ahab wannabes might spot humpbacks, finbacks, minkes, and more.) Hopping one of the region's many ferries is yet another great way to experience the high seas. Prefer to paddle your own canoe or sail your own Sunfish? Rental companies can set you up with almost any kind of watercraft.

## Get to the Art of the Matter

The Cape was a prominent art colony in the 19th century, and today its concentration of galleries is among the highest in the nation. Spend a few hours idly browsing through them. Or take a more organized approach by following one of the Arts & Artisan Trails on Cape Cod, Martha's Vineyard, and Nantucket. Whichever you choose, set aside some time for the Provincetown Art Association and Museum. Because it focuses on artists with a Cape connection, local up-and-comers share wall space with A-listers like John Singer Sargent and Andy Warhol. The PAAM also sponsors a variety of classes year-round for the artistically inclined.

# CAPE COD'S BEST BEACHES

Traditionalists contend that **Nauset Light, Coast Guard, Marconi,** and **Race Point,** all set within the Cape Cod National Seashore, are the quintessential beaches. And it's hard to argue with that assessment. Combining serious surf, sweeping expanses of sand, magnificent dunes, and mesmerizing views, the four biggies do offer the greatest wow factor. Nevertheless, each of us defines the "perfect" beach differently, and there are many more to choose from. Cape Cod alone has more than 150—enough to keep the most inveterate beachcomber busy all year long. So whatever your taste, there is one to fit your criteria.

### For Families
Old Silver—a long crescent of soft white sand in North Falmouth—is more than just another pretty beach. Parents love this Buzzards Bay locale for its comparatively calm, warm water, and kids adore poking around the shallow tidal pools full of sea life.

### For Photographers
Perhaps no beach in this camera-ready region is more photogenic than that below the Aquinnah Cliffs on Martha's Vineyard. It is especially stunning late in the day because these multicolored clay cliffs face west, allowing for gorgeous shots at sunset.

### For Surfers
Wave-blasted Nauset Beach in Orleans (not to be confused with Nauset Light Beach farther north) is one of the preeminent places on the peninsula to Hang 10. If you didn't bring your own board, rentals are readily available at Pump House Surf Co. and Nauset Sports.

### For Sand Castle Connoisseurs
You can play with a shovel and pail anywhere, but beachgoers with architectural aspirations know Jetties Beach on Nantucket has the finest building material. Hordes gather to prove it during Sandcastle & Sculpture Day, held annually in mid-August.

### For History Lovers
In this centuries-old area even a fun-in-the-sun day can double as a history lesson. At Eastham's popular First Encounter Beach, a bronze plaque marks the spot where Myles Standish and his Mayflower buddies first encountered Native Americans in 1620.

### For Freshwater Fans
Don't like bathing in brine? Inland, the Cape has dozens of freshwater kettle holes that were carved in the far-distant past by receding glaciers. Aside from warm, salt-free water, some—like Scargo Lake in Dennis—are also blessed with sandy beaches.

### For Bird-Watchers
On the barrier beaches of the Monomoy National Wildlife Refuge, accessible only by boat, you're bound to see more sandpipers and plovers than people. Summer through early fall, shorebirds and waterfowl flock here to nest, rest, and feast in tidal flats.

### For Night Owls
After hours it's tough to beat Cahoon Hollow Beach in Wellfleet. The water here is chilly. The music at the Beachcomber Bar and Restaurant is, on the other hand, hot. Bands play for an appreciative crowd most nights from Memorial Day to Labor Day.

# CAPE COD'S BEST CLAM SHACKS

If you are what you eat, then most Cape Codders would be a clam...or maybe a lobster roll. It should go without saying that a land named for a type of fish would abound with opportunities to sample tasty seafood, and the region does not disappoint. Some of New England's most talented chefs work in high-end restaurants on the Cape and islands, yet no-frills seafood shacks still have an undeniable appeal. Their food is authentic, their prices are reasonable, and even if their decor leaves something to be desired, most serve up dishes with a side order of scenery.

Since 1976 **Cap'n Frosty's** in Dennis Village has been demonstrating just how diverse the humble clam can be. Whether you have a hankering for clam chowder, clam cakes, clam rolls, fried clams, or a high-heaped clam combo plate, you will find them all at this modest spot.

There is more to the **Clam Shack** in Falmouth than those fresh, fat-bellied mollusks for which it is named. Killer lobster rolls, plump scallops cooked to perfection, and a lovely location right on the harbor have all helped solidify its reputation as a Cape Cod institution.

**Mac's Seafood** in Wellfleet is a hole-in-the-wall take-out joint with perfect views of sailboats and fishing trawlers. For those who can't get enough of its oysters or scallops, Mac's also operates a sit-down restaurant nearby (Mac's Shack), plus three seafood markets.

Don't let the name fool you. Sure the **Kream 'N Kone** serves soft-serve ice cream, but the main course—in fact, the main draw—at this vintage West Dennis eatery is deep-fried seafood. Unless you're concerned about your cholesterol, opt for the clam plate with fries and onion rings.

Sam Vecchione started a chain reaction when he opened the original **Seafood Sam's** in 1974. Now with locations in Harwich, Sandwich, Falmouth, and Yarmouth, Sam's comprehensive menu (which includes broiled seafood and salads) leaves diners clam-oring for more.

**Baxter's Fish 'n' Chips** in Hyannis has been doling out delicious short-order seafood for more than 50 years. Outdoor tables overlook the picturesque harbor, and a passageway also leads to Baxter's Boat House Club, where the same menu is offered in a more upscale atmosphere.

Another memorable place to grab a bite is **The Bite,** a tiny roadside joint on Martha's Vineyard. If the promise of quahog chowder and fresh flounder-and-chips weren't enough to reel you in, the location in the postcard-pretty fishing village of Menemsha would do the trick.

**Arnold's Lobster and Clam Bar** in Eastham is always busy—and once you see the menu, you will understand why. The standard deep-fried fare here is supplemented with shucked-while-you-wait oysters, raw bar clams, steamed lobsters, and New England "chowdah."

# CAPE COD'S BEST ICE CREAM SHOPS

I scream. You scream. We all scream for ice cream. But perhaps nowhere is the collective din heard more clearly than on the Cape and islands. The fascination with ice cream here borders on obsession. Devotees endlessly discuss the merits of traditional hard ice cream versus new-fangled gelato, and waffle cones versus sugar ones. Butterfat content is a hotly debated topic, as is the ratio of add-in to ice cream. Indeed, the only thing aficionados seem to agree on is that the most notable offerings come from mom-and-pop parlors that make their own premium—dare we say artisanal—products. Here's the inside scoop.

**The Ice Cream Smuggler** in Dennis Village prides itself on using only the freshest ingredients, from just-picked berries to spiced apples and rum-soaked raisins. If you're worried about your waistline, frozen yogurts, sorbets, and sugar-free ice cream are on the menu.

In Centerville, **Four Seas Ice Cream** is the sentimental favorite. Established in 1934, this Cape Cod landmark has a retro ambience, efficient service, and back-to-basic flavors (Penuche Pecan is about as fancy as it gets). Occasional Kennedy sightings are an added bonus.

Visitors to Martha's Vineyard aren't left out in the cold. They go crazy for **Mad Martha's Ice Cream Parlors** in Edgartown, Vineyard Haven, and Oak Bluffs. Indecisive eaters who can't choose between the two dozen flavors can always request a 12-scoop Pig's Delight.

Not surprisingly, Dennisport's **Sundae School Ice Cream Parlor** specializes in old-school sundaes. Classic Hot Fudge vies with seasonal options (including fresh blueberry and raspberry) for the "best in class" award. Other locations are in East Orleans and Harwich Port.

The place to go for an ice-cream sandwich is the **Ice Cream Sandwich** in (you guessed it!) Sandwich, where the titular treat consists of a heaping scoop of vanilla wedged between two homemade chocolate chip cookies. Ice-cream cones, cannolis, and cakes are also available.

Need proof that "la vita" really is "dolce" in Provincetown? Just take a look inside the freezer case at **I Dream of Gelato.** More than 160 rotating flavors are made on-site in small batches (amaretto, tiramisu, and sugar-free cappuccino among them), guaranteeing a true taste of Italy.

Since 1889, **Hallet's**—a country drugstore in Yarmouth Port—has served justly famous ice-cream sodas, made from a secret recipe at a marble fountain. Plop yourself down on a swivel stool, place your order; then prepare for a genuine Norman Rockwell moment.

Having opened only in 2005, the **Cape Cod Creamery** is already challenging established favorites for the "crème de la crème" crown. Located in South Yarmouth, it gives frozen concoctions a local twist, dishing out flavors like Craigville Caramel Crunch and Eastham Espresso.

# CAPE COD WITH KIDS

Cape Cod seems almost purpose-designed for families, and though this is slightly less the case on the islands, you will discover plenty of kid-oriented attractions and activities across the region. Beaches aside, the obvious place to visit is Route 28, from about Hyannis to Harwich Port, as it's lined with arcades and minigolf courses. Local museums are also a reliable bet, because most work overtime to engage young guests. **Plimoth Plantation,** for instance, has costumed interpreters who help bring history to life; the **Cape Cod Museum of Art** gives workshops for wee ones; and Nantucket's **Whaling Museum** has its own Children's Discovery Room. Want more? Try these family-tested favorites.

Learning and fun go hand in hand at the hands-on **Cape Cod Children's Museum** in Mashpee. The interactive venue, aimed primarily at the eight-and-under set, comes complete with an indoor planetarium, a puppet theater, and an arghh-rated 30-foot pirate play ship.

Fans of the Peter Cottontail books can see artifacts relating to the author's life—and, in summer, hear some of his timeless stories read—at the **Thornton W. Burgess Museum** in Sandwich. On select days live animals (like those that inspired Burgess) put in an appearance.

Visiting a water park might seem superfluous when you have the Atlantic Ocean lapping at your feet. But fans of **Water Wizz** will beg to differ. The Wareham attraction features a 50-foot-high waterslide with tunnels and dips, plus a wave pool, a river ride, tube rides, and more.

Although most area boat excursions are appropriate for children, some are more engaging than others. The **Discovery Cruise,** operated by OceanQuest in Woods Hole, routinely draws rave reviews because it teaches budding marine biologists all the tricks of the trade.

For more up-close animal encounters visit **Woods Hole Science Aquarium:** America's oldest continuously operating research aquarium. Aside from the expected fish tanks, it has cool touch tanks and a seal pool. You're even welcome behind the scenes to watch staffers work.

Cue the calliope music. Taking a spin on Oak Bluffs' **Flying Horses Carousel,** built in 1876, lets contemporary kids experience life in the past lane. Another antique merry-go-round (this one circa 1912) awaits young riders at the **Heritage Museums and Gardens** in Sandwich.

Culture on the Cape isn't for adults only. Productions at the **Harwich Junior Theatre** are tailor-made for younger audiences, and the **Cape Playhouse** and **Cape Cod Melody Tent** (in Dennis and Hyannis respectively) both host a summer children's theater series.

Don't forget to scan **community calendars** for family-friendly events like the Mashpee Powwow, held annually in early July. Three days of dance contests, drumming, fireball games, and clambakes culminate in the crowning of the Mashpee Wampanoag Indian princess.

---

# FREE & ALMOST FREE

It's easy to spend a fortune on the Cape and islands. It's also unnecessary, because some of the best things in life here actually are free—and you don't have to look far to find them. Take a top-rated site like the **Cape Cod National Seashore.** You may pay to access its swimming beaches—but the Salt Pond Visitor Center houses a free museum, and the park itself hosts a bevy of free programs ranging from tidal flat forays and fishing demos to alfresco yoga classes. Biking the Cape Cod Rail Trail, window-shopping in Wellfleet, people-watching in P'town, gazing at the stars (whether celestial or cinematic) in Edgartown: these activities are priceless, too. Here are some more options for gratuitous fun:

No-cost **summer concerts**—staged weekly in many communities—are music to parsimonious ears. Chatham's town band strikes up on Friday night in Kate Gould Park. Consult local event calendars for noteworthy alternatives.

Frugal fish lovers will be happy to hear that the **Woods Hole Science Aquarium** and **Sandwich State Fish Hatchery** both waive entry fees. In peak season, tours of the **Woods Hole Oceanographic Institution** are free as well.

The **Cape Cod Baseball League** is one of the sporting world's best bargains. Mid-June to mid-August, the "Stars of Tomorrow" suit up with one of 10 teams. And since all are nonprofit, the most you'll have to fork over is a small donation.

Taking self-guided tours of the oh-so-fragrant **Cape Cod Lavender Farm** in Harwich and **Mytoi** (a 14-acre Japanese-inspired garden on Chappaquiddick Island) lets you get a double dose of flower power without dropping a dime.

The upwardly mobile are free to drink in divine vistas from the top of the **Scargo Tower** in Dennis. On a clear day, the 30-foot structure offers unsurpassed views of Scargo Lake, Cape Cod Bay, and distant Provincetown.

Penny-pinching oenophiles, rejoice! **Truro Vineyards** and East Falmouth's **Cape Cod Winery** each offer complimentary tours. Tastings are a deal, too, because the $5–$7 fee includes a souvenir glass.

Anyone hungry for information—or just plain hungry—can take a free tour of the **Cape Cod Potato Chip Factory** in Hyannis. You'll learn how the kettle-cooked, über crunchy chips are made and leave with a sample bag to snack on.

You can peer into the past at **Harris-Black House, Swift-Daley House, Captain Edward Penniman House,** and a handful of other heritage buildings in Brewster and Eastham. Admission is free; however, donations are appreciated.

Put your best foot forward with a free walk around the **Village of Sandwich** or along **Nantucket's Black History Trail.** The former is organized by the Sandwich Glass Museum, the latter by the Friends of the African Meeting House.

# LIKE A LOCAL

Cape residents always know the best hidden beaches, most reliable seafood shacks, and least-crowded spots for shopping strolls and scenic bike rides. If you want to get to know the heart and soul of Cape Cod, and see some of its most alluring diversions, follow the lead of the year-rounders.

## Commune With the Flora and Fauna
Area residents have worked hard to preserve the breathtaking natural beauty and precious wildlife indigenous to the Cape and Islands. For sense of this, visit one of parks and preserves favored by locals, from the Tidal Flats Recreation Area on Cape Cod Canal to Mytoi's serene Japanese-inspired garden on Martha's Vineyard. On the Upper Cape, amble over the Sandwich Boardwalk, a wood-planked promontory spanning a salt marsh and sloping rugosa rose-patch dunes that draw migratory sea birds.

Secret beaches are another locals' draw— try the quietly spectacular Fisher Road Beach in Truro, the tidal pools of secluded Robbin's Hill Beach in Brewster, or dune-backed Chapin Beach in Dennis.

## Shop Where the Regulars Go
The most memorable shops on the Cape eschew touristy T-shirts and knickknacks in favor of high-quality, stylish clothing and crafts that appeal to discerning regulars. Falmouth Center is one of the Cape's top spots for a retail ramble, home to such sophisticated boutiques as Maxwell & Co. and Rosie Cheeks. Main Street in bustling Hyannis is another ground-zero for shopping, having morphed steadily over the years from prosaic to prestigious—check out Oak & Ivory for nautical goods and Puritan of Cape Cod for fine threads. And Provincetown's vaunted Marine Specialties, Inc. is a local institution, thanks to its immense selection of odd lots, salvaged goods, model ships, wooden buoys, and feather boas.

## Grab a Bite at a Down-Home Diner
You'll almost always see a crowd of colorful regulars congregating for breakfast or lunch at Vineyard Haven's vintage ArtCliff Diner, on Martha's Vineyard— try the pecan pancakes in the morning. Just off the Cape in Plymouth, the retro-nostalgic All-American Diner is a favorite venue for Monte Cristo-style egg sandwiches and hearty meat loaf.

Betsy's Diner is a classically gleaming space with a pink-neon sign that lights up downtown Falmouth—it's de rigueur among fans of stick-to-your-ribs diner fare. In Provincetown, locals break away from the crowds to dine at airy and casual Chach, which serves a heavenly fried-chicken salad with buttermilk dressing.

## Attend a Gallery Opening
Visitors often drop by one of the Cape's dozens of galleries—there are especially large concentrations in Provincetown, Wellfleet, Nantucket, and both Edgartown and Vineyard Haven on Martha's Vineyard.

But for a more meaningful local art experience, and a chance to visit with artists, attend a gallery opening. These are most often held Friday and Saturday evenings, and they sometimes feature live music, art lectures, and hors d'oeuvres and wine. Check local newspapers for listings of upcoming gallery events.

# BEST FESTS

### April

Gardeners, this bud's for you! The daffodil—a frilly flower that signals the arrival of spring—takes center stage at Nantucket's **Daffodil Festival Weekend** (508/228–1700, www.nantucketchamber.org) and the **Brewster in Bloom Festival** (800/399–2967, www.brewsterinbloom.org). Both events are "perennial" favorites.

### May

The peninsula celebrates all things nautical during **Cape Cod Maritime Days** (508/362–3225, www.capecodmaritime-days.com). Around 75 events, held Cape-wide throughout May, run the gamut from themed lectures and art exhibits to boatbuilding demos and lighthouse tours. Guided excursions by land or sea are organized as well.

### June

Pilgrims get a lot of press. But they weren't the only European contingent to help shape this region. Provincetown's **Portuguese Festival** (508/487–0500, www.provincetownportuguesefestival.com) honors another with a weekend of food, music, dancing, and fireworks. A boat procession and a blessing of the fleet cap the event.

### July

**Barnstable County Fair** (508/563–3200, www.barnstablecountyfair.org) in East Falmouth has been a Cape tradition since 1844. Some 90,000 people come for nine days of horse pulls, craft displays, 4-H shows, carnival rides, and cotton candy. Grandstand concerts (usually headlined by formerly famous artists) are also on the agenda.

### August

The **Boston Pops Esplanade Orchestra** (888/266–1492, www.bso.org) comes to Hyannis and Nantucket, and the **Cape Cod Symphony Orchestra** (508/362–1111, www.capesymphony.org) plays outdoors in Orleans and Falmouth. More top-caliber music is on tap during the **Cape & Islands Chamber Music Festival** (508/945–8060, www.capecodchambermusic.org).

### September

There's something fishy about September in Cape Cod... Hyannis hosts the **Oyster Festival** (508/775–2201, www.hyannis.com), and Bourne asserts its supremacy with the **Scallop Fest** (508/759–6000, www.bournescallopfest.com).

### October

Leaf peepers drive down to see trees decked out in brilliant fall foliage, but it's the colorful cranberry that makes locals swoon. Get bogged down yourself at the Nantucket Conservation Foundation's one-day **Cranberry Festival** (508/228–2884, www.nantucketconservation.com).

### November

Celebrate Thanksgiving the old-fashioned way with dinner at **Plimoth Plantation** (508/746–1622, www.plimoth.org). Or see the light at Provincetown's **Pilgrim Monument** (508/487–1310, www.pilgrimmonument.org). On Thanksgiving Eve, the tower is festooned with 5,000 bulbs that remain lighted nightly until the New Year.

### December

Many towns on the Cape celebrate Christmas in grand style, but the monthlong **Nantucket Noel** (508/228–1700, www.nantucketchamber.org)—featuring caroling, crafts, and a "Christmas Stroll"—leads the pack.

# RAINY DAY FUN

You can count on plenty of wonderful things in this region: stunning beaches, fresh seafood, bulging boutiques. Great weather, however, isn't always a sure thing. Cape Cod, for example, averages 3 to 4 inches of rain per month, and extended periods of inclement weather aren't unheard of. Happily, rain does not have to put a damper on your fun—even if you're a devoted beach bum. Strolling on the sand can be as enjoyable on a stormy morning, when crowds are sparse and the surf intense, as on a sultry afternoon. Plus, once you've gotten a little wet, you may forget about the showers and enjoy the brooding water views more. Prefer to explore the great indoors? Read on.

Honor the region's rich literary heritage by curling up with a good book. If you didn't pack one, don't panic. The Cape and islands are famous for their **public libraries.** The glorious Nantucket Athenaeum is a good place to start. It's one of the country's oldest.

There are **movie theaters** where cinephiles can catch a matinee on a dreary afternoon. Come dusk, though, nothing compares with a double feature at the nostalgia-inducing Wellfleet Drive-In. Films are shown nightly, rain or shine, late April to mid-September.

Like **live performances?** Each summer the venerable Cape Playhouse in Dennis stages Broadway-style theatricals, and the Cape Cod Melody Tent in Hyannis hosts pop and comedy acts. Vineyard Playhouse on Martha's Vineyard has year-round offerings.

Say "ahhh" at a **spa.** Top destination spas include the Crowne Pointe Inn (Provincetown), Cape Codder Resort (Hyannis), Dan'l Webster Inn (Sandwich), and the Wauwinet and White Elephant (both on Nantucket). The region also boasts a selection of day spas.

The chief charm of Sandwich's **Heritage Museums and Gardens** lies in the fact that—like Cape Cod as a whole—it is at once idyllic and idiosyncratic. Nantucket baskets, primitive paintings, antique autos, and toy soldiers are just some of the items on display.

It's easy to pass time on a rainy day visiting local galleries. But for a one-of-a-kind art encounter, drop by the **Sandwich Glass Museum.** It traces the history of Cape Cod's 19th-century glass industry and holds glassblowing demonstrations throughout the summer.

Thanks to the Cape's prosperous past as a shipping and whaling center, it has an abundance of fine **antiques shops.** So why not indulge in a little treasure hunting? Route 6A between Sandwich and Brewster is a good place to focus your attention.

When the sun's not shining, you can recapture that "one brief shining moment that was known as Camelot" by visiting the **John F. Kennedy Hyannis Museum.** Archival photos and a brief film tell the story of JFK and his Cape connection.

# RIDING THE CAPE COD RAIL TRAIL

In the late 1800s, visitors to Cape Cod could take the train from Boston all the way to Provincetown. However, with the construction of the Sagamore and Bourne bridges in the mid-1930s, the age of the automobile was ushered in. Today, though passenger train service to the Cape has been discontinued, the old railroad right-of-way—now paved and refurbished—is still being put to good use as the peninsula's premier bike path (508/896–3491, www. mass.gov/dcr/parks/southeast/ccrt.htm).

The Cape Cod Rail Trail, constructed in 1978 and extended in the mid-1990s, offers a scenic ride from South Dennis to South Wellfleet over terrain that is easy-to-moderate in difficulty and generally quite flat. Given the good conditions, Rail Trailers who feel the need for speed can cover its 25-mi length in an hour or two. Yet most go at a more leisurely pace, lingering en route at salt marshes, woodlands, cranberry bogs, beaches, ponds, and Nickerson State Park (which maintains the trail and has its own bike path).

Of course, it isn't mandatory to tackle the trail in its entirety. If you are pressed for time—or prone to saddle sores—simply do a segment, perhaps starting in the middle near Nickerson State Park, then looping to one end and back. If you'd rather return to your starting point by public transportation, the easiest way is to set off from Dennis, ride to Orleans, and catch the bike-rack-equipped H20 Line bus back. The Cape Cod Regional Transit Authority has schedules.

The Cape Cod Rail Trail begins at a parking lot off busy Route 134 south of U.S. 6, near Theophilus Smith Road in South Dennis, and ends in South Wellfleet, with a spur leading westward through Har-

wich to Chatham. Free maps are available online (see Web site above) or on the ground at the Dennis Chamber of Commerce and other locations. In addition to distances, these mark amenities such as strategically placed parking lots and restrooms.

### The Wheel Deal

The trail passes through Dennis, Brewster, Orleans, Eastham, and Wellfleet. Bike shops in these towns can provide rental equipment, plus helpful traveling tips. *(See Sports & the Outdoor listings in each chapter for more information.)*

Please note that, under Massachusetts law, children 16 and younger are required to wear bike helmets. This applies whether they are drivers or passengers.

Wheels yield to heels, which means cyclists give walkers the right-of-way. Also remember to pass slower traffic on the left, and call out a warning before you pass.

The trail can get crowded at times. So if you prefer solitude (or cooler temperatures), try heading out earlier in the morning or later in the afternoon.

Nonbikers should note that horseback riding, walking, running, and in-line skating are welcome on the trail's broad unpaved shoulder.

# GREAT ITINERARIES

## CAPE COD IN ONE WEEK: CLASSIC BEACHES & BUSTLING VILLAGES

### Day 1: Falmouth

Begin by crossing the Bourne Bridge and taking Route 28A south through some lovely little towns until you reach Falmouth, an excellent base for exploring the Upper Cape. Here you can stroll around the village green, look into some of the historic houses, and stop at the Waquoit Bay National Estuarine Research Reserve for a walk along the estuary and barrier beach. Take some time to check out the village of Woods Hole, the center for international marine research and the year-round ferry port for Martha's Vineyard. A small aquarium in town has regional sealife exhibits, and there are several shops and museums. If you have any extra time, spend it north of here in the lovely old town of Sandwich, known for the Sandwich Glass Museum and the beautiful grounds and collection of antique cars at Heritage Museums and Gardens.

### Days 2 & 3: Hyannis

The crowded Mid Cape is a center of activity, and its hub is Hyannis. Here you can take a cruise around the harbor or go on a deep-sea fishing trip. There are shops and restaurants along Main Street and plenty of kid-worthy amusements. Kennedy fans shouldn't miss the JFK Museum. End the day with a concert at the Cape Cod Melody Tent. Spend your second day exploring the northern reaches of the Mid Cape with a drive along scenic Route 6, which passes through the charming, slow-paced villages of Barnstable, Yarmouth Port, and Dennis. There are beaches and salt marshes, museums, antiques shops and galleries, and old graveyards along this

route. Yarmouth Port's Bass Hole Boardwalk makes for a particularly beautiful stroll. In Dennis there are historic houses to tour, and the Cape Museum of Fine Arts merits a stop. End the day by climbing 30-foot Scargo Tower to watch the sun set. At night you can catch a film at the Cape Cinema, on the grounds of the Cape Playhouse.

### Days 4 & 5: Chatham

Chatham, with its handsome Main Street, is a perfect base for strolling, shopping, and dining. A trip to the nearby Monomoy Islands is a must for bird-watchers and nature lovers. Back in town, you can watch glassblowing at the Chatham Glass Company, visit the Old Atwood House and Railroad Museums, and drive over to take in the view from Chatham Light. Spend your second day detouring up to Brewster to check out the eclectic mix of antiques shops, museums, freshwater ponds for swimming and fishing, and miles of biking and hiking trails through Nickerson State Park. Don't miss the Cape Cod Museum of Natural History. On the way north from Chatham, take the less-commercial end of Route 28 to Orleans, driving past sailboat-speckled views of Pleasant Bay. On the way up toward Provincetown, stop in Eastham at the National Seashore's Salt Pond Visitor Center.

### Days 6 & 7: Provincetown

Bustling Provincetown sits at the very tip of the Cape, and there's a lot to see and do here. Catch a whale-watch boat and take a trolley tour in town or bike through the National Seashore on its miles of trails. Climb the Pilgrim Monument for a spectacular view of the area—on an exceptionally clear day you can see the Boston skyline. Visit the museums and shops and art galleries, or spend the afternoon swimming and sunning on one of the beaches. To escape the crowds, spend a day driving south through sleepy but scenic Truro and then park your car in Wellfleet's historic downtown, where you'll find a bounty of intriguing shops and galleries. Continue a bit south to historic Marconi Station, which was the landing point for the transatlantic telegraph early in the 20th century. It's also worth walking the short but stunning White Cedar Swamp Trail.

## Alternatives

On Day 2, hop the ferry for a day trip to either Martha's Vineyard or Nantucket. Both islands offer breathtaking scenery and village centers chock-full of great shops and restaurants. And if you're really keen on exploring either island, consider spending the night. Martha's Vineyard requires a shorter ferry ride and is your best choice if time is tight.

On either your first or final day—especially if you're a history buff or you're traveling with kids—pass through Plymouth, on the mainland just north of Sagamore Bridge, and make a visit to Plimoth Plantation, one of the most impressive living-history museums in the country.

## TIPS

❶ Keep in mind that traffic leading onto the Cape is particularly horrendous on Friday, and traffic leading off the Cape is rough on Sunday. Try to time your visit to avoid these times, but if you must travel to or from the Cape on these days, cross as early in the day as possible.

❷ If you're traveling with kids, you might want to pass on some of the itinerary's more adult-oriented highlights described above—such as shopping in Wellfleet and driving along scenic Route 6A from Barnstable to Dennis—and instead set aside some time in the southern sections of Yarmouth and Dennis, where Route 28 passes by countless amusement centers, mini-golf courses, and other kid-friendly amusements.

❸ A car is the best way to explore the Cape, but in the busier town centers—such as Falmouth, Hyannis, Chatham, and Provincetown—you can get around quite easily on foot. Plan to park your car at your accommodation and avoid using it except to explore less densely populated areas of the Cape.

# GREAT ITINERARIES

## MARTHA'S VINEYARD: THE PERFECT THREE-DAY WEEKEND

### Day 1: Vineyard Haven and Oak Bluffs

Start your day in downtown Vineyard Haven with a light morning repast of gourmet espresso and a breakfast "eggwich" at the cozy Beetlebung Coffee House, which is right next to the Martha's Vineyard Chamber of Commerce office, a great source of advice and brochures for exploring the island. Spend some time exploring the historic houses that line William Street, and the many shops and eateries along Main Street.

Once you've worked up an appetite, head just a short walk outside of downtown to Net Results for one of the best lobster rolls on the island. In the afternoon, take a quick jaunt out to West Chop for a great view over Vineyard Sound from the lighthouse.

Head back through Vineyard Haven's downtown toward Oak Bluffs via Beach Road. Spend some time wandering the streets of the Oak Bluffs Campground, where tightly packed pastel-painted Victorian cottages vie with one another for the fanciest gingerbread trim. Then head into the center of Oak Bluffs for a ride on the Flying Horses, the oldest continuously operating carousel in the country. If you have kids in tow, head to the video arcade across the street. Or unwind at the Offshore Ale brewpub, also in Oak Bluffs, where dart enthusiasts can find formidable foes.

### Day 2: Edgartown

Spend your second day on the island exploring historic, dapper Edgartown, where you can start things off with a delicious breakfast at Espresso Love coffeehouse. After downing a vanilla latte and noshing on a homemade raspberry scone, spend the morning browsing the dozens of tony shops and visiting the several museums tracing the town's heritage, including the superb Martha's Vineyard Historical Society and the island's oldest dwelling, the Vincent House Museum.

Grab a lunch at one of the village's many excellent eateries, or grab a hefty sandwich to go from the Edgartown Deli. Then in the afternoon, take the On-Time ferry to Chappaquiddick Island to visit the Mytoi preserve for a stroll. If conservation areas are your thing, the Cape Poge Wildlife Refuge on the island is a must. You'll need a few hours on Chappaquiddick to make the visit worthwhile. Edgartown abounds with superb dinner options upon your return, with Detente leading the pack.

### Day 3: Up-Island

Begin your day with a visit to the West Tisbury farms, some of which have pony rides for kids. Grab breakfast snacks at the nostalgic Alley's General Store. The Mayhew Chapel and Indian Burial Ground are interesting and give an almost eerie look into the past, and Polly Hill Arboretum is a must for horticulture buffs.

Then drive out to Aquinnah Cliffs (formerly Gay Head), one of the most spectacular spots on the island. Go to the lookout at the cliffs for the view, or take the boardwalk to the beach and walk back to see the cliffs and Aquinnah Light from below. Spend some time sunning and swimming at this breathtaking spot. (A note to the modest: the beach attracts

# GREAT ITINERARIES

nude sunbathers; though it's illegal, the officials usually look the other way.)

You can enjoy a nice lunch at the Aquinnah Restaurant, which has stunning views of the sea, or save your appetite for the return drive through the picturesque fishing village of Menemsha, which is one of the best spots in New England to dine on fresh clams, lobsters, and other seafood. Larsen's and The Bite are both good bets for this.

You could also drop by one of the several notable galleries Up-Island, such as the Granary Gallery at the Red Barn, and Martha's Vineyard Glassworks. As the day comes to an end, either pick up some seafood and take it to Menemsha Beach for a sunset picnic, or opt for a considerably fancier dinner at the elegant restaurant at Lambert's Cove Inn.

## Alternatives

If peaceful country lanes and rolling hills bring a smile to your face, skip Oak Bluffs and combine your explorations of Edgartown and Vineyard Haven into one full day. Then spend two days touring Up-Island, allowing extra time to hike the beach below Aquinnah Lighthouse, birdwatch at Sepiessa Point Reservation, or cycle around the part of the island's stunning roads.

Conversely, fans of bustling town centers (and those without a car) might want to skip or drastically shorten any forays Up-Island and instead allocate a full day each for touring Vineyard Haven, Edgartown, and Oak Bluffs. With the extra time in the latter community, you can visit East Chop Lighthouse, and fully avail yourself of the town's growing crop of fine shops.

TIPS

❶ Martha's Vineyard is a sizable island, and for the ultimate freedom to explore the more rural areas Up-Island, it's useful to travel by car. However, the island also has an excellent bus system, and taxis work for getting between the main town centers.

❷ Nature lovers can still find plenty of worthy diversions without venturing Up-Island—just focus your efforts on Chappaquiddick Island, Joseph A. Sylvia State Beach, and Felix Neck Wildlife Sanctuary. Additionally, Island Spirit Sea-Kayak Adventures offers invigorating treks paddles just off-shore.

# GREAT ITINERARIES

## NANTUCKET: THE PERFECT THREE-DAY WEEKEND
### Day 1: An Overview of the Island

If you're new to Nantucket, a great way to spend your first day is simply setting off to explore the different communities on the island, beginning your adventures right in the heart of Nantucket Town, first by enjoying breakfast at the locally revered restaurant Arno's, which is right on Main Street. Stroll around town a bit, perhaps treating yourself to a grand view of the harbor and town from Brant Point Light, at the end of Easton Street.

Next head east across the island to Siasconset, just in time for a memorable lunch in the sun at the Summer House Beachside Bistro. This part of the island is happily free of formal attractions—it's best just to wander about this former fishing village and admire its rose-covered cottages before venturing north a few miles to the even sleepier settlement of Wauwinet. Then head back to Nantucket Town via Polpis Road; along the way you can make detours to check out the Nantucket Life Saving Museum or Windswept Cranberry Bog. If you still have the time an energy, make the 5-mi trip to the island's western community, Madaket Beach, an absolutely breathtaking perch from which to watch the sunset.

### Day 2: Nantucket Town Shopping and Museums

Sophisticated, historic, and relatively bustling—by the peaceful standards of this island—Nantucket Town is an excellent place to spend a full day strolling. There's fine shopping at haute boutiques and esteemed galleries, and a number of museums and historic buildings are within easy strolling distance of the village center.

Kick off day with a hearty breakfast at Black-Eyed Susan's before venturing off to see some of the town's excellent museums. Focus on the properties that are part of the outstanding Nantucket Historical Association, with its ambitiously expanded Whaling Museum. If time allows, get a peek inside the magnificent Nantucket Atheneum, a seminal example of Greek Revival architecture, and the stately First Congregational Church.

For lunch, drop by the reasonably priced Fog Island Cafe, a cheery storefront space in the center of things. Spend your afternoon walking through the commercial district—paying especially close attention to the grid formed by Main, Centre, Broad, and Easy streets—and also drop by the former boathouses of Straight Wharf and Old South Wharf to view the many galleries and boutiques within. The fine shops in this neighborhood proffer everything from whaling artifacts to splashy resort wear to cottage-inspired home furnishings.

### Day 3: Getting to Know Nantucket's Natural Side

It may sound a bit ambitious, but if you're a serious fan of nature, you'll want to head out at dawn to see what the birds are up to. The Downyflake, a homey mid-island breakfast joint, starts serving at 5:30 AM most days (6 AM on Sunday). Pick up a couple of homemade doughnuts for carbo-loading on the road.

The best way to bird is on bike. (Rent one from one of the high-quality island shops.) A couple of miles west of Downyflake, the Nantucket Conservation Foundation maintains a 900-acre preserve comprising

# GREAT ITINERARIES

Sanford Farm, the Woods, and Ram Pasture. To get to here, follow Sparks Avenue to the high school; then it's a scenic zigzag past the Old Mill (consult a bike map, available from the tourism office) to reach the start of the Madaket Bike Path. A few miles farther on the path, just before the intersection with Cliff Road, you'll see a rough-hewn parking lot. From here, 6½ mi of hiking trails (you'll have to ditch your bike—there's a place to lock it up) cross forest and meadow to reach pond and sea, wetlands, and rare sandplain grassland. Figure on at least two hours of walking and gawking.

After emerging from the preserve, bike another 3 mi west along the bike path to Madaket Beach—pausing to pick up a picnic lunch at the Westender—and plod onward along Smith's Point, where the endangered piping plovers dwell. For dinner, retire to Even Keel Cafe in the center of town, where you can dine amid the surprising peace of the patio out back before swooping home on your bike through the cool, starry night.

## Alternatives

If you're truly a history buff and less inclined toward biking and the outdoors, skip all of most of the activities described above for Day 3 and instead tack on an extra day of museum-hopping in Nantucket Town. If you've already seen most of the properties operated by the Nantucket Historical Association, opt instead to tour the attractions that comprise the Maria Mitchell Association, including the aquarium, natural science museum, and two observatories.

> ## TIPS
>
> **1** For exploring Nantucket Town's museums, consider buying a pass for $18 from the Nantucket Historical Association—this gets you into all of the organization's excellent museums and sites.
>
> **2** It's possible to travel between the different communities by shuttle bus or taxi, but for the freedom to turn down intriguing lanes and go at your own pace, traveling by way of your own car (or a rental car) is ideal.

# The Upper Cape

**WORD OF MOUTH**

"In Sandwich there is historical museum which dedicates most of its space to Sandwich glass history and displays. There is a glassblower who will enthrall you with her spiel and skill...Across the street from the museum is an old gristmill to visit, the Thornton Burgess Museum, and a short walk up to the Hoxie House, the oldest house in town...In Falmouth you might want to visit Nobska Light which has a good view out towards Martha's Vineyard."

—irishface

Updated
by Laura V.
Scheel

**THE UPPER CAPE HAS NONE** of the briny, otherworldly breeziness of the Outer Cape and little of the resort feel of Lower Cape cousins like Chatham. The reason is solidly geographical: The Upper Cape's proximity to the mainland yields slightly less-brutal winters than elsewhere on the Cape and, consequently, a substantial year-round population; the region's beaches are intimate; and more of its attractions—freshwater ponds, conservation areas, and small museums—are inland.

If you're collecting superlatives, the Upper Cape is fertile. Sandwich is the oldest town on the Cape, Bourne was the Pilgrims' first Cape Cod settlement and an important trading area, and the first Native American reservation in the United States was established in Mashpee, which still has a large Wampanoag population and a tribal-council governing body.

Being able to find peace and quiet so close to the mainland and the traffic-clogged bridges is an unexpected and much-appreciated characteristic of the Upper Cape. Sandwich, its village streets lined with historic houses and museums, is remarkably well preserved. Heading east, Route 6A meanders past antiques shops, bed-and-breakfasts, and salt marshes. Falmouth, to the south, is an active year-round community, more suburban than seaside, though its easy-to-reach beaches are popular with families. In the villages of North and West Falmouth, along Buzzards Bay, tree-lined country lanes lead to sandy coves, and in East Falmouth and Waquoit, narrow spits of land jut into marshy inlets; plenty of secluded sites for hiking and walking are yours for the taking. Woods Hole, a small but bustling village on the Cape's southwestern tip, is a center for international marine research; it's also the departure point for ferries to Martha's Vineyard.

## EXPLORING THE UPPER CAPE

On the north shore, Sandwich, gracious and lovely, is the Cape's oldest town. Centered inland, Mashpee is a long-standing Native American township in which Native American–owned land is governed by local Wampanoags. Falmouth, the Cape's second-most populous town, is still green and historic, if seemingly overrun with strip malls. Woods Hole, the major port for ferries to Martha's Vineyard, is world renowned for its biological research institutions. Along the west coast, in parts of Bourne and West and North Falmouth, you can find wooded areas ending in secluded coves; the south coast has long-established resort communities.

## ABOUT THE RESTAURANTS

Much like the rest of Cape Cod, the Upper Cape's dining scene ranges from basic seafood shacks to contemporary restaurants that draw inspiration from the far corners of the globe—plus everything in between. Overall, the restaurant options tend toward the traditional, with fried clams, baked scrod, and boiled lobster gracing the most popular menus. Restaurants are more widely scattered in the Upper Cape towns—there are few "restaurant rows"—but if you like to wander and check out your dining options, try Main Street in Falmouth Center or Water Street in Woods Hole.

## ABOUT THE HOTELS

Sandwich and other towns along the north-shore Route 6A Historic District have quiet, traditional villages with an old-Cape feel and charming B&Bs. Along Route 6A you can also find family-friendly motels, ranging from the modest to the better equipped. Historic B&Bs fill the center of Falmouth, and other small inns line the shore and the neighboring streets of Falmouth Heights. Lodging options are fewer in Bourne and West and North Falmouth, but a few B&Bs hidden away on country lanes provide glimpses of old New England. You can also rent modern town houses and condominiums with extensive resort amenities in Mashpee's New Seabury community.

> **TOP 5**
>
> ■ The Upper Cape's many child-friendly freshwater ponds, with sandy beaches and calm waters
>
> ■ Easy bike rides on short trails, especially the Shining Sea Trail between Falmouth and Woods Hole
>
> ■ Summer concerts at Sandwich's Heritage Museums and Gardens
>
> ■ Art galleries and crafts shows, especially in downtown Falmouth and Route 6A in East Sandwich
>
> ■ Walking trails crisscrossing the Ashumet Holly sanctuary and the Mashpee River Woodlands

| WHAT IT COSTS | | | | | |
|---|---|---|---|---|---|
| | ¢ | $ | $$ | $$$ | $$$$ |
| Restaurants | under $10 | $10–$16 | $16–$22 | $22–$30 | over $30 |
| Hotels | under $90 | $90–$140 | $140–$200 | $200–$260 | over $260 |

Restaurant prices are per person for a main course at dinner. Hotel prices are for a standard double room, excluding 6% sales tax (more in some counties) and 1%–4% tourist tax.

## TIMING

Although summer on the Upper Cape is the quintessential New England–vacation experience, the ideal time of year to visit may be early autumn. You can enjoy the beaches and water activities on Cape Cod Bay, Buzzards Bay, and Nantucket Sound in tranquillity between mid-September and late October, when the summer crowds have left but the weather is still mild. The Bourne Scallop Festival takes place in mid-September for three days.

## BOURNE

*6 mi southwest of Sandwich.*

The town of Bourne consists of nine villages—Bourne Village, Bourne-dale, Buzzards Bay, Cataumet, Gray Gables, Monument Beach, Pocasset, Sagamore, and Sagamore Beach—along Buzzards Bay and both sides of the Cape Cod Canal. The villages range from souvenir-shop-dominated commercial districts to bucolic waterfront suburbs. With a mix of year-round and summer residents, the area includes places for learning about the region's marine life and early commercial history, as well as several attractive recreation areas, established and maintained by the Army Corps of Engineers, for biking, hiking, and fishing along the canal.

The Pilgrims established their first Cape Cod settlement in Bourne in 1627, but back then it was still part of Sandwich; Bourne didn't become a separate town until 1884. By that time it had grown into a popular summer colony whose part-time residents included President Grover Cleveland and *Boston Globe* publisher Charles Taylor. Present-day Bourne's maritime orientation was created by the Cape Cod Canal, which opened in 1914. The 17½-mi canal cut the distance for shipping traffic between Boston and New York by 75 mi and eliminated the often-treacherous journey around the Cape. The Army Corps of Engineers took over the canal's operation in the late 1920s and embarked on a project to widen it; the current Bourne and Sagamore bridges were built in the 1930s as part of this project.

☼ The **National Marine Life Center,** on the mainland near the chamber of commerce office, has a small exhibit area devoted to whales, dolphins, seals, and other marine life. In summer there are marine-life educational programs for children and evening lectures about the ocean environment for adults. At this writing, the newly expanded facility for rehabilitating stranded marine animals—which consists of a marine animal hospital and nursery, eight rehabilitation pools, and additional exhibit space—was expected to open in time for the 2009 season. ✉ *120 Main St., Buzzards Bay* ☎ *508/743–9888* ⊕ *www.nmlc.org* ☛ *Free, donations accepted* ☉ *Late May–early Sept., daily 10–5; early Sept.–Columbus Day, weekends 10–5.*

On the mainland side, the **Massachusetts Maritime Academy,** founded in 1891, is the oldest such academy in the country. Future members of the merchant marine receive their training at its 55-acre campus in Buzzards Bay. The library has nautical paintings and scale models of ships from the 18th century to the present and is open to the public at no charge (hours are extensive but vary widely depending on whether school is in session; call ahead). For a 30-to-60-minute tour of the academy (weekdays only; times vary), call 48 hours in advance. The tours are designed for prospective students and their families but are open to all. ✉ *Taylor's Point, Buzzards Bay* ☎ *508/830–5000* ⊕ *www.maritime.edu.*

# The Upper Cape

*Cape Cod Bay*

TO
SCUSSET BEACH &
PLIMOUTH
PLANTATION

Sagamore Bridge

**Sagamore**

Town Neck Beach

East Sandwich Beach

**Sandwich**

130

*Shawme Crowell State Forest*

Green Briar Nature Center

6A

*Buzzards Bay*

25

Cape Cod Canal

Bourne Bridge

Massachusetts Maritime Academy

**Bourne**

Aptucxet Trading Post Museum

**Heritage Museums and Gardens**

6

Old County Rd.

Meetinghouse Rd.

6

Monument Beach

Shore Rd.

28

*Massachusetts Military Reservation*

Peters Pond

Cotuit Rd.

Race La.

Pocasset

*Buzzards Bay*

Cataumet

*Wakeby Pond*

130

**Marstons Mills**

28A

Megansett Beach

Attaquin Park Beach

*Mashpee Pond*

**Mashpee**

**Santuit**

28

North Falmouth

**Coonamessett Farm**

151

*Ashumet Pond*

*Johns Pond*

Mashpee Rotary

**Cotuit**

Old Silver Beach

*Coonamessett Pond*

**Ashumet Holly and Wildlife Sanctuary**

*Popponesset Bay*

28

**Cape Cod Winery**

Sandwich Rd.

Chapoquoit Beach

**Tony Andrews Farm and Produce Stand**

West Falmouth

**East Falmouth**

**Waquoit**

**Popponesset Beach**

Wood Neck Beach

Teaticket

28

Sippewissett Rd.

*Grews Pond*

*Long Pond*

**Waquoit Bay National Estuarine Research Reserve**

Acapesket Rd.

**New Seabury**

**Falmouth**

Surf Drive Beach

*Waquoit Bay*

**Charles D. and Margaret K. Spohr Gardens**

Falmouth Heights Beach

Menauhant Beach

South Cape Beach

**Woods Hole**

Falmouth Beach

Woods Hole Rd.

mail boat

TO HYANNIS

*Nobska Light*

Nobska Pt.

TO MARTHA'S VINEYARD

*Naushon Island*

TO MARTHA'S VINEYARD

*Martha's Vineyard*

**Oak Bluffs**

**Vineyard Haven**

0    2 miles

0    2 kilometers

A monument to the birth of commerce in the New World, the **Aptucxet Trading Post Museum** was erected on the foundation of the original post archaeologically excavated in the 1920s. Here, in 1627, Plimoth Plantation leaders established a way station between the Native American encampment at Great Herring Pond 3 mi to the northeast, Dutch colonists in New Amsterdam (New York) to the south, and English colonists on Cape Cod Bay. Before the canal was built, the Manomet River connected Herring Pond with Buzzards Bay (no, scavengers don't frequent it—it was misnamed for the migrating osprey that do), and a short portage connected the pond to Scusset River, which met Cape Cod Bay. The Native Americans traded furs; the Dutch traded linen cloth, metal tools, glass beads, sugar, and other staples; and the Pilgrims traded wool cloth, clay beads, sassafras, and tobacco (which they imported from Virginia). Wampum (beads made from polished shells) was the medium of exchange.

Inside the post, 17th-century cooking utensils hang from the original brick hearth; beaver and otter skins, furniture, and other artifacts such as arrowheads, tools, and tomahawks are displayed throughout. Also on the grounds are a gift shop in a Dutch-style windmill, a saltworks, herb and wildflower gardens, a picnic area overlooking the canal, and a small Victorian railroad station built for the sole use of President Grover Cleveland, who had a summer home in Bourne. To get here, cross the Bourne Bridge; then take the first right from the Bourne Bridge rotary onto Trowbridge Road and follow the signs. Note that the site is also open on holiday Mondays in season. ⊠ *24 Aptucxet Rd.* ☎ *508/759-9487* ⊕ *www.bournehistoricalsoc.org* ⊒ *$4* ⊗ *Late May–Columbus Day, Tues.–Sat. 10–4, Sun. 2–5.*

☺ A break for energetic children pent up in a car for too many miles, **Cartwheels 2** has a go-kart track, a bumper-boat lagoon, 18 holes of miniature golf, whiffle ball, batting cages, and an arcade with snack bar. Check the Web site for discount coupons. ⊠ *Rte. 28, 2 mi south of Bourne Bridge* ☎ *508/759-2636 or 800/535-2787* ⊕ *www.cartwheels2.com* ⊗ *Apr.–Oct., call for off-season hrs; July–early Sept., daily 10 AM–11 PM.*

A short drive northeast of Bourne proper, the village of **Sagamore** straddles the Cape Cod Canal and is perhaps best known for the bridge, completed in 1935, that bears its name. Primarily a small suburban community, the town has several stores for those interested in bargain hunting or gift shopping.

Watch richly colored lead crystal being handblown at **Pairpoint Glass Company,** America's oldest glass factory (founded in 1837). The shop sells candlesticks, vases, stemware, sun catchers, cup plates, lamps, perfume bottles, and reproductions of original Boston and Sandwich glass pieces. ⊠ *851 Sandwich Rd. (Rte. 6A)* ☎ *508/888-2344 or 800/899-0953* ⊕ *www.pairpoint.com* ⊒ *Free* ⊗ *Showroom weekdays 9–6, Sat. 10–5, Sun. 11–5. Demonstrations May–Dec., weekdays 9–4; Jan.–Apr., call before visiting; demonstration hrs are limited.*

**2**

## WHERE TO STAY & EAT

**$-$$**
SEAFOOD

✕**Chart Room.** Located harborside at the marina in a former cargo barge, this traditional watering hole has been serving seafood classics since 1966. Clam chowder, lobster rolls, broiled scrod, seafood Newburg, baked stuffed shrimp—they're all here, as are sirloin steak, broiled lamb chops, and even grilled cheese-and-tomato sandwiches. ✉*1 Shipyard La., at Kingman Yacht Center, Cataumet* ☎*508/563–5350* ▣*AE, MC, V* ☉*Closed mid-Oct.–mid-May and weekdays late May–late June and early Sept.–mid-Oct.*

**$**
Fodor'sChoice
★
ASIAN

✕**Stir Crazy.** Fresh ingredients with lively Cambodian, Thai, and Vietnamese flavors dominate every dish that graces the menu here (owner Bopha Samms hails from Cambodia). Try the *nhem shross* (an appetizer of vegetables and shrimp) and the refreshing *bar bong* (chilled noodles topped with pork, egg rolls, and coconut-peanut sauce). ✉*570 MacArthur Blvd. (Rte. 28 S), Pocasset* ☎*508/564–6464* ⚏*Reservations not accepted* ▣*MC, V* ☉*Closed Mon. No lunch Sat.–Thurs.*

**$-$$**

▦**Wood Duck Inn.** Behind this cozy B&B, a 17-acre working cranberry bog and acres of conservation land spread out as far as you can see. The small but comfy Cottage Room has lace curtains and a brass bed with a floral comforter, and both suites have a bedroom plus a sitting room that doubles as extra sleeping space. The Garden Suite is done in romantic florals, and the family-friendly Treetops Suite resembles a contemporary apartment in forest green and white; it has a tiny but fully equipped kitchen and sweeping views. The innkeepers deliver breakfast to your door. **Pros:** privacy assured with individual entrances, no common rooms, and breakfast brought to your room; walk to nearby free summer shuttle to island ferry terminals; beautiful pastoral views. **Cons:** suites accessed only by stairs; credit cards not accepted. ✉*1050 County Rd., Cataumet* ☎*508/564–6404* ⊕*www.woodduckinnbb.com* ➭*1 room, 2 suites* ⚑*In-room: no a/c (some), kitchen (some), refrigerator, VCR. In-hotel: Wi-Fi, no-smoking rooms, no elevator* ▣*No credit cards* ⏸*CP.*

**$**

⛰**Scusset Beach State Reservation.** Encompassing 300 acres adjacent to the Cape Cod Canal (there's a fishing pier for anglers), the park has a beach on Cape Cod Bay and 98 RV sites plus 5 tent sites, some wooded. There are cold showers on the beach and hot showers in the campground. ⚑*Beachfront, full hookups* ➭*103 sites* ✉*140 Scusset Beach Rd., off Rte. 3 at Sagamore Bridge rotary* ☎*877/422–6762 campsite reservations, 508/888–0859 general information* ⊕*www.reserveamerica.com* ▣*MC, V.*

## NIGHTLIFE & THE ARTS

The **Army Corps of Engineers** ( ☎*508/759–4431*), which maintains the Cape Cod Canal via a field office in Buzzards Bay, offers free daily programs in summer, including evening campfire programs on canal-related topics (with marshmallow roasting). Call for program details and locations.

In Bourne, Thursday evening **town-band concerts** ( ✉*Main St.* ☎*508/759–6000*) in July and August start at 7 in Buzzards Bay Park.

## SPORTS & THE OUTDOORS

The **Army Corps of Engineers** (☎508/759-4431) sponsors guided walks, bike trips, and hikes, including canal and area natural-history walks.

BASEBALL    The **Bourne Braves** of the collegiate Cape Cod Baseball League play home games at **Upper Cape Tech** (✉*Sandwich Rd.* ⊕*www.bourne braves.org*) from mid-June to mid-August. Players and coaches lead youth clinics in the summer.

BEACHES    **Monument Beach,** off Shore Road, is a small but pretty crescent of sand adjacent to the town dock, facing Buzzards Bay just south of Bourne Bridge. The beach has a snack bar, restrooms, and a parking lot, which is restricted in season to those with resident permits. From Shore Road, turn right onto Emmons Road just past the old train depot.

Sagamore's **Scusset Beach State Reservation** is a pleasant place for a swim, walk, or bike ride near the mainland side of the Sagamore Bridge. The beach sweeps along Cape Cod Bay, and its pier and canal breakwater are popular for fishing and viewing boat traffic; other activities include hiking, picnicking, and camping. There's a parking fee from mid-April to mid-October. ✉*140 Scusset Beach Rd., off Rte. 3 at Sagamore Bridge rotary* ☎*508/888-0859* ⊕*www.mass.gov/dcr* ✉*Mid-Apr.–mid-Oct., parking $7* ⊙*Daily 8–8.*

BICYCLING    An easy, straight trail stretches on either side of the **Cape Cod Canal,** 6½ mi on the south side, 7 mi on the north, with views of the bridges and ship traffic on the canal. Contact the **Army Corps of Engineers** (☎*508/759–4431*) for information about canal trail access and parking.

FISHING    The Cape Cod Canal is a great place to fish—from the service road on either side—for the big blues and striped bass making their way through the passage seasonally (April through November). You don't need a fishing license for saltwater angling, though you will need one for freshwater fishing.

HIKING &    Run by the Army Corps of Engineers, the **Herring Run Visitor Center** (✉*U.*
WALKING    *S. 6, Bournedale* ☎*508/759–4431, 508/759–5991 tides, weather, and special events*), on a bank of the canal with an excellent view, has picnic tables (close to noisy U.S. 6), access to the canal bike path, a herring run through which the fish travel on their spawning run in May, and short self-guided walking trails through the woodland. The visitor center is on the mainland side of the canal, between the bridges.

On the Cape side of the canal, the Army Corps of Engineers manages the **Tidal Flats Recreation Area** (✉*Shore Rd.* ☎*508/759–4431*), a small but peaceful canal-side park near the Cape railroad bridge. It's a pleasant site for picnicking or fishing, with a great view of the canal's ship traffic. There's also access to the canal bike path. In the late afternoon, between 5 and 7, you can watch the bridge lower to allow a service train to cross the canal; these times are approximate and can vary widely because of traffic and bridge work. To reach the recreation area, cross the Bourne Bridge and follow Trowbridge Road to Shore Road.

**ICE-SKATING** **John Gallo Ice Arena** ( ⊠ *231 Sandwich Rd.* ☎ *508/759–8904*) is the place to go for ice skating year-round (except May). Lessons are offered and skate rental is available; admission is $3.

### SHOPPING
**Cape Cod Factory Outlet Mall** ( ⊠ *Factory Outlet Rd., Exit 1 off Rte. 6* ☎ *508/888–8417* ⊕ *www.capecodfactoryoutletmall.com*) has more than 20 outlet stores, including CorningWare-Corelle-Revere, Carter's, Van Heusen, Izod, Bass, and Reebok.

**Christmas Tree Shops** ( ⊠ *Cranberry Hwy. [Rte. 6A], Exit 1 off Rte. 6* ☎ *508/888–7010* ⊕ *www.christmastreeshops.com*) sell dishware and a wide variety of other household goods at bargain prices. There are other locations in Falmouth, Hyannis, West Yarmouth, West Dennis, and Orleans.

## SANDWICH

★  *3 mi east of Sagamore Bridge, 11 mi west of Barnstable.*

A well-preserved New England village, Sandwich wears its history proudly, despite having become increasingly suburban in character over the past few decades and its population soaring to more than 20,000. The oldest town on Cape Cod, Sandwich was established in 1637 by some of the Plymouth Pilgrims and incorporated on March 6, 1638. Driving through town past the white-column town hall, the gristmill on Shawme Pond, the First Church of Christ with its spindlelike spire, and the 18th- and 19th-century homes that line the streets is like driving back in time—you may feel as if you should be holding a horse's reins rather than the steering wheel of a car. When you reach Main Street, park the car and get out for a stroll. Look at old houses on Main Street, stop at a museum or two, and work your way to the delightful Shawme Pond. Unlike other Cape towns, whose deepwater ports opened the doors to prosperity in the whaling days, Sandwich was an industrial town for much of the 19th century. The main industry was the production of vividly colored glass, called Sandwich glass, which is now sought by collectors. The Boston and Sandwich Glass Company's factory here produced the glass from 1825 until 1888, when competition with glassmakers in the Midwest—and finally a union strike—closed it. While you walk, look for etched Sandwich glass from the old factory on front doors. There probably aren't two identical glass panels in town.

The **Sandwich Glass Museum,** with its 9,000 square feet of exhibits, has information about the history of the company, including a diorama showing how the factory looked in its heyday, an "ingredient room" showcasing a wide spectrum of glass colors along with the minerals added to the sand to obtain them, and an outstanding collection of blown and pressed glass in many shapes and shimmering hues. Large glass lamps, vases, and pitchers are impressive, as are the hundreds of candlesticks and small saucers on display. Glassmaking demonstrations are held in summer. A few galleries contain relics of the town's early history (the museum is also the Sandwich Historical Society). The extensive, ornate gift shop sells some handsome reproductions, including some made by local and national artisans. The museum also sponsors several walking tours of the town in July and August. ⊠ *129 Main St., Sandwich Center* ☎ *508/888–0251* ⊕ *www.sandwichglassmuseum.org* ⊠ *$5* ⊙ *Apr.–Dec., daily 9:30–5; Feb. and Mar., Wed.–Sun. 9:30–4*

☾ A lovely place for a stroll or a picnic is the park around **Shawme Pond** ( ⊠ *Water and Grove Sts., Sandwich Center*), a favorite fishing site for children. The ducks and swans love to be fed, though posted signs warn you not to indulge them. Across the way—a perfect backdrop for this setting—stands the spired, white 1848 First Church of Christ, inspired by a design by British architect Christopher Wren.

Where Shawme Pond drains over its dam, a little wooden bridge leads over a watercourse to the waterwheel-powered **Dexter Gristmill**, built in 1654. In season the miller demonstrates the grinding process, talks about the mill's operation, and sells its ground corn. ⊠ *Water and Grove Sts., Sandwich Center* ☎ *508/888–4910 Sandwich Town Hall* ⊠ *$3; combination ticket with Hoxie House $4* ⊙ *Late May and early Sept.–late Sept., Sat. 10–4:45; June–early Sept., Mon.–Sat. 10–4:45.*

**NEED A BREAK?**

The delightful **Dunbar Tea Shop** ( ⊠ **1 Water St. [Rte. 130], Sandwich Center** ☎ **508/833-2485**) is in a former billiards room–carriage house, now converted into a country cottage with paneled walls and assorted antiques and kitschy doodads. Lunch (from a smoked-fish platter with salad to quiche or a salmon tart), English cream tea, and tasty sweets are served from 11 to 5 daily, July through October (until 4:30 the rest of the year). A gift shop sells British tea, specialty foods, and home-decorating items.

☾ The **Thornton W. Burgess Museum** is dedicated to the Sandwich native

**Fodor's Choice** whose tales of Peter Cottontail, Reddy Fox, and a host of other crea-

★ tures of the Old Briar Patch have been part of children's bedtimes for decades. Thornton Burgess (1874–1965), an avid conservationist, made his characters behave true to their species to educate children as he entertained them. Storytelling sessions, often including the live animal that the Burgess story is about, take place regularly in July and August. In the Discovery Room, kids can use their imaginations in the prop-filled classroom. On display are some of Burgess's 170 books (although children are welcome here, the exhibits are of the don't-touch variety). The small gift shop carries puppets, Burgess books, and Pairpoint Crystal cup plates decorated with Burgess characters. ⊠ *4 Water St. (Rte. 130), Sandwich Center* ☎ *508/888–4668* ⊕ *www.thorntonburgess.org* ⊠ *Donations accepted* ⊙ *May–Oct., Mon.–Sat. 10–4, Sun. 1–4.*

Overlooking Shawme Pond is the **Hoxie House**, a remarkable old saltbox virtually unaltered since it was built in 1675. Even though people lived in it until the 1950s, the house was never modernized with electricity or plumbing. Furnishings reflect daily life in the colonial period, with some pieces on loan from the Museum of Fine Arts in Boston. Highlights are diamond-shape lead-glass windows and a collection of antique textile machines. ⊠ *18 Water St. (Rte. 130), Sandwich Center* ☎ *508/888–1173* ⊠ *$3; combination ticket with Dexter Gristmill*

*$4 ⊘ Late May–mid-June, Sat. 10–5, Sun. 1–5; mid-June–mid-Oct., Mon.–Sat. 10–5, Sun. 1–5.*

The **Old Town Cemetery** ( ⊠ *Grove St., Sandwich Center*), on the opposite side of Shawme Pond from Hoxie House, is a classic, undulating New England graveyard. You can stop in for a peaceful moment and trace the genealogy of old Sandwich. On Thursday in July and August, you can hear tales during narrated walking tours about the cemetery's more illustrious inhabitants; call the Sandwich Glass Museum for additional information.

If you're interested in very old houses (by U.S. standards, anyway), there are two worthy examples privately owned yet open for touring. The **Wing Fort House** was built in 1641 and can boast the distinction of being the "oldest house in New England owned and occupied continuously by the same family for over three centuries." The interior reveals changing tastes in decor and architecture over the centuries. ⊠*69 Springhill Rd. (off Rte. 6A), East Sandwich ☎508/833–1540 ⊕www. wingfamily.org ⊠$2 ⊘ Mid-June–late Sept., Tues.–Sat. 10–4.*

Also hailing from the 17th century is the **Benjamin Nye Homestead and Museum,** once the home of one of the first gristmills in the country. Although the mill is long gone, the scenic views are still present, as are the many original details within the home's modest walls. ⊠*85 Old County Rd. (off Rte. 6A), East Sandwich ☎508/888–4213 ⊕www. nyefamily.org ⊠$3 ⊘ Mid-June–mid-Oct., Tues.–Sat. noon–4:30.*

**Heritage Museums and Gardens,** 100 beautifully landscaped acres overlooking the upper end of Shawme Pond, includes gardens and a café as well as an impressive complex of museum buildings with specialty collections ranging from cars to toys. In 1967 pharmaceuticals magnate Josiah K. Lilly III purchased the estate and turned it into a nonprofit museum. A highlight is the Shaker Round Barn, which showcases classic and historic cars—including a 1930 yellow-and-green Duesenberg built for Gary Cooper, a 1919 Pierce-Arrow, a 1915 Milburn Light Electric, and a 1911 Stanley Steamer—as well as art exhibitions. The American History museum houses the Cape Cod Baseball League Hall of Fame as well as antique firearms, a collection of 2,000 hand-painted miniature soldiers, military uniforms, and Native American arts. The art museum has an extensive Currier & Ives collection, Americana (including a mechanical-bank collection), antique toys such as a 1920 Hubley Royal Circus, and a working 1912 Coney Island–style carousel that both adults and little ones can ride as often as they like. A shuttle bus—equipped with a wheelchair lift and space to stow baby strollers—transports visitors every few minutes from the car museum to other exhibit sites.

Paths crisscross the grounds, which include gardens planted with daylilies, hostas, heather, herbs, and fruit trees. Rhododendron enthusiasts will recognize the name of onetime estate owner and hybridizer Charles O. Dexter; the rhododendrons are in full glory from mid-May through mid-June. Daylilies reach their peak from mid-July through early August. Families visiting with youngsters should ask at

Fodor'sChoice
★

the ticket office for Family Funpacks with children's activities, or the Clue tours—scavenger-hunt games for exploring the grounds. In summer, concerts are held in the gardens, often on Wednesday or Saturday evening or Sunday afternoon. The center of the complex is about ¾ mi on foot from the in-town end of Shawme Pond. ⊠ *67 Grove St.* ☎ *508/888-3300* ⊕ *www.heritagemuseumsandgardens.org* ⊠ *$12* ⊙ *Apr.–Nov., daily 10–5; Nov.–Mar., call for very limited hrs.*

At the **Cape Cod Canal Visitor Center,** run by the Army Corps of Engineers, exhibits and video presentations describe the canal's history, area wildflowers, and local "critters." Among the special ranger-led programs are beach and dune walks, as well as evening star watches. The visitor center is opposite the Coast Guard Station, near Joe's Fish Market. ⊠ *Ed Moffitt Dr.* ☎ *508/833-9678* ⊠ *Free* ⊙ *Mid-May–mid-Oct., call for hrs.*

For a view of the bay, you can walk to Town Neck Beach on the **Sandwich Boardwalk,** built over a salt marsh, creek, and low dunes. In 1991 Hurricane Bob and an October nor'easter destroyed the previous boardwalk. Individuals and businesses donated planks to rebuild it, which volunteers then installed. The donors' names; jokes (GET OFF OUR BOARD); thoughts (SIMPLIFY/THOREAU); and memorials to lovers, grandparents, and boats are inscribed on the planks. The long sweep of Cape Cod Bay stretches out around the beach at the end of the walk, where a platform provides fine views, especially at sunset. Stone jetties, dunes, waving grasses, and the entrance to the canal are in the foreground, and you can look out toward Sandy Neck, Wellfleet, and Provincetown or toward the white cliffs beyond Sagamore. The sandy strip on this mostly rocky beach is near the rugosa rose–patch dunes; the flowers have a delicious fragrance, and it's a good place for birding. The creeks running through the salt marsh make for great canoeing. From the town center it's about a mile to the boardwalk; cross Route 6A on Jarves Street, and at its end turn left, then right, and continue to the boardwalk parking lot.

Ⓒ At the **Sandwich Fish Hatchery,** the oldest fish hatchery in the country, you can see more than 200,000 brook, brown, and rainbow trout at various stages of development; they are raised to stock the state's ponds. The mesh over the raceways keeps kingfishers and herons from snagging a free lunch. You can buy feed for 25¢ and watch the fish jump for it. ⊠ *164 Rte. 6A* ☎ *508/888-0008* ⊠ *Free* ⊙ *Daily 9–3.*

**OFF THE BEATEN PATH**

**Green Briar Nature Center and Jam Kitchen.** Is it the soothing pond-side location or its simple earthiness—who's to say? Whatever the reason, this center, owned and operated by the Thornton Burgess Society, is a solid symbol of the old Cape. You pass a wildflower garden on your way in, and the Smiling Pool sparkles out back. Birds flit about the grounds, and great smells waft from vintage stoves in the Jam Kitchen, where you can watch as jams and pickles are made according to Ida Putnam's recipes, used here since 1903 (sun-cooked fruit preserves are especially superb). Come weekdays mid-April through mid-December to see jam being made in the Jam Kitchen; you can even take a jam-making class some evenings or Saturday. The nature center has classes for adults and children, as well as walks, lectures, and a May herb festival, where herbs, wildflowers, and perennials are for sale. The Briar Patch Conservation Area behind the building has nature trails—take a walk and visit the real live animals that inspired Peter Cottontail, Grandfather Frog, and other beloved Thornton Burgess characters. ⊠ *6 Discovery Hill Rd., off Rte. 6A, East Sandwich* ☎ *508/888–6870* ⊕ *www.thorntonburgess.org* ✉ *$2 suggested donation* ☉ *Apr.–Dec., Mon.–Sat. 10–4, Sun. 1–4; Jan.–Mar., Tues.–Sat. 10–4.*

## WHERE TO EAT

**$–$$$**
**★**
ECLECTIC

✕ **Aqua Grille.** At this smart-casual and reasonably priced bistro by the marina, offerings range from Cape basics (clam chowder, fried seafood, boiled lobsters) to more creative contemporary fare, such as nut-crusted halibut with an orange beurre blanc. The excellent lobster salad comprises a hearty serving of greens, tomatoes, avocados, baby green beans, and big, meaty lobster chunks. Sandwiches (salmon burgers, turkey wraps) are also available. ⊠ *14 Gallo Rd., Sandwich* ☎ *508/888–8889* ⊕ *www.aquagrille.com* ▤ *AE, DC, MC, V* ☉ *Closed Nov.–mid-Apr.*

**$–$$**
AMERICAN

✕ **Bee-Hive Tavern.** This informal and friendly colonial-style tavern hasn't been here since Revolutionary times (it opened in the early '90s), but the cozy dark-wood booths and wide-board floors look the part. The kitchen turns out solid American fare, such as burgers and sandwiches, fried seafood, Yankee pot roast, ribs, and steaks. Dinner-size salads are also available. Reservations aren't officially taken, but you can call ahead to make the wait a little easier. ⊠ *406 Rte. 6A, East Sandwich* ☎ *508/833–1184* ▤ *MC, V.*

**$$–$$$**
ECLECTIC

✕ **Hemisphere.** The most striking feature here is the supreme vista: via a generous array of windows, the sun sets over Cape Cod Bay while all manner of boats prepare to make their passage through the Cape Cod Canal. For both lunch and dinner, the menu covers vast ground with everything from fried seafood favorites to the more sophisticated. Try the seared scallops with herbed gnocchi, adorned with grilled prosciutto, watercress, and roasted garlic. Savor items from the raw bar on the outdoor deck for a real seaside experience. There's live entertainment on summer weekends. Stunning views and a full bar make waiting for a table fairly painless (reservations are available only for parties of five or more). ⊠ *98 Town Neck Rd., Sandwich* ☎ *508/888–6166* ▤ *AE, MC, V* ☉ *Closed Nov.–Apr.*

**¢–$**
AMERICAN

✕ **Marshland Restaurant and Bakery.** Sandwich's version of down-home is this homey coffee shop tucked into a parking lot. For breakfast try an Italian omelet, a rich mix of Italian sausage, fresh vegetables, and cheese. The lunch specials—a grilled chicken club sandwich, the Cobb salad, a turkey Reuben, a daily quiche, and the like—are the best choices midday, and for dinner the prime rib does not disappoint. ⊠ *109 Rte. 6A, Sandwich* ☎ *508/888–9824* ▤ *AE, MC, V* ☉ *No dinner Mon.*

**¢–$**
SEAFOOD

✕ **Seafood Sam's.** Fried seafood reigns supreme at Sam's, across from the Coast Guard station and a stone's throw from the Cape Cod Canal. Order from the counter, take a number, and sit in an airy dining room where the munch of fried clams accompanies the sound of lobsters being cracked open. Sam's also has branches in Harwichport, Falmouth, and South Yarmouth. ⊠*6 Coast Guard Rd., Sandwich* ☎*508/888–4629* ⊕*www.seafoodsams.com* ▤*D, MC, V* ⊘*Closed early Nov.–early Mar.*

## WHERE TO STAY

**$$–$$$$**

**Fodor's Choice**
★

🏨**Belfry Inne & Bistro.** This delightful one-of-a-kind inn comprises a 1902 former church, an ornate wood-frame Victorian, and an 1830 Federal-style house clustered on a main campus. Room themes in each building nod to their respective histories—the Painted Lady's charmingly appointed rooms, for example, are named after former inhabitants. The luxurious rooms in the Abbey, named for the six days of creation, have whirlpool tubs and gas fireplaces, and are set along a corridor overlooking the restaurant below. (If it's available, splurge on the Tuesday room—the incredible stained-glass "compass" window will take your breath away.) The Bistro ($$–$$$$) serves dazzling, globally inspired dishes such as black grouper roasted with tamarind-yogurt sauce in a striking setting—look up at the church's original arches and stained glass as you dine. Next door in the Victorian building, the Painted Lady restaurant ($–$$) serves innovative renditions of home-style American favorites, including a delicious baked mac-and-cheese. **Pros:** great in-town location; rooms in the Abbey and the Victorian are especially bright, beautiful, and spacious. **Cons:** many rooms accessible only via steep stairs; some rooms in the Federal-style house can be smallish. ⊠*8 Jarves St., Sandwich* ☎*508/888–8550 or 800/844–4542* ▤*508/888–3922* ⊕*www.belfryinn.com* ↩*20 rooms* ⌂*In-room: no TV (some), Wi-Fi (some). In-hotel: 2 restaurants, bar, no-smoking rooms, no elevator* ▤*AE, D, DC, MC, V* ⍿*BP.*

**$$–$$$$**

🏨**Dan'l Webster Inn and Spa.** Built on the site of a 17th-century inn, the Dan'l Webster is a contemporary hotel within the heart of Sandwich's historic downtown. Rooms are decked out in high-end colonial-inspired cherrywood and mahogany furnishings in traditional colors. You might find a Sheraton reproduction armoire in one room, a pencil-post four-poster bed in another; some units have fireplaces, and most have balconies overlooking the nicely manicured gardens. The restaurant ($$–$$$$) is a longtime favorite. Upscale, modern continental dishes, such as roast rack of lamb stuffed with spinach and olives and served with a cabernet sauce, take their places beside veal Oscar, roast prime rib, and other classics. A casual tavern serves pizzas, burgers, and salads. The spa offers a full slate of massage, facial, and beauty treatments. **Pros:** ideal in-town location, full-service hotel facilities in a tasteful setting. **Cons:** if you're looking for an authentic historic lodging experience with antique detailing and decor, you won't find it here; very popular with business travelers and bus tours. ⊠*149 Main St., Sandwich* ☎*508/888–3622 or 800/444–3566* ▤*508/888–5156* ⊕*www. danlwebsterinn.com* ↩*35 rooms, 13 suites* ⌂*In-room: Wi-Fi. In-hotel: 2 restaurants, room service, pool, spa* ▤*AE, D, DC, MC, V.*

**$**

🏨**Earl of Sandwich Motor Manor.** Single-story Tudor-style buildings form a U around a duck pond and wooded lawn set with lawn chairs. Rooms, attractively if simply furnished, are nicely sized with large windows and dark pine headboards and doors. Many rooms have can-

opy beds. A continental plan is offered from late May to October.
**Pros:** calming countryside setting with picnic areas; reasonable rates;
good location for exploring the area, though not in-town. **Cons:** bathrooms are a little outdated; rooms with two double beds are a bit over-
crowded and dark. ⊠ *378 Rte. 6A, East Sandwich* ☎*508/888–1415 or
800/442–3275* 🖷*508/833–1039* ⊕*www.earlofsandwich.com* 🛏*24
rooms* ⚹*In-room: refrigerator, Wi-Fi. In-hotel: pool, no-smoking
rooms, some pets allowed, no elevator* ▤*AE, D, DC, MC, V* ⧉*CP
☉Closed Dec.–Mar.*

**$$**
**★**
🏠**Inn at Sandwich Center.** Across from the Sandwich Glass Museum, this
18th-century house with fine colonial and Victorian furnishings is listed
on the National Register of Historic Places. In addition to such deco-
rative flourishes as ornate fireplaces and Oriental rugs, rooms contain
high-thread-count linens, robes, and Gilchrist & Soames bath ameni-
ties. A gazebo on a nearby hill houses a secluded spa where you can
arrange to have a professional massage. A hearty breakfast is served
in the keeping room, which contains a fireplace and an antique table
(older than the inn) that seats 10. Gracious hosts Jan and Charlie Preus
know a lot about the region and have created a warm and inviting
inn that's appealing whether you seek quiet seclusion or the oppor-
tunity to mingle with fellow guests. **Pros:** easy access to town center;
some rooms have working fireplaces; intimate and friendly inn. **Cons:**
most rooms accessible only via steep, narrow stairs; Deacon's Room
is on the small side. ⊠ *118 Tupper Rd., Sandwich* ☎*508/888–6958
or 800/249–6949* 🖷*508/888–2746* ⊕*www.innatsandwich.com* 🛏*5
rooms* ⚹*In-room: no phone, DVD (some), no TV (some), Wi-Fi. In-
hotel: no kids under 12, no-smoking rooms, no elevator* ▤*MC, V
☉Closed Jan.–Mar.* ⧉*BP.*

**$$–$$$$**
**★**
🏠**Isaiah Jones Homestead Bed & Breakfast.** Innkeepers Don and Kather-
ine Sanderson may be somewhat new to the lodging business, but with
extensive backgrounds in the global tourism industry, both know how
to give their guests extraordinary service in an equally stellar setting.
The aged Victorian is all graceful lines and high ceilings, adorned with
authentic period antiques and moody stained glass. Despite intricate
wall coverings, sweeping velvet drapes, and canopy beds, the spacious
rooms are uncluttered and welcoming. Recline in the comfortable parlor with afternoon cordials or peruse the DVD library for an in-room
movie. You'll want to rest up after the three-course breakfast that
might include homemade crabmeat quiche. The two suites in the adjacent carriage house have a simpler, cottage style; coffee will be delivered in the morning before breakfast is served in the main house. **Pros:**
easy walk to town center; ultimate in Victorian elegance and design;
beautiful grounds; a pampered experience. **Cons:** most rooms accessible only via steep stairs; some rooms don't have the luxurious bath-
tubs. ⊠ *165 Main St., Sandwich,* ☎*508/888–9115 or 800/526–1625*
🖷*508/888–9648* ⊕*www.isaiahjones.com* 🛏*5 rooms, 2 suites* ⚹*In-
room: no phone, DVD, Wi-Fi. In-hotel: bicycles, no children under 12,
no-smoking rooms, no elevator* ▤*AE, D, MC, V* ⧉*BP.*

**$**
🏠**Sandy Neck Motel.** Like the roadside country motels of old, this white-
shingled motel with cheery blue shutters offers simple and convenient

lodging for a reasonable price. Standard rooms have queen or two double beds, outfitted with white bedspreads and matching wicker furniture. The expansive grounds are dotted with barbecue grills, picnic tables, and Adirondack chairs, set back a bit off Route 6A. The efficiency is a good bet for families on a budget (or who just like to make their own meals) with a full-size kitchen and two bedrooms. The entrance to Sandy Neck Beach is about 1 mi away; for those in search of the entertainment and vacation glitz of Hyannis, it's a mere 15-minute drive. **Pros:** quiet setting with picnic areas; reasonable rates; close to beach. **Cons:** not for those looking for an in-town location. ⊠*669 Rte. 6A, East Sandwich* ☎*508/362–3992 or 800/564–3992* ⊕*www.sandyneck.com* ⊋*11 rooms, 1 efficiency* ⚘*In-room: refrigerator, Wi-Fi. In-hotel: no-smoking rooms, no elevator* ⊟*AE, MC, V* ☺*Closed Nov.–Apr.*

¢ ⚠ **Shawme-Crowell State Forest.** Less than a mile from the Cape Cod Canal, this 742-acre state forest is a good base for local biking and hiking, and campers get free day use of Scusset Beach. Open-air campfires are allowed at the wooded tent and RV (no hookups) campsites. Heated bathroom and shower facilities are a blessing on chilly mornings. The campground is generally open year-round, but if you're planning a winter trip, call to confirm before visiting. ⊠*Rte. 130, Sandwich* ☎*508/888–0351, 877/422–6762 reservations* ⊕*www.reserveamerica. com* ⊋*285 sites* ⊟*MC, V.*

## NIGHTLIFE & THE ARTS

THE ARTS    **Heritage Museums and Gardens** (⊠*67 Grove St.* ☎*508/888–3300*) sponsors jazz and other concerts in its gardens from June to mid-September; bring chairs or blankets. Most concerts are free with admission to the complex. **Town-band concerts** (⊠*Bandstand, Henry T. Wing Elementary School, Rte. 130 and Beale Ave., Sandwich Center* ☎*508/888–5144*) are held Thursday evening from July through late August starting at 7:30.

NIGHTLIFE    **Bobby Byrne's Pub** (⊠*65 Rte. 6A* ☎*508/888–6088*), with other locations in Hyannis and Mashpee, is a comfortable pub, with a jukebox and a good menu.

**British Beer Company** (⊠*46 Rte. 6A* ☎*508/833–9590* ⊕*www.british beer.com*), with other locations in Cedarville, Falmouth, Hyannis, and Plymouth, has a traditional British "public house" atmosphere with a great menu that includes fish, ribs, and pizza. Sunday afternoons feature live, traditional Irish music; a variety of bands play Thursday through Saturday nights.

## SPORTS & THE OUTDOORS

BEACHES    **East Sandwich Beach,** on North Shore Road, lies behind the grass-covered dunes beyond a row of gray-shingle beach cottages. It's a long stretch of sand, but nearby parking is very limited (and restricted to residents between 8 AM and 4 PM in season). From Route 6A follow Ploughed Neck Road to North Shore Road.

**Town Neck Beach,** off Town Neck Road, is a long, dune-backed bay beach with a mix of sand and pebbles. You need a resident parking sticker to leave your car in the large parking area between 8 AM and 4 PM in season. There are restrooms and a snack bar.

GOLF **Sandwich Hollows Golf Club** (✉*1 Round Hill Rd., East Sandwich* ☎*508/888–3384* ⊕*www.sandwichhollows.com*) has an 18-hole, par-71 course that's open to the public.

**Holly Ridge Golf Club** (✉*121 Country Club Rd., Sandwich* ☎*508/428–5577* ⊕*www.hollyridgegolf.com*) has an 18-hole, par-54 course (you can opt to play just 9 holes) that's good for all levels of golfers.

**SHOPPING**

★ The **Brown Jug** (✉*155 Main St., Sandwich* ☎*508/888–4669*) is a tantalizing gourmet-food shop in a cozy brown-shingle house in the center of Sandwich—the perfect place to pick up delicious picnic supplies. You'll find cheeses, chocolate, and all sorts of hard-to-find imported foods; you can also order tasty sandwiches to go.

The **Giving Tree** (✉*550 Rte. 6A, East Sandwich* ☎*508/888–5446 or 888/246–3551* ⊕*www.givingtreegallery.com*), an art gallery and sculpture garden, sells contemporary crafts, jewelry, metal sculpture, and prints. The shop is open Memorial Day through Christmas.

**Joe's Lobster Mart** (✉*Cape Cod Canal* ☎*508/888–2971*), opposite Seafood Sam's and the Coast Guard station, sells fresh-from-the-tank lobsters. Call ahead, and they'll boil your crustaceans to order—a great idea for an easy dinner at your cottage or hotel or for a picnic overlooking the canal. Joe's also sells many varieties of fresh fish.

**Sandwich Auction House** (✉*15 Tupper Rd.* ☎*508/888–1926* ⊕*www.sandwichauction.com*), which auctions antiques, general merchandise, and Oriental rugs, is a great place to spend part of a Wednesday night (Saturday in the off-season); come after 2 PM to preview the items for sale. This local institution has weekly sales. In addition, specialty sales every six to eight weeks feature upscale antiques received during that period. Sales are also held for antique and modern rugs.

Fodor'sChoice **Titcomb's Bookshop** (✉*432 Rte. 6A, East Sandwich* ☎*508/888–2331* ★ ⊕*www.titcombsbookshop.com*) stocks used, rare, and new books, including a large collection of Cape and nautical titles and Americana, as well as an extensive selection of children's books.

EN ROUTE **Route 6A** heads east from Sandwich, passing through the oldest settlements on the Cape. Part of the Old King's Highway historic district, the route is protected from development. Classic inns and enticing antiques shops alternate with traditional gray-shingle homes on this tree-lined road, and the woods periodically give way to broad vistas across the marshes. In autumn the foliage along the way is bright; maples with their feet wet in ponds and marshes put on a good display. Along Route 6A just east of Sandwich Center, you can stop to watch cranberries being harvested in flooded bogs. If you're heading down-Cape and you're not in a hurry, this is a lovely route to take. And if you do wish to take the faster but less-interesting U.S. 6 as your primary route through the region, it's easy to hop off here and there and travel certain stretches of parallel Route 6A.

# FALMOUTH

*2 mi south of West Falmouth, 15 mi south of Bourne Bridge, 4 mi north of Woods Hole.*

Falmouth, the Cape's second-largest town, was settled in 1660 by Congregationalists from Barnstable who had been ostracized by their church and deprived of voting privileges and other civil rights for sympathizing with the Quakers (then the victims of severe repression). The town was incorporated in 1686 and named for Falmouth, England. The Falmouth area, sprawling over 44 square mi, consists of eight villages: Falmouth, North Falmouth, West Falmouth, Hatchville, Teaticket, East Falmouth, Waquoit, and Woods Hole.

Much of Falmouth today is suburban, with a mix of old and new developments and a large year-round population. Many residents commute to other towns on the Cape, to southeastern Massachusetts, and even to Boston. The town has a quaint village center, with a typically old New England village green and a shop-lined Main Street. South of the town center, Falmouth faces Nantucket Sound and has several often-crowded beaches popular with families. To the east, the Falmouth Heights neighborhood mixes inns, B&Bs, and private homes nestled close together on residential streets leading to the sea. Bustling Grand Avenue, the main drag in Falmouth Heights, hugs the shore and the beach. Parks and ponds dot the town; one of the nicest, Grews Pond in Goodwill Park, is north of the town center—it's a lovely site for a picnic on a summer afternoon.

Today attractive old homes, some built by sea captains, flank the **Village Green,** which is listed on the National Register of Historic Places. It served as a militia training field in the 18th century and a grazing ground for horses in the early 19th century. Also on the green is the 1856 **Congregational Church,** built on the timbers of its 1796 predecessor, with a bell made by Paul Revere. The bell's cheery inscription reads THE LIVING TO THE CHURCH I CALL, AND TO THE GRAVE I SUMMON ALL.

**NEED A BREAK?**

**For a region that eagerly fought for independence from Mother England, there sure are a lot of places in Cape Cod to enjoy the oh-so-British pastime of having a spot of tea. Molly's Tea Room ( ⊠ 227 Main St., Falmouth Center ☎ 508/457–1666), right in the center of Falmouth, has dozens of flavors to choose from, as well as a selection of sandwiches, salads, soups, and quiche, should you find yourself a bit hungry as well (try the Queen's Luncheon for a real treat). Non-tea drinkers can partake in the wine or beer offerings. It's a great place to linger on a cloudy, cool day.**

The **Falmouth Museums on the Green** represent life in colonial Cape Cod. The 1790 **Julia Wood House** retains wonderful architectural details—a widow's walk, wide-board floors, leaded-glass windows, and a colonial kitchen with wide hearth. Antique embroideries, baby shoes and clothes, toys and dolls, portraits, furniture, and the trappings of an authentically equipped doctor's office, all from the house's onetime owner, fill the premises. Out back, a re-creation of the Hallett Barn displays antique farm implements, a 19th-century horse-drawn sleigh, and other interesting items. Next door, the smaller **Conant House**, a 1794 half Cape (an asymmetrical 1½-story building), holds military memorabilia, whaling items, scrimshaw, sailors' valentines, and a genealogical- and historical-research library. One collection includes books, portraits, and other items relating to Katharine Lee Bates, the native daughter who wrote "America the Beautiful." The Falmouth Historical Society also owns the 1812 white Cape house where Bates was born, off-site at 16 Main Street. The house is no longer open to the public, but a plaque out front commemorates Bates's birth in 1859.

Guides give tours of the museums, and a formal garden with a gazebo and flagstone paths is adjacent. You can take a break with "Tea in Julia's Garden," which offers tea sandwiches, scones, and other refreshments on Thursday from 1 to 3 in July and August. There are also historical trolley tours in season; call for prices and times. Free walking tours of the town are available Tuesday at 10 mid-June through early October, and free programs demonstrating colonial skills are given on Friday in July and August. You might dip a candle or make butter, weave a basket, or learn some sea chanteys. ⊠ *Village Green, 55 Palmer Ave., Falmouth Center* ☎ *508/548–4857* ⊕ *www.falmouthhistoricalsociety. org* ✉ *Museums $5; tea $12, including museum admission* ☉ *Mid-June–mid-Oct., Tues.–Fri. 10–4, Sat. 10–1.*

The privately owned **Charles D. and Margaret K. Spohr Gardens**, three planted acres on Oyster Pond, are a pretty, peaceful place. The springtime explosion of more than 700,000 daffodils gives way in turn to the tulips, azaleas, magnolias, flowering crab apples, rhododendrons, lilies, and climbing hydrangeas that inspire garden goers in summer. A collection of old millstones, bronze church bells, and ships' anchors decorates the landscape. ⊠ *45 Fells Rd., off Oyster Pond Rd.* ☎ *508/548–0623* ⊕ *www.spohrgardens.org* ✉ *Free* ☉ *Daily sunrise–sunset.*

♻ Video-game rooms and candlepin bowling make the **Leary Family Amusement Center** a great place to take the kids on a rainy day. ⊠ *23 Town Hall Sq., off Rte. 28, Falmouth Center* ☎ *508/540–4877.*

The village of **Woods Hole**, which dangles at the Cape's southwestern tip, has a unique personality shaped by its substantial intellectual community. As a major departure point for ferries to Martha's Vineyard, it draws crowds of through-traffic in season. Well known as a center for international marine research, Woods Hole is home to several major scientific institutions. The National Marine Fisheries Service was here first, established in 1871 to study fish management and conservation. In 1888 the Marine Biological Laboratory (MBL), a center for research and education in marine biology, moved in across the street. Then in 1930 the Woods Hole Oceanographic Institution (WHOI) arrived, and the U.S. Geological Survey's Branch of Marine Geology followed in the 1960s.

Most of the year Woods Hole is a peaceful community of intellectuals quietly going about their work. In summer, however, the basically one-street village overflows with thousands of scientists and graduate students who come from around the globe either to participate in summer studies at MBL, WHOI, or the National Academy of Sciences conference center or to work on independent research projects. A handful of waterside cafés and shops along Water Street compete for the distinction of having the most bicycles stacked up at the door. Parking, limited to a relatively small number of metered spots on the street, can be nearly impossible. If you're coming from Falmouth to wander around Woods Hole, either ride your bicycle down the straight and flat Shining Sea Trail or take the Cape Cod Regional Transit Authority's WHOOSH trolley.

Scientific forces join together at the **Marine Biological Laboratory–Woods Hole Oceanographic Institution Library** ( ✉ *7 Marine Biological Laboratory St., off Water St.* ☎ *508/289–7423* ⊕ *www.mbl.edu*), one of the best collections of biological, ecological, and oceanographic literature in the world. The library has access to more than 200 computer databases and subscribes to more than 5,000 scientific journals in 40 languages, with complete collections of most. During World War II the librarian made arrangements with a German subscription agency to have German periodicals sent to neutral Switzerland and stored until the end of the war. Thus the library's German collections are uninterrupted, whereas even those of many German institutions are incomplete. All journals are always accessible, because they cannot be checked out and because the library is open 24 hours a day. The Rare Books Room contains photographs, monographs, and prints, as well as journal collections that date from 1665.

Unless you are a scientific researcher, the only way you can get to see the library is by taking the **Marine Biological Laboratory tour** ( ☎ *508/289–7623*). The one-hour tours (late June through August, weekdays at 1 and 2), led by retired scientists, include an introductory slide show as well as stops at the library, the Marine Resources Center (where living sea creatures collected each day are kept), and one of the many working research labs. It's a good idea to call for reservations and meeting instructions at least a week in advance.

The **Woods Hole Oceanographic Institution** is the largest independent, private oceanographic laboratory in the world. Several buildings in the village of Woods Hole house its shore-based facilities; others are on a 200-acre campus nearby. During World War II its research focused on underwater explosives, submarine detection, and the development of antifouling paint. Today its $93 million annual budget helps to operate many laboratories with state-of-the-art equipment. A graduate program is offered jointly with the Massachusetts Institute of Technology. WHOI's research vessels roam the world's waters; its staff led the successful U.S.–French search for the *Titanic* (found about 400 mi off Newfoundland) in 1985.

The Woods Hole Oceanographic Institution is open to the public only on guided tours, but you can learn about it at the small **WHOI Exhibit Center,** with videos and exhibits on the institution and its various projects, including its research vessels. **One-hour walking tours** (☎508/289–2252) of the institution and its piers are offered in July and August, weekdays at 10:30 and 1:30; tours begin at the WHOI Information Office at 93 Water Street and are free, but reservations are required. ✉*15 School St.* ☎*508/289–2252* ⊕*www.whoi.edu* 💲*$2 suggested donation* ☾*Call for hrs.*

**THINK TANK**

Woods Hole's incredible concentration of scientific minds is due in part to the variety and abundance of marine life in the area's unpolluted waters and the village's natural deepwater port. Researchers here can easily exchange ideas and information and attend stimulating daily lectures and discussions (many open to the public) given by important scientists. The pooling of resources among the various institutions makes for economies of scale that benefit each while allowing all access to highly sophisticated equipment.

☾ **Fodor's**Choice ★ The compact **National Marine Fisheries Service Aquarium** displays 16 tanks of regional fish and shellfish in several rooms, cramped but nonetheless crammed with stuff to see. Magnifying glasses, a dissecting scope, and mini-squeegees hanging from the frosty tanks (a favorite tool for kids passing through) help you examine marine life. Several hands-on pools hold banded lobsters, crabs, snails, starfish, and other creatures. The top attraction is two harbor seals, on view in the outdoor pool near the entrance in summer; you can watch their feedings weekdays at 11 and 4. ■**TIP**➜**The aquarium's status as a federal facility mandates a check of your driver's license or other valid ID at the door, so come prepared with credentials and expect to wait in line for a few minutes, particularly on rainy days.** ✉*Albatross and Water Sts.* ☎*508/495–2267, 508/495–2001 recorded information* ⊕*www.nefsc.nmfs.gov/nefsc/aquarium* 💲*Free* ☾*June–Aug., Tues.–Sat. 11–4; call for hrs off-season.*

■ **NEED A BREAK?**
**Pie in the Sky** (✉*10 Water St.* ☎*508/540–5475*), a small bakery with indoor and outdoor seating, sells cookies, pastries, and coffees, as well as sandwiches. The Oreo-cookie bars are truly decadent. It's a short walk from the ferry terminal, and a good bet for breakfast.

The **Woods Hole Historical Museum** (formerly known as the Bradley House Museum) is a three-building complex that houses paintings, a restored Woods Hole Spritsail boat, boat models, and a model of the town as it looked in the 1890s. One room is filled with elegant ladies' clothing from the late 1800s. The archives hold old ships' logs, postcards, newspaper articles, maps, diaries, and photographs; more than 200 tapes of oral history provided by local residents; and a 100-volume library on maritime history. Free guided walking tours of the village depart from the museum, which is across from the Martha's Vineyard ferry parking lot, Tuesday at 4 in July and August. ✉*573 Woods Hole Rd.* ☎*508/548–7270* ⊕*www.woodsholemuseum.org* 💲*Free* ☾*Museum* *mid-June–mid-Oct., Tues.–Sat. 10–4; archives year-round, Tues. and Thurs. 10–2.*

The 1888 **Episcopal Church of the Messiah,** a stone church with a coni-cal steeple and a small medicinal-herb garden in the shape of a Celtic cross, is a good place for quiet reflection. The garden, enclosed by a holly hedge, has a bench for meditation. Inscriptions on either side of the carved gate read ENTER IN HOPE and DEPART IN PEACE. ⊠*22 Church St.* ☎*508/548–2145* 🖃*Free* ⊙*Daily sunrise–sunset.*

Impressive **Nobska Light** (⊠*Church St.* ⊕*www.lighthouse.cc/nobska*) has spectacular views from its base of the nearby Elizabeth Islands and of Martha's Vineyard, across Vineyard Sound. The 42-foot cast-iron tower, lined with brick, was built in 1876 with a stationary light. It shines red to indicate dangerous waters or white for safe passage. Since the light was automated in 1985, the adjacent keeper's quarters have been the headquarters of the Coast Guard group commander—a fitting passing of the torch from one safeguarder of ships to another. The lighthouse is open to the public only sporadically for tours; check with the Falmouth Chamber of Commerce for details.

The bucolic villages to the east (well, bucolic once you leave Route 28 and its strip malls) have much to offer nature lovers. **East Falmouth** and **Waquoit** sit on narrow fingers of land that poke out toward Nantucket Sound, so water is never far away here and comes in the form of quiet inlets and marshy bays rather than the crashing surf of the open ocean. Residential neighborhoods, with both seasonal and year-round homes, often end in dirt lanes that lead to the water. Menauhant Beach, the nicest beach in these towns, sits on a thin sliver of land with the sound on one side and a grass-lined cove on the other. Inland, the land is more rural, with a number of farms (and farm stands) still operating.

Overseen by the Massachusetts Audubon Society, **Ashumet Holly and Wildlife Sanctuary** is true to its name and its original plantsman, Wilfred Wheeler, with its 1,000-plus holly trees and shrubs composed of 65 American, Asian, and European varieties. Like Heritage Museums and Gardens in Sandwich, this 45-acre tract of woodland, shady groves, meadows, and hiking trails was purchased and donated by Josiah K. Lilly III to preserve local land. Grassy Pond is home to numerous turtles and frogs, and in summer 35 nesting pairs of barn swallows live in the open rafters of the barn. Maps for self-guided tours cost $1. Tours to nearby Cuttyhunk Island (on a 50-foot sailing vessel) leave Woods Hole every Sunday from mid-July to early October; trips run from 9 to 5 and cost $50. ⊠*286 Ashumet Rd., East Falmouth* ☎*508/362–1426* ⊕*www.massaudubon.org* 🖃*$3* ⊙*Trails daily sunrise–sunset.*

☙ **Waquoit Bay National Estuarine Research Reserve** encompasses 2,500 acres of estuary and barrier beach around the bay, making it a good birding site. **South Cape Beach** is part of the reserve; you can lie out on the sand or join one of the interpretive walks. **Flat Pond Trail** runs through sev-eral different habitats, including fresh- and saltwater marshes. **Washburn Island** (☎*877/422–6762 camping permit*) is accessible by boat (your own) or by Saturday-morning tours (call to reserve). It offers 330 acres

**2**

of pine barrens and trails, swimming, and 11 wilderness campsites (a permit is required). At the **reserve headquarters,** a 23-acre estate, an exhibit center includes displays about the bay's plants and animals, the Cape Cod watershed, and local Wampanoag culture. An interactive exhibit, outside on the lawn, allows you to trace the path of a raindrop; pick up a ball (the pseudo-raindrop) and follow its journey from cloud to land to river and on through the water cycle. In July and August the center has nature programs for children and families, as well as a Saturday-afternoon open house from 2 to 4 PM with family programs and a Tuesday-evening lecture-performance series (you can bring a picnic). ✉ *149 Rte. 28, 3 mi west of Mashpee rotary, Waquoit* ☎ *508/457–0495* ⊕ *www.waquoitbayreserve.org* ⊗ *Exhibit center late June–early Sept., Mon.–Sat. 10–4; late May–late June, weekdays 10–4.*

**Tony Andrews Farm and Produce Stand** has pick-your-own strawberries (June), peas and beans (June and July), herbs (July and August), and tomatoes (August), as well as other produce on the stand. The farm schedules hayrides in fall, and a haunted house is set up in October. You can pick your own pumpkins in fall and choose your Christmas tree in December. ✉ *394 Old Meeting House Rd., East Falmouth* ☎ *508/548–4717* ⊕ *www.tonyandrewsfarmstand.com* ⊗ *June–Oct.; call for hrs and for information about special events.*

☾ ★ **Coonamessett Farm** operates a farm store where you can assemble your own gift baskets or purchase produce and specialty foods, as well as a small café serving breakfast, soups, sandwiches, salads, baked goods, and beverages. Members of the farm's Pick-Your-Own club ($15-per-year membership; non-Cape residents can buy a one-day membership for $5) can pick strawberries, lettuces, herbs, rhubarb, and other fruits and vegetables. Members can also tour the greenhouses and fields, learn about hydroponic-growing systems, and visit the animals (call ahead to arrange tours). The farm also rents canoes for use on the adjacent Coonamessett Pond. On Friday nights in summer, don't miss the wonderful organic vegetarian-buffet dinners with live music. ✉ *277 Hatchville Rd., East Falmouth* ☎ *508/563–2560* ⊕ *www.coonamessettfarm.com* ⊗ *Call for seasonal hrs.*

Rows and rows of grapevines—8,000 in all—line the fields of Kristina and Antonio Lazzari's **Cape Cod Winery.** It now produces seven wines; the Nobska red won a bronze medal at the International Eastern Wine Competition. ✉ *681 Sandwich Rd., East Falmouth* ☎ *508/457–5592* ⊕ *www.capecodwinery.com* ⊗ *July and Aug., tastings Thurs.–Sun. 11–4; late May, June, and Sept.–late Dec., tastings weekends 11–4.*

## WHERE TO EAT

¢–$   ✕**Betsy's Diner.** A classic American treasure, Betsy's is a shiny, happy,
AMERICAN   busy place with a reassuring pink-neon sign urging you to EAT HEAVY. The generous dining room, gleaming counter, and stools and booths by the big windows are done in pretty pastel mauve-and-cream tones. Memorabilia and neon grace the walls. Pancakes, waffles, and omelets are served all day, and typical dinner options include meat loaf and mashed potatoes, knockwurst and sauerkraut, and charbroiled pork

chops. ⊠*457 Main St. (Rte. 28), Falmouth Center, Falmouth* ☎*508/540–0060* ⚑*Reservations not accepted* ▤*AE, D, MC, V* ⊘*No dinner Sun.*

**$$–$$$**
**AMERICAN**

✕**Captain Kidd Restaurant & Bar.** The stately bar, festive atmosphere, and a small number of cozy tables that cluster around a woodstove and overlook Eel Pond make this a year-round favorite for locals. Baked halibut, pan-seared scallops, lemon-herb roasted chicken, lamb medallions, and fried calamari are

a few of the favorites, served in a publike atmosphere. In the bar area, a lighter and less expensive menu is offered, including pizzas, steaks, pastas, fish-and-chips, and fried seafood platters. ⊠*77 Water St., Woods Hole* ☎*508/548–8563* ⊕*www.thecaptainkidd.com* ▤*AE, MC, V.*

**$–$$$**
**★**
**AMERICAN**

✕**Chapoquoit Grill.** Comfortable and bustling, this unassuming local favorite has an Italian slant, starting with creative pastas and wood-fired pizzas. The long list of daily specials might include wood-grilled duck with orange-molasses glaze or sirloin with a tamarind-mango glaze. A fireplace and coral-color walls make the front room intimate, and the larger rear dining room seems vaguely tropical (with a palm tree in the middle). Half portions of many entrées are available for those with smaller appetites. Expect daunting waits for a table on summer weekends; come early or late. ⊠*410 W. Falmouth Hwy. (Rte. 28A), West Falmouth* ☎*508/540–7794* ⚑*Reservations not accepted* ▤*MC, V* ⊘*No lunch.*

**¢–$**
**AMERICAN**

✕**The Clam Shack.** Fried clams top the menu at this basic seafood joint right on Falmouth Harbor. The clams are crisp and fresh; the meaty lobster roll and the fish-and-chips platter are good choices, too. Place your order at the counter and then take your tray to the picnic tables on the roof deck for the best views. More tables are on the dock in back, or you can squeeze into the tiny dining room. Just don't plan on a late night here—the Shack closes most evenings around 8. ⊠*227 Clinton Ave., Falmouth Harbor, Falmouth* ☎*508/540–7758* ▤*No credit cards* ⊘*Closed early Sept.–late May.*

**$–$$$**
**AMERICAN**

✕**Firefly Woodfire Grill and Bar.** Both the menu and the interior change seasonally here, but you can watch your food being prepared in the open kitchen year-round. Much of the food is cooked with the heat of a wood-flame fire, either in the beach-stone oven or on the grill for which the restaurant is named. Try one of the pizzas, or any grilled meat or seafood dish, such as cedar-plank maple-glazed salmon with sweet-potato hash and panfried mushrooms. There's also a full bar with an extensive wine list and beer selection, in addition to colorful cocktails. Pop and folk bands perform here regularly. Lunch is served from late June through August. ⊠*271 Main St. (Rte. 28), Falmouth* ☎*508/548–7953* ⊕*www.fireflywoodfiregrill.com* ▤*AE, D, MC, V.*

**$$–$$$**
**Fodor'sChoice**
**★**
**ITALIAN**

✕**La Cucina Sul Mare.** Northern Italian and Mediterranean cooking is the specialty at this classy, popular place. The staff is friendly and the setting is both intimate and festive, if a bit crowded. Calamari, warm green salad with goat cheese and cranberries, a classic lemon chicken sautéed with shallots and capers, and a variety of specials—including plenty of local fresh fish—adorn the menu. The *zuppa de pesce*, a medley of seafood sautéed in olive oil and garlic and finished in a white wine herb-and-tomato broth, is a specialty. Make sure to come hungry—the portions here are huge—and expect a long wait during prime hours in season (there is also a call-ahead wait list). ✉ *237 Main St. (Rte. 28), Falmouth* ☎ *508/548–5600* ⚓ *Reservations not accepted* ▱ *AE, D, MC, V.*

**$$–$$$$**
**SEAFOOD**

✕**Landfall.** Request a window table overlooking the water at this classic Cape seafood spot, where lobster pots, buoys, and other nautical paraphernalia hang from the ceilings. Lobster, fried clams, and baked scrod lead off the menu of traditional seafood fare. Though the kids will need their restaurant manners, it's still family friendly, and the children's all-you-can-eat specials are a great value. ✉ *2 Luscombe Ave., Woods Hole* ☎ *508/548–1758* ⊕ *www.woodshole.com/landfall* ▱ *AE, MC, V* ✪ *Closed Dec.–Mar.*

**¢–$**
**PORTUGUESE**

✕**Maryellen's Portuguese Bakery.** It's easy to drive right past this no-frills spot hidden behind a Dairy Queen. Take a seat at the counter or at one of the few tables, and then order up breakfast with a Portuguese twist. Try the savory Portuguese omelet, filled with spicy *linguica* (sausage), parsley, onions, and cheese, or the French toast made with Portuguese bread. The lunch menu starts with BLTs and burgers but quickly moves on to kale soup and *cacoilha* (marinated pork). ✉ *829 Main St. (Rte. 28), near Falmouth Heights Rd., Falmouth* ☎ *508/540–9696* ▱ *No credit cards* ✪ *No dinner.*

**¢–$**
**AMERICAN**

✕**Moonakis Café.** Breakfast gets high marks at this humble roadside diner. You'll find all the standards and then some—eggs, pancakes, fruit salad—all nicely done. The chunky hash browns are fried with just the right amount of onions, and if the omelet with roasted tomatoes, olives, and goat cheese is on the menu, it's an excellent choice. Also recommended (if you're not on a diet) are the decadent Belgian waffles buried under strawberries, bananas, and whipped cream. Specials are always offered and change frequently. ✉ *460 Waquoit Hwy. (Rte. 28), Waquoit* ☎ *508/457–9630* ▱ *No credit cards* ✪ *No dinner. No lunch Sunday.*

**$–$$$**
**AMERICAN**

✕**Quarterdeck Restaurant.** Part bar, part restaurant—but all Cape Cod—this spot is across the street from Falmouth's town hall, so the lunch talk tends to focus on local politics. The stained glass is not authentic, but the huge whaling harpoons certainly are. Low ceilings and rough-hewn beams seem a good match for the menu, which includes hearty sandwiches such as Reubens and grilled chorizo at lunch and specials at night. The swordfish kebab, skewered with mushrooms, onions, and green peppers and served over jasmine rice, is especially good. ✉ *164 Main St. (Rte. 28), Falmouth Center, Falmouth* ☎ *508/548–9900* ▱ *AE, D, DC, MC, V.*

$$–$$$$
★
ECLECTIC

X**The RoöBar.** Sibling to the Chatham and Plymouth restaurants of the same name, the RoöBar brings a distinctly urban hipness to Falmouth. The bar is a popular watering hole, and the menu—scallop and smoked-bacon chowder, Asian duck confit pizza, Gorgonzola-crusted filet mignon—draws its inspiration from many cultures. There's also a terrific wine list. ⊠*285 Main St. (Rte. 28), Falmouth Center, Falmouth* ☎*508/548–8600* ⊕*www.theroobar.com* ▤*AE, MC, V* ⊘*No lunch.*

$–$$$
SEAFOOD

X**Shuckers World Famous Raw Bar and Cafe.** Some of the harborside tables at this casual nautical-theme restaurant are so close to the dock that you almost feel as if you're sitting in the bobbing sailboats. The menu ranges from jerk chicken to pasta primavera to lobster ravioli, but it's best to stick with the grilled fish and other simple seafood dishes. The "world-famous" lobster boil—a boiled lobster, steamed clams and mussels, and an ear of corn—is justifiably popular. ⊠*91A Water St., Woods Hole* ☎*508/540–3850* ⊕*www.woodshole.com/shuckers* ▤*AE, D, MC, V* ⊘*Closed Nov.–Apr., and Mon.–Thurs. mid-May– late May and early Sept.–mid-Oct.*

## WHERE TO STAY

$–$$$

▥**Admiralty Inn.** This large roadside motel outside Falmouth Center has several types of rooms and suites, and its child-friendly facilities make it a good bet for families. Standard rooms have two queen-size beds or one queen-size and one Murphy bed. King Jacuzzi rooms have king-size beds and whirlpool tubs in the bedroom. Town-house suites have cathedral ceilings with skylights, two baths (one with whirlpool), a loft with a king-size bed, a living room with a sofa bed, and a queen- or king-size bed. **Pros:** good spot for exploring the Falmouth area and not far from island ferry terminals; good for those traveling with kids. **Cons:** some rooms remain a bit stale and outdated, but the inn is constantly refurbishing. ⊠*51 Teaticket Hwy. (Rte. 28), East Falmouth* ☎*508/548–4240 or 800/341–5700* ☖*508/457–0535* ⊕*www.theadmiraltyinn.com* ⇗*70 rooms, 28 suites* ♿*In-room: microwave (some), refrigerator, VCR (some), Wi-Fi. In-hotel: pools* ▤*AE, D, DC, MC, V* ⊙*CP.*

$$–$$$

▥**Beach Rose Inn.** This rambling 1863 farmhouse sits on more than an acre of peaceful landscape, slightly off the beaten trail but within close distance of local amenities. The outdoor fire pit is a great place to spend cooler evenings, or you can relax in the hot tub. The rooms—some in the main inn, some in the adjacent carriage house—are furnished with quilts, Cape Cod art, and a mix of antiques and reproductions. The Falmouth Suite has an airy, private sunporch. All rooms have private baths, some with whirlpool tubs. A separate, tiny two-bedroom cottage rents by the day and by the week. Ask about planned special events that might include wine tastings, author talks, and artist workshops. **Pros:** idyllic, retreatlike setting; perfect for those who want some quiet indulgence. **Cons:** not an in-town location; must drive to beaches, restaurants, and other attractions. ⊠*17 Chase Rd., off Rte. 28A, West Falmouth* ☎*508/540–5706 or 800/498–5706* ☖*508/540–4880* ⊕*www. thebeachroseinn.com* ⇗*7 rooms, 1 suite, 1 cottage* ♿*In-room: no phone, kitchen (some), refrigerator (some), no TV (some), Wi-Fi. In-*

*hotel: some pets allowed, no kids under 12, no-smoking rooms, no elevator ☰MC, V ⧉BP.*

$$-$$$  ⬚**Cape Wind.** If you're traveling with children who need space to run, this gray-shingle motel on 5 acres is a dependable though modest option. The rooms face a broad green lawn that slopes down to the bay; it's a great place to launch your canoe or kayak, or head out in one of the motel's paddleboats (no charge). The rooms are decidedly basic, with standard motel furnishings that are being continually updated and refreshed. All have refrigerators and coffeemakers, and some have microwaves; others have kitchenettes. The spacious one-bedroom apartment has a private terrace, but its half-basement location makes the interior rather dark. The motel is in a quiet residential neighborhood. **Pros:** beautiful grounds with water views; access to water; babysitting services available; good bet for families. **Cons:** lots of families often means not so quiet. ⊠*34 Maravista Ext., Teaticket, East Falmouth* ☎*508/548–3400 or 800/267–3401* 🖷*508/495–0316* ⊕*www.capewind.com* ⬲*31 rooms, 1 apartment* ⬚*In-room: kitchen (some), refrigerator, Wi-Fi. In-hotel: pool, water sports, some pets allowed, no-smoking rooms, no elevator* ☰*D, MC, V.*

$$  ⬚**Capt. Tom Lawrence House.** A lawn shaded by old maple trees surrounds this pretty white house, which is steps from downtown yet set back from the street enough to feel secluded. Built in 1861 for a whaling captain, the intimate B&B has romantic rooms with antique and painted furniture, Laura Ashley or Ralph Lauren linens, French country wallpaper, and thick carpeting. An efficiency apartment is bright, spacious, and suitable for families, with a fully equipped eat-in kitchen. Breakfast and afternoon snacks are served near the fireplace in the common room. The owners are extremely friendly and helpful. **Pros:** easy walk to Village Green and town center; authentic historic lodging; great breakfasts. **Cons:** rooms accessed via steep, curving staircase; some rooms may feel a little tight. ⊠*75 Locust St., Falmouth* ☎*508/548–9178* 🖷*508/457–1790* ⊕*www.captaintomlawrence.com* ⬲*6 rooms, 1 efficiency* ⬚*In-room: no phone, refrigerator, Wi-Fi. In-hotel: bicycles, no kids under 7 (except in efficiency), no-smoking rooms, no elevator* ☰*AE, MC, V* ⧉*BP* ⊘*Closed Jan.*

$$$–$$$$  ⬚**Chapoquoit Inn.** Four-poster beds, elegant bedcoverings, and garden ★  views fill the rooms at this cozy B&B in a 1739 former Quaker homestead surrounded by woodland and flower beds. Owners Kim and Tim McIntyre (she's a former marketing exec, he's a landscape designer) have furnished their inn with antiques and other family heirlooms. In the sunny breakfast room, which opens to the deck, you might find lemon pancakes or crème brûlée French toast. The sands of Chapoquoit Beach are a short 10-minute walk away. **Pros:** walk to beach (beach chairs and towels available); nearby public tennis courts (innkeepers will provide tennis rackets); intimate and elegant lodging in historic property. **Cons:** not an in-town location, but several amenities nearby. ⊠*495 W. Falmouth Hwy. (Rte. 28A), West Falmouth* ☎*508/540–7232 or 800/842–8994* ⊕*www.chapoquoit.com* ⬲*7 rooms* ⬚*In-room: no phone, VCR (some), no TV (some). In-hotel: bicycles, Wi-Fi, no kids under 12, no-smoking rooms, no elevator* ☰*AE, MC, V* ⧉*BP.*

**$$–$$$$**    ⚆**Coonamessett Inn.** At this delightful old-Cape-style inn-restaurant that's a famous setting for weddings and special occasions, five buildings of one- and two-bedroom suites ring a landscaped lawn that leads to a scenic wooded pond. Rooms are casually decorated, with bleached wood or pine paneling and New England antiques or reproductions. A large collection of Cape artist Ralph Cahoon's work appears throughout the inn. In the main dining room ($$–$$$$)a few contemporary flourishes enhance the traditional menu; you can still find rack of lamb and baked-stuffed lobster, but you might also see cumin-scented scallops with Israeli couscous. Lighter but still excellent food is served in the cozy Eli's Lounge ($). Pros: lush, gardened grounds in historic setting; high marks in romantic-dining setting. Cons: weddings are a constant here—not the place to be if you want to avoid that scene. ✉*311 Gifford St., at Jones Rd., Falmouth* ☎*508/548–2300* 🖷*508/540–9831* ⊕*www.capecodrestaurants.org/coonamessett* ⬐*28 suites, 1 cottage* ♿*In-hotel: restaurant, bar, no-smoking rooms, no elevator* ▤*AE, D, MC, V* ⫯⃝❙*CP.*

**$$–$$$$**    ⚆**Green Harbor Waterfront Lodging.** Although the modest rooms here are clean and adequate, it's the friendly summer camp–like feel that makes this attractive compound great for families. There are old-fashioned lawn swings, a swimming pool, umbrella-topped picnic tables, and barbecue grills, but the main attraction is the waterfront. It's not open ocean here but a peaceful tree-lined inlet, with rowboats and paddleboats for guests' use. (If you've got your own boat, you can launch it here and keep it at the dock.) Some of the no-frills rooms in the 1960s-vintage motel have microwaves and small refrigerators; others have kitchenettes. A spacious three-bedroom cottage has three full baths, an eat-in kitchen, and a living room with a fireplace and two sofa beds. It's down a quiet lane off Route 28. Pros: great for active families; right on the water; a good spot to launch a kayak. Cons: noise and activity levels can be a bit much for those seeking quiet retreat (without kids); rooms could use some updating but are perfectly adequate. ✉*134 Acapesket Rd., East Falmouth* ☎*508/548–4747 or 800/548–5556* 🖷*508/540–1652* ⊕*www.gogreenharbor.com* ⬐*34 rooms, 1 cottage* ♿*In-room: kitchen (some), refrigerator, Wi-Fi. In-hotel: pools, beachfront, water sports, laundry facilities, no-smoking rooms, some pets allowed (fee), no elevator* ▤*AE, D, DC, MC, V* ⊘*Closed Nov.–Apr.*

**$$–$$$$**    ⚆**Holiday Inn.** This chain hotel is a dependable option for families. A tried-and-true comfort formula has been applied here: large rooms with contemporary furnishings, suites with king-size beds, and a large pool area surrounded by patio furniture and greenery. The Kansas City Steakhouse ($$–$$$$) restaurant serves breakfast and dinner year-round. You'll find Cape Cod specialties as well as huge quantities of beef—it's an unexpectedly good restaurant despite its setting inside a chain property. The hotel is adjacent to a pond and is close to Falmouth Center. Pros: big-name dependability; distractions for the kids; not far from town center. Cons: lack of regional character; not for those seeking a Cape Cod experience. ✉*291 Jones Rd., Falmouth* ☎*508/540–2000 or 800/465–4329* 🖷*508/548–2712* ⊕*www.capecodhi.com* ⬐*93 rooms, 5 suites* ♿*In-room: Wi-Fi. In-hotel: restaurant, room service, pool, gym* ▤*AE, D, DC, MC, V.*

**2**

**$$** ⊞**The Inn at Siders Lane.** Housed in a contemporary Federal reproduction building nearly indistinguishable from its authentic neighbors, this elegant B&B blends traditional New England hospitality and 19th-century style with modern amenities. Just steps from downtown's bustle, the Inn feels private and intimate on its quiet corner by the Village Green. Upstairs, the two spacious guest rooms are tastefully appointed with graceful furnishings in pale neutral tones. Each has a queen bed, private bath, and cable TV; the house also has central air-conditioning. Hosts Jim and Maureen Trodden serve a superb hot breakfast, and you can join them again in the afternoon for tea and fresh-baked cookies. **Pros:** easy walk to town activities; intimate setting with few other guests; privacy. **Cons:** rooms are accessible only by stairs; not for those who prefer having many other guests to chat with. ⊠*51 W. Main St., Falmouth* ☎*508/495–4359* ⊕*www.innatsiderslane.com* ➫*3 rooms* ⟳*In-hotel: no children under 10, no-smoking rooms, no elevator* ⊟*MC, V* ⦿*BP.*

**$$$–$$$$** ⊞**Inn on the Sound.** At this understated but stylish inn, perched on
★ a bluff overlooking Vineyard Sound, the living room and most of the guest rooms face the water. Most have queen-size beds, and all contain unfussy, contemporary furnishings such as natural oak tables, unbleached cottons, ample shelf space, and ceiling fans; four have private decks. Common areas include an art-laden living room with a boulder fireplace, oversize windows, and modern white couches; a bistro-like breakfast room; and a porch with more stunning water views. **Pros:** grand water views and nearness to beach (towels and chairs provided); quiet, elegant setting. **Cons:** not an in-town location; must drive to area restaurants and attractions. ⊠*313 Grand Ave., Falmouth Heights* ☎*508/457–9666 or 800/564–9668* 🖷*508/457–9631* ⊕*www.innonthesound.com* ➫*10 rooms* ⟳*In-room: Wi-Fi. In-hotel: beachfront, no kids under 10, no-smoking rooms, no elevator* ⊟*MC, V* ⦿*BP.*

**$$–$$$** ⊞**Mostly Hall B&B.** With its deep, landscaped yard and wrought-iron
★ fence, this elegant inn with a wraparound porch resembles a private estate. (The house got its name when a young guest is said to have exclaimed, "Look! It's mostly hall!") The imposing 1849 Italianate house has an upscale European style with painted wall murals in several bedrooms; the Tuscany Room's walls suggest an intimate Tuscan garden. Three of the rooms are more traditionally decorated, with colonial antiques, and all have canopy beds. Some rooms have the benefit of fireplaces for cool nights. Breakfast is served in the formal parlor or outside on the veranda. Although the inn is steps from the town center, you can lounge in the gardens and feel a world away. **Pros:** walk to town center; ample, parklike grounds; grand home in the Victorian tradition. **Cons:** rooms accessed via steep stairs; bathrooms are a bit small; the bathroom for one room (discounted) is down a set of stairs. ⊠*27 Main St. (Rte. 28), Falmouth* ☎*508/548–3786* 🖷*508/548–5778* ⊕*www.mostlyhall.com* ➫*6 rooms* ⟳*In-room: DVD, Wi-Fi. In-hotel: no kids under 18, no-smoking rooms, no elevator* ⊟*AE, D, MC, V* ⦿*BP.*

$$–$$$$   ⊡ **Palmer House Inn.** This turn-of-the-20th-century Queen Anne home stands on a tree-lined street, just a short stroll from Falmouth's Village Green. The Victorian interior of Falmouth's largest B&B is pretty if slightly over the top, with heavy period furniture, endless lace, and ornate stained-glass windows—many rooms have fireplaces. One good bet is the 3rd-floor Tower Room, which has a view across the treetops. The large rooms in the 1910 carriage house are airier, with more tailored appointments, and four newer rooms, all with whirlpool baths, are less ornate. There's a two-bedroom suite in a separate cottage (where young children are permitted). A candlelight breakfast is served, and afternoon refreshments are available. **Pros:** ideal, walk-to-town location; elegant breakfast. **Cons:** with all the Victorian flourish, the smallish rooms can feel a bit overdone; most rooms (one is ADA compliant) are accessed via steep stairs (especially 3rd-floor rooms). ⊠ *81 Palmer Ave., Falmouth* ☎*508/548–1230 or 800/472–2632* 🖷*508/540–1878* ⊕*www.palmerhouseinn.com* ⏎*16 rooms, 1 cottage* ⚬*In-hotel: bicycles, no-smoking rooms, no elevator* ⊟*AE, D, MC, V* ⫮*BP.*

$$   ⊡ **Sands of Time Motor Inn and Harbor House.** Essentially two lodgings in one, this property on a hill above Woods Hole village houses both a motel and a Victorian-era inn. In the family-friendly motor inn, the furnishings are standard motel-style; the best views, looking out to the water, are from the 2nd-floor rooms, some of which have private balconies. The Harbor House is more eclectic—a canopy bed here, a clawfoot tub there; some rooms have fireplaces or private patios. If you're going to the islands for a night or two, you can keep your car parked free at the inn. **Pros:** can't beat the location for harbor views; short walk to both downtown and island ferry terminals. **Cons:** not for those looking for intimate, historic lodging. ⊠ *549 Woods Hole Rd., Woods Hole* ☎*508/548–6300 or 800/841–0114* 🖷*508/457–0160* ⊕*www. sandsoftime.com* ⏎*35 rooms* ⚬*In-room: refrigerator (some), Wi-Fi. In-hotel: pool, no-smoking rooms, no elevator* ⊟*AE, D, DC, MC, V* ☾*Closed mid-Nov.–mid–Apr.* ⫮*CP.*

$$$–$$$$   ⊡ **Sea Crest Resort.** Location and amenities are strong draws at this modern conference center and resort, whose eight buildings sprawl along one end of beautiful Old Silver Beach—guests enjoy some 700 feet of frontage right along the sand. Rooms, done in dark blues and pastels, are crisp and clean; many have ocean views, and some have gas-log fireplaces. A number of lodging packages are available. The poolside deli, Oscars, is a good bet for a quick burger or sandwich if you don't want to stray far from the beach; it's easily accessible to nonguests. The resort gets high marks for its kids' day camp. **Pros:** a kids' paradise, with pools, beach, and plenty of activities; a popular spot for business conventions; exceptional beachfront location; nightly entertainment in summer. **Cons:** a kids' paradise often translates to less-than-quiet surroundings; not for those seeking an intimate, uncrowded lodging spot. ⊠ *350 Quaker Rd., North Falmouth* ☎*508/540–9400 or 800/225–3110* 🖷*508/548–0556* ⊕*www.seacrest-resort.com* ⏎*258 rooms, 8 suites* ⚬*In-room: refrigerator, Wi-Fi. In-hotel: 2 restaurants, room service, bar, tennis courts, beachfront, water sports, pools, gym, children's programs (ages 3–12; summer only)* ⊟*AE, D, DC, MC, V.*

$$ ★ **Woods Hole Passage.** A century-old carriage house and barn have been converted into a romantic showcase. The large rose-hue common room radiates comfort with its lace curtains and overstuffed furniture. One guest room (the smallest) is in the main house; the others are in the restored barn, where the upstairs rooms have soaring ceilings. Gregarious and helpful owner Deb Pruitt sells Martha's Vineyard ferry tickets at cost so you can avoid lines at the dock. You can enjoy a delicious breakfast on the patio in the lovely yard; early risers can request "breakfast-in-a-bag" to take on the road. Kids are accepted, by prior arrangement. A member of the Green Hotel Association, the inn encourages guests to leave their cars in the lot as much as possible: the town trolley runs right by the inn, heading to Falmouth center or Woods Hole ($2). **Pros:** beautiful gardens; artful lodging in historic structure; extremely helpful innkeeper. **Cons:** not an in-town location; must drive to restaurants, attractions; rooms accessed via steep stairs.  ⊠ *186 Woods Hole Rd., Woods Hole* ☎ *508/548–9575 or 800/790–8976* 🖷 *508/540–4771* ⊕ *www.woodsholepassage.com* ⏎ *5 rooms* ⚷ *In-room: no phone, no TV, Wi-Fi. In-hotel: bicycles, no-smoking rooms, no elevator* ⊟ *AE, D, MC, V* ⫝̸⊙⫝̸*BP.*

## NIGHTLIFE & THE ARTS

THE ARTS  The **College Light Opera Company** ( ⊠ *Highfield Theatre, off Depot Ave., Falmouth* ☎ *508/548–0668* ⊕ *www.collegelightopera.com*) presents nine musicals or operettas for one week each, the results of a summer program involving music and theater majors from colleges around the country. The company consists of more than 30 singers and an 18-piece orchestra. Be forewarned: the quality can vary from show to show.

The **Cape Cod Theatre Project** ( ☎ *508/457–4242* ⊕ *www.capecodtheatreproject.org*) helps develop new American plays through a series of staged readings. Each July the project presents three or four readings, which are followed by audience discussion with the playwright. Productions have included works by Gloucester Stage Company director Israel Horovitz and by Pulitzer Prize winners Lanford Wilson and Paula Vogel. (Readings are not recommended for those under 16 years of age.) Performances take place at **Falmouth Academy** ( ⊠ *7 Highfield Dr., off Depot Ave., Falmouth*)

Performing at the same venue as the College Light Opera Company, the **Falmouth Theatre Guild** ( ⊠ *Highfield Theatre, off Depot Ave.* ☎ *508/548–0400* ⊕ *www.falmouththeatreguild.org*) is a first-rate community theater that presents four plays—a mix of musicals and dramas—from fall through spring.

Falmouth's summer **town-band concerts** ( ⊠ *Scranton Ave.* ☎ *508/548–8500 or 800/526–8532*) are held in Marina Park on Thursday evening starting at 7.

The **Woods Hole Folk Music Society** ( ⊠ *Community Hall, 68 Water St.* ☎ *508/540–0320* ⊕ *www.arts-cape.com/whfolkmusic*) presents professional and local folk and blues in a smoke- and alcohol-free environment, with refreshments available during intermission. Concerts by nationally known performers take place the first and third Sunday of the month from October to May.

**Woods Hole Theater Company** ( ✉ *Community Hall, 68 Water St.* ☎ *508/540–6525* ⊕ *www.woodsholetheater.org*), the community's resident theater group since 1974, presents several productions each year, generally between late spring and early fall.

NIGHTLIFE **Liam Maguire's** ( ✉ *281 Rte. 28, Falmouth Center* ☎ *508/548–0285*) is a festive, authentic Irish pub with nightly Irish and other acoustic music and dependable pub fare.

**Nimrod Inn** ( ✉ *100 Dillingham Ave., Falmouth Center* ☎ *508/540–4132*) presents jazz and contemporary music at least six nights a week year-round. The Nimrod is also a great spot for late-night dining.

**Sea Crest Resort** ( ✉ *350 Quaker Rd., North Falmouth* ☎ *508/540–9400*) has a summer and holiday-weekend schedule of nightly entertainment on the outdoor terrace, including dancing to country, Top 40, reggae, and jazz bands and a big-band DJ.

## SPORTS & THE OUTDOORS

BASEBALL The **Falmouth Commodores** ( ✉ *790 Rte. 28, Falmouth* ☎ *508/432–6909* ⊕ *www.falcommodores.org*) of the collegiate Cape Cod Baseball League play their home games at Guv Fuller Field from mid-June to mid-August. Players and coaches lead youth baseball clinics in June and July.

BEACHES Many town beaches require a parking sticker, or are pay-as-you-go. Weekly nonresident stickers cost $60; two weeks cost $70, three weeks cost $80, and four weeks cost $90. If you're staying at a local lodging establishment, there is the discounted rate of $10 per day. Stickers can be obtained at the Falmouth Town Hall *59 Town Hall Square, 508/548–7611*

**Chapoquoit Beach** ( ✉ *Chapoquoit Rd., West Falmouth*), a narrow stretch of white sand, lines a peninsula that juts dramatically into the bay. Resident parking stickers are required at the beach lot in season, but the surrounding roads are popular with bicyclists. The beach has lifeguards and portable toilets.

**Falmouth Heights Beach** on Grand Avenue is an often-crowded arc of sand on Nantucket Sound, backed by a row of inns and B&Bs. The beach has lifeguards (in summer) and portable toilets. There's a small strip of metered parking on Grand Avenue between Walden Avenue and Crescent Park Avenue.

**Grews Pond** in Goodwill Park, a pretty tree-lined freshwater pond with a sandy beach and swimming area with lifeguard, is popular with local families. You'll find several sites for picnicking, along with restrooms and a volleyball net; there's also a playground nearby. You can enter the park from Route 28 just north of Jones Road or from Gifford Street opposite St. Joseph's Cemetery. Parking is free.

**Megansett Beach** (⊠ *County Rd., North Falmouth*), hidden in a residential neighborhood, is a small, family-friendly location. Weathered gray-shingle homes line the cove, and boats moored at the adjacent yacht club bob in the bay. The beach has lifeguards and a portable toilet but no other services. Resident parking stickers are required at the beach lot in season.

**Menauhant Beach,** on Menauhant Road in East Falmouth, is a long, narrow stretch of sand with a pond in a quiet residential neighborhood. Its slightly more secluded location means it can be a bit less crowded than the beaches near Falmouth Center. The beach has lifeguards, restrooms, outdoor showers, and a small snack bar. Public parking is available; in season the fee is $10.

★ **Old Silver Beach** (⊠ *Off Quaker Rd., North Falmouth*) is a long, beautiful crescent of soft white sand bordered by the Sea Crest Resort at one end. It's especially good for small children because a sandbar keeps it shallow at the southern end and creates tidal pools full of crabs and minnows. The beach has lifeguards, restrooms, showers, and a snack bar. There's a $20 fee for parking in summer.

**Surf Drive Beach,** a family-friendly sandy cove on Surf Drive, faces Nantucket Sound with views out toward the Vineyard. The beach has restrooms and showers as well as lifeguards. Public parking is available; in summer the daily parking fee is $10.

**Wood Neck Beach** (⊠ *Wood Neck Rd., West Falmouth*), in the Sippewisset area, is a sandy bay-side beach backed by grass-covered dunes. At high tide the beach is very narrow, but sandbars and shallow tidal pools make this a good place for children when the tide is out. Resident parking stickers are required in season.

BICYCLING  The **Shining Sea Trail** is an easy 3½-mi route between Locust Street, Falmouth, and the Woods Hole ferry parking lot. It follows the coast, providing views of Vineyard Sound and dipping into oak and pine woods; a detour onto Church Street takes you to Nobska Light. A brochure is available at the trailheads. If you're going to Martha's Vineyard with your bike, you can park your car in one of Falmouth's Steamship Authority lots and ride the Shining Sea Trail to the ferry. (The free shuttle buses between the Falmouth lots and the Woods Hole ferry docks also have bike carriers.) There are plans to eventually extend the trail another 8 mi or so up through West Falmouth.

**Corner Cycle** (⊠ *115 Palmer Ave., Falmouth* ☎ *508/540–4195*) rents bikes (including tandems and children's bikes) by the hour, day, or week. It also rents Burley trailers for carrying small children and does on-site repairs. The shop is two blocks from the Shining Sea Trail. **Holiday Cycles** (⊠ *465 Grand Ave., Falmouth Heights* ☎ *508/540–3549*) has surrey, tandem, and other unusual bikes.

FISHING  Freshwater ponds are good for perch, pickerel, trout, and more; you can obtain the required license (along with rental gear) at tackle shops, such as **Eastman's Sport & Tackle** (⊠ *150 Rte. 28, Falmouth* ☎ *508/548–6900* ⊕ *www.eastmanstackle.com*).

**Patriot Party Boats** ( ✉*227 Clinton Ave., Falmouth Harbor* ☎*508/548–2626 or 800/734–0088* ⊕*www.patriotpartyboats.com*) has deep-sea fishing from party or charter boats. Advance bookings are recommended, particularly for weekend trips.

HORSEBACK RIDING  **Haland Stables** ( ✉*878 Rte. 28A, West Falmouth* ☎*508/540–2552*) offers lessons and trail rides by reservation Monday through Saturday.

ICE SKATING  Skaters take to the ice at the **Falmouth Ice Arena** ( ✉*9 Skating La., off Palmer Ave.* ☎*508/548–7080* ⊕*www.falmouthicearena.com*) fall through spring. You can rent skates from the pro shop.

RUNNING  To run in the world-class **SBLI Falmouth Road Race** ( ✉*Box 732, Falmouth 02541* ☎*508/540–7000* ⊕*www.falmouthroadrace.com*) in mid-August, send a self-addressed, stamped envelope to request an entry form. The race typically closes to entrants in early spring. A crowd of 75,000-plus spectators lines the streets of the 7-mi course, which covers a combination of winding and hilly terrain, flat stretches, and stunning ocean scenery. There are 10,000 registered runners (the spring application window is quite small, and if you cannot run a mile in less than 12 minutes, you are asked not to enter), as well as about 2,000 unofficial ones, making this an immense event for such a small town.

TENNIS & RACQUETBALL  The huge **Falmouth Sports Center** ( ✉*33 Highfield Dr.* ☎*508/548–7433*) has three outdoor and six indoor tennis courts and two racquetball-handball courts, as well as steam rooms and saunas, a full health club, and physical-therapist services. Day and short-term rates are available.

## SHOPPING

★ **Bean & Cod** ( ✉*140 Rte. 28, Falmouth Center* ☎*508/548–8840 or 800/558–8840* ⊕*www.beanandcod.com*), a specialty food shop, sells cheeses, breads, and picnic fixings, along with pastas, coffees and teas, and unusual condiments. The store also packs and ships gift baskets.

**Eight Cousins Children's Books** ( ✉*189 Rte. 28, Falmouth Center* ☎*508/548–5548* ⊕*www.eightcousins.com*) is the place to find reading material for toddlers through young adults. In addition to comprehensive sections on oceans and marine life, Native American peoples, and other Cape topics, the well-stocked shop carries audiotapes, CDs, and games. Author appearances and other special events are scheduled throughout the year, especially in summer.

**Europa** ( ✉*628 Rte. 28, West Falmouth* ☎*508/540–7814*) is a small boutique in a charming old house with a great selection of jewelry, home décor, gifts, and antiques at fair prices. A second room is devoted to lamps and lamp repair.

**Handworks** ( ✉*68 Water St., Woods Hole* ☎*508/540–5291*), tucked in the back of the Community Hall building next to the drawbridge, is a cooperative arts-and-crafts gallery showcasing the work of local artists.

**Howlingbird** ( ✉*91 Palmer Ave., Falmouth Center* ☎*508/540–3787*) stocks detailed hand-silk-screened marine-theme T-shirts and sweatshirts, plus hand-painted cards and silk-screened hats and handbags. An additional retail location in Woods Hole (89 Water St.) is open from mid-April through Christmas.

**Maxwell & Co.** (⊠*200 Main St. (Rte. 28), Falmouth Center* ☎*508/540–8752*) has traditional men's and women's clothing with flair from European and American designers, handmade French shoes and boots, and leather goods and accessories.

**Rosie Cheeks** (⊠*233 Rte. 28, Falmouth Center* ☎*508/548–4572*), whose name was inspired by the owner's daughter, specializes in creative women's clothing and jewelry, with a particularly nice selection of hand-knit sweaters. They also have a branch at Mashpee Commons.

## MASHPEE

*7 mi east of East Falmouth, 10 mi south of Sandwich.*

Mashpee is one of two Massachusetts towns with both municipally governed– and Native American–governed areas (the other town is Aquinnah, formerly known as Gay Head, on Martha's Vineyard). In 1660 the Reverend Richard Bourne, a missionary, gave a 16-square-mi parcel of land to the Wampanoags (consider the irony—an outsider "giving" Native people their own land). Known as the Mashpee Plantation and governed by two local sachems, it was the first Native American reservation in the United States. In 1870 Mashpee was founded as a town. In 1974 the Mashpee Wampanoag Tribal Council was formed to continue its government with a chief, a supreme sachem, a medicine man, and clan mothers. More than 600 residents are descended from the original Wampanoags, and some continue to observe their ancient traditions. Today several residential-resort communities have developed in the Mashpee area; the largest, the Country Club of New Seabury, has one of the best golf courses on the Cape. There are no hotels or inns in Mashpee, although New Seabury does have some home and condo rentals. Mashpee, with its villagelike Mashpee Commons outdoor mall, has also become a popular shopping and dining destination. Yet away from the stores, the town retains a more rural character, with wooded roads, inland ponds, and reminders of the area's original settlers.

The **Old Indian Burial Ground,** near the meetinghouse on Meeting House Road, is an 18th-century cemetery with headstones typical of the period, intricately carved with scenes and symbols and inscribed with witty sayings.

In a cavernous former church building, the **Cape Cod Children's Museum** welcomes kids with interactive play, science exhibits, a 30-foot pirate play ship, a planetarium, and other playtime activities. The museum is best suited for preschoolers and children in the early elementary grades. ⊠*577 Great Neck Rd. S* ☎*508/539–8788* ⊕*www.capecod childrensmuseum.org* ☎*$6* ♥*Memorial Day–Labor Day, Mon.–Sat. 10–5, Sun. noon–5; Labor Day–Memorial Day, Tues.–Thurs. 10–3, Fri. and Sat. 10–5, Sun. noon–5.*

## Powwow, Wampanoag Style

Dancers and drummers re-creating ancient rhythms, and vivid deer-skin costumes decorated with colorful beads and bold plumage are a far cry from the fried clams, shingled saltboxes, and antiques shops that typify Cape Cod, yet they represent the very essence of a culture that has made this area home for thousands of years. It was the Wampanoag tribe who peacefully greeted, assisted, and befriended the Pilgrims who came ashore in 1620. And although their presence is often overlooked amid the luxury resorts and golf courses that dominate the town of Mashpee, the tribe continues to embrace and celebrate their ancestors' way of life.

The Mashpee Wampanoag Powwow, held every year since 1924, is a lively showcase of the tribe's traditions. Open to the public, the early July powwow is a large gathering of local Wampanoags and numerous tribes from throughout the Northeast; some even travel here from the western states. Tents and tables fill the tribal grounds, selling everything from Native American foods to jewelry and T-shirts. A series of intricately costumed dancing and drumming contests takes place during the three-day festival, along with one of the most dramatic events—the fireball ceremony. This ancient healing ritual involves Wampanoag males in what looks a little bit like soccer—except the ball is on fire.

The Mashpee Wampanoag tribal grounds are in Mashpee, off Great Neck Road. For more information, call the **Tribal Council** (☎ 508/477–0208).

Perfect for bird-watching, fishing, or canoeing, the **Mashpee River Woodlands** occupy 391 acres along the Mashpee River. More than 8 mi of trails meander through the marshlands and pine forests. Park on Quinaquisset Avenue, River Road, or Mashpee Neck Road (where there's a public landing for canoe access). Trail maps are available at the Mashpee Chamber of Commerce. The trails are open daily from dawn to dusk.

### WHERE TO EAT

$$–$$$$

**Fodor's Choice**

★

FRENCH

✕ **Bleu.** Chef Frederic Feufeu, a native of the Loire Valley, brings the flavors of France to this urbane restaurant in the pseudo-quaint Mashpee Commons retail and entertainment village. From bistro classics to haute cuisine and sophisticated lunch sandwiches to decadent desserts, the flavors are astounding. Seasonal specialties include roasted filet mignon with poached foie gras, fingerling potatoes, candied shallots, and bordelaise sauce. Shrimp tempura with miso mustard sauce and Asian slaw is one of the tempting lighter and less expensive dishes served in the natty bar. There's also a jazz brunch on Sunday, from Labor Day to Memorial Day. ⊠7 Market St., Mashpee Commons, Mashpee ☎508/539–7907 ⊟AE, D, MC, V.

$$–$$$$

AMERICAN

✕ **Popponesset Inn.** The surroundings, more so than the lobster rolls, burgers, grilled swordfish, steaks, and other straightforward offerings, are exceptional here. The site is a gem, with old Cape Cod saltbox houses nearby, lovely Nantucket Sound in the background, and perfect

2

light in the evening. The restaurant has a lounge called Poppy's and comprises several small dining rooms, some with skylights and others looking over the water through glass walls. Sit outside, either under the tent or at one of the umbrella tables. ⊠*95 Shore Dr., The Country Club of New Seabury, Mashpee* ☎*508/477–1100* ▭*AE, DC, MC, V* ⊗*Closed mid-Oct.–late Apr. Closed Mon.–Thurs. Sept. and Oct. No lunch.*

¢–$$    ✕**The Raw Bar.** At this funky little seafood joint you can pull up a bar
SEAFOOD    stool and chow down on giant lobster rolls, littlenecks, cherrystones, oysters, steamers, and peel-your-own shrimp, all easily washed down with a local brew or a rum punch. Despite a few picnic tables out back, the scene here is more "bar" than "seafood shack." There's live music some nights, too, at the Marketplace. ⊠*Popponesset Market Pl., Mashpee* ☎*508/539–4858* ▭*AE, MC, V* ⊗*Closed late Oct.–early Apr.*

$–$$$    ✕**Siena.** A boisterous, high-ceilinged space at Mashpee Commons, this
★    modern Italian restaurant warms the hearts of patrons with its genu-
ITALIAN    inely friendly service and well-crafted Tuscan cuisine. You might start with the exceptional buffalo mozzarella salad before moving on to a wood-grilled veal chop with marsala sauce, or linguine with sautéed littleneck clams, white wine, garlic, and parsley. Several fine brick-oven pizzas are offered, too. Grand Marnier flourless chocolate cake makes for a magnificent ending. In warm weather, you can dine on the ample patio. ⊠*11A Steeple St., Mashpee Commons, Mashpee* ☎*508/477–5929 or 877/477–5929* ▭*AE, D, MC, V.*

### NIGHTLIFE & THE ARTS

**Bobby Byrne's Pub** ( ⊠*Mashpee Commons, Rtes. 28 and 151* ☎*508/477–0600*) is a comfortable pub with an outdoor café, a jukebox, and reliable pub fare.

The 90-member **Cape Cod Symphony Orchestra** ( ☎*508/362–1111* ⊕*www.capesymphony.org*) comes to Mashpee in July for its annual Sounds of Summer Pops Concert (it also performs an August concert in Orleans). The performance takes place at the Mashpee Commons.

### SPORTS & THE OUTDOORS

BEACHES    **Attaquin Park Beach** ( ⊠*End of Lake Ave. off Rte. 130, near Great Neck Rd. N*) is a pretty, sandy place with a spectacular view of the interconnecting Mashpee and Wakeby ponds, the Cape's largest freshwater expanse. It's popular for swimming, fishing, and boating, but resident parking stickers are required in season.

**South Cape Beach** is a 2½-mi-long state and town beach on warm Nantucket and Vineyard sounds, accessible via Great Neck Road south from the Mashpee rotary. You can walk to get a bit of privacy on this beach, which is wide, sandy, and pebbly in parts, with low dunes and marshland. The only services are portable toilets, although lifeguards are on duty in season. A hiking trail loops through marsh areas and ponds, linking it to the Waquoit Bay National Estuarine Research Reserve. Resident parking stickers are required for the town-beach parking section, but anybody may park at the state-beach section for $7 per day late May through early September (it's free off-season).

GOLF    **Quashnet Valley Country Club** ( ✉ *309 Old Barnstable Rd., Mashpee* ☎ *508/477–4412*) has a beautiful course in an area of cranberry bogs, the Quashnet River, ponds, and mature trees. It's a 6,601-yard, par-72 championship layout.

HIKING &    The 4 mi of walking trails at 135-acre **Lowell Holly Reservation** ( ✉ *S.*
WALKING    *Sandwich Rd. off Rte. 130* ☎ *508/679–2115* ⊕ *www.thetrustees.org*), administered by the Trustees of Reservations, wind through American beeches, hollies, white pines, and rhododendrons on a peninsula between Mashpee and Wakeby ponds. The reservation has picnic tables and a little swimming beach. A small free parking area is open year-round, and an additional parking lot opens from late May to early September ($6). You can also launch a boat from the landing ($6 per day).

In summer the **Mashpee Conservation Commission** ( ☎ *508/539–1400 Ext. 540 for schedules*) has information about free naturalist-led guided walks of Mashpee's woods and conservation areas. Family nature walks, animal scavenger hunts, and "pond scoops" to explore aquatic life are a few of the activities offered for kids and their parents; sunrise walks on South Cape Beach and natural-history tours of the Lowell Holly Reservation are also on the program.

## SHOPPING

**Mashpee Commons** ( ✉ *Junction of Rtes. 28 and 151* ☎ *508/477–5400* ⊕ *www.mashpeecommons.com*) has about 80 mostly upscale stores, including restaurants, art galleries, and a mix of local boutiques and national chains, in an attractive village square. There's also a multi-screen movie theater and free outdoor entertainment in summer. Some of the more unique shops are **M. Brann & Co.** ( ☎ *508/477–0299*), a creative home-and-gift shop that carries everything from funky refrigerator magnets and unusual candlesticks to handcrafted glassware, one-of-a-kind lamps, mirrors, and furniture, with many works by New England artists; **Soft As A Grape** ( ☎ *508/477–5331*), an elegant but sporty men's and women's clothier with several branches around the Cape; and **Cape Cod Toys** ( ☎ *508/477–2221*), crammed full of anything the children might possibly need, including beach toys, board games, and science projects.

**Popponesset Marketplace** ( ✉ *Off Great Neck Rd. S, New Seabury* ⊹ *2½ mi south of Rte. 28 from Mashpee rotary* ☎ *508/477–9111* ⊕ *www. popponessetmarketplace.com*), open from late spring to early fall, has 20 shops (boutique clothing, home furnishings), eating places (a raw bar, pizza, ribs, Ben & Jerry's), miniature golf, and weekend entertainment (bands, fashion or puppet shows, sing-alongs).

# THE UPPER CAPE ESSENTIALS

*To research prices, get advice from other travelers, and book travel arrangements, visit ⊕www.fodors.com.*

## TRANSPORTATION

### BY BOAT & FERRY
Year-round ferries to Martha's Vineyard leave from Woods Hole. Seasonal Vineyard ferries leave from Falmouth. *For details ⇨Boat & Ferry Travel in Essentials in the back of this book.*

### BY BUS
Peter Pan Bonanza offers direct bus service to Bourne, Falmouth, and the Woods Hole steamship terminal from Boston's Logan Airport, downtown Boston, Providence (Rhode Island), Fall River, and New Bedford, as well as connecting service from New York, Connecticut, and Providence's T.F. Green Airport. Some of the buses from Boston also make stops in Wareham. Bonanza runs a service between Bourne, Falmouth, and Woods Hole year-round. Plymouth & Brockton Street Railway provides bus service to Provincetown from downtown Boston and Logan Airport, with stops en route. The Logan Direct airport express service bypasses downtown Boston and stops in Plymouth, Sagamore, Barnstable, and Hyannis.

The Cape Cod Regional Transit Authority's SeaLine, H2O Line, Barnstable Villager, and Hyannis Villager buses travel between the Upper and Lower Cape. Service is not frequent—buses depart once every hour or two, depending on the time of day—so check the schedule before you set out. To travel between Falmouth and Woods Hole, the WHOOSH trolley, also run by the Cape Cod Regional Transit Authority, is convenient. *For more information, see ⇨Bus Travel in Essentials in the back of this book.*

Bus Depots **Bonanza Bus Terminals** ( ⊠ *South Station Bus Terminal, 700 Atlantic Ave., Boston* ☎ *617/720–4110* ⊠ *Depot Ave., Falmouth* ☎ *508/548–7588* ⊕ *www.peterpanbus.com* ⊠ *Steamship Authority Piers, Woods Hole* ☎ *508/548–5011* ⊕ *www.islandferry.com).* **Hyannis Transportation Center** ( ⊠ *215 Iyannough Rd., Hyannis* ☎ *508/775–8504).* **Plymouth & Brockton Street Railway Terminals** ( ⊠ *South Station Bus Terminal, 700 Atlantic Ave., Boston* ☎ *508/746–0378* ⊕ *www.p-b.com).*

Bus Lines **Bonanza Bus Lines (division of Peter Pan Bus)** ( ☎ *888/751–8800* ⊕ *www.peterpanbus.com).* **Cape Cod Regional Transit Authority** ( ☎ *800/352–7155* ⊕ *www.capecodtransit.org).* **Plymouth & Brockton Street Railway** ( ☎ *508/746–0378* ⊕ *www.p-b.com).*

### BY TAXI
Taxi Company **Falmouth Taxi** ( ⊠ *Falmouth* ☎ *508/540–7200).*

## CONTACTS & RESOURCES

### CONDO & HOUSE RENTALS
Donahue Real Estate lists both apartments and houses for rent in the Falmouth area. Real Estate Associates lists properties (some pricey)

ranging from beach cottages to waterfront estates, with a focus on more expensive houses. It covers Falmouth, Bourne, and Mashpee.

Local Agents **Donahue Real Estate** (⊠ *Falmouth* ☎ *508/548–5412* ⊕ *www.falmouthhomes.com*). **Real Estate Associates** (⊠ *Falmouth, Mashpee, Sandwich* ☎ *508/540–5545* 🖷 *508/563–6943* ⊕ *www.uppercaperentals.com*).

## VISITOR INFORMATION

The year-round visitor information center on Route 25, in a rest area about 3 mi west of the Bourne Bridge, is open daily 9 to 5 (with extended hours 8 AM to 10 PM from late May to mid-October). The Cape Cod Canal Region, which includes Sandwich, Bourne, and Wareham, has information centers at the Sagamore rotary, at a train depot in Buzzards Bay, and on Route 130 in Sandwich (near U.S. 6 intersection).

Tourist Information **Cape Cod Canal Region Chamber of Commerce** (⊠ *70 Main St., Buzzards Bay* ☎ *508/759–6000* ⊕ *www.capecodcanalchamber.org*). **Falmouth Chamber of Commerce** (⊠ *20 Academy La., Falmouth* ☎ *508/548–8500 or 800/526–8532* ⊕ *www.falmouthchamber.com*). **Mashpee Chamber of Commerce** (⊠ *520 Main St. (Rte. 130)* ☎ *508/477–0792, 800/423–6274 outside Massachusetts* ⊕ *www.mashpeechamber.com*). **Sandwich Chamber of Commerce** (⊠ *Rte. 130, Box 744,* ☎ *508/833–9755* ⊕ *www.sandwichchamber.com*).

# The Mid Cape

## WORD OF MOUTH

"If possible I would try to stay in one of villages of Dennis, and I would go to Mayflower Beach in Dennis... Staying in Dennis affords you the opportunity to see both the 6A side, quieter but quaint, or the 28 side, with lots of things to do (lots of traffic as well)... Capt Frosty's is a Dennis tradition, wonderful fried clams, etc. Lots of restaurants on the 28 side. Sundae School, great ice cream and always crowded. Kreme N Kone seems to be a favorite for lots of people."

—mahs

Updated
by Laura V.
Scheel

**MORE A COLLOQUIALISM THAN A** proper name, the designation "Mid Cape" refers to central Cape Cod, the most heavily populated—and touristed—part of the peninsula. To the north lies tranquil Cape Cod Bay, laced with wide beaches, inlets, creeks, and marshes. The tides on the bay are dramatic—at dead low some beaches double in size as tidal flats stretch out for hundreds to thousands of feet. The calmer waters on the bay side make these beaches particularly suitable for kids, and when the tide is out, they can explore and play in the tidal pools left behind.

The main thoroughfare through the north side of the Mid Cape is Route 6A, a scenic section that dates from 1684, making it one of the first major roads constructed on Cape Cod. Alternately called Old King's Highway, Main Street, and Hallet Street, the road winds through the villages of West Barnstable, Barnstable, Cummaquid, Yarmouth Port, and Dennis, with north-side harbors and beaches just a short drive from village centers. A residential and commercial mix, Route 6A is lined with antique captains' mansions and farmhouses that are now private homes, bed-and-breakfasts, art galleries, restaurants, and antiques shops. Protected by a historical society, colors and architecture along the road are kept to the standards set by early settlers.

On the south side of the Mid Cape, sunbathers flock to the expansive beaches along Nantucket Sound. The main thoroughfare here is the busy and overdeveloped Route 28, which passes through Centerville, Osterville, Hyannis, West and South Yarmouth, and Dennisport. This stretch is particularly unpleasant and tawdry between West Yarmouth and Dennisport, where it's lined with strip motels, clam shacks, miniature-golf courses, ice-cream parlors, and tacky T-shirt outlets. A draw for families in its 1960s heyday, the area hasn't seen much renovation since. However, if you stray from the congestion of Route 28, the serenity of soft sand and quiet back roads awaits. It's hard to get too lost on the Cape—you can't go far off the main roads without hitting water—so poking around is worth the risk.

Between routes 6A and 28 is the "mid" of the Mid Cape, a mostly residential area with some historic sections, a few quiet freshwater ponds, and the commercial sections of Hyannis. Nearby are tony Osterville and Hyannis Port, a well-groomed enclave and site of the Kennedy compound.

## EXPLORING THE MID CAPE

The Mid Cape includes the towns of Barnstable, Yarmouth, and Dennis, each divided into smaller townships and villages. The town of Barnstable, for example, consists of Barnstable Village, West Barnstable, Cotuit, Marstons Mills, Osterville, Centerville, and Hyannis, with the smaller quasi villages (distinguished by their separate postal codes) of Craigville, Cummaquid, Hyannis Port, West Hyannis Port, and Wianno. Yarmouth contains Yarmouth Port, along the north shore, and the mid- and south villages of West Yarmouth and South Yarmouth. The town of Dennis's villages are easy to remember:

Dennis, West Dennis, South Dennis, East Dennis, and Dennisport. Route 6A winds along the north shore through tree-shaded scenic towns and village centers, and Route 28 dips south through some of the more overdeveloped parts of the Cape. Generally speaking, if you want to avoid malls, heavy traffic, and cheesy motels, stay away from Route 28 from Falmouth to Chatham.

**3**

> ### TOP 5
>
> ■ The gentle surf of Sandy Neck Beach, along the north side of Barnstable Harbor
>
> ■ Biking along the scenic 25-mi Cape Cod Rail Trail, which begins in South Dennis and ends in South Wellfleet
>
> ■ Summertime performances at the Cape Cod Melody Tent in Hyannis
>
> ■ Sightseeing, fishing, and clamming at Bass River
>
> ■ Shopping the boutiques, crafts shops, bookstores, antiques centers, candy shops, and galleries along Route 6A

## ABOUT THE RESTAURANTS

The Mid Cape is chock-full of eateries, ranging from sedate, high-end haute cuisine houses such as Hyannis's Paddock, the Regatta of Cotuit, and Dennis's Red Pheasant to such family-friendly places as the Red Cottage in Dennis. Expect good fun and great eats at the area's dozens of clam shacks and other super-casual restaurants along Route 28 in Yarmouth and Dennis. If you simply want lots of choices, head to Barnstable and its villages, particularly Hyannis, where a stroll down Main Street will bring you to a dozen fine restaurants ranging from lunch joints to Thai, Italian, Cajun, and upscale American dining establishments.

## ABOUT THE HOTELS

On the northern (bay) side, Route 6A from Barnstable to Dennis has dozens of B&Bs, many in the elegant former homes of sea captains. In contrast, Route 28 on the south side has row after row of lodgings, from tacky roadside motels to medium-range family hotels, with larger seaside resorts along the side roads on Nantucket Sound. Main Street, Hyannis, is lined with motels, and several inns and B&Bs perch on side streets leading to Hyannis Harbor and Lewis Bay.

| WHAT IT COSTS | | | | | |
|---|---|---|---|---|---|
| | $$$$ | $$$ | $$ | $ | ¢ |
| RESTAURANTS | over $30 | $22–$30 | $16–$22 | $10–$16 | under $10 |
| HOTELS | over $260 | $200–$260 | $140–$200 | $90–$140 | under $90 |

Restaurant prices are per person for a main course at dinner. Hotel prices are for a standard double room, excluding 6% sales tax (more in some counties) and 1%–4% tourist tax.

## TIMING

In summer the Mid Cape bustles with tourists. But from Columbus Day weekend through April the area is a peaceful collection of towns and villages, with beaches (no fees) for strolling, trails for walking and biking, and a wealth of shopping and entertainment. Although the year-round population has ballooned in the last decade, the off-season is still a laid-back and welcome time to catch the best of the Cape minus the crowds. Fall sees bursts of color in the easily accessed forests and marshes; winter brings a slower pace of life and a holiday spirit that locals love to celebrate with Christmas strolls featuring tours of shops, B&Bs, and old homes. Spring is also quiet, as the Mid Cape awakens to blooming trees, warmer days, reopened B&Bs, newly landscaped golf courses, and flower festivals. Boats come out of hibernation—Hyannis Whale Watcher Cruises, for instance, starts its program in May.

## BARNSTABLE

*Barnstable Village is 11 mi east of Sandwich; Hyannis is 11 mi east of Mashpee.*

With nearly 50,000 year-round residents, Barnstable is the largest town on the Cape, extending from the bay to the sea and comprising several prominent villages, including Centerville, Cotuit, and Osterville. The community of Hyannis feels like its own distinct municipality, but is actually a village within Barnstable.

Barnstable is also the second-oldest town on the Cape—it was founded in 1639, two years after Sandwich. You can sense its history in **Barnstable Village,** on and near Main Street (Route 6A), a lovely area of large old homes dominated by the Barnstable County Superior Courthouse. In the Village Hall is the Barnstable Comedy Club, one of the oldest community theater groups in the country. Just north of the village are the marshes and beaches of Cape Cod Bay, including beautiful Sandy Neck Beach, as well as busy Barnstable Harbor. The Cape Cod Conservatory of Music and Arts and Cape Cod Community College are also in the vicinity.

The **Olde Colonial Courthouse,** built in 1772 as the colony's second courthouse, is the home of **Tales of Cape Cod** ( ⊠ *3018 Rte. 6A, Barnstable* ☎ *508/362–8927* ⊕ *www.talesofcapecod.org*). The historical society holds a weekly slide-illustrated lecture on Tuesday in July and August, plus special events in the shoulder seasons: in May there's a lecture during Maritime Week, and in June there's one during Heritage Week. In September, a "mystery" bus trip takes visitors to areas of historic interest. While you're here, take a peek across the street at the old-fashioned English gardens at St. **Mary's Episcopal Church.**

The **Sturgis Library,** established in 1863, is in a 1644 building listed on the National Register of Historic Places. Its holdings date from the 17th century and include hundreds of maps and land charts, the definitive collection of Cape Cod genealogical material, and an extensive maritime history collection. ⊠ *3090 Main St. (Rte. 6A), Barnstable*

# The Mid Cape

## KEY
🚲 Cape Cod Rail Trail

Cape Cod Bay

Sandy Neck Beach

Sandy Neck Rd.

Sandy Neck

Barnstable Harbor

West Barnstable

6A

149

149

Marstons Mills

28

South County Rd.

TO COTUIT

BARNSTABLE

132

Cape Cod Community College

Barnstable Village

Cummaquid

Shoot Flying Hill Rd.

Wequaquet Lake

Centerville

Osterville

Craigville Beach

TO DOWSES BEACH

Keveney Bridge

Mill Pond

Hathaway's Pond

Yarmouth Port

Dennis Pond

Willow St.

Yarmouth Rd.

W. Main St.

Barnstable Municipal Airport

Hyannis
see detail map

Hyannis Port

Lewis Bay

Kalmus Park Beach

Chapin Beach

Bass Hole Boardwalk

Corporation Beach

Center St.

Union St.

Dennis Village

6A

Yarmouth

YARMOUTH

Higgins Crowell Rd.

Buck Island Rd.

West Yarmouth

Winslow Gray Rd.

28

Seagull Beach

Swan Pond

Yarmouth Boardwalk

Parker's River Beach

South Yarmouth

Yarmouth

Station Ave.

Flax Pond

Follins Pond

Cape Playhouse

Scargo Tower

134

Scargo Hill Rd.

Scargo Lake

Old Bass River Rd.

6

South Dennis

DENNIS

Bass River

West Dennis

West Dennis Beach

28

Lower County Rd.

Dennisport

🚲🚲

TO HARWICH

Great Western Rd.

Swan Pond

Clough Rd.

Upper Mill Pond

Setucket Rd.

Stony Brook Rd.

Tubman Rd.

Seymour Pond

0    2 miles

0    2 kilometers

☎508/362–6636  ⊕www.sturgislibrary.org  ⊘Mon., Wed., Thurs., and Fri. 10–5, Tues. 1–8, Sat. 10–4.

The **Coast Guard Heritage Museum,** housed in the old Trayser Building, is continually evolving and expanding. The structure itself is on the National Register of Historic Places, and the museum is filled with all things related to this seafaring branch of the U.S. military. Artifacts and displays also highlight early lifesaving and lighthouse histories, and a small shop sells related books and items. Elsewhere on the grounds is the circa 1690 jail, with two cells bearing former inmates' graffiti. Call for the ongoing schedule of lectures and events. ⊠3353 Main St. (Rte. 6A), Barnstable ☎508/362–8521 ⊠$4 ⊘Mid-May–mid-Oct., Tues.–Sat. 10–3.

If you're interested in Cape history, the **Nickerson Memorial Room** at **Cape Cod Community College** has the largest collection of Cape Cod information, including books, records, ships' logs, oral-history tapes, photographs, and films. It also has materials on the neighboring islands of Martha's Vineyard and Nantucket. ⊠2240 Iyanough Rd., off Rte. 132, West Barnstable ☎508/362–2131 Ext. 4445 ⊕www.capecod. mass.edu ⊘Mon., Wed., and Fri. 8:30–4:30.

About 7 mi southwest of Barnstable Village, **Centerville** was once a busy seafaring village, its history evident in the 50 or so shipbuilders' and sea captains' houses along its quiet, tree-shaded streets. Offering the pleasures of sheltered ocean beaches on Nantucket Sound, such as **Craigville Beach,** and of freshwater swimming in Lake Wequaquet, it has been a popular vacation area since the mid-19th century. Shoot Flying Hill Road, named by Native Americans, is the highest point of land on the Cape, with panoramic views of Plymouth and Provincetown to the north and Falmouth and Hyannis to the south.

In a 19th-century house, the **Centerville Historical Society Museum** has furnished period rooms, Sandwich glass, miniature carvings of birds by Anthony Elmer Crowell, models of ships, marine artifacts, military uniforms and artifacts, antique tools, perfume bottles (dating from 1760 to 1920), historic costumes and quilts, and a research library. Each summer there are special costume exhibits or other shows. ⊠513 Main St., Centerville ☎508/775–0331 ⊕www.centervillehistoricalmuseum. org ⊠$5 ⊘May–mid-Dec., Tues.–Sat. noon–4.

The **1856 Country Store** ( ⊠555 Main St., Centerville ☎508/775–1856 or 888/750–1856 ⊕www.1856countrystore.com) still sells penny candy, except that these days each candy costs at least 25 pennies. The store also carries newspapers, coffee, crafts, jams, and all kinds of gadgets and toys. You can sip your coffee—and take a political stance—by choosing a wooden bench out front: one is marked DEMOCRAT, and the other REPUBLICAN.

**NEED A BREAK?**

Sample a variety of creamy homemade flavors at **Four Seas Ice Cream** ( ⊠360 S. Main St., Centerville ☎508/775–1394), a tradition for generations of summer visitors. The kitchen also turns out short-order lunch and dinner fare. It's open from late May to mid-September until 10:30 PM.

The **Centerville Library** ( ⊠*585 Main St., Centerville* ☎*508/790–6220* ⊕*www.centervillelibrary.org*) has a 42-volume noncirculating set of transcripts of the Nuremberg Trials. The library is open Monday and Wednesday 9:30 to 5; Tuesday and Thursday 9:30 to 7; Friday 9:30 to 3; and Saturday 10 to 2; it's closed on Sunday.

From Centerville, head west about 7 mi to reach **Cotuit,** a charming little community formed around seven homesteads belonging to the family of 18th-century trader Winslow Crocker. Much of the town lies along and just south of Route 28, west of Osterville and east of Mashpee, and its center is not much more than a crossroads with a post office, an old-time coffee shop, a pizza parlor, and a general store, which all seem unchanged since the 1940s. Large waterfront estates line sections of Main Street and Ocean View Drive, where small coves hide the uncrowded Loop Beach and Ropes Beach. It's best to get to the beaches by bike, because traffic is light and beach parking is for residents only.

The **Cahoon Museum of American Art** is in one of the old Crocker family buildings, a 1775 Georgian colonial farmhouse that was once a tavern and an overnight way station for travelers on the Hyannis–Sandwich stagecoach line. Displays include selections from the permanent collection of American primitive paintings by Ralph and Martha Cahoon, along with other 19th- and early-20th-century artists. Special exhibitions, classes, talks, and demonstrations are held throughout the summer. The museum store is full of interesting treasures. ⊠*4676 Falmouth Rd. (Rte. 28), Cotuit* ☎*508/428–7581* ⊕*www.cahoonmuseum.org* ⊠*$5* ☾*Feb.–Dec., Tues.–Sat. 10–4, Sun. 10–4.*

The first motor-driven fire-fighting apparatus on Cape Cod, a 1916 Model T chemical-fire engine, is in the **Santuit-Cotuit Historical Society Museum,** behind the **Samuel Dottridge Homestead,** which itself dates from the early 1800s. ⊠*1148 Main St., Cotuit* ☎*508/428–0461* ⊠*Free* ☾*Mid-June–mid-Oct., Sat. and Sun. 1–5.*

**Cotuit Library** ( ⊠*871 Main St., Cotuit* ☎*508/428–8141* ⊕*www.library. cotuit.ma.us*) has a noncirculating set of luxurious leather-bound classics. Library hours are 1:30 to 5:30 and 7 to 8:30 Monday; 9:30 to 5:30 Tuesday and Friday; 1:30 to 5:30 Wednesday; 9:30 to 5:30 and 7 to 8:30 Thursday; and 10 to 4 Saturday. The library is closed Sunday.

A wealthy Barnstable enclave 5 mi east of Cotuit, **Osterville** is lined with elegant waterfront houses, some of which are large "cottages" built in the 19th century when the area became popular with the moneyed set. You'll find that most beaches in the village, including the impressive **Dowses Beach,** are restricted to residents-only parking. Despite its haute homes, the village of Osterville retains the small-town charm that permeates the Cape; its Main Street and Wianno Avenue area has a collection of trendy boutiques and jewelry shops mixed with a library, a post office, and country stores. The village's festivals of Daff O'ville Day (late April) and Christmas Stroll (mid-December) are heavily attended.

The **Osterville Historical Society Museum,** in an 1824 sea captain's house, has antiques, dolls, and exhibits on Osterville's history. Two wooden-boat museums—each showcasing various sailing vessels—and the late-18th-century Cammett House are also on the lovely, rambling 2-acre property. Special events include a large outdoor antiques show in mid-August. During December's Christmas Stroll, the museum reopens decorated in holiday splendor, with music and refreshments. ⊠*155 W. Bay Rd., Osterville* ☎*508/428–5861* ⊠*$5* ☉*Mid-June–mid-Sept., Thurs.–Sun. 1:30–4:30.*

**NEED A BREAK?**

**Gone Chocolate** (⊠*858 Main St.Osterville* ☎*508/420–0202*) will tempt you with old-fashioned chocolate-pecan turtles, saltwater taffy, ice cream, and other confections.

**Hyannis** was named for the Native American sachem Iyanno, who sold the area for £20 and two pairs of pants. Perhaps he would have sold it for far more had there been any indication that Hyannis would become known as the "home port of Cape Cod" or that the Kennedys would pitch so many tents here. Hyannis is effectively the transportation center of the Cape: it's near the airport, and ferries depart here for Nantucket and (in season) Martha's Vineyard. The busy roads feeding into the town are lined with a few of the same big-box stores you'd find anywhere.

A bustling year-round hub of activity, Hyannis has the Cape's largest concentration of businesses, shops, malls, hotels and motels, restaurants, and entertainment venues. Main Street is lined with used-book and gift shops, jewelers, clothing stores, summer-wear and T-shirt shops, and ice-cream and candy stores. The street can have a somewhat forlorn, down-at-the-heels feeling, as the malls outside downtown have taken their toll on business, but there are plenty of good-fun and fancy eateries here.

Perhaps best known for its association with the Kennedy clan, the Hyannis area was also a vacation site for President Ulysses S. Grant in 1874 and later for President Grover Cleveland. Today Hyannis is making an effort to preserve its historical connection with the sea. By 1840 more than 200 shipmasters had established homes in the Hyannis–Hyannis Port area. Aselton Park (at the intersection of South and Ocean streets) and the Village Green on Main Street are the sites of events celebrating this history, and Aselton Park marks the starting point of the scenic Walkway to the Sea, which extends to the dock area.

Three parallel streets run through the heart of town. Busy, shop-filled Main Street runs one-way from east to west; South Street runs from west to east; and North Street is open to two-way traffic. The airport rotary connects with heavily trafficked routes 132 and 28 and with U.S. 6. Off Ocean Street and Sea Street lie several excellent beaches, including Kalmus Park Beach, renowned for its stiff winds and hordes of windsurfers, and the smaller Veterans Park Beach, next to the Kennedy Memorial.

# Hyannis

TO RTES.
132 & 28

TO
CAPE COD
POTATO CHIPS
FACTORY

TO RTES.
132 & 28

TO RTES.
6 & 6A

Megan Rd.

Bearses Way

Stevens St.

Winter St.

Barnstable Rd.

Ridgewood Rd.

Yarmouth Rd.

Hyannis
Public
Library

North St.

Main St.

Pleasant St.

Village
Green

Steamship
docks

TO RTE. 28

Fawcetts
Pond

W. Main St.

Aunt
Betty's
Pond

Ryan Family
Amusement

Aselton
Park

Cape Cod
Melody
Tent

West
End
Rotary

South St.

Ocean St.
docks

Bismore
Park

Pitchers Way

Sea St.

Old Colony Rd.

Simmons
Pond

Greenwood Ave.

Gosnold St.

Ocean St.

Lewis
Bay

Veterans
Park
Beach

Scudder Ave.

Hyannis Ave.

Ocean Ave.

Sea St.
Beach

Kalmus Park
Beach

Wachusett
Ave.

Irving Ave.

Iyanough
Ave.

Hyannis
Harbor

0          500 yards

0          500 meters

① In Main Street's Old Town Hall, the **John F. Kennedy Hyannis Museum**
explores JFK's Cape years (1934–63) through enlarged and annotated
photographs culled from the archives of the JFK Library near Boston,
as well as a seven-minute video narrated by Walter Cronkite. The gift
shop sells mugs, T-shirts, and presidential memorabilia. Newly opened
in summer 2008 is the **Cape Cod Baseball League Hall of Fame and
Museum,** housed in several rooms in the basement of the JFK museum
(which is appropriately referred to as "The Dugout"). Plaques of Hall
of Famers, autographed items from former players who went on to play
professional ball, and other Cape League memorabilia are on view; several films about the league and baseball itself are played continuously.
The baseball museum shares hours with the JFK museum. A joint ticket
($8 adults) allows admission to both museums; otherwise admission
is $5 (kids under 10 are admitted free). ⊠ *397 Main St., Downtown
Hyannis* ☎*508/790–3077* ⊕*www.jfkhyannismuseum.org* ⌨*$5; $8
for joint admission with Cape Cod Baseball League Hall of Fame and
Museum* ☯*Memorial Day–mid-Oct., Mon.–Sat. 9–5, Sun. noon–5;
mid-Oct.–Nov., Mon.–Sat. 10–4, Sun. noon–4; Nov.–early Dec. and
mid-Feb.–mid-Apr., Thurs.–Sat. 10–4, Sun. noon–4.*

② The **St. Francis Xavier Church** ( ⊠*347 South St., Downtown Hyannis*
☎*508/771–7200* ⊕*stfrancishyannis.homestead.com*) is where Rose

Kennedy and her family worshipped during their summers on the Cape; the pew that John F. Kennedy used regularly is marked with a plaque. Mass is given in English, Spanish, or Portuguese (at different times).

NEED A
BREAK?

In an unlikely spot amid several industrial buildings near the airport, **Pain D'Avignon** (⊠ *15 Hinckley Rd.*   ☎ *508/778–8588*   ⊕ *www.paindavignon. com*) is nevertheless worth seeking out, especially if you're planning a picnic (although you can dine here at one of the few stainless-steel tables and chairs on a small patio). This quirky old-world-style bakery produces fine artisan breads that end up at some of the finest restaurants and gourmet shops in Boston. Drop in for delectable raisin-pecan or calamata-olive breads, cranberry bagels, chocolate-chip cookies, panini sandwiches, and fine gourmet supplies, such as cheeses, oils, and sauces.

❸ Beyond the bustling docks where waterfront restaurants draw crowds and ferries, harbor-tour boats, and deep-sea fishing vessels come and go, the quiet esplanade by the **John F. Kennedy Memorial** ( ⊠ *Off Ocean St. south of Channel Point, Hyannis Harbor*) overlooks boat-filled Lewis Bay. JFK loved to sail these waters, and in 1966 the people of Barnstable erected a plaque and fountain pool here in his memory. Adjacent to the memorial is **Veterans Park,** with a beach, a tree-shaded picnic and barbecue area, and a playground.

**Bismore Park** ( ⊠ *Off Ocean St., Hyannis Harbor*) is part of a continuing and avid effort to revitalize downtown Hyannis and encourage folks to linger here and explore. In the summer season the green is populated with modest wood sheds—"shanties"—that artisans and artists rent and use as small workshops and stores.

❹ Hyannis Port became a hot spot for Americans during the Kennedy presidency, when the **Kennedy Compound** became the summer White House. The days of hordes of Secret Service agents and swarms of tourists trampling down the bushes are gone, and the area is once again a community of quietly posh estates—though the Kennedy mystique is such that tourists still seek it out. The best way to get a glimpse of the compound is from the water on one of the many harbor tours or cruises.

Joseph P. and Rose Kennedy bought their house here—the largest one, closest to the water—in 1929 as a healthful place to summer with their soon-to-be-nine kids. (Son Ted bought the house before his mother's death in 1995.) Sons Jack and Bobby bought neighboring houses in the 1950s. Jack's is the one at the corner of Scudder and Irving, with the 6-foot-high stockade fence on two sides. Bobby's is next to it, with a white fieldstone chimney. Ted bought a home on Squaw Island, a private island connected to the area by a causeway at the end of Scudder Avenue. It now belongs to his ex-wife, Joan. Eunice (Kennedy) and Sargent Shriver have a house near Squaw Island, on Atlantic Avenue.

The compound is relatively self-sufficient in terms of entertainment: Rose Kennedy's former abode (with 14 rooms and 9 baths) has a movie theater, a private beach, a boat dock, a swimming pool, a tennis court, and a sports field that was the scene of the famous Kennedy touch-football matches. Maria Shriver, Caroline Kennedy Schlossberg, and other family members have had their wedding receptions here. In the summer of 1999 family members waited at the compound, with local and international media lining the streets, for confirmation of John F. Kennedy Jr.'s death in a plane crash off Martha's Vineyard. He and his wife, Carolyn Bessette Kennedy, were flying her sister Lauren Bessette to the Vineyard before continuing on to a cousin's wedding in Hyannis; all three were killed.

**OFF THE BEATEN PATH**

**Cape Cod Potato Chips Factory.** There's a standing invitation on the back of the bag: come for a free tour of the factory and get free samples of the crunchy all-natural chips hand-cooked in kettles in small batches. ⊠*Independence Dr. (opposite Cape Cod Mall) to Breed's Hill Rd., off Rte. 132* ☎*508/775–3358* ⊕*www.capecodchips.com* ☺*Weekdays 9–5.*

**Hyannis Public Library** ( ⊠*401 Main St., Downtown Hyannis* ☎*508/775–2280* ⊕*www.hyannislibrary.org*) has a case full of books on JFK. Summer library hours are 11 to 5 Monday, Thursday, and Friday, and 11 to 8 Tuesday and Wednesday. The library is closed weekends in summer (Sunday and Monday in winter).

Perfect for a rainy day, **Ryan Family Amusement** is replete with bowling lanes, video-game rooms, and that old seaside favorite, Skee-Ball. ⊠*441 Main St., Downtown Hyannis* ☎*508/775–3411* ☺*Daily; hrs vary.*

## WHERE TO EAT

**$–$$$**

**AMERICAN**

✕**Barnstable Tavern & Grille.** This handsome old building right in the village center, across from the courthouse and Barnstable Comedy Club, holds both a formal restaurant and a more relaxed tavern. Fresh seafood dishes and the Tavern Keeper's Special (a medley of seafood in a casserole) are local favorites. Lighter lunch fare includes burgers, salads, and sandwiches. Look for live music on the patio Friday night. ⊠*3176 Main St. (Rte. 6A), Barnstable* ☎*508/362–2355* ⊟*AE, MC, V.*

**¢–$$$**

**SEAFOOD**

✕**Baxter's Fish 'n' Chips.** Since fried seafood is a Cape staple, you may want to pay homage to one of the best Fry-o-lators around. Right on Hyannis Harbor, it's been a favorite of boaters and bathers alike since 1955. Generous portions of fried clams are delicious and cooked hot to order. The picnic tables outside, some set up on an old floating ferry, allow you to catch some rays while enjoying lobster, fish-and-chips, or something from the raw bar. If the weather's not on your side, there's indoor seating overlooking the harbor. A passageway off the dining room leads to Baxter's Boat House Club, a slightly more upscale space that has the same menu. ⊠*Pleasant St., Hyannis Harbor, Hyannis* ☎*508/775–4490* ⊕*www.baxterscapecod.com* ⚓*Reservations not accepted* ⊟*AE, DC, MC, V* ☺*Closed mid-Oct.–Apr. and weekdays early Sept.–mid-Oct.*

**¢–$$**

**Fodor's**Choice

★

**BRAZILIAN**

✕**Brazilian Grill.** The Cape has a large Brazilian population, and you can find many of these residents, plus plenty of satisfied visitors, at this all-you-can-eat *churrascaria* (Brazilian barbecue). Waiters circulate through the dining room offering more than a dozen grilled meats—

## The New Face of Hyannis

More than 1 million people travel to Hyannis each year—but many are merely passing *through* the town on their way to its ferry docks and boats to the outlying islands. For decades, townsfolk wished that these travelers would spend a little bit of time—and money—in Hyannis, but there wasn't much to entice them to stay.

But today, changes are afoot. In a move to become more family-friendly, sophisticated, and appealing, Hyannis has been revitalizing its downtown and waterfront areas. One pleasant improvement is the "Walkway to the Sea," a wave-patterned brick path that winds from Main Street at the Village Green all the way down to Bismore Park at Hyannis Harbor. Along the way are colorful art installations of lobster buoys, complete with educational

information about the fishing industry. The Village Green itself is now host to a weekly farmers' market, free movie showings, and band concerts in the summer.

As part of the "Harbor Your Arts" initiative, a series of wood "shanties" now populate Aselton Park along the Walkway to the Sea. Juried artists and artisans rent the sheds as both work space and selling arenas for their products. There's also a seasonal stage, where free musical and theatrical performances are held in summer.

The entire downtown corridor is abuzz with building restorations, improvements, expansions, creative landscaping, new sidewalks, and spruced-up storefronts. You may just want to linger before catching your ferry.

beef, pork, chicken, sausage, even quail—on long swordlike skewers. You can help yourself to a buffet of salads and side dishes, including *farofa* (a couscouslike dish made of manioc [also known as cassava or yuca]), plantains, rice, and beans. The atmosphere is often loud and jovial. For dessert, the homemade flan is the best anywhere. Dine on the redbrick patio in warm weather. ⊠ *680 Main St., West End, Hyannis* ☎ *508/771–0109* ▤ *AE, D, DC, MC, V.*

**$$–$$$**  ✕ **Dolphin Restaurant.** For the scoop on local politics, eavesdrop at the
**AMERICAN**  Dolphin. A popular spot among local political figures, for decades this has been the place in town where opinions clash and deals are cut. The dark, inviting interior has a colonial feel. Lunch favorites include the shrimp-and-crab melt, rib-eye steak, and fish-and-chips. Dinner consists of a straightforward, well-prepared roster of traditional steaks, chops, and seafood grills and sautés. The small but welcoming bar is a good spot to chow down if you're dining solo. ⊠ *3250 Main St. (Rte. 6A), Barnstable* ☎ *508/362–6610* ▤ *AE, DC, MC, V* ☉ *No lunch Sun.*

**$–$$**  ✕ **Fazio's Trattoria.** Set in an old Italian-bakery building, swank but
**★**  affordable Fazio's looks like the trattoria it is, with wood floors, high
**ITALIAN**  ceilings, and a deli case full of fresh pasta, breads, and cheeses. There's also an espresso and cappuccino bar. Chef Tom Fazio's menu leans on fresh ingredients and herbed pastas, such as basil fettuccine with shrimp, lemon, and plum tomatoes. All ravioli, pastas, and breads are homemade, and the brick-oven pizzas are delicious. Take home some fresh cannoli for dessert. ⊠ *294 Main St., Downtown, Hyannis* ☎ *508/775–9400* ⊕ *www.fazio.net* ▤ *AE, MC, V*

**Where to Stay & Eat in Hyannis**

Restaurants ▼

Baxter's Fish 'n' Chips ..... **1**
Brazilian Grill .... **8**
Fazio's Trattoria ......... **2**
Hannah Fusion Bar & Bistro ...... **7**
Harry's ........... **9**
Misaki .......... **11**
Naked Oyster .... **5**
The Paddock ... **10**
Roadhouse Café .............. **6**
Sam Diego's ..... **4**
Ying's ........... **3**

Hotels ▼

Anchor-In ....... **1**
Breakwaters ..... **5**
Cape Cod Inn .... **2**
Cape Codder Resort ............ **8**
Capt. Gosnold Village .......... **4**
Comfort Inn Cape Cod ........ **9**
Hyannis Inn Motel ............ **3**
Resort & Conference Center at Hyannis .......... **6**
Simmons Homestead Inn .. **7**

KEY
① Hotels
❶ Restaurants

$$$–$$$$
ECLECTIC

✕**Five Bays Bistro.** With its stylish feel and creative menu, this contemporary bistro wouldn't be out of place in Boston or Manhattan. Dishes such as Asian spring rolls or tuna with wasabi sauce draw inspiration from the East, whereas others—perhaps a linguine, duck, and artichoke appetizer or an entrée of seared halibut with shallot risotto—have a more Mediterranean flavor. ⊠ *825 Main St., Osterville* ☎ *508/420–5559* ⊕ *www.fivebaysbistro.com* ▭ *AE, D, MC, V* ☉ *No lunch.*

$$$–$$$$
★
ASIAN

✕**Hannah Fusion Bar & Bistro.** Known and loved for its hip city atmosphere, intriguing and stylish drinks—ever had a saki martini?—and artful blend of Far East and American flavors, this funky spot has staked a mighty claim on Main Street. The lunch menu features some hearty and intriguing sandwiches such as the Chino-Latino pork sandwich—made from grilled spiced pork loin—or the Cuban ham panini with garlic-parmesan aioli and hand-carved Swiss. There's an ample bar menu (half-price appetizers daily from 5 to 7) that tempts with everything from grilled-cheese pizza to edamame. For dinner, favorites include the Mongolian coffee-encrusted pork tenderloin or, for seafood lovers, baked prawns stuffed with lobster and sea scallops. A lively bar crowd lingers long after the kitchen closes. ⊠ *615 Main St., Downtown, Hyannis* ☎ *508/778–5565* ⊕ *www.hannahsbistro.com* ▭ *AE, DC, MC, V*

¢–$$$ ✕**Harry's.** This lovably divey-looking place serves sizable portions of
SOUTHERN Cajun and creole dishes with great spices. The menu includes a number
of meal-size sandwiches and burgers as well as blackened local fish that's
done to perfection. The jambalaya will make you wonder if there's a bayou
nearby. It's also a prime location for music: you can hear blues, zydeco,
and folk music nightly year-round. ⊠*700 Main St., West End, Hyannis*
☎*508/778–4188* ⌖*Reservations not accepted* ▤*AE, DC, MC, V.*

$–$$$ ✕**Misaki.** Tucked away on quiet West Main Street, frantically popular
JAPANESE Misaki serves authentic Japanese food in an intimate space with tables
arranged closely together. The menu has a diverse array of traditional
Japanese dishes, such as vegetable tempura, yaki soba, and chicken or
beef teriyaki, but the sushi and sashimi—prepared by an experienced
master sushi chef—are the real stars here. Try the tuna rolls, which are
delectably soft and silky. Two traditional Japanese "sitting booths"
are available by reservation. ⊠*379 W. Main St., Hyannis* ☎*508/771–
3771* ▤*AE, MC, V.*

$$$–$$$$ ✕**Naked Oyster.** The big draw at this dapper restaurant with dark-
Fodor'sChoice wood-paneled walls and soft lighting is the extensive list of weekly
★ changing specials, which truly show off the kitchen's estimable talents.
ECLECTIC You'll always find several raw and "dressed" oyster dishes (such as
barbecue oysters on the half shell with bleu cheese, caramelized onions,
and bacon) plus a nice range of salads and appetizers. Among the main
dishes, consider the superb sliced duck breast with a port-wine and
Rainier cherry sauce, or the sautéed shrimp in a piquant Thai peanut-
cashew sauce over noodles. The oyster stew is also out of this world.
⊠*20 Independence Dr., off Rte. 132, Hyannis* ☎*508/778–6500*
▤*AE, D, DC, MC, V* ☉*No lunch weekends.*

¢–$$ ✕**Osterville Fish Too.** This combination seafood market/casual restaurant
★ sits right on Barnstable Harbor at Millway Marina, giving it access
SEAFOOD to the freshest seafood around. It's tiny, with a fistful of outside picnic tables on a wooden deck and limited parking, but the fried clams
and fish sandwiches are worth the inevitable wait. Arrive hungry and
try the fat onion rings or the prodigious seafood platters (piled high
with sole, shrimp, scallops, and clams). ⊠*275 Mill Way, Barnstable*
☎*508/362–2295* ▤*MC, V* ☉*Closed Oct.–Mar.*

$$–$$$$ ✕**The Paddock.** The Paddock is synonymous with tried-and-true formal
★ dining on the Cape. Sumptuous upholstery in the main dining room
CONTINENTAL and old-style wicker on the breezy summer porch create authentic Vic-
torian ambience. The menu is traditional yet subtly innovative, and
fresh ingredients are combined in novel ways: baked grey sole with
cranberry-and-thyme crust and lemon aioli, for example. The steak
au poivre, with several varieties of crushed peppercorns, is masterful;
the fire-roasted salmon is stuffed with lobster, goat cheese, and mush-
rooms, topped with avocado-compound butter. ⊠*20 Scudder Ave.,
West End, Hyannis* ☎*508/775–7677* ⊕*www.paddockcapecod.com*
▤*AE, DC, MC, V* ☉*Closed mid-Nov.–Mar.*

$$$–$$$$ ✕**Regatta of Cotuit.** It's worth driving out of your way to this refined res-
Fodor'sChoice taurant in a handsomely restored cinnamon-hued stagecoach inn filled
★ with wood, brass, and Oriental rugs. Chef-owner Weldon Fizell turns out
AMERICAN wonderfully inventive versions of classic regional American fare, such

as roasted Atlantic halibut atop a basil pasta flan, dressed with lump crabmeat, asparagus, button mushrooms, fresh tomato, and herbed pan sauce. The signature premium fillet of North Dakota buffalo tenderloin is prepared differently each night, with seasonal starches and vegetables. The cozy taproom has its own bar menu (a bit more modestly priced), offering such treats as a fresh lobster pizzetta with herb goat cheese, caramelized onion, and arugula pesto. Try tackling the half-pound Tap Burger with bleu cheese, grilled Vidalia onion, and barbecue sauce. There's also an assortment of colorful cocktails (prickly-pear margaritas, appletinis); in warmer months there's a nice view from the outdoor terrace. ⊠*4631 Falmouth Rd. (Rte. 28), Cotuit* ☎*508/428–5715* ⊕*www. regattaofcotuit.com* ⚑*Reservations essential* ⊟*AE, MC, V.*

**$$–$$$$** ✕**Roadhouse Café.** Candlelight flickers off the white-linen tablecloths
★ and dark-wood wainscoting at the Roadhouse Café, a smart choice for
ECLECTIC a night out. Popular dishes include the roasted pepper–and–goat cheese appetizer and shrimp and basil pesto over linguine. In the more casual bistro and the mahogany bar, you can order from a separate menu, which includes thin-crust pizza as well as burgers and lighter fare. Listen to excellent straight-ahead jazz on Monday night year-round in the bistro. There's a piano bar the rest of the week from early July to early September and on Friday and Saturday in the off-season. ⊠*488 South St., Downtown, Hyannis* ☎*508/775–2386* ⊕*www.roadhousecafe. com* ⚑*Reservations essential* ⊟*AE, D, MC, V* ⊙*No lunch.*

**$–$$** ✕**Sam Diego's.** The bar has a busy social scene, and the menu has sat-
MEXICAN isfying—if predictable—Tex-Mex burritos, enchiladas, and fajitas. Crispy deep-fried ice cream served in a giant goblet is a house favorite; the margaritas, which come in several flavors, are another crowd-pleaser. The prop-shop furnishings may be a little cheesy—sombreros, Aztec birds, and the like—but the place is fun, friendly, and popular with families. Weekday lunch options include an all-you-can-eat chili and taco bar, and dinner is served nightly until midnight. ⊠*950 Iya-nough Rd. (Rte. 132) , Hyannis* ☎*508/771–8816* ⊕*www.samdiegos. com* ⊟*AE, D, MC, V.*

**¢–$** ✕**Sweet Tomatoes.** Don't be put off by the prosaic setting of this small
★ pizza place. Sweet Tomatoes serves absolutely tantalizing pizza made
PIZZA with whole-wheat dough, plus a slew of calzones, panini sandwiches, grinders, and wraps, all with fresh, creative ingredients. Top picks among the pies include the Dirty Bomb, with shaved steak, porto-bello mushrooms, onions, peppers, mozzarella, and red sauce; and the tangy white three-cheese with mozzarella, ricotta, asiago, and garlic (try ordering it with anchovies for a little extra kick). The Mediter-ranean salad makes for a delicious starter. ⊠*770 Main St., Osterville* ☎*508/420–1717* ⊟*MC, V.*

**¢** ✕**Whistleberries.** Most people settle for takeout from this tiny sandwich
CAFE shop, but the lucky few who manage to grab one of the three coun-ter spots or two tables are in for an olfactory treat. Breakfast options include fresh muffins; "scrambled" eggs (they're actually steamed by the cappuccino machine); bagels; or burrito sandwiches stuffed with cheese, bacon, vegetables, rice, beans, and sour cream. For lunch, try a wrap—there are many tempting choices, from barbecued chicken to

Mediterranean: red pepper, hummus, tabbouleh, tomato, onion, and feta cheese folded up in a spinach tortilla. ⊠*3261 Main St. (Rte. 6A), Barnstable* ☎*508/362–6717* ▭*No credit cards* ⊘ *No dinner.*

**$–$$$**
SEAFOOD

✕**Wimpy's.** No, this is not a fast-food hamburger joint—it's a Cape standby with an extensive menu that favors Italian food and lots of fish, from swordfish to salmon. There's also a good dose of meat entrées, pasta, and chicken. Wimpy's loyal clientele fills a big family dining room, a sunny atrium, and a dark traditional tavern that has cozy booths and a fine old bar. Opt for the more inventive specials, such as tortilla-crusted salmon topped in a caper sauce, or try a simple prime rib (when available). You can get takeout here, too. Sunday brunch is filled with traditional offerings such as Belgian waffles, crepes, and eggs Benedict prepared six different ways. ⊠*752 Main St., Osterville* ☎*508/428–6300, 508/428–3474 takeout* ▭*AE, DC, MC, V.*

**¢–$$**
ASIAN

✕**Ying's.** The huge menu at this little pan-Asian place presents Thai, Korean, and Japanese cuisines. Ying's sushi and sashimi combos are artful, and its many curried Thai seafood, noodle, and fried-rice dishes range from spicy to, well, really spicy. For something different, try the Korean *bibimbap* (vegetables, beef, and egg on rice with hot sauce). Tables are set up by the windows, and there's a sushi bar and a small lounge area with a selection of Asian beers. Try the sweet and thick Thai iced tea—you won't need dessert (but if you do, the fried ice cream is a treat). For more American-style food (as well as some Asian specialties) and nightly entertainment, check out Ying's other restaurant, the **Blue Anchor Cafe,** at 453 Main Street. ⊠*59 Center St., East End, Hyannis* ☎*508/790–2432* ▭*AE, MC, V.*

## WHERE TO STAY

**$$–$$$**

🎃**Acworth Inn.** This 1860 house 1 mi east of Barnstable Village has four large rooms and a spacious two-room suite. Rooms are decorated with soft pastels, lacy designer linens, and tasteful hand-painted furniture. The suite, with modern furnishings, also has a fireplace, whirlpool tub, TV–VCR, and refrigerator. Breakfast is family-style and includes granola, fresh muffins or homemade coffee cake, fruit, yogurt, and an entrée that might use herbs from the inn's gardens. Although the inn is not designed for small children, you can inquire about bringing older kids. **Pros:** comfortable, intimate setting; good spot for exploring nearby towns along historic Route 6A; can arrange in-room spa treatments. **Cons:** some rooms have tiny stall showers; rooms accessed via steep stairs. ⊠*4352 Main St. (Rte. 6A), Cummaquid* ⌂*Box 256, Cummaquid 02637* ☎*508/362–3330 or 800/362–6363* ☎*508/375–0304* ⊕*www.acworthinn.com* ➪*4 rooms, 1 suite* ⌂*In-room: no phone, refrigerator (some), DVD (some), no TV (some), Wi-Fi. In-hotel: no kids under 12, no-smoking rooms, no elevator* ▭*AE, D, MC, V* ⦿*BP.*

**$$–$$$$**

🎃**Anchor-In.** Most rooms at this pale-green motel on the north end of Hyannis Harbor have harbor views and small balconies overlooking the water. Its simple street-side appearance belies its spacious accommodations and extensive grounds. Recent and continual upgrades to the rooms have enhanced the quality factor with down comforters, terry robes, triple sheets, king-size beds, and flat-screen televisions. Some rooms have refrigerators, and the larger deluxe and executive rooms have wraparound porches. Lisa and Skip Simpson deliver the warm, personal service of a small B&B. Ferries to Nantucket and Martha's Vineyard are just around the corner. **Pros:** easy walk to downtown activity, island ferry terminals, and several waterfront restaurants; great harbor views from many rooms. **Cons:** 2nd-floor rooms accessed via stairways. ✉*1 South St., Hyannis* 🕾*508/775–0357* 🖷*508/775–1313* ⊕*www.anchorin.com* ⬤*43 rooms* ⭢*In-room: refrigerator (some), DVD (some), Wi-Fi. In-hotel: pool, no elevator* ▭*AE, D, MC, V* ⏏*CP.*

**$$–$$$** 🏨 **Ashley Manor.** Set behind hedges and a wide lawn, this B&B is a short walk from the village center. The 1699 inn has preserved its antique wide-board floors and has open-hearth fireplaces (one with a beehive oven) in the living room, the dining room, and the keeping room. The rooms are toasty, too—all but one have working fireplaces, and the suites have whirlpool tubs. Antique and country furnishings, Oriental rugs, and glimmers of brass and crystal create an elegant feel. Breakfast is served on the backyard terrace or in the formal dining room. **Pros:** less than 1 mi to restaurants and shops of Barnstable Village; spacious, authentically decorated rooms; working fireplaces for cooler nights; in-room spa treatments available. **Cons:** rooms are on 2nd floor, accessed via very steep stairs. ✉*3660 Main St. (Rte. 6A), Box 856, Barnstable* 🕾*508/362–8044 or 888/535–2246* ⊕*www.ashleymanor.net* ⬤*2 rooms, 4 suites* ⭢*In-room: DVD, Wi-Fi. In-hotel: tennis court, no kids under 14, no-smoking rooms, no elevator* ▭*AE, D, MC, V* ⏏*BP.*

**$$** 🏨 **Beechwood Inn.** Debbie and Ken Traugot's yellow-and-pale-green
★ 1853 Queen Anne house has gingerbread trim and is wrapped by a wide porch with wicker furniture and a glider swing. Named for the property's two magnificent and aged beech trees (one grand weeping, the other copper), the inn emphasizes its Victorian splendor. Although the parlor is pure mahogany-and-red-velvet Victorian, guest rooms (all with queen- or king-size beds) have antiques in lighter Victorian styles; several have fireplaces, and one has a bay view. Bathrooms have pedestal sinks and antique lighting fixtures. Breakfast is served in the dining room, which has a pressed-tin ceiling, a fireplace, and lace-covered tables. Afternoon tea and homemade snacks are also available, best enjoyed on the vast veranda furnished with comfortable chairs, under the shade of the big beech. **Pros:** exquisite lodging in historic Victorian; spacious rooms; choose from seven different beaches within a 5-mi radius. **Cons:** most rooms accessed via narrow, curved stairs. ✉*2839 Main St. (Rte. 6A), Barnstable* 🕾*508/362–6618 or 800/609–6618* 🖷*508/362–0298* ⊕*www.beechwoodinn.com* ⬤*6 rooms* ⭢*In-room: no phone, refrigerator, Wi-Fi. In-hotel: bicycles, no kids under 12, no-smoking rooms, no elevator* ▭*AE, D, MC, V* ⏏*BP.*

**$$** 🏨 **Breakwaters.** These privately owned, weathered gray-shingle cottages rent by the week in summer (or nightly in spring and fall). It's a relaxed place, set on a quiet dead-end lane. Cottages are divided into one-, two-, and three-bedroom units and offer all the comforts of home. Each unit has one or two full baths; a kitchen with microwave, coffeemaker, refrigerator, toaster, and stove; TV and phone (local calls are free); and a deck or patio with a grill and picnic table. Most units have water views. An in-ground heated pool is less than 200 feet from the lifeguarded town beach on Nantucket Sound. Excluding Sunday, there is daily maid service. **Pros:** excellent waterfront location; ideal for families and groups traveling together. **Cons:** hard to reserve unless you're staying for a week; not the place for a quiet, private getaway (unless it's spring or fall). ⊠ *432 Sea St., Box 118, Hyannis* ☎☎*508/775– 6831* ⊕*www.thebreakwaters.com* ⇰*19 cottages* ⌂*In-room: no a/c, kitchen. In-hotel: pool, beachfront, no-smoking rooms, no elevator, public Wi-Fi* ☰*No credit cards* ⊘*Closed mid-Oct.–Apr.*

¢–$$    ☒**Cape Cod Inn.** This centrally located inn on downtown Main Street is within walking distance of all of Hyannis's major sights. The no-frills rooms have large double beds; most, unfortunately, have views of a drab parking lot. The inn is attached to the Duck Inn Pub, a popular local hangout where breakfast is served. **Pros:** right in the midst of downtown action; good spot for families (there's even a bowling alley next door); very reasonable rates. **Cons:** not the place for a serene getaway; less-than-ideal views. ⊠ *447 Main St., Hyannis* ☎*508/775– 3000* ☎*508/771–1457* ⊕*www.capecodinnhyannis.com* ⇰*37 rooms, 3 suites* ⌂*In-room: Wi-Fi. In-hotel: restaurant, bar, pool, no elevator* ☰*AE, D, MC, V* ☜❘*CP.*

$$–$$$$    ☒**Cape Codder Resort.** Don't let the kids spy the indoor wave pool here—a fantasy of waves, waterfalls, and waterslides—or you'll never get out to see anything else on the Cape. Although it's set on an unattractive stretch of Route 132, this sprawling, family-friendly compound has quite a few amenities, including an excellent spa. Rooms range from basic to more elaborate—the Cape Codder rooms are more upscale than the standard "deluxe" ones. The best rooms face the inner courtyard, overlooking the lawn or the "beach" (a stretch of sand that's used for seasonal clambakes). The suites are huge; several have spiral staircases that lead up to a sleeping loft. Note that the hotel is sometimes packed with conventioneers and that there's no conventional pool for swimming, apart from the kid-oriented wave pool. **Pros:** good for those seeking a larger resort with many amenities for kids and adults; close to downtown, restaurants, and shopping. **Cons:** not the place for peaceful poolside contemplation; not for those looking for a regional lodging experience. ⊠ *1225 Iyanough Rd. (Rte. 132), Hyannis* ☎*508/771– 3000 or 888/297–2200* ☎*508/771–6564* ⊕*www.capecodderresort. com* ⇰*252 rooms, 8 suites* ⌂*In-room: Wi-Fi. In-hotel: 2 restaurants, room service, bar, gym, tennis court, spa* ☰*AE, D, DC, MC, V.*

$$–$$$$    ☒**Capt. Gosnold Village.** An easy walk from Kalmus Beach and town,
★    this peaceful, low-key colony of motel rooms and pink-shutter cottages is ideal for families. Kids can ride their bikes around the quiet street, and the pool is fenced in and watched over by a lifeguard. In some rooms, walls are attractively paneled with painted pine; floors are carpeted, and simple furnishings are colonial or modern. All cottages have decks and gas grills and receive maid service. Choose from efficiency units or one- to three-bedroom cottages. The cottages aren't air-conditioned, but you can rent an air-conditioning unit. **Pros:** a good bet for families; short walk to nearby beach. **Cons:** not quite an in-town location; no water views. ⊠ *230 Gosnold St., Hyannis* ☎*508/775–9111* ⊕*www.*

*captaingosnold.com* ⤷*23 units* ⚲*In-room: no a/c, kitchen (some). In-hotel: pool, no elevator* ▤*MC, V* ⊘*Closed Nov.–mid-Apr.*

**$$** ⛊**Centerville Corners Motor Lodge.** One of the few Mid Cape motels that's not on a traffic-choked, crassly developed road, this attractive redbrick and shingled motor lodge is in the heart of peaceful Centerville Village, facing the wonderful Four Seas Ice Cream parlor. Although the rooms are dull and the furnishings are dated, you can't beat the location. Golf packages are available. **Pros:** good location; about ½ mi to Craigville Beach; affordable, off-season golf packages. **Cons:** outdated decor; most rooms have a view of the parking lot. ✉*1338 Craigville Beach Rd., Centerville* ⌂*Box 507, 02632* ☏*508/775–7223 or 800/242–1137* 🖷*508/775–4147* ⊕*www.centervillecorners.com* ⤷*48 rooms* ⚲*In-room: kitchen (some), Wi-Fi. In-hotel: pool, no-smoking rooms, some pets allowed (fee), no elevator* ▤*AE, D, MC, V* ⊘*Closed Nov.–Apr.* �[O]*CP.*

**$$–$$$** ⛊**Comfort Inn Cape Cod.** All the rooms at this midrange chain motel have white-oak-veneer furnishings and include one king-size or two double beds, a table and chairs or a desk and chair, and a wardrobe. Some king rooms have sofa beds. The quietest rooms are on the top floor, facing the pond and woods; all have free HBO and Nintendo, and pets are allowed. Although the location is fairly convenient to U.S. 6, the Comfort Inn is a few miles north of downtown Hyannis up traffic-choked Route 132—it is quiet and set well back from the road, though. **Pros:** good package deals for travelers looking for deals; not far from downtown shopping, restaurants, and activities; good for travelers who like the large chain-motel experience. **Cons:** set along busy, heavily trafficked road; no views or peaceful settings. ✉*1470 Rte. 132, Hyannis* ☏*508/771–4804, 800/228–5150 reservations* 🖷*508/790–2336* ⊕*www.comfortinn-hyannis.com* ⤷*103 rooms, 1 suite* ⚲*In-room: Wi-Fi. In-hotel: pool, gym, no-smoking rooms, some pets allowed* ▤*AE, D, DC, MC, V* ⎸O⎹*CP.*

**$$$** ⛊**The Highpointe Inn.** Debbie and Rich Howard's intimate haven is nestled high on a hill overlooking dunes, the Great Salt Marsh, and the Bay at Sandy Neck. Although it's just minutes from historic Route 6A, the light and airy B&B transports you to a dreamlike getaway, offering casual luxury at its best. Each of the inn's three rooms inspires serenity with comforting colors, decor, and magical views. Breakfast offers a choice of five hot entrées and may include Rich's famed French toast and Debbie's homemade goodies. **Pros:** immaculate and sophisticated lodging; can arrange for in-room spa services; serene and private setting. **Cons:** not for those looking for a busy, in-town location or lodging in an antique home. ✉*70 High St.* ⌂*Box 346, West Barnstable 02668* ☏*508/362–4441 or 888/362–4441* 🖷*508/362–4401* ⊕*www. thehighpointeinn.com* ⤷*3 rooms* ⚲*In-room: no phone, DVD, refrigerator, Wi-Fi. In-hotel: gym, no kids under 12, no-smoking rooms, no elevator* ▤*AE, D, MC, V* ⎸O⎹*BP.*

**FodorsChoice** ★

**$$–$$$** ⛊**Honeysuckle Hill.** Innkeepers Freddy and Ruth Riley provide plenty of little touches here: fresh flowers and chocolate truffles in every room, a guest fridge stocked with beverages (including wine and beer), beach chairs with umbrellas (perfect for nearby Sandy Neck Beach), and an

**FodorsChoice** ★

3

always-full cookie jar. Additional indulgences include the self-serve liquor and cordial trays in the parlor. Guests are often seen carrying their evening cocktails to the gazebo for a game of cards. The airy, country-style guest rooms in this 1810 Queen Anne–style cottage have lots of white wicker, featherbeds, checked curtains, and pastel-painted floors. The spacious 2nd-floor Wisteria Room overlooking the lush yard is a particularly comfortable retreat, and the screened-in porch is a peaceful place to sip early-morning coffee. **Pros:** gracious and generous innkeepers; lush gardens on the grounds; tasteful, large rooms; very short drive to Sandy Neck Beach. **Cons:** most rooms are accessed via steep stairs. ⊠ *591 Main St. (Rte. 6A), West Barnstable* ☎ *508/362–8418 or 866/444–5522* 🖶 *508/362–8386* ⊕ *www.honeysucklehill. com* ➭*4 rooms, 1 suite* ⌂*In-room: no phone, VCR (some), Wi-Fi. In-hotel: bicycles, no kids under 12, no-smoking rooms, no elevator* ⊟*AE, MC, V* ⏁❙*BP.*

$–$$ 🛏️**Hyannis Inn Motel.** The main building of this second-oldest motel in Hyannis, a modest two-story spread, served as press headquarters during JFK's presidential campaign. Today, it's right in the heart of the downtown shopping and retail action. The main building's immaculate rooms have double, queen-size, or king-size beds; some have whirlpool tubs. Other deluxe rooms in a separate wing out back are larger, sunnier, and quieter (they don't face Main Street) and have queen- or king-size beds, sleeper sofas, walk-in closets, and refrigerators. The restaurant serves breakfast only. **Pros:** great for those who want to leave their cars and be right in the thick of downtown; spacious rooms (those in the separate wing are especially suited for families); nice outside sundecks for relaxing. **Cons:** not a beachfront spot or one with water views; not for those who are seeking a more peaceful, countryside setting. ⊠*473 Main St., Hyannis* ☎*508/775–0255 or 800/922–8993* 🖶*508/771–0456* ⊕*www.hyannisinn.com* ➭*77 rooms* ⌂*In-room: refrigerator (some), Wi-Fi. In-hotel: restaurant, bar, pool, no elevator* ⊟*AE, D, MC, V* ⊘*Closed early Nov.–late Mar.*

$$ 🛏️**Josiah Sampson House.** Guest rooms in this stunning 1793 Federal-style home near Cotuit's tranquil (and diminutive) village center have canopy beds, needlepoint rugs, antiques, and air-conditioning; most have fireplaces. Hannah's Room, the most spacious, has a queen-size four-poster bed and built-in window seats. The Sampson Room has an extra-large bathroom and a view of the backyard and handsome grounds. Tennis privileges ($8 for 1½ hours) are available at the Kings Grant Racquet Club next door. **Pros:** very quiet and pastoral setting yet near Route 28; proximity to area beaches and Cape Cod Baseball League games. **Cons:** not an in-town location, though a good base from which to explore area; one room's bathroom is a short walk down the hall. ⊠*40 Old Kings Rd., off Main St., Cotuit* ☎*508/428–8383* ⊕*www.josiahsampson.com* ➭*6 rooms* ⌂*In-room: no phone, no TV, Wi-Fi. In-hotel: bicycles, no kids under 12, no-smoking rooms, no elevator* ⊟*AE, MC, V* ⏁❙*BP.*

$$–$$$ 🛏️**Lamb and Lion Inn.** Lamb and Lion occupies a 1740 farmhouse and barn, as well as several additions, with rooms and suites gathered around a courtyard and large swimming pool. Inside, some rooms

are summery, with blue-and-white-stripe wallpaper and wicker chairs, whereas others are more staid, furnished with antiques and dark woods. The Innkeeper's Pride Suite has a fireplace and Jacuzzi tub that opens to a private deck; the rustic Barn-Stable, in the original barn, has three sleeping lofts that can accommodate six. Amenities include pickups and drop-offs from local ferries and the Barnstable Municipal Airport. If you're up for exploring, the innkeepers have designed several themed driving tours. **Pros:** convenient location for area exploring; island ferry drop-offs a real bonus. **Cons:** not for those looking for an in-town location or the antique-home experience. ⊠*2504 Main St. (Rte. 6A), Box 511, Barnstable* ☎*508/362–6823 or 800/909–6923* 🖷*508/362–0227* ⊕*www.lambandlion.com* ⟿*4 rooms, 6 suites* ♿*In-room: DVD, kitchen (some), Wi-Fi. In-hotel: pool, airport shuttle, no kids under 10 (in summer), some pets allowed (fee), no elevator* ▭*MC, V* ⦿*CP.*

**$$$** 🏨 **Resort & Conference Center at Hyannis.** Formerly the Four Points Sheraton, this expansive property finished a complete $12 million renovation in May 2008. Sparklingly new and sleek, contemporary-style rooms have granite counters in the bathrooms and tasteful neutral color schemes. Rooms face either the golf course or the nicely maintained courtyard. Deluxe rooms and suites with separate sitting areas are also available, though all rooms are generously sized and have their own private balcony or patio. Dining options range from casual pub-style to more formal dinners, or alfresco under the cabana tent by the pool. Guests also have complimentary access to the on-site Atlantis Sports Club. **Pros:** ideal for those who prefer the amenities of a full-service hotel; great for business travelers; easy access to bustle of downtown. **Cons:** not for those seeking a regional lodging experience. ⊠*35 Scudder Ave., West End rotary, Hyannis* ☎*508/862—6920 or 866/828–8259* ⊕*www.capecodresortandconference.com* ⟿*232 rooms* ♿*In-room: refrigerator, Wi-Fi. In-hotel: 4 restaurants, room service (summer months), bars, golf course, pools, gym, spa, concierge (summer months), executive floor* ▭*AE, D, DC, MC, V.*

**$$–$$$** 🏨 **Simmons Homestead Inn.** At this 1820 former sea captain's estate, each room in the main house or the detached barn is named for an animal and decorated (somewhat excessively) accordingly. This offbeat and casual inn has rooms with antique, wicker, or canopied four-poster beds topped with brightly colored quilts; some have fireplaces, and some, such as the large, cheery Bird Room, have private decks. You can borrow 10-speed mountain bikes, and Simmons Pond is a short jaunt on the property's trail. Gregarious innkeeper Bill Putman encourages you to return each evening for a wine-and-socializing hour. He'll also be happy to show you his collection of nearly 60 vintage cars or his roughly 500 vintages of single-malt Scotch. About three dozen friendly cats roam about the property. If you're flying into Hyannis, you can arrange to be picked up in one of Bill's classic cars: a stunning 1967 Bentley sedan. **Pros:** good place for people with pets; ample grounds and pond on the property; socializing among guests greatly encouraged with happy hours; great car collection. **Cons:** if you're not a cat lover, stay clear. ⊠*288 Scudder Ave., Box 578, Hyannis Port*

☎ *508/778–4999 or 800/637–1649* 🖶 *508/790–1342* ⊕ *www.sim-monshomesteadinn.com* ⇄ *12 rooms, 2 suites* ⊘ *In-room: no phone, no TV. In-hotel: bicycles, no-smoking rooms, some pets allowed (fee), no elevator* ▤ *AE, D, MC, V* ⦿|*BP.*

## NIGHTLIFE & THE ARTS

THE ARTS    The **Boston Pops Esplanade Orchestra** ( ☎ *508/362–0066* ⊕ *www.arts-foundationcapecod.org*) wows the crowd with its annual Pops by the Sea concert, held in August at the Hyannis Village Green. Each year a celebrity guest conductor strikes up the band for a few selected numbers; past baton bouncers have included Olympia Dukakis, Joan Kennedy, Mike Wallace, Art Buchwald, Maya Angelou, and Sebastian Junger.

In 1950 actress Gertrude Lawrence and her husband, producer-manager Richard Aldrich, opened the **Cape Cod Melody Tent** ( ⊠ *21 W. Main St., at West End rotary, Hyannis* ☎ *508/775–5630, 800/347–0808 for tickets* ⊕ *www.melodytent.com*) to showcase Broadway musicals and concerts. Today it's the Cape's top venue for pop concerts and comedy shows. Performers who have played here, in the round, include the Indigo Girls; Lyle Lovett; Tony Bennett; Bill Cosby; and Crosby, Stills & Nash. The Tent also holds an 11 AM Wednesday children's theater series in July and August.

**Cape Cod Opera**( ☎ *508/398–1068* ⊕ *www.capecodopera.org*) puts on several performances a year, usually in August, December, and February. Operas are held at the Tilden Arts Center at Cape Cod Community College, Route 132, Barnstable.

The 90-member **Cape Cod Symphony Orchestra,** under talented and passionate conductor Jung-Ho Pak, gives regular classical and children's concerts with guest artists September through May. Performances are held at the Barnstable Performing Arts Center at **Barnstable High School** ( ⊠ *744 W. Main St., Hyannis* ☎ *508/362–1111* ⊕ *www.cape symphony.org*).

**Harbor Your Arts** ( ☎ *508/862–4990* ⊕ *harboryourarts.com*) is a great program of visual and performing arts sponsored by the town of Hyannis and local businesses. Early evenings in July and August come alive with various free programs. Bring your beach chairs and blankets for the family-friendly Shakespeare by the Sea series, Sunday at 5 PM. The Citizens Bank Concert Series features local musicians—folk, jazz, and everything in between—on Tuesday at 6 PM. Friday night gets extra lively with the Reggae, Rhythm and Blues Summer Concert Series, beginning at 6 PM. All events take place at Aselton Memorial Park, at the intersection of South and Ocean streets.

**Opera New England of Cape Cod** ( ☎ *508/771–3600* ⊕ *www.operanecc. org*) hosts two or three performances a year, in spring and fall, by the National Lyric Opera Productions. Operas are held at the Tilden Arts Center at Cape Cod Community College, Route 132, in Barnstable.

In July and August **town-band concerts** ( ☎ *508/362–5230 or 877/492–6647* ) are held on Wednesday evening at 7:30 on the Town Green on Main Street, Hyannis.

NIGHTLIFE   Hyannis is Barnstable's nightlife hub, with more than a dozen popular bars and taverns, most of them along Main Street in the heart of downtown. Elsewhere in this otherwise lightly developed town, bars and clubs are few and far between.

The **Barnstable Comedy Club** ( ✉ *Village Hall, Rte. 6A, Barnstable* ☎ *508/362–6333* ⊕ *www.barnstablecomedyclub.com* ), the Cape's oldest amateur theater group (it was founded in the 1920s), gives much-praised musical and dramatic performances throughout the year; the season generally runs from late October to May. Folks who appeared here before they made it big include Geena Davis, Frances McDormand, and Kurt Vonnegut, a past president of the BCC.

**The British Beer Company** ( ✉ *412 Main St., Hyannis* ☎ *508/771–1776* ⊕ *www.britishbeer.com* ) has a hearty selection of beers, from stouts to pilsners; most nights there's also live entertainment—usually local rock bands. The BBC also has branches on the Cape in Sandwich and Falmouth.

**Bud's Country Lounge** ( ✉ *3 Bearses Way, at Rte. 132, Hyannis* ☎ *508/771–2505* ) has pool tables and live music, dancing, and karaoke year-round.

**Club 477/Mallory Dock** ( ✉ *477 Yarmouth Rd., Hyannis* ☎ *508/771–7511* ), in the old Hyannis train station, is the Cape's only gay club outside Provincetown. There's a piano bar on the lower level and a dance bar on the upper floor with music almost as hot as the crowd.

**The Comedy Lounge** ( ✉ *Radisson Hotel Hyannis, Rte. 28, Hyannis* ☎ *877/548–3237* ⊕ *www.comedylounge.com* ), despite its location in a ubiquitous chain hotel, pulls in top comedy acts from throughout the Northeast. Shows are held Friday and Saturday night June to September; only on Friday otherwise.

★   **Harry's Blues Bar** ( ✉ *700 Main St., Hyannis* ☎ *508/778–4188* ) is hopping nearly every night year-round, drawing blues lovers of all ages. Expect to see 21-year-olds and 70-year-olds dancing up a sweat side by side. Owner Laddie Durham fills the creole joint with crowd-pleasing bands and top-notch hospitality. In summer, crowds spill over from inside onto the two decks.

**The Island Merchant** ( ✉ *302 Main St., Hyannis* ☎ *508/771–1337 www.theislandmerchant.com* ) showcases a fine range of acoustic, blues, open jazz jams, and rock. There's even a dinner music series. The food is pretty tasty, too; look for some good island-influenced items like the West Indian pumpkin bisque, and jerked chicken. If you're staying late for the music and get a bit hungry, there are $2 burgers served from 10 PM to closing (1 AM). They're closed Tuesday.

**Pufferbellies** ( ✉ *183 Rte. 28, Hyannis* ☎ *508/790–4300 or 800/233–4301* ), in an old railroad roundhouse by the Hyannis tracks, is the

Mid Cape's largest dance club, with several dance floors (including the club's own go-go dancers on their own stages), as well as eats, Internet terminals, and even volleyball courts. Listen for lots of reggae, hip-hop, techno, and even Irish music. Several large concert events are held throughout the year.

★ After dinner, **RoöBar** ( ⊠*586 Main St., Hyannis* ☎*508/778–6515*) turns up the music and morphs into *the* place to see and be seen on Cape Cod. The Manhattan-esque haunt draws large crowds of attractive twenty- and thirtysomethings; expect to see lines of people out the door in summer. Personable bartenders and staff boost the already lively atmosphere.

### SPORTS & THE OUTDOORS

BASEBALL The **Cotuit Kettleers** of the collegiate Cape Cod Baseball League play home games at **Lowell Park** ( ⊠*Lowell Ave., 2 mi south of Rte. 28, Cotuit* ☎*508/428–3358* ⊕*www.kettleers.org*) from mid-June to mid-August. The team also puts on youth and advanced baseball clinics in the summer.

The **Hyannis Mets** ( ☎*508/420–0962* ⊕*www.hyannismets.org*) of the collegiate Cape Cod Baseball League play home games at **McKeon Field** ( ⊠*High School Rd., Downtown Hyannis*) from mid-June to mid-August. Interested 5–17-year-olds can sign up with the Hyannis Mets Youth Baseball Academy.

BEACHES ⚠ **Daily parking fees at Barnstable beaches are $15 in season. Note: At this writing, the town of Barnstable is considering a townwide smoking ban on all of its ocean beaches.**

Hovering above Barnstable Harbor and the 4,000-acre **Great Salt Marsh, Sandy Neck Beach** stretches some 6 mi across a peninsula that ends at **Sandy Neck Light.** The beach is one of the Cape's most beautiful—dunes, sand, and sea spread endlessly east, west, and north. The marsh used to be harvested for salt hay; now it's a haven for birds, which are out and about in the greatest numbers in morning and evening, during low tide, and during spring and fall migrations. The lighthouse, standing a few feet from the eroding shoreline at the tip of the neck, has been out of commission since 1952. It was built in 1857 to replace an 1827 light, and it used to run on acetylene gas. It's now privately owned and no longer accessible from the beach. If you like to hike, ask at the ranger station for a trail brochure. The main beach at Sandy Neck has lifeguards, a snack bar, restrooms, and showers. As you travel east along Route 6A from Sandwich, Sandy Neck Road is just *before* the Barnstable line, although the beach itself is in West Barnstable. ⊠*Sandy Neck Rd., West Barnstable* ⊙*Daily 8* AM–9 PM, *but staffed only until 5* PM.

**Hathaway's Pond** ( ⊠*Off Phinney's La., Barnstable*) is a freshwater pond with a beach, restrooms, and a lifeguard (in season).

**Craigville Beach,** on Craigville Beach Road in Centerville, is a long, wide strand that is extremely popular with the collegiate crowd. The beach has lifeguards, showers, and restrooms, and there's food nearby.

**Kalmus Park Beach,** at the south end of Ocean Street in Hyannis, is a fine, wide sandy beach with an area set aside for windsurfers and a sheltered area that's good for kids. It has a snack bar, restrooms, showers, and lifeguards.

Also in Hyannis, **Veterans Park,** next to the John F. Kennedy Memorial on Ocean Street, has a small beach that's especially good for kids; it's sheltered from waves and fairly shallow. There are picnic tables, barbecue facilities, showers, and restrooms.

BICYCLING **Cascade Motor Lodge** ( ⊠ *201 Main St., Downtown Hyannis* ☎ *508/775–9717*), near the bus and train station, rents three-speed and mountain bikes by the half day, full day, and week.

BOATING **Eastern Mountain Sports** ( ⊠ *1513 Rte. 132, Hyannis* ☎ *508/362–8690*) rents kayaks and camping gear.

The catboat *Eventide* ( ⊠ *Ocean St. Dock, Hyannis* ☎ *508/775–0222 or 800/308–1837* ⊕ *www.catboat.com*) sails in Hyannis Harbor and out into Nantucket Sound on several one- and two-hour cruises; options include a nature tour and a sunset cruise.

**Hy-Line** ( ⊠ *Ocean St. Dock, Hyannis* ☎ *508/790–0696* ⊕ *www. hy-linecruises.com*) offers cruises on reproductions of old-time Maine coastal steamers. The one-hour tours of Hyannis Harbor and Lewis Bay include a view of the Kennedy compound and other points of interest.

FISHING **Aquarius Charters Inc.** ( ⊠ *Barnstable Harbor* ☎ *508/362–9617* ⊕ *www. aquariussportfishing.com*) supplies all gear on its 35-foot boat and offers four-, six-, and eight-hour trips for up to six people to catch bass, blues, tuna, and shark. Reservations are recommended.

**Hy-Line** ( ⊠ *Ocean St. Dock, Hyannis* ☎ *508/790–0696* ⊕ *www. hy-linecruises.com*) leads fishing trips on a walk-on basis in spring and fall, but reservations are mandatory in summer.

GOLF **The Resort and Conference Center at Hyannis** ( ⊠ *35 Scudder Ave., Hyannis* ☎ *508/862–6980* ⊕ *www.twinbrooksgolf.net*) is a beautifully landscaped, challenging 18-hole, par-3 course called Twin Brooks; it's a public course. You may bump into some famous faces; many performers from the Cape Cod Melody Tent tee off here while they're in town.

HEALTH & **Cape Cod Fitness Center** ( ⊠ *Radisson Hotel, 287 Iyannough Rd. (Rte.*
FITNESS CLUBS *28), Hyannis* ☎ *508/790—4477* ⊕ *www.capecodfitnesscenter.com*) has an indoor pool, a large selection of the latest workout machines, weights, and a regular schedule of fitness, yoga, and Pilates classes. Day and short-term memberships are available.

**Atlantis Sports Club** ( ⊠ *Resort and Conference Center at Hyannis, 35 Scudder Ave., West End rotary, Hyannis* ☎ *508/862–2535*) has a fitness club, a full schedule of fitness and yoga classes, and indoor and outdoor pools. Day and short-term memberships are available.

HORSEBACK
RIDING

**Holly Hill Farm** (⊠*240 Flint St., Marstons Mills* ☎*508/428–2621* ⊕*www.hollyhillstable.com*) offers horseback-riding instruction and a day camp but no trail rides.

ICE-SKATING

The **Joseph P. Kennedy Jr. Memorial Skating Rink** (⊠*141 Bassett La., Hyannis* ☎*508/790–6345*), named

**WORD OF MOUTH**

"Hyannis is now quite a busy city, good for shopping—the mother of all Christmas Tree Shops is there, for one." —Reeder

for the late Kennedy scion and war hero, offers skating October through March, with special times reserved for teenagers, youngsters, and families; skate rentals are available.

WHALE-
WATCHING

On **Hyannis Whale Watcher Cruises** out of Barnstable Harbor, a naturalist narrator comments on whale sightings and the natural history of Cape Cod Bay. Trips last about four hours, and there are concessions on board. In July and August you can cruise at sunset, too; go for a real treat and sign on for a clambake cruise that includes a traditional dinner of steamed lobster, corn on the cob, steamers, linguica, potatoes, onions, and Bailey's bread pudding. Prices for adults are about $65; reservations are recommended. ⊠*Millway Marina, off Phinney's La., Barnstable* ☎*508/362–6088 or 888/942–5392* ⊕*www.whales. net* ◻*$45* ☉*May–Oct.*

### SHOPPING

Main Street in downtown Hyannis has gradually been gentrified in recent years and has become one of the top shopping destinations on the Cape, buzzing with several art galleries and antiques shops, numerous clothiers, and a slew of other, mostly independent, boutiques and gift emporia. You'll also find quite a few restaurants along this walkable stretch, including several cafés that are nice for a cup of coffee or a light snack. Heading through the villages of Barnstable along Route 6A, you'll find no shortage of intriguing art galleries and rustic antiques shops.

**Cape Cod Mall** (⊠*Between Rtes. 132 and 28, Hyannis* ☎*508/771–0200* ⊕*www.capecodmall.com*), the Cape's largest, has 120 mid- to upper-end mostly chain shops, including department stores such as Macy's and Sears; smaller anchor stores such as Marshalls, Barnes & Noble, and Best Buy; and a 12-screen movie complex.

**Cape Cod Weathervane Company** (⊠*379 Iyannough Rd. [Rte. 28], Hyannis* ☎*508/775–9100* ⊕*www.capecodweathervanes.com*) has a huge selection of weather vanes, both traditional and unusual (just think what the neighbors will say about the pig holding a martini on your roof…) You'll also find bird feeders, door plaques, wind chimes, and all sorts of items for your home and garden.

**Christmas Tree Shops** (⊠*655 Iyanough Rd. [Rte. 132], Hyannis* ☎*508/778–5521* ⊕*www.christmastreeshops.com*), a Cape mainstay, are a bargain shoppers' haven. Take home Cape souvenirs at a great discount along with just about anything you might need—or not need—to decorate your home. The Hyannis store is the largest on the Cape.

★ **Oak & Ivory** (✉*1112 Main St., Osterville* ☎*508/428–9425* ⊕*www.oakandivory.com*) specializes in Nantucket lightship baskets made on the premises, as well as gold miniature baskets and scrimshaw. China, gold jewelry, and other gifts round out the selection.

The handsome flagship **Puritan of Cape Cod** (✉*408 Main St., Hyannis* ☎*508/775–2400*) store carries upscale clothing brands, from North Face to Eileen Fisher and Ralph Lauren; they also sell outdoor gear. Service is great here, and they also have several other stores around the Cape.

The **Sow's Ear Antique Company** (✉*4698 Falmouth Rd. [Rte. 28], Cotuit* ☎*508/428–4931*), in a late-1600s house next to the Cahoon Museum, specializes in folk art—dolls, ship models, wood carvings, antique quilts, and paintings.

**West Barnstable Tables** (✉*2454 Meetinghouse Way [Rte. 149], West Barnstable* ☎*508/362–2676*) has exquisite handcrafted tables, chairs, chests, and other furniture made from the finest woods.

The decor changes seasonally at **Whippletree** (✉*660 Main St. [Rte. 6A], West Barnstable* ☎*508/362–3320* ⊕*www.thewhippletree.com*), a 1779 barn where Christmas decorations and country gift items hang from the rafters year-round. Goods include German nutcrackers, from Prussian soldiers to Casanovas.

For stunning arts and crafts imported from Africa, check out **Zizini** (✉*382 Main St., Hyannis* ☎*508/790–2109* ⊕*www.zizini.com*), which carries colorful ceramic and bead necklaces, handwoven pocketbooks, carved wooden masks, and abstract soapstone carvings. The store operates on a fair-trade policy, helping to support artisans who create the goods.

## YARMOUTH

*Yarmouth Port is 3 mi east of Barnstable Village; West Yarmouth is 2 mi east of Hyannis.*

Once known as Mattacheese, or "the planting lands," Yarmouth was settled in 1639 by farmers from the Plymouth Bay Colony. The town's northernmost village of **Yarmouth Port** wasn't established as a distinct village until 1829. By then the Cape had begun a thriving maritime industry, and men turned to the sea to make their fortunes. Many impressive sea captains' houses—some now B&Bs and museums—still line enchanting Route 6A and nearby side streets, and Yarmouth Port has some real old-time stores in town. A mile's drive north of Route 6A is the small but lovely Gray's Beach, where a boardwalk at Bass Hole stretches hundreds of feet over the wide marsh and the Callery-Darling conservation land trails loop through forest and marshland.

Visit the **Edward Gorey House Museum** to explore the eccentric illustrations and offbeat humor of the late acclaimed artist. The regularly changing exhibitions, arranged in the downstairs rooms of Gorey's former home, include drawings of his oddball characters and reveal the mysterious psyche of the sometimes dark but always playful illustrator. Kids enjoy the section of the house with interactive exhibits that promote Gorey's lifelong dedication to animal welfare. ⊠ *8 Strawberry La., Yarmouth Port* ☎ *508/362–3909* ⊕ *www.edwardgoreyhouse.org* ⊠ *$5* ☉ *Mid-Apr.–mid-Dec., Thurs.–Sat. 11–4, Sun. noon–4; July–early Oct., Wed.–Sat. 11–4, Sun. noon–4; mid-Oct.–late Dec., Fri. and Sat. 11–4, Sun. noon–4; closed mid-Dec.–mid-Apr. Call ahead to confirm off-season hours.*

★ For a peek into the past, make a stop at **Hallet's,** a country drugstore preserved as it was in 1889 when it was opened by Thacher Hallet, the current owner's grandfather. Hallet served not only as druggist but also as postmaster and justice of the peace. Sit at a swivel stool at the all-marble soda fountain and order their secret-recipe ice-cream soda and, in season, an inexpensive breakfast or lunch. ⊠ *139 Main St. (Rte. 6A), Yarmouth Port* ☎ *508/362–3362* ☉ *Apr.–mid-Nov.; call for hrs.*

Above Hallet's Store, the **Thacher Taylor Hallet Museum** displays photographs and memorabilia of Yarmouth Port and the Hallet family. ⊠ *139 Main St. (Rte. 6A), Yarmouth Port* ☎ *508/362–3362* ⊠ *Donations accepted for museum* ☉ *Apr.–mid-Nov.; call for hrs.*

The 1886 **Village Pump** ( ⊠ *220 Rte. 6A, Yarmouth Port*), a black wrought-iron mechanism long used for drawing household water, is topped by a lantern and surrounded by ironwork with cutouts of birds and animals. In front is a stone trough that was used for watering horses. It's across from the Parnassus Book Service.

The 1696 **Old Yarmouth Inn** ( ⊠ *Rte. 6A, near Summer St., Yarmouth Port* ☎ *508/362–9962*), near the village pump, is the Cape's oldest inn and a onetime stagecoach stop *(see Where to Stay & Eat, Yarmouth Port, below).*

The **Botanical Trails of the Historical Society of Old Yarmouth,** behind the **post office** ( ⊠ *231 Main St., Yarmouth Port*), consists of 50 acres of oak and pine woods and a pond, accented by blueberries, lady's slippers, Indian pipes, rhododendrons, and hollies. Stone markers and arrows point out the 2 mi of trails; you'll find trail maps in the gatehouse mailbox. Just beyond the historical society's trails, you can find **Kelley Chapel,** built in 1873 by a father for his daughter, who was grieving over the death of her child. An iron woodstove and a pump organ dominate the simple interior. ⊠ *Off Rte. 6A* ⊠ *$1 suggested donation* ☉ *Gatehouse July and Aug., daily 1–4. Trails during daylight hrs year-round.*

The 1780 **Winslow Crocker House** is an elegantly symmetrical two-story Georgian with 12-over-12 small-pane windows and rich paneling in every room. Crocker was a well-to-do trader and land speculator; after his death, his two sons built a wall dividing the house in half. The structure was moved here from West Barnstable in 1936 by Mary Thacher, who donated it—along with her collection of 17th-to-19th-century furniture, pewter, hooked rugs, and ceramics—to Historic New England (formerly the Society for the Preservation of New England Antiquities), which operates it as a museum. ⊠ *250 Main St. (Rte. 6A), Yarmouth Port* ☎ *617/227–3956* ⊕ *www.historicnewengland.org* ✉ *$5* ⊙ *June–mid-Oct., 1st and 3rd Sat. of month, tours at 11, noon, 1, 2, 3, and 4.*

Built in 1840 onto an existing 1740 house for a sea captain in the China trade, the **Captain Bangs Hallet House** is a white Greek Revival building with a hitching post out front and a weeping beech in back. The house and its contents typify a 19th-century sea captain's home, with pieces of pewter, china, nautical equipment, antique toys, and clothing on display. The kitchen has an original 1740 brick beehive oven and butter churns. Tour guides relate salty sea captains' stories from the 19th century. ⊠ *11 Strawberry La., off Rte. 6A, Yarmouth Port* ☎ *508/362–3021* ⊕ *www.hsoy.org* ✉ *$3* ⊙ *June–mid-Oct., Thurs.–Sun. 1–4, tours at 1, 2, and 3.*

Purchased in 1640 and established as a prosperous farm in the late 1700s, the **Taylor-Bray Farm** ( ⊠ *Bray Farm Rd., Yarmouth Port* ☎ *508/385–9407* ⊕ *www.taylorbrayfarm.org*) is listed on the National Register of Historic Places. Now a working farm for educational purposes, it hosts special events, such as an annual sheep shearing, a fall festival, and a crafts fair. The public is welcome to take advantage of the farm's picnic tables, walking trails, and great views of the tidal marsh year-round from dawn to dusk. Call for more information.

For a scenic loop with little traffic, turn north off Route 6A in Yarmouth Port onto Church Street or Thacher Street, then left onto Thacher Shore Road. In fall this route is especially beautiful, with impressive stands of blazing-red burning bush. Wooded segments alternate with open views of the marsh. Keep bearing right, and at the WATER STREET sign, the dirt road on the right will bring you to a wide-open view of marshland as it meets the bay. Don't drive in too far, or you may get stuck. As you come out, a right turn will take you to **Keveney Bridge,** a one-lane wooden bridge over marshy Mill Pond, and back to Route 6A.

One of Yarmouth Port's most beautiful areas is Bass Hole, which stretches from Homer's Dock Road to the salt marsh. **Bass Hole Boardwalk** ( ⊠ *Trail entrance on Center St. near Gray's Beach parking lot*) extends over a marshy creek; amid the salt marshes, vegetated wetlands, and upland woods meander the 2½-mi **Callery-Darling nature trails.** Gray's Beach is a little crescent of sand with still water good for kids—but don't go beyond the roped-in swimming area, the only section where the current isn't strong. At the end of the boardwalk, benches provide a place to relax and look out over abundant marsh life and, across the creek, the beautiful, sandy shores of Dennis's Chapin Beach. At low tide you can walk out on the flats for almost a mile. It's a far cry from the 18th century, when a harbor here was the site of a schooner shipyard.

About 4 mi south of Yarmouth Port and directly east of Hyannis, you'll find **West Yarmouth**. The commercial hub (and the major road through the community) is, for better or worse, Route 28—the part of the Cape people love to hate. As you pass through the area—probably very slowly in summer traffic—it's one motel, strip mall, nightclub, and miniature-golf course after another. In 1989, as *Cape Cod Life* magazine put it, "the town [began] to plant 350 trees in hopes that eventually the trees' leaves, like the fig leaf of Biblical lore, [would] cover the shame of unkempt overdevelopment." Regardless of the glut of tacky tourist traps, there are some interesting sights in the little villages along the way. So take Route 28 if you want to intersperse amusements with your sightseeing, because you really can amuse yourself to no end here. If you want to avoid this road entirely, a sensible option is to take speedy U.S. 6 to the exit nearest what you want to visit and then cut south across the interior. If you must travel the Route 28 area, take Buck Island Road, which runs north of and parallel to much of the busy route in West and South Yarmouth.

Yelverton Crowe settled the village of West Yarmouth in 1643 after acquiring the land from a Native American sachem. The deal they struck was that Crowe could have as much land as he could traverse in an hour in exchange for an "ox-chain, a copper kettle...and a few trinkets." The first settlers were farmers; when Central Wharf near Mill Creek was built in the 1830s, the town turned to more commercial ventures as it became headquarters for the growing packet service that ferried passengers from the Cape to Boston.

Listed on the National Register of Historic Places, the 1710 **Baxter Grist Mill,** by the shore of Mill Pond, is the only mill on Cape Cod powered by an inside water turbine; the others use either wind or paddle wheels. The mill was converted to the indoor metal turbine in 1860 because of the pond's low water level and the damage done to the wooden paddle wheel by winter freezes. The original metal turbine is displayed on the grounds, and a reproduction powers the restored mill. A videotape tells the mill's history. There are no scheduled hours or tours, but feel free to walk around the grounds. ⊠ *Rte. 28, across from Baxter Ave., West Yarmouth* ☎ *508/362–3021* ⊕ *www.hsoy.org/historic/baxtermill.htm.*

A unique and lovely walking trail, the **Yarmouth Boardwalk** ( ⊠ *Off Meadowbrook La., West Yarmouth*) stretches through swamp and marsh and leads to the edge of pretty Swan Pond, which is ringed with woods. To get here, take Winslow Gray Road northeast from Route 28, turn right on Meadowbrook Lane, and take it to the end.

☾ An entertaining, educational, and occasionally hokey stop for kids, **ZooQuarium** has sea-lion shows, a petting zoo with native wildlife, a touch-friendly tidal pool, wandering peacocks, aquariums, and educational programs, plus pony rides in summer. The Children's Discovery Center presents changing exhibits such as *What's the Buzz on Bees* and *What's for Lunch* (for which kids can prepare meals for animals).

✉ *674 Main St. (Rte. 28), West Yarmouth* ☎ *508/775–8883* ⊕ *www. zooquariumcapecod.net* ⌦ *$10* ☉ *Late June–Labor Day, daily 9:30– 5; Labor Day–Nov., Thurs.–Mon. 9:30–4; Dec.–mid-Feb., weekends 9:30–3; mid-Feb.–June, Wed.–Mon. 9:30–5.*

**NEED A BREAK?**

**Jerry's Seafood and Dairy Freeze** ( ✉ **654 Main St. [Rte. 28], West Yarmouth** ☎ **508/775–9752), open year-round, serves fried clams and onion rings, along with thick frappes (milk shakes), frozen yogurt, and soft-serve ice cream at good prices.**

A few miles east of West Yarmouth, you'll reach its similarly exuberant sister village, **South Yarmouth.** Here you can find charter boats, a river cruise, and boat and kayak rentals, plus seafood restaurants and markets. Like West Yarmouth, South Yarmouth has a stretch of blight and overdevelopment on Route 28, but it also has some nice beaches that are good for families. For a good indication of what the town looked like in the late 19th century, take a drive down Pleasant Street and the Main Street section south of Route 28 to view old homes in the Federal and Greek Revival styles. This section along Bass River was once home to the village's elite businessmen, bankers, and sea merchants. Adding to the pastoral aura of the area is the **Judah Baker Windmill**; the grounds here are pretty and peaceful. For a closer look, the windmill is open Tuesday and Thursday during summer.

South Yarmouth was once known as Quaker Village for the large numbers of Quakers who settled the area in the 1770s after a smallpox epidemic wiped out the local Native American population. The 1809 **Quaker Meeting House** is still open for worship. Two separate entrance doors and the partition down the center were meant to divide the sexes. The adjacent cemetery has simple markers with no epitaphs, an expression of the Friends' belief that all are equal in God's eyes. Behind the cemetery is a circa-1830 one-room Quaker schoolhouse. ✉ *58 N. Main St., South Yarmouth* ☎ *508/398–3773* ☉ *Meeting for worship Sun. at 10.*

**Pirate's Cove** is the most elaborate of the Cape's many miniature-golf setups, with a hill, a waterfall, a stream, and the 18-hole Blackbeard's Challenge course. ✉ *728 Main St. (Rte. 28), South Yarmouth* ☎ *508/394–6200* ☉ *July and Aug., daily 9 AM–11 PM; late Apr.–June, Sept., and Oct., most days 10–8, but call.*

For rainy-day fun, **Ryan Family Amusements** offers video-game rooms, Skee-Ball, and bowling. There's a snack bar that serves pizza, sandwiches, and beer and wine. ✉ *1067 Main St. (Rte. 28), South Yarmouth* ☎ *508/394–5644* ☉ *Daily; hrs vary.*

## WHERE TO EAT

$$–$$$$
★
ITALIAN

✕ **Abbicci.** Set inside a creamy yellow 1755 house nestled beneath towering shade trees, Abbicci is an airy, smartly decorated space with a handsome black-slate bar. One of the first to bring northern Italian cooking to Cape Cod, owner Marietta Bombardieri has remained true to tradition, offering fish and elegant pastas during summer and heartier dishes in the winter months. Expect to find rich and full-tasting fare; one of the most pleasing is roast rack and grilled leg of lamb with a Cabernet mint demi-glace. The menu changes seasonally, so there is always something new. A creative tapas menu makes this a great choice for grazing and sipping wine. The Sunday brunch menu strays nicely from the typical; try the organic hanger steak with a fried duck egg or the thyme and hazelnut pancakes. ⊠ *43 Main St. (Rte. 6A), Yarmouth Port* ☎ *508/362–3501* ⊕ *www.abbicci.com* ▤ *AE, D, DC, MC, V.*

> **LAY OF THE LAND**
>
> Locals sometimes refer to South Yarmouth as Bass River, after the river that separates the village from West Dennis.

¢–$$$ ✕ **Ardeo.** Despite its unpromising location in a shopping plaza, this
MEDITERRANEAN smart-casual Mediterranean bistro has built a local following for its pizzas, pastas, salads, panini sandwiches, and Middle Eastern fare. Some may find the food more Americanized than authentic, but it's tasty nonetheless. There's something for everyone here—you could bring the kids, or your grandparents, or a group of pals, and it's a good choice for vegetarians, too. As testament to its popularity, additional locations have sprouted on Hyannis's Main Street and in Yarmouth and Brewster. ⊠ *23 V Whites Path, Union Station Plaza, South Yarmouth* ☎ *508/760–1500* ⊕ *www.ardeocapecod.com* ▤ *AE, D, MC, V.*

$–$$$ ✕ **Inaho.** Yuji Watanabe, chef-owner of the Cape's best Japanese restau-
Fodor'sChoice rant, makes early-morning journeys to Boston's fish markets to shop
★ for the freshest local catch. His selection of sushi and sashimi is vast
JAPANESE and artful, and vegetable and seafood tempura come out of the kitchen fluffy and light. If you're a teriyaki lover, you can't do any better than the chicken's beautiful blend of sweet and sour. One remarkable element of the restaurant is its artful lighting: small pinpoint lights on the food accentuate the presentation in a dramatic way. Can't decide what to order? Try the Omakase Kaiseki dinner: for $100 and up per person, the chef designs a varied and generous tasting menu (advanced notice is necessary). The serene and simple Japanese garden out back has a traditional koi pond. ⊠ *157 Main St. (Rte. 6A), Yarmouth Port* ☎ *508/362–5522* ▤ *MC, V.* ⊗ *Closed Sun.*

¢–$ ✕ **Keltic Kitchen.** If you like to start your day with a substantial meal,
★ stop in at this friendly café for a traditional Irish breakfast—eggs, sau-
CAFE sage, rashers (bacon), black-and-white pudding, home fries or beans, tomato, and brown bread or scones. The potato pancakes with sour cream and scallions are also tasty, as are the more "American" options, including French toast and omelets. At midday, you can still get breakfast, or choose from an assortment of sandwiches that might include corned beef or burgers. Just don't come by too late—the kitchen closes around 2 PM. ⊠ *415 Main St. (Rte. 28), West Yarmouth* ☎ *508/771–4835* ▤ *AE, MC, V* ⊗ *No dinner.*

$$–$$$$ ✕ **Old Yarmouth Inn Restaurant & Tavern.** Established in 1696, this inn—
AMERICAN the oldest on Cape Cod—now primarily functions as a restaurant (rooms are available in season). It comprises a main dining room, which is bright and airy, and two smaller and more intimate ones, plus the wood-paneled Tavern, which has a full bar and serves more casual fare. Fresh ingredients are a priority, so the menu changes seasonally; the wide range of meat, poultry, seafood, and pasta dishes infused with

clever combinations of familiar flavors offers something for just about everyone. The Sunday brunch is popular. ⊠*223 Main St. (Rte. 6A), Yarmouth Port* ☎*508/362–9962* ⊕*www.oldyarmouthinn.com* ▤*AE, D, MC, V* ☉*Closed Mon., Jan.–May. No lunch Sun. or Mon.*

¢–$$  ✕ **The Optimist Café.** From the outside, this bold Gothic Victorian looks
BRITISH like something out of a Brothers Grimm tale, with its steeply pitched roof, turrets, elaborate gingerbread trim, and deep rose-and-green paint job. Inside, vibrant yellow walls help convey the café's mission to "turn a frown upside down." Chances are you'll be delighted with the great selection for breakfast (served all day) and lunch, featuring traditional English fare like the Ploughman's Lunch. Other British Isles favorites include several curries, smoked fish options, scones, and crumpets. Royalty or no, you're bound to be most pleased with the afternoon tea. Go all out with The Majesty: scones with clotted cream and preserves, a selection of finger sandwiches and desserts, a pot of tea, and a flute of champagne. ⊠ *134 Main St. (Rte. 6A) Yarmouth Port* ☎*508/362–1024* ▤ *AE, D, MC, V* ☉*No dinner.*

$$–$$$  ✕**The Skipper.** This classic Cape restaurant has been around since 1936.
SEAFOOD Sit downstairs in the nautical-theme main room or upstairs on the outside deck, which has terrific views of nearby Nantucket Sound. The kitchen turns out an appealing mix of fish and shellfish dishes, plus a handful of Italian specialties and landlubber options (such as Yankee pot roast and prime rib au jus). Try the seared chili-garlic scallops or the Thai coconut shrimp-and-chicken over rice. ⊠*152 S. Shore Dr.South Yarmouth* ☎*508/394–7406* ⚑*Reservations not accepted* ▤*AE, D, MC, V* ☉*Closed Nov.–mid-Apr.*

$–$$$$  ✕**Yarmouth House Restaurant.** This festive, family-owned, green-shingle
AMERICAN restaurant has built a devoted local following over the years. The menu has classic Italian dishes such as chicken Parmesan and veal marsala, as well as traditional grilled steaks and plenty of fresh seafood dishes. Try the filet mignon à la Neptune (topped with lobster meat and hollandaise sauce), and accompany your meal with a selection from their long list of beers, wines, and specialty cocktails. Early-bird specials, Sunday specials, and a kids' menu are available. ⊠*335 Main St. (Rte. 28), West Yarmouth* ☎*508/771–5454* ⊕*www.yarmouthhouse.com* ▤*AE, D, MC, V.*

**WHERE TO STAY**

$–$$  🏠**All Seasons Motor Inn.** This well-cared-for motor lodge in downtown
South Yarmouth ranks above the others in town because of its great staff, a lovely outdoor pool with attractive grounds and patio furniture, and large guest rooms with clean and updated fixtures and furnishings—many have balconies or patios overlooking the pool and courtyard. Plus, it's right by the Cape Cod Creamery ice-cream shop. The dining room serves lunch by the pool during the summer season. Be sure to ask for a discounted parking pass to Yarmouth-area beaches. **Pros:** easy access to all the activities and amenities of busy Route 28; reasonable prices for well-equipped rooms; two pools. **Cons:** not for a quiet romantic getaway (very popular with families with small children); no water views; not beachfront. ⊠*1199 Main St. (Rte. 28), South Yarmouth* ☎*508/394–7600 or 800/527–0359* 🖷*508/398–7160*

⊕*www.allseasons.com* ⟋*114 rooms* ⟠*In-room: refrigerator, DVD, Wi-Fi. In-hotel: pools, gym, no-smoking rooms, no elevator* ⊟*AE, D, MC, V* ⦿*CP.*

**$–$$$**   **Bayside Resort.** A bit more upscale than most of the properties along
★   Route 28, but still with extremely reasonable rates, the Bayside over-
looks pristine salt marshes and, beyond them, Lewis Bay. Although
it's not right on the water, there is a small beach and a large outdoor
pool with a café (there's also an indoor pool). Rooms have contem-
porary light-wood furnishings, and several have cathedral ceilings,
whirlpool tubs, and views toward the bay. Many members of the staff
have worked here for years, which helps to explain the resort's fam-
ily-friendly vibe. The Bayside Resort also offers a number of package
deals related to everything from golf to day trips to Martha's Vineyard
and Nantucket. **Pros:** ideal for families with children (organized kids'
programs available); close to attractions of busy Route 28; reason-
able rates; some water views; lots of specialized package deals. **Cons:**
beach is more like a sandy tanning area; no swimming; not for those
seeking quiet and intimate surroundings. ⊠*225 Main St. (Rte. 28),
West Yarmouth* ☎*508/775–5669 or 800/243–1114* 🖷*508/775–8862*
⊕*www.baysideresort.com* ⟋*128 rooms* ⟠*In-room: refrigerators,
Wi-Fi. In-hotel: bar, pools, gym, beachfront, no elevator* ⊟*AE, D,
MC, V* ⦿*CP.*

**$–$$$**   **Cape Point Hotel.** Families flock to this sensibly priced miniresort, tak-
ing advantage of the many amenities, large rooms, patient and friendly
staff, and the fact that kids are nearly always certain to find plenty of
other playmates here, especially in summer. Rooms contain simple but
updated modern furniture. The poolside Cabana Grill serves lunch in
July and August (it's open until 4:30). After one overnight visit here,
you're eligible to receive the Cape Point's unbelievably low-price off-
season specials. The hotel puts together some great golf packages with
a number of local clubs, and the same owners run the Mariner Motor
Lodge *(⇨ below)* and the even more affordable Town 'N Country
Motor Lodge. **Pros:** great for families with kids; reasonable and attractive golf package deals; close to all area attractions and restaurants.
**Cons:** not for those looking for a quiet retreat; no beachfront or water
views. ⊠*476 Main St. (Rte. 28), West Yarmouth* ☎*508/778–1500 or
800/323–9505* 🖷*508/778–5516* ⊕*www.capepointhotel.com* ⟋*116
rooms* ⟠*In-room: DVD, Wi-Fi. In-hotel: restaurant, bar, pools, gym*
⊟*AE, D, MC, V.*

**$$–$$$$**   **Capt. Farris House.** Steps from the Bass River Bridge and a short spin
FodorsChoice   away from congested Route 28 sits this imposing 1845 Greek Revival
★   home. Thoughtful amenities abound, from the plush bathrobes, beach
supplies, and fresh flowers in each room to a selection of complimentary
cordials. The large rooms and suites have either antique or canopied
beds, plush comforters, fancy drapes, and deep tile baths (all but one
with a whirlpool tub). Some have fireplaces and sundecks. Breakfast is
served in the formal dining room or the greenhouse-style interior court-
yard and might include quiche with pumpkin-pecan scones or thick
French toast. Baked goods and coffee are available after hours. **Pros:**
exquisite aged inn with beautiful grounds; ideal location for exploring

Mid Cape area; close to area restaurants and attractions. **Cons:** many rooms on 2nd floor (no elevator); not an in-town or on-beach location. ✉ *308 Old Main St., Bass River Village* ☎ *508/760–2818 or 800/350–9477* 🖷 *508/398–1262* 🌐 *www.captainfarris.com* 🛏 *6 rooms, 4 suites* ⌂ *In-room: VCR, Wi-Fi. In-hotel: no kids under 12, no-smoking rooms, no elevator* ⊟ *AE, D, MC, V* ⏃❙ *BP* ⊘ *Closed Jan.*

$$–$$$    🏠 **The Inn at Cape Cod.** A stately Greek Revival building with imposing columns, the inn has one of the most dramatic facades of any house on the Cape; it sits near the Botanical Trails and has its own fine gardens, patios, and tree-shaded lawns. On the 1st floor, the Joshua Sears Room, with a mahogany king-size four-poster bed and antique furnishings, is a traditional Victorian chamber. Upstairs, the romantic Village Suite, with an Italian armoire and cherrywood writing desk, opens to the front porch; the frilly Victorian Room has its own fireplace. Some smaller rooms, particularly the basic Guest Room, are pint-size. **Pros:** elegant and intimate historic lodging; close to attractions of scenic Route 6A. **Cons:** some rooms a bit small; no water views or direct beach access; some rooms accessed via steep stairs. ✉ *4 Summer St., Yarmouth Port* ☎ *508/375–0590 or 800/850–7301* 🖷 *508/362–9520* 🌐 *www.innatcapecod.com* 🛏 *7 rooms, 2 suites* ⌂ *In-room: DVD, VCR, Wi-Fi. In-hotel: no-smoking rooms, no elevator* ⊟ *AE, D, DC, MC, V* ⏃❙ *BP.*

$$    🏠 **Inn at Lewis Bay.** Affordable and beautiful, this 1920s Dutch Colonial
★    overlooks Lewis Bay, a short walk from the beach. Janet Vaughn, who owns the inn with her husband, David, is an avid quilter; her works top the antique or canopy beds and adorn the walls in the country-style rooms. Each room has a name and a theme; Whale Watch, with its distinctive navys and maroons, is one of two rooms with water views. Bountiful breakfasts are served in the dining room or on the spacious front porch, which is also a pleasant place for afternoon tea and home-baked cookies. It's in a quiet residential neighborhood south of the Route 28 fray. **Pros:** only one block to beach; friendly and appealing B&B feel; peaceful surroundings. **Cons:** some rooms up a set of stairs; not an in-town location. ✉ *57 Maine Ave., West Yarmouth* ☎ *508/771–3433 or 800/962–6679* 🖷 *508/790–1186* 🌐 *www. innatlewisbay.com* 🛏 *6 rooms* ⌂ *In-room: no phone, no TV (some), Wi-Fi. In-hotel: no kids under 12, no-smoking rooms, no elevator* ⊟ *AE, MC, V* ⏃❙ *BP.*

$$–$$$    🏠 **Liberty Hill Inn.** Smartly but traditionally furnished common areas—
Fodor's Choice    including the high-ceiling parlor, the formal dining room, and the wrap-
★    around porch—are a major draw to this dignified 1825 Greek Revival house. Guest rooms in both the main building and the carriage house are filled with a mix of old-world romantic charm and modern amenities; each is uniquely decorated, and some have whirlpool tubs and fireplaces for those chilly evenings. Breakfast might include blueberry French toast or a frittata, and afternoon tea is also available. If you're traveling with children under five, please make advanced arrangements with the innkeepers. **Pros:** elegant, historic, and tasteful surroundings; beautiful grounds; romantic and intimate setting. **Cons:** some rooms accessed only via some steep stairs; some bathrooms have only small

shower stalls; not a waterfront location. ✉ *77 Main St. (Rte. 6A), Yarmouth Port* ☎ *508/362–3976 or 800/821–3977* 🖷 *508/362–6485* ⊕ *www.libertyhillinn.com* ⬅ *8 rooms, 1 suite* ⚙ *In-room: Wi-Fi. In-hotel: no-smoking rooms, no elevator* ⊟ *AE, D, MC, V* ◯|*BP.*

$    🏠 **Mariner Motor Lodge.** Although crowded Route 28 is more commercial than serene, it's also home to several value-packed hotels. The Mariner is a good family lodging and a bargain. Although the rooms are standard-issue motel—think basic furnishings such as floral bedcovers and carpets that can take a direct hit from a spilled soft drink—the outdoor pool is heated and large, and a heated indoor pool, with an oversize whirlpool hot tub, is great for rainy days. Also on-site are a miniature-golf course and vending machines for snacks. Kids stay free, and weekday rates are reduced. **Pros:** ideal for those traveling with children; great golf packages; reasonable rates; close to attractions and restaurants. **Cons:** not for a quiet retreat; no beachfront or water views. ✉ *573 Main St. (Rte. 28), West Yarmouth* ☎ *508/771–7887 or 800/445–4050* 🖷 *508/771–2811* ⊕ *www.mariner-capecod.com* ⬅ *100 rooms* ⚙ *In-room: safe, refrigerator. In-hotel: restaurant, pools, no-smoking rooms, public Wi-Fi, no elevator* ⊟ *AE, D, MC, V.*

$$–$$$$    🏠 **Ocean Mist.** This three-story, motel-style resort sits on its own private (if tiny) beach on Nantucket Sound. The rooms have generic modern furnishings, cable TV, and either wet bars (with sink and refrigerator) or fully stocked kitchenettes. The duplex loft suites are a step above, with cathedral ceilings, sitting areas with pullout sofas, skylights, and one or two private balconies overlooking the water; more than half the rooms here have water views. **Pros:** great beachfront location; a good bet for those with children; rooms are well equipped. **Cons:** not for those looking for a quiet ocean-side retreat. ✉ *97 S. Shore Dr., South Yarmouth* ☎ *508/398–2633 or 800/248–6478* 🖷 *508/760–3151* ⊕ *www.capecodoceanresorts.com* ⬅ *32 rooms, 31 suites* ⚙ *In-room: kitchen (some), refrigerator. In-hotel: pool, beachfront, laundry facilities, no-smoking rooms, no elevator* ⊟ *AE, D, MC, V* ◯ *Closed Dec.–mid-Feb.*

$$–$$$$    🏠 **Seaside Cottages.** Right on Nantucket Sound, this 5-acre village of Cape-style cottages (studios and one- or two-bedroom units) has a view of scalloped beaches in both directions. Seaside was built in the 1940s, and the furnishings vary from cottage to cottage, since each is individually owned. All have kitchens or kitchenettes, and many have wood-burning fireplaces. The oceanfront cottages, right off a strip of grass set with lounge and Adirondack chairs, have the best views. Cottages in the adjacent pine grove are generally very pleasant, too. Rentals are by the week in summer; cottages can be rented by the night in late spring and fall. **Pros:** great beachfront location; linens and towels provided; daily housekeeping; spacious grounds. **Cons:** cottages are very close together; not for those seeking ultimate privacy; very popular with families with small children; nightly reservations hard to come by. ✉ *135 S. Shore Dr., South Yarmouth* ☎ *508/398–2533* 🖷 *508/398–2523* ⊕ *www.seasidecapecod.com* ⬅ *42 cottages* ⚙ *In-room: no a/c, no phone, kitchen (some). In-hotel: beachfront, public Wi-Fi, no elevator* ⊟ *MC, V* ◯ *Closed mid-Oct.–Apr.*

## NIGHTLIFE & THE ARTS

**Cape Cod Irish Village** ( ✉ *512 Main St. (Rte. 28), West Yarmouth* ☎ *508/771–0100*) has dancing to two- or three-piece bands performing traditional and popular Irish music year-round. The crowd is mostly couples and people over 35.

**Oliver's** ( ✉ *6 Bray Farm Rd., off Rte. 6A, Yarmouth Port* ☎ *508/362–6062*) has live music in a variety of genres in its tavern on weekends year-round.

West Yarmouth's summertime **town-band concerts** are held on Monday in July and August at 7 PM at **Mattacheese Middle School** ( ✉ *Off Higgins Crowell Rd., West Yarmouth* ☎ *508/778–1008*).

## SPORTS & THE OUTDOORS

BASEBALL  The **Yarmouth-Dennis Red Sox** of the collegiate Cape Cod Baseball League play home games at Dennis-Yarmouth High School's **Red Wilson Field** ( ✉ *Station Ave., South Yarmouth* ☎ *508/394–9387* ⊕ *www.ydredsox. org*) from mid-June to mid-August. Baseball clinics for girls and boys age five and up run throughout the season.

BEACHES  Parking at Yarmouth beaches for nonresidents is $12 on weekdays and $15 on weekends Memorial Day through Labor Day. Weekly stickers are also available for $50 and can be purchased right at most beach booths.

**Dennis Pond** ( ✉ *Off Summer St., Yarmouth Port*) is a freshwater pond with a sandy beach, restrooms, and a seasonal snack bar. In season, a resident parking sticker is required.

The **Flax Pond** ( ✉ *N. Main St. between High Bank and Great Western Rds., South Yarmouth*) recreation area has freshwater swimming, a lifeguard, and ducks, but no sand beach, just pine needle–covered ground. There's a pine-shaded picnic area with grills, as well as tennis and basketball courts and plenty of parking.

**Parker's River Beach** ( ✉ *South Shore Dr., South Yarmouth*), a flat stretch of sand on warm Nantucket Sound, is perfect for families. It has a lifeguard, a concession stand, a gazebo and picnic area, a playground, outdoor showers, and restrooms.

**Seagull Beach** ( ✉ *Seagull Rd. off South Sea Ave., West Yarmouth*), a long, wide beach along Nantucket Sound, has restrooms and a seasonal concession stand.

BIKE RENTAL  **Bike Zone Inc.** ( ✉ *1124 Rte. 28, South Yarmouth* ☎ *508/398–5550*) rents and sells bicycles; it's also a good local resource for all things related to cycling on the Cape.

BOATING  **Great Marsh Kayak Tours** ( ✉ *Rte. 28, West Yarmouth* ✛ *Next to ZooQuarium* ☎ *508/775–6447 or 866/395–2925* ⊕ *www.greatmarsh kayaktours.com*) offers a range of great excursions along the water, from fly-fishing trips to sunset jaunts—you can also customize your own itinerary.

FISHING **Truman's** ( ⊠ *608 Rte. 28, West Yarmouth* ☎ *508/771–3470*) can supply you with a required freshwater license and rental gear.

GOLF **Blue Rock Golf Course** ( ⊠ *Off Great Western Rd., South Yarmouth* ☎ *508/398–9295*) is a highly regarded, easy-to-walk 18-hole, par-3, 3,000-yard public course crossed by a pond. The pro shop rents clubs; reservations are mandatory in season.

HEALTH & **Mid Cape Racquet Club** ( ⊠ *193 White's Path, South Yarmouth*
FITNESS CLUBS ☎ *508/394–3511* ⊕ *www.midcaperacquet.com*) has one racquetball, one squash, and nine indoor tennis courts; indoor basketball; a sauna, steam room, and whirlpools; massage services; and a free-weight and cardiovascular room—plus day care. It also offers Spinning, kickboxing, and body blast classes. Daily rates are available.

### SHOPPING

**Cummaquid Fine Arts** ( ⊠ *4275 Main St. [Rte. 6A], Cummaquid* ☎ *508/362–2593*) has works by contemporary resident Cape Cod artists, all beautifully displayed in an old home.

**Design Works** ( ⊠ *159 Main St. [Rte. 6A], Yarmouth Port* ☎ *508/362–9698*) specializes in home furnishings, from luxurious linens, bath products, and antique furniture (especially Scandinavian) to high-end women's accessories, baby items, and glassware. If it's furniture you're after, ask to make an appointment to tour their large warehouse in nearby Hyannis.

**Parnassus Book Service** ( ⊠ *220 Rte. 6A, Yarmouth Port* ☎ *508/362–6420*), occupying a three-story 1840 former general store, has a huge selection of old and new books—Cape Cod, maritime, Americana, antiquarian, and others—and is a great place to browse. Its bookstall, outside on the building's side, is open 24 hours a day and works on the honor system—tally up your purchases and leave the money in the mail slot. Parnassus also carries Robert Bateman's nature prints.

**Peach Tree Designs** ( ⊠ *173 Rte. 6A, Yarmouth Port* ☎ *508/362–8317*) carries home furnishings and decorative accessories; some are from local craftspeople, all are beautifully made.

**Wild Birds Unlimited** ( ⊠ *1198 Main St. [Rte. 28], Yarmouth* ☎ *508/760–1996*) sells all things bird related, from bird-watching tools to feeders, seed, and suet. You'll also find bird- and nature-themed gifts, garden accents, T-shirts, birdbaths, and all sorts of avian treasures.

## DENNIS

*Dennis Village is 4 mi east of Yarmouth Port; West Dennis is 1 mi east of South Yarmouth.*

Like Yarmouth, Dennis has a split personality. The town's southern villages, such as Dennis Port and West Dennis, tend to be heavily developed and commercialized and are more popular with families, whereas the northern section, anchored by historic **Dennis Village,** is peaceful and dignified, with countless old homes and inns lining Route 6A.

The backstreets of Dennis Village still retain the colonial charm of its seafaring days. The town, which was incorporated in 1793, was named for the Reverend Josiah Dennis. There were 379 sea captains living here when fishing, salt making, and shipbuilding were the main industries, and the elegant

WORD OF MOUTH

"Don't forget to play minigolf. It's illegal to leave the Cape without having played at least one round."

—bennnie

3

houses they constructed—now museums and B&Bs—still line the streets. In 1816, resident Henry Hall discovered that adding sand to his cranberry fields' soil improved the size of his harvest and the quality of the fruit. The following decades saw cranberry farming and tourism become the Cape's main commercial enterprises. Dennis has a number of conservation areas and nature trails and numerous freshwater ponds for swimming. The village center has antiques shops, general stores, a post office, and ice-cream shops. There's also a village green with a bandstand, the site of occasional summer concerts.

The **Josiah Dennis Manse,** a saltbox house with add-ons, was built in 1736 for the Reverend Josiah Dennis. Inside, the home reflects life in the Reverend Dennis's day. A child's room includes antique furniture and toys, the keeping room has a fireplace and cooking utensils, and the attic exhibits spinning and weaving equipment. Throughout you'll see china, pewter, and portraits of sea captains. The Maritime Wing has ship models, paintings, and nautical artifacts. On the grounds is a 1770 one-room schoolhouse, furnished with wood-and-wrought-iron desks and chairs. Events throughout the summer include guided cemetery walking tours, an old-fashioned pie sale, a Victorian tea party, and open houses with costumed interpreters plying old-time 19th-century home skills. ⊠ *77 Nobscussett Rd., at Whig St., Dennis Village* ☎ *508/385–2232* ⊕ *www.dennishistsoc.org* ✉ *Donations accepted* ☉ *Late June–Sept., Tues. 10–noon, Thurs. 2–4.*

On a clear day, you'll have unbeatable views of Scargo Lake, Dennis Village's scattered houses below, Cape Cod Bay, and distant Provincetown from the top of **Scargo Tower.** A wooden tower built on this site in 1874 was one of the Cape's first tourist attractions; visitors would pay 5¢ to climb to the top for the views. That tower burned down, and the present all-stone 30-foot tower was built in 1901 to replace it. Winding stairs bring you to the top; don't forget to read the unsightly, but amusing, graffiti on the way up. Expect crowds at sunrise and sunset. ⊠ *Scargo Hill Rd., off Rte. 6A or Old Bass River Rd., Dennis Village* ✉ *Free* ☉ *Daily sunrise–sunset.*

**NEED A BREAK?** **Dip into homemade ice cream and frozen yogurt at the Ice Cream Smuggler** ( ⊠ *716 Rte. 6A, Dennis Village* ☎ *508/385–5307*)**, across the street from the town green and cemetery. The ginger ice cream is a specialty, but order the triple hot-fudge sundae for the ultimate decadence.**

☺ For Broadway-style dramas, comedies, and musicals, as well as kids'
FodorśChoice    plays, you can attend a production at the **Cape Playhouse,** the oldest pro-
★    fessional summer theater in the country. In 1927 Raymond Moore, who
had been working with a theatrical troupe in Provincetown, bought an
1838 former Unitarian meetinghouse and converted it into a theater.
The original pews still serve as seats. The opening performance was *The
Guardsman,* starring Basil Rathbone. Other stars who performed here
in the early days—some in their professional stage debuts—include Bette
Davis (who first worked here as an usher), Gregory Peck, Lana Turner,
Ginger Rogers, Humphrey Bogart, Tallulah Bankhead, and Henry
Fonda, who appeared with his then-unknown 20-year-old daughter,
Jane. Cape resident Shirley Booth was such an admirer of the playhouse
that she donated her Oscar (for *Come Back, Little Sheba*) and her Emmy
(for *Hazel*) to the theater; both are on display in the lobby during the
season. Behind-the-scene tours are also given in season; call for a schedule. The playhouse offers children's theater on Friday morning during
July and August. Also on the 26-acre property, now known as the Cape
Playhouse Center for the Arts, are a restaurant, the **Cape Cod Museum
of Art,** and the **Cape Cinema,** whose exterior was designed in the style
of the Congregational church in Centerville. Inside, a 6,400-square-foot
mural of heavenly skies—designed by Massachusetts artist Rockwell
Kent, who also designed the gold-sunburst curtain—covers the ceiling.
✉*820 Rte. 6A, Dennis Village* ☎*508/385–3911 or 877/385–3911*
⊕*www.capeplayhouse.com* ☾*Call for tour schedule.*

NEED A
BREAK?    Indulge in sumptuous baked goods at **Buckie's Biscotti** (✉*780 Main St.
[Rte. 6A], Dennis Village* ☎*508/385–4700*), just behind the Dennis Post
Office near the Cape Playhouse. Have a slice of pie—try the Italian home-
style ricotta or the key lime, arguably the Cape's best—or another tasty treat,
then wash it all down with a cappuccino or latte.

The **Cape Cod Museum of Art** has a permanent collection of more than
850 works by Cape-associated artists. Important pieces include a portrait of a fisherman's wife by Charles Hawthorne, the father of the
Provincetown art colony; a 1924 portrait of a Portuguese fisherman's
daughter by William Paxton, one of the first artists to summer in Provincetown; a collection of wood-block prints by Varujan Boghosian,
a member of Provincetown's Long Point Gallery cooperative; an oil
sketch by Karl Knaths, who painted in Provincetown from 1919 until
his death in 1971; and works by abstract expressionist Hans Hoffman
and many of his students. The museum also plays host to interesting
temporary exhibitions, film festivals, lectures, art classes, and trips.
The outdoor sculpture garden has an eclectic collection on display;
it's a pleasant place to take a short stroll. Admission is by donation on
Thursday. ✉*60 Hope La., on grounds of Cape Playhouse, off Rte. 6A,
Dennis Village* ☎*508/385–4477* ⊕*www.ccmoa.org* ☜*$8* ☾*Mon.–
Wed., Fri., Sat. 10–5, Thurs. 10–8, Sun. noon–5* ☾*Closed Mon. mid-
Oct–late May.*

In another one of those tricks of Cape geography, the village of **West
Dennis** is actually south of South Dennis, on the east side of the Bass

River. Dennisport is farther east, near the Harwich town line. If you're driving between West Dennis and Harwich, Lower County Road, with occasional glimpses of the sea between the cottages and beachfront hotels, is a more scenic alternative to overdeveloped Route 28.

The Mid Cape's last southern village is **Dennisport,** a prime summer-resort area, with gray-shingle cottages, summer homes and condominiums, and lots of white-picket fences covered with rambling roses. The Union Wharf Packing Company operated here in the 1850s, and sailmakers and ship chandlers lined the shore. Sunbathers now pack the sands where sea clams once laid primary claim.

**NEED A BREAK?**

Set in a rustic mid-19th-century barn decorated with a working nickelodeon, the **Sundae School Ice Cream Parlor** ( ✉ *387 Lower County Rd., Dennisport* ☎ *508/394-9122*), open mid-April through mid-October, serves great homemade ice cream, frozen yogurt, real whipped cream, and old-fashioned sarsaparilla and cream soda from an antique marble soda fountain.

## WHERE TO EAT

$–$$
Fodor'sChoice
★
SEAFOOD

✕ **Cap'n Frosty's.** A great stop after the beach, this is where locals go to get their fried seafood. This modest joint has a regular menu that includes ice cream, a small specials board, and a counter where you order and take a number written on a french-fries box. The staff is young and hardworking, pumping out fresh fried clams and fish-and-chips on paper plates. All frying is done in 100% canola oil, and rice pilaf is offered as a substitute for fries. There's seating inside as well as outside on a shady brick patio. ✉ *219 Main St. (Rte. 6A), Dennis Village* ☎ *508/385-8548* ⌖ *Reservations not accepted* ☐*MC, V* ⊘ *Closed early Sept.–Mar.*

$–$$
AMERICAN

✕ **Clancy's.** A local landmark on the bucolic Swan River, Clancy's is popular—the parking lot is often jammed by 5 PM, so expect a substantial wait during peak hours in season. This is an enormous operation, with long family tables, round tables, booths, a deck overlooking the river, and two bars. On the seemingly endless menu are several variations of nachos, salads, and chili. Clancy's likes to be creative with the names of its dishes, so you can find items such as steak Lucifer (sirloin topped with lobster, asparagus, and béarnaise sauce) and a Sunday-brunch menu with the likes of crab, steak, or eggs Benny. ✉ *8 Upper County Rd., Dennisport* ☎ *508/394-6661* ⌖ *Reservations not accepted* ☐*AE, DC, MC, V.*

$$–$$$
★
ITALIAN

✕ **Gina's by the Sea.** Some places are less than the sum of their parts; Gina's is more. This funky old building is tucked into a sand dune, so that the aroma of fine northern Italian cooking blends with a fresh breeze off the bay. The dining room is tasteful, cozy, and especially wonderful in fall when the fireplace is blazing. Blackboard specials could include angel-hair pasta or linguine with clams. If you don't want a long wait, come early or late. An enthusiastic staff rounds out the experience. ✉ *134 Taunton Ave., Dennis Village* ☎ *508/385-3213* ⌖ *Reservations not accepted* ☐*AE, MC, V* ⊘ *Closed Dec.–Mar. and Mon.–Wed.*

¢–$
AMERICAN

✗**Grumpy's Restaurant.** This airy diner consistently packs its tables and counter space year-round, and for good reason. From baked goods to waffles and eggs done any way you like them, Grumpy's jump-starts your day with generous portions for breakfast and lunch. Get here early to avoid a line that often curls out the door. ⊠*1408 Main St. (Rte. 6A), Dennis Village* ☎*508/385–2911* ⚘*Reservations not accepted* ▤*MC, V* ⊘*No dinner.*

¢–$$
SEAFOOD

✗**Kream 'N Kone.** The Kream 'N Kone has been going strong since 1953: order up some fried clams and a shake or a soda, get a number, wait five minutes, and sit down to some of the best fast food anywhere. Fried food will overflow your paper plate onto a plastic tray, but it's so good that what you thought you'd never be able to finish somehow vanishes. The onion rings in particular are a knockout. At times the prices seem surprisingly high, but the quality and quantity of what you get are well worth the splurge. ⊠*Corner of Rtes. 134 and 28, West Dennis* ☎*508/394–0808* ▤*MC, V* ⊘*Closed Nov.–Jan.*

$$–$$$$
Fodor'sChoice
★
ECLECTIC

✗**Ocean House.** Overlooking Nantucket Sound, this noisy but superb restaurant has views to match the spectacular food and service. For dinner, try apple mustard–glazed Atlantic salmon with creamy cheddar grits, followed by caramelized sugar–encrusted vanilla-bean crème brûlée. Chef Anthony Silvestri changes the menu seasonally. There are plenty of decadent options to choose from. Half plates are available for many entrées, ideal for smaller appetites or sharing. ⊠*End of Depot St., Dennisport* ☎*508/394–0700* ▤*AE, D, MC, V* ⊘*Closed Mon. (and Tues. in spring and fall); no lunch. Closed Jan. and Feb.*

$$–$$$
SEAFOOD

✗ **The Oyster Company.** Surprise, surprise: oysters are the big stars at this popular, lively restaurant. The owners have their own oyster farm out in Dennis waters, and oysters from other towns are also well represented—as are clams—and can be had a variety of ways (though raw on the half shell is the best way to enjoy these super-fresh bivalves). Seafood dominates the menu, from salmon to a great cioppino, with lobster, shrimp, mussels, and littlenecks in a lobster saffron broth. There's also some hearty land fare, from organic beef and duck to lamb. A roster of fancy martinis are nearly as popular as the oysters. It's a fun place all around, with great food and a boisterous atmosphere. ⊠ *202 Depot St. Dennisport, Dennisport* ☎*508/398–4600* ▤ *AE, MC, V* ⊘*No lunch.*

¢
Fodor'sChoice
★
AMERICAN

✗**Red Cottage Restaurant.** Up Old Bass River Road ½ mi north of the town hall, the Red Cottage is indeed a red cottage and serves breakfast and lunch year-round. Locals pack this place even in the off-season, and you can expect a wait in the summer. The cottage is a no-frills, friendly place with food that runs the gamut from decadent stuffed French toast specials to a list of health-conscious offerings with egg whites, "lite" cheese, and turkey bacon. The grill is in plain view; if you want to watch your meal being cooked, the swivel stools at the counter have the best angle. Bottomless cups of coffee are served in an interesting collection of mismatched mugs. The breakfasts are better than the lunches, but both are no-nonsense and just plain reliably good. ⊠*36 Old Bass River Rd., Dennis Village* ☎*508/394–2923* ⚘*Reservations not accepted* ▤*No credit cards* ⊘*No dinner.*

**3**

**$$–$$$$** ✕**Red Pheasant.** This is one of the Cape's best cozy country restau-
**Fodor's**Choice rants, with a consistently good kitchen where creative American food
★ is prepared with elaborate sauces and herb combinations. For instance,
AMERICAN organic chicken is served with an intense preserved-lemon and fresh
thyme sauce, and exquisitely grilled veal chops come with a dense red
wine–and–portobello mushroom sauce. In fall, look for the specialty
game dishes, including venison and quail. Try to reserve a table in the
more intimate Garden Room. The expansive wine list is excellent. A
nice Sunday brunch is served from mid-October to June. Those with
little ones in tow may want to go elsewhere for dinner; this is not the
place for a family meal. ✉*905 Main St. (Rte. 6A), Dennis Village* ✆
☎*508/385–2133* ⊕*www.redpheasantinn.com* ⌖*Reservations essen-
tial* ☐*AE, D, MC, V* ⊘*No lunch.*

**$$–$$$$** ✕**Scargo Café.** With the Cape Playhouse right across the street, this
AMERICAN upscale contemporary American restaurant is a favorite before- and
after-show haunt. There's plenty of seafood on the eclectic menu, which
includes Seafood Strudel with crab, shrimp, and scallops baked in a
pastry crust and topped with Newburg sauce and shrimp. Carnivores
will take delight in dishes like pan-seared pork medallions, rack of
lamb, and tenderloin à la chevre. Lighter meals include a ginger shrimp
salad and an Asian-style fish sandwich served with seaweed salad. An
added plus: the kitchen stays open until 11 PM in summer. ✉*799 Main
St. (Rte. 6A), Dennis Village* ☎*508/385–8200* ⊕*www.scargocafe.com*
☐*AE, D, MC, V.*

**$–$$$** ✕**Swan River Seafood Restaurant.** From the right table you can have a
SEAFOOD beautiful view of the Swan River marsh and Nantucket Sound beyond
at this informal little eatery, which turns out great fresh fish in both
traditional and creative preparations. Besides the usual fried and
broiled choices, try mako shark au poivre or scrod San Sebastian,
simmered in garlic broth with littleneck clams. There's also a take-
out window. ✉*5 Lower County Rd., Dennisport* ☎*508/394–4466*
☐*AE, MC, V* ⊘*Closed mid-Sept.–late May. No lunch weekdays late
May–mid-June.*

**WHERE TO STAY**

**$$–$$$$** 🏠**The Corsair and Cross Rip.** These motels, built side by side, offer clean
and crisp rooms, many with captivating beach views. Rooms in the
main motel buildings range from smaller "value" units with one queen
bed to pricier deluxe accommodations with kitchenettes and sitting
areas, plus a few spacious condo-style suites. Three large three- and
four-bedroom vacation houses are also available for rent; they can sleep
up to 12 and are fully equipped with luxurious amenities. Decor in the
motel buildings is more basic, but between the oceanfront location
(there are three private beaches) and the extensive facilities, you probably won't be spending much time in your room. There are also laundry facilities on-site. Suites and houses require a one-week minimum
stay in season. **Pros:** right on the beach; plenty of activities and three
pools to choose from; great for families. **Cons:** not for those seeking a
quiet retreat (big family destination). ✉*33 and 41 Chase Ave., Dennisport* ☎*508/398–2279 or 800/889–8037* ⊕*www.corsaircrossrip.com*
⇨*37 rooms, 6 suites* ♿*In-room: kitchen (some), refrigerator, Wi-Fi.*

*In-hotel: beachfront, pools, laundry facilities, no-smoking rooms, no elevator* ⊟*AE, D, MC, V* ⊘*Closed late Oct.–Mar.*

**$$** ▣ **English Garden Bed & Breakfast.** Anita and Joe Sangiolo—she's a former actress and he's a retired engineer—have turned their comfortable 1922 home into an equally comfortable B&B. The eight rooms are done in a cheerful country style, with quilts, four-poster or iron beds, and pine armoires; four rooms have ocean views. The adjacent carriage house has two modern suites, each with a bedroom, separate living area with gas fireplace, in-room laundry, and kitchenette—these are available on a weekly basis. Beach chairs and towels are provided (the house is a block from the sand), and Joe has put together a meticulously detailed notebook of things to do. Film buffs take note: one of the two guest parlors has a TV–VCR and a collection of classic movies. **Pros:** walk to beach; quiet area; gracious, helpful innkeepers; many ocean-view rooms. **Cons:** not an in-town location; rooms on 2nd and 3rd floors via stairs. ⊠*32 Inman Rd., Dennisport* ☎*508/398–2915 or 888/788–1908* ⊟*508/398–2852* ⊕*www.anenglishgardenbb.com* ⟋*9 rooms, 2 suites* ⟁*In-room: kitchen (some). In-hotel: Wi-Fi, no kids under 10 (except in suites), no-smoking rooms, no elevator* ⊟*D, MC, V* ⊘*Closed Nov.–mid-Apr.* ⦿|*BP.*

**$–$$** ▣ **The Garlands.** Old Wharf Road in Dennisport is lined with strip motels and cottage colonies, but few places provide comfort and views to match this bi-level motel-style complex. There are 20 units in all; 18 are two-bedroom suites. Each unit has a fully equipped kitchen, private sundeck or patio, and daily maid service. The oceanfront VIP suites, simply named A and B (two bedrooms) and C and D (one bedroom), are the best picks here—the nearly floor-to-ceiling windows offer unobstructed water views; at high tide you're almost in the surf. **Pros:** ideal beachfront location; fully equipped units for convenience. **Cons:** not an in-town location; no credit cards. ⊠*117 Old Wharf Rd., Box 506, Dennisport* ☎*508/398–6987* ⊕*www.thegarlandscapecod.com* ⟋*20 suites* ⟁*In-room: no a/c, kitchen. In-hotel: beachfront, no kids under 5, no elevator* ⊟*No credit cards* ⊘*Closed mid-Oct.–mid-Apr.*

**$–$$$**      ▣ **Isaiah Hall B&B Inn.** Lilacs and pink roses trail along the white-picket
**Fodor's Choice**  fence outside this 1857 Greek Revival farmhouse on a quiet residential
★       road near the bay. Innkeepers Jerry and Judy Neal set the scene for a romantic getaway with guest rooms that have country antiques, floral-print wallpapers, and homey touches, such as quilts and Priscilla curtains. In the attached carriage house, rooms have three walls stenciled white and one paneled with knotty pine, and some have small balconies overlooking a wooded lawn with gardens, grape arbors, and berry bushes. The Isaiah Hall Suite, with king bed and fireplace, can connect with another room to create a good-size two-bedroom/two-bath unit. The carriage-house suite has a king-size bed, a separate sitting area with a pullout couch, and a refrigerator. Common areas such as the dining room are elegant. Make-it-yourself popcorn, tea, coffee, and soft drinks are always available. **Pros:** beautiful grounds in very quiet, historic setting; not far from area beaches and attractions. **Cons:** many rooms accessed via very steep steps; some rooms are on the small side. ⊠*152 Whig St., Box 1007, Dennis Village* ☎*508/385–9928 or*

*800/736–0160* 🖷*508/385–5879* ⊕*www.isaiahhallinn.com* 🛏*10 rooms, 2 suites* ♿*In-room: DVD, Wi-Fi. In-hotel: no kids under 7, no-smoking rooms, no elevator* ▤*AE, D, MC, V* ⦿|*BP.*

$$$–$$$$ 🏨**Lighthouse Inn.** On a small private beach adjacent to West Dennis Beach, this venerable Cape resort has been in family hands since 1938. The main inn was built around a still-operational 1855 lighthouse. Along a landscaped lawn are 23 individual one-to-three-bedroom shingled cottages and five larger buildings with multiple guest rooms. Cottages have decks, fireplaces, two double (or one double and one king-size) beds, and sitting areas (but no kitchens). In the main inn are five guest rooms, a living room, a library, and a waterfront restaurant serving New England fare. In summer, supervised kids' activities give parents some private time. **Pros:** good beachfront location; tons of activities for those traveling with children. **Cons:** not for those seeking quiet, intimate lodging (lots of kids about). ✉*1 Lighthouse Rd., Box 128, West Dennis* ☎*508/398–2244* 🖷*508/398–5658* ⊕*www. lighthouseinn.com* 🛏*40 rooms, 23 cottages* ♿*In-room: refrigerator, Wi-Fi. In-hotel: restaurant, room service, bar, tennis court, pool, beachfront, children's programs (ages 3–12), no elevator* ▤*MC, V* ⊗*Closed mid-Oct.–mid-May* ⦿|*BP, MAP.*

$$–$$$ 🏨**Scargo Manor.** This 1895 sea captain's home has a prime location on Scargo Lake, with a private beach and dock. Inside, innkeepers Larry and Debbie Bain display a collection of art and antiques amid the Victorian furnishings. There's plenty of room to spread out on the big screened porch, in the sitting room or more formal living room, or in the cozy 3rd-floor reading room. If you want a lake view, choose the cozy all-blue Hydrangea Room, with a pineapple-top four-poster bed and a skylight overhead. For more space, the Captain Howe's Suite has a king-size canopy bed, plus a separate sitting room with a working fireplace that's bigger than the guest rooms at many other B&Bs. Kids five and up are welcome. **Pros:** great freshwater lakefront location for swimming and boating; many rooms have water views; historic lodging. **Cons:** rooms are accessed via steep stairs; some rooms have small shower stalls. ✉*909 Main St. (Rte. 6A), Dennis Village* ☎*508/385–5534 or 800/595–0034* 🖷*508/385–9791* ⊕*www.scargomanor.com* 🛏*4 rooms, 2 suites* ♿*In-room: no phone, Wi-Fi. In-hotel: beachfront, bicycles, no-smoking rooms, no elevator* ▤*D, MC, V* ⦿|*BP.*

$–$$ 🏨**Shady Hollow Inn.** Dedicated vegetarians, owners Ann Hart and David Dennis found B&B travel a challenge, so they opened their own vegetarian-friendly inn in tranquil South Dennis, well off the beaten path. Their breakfasts, which might include omelets, dairy-free baked goods, or a tofu quiche, are designed to appeal to anyone, from foodies to strict vegans. By prior arrangement, they can also prepare vegetarian dinners. Furnishings in their comfortable home are Mission-style; the guest rooms have quilt-topped beds, and the largest—the airy 1st-floor Westwind—has a striking painted mantel. The upstairs Lookout Room (two twin beds) can be joined with the Seabreeze (queen bed) for a suite that shares a large bathroom. Two kayaks are available on a first-come, first-served basis (the innkeepers will even take you to the nearby landing at Bass River); two bicycles are also available. **Pros:** in historic district; intimate and peaceful lodging in comfortable setting. **Cons:** some rooms accessed via stairs; not an in-town or beachfront location. ⊠*370 Main St., South Dennis* ☎*508/394–7474* ⊕*www. shadyhollowinn.com* ⇨*4 rooms, 3 with bath* ♨*In-room: no phone, VCR. In-hotel: bicycles, no kids under 10, no-smoking rooms, no elevator* ▤*MC, V* ⚬|*BP.*

### NIGHTLIFE & THE ARTS

The **Cape Playhouse** (⊠*820 Main St. (Rte. 6A), Dennis Village* ☎*508/385–3911 or 877/385–3911* ⊕*www.capeplayhouse.com*), an 1838 former Unitarian meetinghouse, is the oldest professional summer theater in the country. Top stars appear here each summer, and the playhouse also mounts kids' shows on Friday morning in July and August. On the grounds of the Cape Playhouse is the artsy **Cape Cinema** (⊠*508/385–2503* ⊕*www.capecinema.com*), which shows foreign and first-run films throughout the summer.

**Harvest Gallery Wine Bar** (⊠*776 Main St., Dennis Village* ☎*508/385–2444*) is right at home near the Cape Cod Museum of Art, Cape Cod Cinema, and the Cape Playhouse. There's an extensive wine list; a good variety of hors d'oeuvres, salads, and desserts; eclectic artwork; and live music. They're closed Tuesday.

**Improper Bostonian** (⊠*Rte. 28, Dennisport* ☎*508/394–7416*), open only in summer, has a mix of live music and DJ-spun dance tunes several nights a week and attracts a young crowd.

**Lost Dog Pub** (⊠*1374 Rte. 134, Dennis Village* ☎*508/385–6177*) offers basic pub eats and a relaxed social atmosphere; it's a popular place for locals and visitors to grab a beer after a long day. There's live music at least once a week.

**The Screening Room** (⊠*60 Hope La., Dennis Village* ☎*508/385–4477*), at the Cape Cod Museum of Art, shows avant-garde, classic, art, and independent films throughout the year. Call for a schedule.

The **Sand Bar** (⊠*Lighthouse Rd., West Dennis* ☎*508/398–7586*) presents the boogie-woogie piano playing of local legend Rock King, who's been tickling the ivories—and people's funny bones—since the 1960s. The club is closed from mid-October to mid-May.

In season, you can dance to a DJ and live bands at **Sundancer's** (⊠*116 Main St. [Rte. 28], West Dennis* ☎*508/394–1600*). It's closed December and January.

### SPORTS & THE OUTDOORS

BEACHES  Parking at all Dennis beaches is $15 a day in season for nonresidents.

**Chapin Beach** (⊠*Chapin Beach Rd., Dennis Village*) is a lovely dune-backed bay beach with long tidal flats—you can walk really far out at low tide. It has no lifeguards or services.

**Corporation Beach** (⊠*Corporation Rd., Dennis Village*) has lifeguards, showers, restrooms, and a food stand. Once a packet landing owned by a corporation of the townsfolk, the beautiful crescent of white sand backed by low dunes now serves a decidedly noncorporate purpose as a public beach.

**Mayflower Beach** ( ⊠*Dunes Rd. off Bayview Rd., Dennis Village*) reveals hundreds of feet of tidal flats at low tide. The beach has restrooms, showers, lifeguards, and a food stand.

For freshwater swimming, **Scargo Lake** ( ⊠*Access off Rte. 6A or Scargo Hill Rd., Dennis Village*) has two beaches with restrooms, playgrounds, and a picnic area. The sandy-bottom lake is shallow along the shore, which is good for kids. It's surrounded by woods and is stocked for fishing.

The **West Dennis Beach** ( ⊠*Lighthouse Rd. off Lower County Rd., West Dennis*) is one of the best on the south shore. A breakwater was started here in 1837 in an effort to protect the mouth of Bass River, but was abandoned when a sandbar formed on the shore side. It's a long, wide, and popular sandy beach, stretching for 1½ mi, with marshland and the Bass River across from it. Popular with windsurfers, the beach also has bathhouses, lifeguards, a playground, concessions, and parking for 1,000 cars.

BICYCLING   You can pick up the 25-mi Cape Cod Rail Trail at several points along its path. In fact, riding the entire trail in one day doesn't do justice to its sights and side trips (though it certainly can be done). Many cyclists, especially those with small kids, prefer the piecemeal method because they can relax and enjoy the sights—and not turn their legs into jelly.

The ride in Dennis starts as a flat, straight spin through a small pine forest—a good warm-up exercise. Your first road crossing is at busy Great Western Road, one of the town's major thoroughfares, after which you'll pass Sand Pond and Flax Pond in Harwich. The Dennis part of the trail is short, but it's worth starting here for the ample parking at the trail's entrance and for the several bike-rental places that set up shop on Route 134.

A guidebook published by the Dennis Chamber of Commerce includes bike tours and maps. You can rent bikes from a number of places along the Cape Cod Rail Trail. **Barbara's Bike Shop** ( ⊠*430 Rte. 134, Dennis Village* ☎*508/760–4723*) is at the Rail Trail entrance.

BOATING   **Cape Cod Waterways** ( ⊠*16 Rte. 28, Dennisport* ☎*508/398–0080*) rents canoes, kayaks, and electric paddleboats for leisurely travel on the Swan River.

FISHING   Sesuit Harbor, on the bay side of Dennis off Route 6A, is busy with fishing and pleasure boats; several are available for fishing charters. The *Prime Rate* ( ⊠*Sesuit Harbor* ⌖ *East Dennis* ☎*508/385–4626*) makes four-, five-, and six-hour fishing excursions. Hannah C. Charters ( ⊠*Sesuit Harbor* ⌖*, East Dennis* ☎*508/385–8150* ⊕*www. hannahccharters.com*) runs half- or full-day trips in search of stripers and bluefish with up to six people.

ICE SKATING  You can ice-skate at the **Tony Kent Arena** ( ✉ *8 Gages Way, South Dennis* ☎ *508/760–2400* ⊕ *www.tonykentarena.com*) fall though spring and on Saturday in summer. Rental skates are available.

JOGGING  **Lifecourse** ( ✉ *Bob Crowell Rd. and Old Bass River Rd., South Dennis*) is a 1½-mi jogging trail through the woods, with 20 exercise stations along the way. It's part of a recreation area that includes basketball and handball courts, ball fields, a playground, and a picnic area.

## SHOPPING

**Antiques Center of Cape Cod** ( ✉ *243 Main St. [Rte. 6A], Dennis Village* ☎ *508/385–6400*) is a large and busy market populated by more than 160 dealers offering furniture, artwork, jewelry, china, clocks, books, antique dolls, and other collectibles.

**Armchair Bookstore** ( ✉ *619 Main St. [Rte. 6A], Dennis Village* ☎ *508/385–0900*) carries a large selection of new releases, plus numerous books about Cape lore, history, and sights. Also on hand are cards and knick-knacks and a kids' section with books, games, and toys.

**Cape Cod Shoe Mart** ( ✉ *271 Main St. [Rte. 28], Dennisport* ☎ *508/398–6000*) has such brand names as Capezio, Dexter, Clark, Esprit, Nike, Reebok, L. A. Gear, and Rockport.

**Dick & Ellie's Flea Market** ( ✉ *Theophilus Smith Rd., off Rte. 134, next to Patriot Square Plaza, Dennis* ☎ *508/394–6131* ⊕ *www.capecod outdoormarket.com*) has vendors selling clothing, jewelry, handbags, crafts, plants, and even lobsters, in a large outdoor market. There's a kids' "Playland" on-site, free with admission ($1). They're open Thursday through Monday from late June to Labor Day, weekends through Columbus Day.

**Emily's Beach Barn** ( ✉ *708 Main St. [Rte. 6A], Dennis Village* ☎ *508/385–8328*) has fashionable women's beachwear, from bathing suits and wraps to sun hats and summer dresses and tops.

★ **Robert C. Eldred Co.** ( ✉ *1483 Rte. 6A, East Dennis* ☎ *508/385–3116* ⊕ *www.eldreds.com*) holds more than two dozen auctions per year, dealing in Americana; estate jewelry; top-quality antiques; marine, Asian, American, and European art; tools; and dolls. Its "general antiques and accessories" auctions put less-expensive wares on the block.

**Ross Coppelman, Goldsmith** ( ✉ *1439 Rte. 6A, East Dennis* ☎ *508/385–7900* ⊕ *www.rosscoppelman.com*) sells original jewelry in high-karat gold, semiprecious gemstones, and other materials (customized wedding bands are a specialty). The pieces are designed by Coppelman, a self-taught goldsmith who has been honing his craft for more than 30 years. Be sure to take a peek into the tiny workshop as you enter the showroom.

Fodor'sChoice  **Scargo Pottery** ( ✉ *30 Dr. Lord's Rd. S, off Rte. 6A, Dennis Village*
★ ☎ *508/385–3894* ⊕ *www.scargopottery.com*) is in a pine forest, where potter Harry Holl's unusual wares—such as his signature castle birdhouses—sit on tree stumps and hang from branches. Inside are the

workshop and kiln, plus work by Holl's four daughters. With luck you can catch a potter at the wheel; viewing is, in fact, encouraged.

# THE MID CAPE ESSENTIALS

*To research prices, get advice from other travelers, and book travel arrangements, visit ⊕www.fodors.com.*

### TRANSPORTATION

### BY BOAT & FERRY

Ferries to Nantucket and Martha's Vineyard leave from Hyannis year-round. *For details, see ⇨ Boat & Ferry Travel in Essentials in the back of this book.*

### BY BUS

Hyannis is the Cape's transit hub, and is served by a number of bus routes, including the local Hyannis Villager and the Barnstable Villager lines. Buses also link Hyannis with Orleans, Woods Hole, Provincetown, Plymouth, downtown Boston, and Logan airport, as well as various towns on each route. *For more information, see ⇨ Bus Travel in Essentials in the back of this book.*

**Bus Depots Hyannis Transportation Center** ( ✉ *215 Iyanough Rd., Hyannis* ☎ *508/775-8504* ⊕ *www.capecodtransit.org*). **Plymouth & Brockton Street Railway Terminals** ( ✉ *South Station Bus Terminal, 700 Atlantic Ave., Boston* ☎ *508/746-0378*).

### BY TAXI

There are taxi stands at the Hyannis airport, the Hyannis bus station, the ferry terminals, and the Capetown Mall, across the street from the Cape Cod Mall. In Hyannis, call Checker Taxi for pickups. Dick's Taxi will pick you up and has a stand at the airport. John's Taxi & Limousine picks up in Dennis and Harwich only but will take passengers all over the Cape. Town Taxi is found at several locations around Hyannis, including Capetown Mall, the bus station, and on West Main Street.

**Taxi Companies Checker Taxi** ( ☎ *508/771-8294*). **Dick's Taxi** ( ☎ *508/428-4918*). **John's Taxi & Limousine** ( ☎ *508/394-3209*). **Town Taxi** ( ☎ *508/771-5555 or 888/771-8696*).

### CONTACTS & RESOURCES

### CONDO & HOUSE RENTALS

Century 21, Sam Ingram Real Estate handles rentals throughout the Mid Cape region. Mid-Cape Rentals offers properties throughout the villages of Dennis, Yarmouth, and Harwich. Peter McDowell Associates offers a wide selection of properties for rent by the week, month, or season; the company also rents larger homes for family reunions and other gatherings. Most places are in Dennis. Waterfront Rentals covers Bourne to Truro, listing everything from condos to estates.

**Local Agents Century 21, Sam Ingram Real Estate** ( ✉ *938 Rte. 6A, Yarmouth*

Port ☎508/362–1191 or 800/676–3340 🖷508/362–7889 ⊕summerrentalscape
cod.com). **Mid-Cape Rentals** (✉598 Route 28, West Dennis ☎888/394–6588
⊕www.midcaperentals.com). **Peter McDowell Associates** (✉585 Main St.
[Rte. 6A], Dennis ☎508/385–9114 or 888/385–9114 ✉11 Main St. [Rte. 28],
Dennisport ☎508/394–5400 or 800/870–5401 ⊕www.rentcapecodproperties.
com). **Waterfront Rentals** (✉20 Pilgrim Rd., West Yarmouth ☎508/778–1818
🖷508/771–3563 ⊕www.waterfrontrentalsinc.com).

## TOURS

Cape Cod Soaring Adventures offers glider flights and lessons out of
Marstons Mills. Fully narrated history tours of the downtown Hyannis area are conducted on old-time trolleys with Olde Barnstable Trolley. Hour-long tours leave from behind the JFK museum at 397 Main
Street; combo tickets are available with the museum.

**Information** **Cape Cod Soaring Adventures** (☎508/420–4201 ⊕www.
capecodsoaring.com).**Olde Barnstable Trolley** (☎508/771–8687 ⊕www.olde
barnstabletrolley.com).

## VISITOR INFORMATION

The Cape Cod Chamber of Commerce is open year-round, Monday
through Saturday 9 to 5 and Sunday 10 to 4.

**Tourist Information** **Cape Cod Chamber of Commerce** (✉Junction of U.S. 6
and 132 📮Box 790, Hyannis 02601 ☎508/362–3225 or 888/332–2732 ⊕www.
capecodchamber.org). **Dennis Chamber of Commerce** (✉238 Swan River Rd.,
West Dennis 📮Box 1001, West Dennis 02670 ☎508/398–3568 or 800/243–9920
⊕www.dennischamber.com). **Hyannis Chamber of Commerce** (✉397 Main St.
📮Box 100, Hyannis 02601 ☎508/775–2201 or 877/492–6647 ⊕www.hyannis.
com). **Yarmouth Chamber of Commerce** (✉425 Rte. 28, West Yarmouth02673
📮Box 476, South Yarmouth 02664 ☎508/778–1008 or 800/732–1008 ⊕www.
yarmouthcapecod.com Information center ✉U.S. 6 heading east between exits
6 and 7 ☎508/362–9796).

# The Lower Cape

**WORD OF MOUTH**

"I'll second Fort Hill Bed and Breakfast. We have stayed at a number of other B+B's over the years on the outer Cape but none compare to the location, privacy, space and friendliness that we found at Fort Hill. The cottage has ocean views, gas fireplace and private gardens. It is very private and is decorated with a "Maine Cottage" look. You know, sea-grass rug, painted wainscoating, bluestone floors and country-check sofa and chair. It is the only lodging that is inside the National Seashore, away from the hustle of the main roads, but just a couple of minutes from Orleans and 30 minutes from Provincetown."

—yellowbyrd

Updated
by Laura V.
Scheel

**SPECKLED WITH STILL-ACTIVE CRANBERRY BOGS,** sturdy trees, and pastures, the Lower Cape exudes a peaceful residential aura. You won't find roadways cluttered with minigolf complexes, trampolines, or bumper boats here. And although an influx of year-round residents has transformed much of the Upper Cape into a commuter's haven, the Lower Cape still has a quiet sense of history and simple purpose.

Rich in history and Cape flavor, Brewster and Harwich stand opposite each other in the area just shy of the Cape's elbow. Harwich, farther inland, has antique homes, rambling old burial grounds, and a modest town center with shops, restaurants, museums, churches, and public parks. Brewster is similarly historic; examples of Victorian, Greek Revival, and colonial architecture abound, most meticulously preserved. Many homes have been converted to welcoming guesthouses and bed-and-breakfasts, whereas others are privately owned.

The traditional, elegant town of Chatham perches dramatically at the end of the peninsular elbow. It's here that the Atlantic begins to wet the shores of the Cape, sometimes with frightening strength. Chatham has shown its vulnerability to the forces of nature over the years, as little by little the town's shores have succumbed to the insatiable sea.

North of Chatham is Orleans, supply center of the Lower and Outer Capes, replete with large grocery chains and shopping plazas. The famed Nauset Beach is here, its dune-backed shores crammed with sun-seeking revelers in summer. Orleans also has a rich history—you just have to leave the maze of industry to find it. Continuing north, you can reach Eastham, a town often overlooked because of its position on busy U.S. 6. It too is perfectly charming, if you know where to look.

The Lower Cape is blessed with large tracts of open space, set aside for conservation. South of Chatham, the Monomoy National Wildlife Refuge is a twin-island bird sanctuary. Here dozens of species of birds are free to feed, nest, and expand their numbers without human meddling. Recreation seekers should head straight to Nickerson State Park in Brewster to frolic in freshwater ponds or enjoy a serene bike ride under the shade of stately white pine, oak, and maple trees. In Eastham, where the Cape Cod National Seashore officially begins, the Salt Pond Visitor Center has a wealth of area information, educational programs, and guided tours.

## EXPLORING THE LOWER CAPE

The towns of Harwich, Chatham, Brewster, Orleans, and Eastham make up the Lower Cape. Of these, only Brewster and Orleans touch Route 6A. Harwich, Chatham, and Orleans span Route 28—but have no fear. Although it's known for traffic, Route 28's congestion eases as the road winds toward the Lower Cape. Eastham sits along U.S. 6, which is the fastest way to get to all the towns—but if you're concerned about the journey as well as the destination, it's worthwhile to amble along Route 28 or 6A. Along the way, picturesque harbors, scenic side roads, and the towns' main streets, antiques stores, romantic inns, and colonial homes dot the landscape. Follow Route 28 into Chatham and make your way to the Chatham Lighthouse for breathtaking views of Nantucket Sound.

## ABOUT THE RESTAURANTS

Each town has its own batch of treasured and traditional restaurants, and all will be crowded in summer. A significant number of restaurants close their doors once the crowds thin in October—including the beloved fried-seafood shacks—but plenty remain open throughout the year. Fresh seafood is a major staple.

| TOP 5 |
| --- |
| ■ Shelling Cape Cod Bay's beaches at low tide |
| ■ Walking the forested trails of Nickerson State Park in Brewster |
| ■ Browsing the art galleries on Chatham's Main Street |
| ■ Cheering on the teams of the Cape Cod Baseball League, made up of the nation's top college players |
| ■ Devouring the lobster roll at Brax Landing in Harwich Port |

4

If you are celebrating a milestone or hoping to delight someone special, Brewster's Chillingsworth impresses with French-country elegance. The Chatham Bars Inn recalls an era of gentle tranquillity. If you're undecided, a stroll down Chatham's Main Street will tempt your palate. The restaurants in Orleans, Brewster, Harwich, and Eastham are spread out through the towns, but top restaurants such as the Brewster Fish House are worth finding.

Most Cape towns—including Chatham, Orleans, Eastham, Brewster, and Harwich—have banished smoking from restaurants and bars; smokers can retreat for a break outdoors.

## ABOUT THE HOTELS

Money made in early maritime fortunes helped build exquisite homes, many of which are now unique and lovely inns. Chatham is blessed with dozens of these aged beauties, most with all the modern conveniences. B&Bs and intimate guesthouses are the primary lodging choices, but even larger hotels such as Chatham Bars Inn and the Chatham Wayside Inn capture the charm of Old Cape Cod. Expect fewer hotel and motel options on this part of the Cape. However, there are a few roadside or waterfront hotels outside the town centers. These complexes, which usually welcome families with small children, can be a bit softer on the wallet.

Brewster is essentially a B&B kind of town, offering lodging in former sea captains' homes. Harwich and Orleans have a mixture of both family-friendly hotel complexes and lovingly restored inns. Eastham has quite a few large-scale hotels along U.S. 6, including a Sheraton. Don't expect to find bargains here during the high season.

Other options include camping or weekly cottage rentals—all towns have the Cape's trademark cottage colonies. Note that in summer these must be secured well in advance, usually through a local real-estate agent.

## TIMING

Although the crowds of summer are testament to the appeal of the Lower Cape and its spectacular beaches, outdoor pursuits, crafts and art shows, concerts, and special events, the region is becoming a popular year-round destination. Because of its ocean-side climate, spring and fall are simply lesser shades of full-blown summer. Seasonal businesses reopen in late May and early June, but lodging rates remain less pricey than during the high season, and the agonies of summertime traffic, long waits at restaurants, and parking restrictions at area beaches can be avoided. September, October, and even November are the same. The waters usually remain warm enough to swim well into October, and many shops attempt to rid their stocks of merchandise by having generous sales.

You won't get the expected splendors of New England foliage on the Lower Cape, because the landscape changes are subtle. Swaying salt-marsh grasses turn golden, cranberry bogs explode into ruby-red quilts, and the ocean relaxes into a deep, deep blue. The light becomes softer and its patterns more dramatic on both land and sea. In the towns of Harwich, Brewster, and Orleans, where the soil is substantial enough to support mighty oaks and maples, the colors of autumn do peer through. A drive along Route 6A under the canopy of changing leaves is just as breathtaking as a summer jaunt past blooming gardens.

| WHAT IT COSTS | | | | |
|---|---|---|---|---|
| $$$$ | $$$ | $$ | $ | ¢ |
| RESTAURANTS over $30 | $22–$30 | $16–$22 | $10–$16 | under $10 |
| HOTELS over $260 | $200–$260 | $140–$200 | $90–$140 | under $90 |

Restaurant prices are per person for a main course at dinner. Hotel prices are for a standard double room in high season, excluding 6% state tax, local taxes, and gratuities. Some inns add a 15% service charge.

## BREWSTER

*6 mi north of Chatham, 5 mi west of Orleans, 20 mi east of Sandwich.*

Brewster calls itself the Sea Captains' Town, honoring its rich heritage as a seafaring community. Historic Route 6A, the Old King's Highway, winds through its center. This road, the old stagecoach route, was once nearly the only one at this end of the Cape, and residents and legislators alike are determined to keep it well preserved. Homes and businesses must adhere to historic detail: there are no neon signs, no strip malls—only the gentle facades of a graceful era.

Named for Plymouth leader William Brewster, the area was settled in 1659 but was not incorporated as a separate town until 1803. In the early 1800s, Brewster was the terminus of a packet cargo service from Boston. In 1849 Henry David Thoreau wrote that "this town has more

# The Lower Cape

## Cape Cod Bay

### KEY
🚲 Cape Cod Rail Trail
⛴ Ferry

**CAPE**
**COD**
**NATIONAL**
**SEASHORE**

ATLANTIC OCEAN

North Truro

Castle Rd.

Ballston Beach

Truro

Old Country Rd.

6

Griffin Island Rd.

Chequesset Neck Rd.

Gull Pond

Long Pond

Newcomb Hollow Beach

Cahoon Hollow Beach

White Crest Beach

LeCount Hollow Beach

Wellfleet

Great Pond

South Wellfleet

Great Island

Wellfleet Harbor

6

Marconi Beach

North Eastham

Nauset Light

Nauset Light Beach

Coast Guard Beach

Salt Pond Visitor Center

Eastham

Nauset Marsh

First Encounter Beach

Fort Hill Area

Rock Harbor

Nauset Harbor

Skaket Beach

Orleans

Beach Rd.

Nauset Beach

Pilgrim Lake

28

### Detail map (Brewster area)

Brewster Historical Society Museum

Linnell Landing

Crosby Beach

Breakwater Landing

East Brewster

Cape Cod Museum of Natural History

Brewster Store

6A

Brewster

Brewster Ladies' Library

6A

Stony Brook Rd.

West Brewster

Tubman Rd.

---

see detail map above

Brewster

East Brewster

West Brewster

Flax Pond

Nickerson State Park

Millstone Rd.

Long Pond Rd.

6

39

Pleasant Bay

Paine's Creek Beach

6A

East Dennis

Dennis

Stony Brook Grist Mill

Punkhorn Parklands

124

Long Pond

Setucket Rd.

134

6

South Dennis

East Harwich

Chatham see detail map

North Beach

Chatham Light

39

137

West Chatham

South Yarmouth

Harwich

28

West Dennis

Dennisport

Harwich Port

South Harwich

Harding's Beach

Morris Island

South Beach

May-Oct.

Monomoy National Wildlife Refuge

0    2 miles
0    2 kilometers

mates and masters of vessels than any other town in the country." Many mansions built for sea captains remain, and quite a few have been turned into handsome B&Bs (though in recent years, more than a few of these have reverted to private homes). In the 18th and 19th centuries, the bay side of Brewster

was the site of a major salt-making industry. Of the 450 saltworks operating on the Cape in the 1830s, more than 60 were here.

Brewster's location on Cape Cod Bay makes it a perfect place to learn about the region's ecology. The Cape Cod Museum of Natural History is here, and the area is rich in conservation lands, state parks, forests, freshwater ponds, and brackish marshes. When the tide is low in Cape Cod Bay, you can stroll the beaches and explore tidal pools up to 2 mi from the shore on the Brewster flats. When it's high tide, the water is relatively warm and very calm for swimming. Both Nickerson State Park and the Punkhorn Parklands have thousands of acres through which to wander.

Windmills used to be prominent in Cape Cod towns; the Brewster area once had four. The 1795 **Higgins Farm Windmill** ( ⊠ *Off Rte. 6A, Drummer Boy Park, just west of the Cape Cod Museum of Natural History, West Brewster* ☎ *508/896–9521* ⊕ *www.brewsterhistoricalsociety.org* ☺ *July–Sept., Thurs.–Sat. 1–4*)—an octagonal-type mill shingled in weathered pine with a roof like an upturned boat—was moved here in 1974 and has been restored. The millstones are original. At night the mill is often spotlighted, which makes for quite a sight.

On the grounds of the Higgins Farm Windmill in Drummer Boy Park, the one-room **Harris-Black House** dates to 1795. Today, the restored building is partially furnished and is dominated by a brick hearth and original woodwork. ⊠ *Off Rte. 6A, Drummer Boy Park, just west of Cape Cod Museum of Natural History, West Brewster* ☎ *508/896–9521* ⊕ *www. brewsterhistoricalsociety.org* ☐ *Free* ☺ *July–Sept., Thurs.–Sat. 1–4.*

A short drive from Route 6A is the **Stony Brook Grist Mill,** a restored, operating 19th-century fulling mill (a mill that shrinks and thickens cloth), now also a museum. The old mill's waterwheel slowly turns in a small, tree-lined brook. Inside, exhibits include old mill equipment and looms; you can watch cornmeal being stone-ground and get a lesson in weaving on a 100-year-old loom. Out back, across wooden bridges, a bench has a view of the pond and of the sluices leading into the mill area.

Early each spring, in April and early May, Stony Brook's **Herring Run** boils with alewives (herring) making their way to spawning waters; it's an amazing sight. The fish swim in from Cape Cod Bay up Paine's Creek to Stony Brook and the ponds beyond it. The herring run, a rushing stream across the street from the mill, consists of ladders that help the fish climb the rocky waters. Seagulls swarm in and pluck herring from the run into midair. Sadly, disturbingly low numbers of returning herring have prompted the state to issue a three-year moratorium on fish harvests at the run. Tentatively ending in the spring of 2009, it says that no herring can be taken from the stream, ending a long-standing tradition in hopes of increasing fish stocks. Farther down the path to the stream, there's an ivy-covered stone wishing well and a wooden bridge with a bench. ✉*Stony Brook Rd., West Brewster* ✛*Off Rte. 6A* ☎*No phone* 🎫*Donations accepted* ⊙*June–Aug., Sat. 10–2.*

♻ For nature enthusiasts, a visit to the **Cape Cod Museum of Natural History** is a must; it's just a short drive west from the heart of Brewster along Route 6A. The spacious museum and pristine grounds include guided field walks, a shop, a natural-history library, lectures, classes, nature and marine exhibits such as a working beehive, and a pond- and sea-life room with live specimens. Walking trails wind through 80 acres of forest, marshland, and ponds, all rich in birds and other wildlife. The exhibit hall upstairs has a wall display of aerial photographs documenting the process by which the famous Chatham sandbar was split in two. The museum also has guided canoe and kayak trips from May through September and several cruises that explore Cape waterways. Onboard naturalists point out the wildlife and relay historical information about each habitat. Call for tour times and fees, and sign up as early as you can. There are children's and family activities in summer, including guided field walks, nature programs, full- and half-day workshops, and one- and two-week day camps consisting of art and nature classes for preschoolers through ninth graders. ✉*869 Main St. (Rte. 6A), West Brewster* ☎*508/896–3867, 800/479–3867 in Massachusetts* ⊕*www. ccmnh.org* 🎫*$8* ⊙*Oct.–Dec. and Feb.–Mar., Wed.–Sun. noon–4; Apr. and May, Wed.–Sun. 10–4; June–Sept., daily 9:30–4; closed Jan.*

*Fodor's*Choice
★

4

The **Brewster Ladies' Library** ( ✉*1822 Main St. (Rte. 6A)* ☎*508/896–3913* ⊕*www.brewsterladieslibrary.org*) is in a restored Victorian building with a more modern addition; both are painted in the historically accurate and eye-catching hues of deep cranberry and creamy yellow. The library is host to a full schedule of regular events for all ages, including book discussion groups, lectures, readings, and craft programs for children.

At the junction of Route 124, the **Brewster Store** ( ✉*1935 Main St. [Rte. 6A]* ☎*508/896–3744* ⊕*www.brewsterstore.com*) is a local landmark. Built in 1852 as a church, it's a typical New England general store with such essentials as the daily papers, penny candy, and benches out front for conversation. Out back, the Brewster Scoop serves ice cream mid-June through early September. Upstairs, the old front of the store has been re-created, and memorabilia from antique toys to World War II bond posters are displayed. Downstairs there's a working antique nickelodeon; locals warm themselves by the old coal stove in the colder months.

**NEED A BREAK?**

If you need a quick break, **Hopkins House Gift and Bakery** ( ✉*2727 Main St. [Rte. 6A], East Brewster* ☎*508/896–9337*) is the perfect pit stop. Wash down a chewy hermit cookie, baked with molasses and raisins, with some strong, hot coffee. A home-furnishings shop attached to the bakery might tempt you to stretch your legs a while longer.

Known as the Church of the Sea Captains, the handsome **First Parish Church** (✉ *1969 Main St. [Rte. 6A]* ☎ *508/896–5577*), with Gothic windows and a capped bell tower, is full of pews marked with the names of famous Brewster seamen. Out back is an old graveyard where militiamen, clergy, farmers, and sea captains rest side by side. The church is the site of a summer musical program, which includes the ever-popular Tanglewood marionette show, Tuesday through Thursday mornings at 9:30.

The **Brewster Historical Society Museum,** in an 1830s house, has a sea captain's room with paintings and artifacts, an 1890 barbershop, a child's room with antique toys and clothing, a room of women's period gowns and accessories, and other exhibits on local history and architecture. Out back, a ¼-mi nature trail over dunes leads to the bay. ✉ *3171 Rte. 6A, East Brewster* ☎ *508/896–9521* ⊕ *www.brewsterhistoricalsociety. org* ☞ *Free (donations accepted)* ☉ *July and Aug., Thurs.–Sat. 1–4.*

For a lovely hike or run through the local wilds, try the **Punkhorn Parklands,** with freshwater kettle-hole ponds and 45 mi of scenic trails meandering through 800 acres of meadows, marshes, and pine forests. ✉ *End of Run Hill Rd., off Stony Brook Rd., West Brewster.*

☽ **Nickerson State Park**'s 1,961 acres were once part of a vast estate belonging to Roland C. Nickerson, son of Samuel Nickerson, a Chatham native who became a multimillionaire and founded the First National Bank of Chicago. Today the land is open to the public for recreation. Roland and his wife, Addie, lavishly entertained such visitors as President Grover Cleveland at their private beach and hunting lodge in English country-house style, with coachmen dressed in tails and top hats and a bugler announcing carriages entering the front gates. Like a village unto itself, the estate gardens provided much of the household's food, supplemented by game from its woods and fish from its ponds. It also had its own electric plant and a 9-hole golf course by the water. The enormous mansion Samuel built for his son in 1886 burned to the ground 20 years later, and Roland died two weeks after the event. The grand stone mansion built to replace it in 1908 is now part of the Ocean Edge resort. In 1934 Addie donated the land for the state park in memory of Roland and their son, who died during the 1918 flu epidemic.

The park consists of acres of oak, pitch pine, hemlock, and spruce forest speckled with seven freshwater kettle ponds formed by glacial action. Some ponds are stocked with trout for fishing. You can swim in the ponds, canoe, sail, kayak, bicycle along 8 mi of paved trails that have access to the Cape Cod Rail Trail, picnic, and cross-country ski in winter. Bird-watchers seek out the thrushes, wrens, warblers, woodpeckers, finches, larks, Canada geese, cormorants, great blue herons, hawks, owls, ospreys, and other species that frequent the park. Occasionally, red foxes and white-tailed deer are spotted in the woods. Both tent and RV camping are extremely popular here, and nature programs are offered in season. A map of the park is available on-site. ✉ *3488 Rte. 6A, East Brewster* ☎ *508/896–3491* ⊕ *www.mass.gov/dcr* ✉ *Free* ⊙ *Daily dawn–dusk.*

**NEED A BREAK?** Looking for a little south-of-the-border zing? Then stop in at **El Guapo's Taqueria** ( ✉ *239 Underpass Rd. near Cape Cod Rail Trail crossing South Brewster* ☎ *508/896–3338*) for a quick lunch or dinner. It's mostly a take-out place (there are a few tiny tables inside; several picnic tables outside) where you can choose from basic but tasty Mexican standards like tacos—the fish tacos are especially good—quesadillas, generous burritos, enchiladas, and fajitas. For milder fare, you'll find burgers and even some barbecue specials. There's also an ice-cream window out back.

## WHERE TO EAT

$$$$
★
ECLECTIC
✗ **Bramble Inn.** Inside an inviting 1860s white house in Brewster's historic village center, this romantic property presents well-crafted, globally inspired contemporary fare in five dining rooms with floral wallpaper or wood-paneled walls, hung with gilt-framed mirrors and watercolor and oil paintings (much of the artwork is for sale). During the warmer months, dine on a patio amid fragrant flower beds. The four-course prix-fixe menu changes often but always includes the assorted seafood curry—the house favorite—which combines lobster, shrimp, scallops, and cod in a light curry sauce with grilled banana, toasted coconut, sliced almonds, and house chutney. If you're not up for the four-course meal, you can also order à la carte from a lighter bistro menu, which is served in the bar as well as on one of the garden patios. There are also a few attractive overnight rooms. ✉ *2019 Main St. (Rte. 6A), East Brewster* ☎ *508/896–7644* ⊕ *www.brambleinn.com* ☐ *AE, D, MC, V* ⊙ *Closed Mon. and Tues. Closed Jan.–Mar. No lunch.*

$$–$$$$
SEAFOOD
✗ **Brewster Fish House.** Humble on the outside yet vibrant and flavorful within, the Fish House has carved a niche for itself: Cape Cod standards such as classic scrod and New England boiled dinner share billing with both traditional and more inspired preparations of duck, rack of lamb, Cornish hen, and tenderloin of beef. Locals are known to drive from all points of the Cape to this lovably rickety restaurant for the super-fresh fish. It can be noisy and it's always crowded in summer, but it's worth the wait. The wine list includes a flavorful selection of by-the-glass offerings. ✉ *2208 Main St. (Rte. 6A) Brewster* ☎ *508/896–7867* ✐ *Reservations not accepted* ☐ *MC, V.*

$–$$
AMERICAN
✗ **Brewster Inn and Chowder House.** The consistently excellent food at this long-standing Cape institution continues to live up to its great reputation among locals. Home cooking in the traditional New England style is the rule; you'll find no fancy or fussy fusion recipes here—just comfort food. Look for simple but tasty meat and seafood standards, and don't miss the rich and full-bodied New England clam chowder. The

service is friendly, the prices are kind, and you won't leave hungry. The restaurant serves lunch and dinner daily year-round. ✉*1993 Main St. (Rte. 6A)* ☎*508/896–7771* ▤*MC, V.*

**$$$$**
**Fodor's**Choice
★
FRENCH

✕**Chillingsworth.** One of the crown jewels of Cape restaurants, Chillingsworth combines formal presentation with an excellent French menu and a diverse wine cellar to create a memorable dining experience. Super-rich risotto, roast lobster, and grilled Angus sirloin are favorites. Dinner in the main dining rooms is prix-fixe and includes seven courses—appetizer, soup, salad, sorbet, entrée, "amusements," and dessert, plus coffee or tea. Less expensive à la carte options for lunch, dinner, and Sunday brunch are served in the more casual, patio-style Bistro. There are also a few guest rooms here for overnighting. ✉*2449 Main St. (Rte. 6A), East Brewster* ☎*508/896–3640* ⊕*www.chillingsworth. com* ▤*AE, DC, MC, V* ⊙*Closed Thanksgiving–mid-May.*

**¢–$$**
AMERICAN

✕**JT's Seafood.** Fresh and ample portions of fried seafood take center stage at this casual joint, which is very popular with families. Pick from several seafood platters, or gnaw on baby back ribs or burgers if you need a break from the fruits of the sea. Several items, including corn dogs, grilled cheese (lunch only), and peanut butter and jelly, are good kid-friendly choices. Place your order at the counter and sit inside or out. Leave your mark by sticking a pin in your town's name on the big map by the order counter. Takeout is also available. ✉*2689 Main St. (Rte. 6A)* ☎*508/896–3355* ⬧*Reservations not accepted* ▤*MC, V* ⊙*Closed mid-Oct.–mid-Apr.*

**¢–$**
AMERICAN

✕**Laurino's Tavern.** There's something timeless about this noisy pizza joint and American eatery with warm wood paneling, generous booth-style seating, and red-and-white-checked tablecloths, plus a big patio and a playground for kids. Meatball grinders, steak-and-cheese sandwiches, and specialty pizzas are mainstays. Try a buffalo-chicken pizza, topped with wing sauce and cheddar cheese, with a bleu cheese dipping sauce. Lasagna, shrimp scampi, and mussels marinara are popular choices. The long, friendly bar is a great place to sit with a buddy over a beer and a big plate of Macho Nachos. In summer live music serenades the late-night crowd. ✉*3668 Main St. (Rte. 6A), East Brewster* ☎*508/896–6135* ⬧*Reservations not accepted* ▤*AE, MC, V.*

**$$–$$$**
FRENCH

✕**Peddler's Restaurant.** The husband-and-wife team Alain and Beth have been quietly serving French bistro fare to a loyal (and tight-lipped) crowd of very satisfied locals. A lack of advertising and generous word-of-mouth following have kept this lovely little spot somewhat shrouded in mystique; and wisteria vines—which cover the building so entirely that it's hard to find the front door—help keep the place a secret. Inside, about a dozen tables dressed in white linen are illuminated by the glow of candles and dangling white lights, setting the stage for a meal that should be savored slowly. French-born Alain uses his native culinary training to prepare a host of patés, escargots, flounder meuniére, and the house favorite, duck à l'orange with a Grand Marnier sauce. The menu changes daily; it's handwritten on a blackboard on a side wall. Finish your memorable meal with the homemade pistachio ice cream with chocolate ganache. ✉*67 Thad Ellis Rd., East Brewster*

☎508/896–9300 ☜ *Reservations not accepted* ▤ *MC, V* ☯ *Closed Sun. and Mon. in Aug. Closed Sun.–Wed. Sept.–July. No lunch.*

### WHERE TO STAY

$$–$$$$   🔲**Brewster By The Sea Inn & Spa.** Weather permitting, a three-course breakfast is served on the patio overlooking a swimming pool and 2 acres of landscaped gardens at this restored, beautifully decorated 1846 farmhouse on historic Route 6A. A fireplace is the focal point in one guest room, and another has a king-size canopy bed and sliders that open onto a private deck. Three more guest rooms, furnished with authentic and reproduction antiques, fireplaces, and hot tubs, are in an adjacent carriage house. Afternoon tea is included. Some off-season weekends are centered on cooking workshops and murder-mystery sleuths; ask about spa and/or dinner packages. **Pros:** intimate lodging; ideal for those who want to fully relax while away from busy distractions. **Cons:** not an in-town or beachside location; not for those traveling with children. ⊠*716 Main St. (Rte. 6A),* ☎*508/896–3910 or 800/892–3910* 🖷*508/896–4232* ⊕*www.brewsterbythesea.com* ⇨*6 rooms, 2 suites* ♿*In-room: Wi-Fi. In-hotel: pool, spa, no kids under 16, no-smoking rooms, no elevator* ▤*AE, D, MC, V* ⍩*BP.*

$$   🔲**Candleberry Inn.** This 1790s Georgian mansion sits along scenic Main Street (Route 6A) and was once the home of writer Horatio Alger. The sun-filled rooms are unfussy but elegant, with Oriental rugs, wide-plank floors, original woodwork, and tall windows with the original wavy glass. Several have working fireplaces, and two particularly cozy units—the Seabreeze and Treetops rooms—have pitched ceilings and access to a deck overlooking the leafy grounds and fragrant gardens. The Seacroft Suite has French doors leading to a large sitting area. Gracious innkeepers Stuart and Charlotte Fyfe serve a delicious full breakfast out by the garden in summer and in a cozy dining room during the cooler months. For added pampering, book an in-house massage session. Spring and fall guests may want to sign up for weekend herb workshops. **Pros:** in the heart of historic Brewster village; authentic historic lodging; spacious gardens and grounds. **Cons:** many rooms accessed via steep stairs; some rooms are on the smaller size because of the home's age. ⊠*1882 Main St. (Rte. 6A),* ☎*508/896–3300 or 800/573–4769* 🖷*508/896–4016* ⊕*www.candleberryinn.com* ⇨*7 rooms, 1 suite* ♿*In-hotel: no kids under 10, no-smoking rooms, no elevator* ▤*AE, D, DC, MC, V* ⍩*BP.*

$$   🔲**Isaiah Clark House.** This former 18th-century sea captain's residence, just west of the town proper, retains its wide-plank flooring and low, sloping ceilings and has a varied selection of antiques. The original inhabitants have left their mark all over the house, from the scrawled signature of 13-year-old son Jeremiah in a closet to the framed historic documents and photographs on the walls to the namesake of each of the rooms (all Clark family women). Most rooms have queen-size four-poster or canopy beds, braided rugs, and fireplaces. The extensive gardens yield some of the fruit used in the homemade pies, muffins, and breads that are served at breakfast. **Pros:** beautifully maintained, historic lodging; outdoor shower available for post-beach refresher; beaches and town center just a few minutes away. **Cons:** not for those traveling

with younger children. ⊠*1187 Main St. (Rte. 6A),* ☎*508/896–2223 or 800/822–4001* ⊕*www.isaiahclark.com* 📞*7 rooms* 🖫*In-room: no phone, Wi-Fi. In-hotel: no kids under 13, no-smoking rooms, no elevator* ⊟*AE, MC, V* ⊙|*BP. Closed Dec.–mid-Apr.*

$$$–$$$$   ⊞**Ocean Edge.** One of the Cape's few full-service resorts, Ocean Edge
★   is a luxury community straddling both sides of Route 6A—it borders Cape Cod Bay on the west, and its champion 18-hole golf course is on the east side. Accommodations range from hotel rooms in the conference center to one-to-three-bedroom condominiums in the woods and two- to three-bedroom beachfront villas. Condominiums have full kitchens and washer-dryers; some units have fireplaces, and many have ocean views. All rooms and condos have balconies or patios. In addition to the golf course, there are several pools, basketball, volleyball, and tennis courts. Clambakes, concerts, and tournaments take place throughout the summer. **Pros:** great for golfers; many rooms on Cape Cod Bay side with beach access and water views; full-service resort. **Cons:** not for those looking for intimate lodging experience. ⊠*2907 Main St. (Rte. 6A),* ☎*508/896–9000 or 800/343–6074* 🖷*508/896–9123* ⊕*www.oceanedge.com* 📞*292 condominium units, 90 rooms* 🖫*In-room: Wi-Fi. In-hotel: 4 restaurants, room service, bar, tennis courts, pools, gym, beachfront, bicycles, concierge, kids' programs (ages 4–17), laundry facilities* ⊟*AE, D, DC, MC, V.*

$–$$   ⊞**Old Sea Pines Inn.** With its white-column portico and wraparound
Fodor's Choice   veranda overlooking a broad lawn, Old Sea Pines, which housed a
★   young ladies' boarding school in the early 1900s, resembles a vintage summer estate. Climb the sweeping staircase to guest rooms decorated with reproduction wallpaper, antiques, and framed old photographs. Some are quite large; others have fireplaces. One of the more popular rooms has a sitting area in an enclosed sunporch. Rooms in a newer building are simple, with bright white modern baths and cast-iron queen-size beds. Some rooms have shared bathrooms. The inn also holds a Sunday night Broadway musical dinner revue from mid-June through mid-September. **Pros:** not far from town center; beautiful grounds; reasonable rates in historic setting. **Cons:** some rooms have shared baths; many rooms accessed steep stairway on upper floors. ⊠*2553 Main St. (Rte. 6A), Box 1070,* ☎*508/896–6114* 🖷*508/632–0084* ⊕*www.oldseapinesinn.com* 📞*24 rooms, 19 with bath, 5 suites* 🖫*In-room: no phone, no TV (some), Wi-Fi. In-hotel: no kids under 8 (except for family suites), no-smoking rooms, no elevator* ⊟*AE, D, MC, V* ⊙*Closed Jan.–Mar.* ⊙|*BP.*

¢   ⚠**Nickerson State Park.** Shaded by a canopy of white pine, hemlock, and spruce, Nickerson State Park is a nature lover's haven. Encompassing close to 2,000 acres of wooded landscape teeming with wildlife, the park is the Cape's largest and most popular camping site. While away a summer afternoon trout fishing, walking, biking on 8 mi of paved trails (which connect to the Cape Cod Rail Trail), canoeing, sailing, kayaking, or bird-watching; there are four ponds for swimming, plus ocean beaches nearby. RVs must be self-contained. Maps and schedules of park programs are available at the park entrance. Long-awaited upgrades in electric and water systems were completed in mid-2008 and have improved camp services significantly. Camp-ground reservations are accepted six months in advance, mid-April through mid-October, and sites are available on a walk-in basis only the rest of the year. There's a $9.50 fee per advanced reservation; note that camping fees are slightly lower for in-state residents. Reservations can be made by phone or online at www.ReserveAmerica.com. ⚒️ *Flush toilets, dump station, drinking water, showers, fire grates, grills, picnic tables, public telephone, general store, ranger station, play area, swimming (ponds)* ⟳ *420 sites, some yurts* ✉ *3488 Rte. 6A,* ☎ *508/896–3491, 877/422–6762 reservations* 🖷 *508/896–3103* ⊕ *www.mass.gov/dcr* ⊟ *No credit cards.*

### NIGHTLIFE & THE ARTS

The **Cape Cod Repertory Theatre Co.** ( ✉ *3299 Rte. 6A, East Brewster* ☎ *508/896–1888* ⊕ *www.caperep.org*) performs several impressive productions, from original works to classics, in its indoor Arts and Crafts–style theater way back in the woods. The season runs from May to November. Mesmerizing entertainment for children, in the form of lively outdoor (and often interactive) theater, is provided here, too. One-hour puppet shows and age-appropriate productions are given Monday through Wednesday mornings at 10 from late June through August. The theater is just west of Nickerson State Park.

Sunday evenings by the bay are filled with the sounds of the **town-band concerts** ( ✉ *Rte. 6A, West Brewster*), held in the gazebo on the grounds of Drummer Boy Park. The park is about ½ mi west of the Cape Cod Museum of Natural History, on the western side of Brewster. Families with little ones will delight in the park's playground with its ornate wood facilities.

The **Woodshed** ( ✉ *1993 Main St. [Rte. 6A]* ☎ *508/896–7771*), the rustic bar at the Brewster Inn, is a good place to soak up local color and listen to pop duos or bands that perform nightly. It's open from May through October.

### SPORTS & THE OUTDOORS

BASEBALL   The **Brewster Whitecaps** ( ☎ *508/385–5073* ⊕ *www.brewsterwhitecaps. com*) of the collegiate Cape Cod Baseball League play home games at **Stony Brook School** ( ✉ *Underpass Rd., Brewster*) from mid-June to mid-August.

BEACHES   **Flax Pond** ( ✉ *3488 Main St. [Rte. 6A], East Brewster* ☎ *508/896–3491*) in Nickerson State Park, surrounded by pines, has picnic areas, a bath-house, and water-sports rentals.

Brewster's bay beaches all have access to the flats that at low tide make for very interesting tidal-pool exploration. Eponymous roads to each beach branch off Route 6A; there's limited parking. All of the bay beaches require a daily, weekly, or seasonal parking pass (which for nonresidents cost $15, $50, and $125, respectively); these can be purchased at the town hall ( ☎ *508/896–4511*). **Breakwater Landing** is one of the most popular beaches in town and has an ample parking area. **Linnell Landing** has a smaller lot and tends to fill up quickly. A favorite among the toddler crowd and the sunset seekers, **Paine's Creek** also lacks a large lot, but if you get there early enough, you can find a spot. Harder to find down a dead-end street but worth it, **Robbin's Hill** is known for its intriguing tidal pools. Farther east off Route 6A is **Crosby Beach,** ideal for beach walkers—you can trek straightway to Orleans if you so desire.

BICYCLING   The **Cape Cod Rail Trail** has many access points in Brewster, among them Long Pond Road, Underpass Road, and Nickerson State Park.

**Brewster Bike** ( ⊠*442 Underpass Rd.*  ☎*508/896–8149*) carries a large selection of bikes for rent.

The **Rail Trail Bike and Kayak** ( ⊠*302 Underpass Rd.*  ☎*508/896–8200*) rents bikes, including children's bikes, and in-line skates. Parking is free, and there's a picnic area with easy access to the Rail Trail.

FISHING   Many of Brewster's freshwater ponds are good for catching perch, pickerel, and other fish; five ponds are well stocked with trout. Especially good for fishing is Cliff Pond in Nickerson State Park. You'll need a **fishing license,** available from just about any local bait and tackle shop. To get your fishing license online, visit the Massachusetts Department of Fish and Game Web site at www.sport.state.ma.us.

GOLF   The **Captain's Golf Course** ( ⊠*1000 Freeman's Way, east of Rte. 6* ☎*508/896–1716 or 877/843–9081* ⊕ *www.captainsgolfcourse.com*) is an excellent public facility with two fine 18-hole courses—*Golf Digest* has named it one of the leading public courses in the nation.

HORSEBACK   **Woodsong Farm** ( ⊠*121 Lund Farm Way, South Brewster* ☎*508/896–*
RIDING   *5800* ⊕*www.woodsongfarm.com*) has instruction and day programs, but no rentals or trail rides; it also has a horsemanship day-camp program for kids 5 to 18.

TENNIS   Run by the town and open to the public at no charge are four **public tennis courts,** all just behind the fire and police stations on 1673 Route 6A. Two basketball courts are also available for public use.

WATER   **Cape Cod Sea Camps** ( ⌂*Box 1880, Brewster 02631* ☎*508/896–3451*
SPORTS   ⊕*www.capecodseacamps.com*) teache team sports, archery, art, drama, sailing, and water sports to kids ages 4 to 17.

**Jack's Boat Rentals** ( ⊠*Flax Pond, Nickerson State Park, Rte. 6A, East Brewster* ☎*508/896–8556*) rents canoes, kayaks, Seacycles, Sunfish, pedal boats, and sailboards.

**SHOPPING**

**B. D. Hutchinson** ( ⊠*1274 Long Pond Rd., South Brewster* ☎*508/896–6395*), a watch and clock maker, sells antique and collectible watches, clocks, and music boxes.

★ **Brewster Book Store** ( ⊠*2648 Main St. [Rte. 6A], East Brewster* ☎*508/896–6543 or 800/823–6543*) prides itself on being a special Cape bookstore. It's filled to the rafters with all manner of books by local and international authors and has an extensive fiction selection and kids section. A full schedule of author signings and children's story times continues year-round.

**Countryside Antiques** ( ✉ *2052 Main St. [Rte. 6A], Brewster* ☎ *508/896–1444*) specializes in European and Asian antique furniture, home-accent pieces, china, and silver.

**HandCraft House** ( ✉ *3996 Rte. 6A, East Brewster* ☎ *508/240–1412*) has "handmade in the USA" art for the home and garden, wood sculptures, handblown glass, stoneware, watercolors, and jewelry.

**Kings Way Books and Antiques** ( ✉ *774 Main St. [Rte. 6A], West Brewster* ☎ *508/896–3639*) sells out-of-print and rare books—they have a large medieval section—plus small antiques, china, glass, silver, coins, and linens.

**Lemon Tree Village** ( ✉ *1069 Main St. [Rte. 6A]*) is a cheery complex filled with many unusual stores. You can find garden statuary, top-of-the-line cooking implements, locally made arts and crafts, pottery, birding supplies, clothing, gifts, jewelry, and toys. There's even a café next door if all that shopping makes you hungry.

Open from April through October, the **Satucket Farm Stand** ( ✉ *76 Harwich Rd. [Rte. 124], off Rte. 6A* ☎ *508/896–5540*) is a real old-fashioned farm stand and bakery. Most produce is grown on the premises, and you can fill your basket with home-baked scones and breads, fruit pies, produce, herbs, and flowers.

The **Spectrum** ( ✉ *369 Main St. [Rte. 6A], West Brewster* ☎ *508/385–3322*) carries a great selection of imaginative American arts and crafts, including pottery, stained glass, and art glass.

★ **Sydenstricker Galleries** ( ✉ *490 Main St. [Rte. 6A], West Brewster* ☎ *508/385–3272*) stocks glassware handcrafted by a unique process, which you can watch while you're in the shop.

## HARWICH

*6 mi south of Brewster, 5 mi east of Dennis.*

Originally known as Setucket, Harwich separated from Brewster in 1694 and was renamed for the famous English seaport. Like other townships on the Cape, Harwich is actually a cluster of several small villages, including Harwich Port. Historically, the villages of Harwich were marked by their generous number of churches and the styles of worship they practiced—small villages often sprang up around these centers of faith.

Harwich and Harwich Port are the commercial centers, and although the two have very different natures, both have graceful old architecture and rich histories. Harwich Port is the more bustling of the two: brimming with shops, calm-water beaches, restaurants, and hotel complexes, it packs all manner of entertainment and frivolity along its roadways. Harwich is more relaxed; its commerce is more centered, and its outlying areas are graced with greenery, large shade trees, and historic homesteads. The Harwich Historical Society has a strong presence here, maintaining exhibits and artifacts significant to the town's past.

The Cape's famous cranberry industry took off in Harwich in 1844, when Alvin Cahoon was its principal grower. Today you'll still find cranberry bogs throughout Harwich, and each September the town holds a **Cranberry Festival** to celebrate the importance of this indigenous berry; the festival is usually scheduled during the week after Labor Day.

Three naturally sheltered harbors on Nantucket Sound make the town, like its English namesake, popular with boaters. You'll find dozens of elegant sailboats and elaborate yachts in Harwich's harbors, plus plenty of charter-fishing boats. Each year in August the town pays celebratory homage to its large boating population with a grand regatta, Sails Around the Cape.

Beaches are plentiful in Harwich, and nearly all rest on the warm and mild waters of Nantucket Sound. Freshwater ponds, ideal for swimming as well as small-scale canoeing and kayaking, also speckle the area. Several conservation areas have miles of secluded walking trails, many alongside vivid cranberry bogs.

Once the home of a private school offering the first high school–level curriculum in Harwich, the pillared 1844 Greek Revival building of the **Brooks Academy Museum** now houses the museum of the **Harwich Historical Society**. In addition to a large photo-history collection and exhibits on artist Charles Cahoon (grandson of cranberry grower Alvin), the socio-technological history of cranberry culture, and shoe making, the museum has antique clothing and textiles, china and glass, fans, and toys. There's also an extensive genealogical collection for researchers (open by appointment). On the grounds is a powder house used to store gunpowder during the Revolutionary War, as well as a restored 1872 outhouse that could spur your appreciation for indoor plumbing. On the schedule throughout the season are historic lectures, children's programs, and special events such as the annual Civil War reenactment. ✉*80 Parallel St.* ☎*508/432–8089* ⊕ *www.harwich historicalsociety.org* ✉*Donations accepted* ⊙*Late June–mid-Oct., Thurs.–Sat. 1–4.*

� **Brooks Park** on Main Street (Route 28) is a good place to stretch your legs; it has a playground, picnic tables, a ball field, tennis courts, and a bandstand where summer concerts are held.

☺ For children who have spent too much time in the car watching you drive, a spin behind the wheel of one of 20 top-of-the-line go-karts at **Bud's Go-Karts** may be just the thing. ✉*9 Sisson Rd., off Rte. 28, Harwich Port* ☎*508/432–4964* ⊙*June–early Sept., Mon.–Sat. 9 AM–11 PM, Sun. 10 AM–11 PM.*

☺ **Grand Slam Entertainment** has softball- and baseball-batting cages and pitching machines, including one with fastballs up to 80 mph and a Wiffle-ball machine for younger kids, plus a bumper-boat pool and a video-arcade room. ✉*322 Main St. (Rte. 28), Harwich Port*

☎*508/430–1155* ⊕*www.grandslamentertainment.com* ⊙*Apr., May, and Sept.–mid-Oct., Mon.–Sat. 11–7, Sun. 11–9; June–Aug., daily 9* AM*–10* PM.

☺ The **Trampoline Center** has 12 trampolines set up at ground level over pits for safety. ⊠*296 Main St. (Rte. 28), West Harwich* ☎*508/432–8717* ⊙*Apr.–mid-June, weekends, hrs vary widely, call ahead; mid-June–early Sept., daily 9* AM*–10* PM.

## WHERE TO EAT

$$
SEAFOOD

✕**Brax Landing.** In this local stalwart perched alongside busy Saquatucket Harbor, you can get a menu tip-off as you pass by tanks full of lobsters in the corridor leading to the dining room. The restaurant sprawls around a big bar that serves specialty drinks such as the Banzai (frozen piña colada with a float of dark rum). The swordfish with pineapple-mango salsa and the herb-crusted Chatham scrod are favorites, both served simply and well. And if you've been after the ultimate lobster roll—and never thought you could get full on one—sample the one at Brax Landing, bursting with the meat of a 1¼-pound lobster. There's also a notable children's menu, and Sunday brunch is an institution. ⊠*705 Main St. (Rte. 28 at Saquatucket Harbor), Harwich Port* ☎*508/432–5515* ⌂*Reservations not accepted* ▭*AE, DC, MC, V* ⊙*Restaurant closed Jan. and Feb.; bar open year-round.*

$$–$$$
★
ITALIAN

✕**Buca's Tuscan Roadhouse.** This romantic roadhouse near the Chatham border, with a vintage Ford station wagon parked out front, has crisp red-and-white-checked tablecloths and a vibe that might just transport you to Italy—and if it doesn't, the food will. From *zuppa* (soup) to aged pecorino, Gorgonzola, and ricotta salad with figs to veal with red wine, balsamic butter, sun-dried cherries, and roasted tomatoes, this is mouthwatering Italian fare taken far beyond traditional home cooking. ⊠*4 Depot Rd., Harwich* ☎*508/432–6900* ⊕*www.bucasroadhouse. com* ▭*MC, V* ⊙*No lunch.*

$$$–$$$$
★
AMERICAN

✕**Cape Sea Grille.** Sitting primly inside a dashing Gothic Victorian house on a side street off hectic Route 28, this gem with distant sea views cultivates a refined ambience with fresh flowers, white linens, and vibrant wall murals. Specialties from the ever-changing menu include crispy duck confit with Swiss chard, roasted beets, and a red-wine glaze; and grilled Atlantic salmon wrapped in prosciutto with melon, cucumbers, toasted Israeli couscous, and a wild-blackberry vinaigrette. Chef-owner Douglas Ramler (formerly of Boston's noted Hamersley's Bistro) relies on the freshest ingredients. ⊠*31 Sea St., Harwich Port* ☎*508/432–4745* ⊕*capeseagrille.com* ▭*AE, D, MC, V* ⊙*Closed mid-Dec.–early Apr. No lunch.*

$$$–$$$$
AMERICAN

✕**Circadia Bistro.** The abundant gardens outside this large 1830 Cape provide many of the flavors for the New American bistro cuisine served within. Two menus—the more formal bistro and the more rustic tavern—feature local seafood and seasonal ingredients. From the bistro side, you might start out with the soft-shell crab tempura, with black bean Asian salsa and chili garlic sauce; or day-boat scallops with a creamy herb risotto, white truffle oil, and frizzled leeks. The tavern menu is no less globally inspired, and features a selection of intriguing "small plates" as well as regular-size dinners, with a gentler price tag. Surrounded by aged wood floors, multiple fireplaces, white linens, and candlelight, this is a place to go if you're looking for a memorable evening out. ⊠*86 Sisson Rd., Harwich Port* ☎*508/432–2769* ⊕*www. circadiabistro.com* ▭*MC, V*

¢–$$ ✕ **400 East.** This big, dark restaurant buzzing with conversation is in a

AMERICAN nondescript shopping plaza. The menu includes teriyaki chicken, prime rib, lobster ravioli, burgers, and baked scrod, but also has excellent pizza, with toppings such as wild mushrooms, bleu cheese, and chicken sausage. Eating at the busy, U-shape bar is a good alternative to waiting for a table. The 400 has a cousin restaurant (also called the 400) downtown on Main Street. ⊠*1421 Orleans Rd. (Rte. 39)* ☎*508/432–1800* ▭*AE, D, MC, V.*

$$$–$$$$ ✕ **L'Alouette Bistro.** Owners Alan and Gretchen Champney serve authen-

FRENCH tic French food in this unassuming gray-shingle house with a loyal following among foodies in the know. Look for traditional and contemporary selections such as butter-poached lobster with a saffron-vanilla sauce, Moroccan braised lamb with preserved lemon and mint, and sun-dried-tomato-crusted halibut with a lemon, roasted garlic, and sage sauce and wilted spinach. Desserts here are a particular delight, especially the light and not-too-sweet tarte tatin. There's also a superb wine list. ⊠*787 Main St. (Rte. 28), Harwich Port* ☎*508/430–0405* ⊕*www.lalouettebistro.com* ▭*AE, DC, MC, V* ⊗*No lunch.*

$$–$$$ ✕ **The Port.** An urbane and homey storefront café in downtown Har-

★ wich Port, the kitchen focuses on fairly traditional American fare, espe-

SEAFOOD cially seafood, but with some inventive interpretations. You might, for instance, sample pistachio-crusted halibut with baby spinach and lemongrass rice, finished with an orange beurre blanc; or the panfried rainbow trout, topped with toasted almonds and a lemon–white wine sauce. The Thai-style lobster-crab cake with wasabi sour cream makes for a nice starter, or choose from a variety of local oysters from the raw bar. The menu is long and ambitious, and there's also an extensive, well-chosen wine list. ⊠*541 Main St. (Rte. 28)* ☎*508/430–5410* ▭*AE, MC, V* ⟀*Reservations only for parties of 5 or more* ⊗*Closed Dec.–Apr. No lunch.*

## WHERE TO STAY

$$$–$$$$ 🏨 **Dunscroft by-the-Sea.** This charming, luxurious beach house sits a half

★ block from Nantucket Sound and within walking distance of several restaurants, yet it's on a peaceful street away from the crowds. The rooms have many romantic amenities, including king- and queen-size lace-canopy and four-poster beds, whirlpool tubs, luxury linens, cotton robes, and working fireplaces in some rooms. The cottage suite has a living room with a fireplace, kitchenette, and Jacuzzi. In the common gathering room you'll find a baby grand piano and extensive library. Innkeeper Alyce's full breakfasts are fantastic (she makes killer French toast). **Pros:** walk to beach; elegant and romantic lodging in a quiet setting; grand breakfasts. **Cons:** some rooms accessed via steep stairs; no water views. ⊠*24 Pilgrim Rd., Harwich Port* ☎*508/432–0810 or 800/432–4345* ⊕*www.dunscroftbythesea.com* 🛏*8 rooms, 1 cottage*

🛍 *In-room: kitchen (some), Wi-Fi. In-hotel: no kids under 14, no eleva-tor* ⊟*AE, MC, V* ⦾*BP.*

**$–$$$**  🛏 **Lion's Head Inn.** Actually a bit closer to Dennisport than to Harwich and Harwich Port, this well-maintained early-19th-century sea cap-tain's home sits along a quiet street in a peaceful neighborhood a little less than a mile north of the sea. Innkeepers Marilyn and Tom Hull run this low-key, reasonably priced B&B and also rent out a pair of one-bedroom cottages with full kitchens and living rooms with double futons (so each can sleep a total of four); the cottages are available weekly in summer and for shorter stays the rest of the year. Rooms are modestly but tastefully appointed, with country quilts and a smatter-ing of antiques. A big plus here is the large outdoor pool and attractive patio. **Pros:** set back off busy Route 28 yet not far from area attrac-tions; good location for exploring Dennis and Harwich areas; large outdoor pool. **Cons:** many rooms accessed via steep stairs; room decor could use a little freshening, though comfortable; not an in-town or beachfront location. ✉*186 Belmont Rd., West Harwich* ☎*508/432–7766 or 800/321–3155* ⊕*www.capecodinns.com* ⇆*5 rooms, 1 suite, 2 cottages* 🛍*In-room: no TV (some). In-hotel: pool, no elevator, public Wi-Fi* ⊟*D, MC, V* ⦾*CP.*

**$$$$**  🛏 **Wequassett Inn Resort & Golf Club.** Twenty Cape-style cottages and an
**Fodor's Choice** attractive hotel make up this traditionally elegant resort by the sea.
★ Set on 22 acres of shaded landscape partially surrounded by Pleas-ant Bay, the Wequassett is an informally upscale resort. An attentive staff, evening entertainment, fun in the sun, and golf at the exclusive Cape Cod National Golf Club are just a few of the benefits you can count on at Wequassett. Chef Bill Brodsky's creative globally inspired cuisine graces the menus of the three restaurants—the star being the sophisticated 28 Atlantic ($$$–$$$$), which is one of the top destina-tion restaurants on the Cape, serving such stellar creations as yellowfin and salmon tartare, and caramelized skate wing with beet-daikon-horseradish salad and watercress jus. The Outer Bar & Grill serves cocktails, beverages, snacks, and light lunch fare poolside. After a day at the beach or on the links, retire to your spacious room and relax amid fresh pine furniture, floral bedcovers or handmade quilts, and overflowing window boxes. Or sip a cocktail on the lawn out-side your private cottage-style room overlooking Pleasant Bay. A 2008 project created additional lodging; the new rooms and suites in the resort's "Signature Collection" have upped the ante in style, ameni-ties, and price: the one-bedroom Round Cove Suite lists two balconies, two fireplaces, incredible water views, and a separate sitting parlor among its attributes. It's nearly 1,200 square feet—and yours for a mere $3,500 per night in summer. **Pros:** full-service resort in idyllic, waterfront setting; activities and programs for all ages; babysitting services on-site; elegant surroundings. **Cons:** rates are very steep; not an in-town location. ✉*2173 Orleans Rd. (Rte. 28)* ☎*508/432–5400 or 800/225–7125* 🖷*508/432–5032* ⊕*www.wequassett.com* ⇆*115 rooms, 7 suites* 🛍*In-hotel: 3 restaurants, room service, bar, tennis courts, pool, gym, water sports, children's programs (ages 4–12), no elevator* ⊟*AE, D, DC, MC, V* ⦾*Closed Nov.–Mar.* ⦾*FAP.*

**$$$–$$$$**    🏠**Winstead Inn and Beach Resort.** Comprising two distinct properties,
★    the Winstead Inn and Beach Resort offer a two-for-one Cape Cod expe-
rience. Harking back to an earlier era, the airy, attractive Beach Resort
sits on a private beach overlooking Nantucket Sound. You can gaze at
the sweep of coast and surrounding grasslands while enjoying a gener-
ous continental breakfast from rockers and umbrella tables on the deck
and wraparound porches. At the other end of the spectrum, the Win-
stead Inn sits along a quiet street on the edge of downtown. Greenery
surrounds this Gothic Victorian house, and many of the rooms have a
view of the outdoor pool. Guests at either property can use the ameni-
ties and facilities at both locations. **Pros:** one property sits right on the
sand of private beach and most rooms have water views; pool privi-
leges at sister property; spacious, elegant rooms. **Cons:** many rooms up
steep stairs; not for those on a budget. ✉*114 Parallel St.,* ✉*4 Brad-
dock La., Harwich Port* ☎*508/432–4444 or 800/870–4405* ⊕*www.
winsteadinn.com* 🛏*18 rooms, 4 suites* ♿*In-room: Wi-Fi. In-hotel:
pool, no-smoking rooms, no elevator* ▭*AE, MC, V* ⦿*CP.*

### NIGHTLIFE & THE ARTS

THE ARTS    The **First Congregational Church** (✉*Main St. at corner of Rtes. 39 and
124, Harwich* ☎*508/432–1053*) closes its day of worship with Sunday-
evening Candlelight Concerts at 7:30 from July through September.

**Harwich Junior Theatre** (✉*105 Division St., West Harwich* ☎*508/432–
2002* ⊕*www.hjtcapecod.org*) gives theater classes for kids year-round
and presents 12 family-oriented productions.

**Town-band concerts** (☎*508/432–1600*) in Harwich take place in sum-
mer on Tuesday evening at 7:30 in Brooks Park.

NIGHTLIFE    The **Hot Stove Saloon** (✉*551 Main St. [Rte. 28], Harwich Port*
☎*508/432–9911*) is a convivial spot for tasty pub fare and a wide
selection of beers and cocktails. The baseball-theme tavern also airs
sporting events on TV.

**Irish Pub** (✉*126 Main St. [Rte. 28], West Harwich* ☎*508/432–8808*)
has dancing to bands—playing Irish, American, and dance music—as
well as sing-alongs, pool, darts, sports TV, and pub food in the bar.

**Jake Rooney's Pub** (✉*119 Brooks Rd., off Rte. 28, Harwich Port*
☎*508/430–1100*) is a comfortable watering hole. Keno and live
entertainment three nights a week make it a fun place to hang out
with friends.

**Wequassett Inn Resort & Golf Club** (✉*173 Orleans Rd. [Rte. 28], Pleas-
ant Bay* ☎*508/432–5400*) has a jazz duo or piano music nightly in its
lounge in July and August (jacket requested).

### SPORTS & THE OUTDOORS

BASEBALL    The **Harwich Mariners** (✉*Harwich High School, Oak St.* ☎*508/432–
2000* ⊕*www.harwichmariners.org*) of the collegiate Cape Cod Base-
ball League play home games at Whitehouse Field on Oak Street from
mid-June through mid-August.

BEACHES    Harwich has 21 beaches, more than any other Cape town. Most of the ocean beaches are on Nantucket Sound, where the water is a bit calmer and warmer. Freshwater pond beaches are also abundant. Nonresident beach parking stickers, sold at the **Harwich Community Center** ( ⊠ *100 Oak St.* 🕾 *508/432–7638*), cost $55 for one week, and $125 for the season, which runs from June through Labor Day. Ask for the free map of the town's beaches when you get your sticker.

BICYCLING    The **Bike Depot** ( ⊠ *500 Depot St.* 🕾 *508/430–4375*) has rentals, including some antique bikes. It's in North Harwich, right off the bike trail.

BOATING    Whether you're in the mood to sail under the moonlight, hire a private charter, or learn to navigate yourself, **Cape Sail** ( ⊠ *337 Saquatucket Harbor, off Rte. 28, Harwich Port* 🕾 *508/896–2730*) can accommodate any whim.

**Nauti Jane's** ( ⊠ *Off Rte. 28 at Wequassett Inn, East Harwich* 🕾 *508/430–6893*) has Day Sailers, powerboats, or peaceful kayaks for rent.

FISHING    Fishing trips are operated on a walk-on basis from spring through fall on the *Golden Eagle* ( ⊠ *Wychmere Harbor, Harwich Port* 🕾 *508/432–5611*).

The *Yankee* ( ⊠ *Saquatucket Harbor, Harwich Port* 🕾 *508/432–2520*) invites passengers in search of fluke, scup, sea bass, and tautog aboard its 65-foot party boat. Two trips depart daily Monday through Saturday in season; there's also one on Sunday. Reservations are recommended.

GOLF    **Cranberry Valley Golf Course** ( ⊠ *183 Oak St.* 🕾 *508/430–5234* ⊕ *www.cranberrygolfcourse.com*) has a championship layout of 18 well-groomed holes surrounded by cranberry bogs.

**Harwich Port Golf Club** ( ⊠ *South and Forest Sts., Harwich Port* 🕾 *508/432–0250* ⊕ *www.harwichportgolf.com*) has a 9-hole course that's great for beginners.

### SHOPPING

**Cape Cod Braided Rug Co.** ( ⊠ *537 Rte. 28, Harwich Port* 🕾 *508/432–3133*) makes braided rugs in all colors, styles, and sizes.

★    **Cape Cod Lavender Farm** ( ⊠ *Corner of Rte. 124 and Weston Woods Rd., off U.S. 6, Exit 10, Harwich* 🕾 *508/432–8397* ⊕ *www.capecod-lavenderfarm.com*) consists of some 14,000 lavender plants, making it one of the largest such farms on the East Coast. Harvesttime is usually around late June and July, when you'll see acres and acres of stunning purple waves. Apart from the plants themselves, the farm makes and sells soaps and bath salts, candles, potpourri, marmalade, lemonade, and many other lavender-infused goods and gifts. Keep your eyes peeled for their sign (on the right) as you're driving south on Route 124—it's easy to miss.

**Cedar Spring Herb Farm** ( ⊠ *159 Long Pond Dr., Harwich* 🕾 *508/430–4372* ⊕ *www.cedarspringherbfarm.com*) spreads out over 7 acres of walking trails, picnic areas, and fragrant, lush herb gardens. The emphasis here is health, both of the spiritual and physical sort; all herb products for sale are made from organic plants, and there is a full schedule of lectures, classes, and ceremonial healings and events. The farm is open from May to November.

**820 Main Gallery** (⊠*820 Main St. [Rte. 28], Harwich Port* ☎*508/430–7622*) sells original works in oil, acrylics, watercolors, and photography, as well as limited-edition prints by established local artists. The gallery specializes in regional land- and seascapes.

## WORD OF MOUTH

"Chatham is a great little town on The Cape. The Main Street area is so cute, lots of shops and restaurants. Really good food at The Impudent Oyster. Also stop into The Chatham Squire—you can't miss these places. Check out the Lighthouse, Chatham Bars Inn, and Fish Pier."

—Patty B

The **Potted Geranium** (⊠*188 Main St. [Rte. 28], West Harwich* ☎*508/432–1114*) stocks country-inspired home-related gifts, including colorful wind flags, handcrafted items, and wind chimes.

## CHATHAM

*5 mi east of Harwich, 8 mi south of Orleans.*

Low-key, well-heeled Chatham feels like a sliver of Nantucket that's floated over to the Cape. It's neatly groomed and blue-blooded yet artsy, prim but eccentric, straight-arrow but with loads of personality. Originally populated by Native Americans, Chatham came into the hands of white settlers from Plymouth in 1656, when William Nickerson traded a boat for the 17 square mi of land that make up the town. In 1712 the area separated from Eastham and was incorporated as a town; the surnames of the Pilgrims who first settled here still dominate the census list. Although Chatham was originally a farming community, the sea finally lured townspeople to turn to fishing for their livelihood, and the industry has held strong to this day.

At the bent elbow of the Cape, with water nearly surrounding it, Chatham has all the charm of a quietly posh seaside resort, with plenty of shops but none of the crass commercialism that plagues some other towns on the Cape. And it's charming: the town has gray-shingle houses with tidy awnings and cheerful flower gardens, an attractive Main Street with crafts and antiques stores alongside dapper cafés, and a five-and-dime. It's a traditional town (said to have more registered Republican voters than any other town on Cape Cod), where elegant summer cottages share the view with stately homes rich in Yankee architectural detail. In fact, this tiny town by the sea is where you'll find some of the finest examples of bow-roof houses in the country. Chatham's nowhere near as kitschy as Provincetown, but it's not overly quaint, either—it's casual and fun, in a refined New England way.

Because of its location at the elbow, Chatham is not a town you just pass through—it's a destination in itself. During summer months, the

Chatham

Atwood House Museum .........2
Chatham Light ...4
Fish Pier .........6
Monomoy National Wildlife Refuge headquarters ....5
Old Grist Mill ....3
Railroad Museum .........1

Emery La.

28

Tern Island

Chatham Harbor

Stony Hill Rd.

Crowell Rd.

Barcliff Ave.

Old Harbor Rd.

Shore Rd.

6

TO WEST CHATHAM
28

28

1
♦ Veteran's Field

Depot Rd.

♦ Monomoy Theatre

TO HARDING'S BEACH

Queen Anne Rd.

Seaview St.

Kate Gould Park

Chatham Bars Ave.

Main St.

Oyster Pond

Stage Harbor Rd.

Cross St.

Chase Park

Shattuck Pl.

Old Mill Dr.

3

Mill Pond

Water St.

4

Cedar St.

2

Bridge St.

Morris Island Rd.

Champlain Rd.

Stage Island Rd.

TO NORTH BEACH

Stage Harbor

Morris Island

Tisquantum Rd.

Chatham Harbor

Monomoy National Wildlife Refuge

5

South Beach

0        750 yards

0        750 meters

North Monomoy

Monomoy National Wildlife Refuge

town bursts into bloom as hydrangeas blossom in shades of cobalt blue, indigo, and deep violet. And although it can get crowded in high season—and even on weekends during shoulder seasons—Chatham remains a true New England village.

**1** Authentic all the way, the **Railroad Museum** is in a restored 1887 depot. Exhibits include a walk-through 1910 New York Central caboose, old photographs, equipment, thousands of train models, and a diorama of the 1915 Chatham rail yards. *⊠153 Depot Rd., West Chatham ☎No phone ⊠Free ⊙Mid-June–mid-Sept., Tues.–Sat. 10–4.*

On **Queen Anne Road** around Oyster Pond, half-Cape houses, open fields, and rolling pastures reveal the area's colonial and agricultural history.

**2** Built by sea captain Joseph C. Atwood in 1752 and occupied by his ★ descendants until it was sold to the Chatham Historical Society in 1926, the **Atwood House Museum** has a gambrel roof, variable-width floor planks, fireplaces, an old kitchen with a wide hearth and a bee-hive oven, and some antique dolls and toys. The New Gallery displays portraits of local sea captains. The Joseph C. Lincoln Room has the manuscripts, first editions, and mementos of the Chatham writer, and there is an antique tool room in the basement. The 1974 Durand Wing has collections of seashells from around the world and threaded Sand-wich glass, as well as Parian-ware figures, unglazed porcelain vases, figurines, and busts. In a remodeled freight shed are the stunning and provocative murals (1932–45) by Alice Stallknecht Wight portraying religious scenes in Chatham settings. On the grounds are an herb gar-den, the old turret and lens from the Chatham Light, and a simple camp house rescued from eroding North Beach. *⊠347 Stage Harbor Rd., West Chatham ☎508/945–2493 ⊕www.chathamhistoricalsociety. org ⊠$5 ⊙Mid-June–Oct., Tues.–Sat. 1–4 (opens at 10 AM on rainy days); July and Aug., Tues.–Sat. 10–4.*

**3** The **Old Grist Mill**, one of a number of windmills still on the Cape, was built in 1797 by Colonel Benjamin Godfrey for the purpose of grinding corn. How practical the mill actually was is a matter of debate: for it to work properly, a wind speed of at least 20 mph was necessary, but winds more than 25 mph required the miller to reef the sails or to quit grinding altogether. The mill was moved to its present location from Miller Hill in 1956 and extensively renovated. *⊠Old Mill Dr. near Mill Pond ⊠Free ⊙July and Aug., weekdays 10–3.*

**Mill Pond** is a lovely place to stop for a picnic. There's fishing from the bridge, and you'll often see bullrakers at work, plying the pond's muddy bottom with 20-foot rakes in search of shellfish.

**Stage Harbor,** sheltered by Morris Island, is where Samuel de Cham-plain anchored in 1606. The street on its north side is, not surpris-ingly, called Champlain Road. A skirmish here between Europeans and Native Americans marked the first bloodshed in New England between Native people and colonial settlers.

❹ The famous view from **Chatham Light** (✉ *Main St. near Bridge St.,*
★ *West Chatham*)—of the harbor, the offshore sandbars, and the ocean
beyond—justifies the crowds that gather to share it. The lighthouse
is especially dramatic on a foggy night, as the beacon's light pierces
the mist. Coin-operated telescopes allow a close look at the famous
"Chatham Break," the result of a fierce 1987 nor'easter that blasted
a channel through a barrier beach just off the coast; it's now known
as North and South beaches. The Cape Cod Museum of Natural History in Brewster has a display of photos documenting the process of
erosion leading up to and following the break. The U.S. Coast Guard
auxiliary, which supervises the lighthouse, offers tours April through
September on most Wednesdays of each month. The lighthouse is also
open by appointment and on three special occasions during the year:
Seafest, an annual tribute to the maritime industry held in mid-October; mid-May's Cape Cod Maritime Week; and June's Cape Heritage
Week. There is free but limited parking in front of the lighthouse facing
the beach: the 30-minute time limit is closely monitored; linger much
longer and you're likely to get a ticket.

Fodor'sChoice  **Monomoy National Wildlife Refuge** is a 2,500-acre preserve including the
★ Monomoy Islands, a fragile 9-mi-long barrier-beach area south of Chatham. Monomoy's North and South islands were created when a storm
divided the former Monomoy Island in 1978. Monomoy was itself
separated from the mainland in a 1958 storm. A haven for bird-watchers, the island is an important stop along the North Atlantic Flyway for
migratory waterfowl and shorebirds—peak migration times are May
and late July. It also provides nesting and resting grounds for 285 species, including gulls—great black-backed, herring, and laughing—and
several tern species. White-tailed deer also live on the islands, and harbor and gray seals frequent the shores in winter. The only structure on
the islands is the **South Monomoy Lighthouse,** built in 1849.

Monomoy is a quiet, peaceful place of sand and beach grass, tidal flats,
dunes, marshes, freshwater ponds, thickets of bayberry and beach plum,
and a few pines. Because the refuge harbors several endangered species,
activities are limited. Certain areas are fenced off to protect nesting
areas of terns and the threatened piping plover. Several groups conduct tours of the islands, including the Massachusetts Audubon Society in South Wellfleet and the Cape Cod Museum of Natural History
in Brewster, many with a focus on bird-watching. Most of these tours
cost about $20 to $35 per person, depending on the length of the tour
and the itinerary. In season, the *Rip Ryder* (☎ *508/945–5450* ⊕ *www.*
*monomoyislandferry.com*) will take you over from the Wildlife Refuge
headquarters (off Morris Island Road) for bird- or seal-watching tours;
private charters are also available. Another excellent option is **Monomoy**
**Island Excursions** (☎ *508/430–7772* ⊕ *www.nantucketislandferry.com*),
which offers seal and seabird tours and boat trips out around Monomoy Island, leaving from Saquatucket Harbor on a 43-foot high-speed
catamaran. **Outermost Adventures** (☎ *508/945–5858* ⊕ *www.outermos-*
*tharbor.com*) also provides water-taxi services out to Monomoy Island
and offers fishing, birding, and seal-watching cruises.

**⑤** The **Monomoy National Wildlife Refuge headquarters** ( ✉ *Off Morris Island Rd., Morris Island* ☎ *508/945–0594* ⊕ *www.fws.gov/northeast/monomoy/*), on the misleadingly named Morris Island (it's connected to the mainland), has a visitor center and bookstore, open daily 8 to 4, where you can pick up pamphlets on Monomoy and the birds, wildlife, and flora and fauna found there. A ¾-mi interpretive walking trail around Morris Island, closed at high tide, gives a good view of the refuge and the surrounding waters. The area itself is open daily for exploring from dawn to dusk. Nature's prowess is evident and perpetual in this fragile spot: in November 2006 a fierce storm recrafted the waterways, actually linking, by land, the tip of nearby South Beach to South Monomoy Island. This natural land bridge has enabled hikers to walk the distance—something that hadn't been possible for nearly half a century.

**⑥** The **Fish Pier** ( ✉ *Shore Rd. and Barcliff Ave., North Chatham*) bustles with activity when Chatham's fishing fleet returns, sometime between noon and 2 PM daily, depending on the tide. The unloading of the boats is a big local event, drawing crowds who watch it all from an observation deck. From their fishing grounds 3 to 100 mi offshore, fishermen bring in haddock, cod, flounder, lobster, halibut, and pollack, which are packed in ice and shipped to New York and Boston or sold at the fish market here. You might also see sand sharks being unloaded. Typically they are sent, either fresh or frozen, to French and German markets. Also here is *The Provider,* a monument to the town's fishing industry, showing a hand pulling a fish-filled net from the sea.

The **Eldredge Public Library** ( ✉ *564 Main St.* ☎ *508/945–5170* ⊕ *www. eldredgelibrary.org*) has a special genealogy department as well as story times for kids, book-discussion groups, and special programs and lectures.

Known for their artful contemporary treatment of blown glass, Jim Holmes and Deborah Doane of the **Chatham Glass Company** create everything from candleholders to unique vases in a vast spectrum of colors. You can watch them perform the fascinating process of glassblowing here. ✉ *758 Main St.* ☎ *508/945–5547* ⊕ *www.chathamglass.com* ☺ *Late May–early Sept., Mon.–Sat. 10–5; early Sept.–late May, daily 10–5.*

**NEED A BREAK?**

If you're looking for a fat and fancy sandwich, a morning bagel, or an afternoon cappuccino pick-me-up, stop in at the **Chatham Village Cafe** ( ✉ *400 Main St.* ☎ *508/945-2525*). Eat inside at one of the few tables for some good street-side people-watching, or head over to the Village Green for an impromptu picnic. Head to **Buffy's** ( ✉ *456 Main St.* ☎ *508/945-5990*) for Chatham's finest (and only homemade) ice cream. You can nosh on your cone at one of the tables set along the lawn outside, beneath a prodigious apple tree. Don't overlook the fresh-squeezed lime rickies and tangy smoothies. **Carmine's** ( ✉ *595 Main St.* ☎ *508/945-5300*) serves some of the best New York–style pizza (by the slice or the pie) outside New York. There are just a handful of tables inside this storefront eatery in the heart of downtown, which is also an excellent source for grinders and mouthwatering gelato.

Although it's open only on Wednesday morning, it's worth stopping by the **Caleb House**, a 1772 1½-story Cape cottage that nearly faced the wrecking ball in 2001 but was saved and converted into a modest house-museum. The house contains original wainscoting and artful handcrafted woodworking as well as three working fireplaces, a beehive oven, and wide-plank pine floors. Caleb House offers a variety of classes on such colonial activities as chair caning, spinning and weaving, open-hearth cooking, and kitchen gardening. It's on Route 28, headed north toward Orleans. ✉*1107 Orleans Rd., Chathamport* ☎*508/945–6086* ⊕*www.nickersonassoc.org* ✉*Free* ⊙*Mid-June–late Sept., Wed. 9–1.*

> ### ROUGH NEIGHBORHOOD
>
> Chatham's position on the confluence of Nantucket Sound and the Atlantic Ocean makes the town especially vulnerable to the destructive wrath of stormy seas. Many a home and beachfront have been lost to the tumultuous waters. But like any stalwart New England character, Chatham will continue to hold on to its fortunes, its past, and its future.

## WHERE TO EAT

**$$–$$$**
**ITALIAN**
✕**Campari's Bistro.** It's just a short drive north of downtown, toward Pleasant Bay, to reach this reliable spot known for good regional Italian fare. The softly lighted dining room has large and comfy booths and wood paneling, and you can also dine in the casual tavern, which is more appropriate for families. Nice starters include lemon-poached shrimp wrapped in prosciutto, and crab cakes with creole mustard aioli. Seafood Florentine and veal-and-spinach-stuffed cannelloni rank among the better entrées, but the wood-fired thin-crust pizzas steal the show here. ✉*323 Orleans Rd. (Rte. 28), North Chatham* ☎*508/945–9123* ⊕*www.camparis.com* ✉*AE, D, DC, MC, V* ⊙*No lunch.*

**$$**
**SEAFOOD**
✕**Chatham Squire.** If you order anything local here from the long list of tried-and-true American standbys, you won't go wrong. The fish is as fresh and good as you get on Cape Cod, and the kitchen continues to innovate while still remaining true to its Cape roots. The calamari is always tender, the New England smoked-fish plate is delicious, and the clam chowder is a must. Expect a long wait in season, in which case you can visit the bar and pick up on the local gossip. ✉*487 Main St.* ☎*508/945–0945* ⊕*www.thesquire.com* ⌂*Reservations not accepted* ✉*AE, D, MC, V.*

**$–$$$**
★
**SEAFOOD**
✕**Impudent Oyster.** A cozy, festive locals' tavern with an unfailingly cheerful staff and superb but reasonably priced seafood, this always-packed restaurant sits inside a dapper house just off Main Street. It's a great place for a romantic meal or dinner with friends or kids, and the menu offers light burgers and sandwiches as well as more substantial fare. Mussels with white-wine sauce is a consistent favorite. The dining room is split-level, with a bar in back on the lower level. There's not a ton of seating, so reserve early on weekends. ✉*15 Chatham Bars Ave.* ☎*508/945–3545* ✉*AE, MC, V.*

**$–$$$**
**ECLECTIC**
✕**Marley's.** You'll find traditional New England fare—often served with a decidedly international flair—at Marley's, one of the best family res-

# Where to Stay & Eat in Chatham

500 Yards
500 meters

**Restaurants** ▼

Campari's
Bistro ...........**5**

Chatham
Squire ...........**2**

Impudent
Oyster ...........**1**

Marley's .........**6**

Pisces ...........**7**

Red Nun
Bar & Grille .....**4**

Vining's
Bistro ...........**3**

**Hotels** ▼

Captain's
House Inn .......**7**

Carriage
House Inn .......**8**

Chatham
Bars Inn .........**3**

Chatham
Wayside Inn .....**4**

Cranberry Inn ...**1**

Hawthorne
Motel ...........**2**

Old Harbor
Inn .............**5**

Queen Anne
Inn .............**6**

Emery La.

28

Stony Hill Rd.

Crowell Rd.

Barcliff Ave.

Old Harbor Rd.

TO WEST
CHATHAM

Depot Rd.

28

TO HARDING'S
BEACH

Queen Anne Rd.

**Railroad
Museum**

**Monomoy
Theatre**

**Veteran's Field**

Seaview St.

**Kate
Gould
Park**

Chatham Bars Ave.

Main St.

Shore Rd.

**Fish Pier**

*Chatham
Harbor*

*Tern
Island*

Cross St.

Shattuck Pl.

Old Mill Dr.

**Old Grist
Mill**

Water St.

**Chatham
Light**

*Chase
Park*

*Mill
Pond*

Stage Harbor Rd.

Cedar St.

**Atwood
House
Museum**

Bridge St.

Morris Island Rd.

Champlain Rd.

*Oyster
Pond*

*Chatham
Harbor*

Stage Island Rd.

*Stage
Harbor*

*Morris Island*

TO NORTH
BEACH →

**KEY**

① *Hotels*

❶ *Restaurants*

taurants in the area. Scallops prepared with pineapple, rum, and brown sugar and topped with a coconut-macaroon crust are a favorite. Crab cakes and Cajun blackened salmon served with poached shrimp and crabmeat are house specialties. Steak, prime rib, chicken potpie, lobster, and steamers round out the menu, which also includes several vegetarian dishes. ⊠*1077 Main St., West Chatham* ☎*508/945–1700* ⊟*AE, MC, V* ⊘*No lunch.*

**\$\$–\$\$\$**
Fodor'sChoice
★
SEAFOOD
✕**Pisces.** An intimate dining room inside a simple yellow house not far from the Harwich border, Pisces, as its name suggests, serves coastal-inspired fare—if it swims in local waters, you can probably sample it here. A rich chowder of lobster, butternut squash, and corn is a terrific way to start your meal. Move on to Mediterranean-style fisherman's stew in saffron-lobster broth, or roasted cod with a simple but flavorful dressing of tomatoes, capers, lemon, and olive oil. Complement your dinner with a selection from the extensive wine list, which offers more than 20 vintages by the glass. ⊠*2653 Main St., South Chatham* ☎*508/432–4600* ⊕*www.piscesofchatham.com* ⊟*MC, V* ⊘*Closed Dec.–Mar. No lunch.*

**¢–\$**
AMERICAN
✕**Red Nun Bar & Grille.** It's easy to find this vibrant red restaurant, just out of the thick of downtown Chatham as you're heading toward Harwich Port. Inside this diminutive and friendly pub you'll find nothing fancy—just a few tried-and-true favorites like New England clam chowder, stuffed quahogs, basic salads, a great half-pound burger, and hefty, hot sandwiches. For something a little different, try the fish tacos, made with local cod. For dinner selections, check out the mixed grill, which changes daily. Blackboard specials for lunch and dinner are numerous and varied, the food is satisfying, and the prices are reasonable. Sports fans will be happy with multiple televisions, QB1, and NTN Buzztime. ⊠ *746 Main St., Chatham* ☎*508/348–0469* ⊟*AE, D, MC, V.*

**\$\$–\$\$\$**
ECLECTIC
✕**Vining's Bistro.** An exceptionally inventive menu and a determination not to rest on its laurels make this restaurant a standout. The wood grill infuses many dishes with a distinctive flavor heightened further by the chef's use of zesty rubs and spices from all over the globe. The Thai-style crab cakes come with a sharp chili-cucumber vinaigrette, and pan-roasted sea scallops are served with smoked bacon, mixed mushrooms, and caramelized red-onion confit. The restaurant is upstairs at the Gallery Building, and many windows look out on the art below. Though the atmosphere is casual, this is not a family place; there is a deliberate lack of high chairs, booster seats, and kiddie-meal options. ⊠*595 Main St.* ☎*508/945–5033* ⌔*Reservations not accepted* ⊟*AE, MC, V* ⊘*Closed Jan.–mid-Apr.*

## WHERE TO STAY

**\$\$\$–\$\$\$\$**
★
▥**Captain's House Inn.** A Victorian tile ceiling, wide-board floors, and elaborate moldings and wainscoting are just part of what makes Jill and James Meyer's inn one of the Cape's most popular. Each room has its own personality; some are quite large, and all have fireplaces. The Hiram Harding Room, in the bow-roof Captain's Cottage, has 200-year-old hand-hewn ceiling beams, a wall of raised walnut paneling, and a large, central working fireplace. Suites in the former stables are spacious and have hot tubs, fireplaces, TV–DVDs, mini-refrigerators,

and private patios or balconies. A young staff of British hospitality students serves an over-the-top full breakfast each morning and high tea in the afternoon. The herb and flower gardens and neatly trimmed lawns are stunning. **Pros:** elegant lodging in authentic historic setting; beautiful grounds ideal for croquet (accoutrements provided); pampered service. **Cons:** many rooms accessed via steep stairs; not an in-town or beachfront location. ⊠*369 Old Harbor Rd.* ☎*508/945–0127 or 800/315–0728* 🖷*508/945–0866* ⊕*www.captainshouseinn.com* 🛏*12 rooms, 4 suites* ♿*In-room: refrigerator (some), DVD, Wi-Fi. In-hotel: pool, gym, laundry service, no kids under 10, no-smoking rooms, no elevator* ▤*AE, D, MC, V* ⏍⎮*BP.*

$$$–$$$$
★
**Carriage House Inn.** Innkeepers Paula and Tim Miller have brought a sense of fresh, beach-resort elegance to this aged inn just outside of Chatham's town center. Rooms throughout the inn are a blend of contemporary with a distinct Cape Cod feel; walls are painted in soothing hues of cream, soft blues, and greens, and each is blessedly uncluttered with unnecessary frills. The former stables contain three larger and more secluded rooms with high-pitched ceilings, fireplaces, and French or sliding-glass doors leading to private outdoor areas. Paula brings her extensive spa experience to the mix; you can indulge in an array of luxury treatments in the privacy of your room. Each morning a delicious full breakfast begins the day, which might include Tim's special blueberry baked French toast. The beach is a mile away. **Pros:** beautifully appointed, spacious rooms; added decadence of in-house spa services; ample and well-maintained grounds; romantic and intimate setting. **Cons:** near a busy intersection though not very loud; long walk to town; no water views or beachfront. ⊠*407 Old Harbor Rd.* ☎*508/945–4688 or 800/355–8868* ⊕*www.thecarriagehouseinn.com* 🛏*6 rooms* ♿*In-room: DVD, Wi-Fi (some). In-hotel: spa services, no kids under 10, public Wi-Fi, no-smoking rooms, no elevator* ▤*AE, D, MC, V* ⏍⎮*BP.*

$$$$
**Chatham Bars Inn.** Overlooking Pleasant Bay from atop a windswept bluff, Chatham Bars Inn is a grande-dame hotel that has long been one of the Cape's most coveted retreats. The ground-floor lobby gives way to the formal restaurant on one side and a porch-fronted lounge on the other. Elegant guest rooms in the resort's main inn, and multiple buildings and cottages spread far and wide are filled with hand-painted furnishings by local artists and colorful fabrics depicting sunny seaside scenes. Adding to the well-heeled flavor of the inn is an additional massive spa complex, complete with a 4,000-square-foot hydrotherapy pool. If you'd like to be as close as possible to this pampering palace, you can stay in one of the lavishly appointed suites within the new space. **Pros:** many rooms look out to serene ocean waters; well-appointed rooms in a full-service resort; plenty of activities for all ages. **Cons:** not an in-town location; not for those looking for smaller, more intimate lodging establishments; rates are fairly steep. ⊠*297 Shore Rd.* ☎*508/945–0096 or 800/527–4884* 🖷*508/945–5491* ⊕*www.chathambarsinn.com* 🛏*149 rooms, 68 suites* ♿*In-room: DVD, Wi-Fi. In-hotel: 4 restaurants, bar, tennis courts, pools, gym, spa, beachfront, children's programs (ages 4–14)* ▤*AE, D, MC, V.*

**$$$$** ⊡**Chatham Wayside Inn.** Once a stop on a turn-of-the-20th-century stage-coach route, this venerable inn is still an oasis for weary travelers. Everything is crisp and colorful here, from the floral comforters and wallpapers to freshly painted walls and bright carpeting. Some rooms have balconies, fireplaces, and hot tubs. With a great location smack-dab in the center of town, you may not have to leave your room to hear the sounds of the weekly town-band concerts. The restaurant serves reliable contemporary American fare and a very good Sunday brunch. Guests staying in the spring and fall seasons can enjoy a complimentary continental breakfast with their room rate. **Pros:** right in the center of town; many amenities and services; spacious and efficient rooms. **Cons:** not for those seeking authentic historic lodging—more of an upscale feel than an old inn; no water views or beachfront. ⊠*512 Main St.* ☎*508/945–5550 or 800/242–8426* 🖷*508/945–3407* ⊕*www.waysideinn.com* 📞*56 rooms* ♨*In-room: VCR (some), DVD (some), Wi-Fi. In-hotel: gym, restaurant, pool* ⊟*D, MC, V* ⊘*Closed Jan.*

**$$$–$$$$** ⊡**Cranberry Inn.** This grand 1830s inn is a short walk east of the commercial span of Main Street, near the heart of downtown—but it has a protected marsh in its backyard. Billed as the oldest continuously operating lodging establishment in Chatham, the inn is filled with antique and reproduction furniture, plus handmade quilts, braided rugs, and other homey touches. The 18 rooms and suites come in a wide variety of shapes and sizes, some of them accommodating as many as six guests. Several rooms have fireplaces, wet bars, and private balconies. Breakfast, which is also available to the public by reservation, is served in a lovely dining room that doubles as the setting for an informal afternoon tea with delicious sweets and treats. An intimate pub with a wood-burning fireplace has a full liquor license and is open to the public. On hot days you can cool off on the great big north-facing veranda overlooking Main Street. **Pros:** fine location and an easy walk to town center; spacious rooms, many with fireplaces for chilly nights; gym privileges at local club (fee). **Cons:** no water views or beachfront; not for those traveling with young children. ⊠*359 Main St.* ☎*508/945–9232 or 800/332–4667* 🖷*508/945–3769* ⊕*www.cranberryinn.com* 📞*15 rooms, 3 suites* ♨*In-room: Wi-Fi. In-hotel: bar, no kids under 12, no-smoking rooms, no elevator* ⊟*AE, D, MC, V* ⊙*BP.*

**$$$–$$$$** ⊡**Hawthorne Motel.** Beyond the Hawthorne Motel's modest roadside appearance extends a private beach overlooking Pleasant Bay, the Atlantic, and Chatham Harbor. Nearly all the rooms have stunning water views. Choose from spotless, no-nonsense, simply decorated motel rooms or kitchenette efficiency units with small refrigerators, two heating plates, and a countertop-sink work area. There's also a two-bedroom cottage (rented by the week in season) with full kitchen and a separate living-dining room, plus amenities such as a VCR and an outdoor grill. The center of town is just a short walk away. Long-distance calls within the Lower 48 states are free, and the lobby has a computer with high-speed Internet access, fresh-brewed coffee, and complimentary morning newspapers. **Pros:** supreme waterfront location (most rooms have direct views); easy access to nearby attractions and activities; pretty reasonable for the area. **Cons:** rooms are pretty standard motel fare though clean and comfortable; a 10-to-15-minute walk to town center. ✉*196 Shore Rd.* ☎*508/945–0372* ⊕*www. thehawthorne.com* ⤳*16 rooms, 10 efficiencies, 1 cottage* ♿*In-room: kitchen (some), refrigerator, Wi-Fi. In-hotel: public Internet, no-smoking rooms, no elevator* ⊟*MC, V* ⊗*Closed mid-Oct.–mid-May.*

$$$–$$$$    🏠**Old Harbor Inn.** Congenial, thoughtful hosts Ray and Judith Braz run this cheery B&B set inside a handsome 1930s colonial-revival house a few steps from Main Street and downtown shopping. You'll receive plenty of extras and treats, from in-room snack baskets and extensive complimentary bath products to hair dryers and fluffy robes. Most rooms feel distinctly Victorian in flavor—the cozy yet spacious Port Fortune room has exposed beams, pitched ceilings, white wicker furniture, and Laura Ashley linens. If it's luxury you're after, book the Stage Harbor Suite, which has a two-person Jacuzzi and separate shower. Relax out back on the deck or in the verdant, shaded garden. **Pros:** quick walk to center of town; well-appointed rooms with plenty of amenities. **Cons:** not a beachfront location. ✉*22 Old Harbor Rd.* ☎*508/945–4434 or 800/942–4434* ⊕*www.chathamoldharborinn. com* ⤳*7 rooms, 1 suite* ♿*In-room: no phone, refrigerator, VCR. In-hotel: gym, public Wi-Fi, no-smoking rooms, no kids under 12, no elevator* ⊟*MC, V* ⧖*BP.*

$$$–$$$$    🏠**Queen Anne Inn.** Built in 1840 as a wedding present for the daughter
★       of a famous clipper-ship captain, the Queen Anne first opened as an inn in 1874. Some of the large guest rooms have working fireplaces, balconies, and hot tubs. The lavish studio rooms in the Victorian cottage are particularly dashing and convey more of a colonial Caribbean flair. Lingering and lounging are encouraged—around the large heated outdoor pool, at the tables on the veranda, in front of the fireplace in the sitting room, or in the plush parlor. A licensed massage therapist is on hand, should you wish to indulge in a treatment. The place has a wonderful, cozy feel in winter, making it a great year-round option, though the restaurant is closed in winter. Run by locally renowned chef Toby Hill, the Eldredge Room ($$$–$$$$; closed Jan.–Apr., no lunch) turns out sublime regional American fare, including an updated fish-and-chips consisting of truffle-crusted flounder, frites, truffle tartar sauce, and malt vinaigrette, and crispy honey-Dijon venison "lollipops" with a chocolate-zinfandel dipping sauce. There's also an extensive American caviar menu. **Pros:** spacious and thoughtfully decorated rooms in historic setting; well suited for relaxing with hot tubs and fireplaces. **Cons:** it's a generous walk to the town center; rooms accessed via steep stairs. ✉*70 Queen Anne Rd.* ☎*508/945–0394 or 800/545–4667* 🖷*508/945–4884* ⊕*www.queenanneinn.com* ⤳*33 rooms* ♿*In-room: Wi-Fi. In-hotel: restaurant, bar, tennis courts, pool, no-smoking rooms, no elevator* ⊟*AE, D, MC, V* ⊗*Closed Jan.–Mar.*

## NIGHTLIFE & THE ARTS

THE ARTS   **Chatham Drama Guild** (✉*134 Crowell Rd.* ☎*508/945–0510* ⊕*www. chathamdramaguild.com*) stages productions year-round, including musicals, comedies, and dramas.

The **Creative Arts Center** (⊠*154 Crowell Rd.* ☎*508/945–3583* ⊕*www. capecodcreativearts.org*) thrives year-round with classes, changing gallery exhibitions, demonstrations, lectures, and other activities.

In July and August the **Guild of Chatham Painters** presents an outdoor art gallery on Thursday and Friday from 9:30 to 5 on the Main Street School's lawn. ⊠*Main St.*

The **Monomoy Theatre** (⊠*776 Main St.* ☎*508/945–1589* ⊕*www. monomoytheatre.org*) stages summer productions—thrillers, musicals, classics, and modern drama—by the Ohio University Players.

Chatham's summer **town-band concerts** (⊠*Kate Gould Park, Main St.* ☎*508/945–5199*) begin at 8 PM on Friday and draw up to 6,000 people. As many as 500 fox-trot on the roped-off dance floor, and there are special dances for children and sing-alongs for all.

NIGHTLIFE   **Chatham Squire** (⊠*487 Main St.* ☎*508/945–0945*), with four bars—including a raw bar—is a rollicking year-round local hangout, drawing a young crowd to the bar side and a mixed crowd of locals to the restaurant.

After great success in Hyannis and Falmouth, the owners of the **RoöBar** (⊠*907 Main St.* ☎*508/945–9988* ⊕*www.theroobar.com*) opened a third location in Chatham, transforming what was once a Friendly's into an elegant bar and bistro. Patrons enjoy an extensive wine list, great mixed drinks, and varied entertainment—usually rock music—on weekends.

## SPORTS & THE OUTDOORS

BASEBALL   The **Cape Cod Baseball League,** begun in 1885, is an invitational league of college players that counts Carlton Fisk, Ron Darling, Mo Vaughn, Nomar Garciaparra, and the late Thurman Munson as alumni. Considered the country's best summer league, it's scouted by every major-league team. The 10 teams of the Cape Cod Baseball League play a 44-game season from mid-June to mid-August; games held at all 10 fields are free. The **Chatham A's** (⊠*Veterans' Field, Main and Depot Sts. by rotary* ☎*508/996–5004* ⊕*www.chathamas.com*) games are great entertainment.

**Baseball clinics** (⊠*Veterans' Field, Main and Depot Sts. by rotary* ☎*508/432–6909*)—for kids 6 through 8, 9 through 12, and 13 through 17—are offered in one-week sessions by the Chatham A's in summer. The other nine town teams in the Cape league also conduct clinics (☎*508/996–5004 information*).

BEACHES   **Outermost Harbor Marine** (⊠*Morris Island Rd., Morris Island* ☎*508/945–2030*) runs shuttles to South Beach; rides cost $20 round-trip for adults (including parking).

**Beachcomber** (⊠*Crowell Rd., Chatham* ☎*508/945–5265*) runs a fleet of bright yellow boats for beach shuttles to North Beach from the Fish Pier (off Shore Road), seal-watching trips, and sunset cruises. A free old-fashioned trolley (it's green) runs from the satellite parking lot (also free) on Crowell Road, at the Chatham Boat Company.

CLOSE UP

# The Cape Cod Baseball League

At the Baseball Hall of Fame in Cooperstown, New York, you can find a poster announcing a showdown between archrivals Sandwich and Barnstable. The date? July 4, 1885. In the 120-plus years since that day, the Cape's ball-playing tradition has continued unabated. To see a game on the Cape today is to come into contact with baseball's roots—you'll remember why you love the sport.

As they have since the 1950s, top-ranked college baseball players from around the country descend on the Cape when school lets out, just in time to begin the season in mid-June. Each player joins one of the league's 10 teams, each based in a different town: the Bourne Braves, Wareham Gatemen, Falmouth Commodores, Cotuit Kettleers, Hyannis Mets, Dennis-Yarmouth Red Sox, Harwich Mariners, Brewster Whitecaps, Chatham Athletics (A's), and Orleans Cardinals.

Players lodge with local families and work day jobs cutting lawns, painting houses, or giving baseball clinics in town parks. In the evening, though, their lives are given over to baseball.

The Cape League's motto is "Where the Stars of Tomorrow Shine Tonight." By latest count, one of every eight active major-league ballplayers spent a summer in the Cape League on the way up. You could build an all-star roster with names such as Nomar Garciaparra, Frank Thomas, Jeff Bagwell, Todd Helton, and Barry Zito.

To enshrine these heroes past, the Cape League inducted the first members into its Hall of Fame at the Heritage Museums & Gardens in Sandwich in January 2001. Among the 12 players honored were Thurman Munson, Mike Flanagan, Jeff Reardon, Mo Vaughn, and Frank Thomas.

Yet as good as the baseball is—you'll often see major-league scouts at a game—another great reason to come out to the ballpark is...the ballpark. Chatham's Veterans Field is the Cape's Monster Park at Candlestick Point: much like the San Francisco park, fog tends to engulf the games here. Orleans's Eldredge Park is a local favorite—immaculate, cozy, and comfortable. Some parks have bleachers; in others, it's up to you to bring your own chair or blanket and stretch out behind a dugout or baseline. Children are free to roam and can even try for foul balls—which they are, however, asked to return because, after all, balls don't grow on trees. When hunger hits, the ice-cream truck and hot-dog stand are never far away.

Games start at either 5 or 7, depending on whether the field has lights; occasionally there are afternoon games. Each team plays 44 games in a season, so finding one is rarely a problem (⊕ www.capecodbaseball. org has information). And, best of all, they're always free. The Cape's baseball scene is so American, the ambience so relaxed and refreshing, it's tempting to invoke the old *Field of Dreams* analogy. But the league needs no Hollywood comparison. This is the real thing.

–Seth Rolbein

**Harding's Beach** (✉*Harding's Beach Rd., off Barn Hill Rd., West Chatham*), west of Chatham center, is open to the public and charges daily parking fees to nonresidents in season. Lifeguards are stationed here in summer. This beach can get crowded, so plan to arrive early or late. Nonresident parking fees at Chatham beaches are $15 daily, $60 weekly, and $125 seasonally.

**Cockle Cove Beach** (✉*Cockle Cove Rd. off Rte. 28, South Chatham*) is a favorite with families because of its gentle waves and the warmer waters of Nantucket Sound. It's a good, large beach for strolling and exploring. There are lifeguards and restrooms. Nonresident parking fees are in effect *(see above)*.

**Ridgevale Beach** (✉*Ridgevale Rd. off Rte. 28, West Chatham*) is very popular in summer; there are lifeguards, a snack bar, boat rentals, and restrooms. Nonresident parking fees are in effect *(see above)*.

4

BICYCLING    All manner of bikes are available for rent at **Chatham Cycle** (✉*193 Depot Rd.* ☎*508/945–8981*).

BOATING    **Monomoy Sail & Cycle** (✉*275 Orleans Rd., North Chatham* ☎*508/945–0811*) rents sailboards and kayaks. You'll need your own roof rack; this location is not on the water.

*Rip Ryder* (☎*508/945–5450*) boat tours offers naturalist-led trips that leave from the Monomoy National Wildlife Refuge area to view birds and seals and explore the rich and ever-changing habitat of the North and South Monomoy Island areas.

**Nauti Jane's** (✉ *Ridgevale Beach at Ridgevale Rd., Chatham* ☎*508/432–4339*) has Sunfish and kayaks for rent.

GOLF    **Chatham Seaside Links** (✉*Seaview St., West Chatham* ☎*508/945–4774*), a 9-hole course, is good for beginners.

SURFING    The Lower and Outer Cape beaches, including North Beach in Chatham, are the best on the peninsula for surfing, which is tops when there's a storm offshore. Chatham does not have any surf shops, but you'll find them in nearby Orleans.

TENNIS    **Chatham Bars Inn** (✉*297 Shore Rd.* ☎*508/945–0096 Ext. 6759*) offers three waterfront all-weather tennis courts, which are open to the public by reservation for $35 an hour. You can also take lessons and visit the pro shop.

The town maintains two public tennis parks, one on Depot Road next to the Railroad Museum at No. 153 and the other at the middle school on Crowell Road.

## SHOPPING

**Main Street** is a busy shopping area with a diverse range of merchandise, from the pocketbook-friendly to the pricier and more upscale. Here you'll find galleries, crafts, clothing stores, bookstores, and a few good antiques shops.

★ **Chatham Jam and Jelly Shop** ( ✉ *10 Vineyard Ave., at Rte. 28, West Chatham* ☎ *508/945–3052 or 877/526–7467*) sells delicious concoctions like rose-petal jelly, apple-lavender chutney, and beach-plum jam, as well as all the old standbys. All preserves are made on-site in small batches, and about 75 of the 120-plus varieties are available for sampling (which is encouraged).

The **Crooked Fence** ( ✉ *593 Main St.* ☎ *508/945–4622*), tucked inconspicuously behind Dunkin' Donuts, stocks eclectic, well-chosen home furnishings and gifts, such as cast-iron planters, Nantucket baskets, wind chimes, imported Tuscan tableware, and models of vintage planes and boats.

The **East Wind Silver Co.** ( ✉ *878 Main St.* ☎ *508/945–8935*) specializes in artful silver jewelry but also sells watercolor paintings, pottery, fountains, and Tiffany-style lighting.

**Maps of Antiquity** ( ✉ *1409 Main St. [Rte. 28], Chatham* ☎ *508/945–1660* ⊕ *www.mapsofantiquity.com*) sells original and reproduction maps of Cape Cod, New England, and other parts of the world. Some date to the 1700s. Above the shop in this restored 18th-century home are several guest rooms and suites for rent ($95–$165).

**Marion's Pie Shop** ( ✉ *2022 Main St. [Rte. 28], West Chatham* ☎ *508/432–9439*) sells homemade and home-style fruit breads, pastries, prepared foods such as lasagna, Boston baked beans, and chowder base, and, of course, pies, both savory and sweet.

**S. Wilder & Co.** ( ✉ *309 Orleans Rd. [Rte. 28], North Chatham* ☎ *877/794–5337*), also known as Cape Cod Lanterns, displays old-style colonial crafts. Handcrafted brass and copper lanterns are made here.

**Tale of the Cod** ( ✉ *450 Main St., Chatham* ☎ *508/945–0347*) has a wide selection of Chatham-related gifts for the home or individual, including painted furniture; specialty dolls; and Chatham-themed rugs, throws, and glass.

**Yankee Ingenuity** ( ✉ *525 Main St.* ☎ *508/945–1288*) stocks a varied selection of unique jewelry and lamps and a wide assortment of unusual, beautiful trinkets at reasonable (especially for Chatham) prices.

**Yellow Umbrella Books** ( ✉ *501 Main St.* ☎ *508/945–0144*) has an excellent selection of new books, many about Cape Cod, as well as used books.

**EN ROUTE** North of Chatham and on the way to Orleans, you'll encounter perhaps the most beautiful stretch of Route 28, the road that's so blighted by overdevelopment in Harwich, Dennis, and Yarmouth. Along here, the narrow road twists and turns alongside the western shoreline of rippling **Pleasant Bay.** Turn east onto any number of peaceful country roads, and you'll end up near the water and within view of Nauset Spit and Pleasant Bay's several islands. This is excellent biking and jogging territory—but keep in mind that Route 28 is fairly narrow along this span, with a tiny shoulder, so keep your eye out for oncoming traffic.

# ORLEANS

*8 mi north of Chatham, 35 mi east of Sagamore Bridge.*

Named for Louis-Philippe de Bourbon, *duc d'Orléans* (duke of Orléans), who reputedly visited the area during his exile from France in the 1790s, Orleans was incorporated as a town in 1797. Historically, it has the distinction of being the only place in the continental United States to have received enemy fire during either world war. In July 1918 a German submarine fired on commercial barges off the coast. Four were sunk, and one shell is reported to have fallen on American soil.

Today Orleans is part quiet seaside village and part bustling center with strip malls. The commercial hub of the region, Orleans is one of the more steadily populated areas, year-round, of the Lower Cape. Yet the town retains a fervent commitment to preserving its past, and residents, in support of local mom-and-pop shops, maintain an active refusal policy of many big-time corporations.

Orleans has a long heritage in fishing and seafaring, and many beautifully preserved homes remain from the colonial era. Many are found in the small village of East Orleans, home of the town's Historical Society and Museum. In other areas of town, such as down by Rock Harbor, more modestly grand homes stand near the water's edge.

As you head north, this is the first Cape town to touch both Cape Cod Bay and the Atlantic Ocean. Nauset Beach, on the Atlantic, is enormously popular. Backed by towering dunes dotted with sea grass and colorful *rosa Rugosa*, this beach could be the starting point for a long but beautiful trek clear to the very tip of the Cape. Skaket Beach, just south of Rock Harbor, is the main bay-side beach and affords both scenic views and calm, warm waters for swimming.

A walk along Rock Harbor Road, a winding street lined with gray-shingle Cape houses, white-picket fences, and neat gardens, leads to the bay-side **Rock Harbor,** site of a War of 1812 skirmish in which the Orleans militia kept a British warship from docking. In the 19th century Orleans had an active saltworks, and a flourishing packet service between Rock Harbor and Boston developed. Today the former packet landing is the base of charter-fishing and party boats in season, as well as of a small commercial fishing fleet whose catch hits the counters at the fish market and small restaurant here. Sunsets over the harbor are spectacular. Don't be surprised to see a line of trees (real, though not thriving) marking the narrow boat channel out to the bay. New markers are installed each season.

The Community of Jesus, a religious community whose members come from a variety of Christian traditions, owns a large chunk of the Rock Harbor area. Their dramatic cathedral, the **Church of the Transfiguration,** showcases the work of local and international artisans, and reflects the community's dedication to the arts. Inside there's an organ with thousands of pipes, authentic frescoes depicting biblical scenes, colorful stained-glass windows, and gorgeous, intricate mosaic work mixing religious themes with images of local flora and fauna. ⊠*Rock Harbor Rd. across from Rock Harbor* ☎*508/255–1054, 508/255–6204 tours* ⊕*www.communityofjesus.org* ✉*Free, donations accepted* ☉*Tours Tues., Fri., and Sat. at 3, Thurs.–Tues. at sunset; services are open to public.*

**NEED A BREAK?**

The **Cottage St. Bakery** ( ⊠*5 Cottage St.* ☎*508/255–2821*) prepares delicious artisanal breads, pastries, cakes, and sweets, as well as healthful breakfast and lunch fare, from homemade granola to hefty sandwiches.

The 1890 **French Cable Station Museum** was the stateside landing point for the 3,000-mi-long transatlantic cable that originated in Brittany. Another cable laid between Orleans and New York City completed the France–New York link, and many important messages were communicated through the station. During World War I, when it was an essential connection between army headquarters in Washington and the American Expeditionary Force in France, the station was under guard by the marines. By 1959 telephone service had rendered the station obsolete, and it closed—but the equipment is still in place. ⊠*41 S. Orleans Rd., Orleans* ☎*508/240–1735* ⊕*www.frenchcablestationmuseum.org* ✉*Donations accepted* ☉*June and Sept., Fri.–Sun. 1–4; July and Aug., Thurs.–Sat. 1–4.*

The **Jonathan Young Windmill,** a pretty if somewhat incongruous sight on the busy highway, is a landmark from the days of salt making in Orleans, when it would pump saltwater into shallow vaults for evaporation. A program explaining the history and operation of the mill demonstrates the old millstone and grinding process. ⊠*Rte. 6A and Town Cove, Orleans* ☉*July and Aug., daily 11–4; June and Sept., weekends 11–4.*

**NEED A BREAK?**

Grab a baked treat, chocolates of all varieties, and any number of coffee concoctions at the **Chocolate Sparrow** ( ⊠*5 Old Colony Way* ☎*508/240–2230*), right by the Cape Cod Rail Trail. The adjacent Ice Cream at the Sparrow serves tasty hard and soft ice cream.

The **Academy of Performing Arts** ( ⊠*5 Giddiah Hill Rd.* ☎*508/255–5510 or 508/255–1963* ⊕*www.apacape.org*) offers two-week sessions of theater, music, and dance classes to kids ages 8 to 12, with a show at the end of each session. It also schedules year-round classes for ages four to adult in dance, music, and drama. The academy's theater is at 120 Main Street.

**Snow Library** ( ⊠*Main St. and Rte. 28* ☎*508/240–3760* ⊕*www.snowlibrary.org*) has been in operation since around 1876; today there are kids' story hours and numerous lecture programs.

CLOSE UP

# Rotary 101

The English cheerfully call them "roundabouts," and although that lighthearted moniker might sound like it describes a fun (albeit slightly nauseating) carnival ride, rotaries are serious business. Uninitiated drivers are often so confused upon entering one that they either ignore all rules of the road or freeze up completely. Both reactions will likely cause horns to blare and the fists and fingers of your fellow motorists to come out in full force. But it doesn't have to be this way. Follow a few simple rules, and you'll be swinging around traffic circles like a local. The most important thing to remember is that drivers who are already in the rotary have the right of way: those entering must yield to the traffic in the rotary. This means that if you're approaching the rotary, you must wait until there is enough space for you to enter—you can't just hit the gas and hope for the best. Because if you do, you probably just caused a fellow motorist to commit another cardinal sin: stopping while in the rotary. Either that, or he just hit you. Using a rotary is actually a very simple concept. Now that you know the rules, you may even grow to appreciate their exquisite logic (at the very least, you'll see fewer unfriendly hand gestures). —Laura V. Scheel

4

## WHERE TO EAT

$$–$$$$
★
MEDITERRANEAN

✕**Abba.** Abba serves inspired pan-Mediterranean cuisine in an elegant and intimate setting. Chef and co-owner Erez Pinhas skillfully combines Middle Eastern, Asian, and Southern European flavors in such dishes as herb-crusted rack of venison with shiitake risotto and asparagus in port sauce, and grilled tuna with vegetable nori roll tempura in a balsamic miso and mustard sauce. Cushy pillows on the banquettes and soft candlelight flickering from Moroccan glass votives add a touch of opulence. Reservations suggested. ⊠ *Old Colony Way and West Rd.* ☎ *508/255–8144* ⊕ *www.abbarestaurant.com* ⊟ *AE, D, MC, V* ⊗ *No lunch.*

$$–$$$
CONTINENTAL

✕**Academy Ocean Grill.** Academy Ocean Grill occupies a stately shingle house surrounded by gardens—in warm weather, you can dine on the patio amid the flowers and greenery. It's a nice place for a relaxed and elegant luncheon; do try the tasty crab melt. Top dishes include chunky crab cakes; roasted monkfish simmered in a Cajun clam broth with andouille, tomatoes, and scallions, served with lobster ravioli; and traditional veal saltimbocca. An exceptional wine list rounds out the offerings. There's also a Sunday brunch. ⊠ *2 Academy Pl., off Rte. 28* ☎ *508/240–1585* ⊟ *AE, D, MC, V* ⊗ *Closed Mon. Closed mid-Jan.–early Apr.*

$$–$$$
ECLECTIC

✕**The Beacon Room.** Adorned with crisp linens, frilly curtains, and wood furnishings, this homey cottage bistro serves up a nice mix of seafood and meats enhanced with sophisticated and inventive flavors. Start with the Gorgonzola, sun-dried cranberry, and walnut salad, then move on to sesame-crusted salmon with cilantro oil or pecan-crusted venison with a sauce of red zinfandel and pan drippings. In warmer months, dinner on the garden patio is particularly urbane. An ambitious wine list complements the fine selection. Reservations aren't taken, although there is a call-ahead waiting list for busy summer nights. ✉ *23 West Rd.* ☎ *508/255–2211* ⌁ *Reservations not accepted* ▤ *MC, V.*

$$–$$$$
★
CONTINENTAL

✕ **Captain Linnell House.** Sea captain Eben Linnell built this stunning mansion in 1840, basing its design on a neoclassical villa he'd once visited in the South of France. Linnell's masterpiece now contains one of the Cape's most esteemed formal restaurants, a longtime favorite for celebrating special occasions. A competent and polite staff serves Continental cuisine, which is consistently superb. The kitchen tends to stick with tried-and-true classics, such as herb-and-mustard-crusted rack of lamb with a pinot-noir reduction, and grilled Black Angus steak au poivre with a zinfandel-peppercorn sauce. Considering the fine ingredients and opulent surroundings, it's an excellent value. ✉ *137 Skaket Beach Rd.* ☎ *508/255–3400* ⊕ *www.linnell.com* ▤ *AE, MC, V* ◷ *No lunch.*

¢–$$
★
AMERICAN

✕ **Land Ho!** Tried-and-true tavern fare is the rule at Orleans' flagship local restaurant. The scene is usually fun and boisterous; dozens of homemade wooden signs hang from the rafters above the red-checked tablecloths. The burgers and the sea-clam pie are both excellent, and the blackboard specials change daily. This is a good place for a rainy-day lunch. On weekend nights, it livens up even more with the music of local bands. ✉ *38 Cove Rd. (Rte. 6A)* ☎ *508/255–5165* ⌁ *Reservations not accepted* ▤ *AE, MC, V.*

$$–$$$
★
ECLECTIC

✕ **Mahoney's Atlantic Bar and Grill.** Chef-owner Ted Mahoney cooked for years at one of Provincetown's busiest restaurants before opening this always-hopping downtown spot that serves commendable dinner fare and draws big crowds for cocktails and appetizers. The menu emphasizes seafood, with such favorites as tuna sashimi, scallops, and a classic bouillabaisse brimming with shrimp, scallops, squid, haddock, littlenecks, and mussels in an herbed saffron broth, served over pasta. There are a few good vegetarian options as well, and several good steak, lamb, and chicken dishes. The bar is long and comfortable, and on many evenings you can sip your martini or California wine to live music. ✉ *28 Main St.* ☎ *508/255–5505* ⊕ *www.mahoneysatlantic.com* ▤ *AE, MC, V.*

$$–$$$$
★
ITALIAN

✕ **Nauset Beach Club.** Locals have long favored this upscale but casual trattoria on the road leading out to Nauset Beach. The kitchen produces seasonally inspired northern Italian food, with an emphasis on locally harvested seafood and produce. Choose from a fixed-price option (offered nightly starting at about $20 for three courses), or the à la carte menu, which includes favorites like veal alla Milanese, and sun-dried-tomato-crusted halibut in a lobster essence reduction. Known for their extensive wine list (they won a Wine Spectator award of excellence for their collection of Italian and American wines), the restaurant creates themed dinners with wine pairings throughout the year. ✉ *222 Main St., East Orleans* ☎ *508/255–8547* ⊕ *www.nausetbeachclub.com* ▤ *AE, D, DC, MC, V* ◷ *No lunch.*

$–$$$
ECLECTIC

✕ **Saltwater Grille.** Although it has seen many transformations over the last few years, this spot has finally found its niche. The former Binnacle Tavern has been eliminated, though its spirit lives on in the menu, where old favorites like delicious pizzas with some inventive toppings (apples, linguica sausage, pine nuts, Brie), generous burgers, specialty sandwiches, and an extensive menu of designer martinis can be had. Inside, it's a bit like eating in your favorite bright beach house. You'll find grilled meats and seafood aplenty here, as well as a good selection of pastas and salads. ✉ *20 S. Orleans Rd. (Rte. 28)* ☎ *508/255–5149* ▭ *AE, MC, V* ⚏ *Reservations not accepted* ⊗ *No lunch.*

**¢–$**
**SEAFOOD**
✕ **Sir Cricket's Fish and Chips.** For a beautifully turned-out fish sandwich, pull into this tiny local favorite, a hole-in-the-wall attached to Nauset Fish & Lobster Pool. Built mainly for takeout, this no-frills fish joint does have three or four tiny tables and a soda machine. Try the fresh oyster roll or go for a full fisherman's platter. As you eat, check out the chair seats—each is an exquisitely rendered mini-mural of Orleans history or a personality painted by legendary local artist Dan Joy. ✉ *39 Cranberry Hwy. (Rte. 6A)* ☎ *508/255–4453* ⚏ *Reservations not accepted* ▭ *No credit cards.*

## WHERE TO STAY

**$$–$$$**
**★**
▦ **Cove Motel.** Consisting of two main buildings overlooking Orleans Town Cove, this tidy but prosaic year-round motel has large rooms, most with decks or patios overlooking the water. Furnishings are undistinguished but updated and pleasant, and rooms have tasteful, neutral color schemes. Some units have fireplaces and kitchens, and two-room suites can comfortably accommodate four guests. An attractive picnic area overlooks the heated pool. You can't beat the location, and in summer you'll receive a complimentary boat tour around Town Cove. **Pros:** many water-view rooms; right on Town Cove; easy walk throughout town. **Cons:** sits right on semi-busy road; not for those looking for authentic historic lodging. ✉ *13 S. Orleans Rd. (Rte. 28), Box 279* ☎ *508/255–1203 or 800/343–2233* ⊕ *www.thecoveorleans.com* ⮌ *37 rooms, 10 suites* ⚏ *In-room: kitchen (some), refrigerator, DVD. In-hotel: pool, public Wi-Fi, no elevator* ▭ *AE, D, MC, V.*

**$$$–$$$$**
**Fodor's**Choice
**★**
▦ **A Little Inn on Pleasant Bay.** Run by sisters Sandra Zeller and Pamela Adam and Sandra's husband, Bernd Zeller—all of whom have extensive corporate and hospitality backgrounds—this gorgeously decorated inn occupies a 1798 building on a bluff beside a cranberry bog, across Route 28 from the bay for which it's named. The main house has four rooms, and two adjoining nearby buildings contain another five rooms. Many of the accommodations look clear out to the bay, and others face the lush gardens. The Mercury room has French doors leading out to a private garden patio, and the spacious Wianno room is warmed by a fireplace and has a lovely sitting area. The roomy, modern bathrooms are among the nicest of any hotel on the Cape. The breakfast buffet includes a dazzling variety of fresh fruits, baked goods, smoked fish, cold cuts, fine cheeses, yogurts, cereals, and other treats. It's more substantial than many full breakfasts, and you can enjoy it while sitting on the pretty patio, admiring Pleasant Bay in the distance. Walk across the street to a small private beach with its own dock. **Pros:** peaceful, pastoral setting with great water views; abundant buffet breakfast; spacious, well-appointed rooms. **Cons:** not an in-town location; must drive a distance to either Orleans or Chatham. ✉ *654 S. Orleans Rd., Box 190, South Orleans* ☎ *508/255–0780 or 888/332–3351* ⊕ *www.alittleinn onpleasantbay.com* ⮌ *9 rooms* ⚏ *In-room: no phone, no TV, Wi-Fi.*

**4**

*In-hotel: no kids under 10, no-smoking rooms, no elevator* ⊟AE, MC, V ⏐⊙⏐CP ⊙ *Closed Nov.–Apr.*

**$–$$** 🏠**Nauset House Inn.** You could easily spend a day trying out all the places to relax in this early-19th-century farmhouse. There's a parlor with comfortable chairs and a large fireplace, an orchard set with picnic tables, and a lush conservatory with a weeping cherry tree in its center. Rooms in both the main building and the adjacent Carriage House have stenciled walls, quilts, and unusual antique pieces, as well as hand-painted furniture, stained glass, and prints done by one of the owners. The beach is ½ mi away (they'll set you up with beach chairs and towels), and the attractions of town are close—but not too close. Those rooms with a shared bath all cost $95 or less. In early evening, wine and snacks are served to guests in the main house. **Pros:** authentic historic lodging in peaceful setting; ideal for relaxing and getting away from distractions; can walk to excellent ocean beach. **Cons:** many rooms must share a bath (though discounted); some rooms accessed via steep stairways. ⊠*143 Beach Rd., Box 774, East Orleans* ☎*508/255–2195, 800/771–5508* ⊕*www.nausethouseinn.com* 🛏*14 rooms, 8 with bath* ⚐ *In-room: no phones, no TV, no a/c, Wi-Fi (some). In-hotel: public Wi-Fi, no kids under 12, no-smoking rooms, no elevator* ⊟D, MC, V ⊙ *Closed Nov.–mid-Apr.* ⏐⊙⏐BP.

**$$–$$$$** 🏠**Orleans Inn.** This bustling inn and restaurant, housed in an 1875 sea
**Fodor'sChoice** captain's mansion, is run with warmth and enthusiasm by the large
★ Maas family. The imposing, turreted structure has two distinct faces: one is turned toward a busy intersection and a large shopping plaza, whereas the other looks longingly over tranquil Town Cove. Rooms here are simply but charmingly appointed (look for your complimentary gift basket filled with regional treats) with classic wood furniture and floral quilts on the beds; the larger waterfront suites have sitting areas and great views of the harbor. Common areas include a kitchenette with a microwave and toaster oven and a sitting room in the basement with a large TV and videos. The restaurant ($–$$$), which uses some creative ingredients in its traditional standbys, serves large portions of fish-and-chips, grilled sirloin, and grilled salmon with orange-honey glaze. There's also an excellent Sunday brunch. Remarkably, the inn has no cancellation fee: you must pay in full for your stay at the time of booking, but even if you cancel the day of arrival, you'll receive a full refund. Local and long-distance phone calls are complimentary, too. On Friday evenings the tavern is filled with the sounds of live traditional Irish music, played by local musicians. **Pros:** great waterfront location; outdoor dining overlooking the cove (about the only place in town); gracious hosts; many amenities. **Cons:** some rooms face busy intersection rather than the water; rooms accessed via steep stairs. ⊠*3 Old County Rd., ⏐Box 188, Orleans* ☎*508/255–2222 or 800/863–3039* 🖶*508/255–6722* ⊕*www.orleansinn.com* 🛏*8 rooms, 3 suites* ⚐*In-room: VCR, DVD, refrigerator, Wi-Fi. In-hotel: restaurant, bar, no-smoking rooms, no elevator* ⊟AE, MC, V ⏐⊙⏐BP.

**$$** 🏠**Skaket Beach Motel.** Rooms in this convenient-to-everything inland motel overlooking a busy intersection are well sized; a handful of suites have kitchens and two or three bedrooms. Outdoor facilities include horseshoes, a heated pool, and grills. **Pros:** tasty homemade blueberry muffins in the morning; central location for exploring the area; good for those traveling with children (pool, lawn games). **Cons:** faces very busy intersection; pool area can be loud with nearby traffic. ✉*203 Cranberry Hwy. (Rte. 6A)* ☎*508/255–1020 or 800/835–0298* 🖷*508/255–6487* ⊕*www.skaketbeachmotel.com* 🛏*40 rooms, 6 suites* ♿*In-room: kitchen (some), refrigerator, Wi-Fi (some). In-hotel: pool, laundry, public Wi-Fi, no elevator* ☰*MC, V* ☾*Closed late Nov.–mid-Mar.* ¶◯*CP.*

### NIGHTLIFE & THE ARTS

The **Academy Playhouse** ( ✉*120 Main St.* ☎*508/255–1963* ⊕*www.apa1.org*), one of the oldest community theaters on the Cape, stages 12 or 13 productions year-round, including original works.

**4**

The **Stages Theatre Company** ( ☎*508/255–3999* ⊕*www.gdaf.org*) puts on music and theater events several times a year. The group is affiliated with the Community of Jesus; performances are held on the Community's grounds at Rock Harbor.

**Land Ho!** ( ✉*38 Cove Rd. [Rte. 6A]* ☎*508/255–5165*) has live local bands frequently throughout the year.

**Mahoney's Atlantic Bar and Grill** ( ✉*28 Main St.* ☎*508/255–5505*) regularly has live jazz and blues in the bar area; call for times.

Free ocean-side concerts are held in the gazebo at **Nauset Beach** each Monday evening from 7 to 9 in July and August. The resident fried-clam shack stays open until 10.

### SPORTS & THE OUTDOORS

BASEBALL The **Orleans Cardinals** ( ☎*508/255–0793* ⊕*www.orleanscardinals.com*) of the collegiate Cape Cod Baseball League play home games at **Eldredge Park** ( ✉*Rte. 28*) from mid-June to mid-August.

BEACHES The town-managed **Nauset Beach** ( ✉*Beach Rd., Nauset Heights* ☎*508/240–3780*)—not to be confused with Nauset Light Beach on the National Seashore—is a 10-mi sweep of sandy ocean beach with low dunes and large waves good for bodysurfing or board surfing. The beach has lifeguards, restrooms, showers, and a food concession. Despite its size, the massive parking lot often fills up when the sun is strong; arrive quite early or in the late afternoon if you want to claim a spot. The beach is open to off-road vehicles with a special permit. Daily parking fees are $15; a one-week pass costs $50, and a season pass is $110. Entrance is free with a resident sticker. For more information, call the parks department.

Freshwater seekers can access **Pilgrim Lake** ( ✉*Pilgrim Lake Rd. off Monument Rd. and Rte. 28, South Orleans*), which has the same parking and sticker fees as Nauset Beach.

**NEED A BREAK?** For a quick fix for your sweet tooth or something more substantial like a cup of homemade soup, grilled panini, or other great sandwiches, head to **Cape Cup** ( ✉*54 Main St.* ☎*508/255–1989*). It's also a great spot for a hot blast of espresso when you need a jolt or a breakfast treat.

**Skaket Beach** ( ⊠*Skaket Beach Rd., Namskaket* ☎*508/240–3775*) on Cape Cod Bay is a sandy stretch with calm, warm water good for children. It's a good place to watch motorboats, fishing charters, and sailboats as they leave the channel at Rock Harbor or take in the spectacular evening sunsets. There are restrooms, lifeguards, and a snack bar. Daily parking fees are the same as at Nauset Beach.

BOATING **Arey's Pond Boat Yard** ( ⊠*43 Arey's La., off Rte. 28, South Orleans* ☎*508/255–0994*) has a sailing school with individual and group lessons.

FISHING Many of Orleans's freshwater ponds offer good fishing for perch, pickerel, trout, and more. The required fishing license, along with rental gear, is available at the **Goose Hummock Shop** ( ⊠*15 Rte. 6A* ☎*508/255–0455*), which also rents kayaks and gives kayaking lessons and tours.

**Rock Harbor Charter Boat Service** ( ⊠*Rock Harbor* ☎*508/255–9757, 800/287–1771 in Massachusetts* ⊕*www.rockharborcharters.com*) goes for bass and blues in the bay from spring through fall. Walk-ons and charters are both available.

HEALTH & **Willy's Gym** ( ⊠*21 Old Colony Way* ☎*508/255–6826* ⊕*www.willys*
FITNESS CLUBS *gym.com*) is one of the Cape's top fitness facilities, with state-of-the-art cardio and weight-training equipment and studios for yoga, Pilates, martial arts, aerobics, and dance classes. Daily, weekly, and monthly passes are available. The on-site Kembali Spa offers a wide range of massage and treatment options. This 27,000-square-foot location is the original Willy's; the one in Eastham is even larger.

SPAS **Heaven Scent You** ( ⊠*13 Cove Rd.* ☎*508/240–2508*) offers massage, spa services, and beauty treatments—everything you need for some relaxation and rejuvenation.

Housed in a beautifully restored aged Victorian, the elegant day spa **Welstar** ( ⊠*42 S. Orleans Rd.* ☎*508/240–1422 or 800/893–6008* ⊕*www.dayspacapecod.com*) sits right on busy Route 28 in the center of Orleans. Decadent specialty treatments include crystal balancing (for refocusing the body's energy), seaweed contouring masks, warm stone massages, facials, manicures, pedicures, and many more esoteric treats.

SPORTING For bike rentals just across the way from the Cape Cod Rail Trail, head
GOODS— to **Orleans Cycle** ( ⊠*26 Main St.* ☎*508/255–9115*).
RENTALS
**Idle Times Bike Shop** ( ⊠*29 Main St.* ☎*508/240—1122)*is close to the Cape Cod Rail Trail.

SURFING The Lower and Outer Cape beaches, including Nauset Beach in Orleans, are the best spots for surfing, especially when there's a storm offshore. For a surf report—water temperature, weather, surf, tanning factor—call ☎*508/240–2229*.

**Pump House Surf Co.** ( ⊠*9 Rte. 6A* ☎*508/240–2226*) rents wet suits and surfboards, and sells boards and gear.

**Nauset Sports** (⊠*Jeremiah Sq., Rte. 6A at rotary* ☎*508/255–4742*) rents surf-, body-, skim-, and wake boards as well as wet suits.

## SHOPPING

Orleans's Main Street, between Route 6A and Route 28, is lined with a good number of specialty shops. It's a great area for browsing or taking a break on a park bench.

**Baseball Shop** (⊠*26 Main St.* ☎*508/240–1063*) sells licensed products relating to baseball and other sports—new and collectible cards (and nonsports cards) as well as hats, clothing, and videos.

**Bird Watcher's General Store** (⊠*36 Rte. 6A* ☎*508/255–6974 or 800/562–1512*) stocks nearly everything avian but the birds themselves: feeders, paintings, houses, books, binoculars, calls, bird-theme apparel, and more.

**Karol Richardson** (⊠*47 Main St.* ☎*508/255–3944*) sells fine contemporary clothing, plus silk wraps and scarves, hats, shoes, handbags, and handcrafted jewelry. You'll usually pay more for the quality goods here, but bargains can be found at the shop's off-season warehouse sales.

**Kemp Pottery** (⊠*9 Cranberry Hwy. [Rte. 6A]* ☎*508/255–5853*) features the often whimsical works of a father and son team—including functional and decorative stoneware and porcelain—often with natural and fantastical themes. They also have fountains, garden sculpture, pottery sinks, and stained glass.

**Oceana** (⊠*1 Main St. Sq.* ☎*508/240–1414*) has a beautiful selection of nautical-theme home accents, gifts, and jewelry, as well as colorful hooked rugs made by Cape artist Claire Murray.

The **Orleans Farmers' Market** (⊠*Old Colony Way across from Capt'n Elmers* ☎*508/255–0951*) is the place to go for local delicacies such as fresh produce, flowers, and homemade goodies. It's open 8 AM to noon Saturday morning throughout the summer. Be forewarned—early birds get the best selection, and things tend to disappear quickly.

**Village Farm Market** (⊠*199 Main St., East Orleans* ☎*508/255–1949*) sells local produce, fresh sandwiches and roll-ups, salads (salad bar or prepared varieties), homemade soup, ice cream, fresh-baked breads, and other supplies for a great picnic. There's also a full-service butcher counter and fish market. A wide assortment of flowers, both dried and fresh, are sold, adding great color to the beautiful, beamed old-style barn.

ART & CRAFTS
GALLERIES
The **Addison Art Gallery** (⊠*43 S. Orleans Rd. [Rte. 28]* ☎*508/255–6200*), in four rooms of a brick-red Cape house, represents more than two dozen regional artists. Peruse the collection of contemporary works, many of which were inspired by life on Cape Cod. The sculpture garden in the side yard is a perfect complement to the tasteful gallery. Receptions, where you can often meet the week's featured artist, are held year-round from 5 to 7 on Saturday night.

**Gallery 31** (✉*31 Main St.* ☎*508/247–9469*) is a partnership of nearly one dozen local artists, representing a wide range of mediums and styles.

**Left Bank Gallery** (✉*8 Cove Rd.* ☎*508/247–9172*) carries an eclectic mix of handcrafted jewelry, fine art by both local and national artists, hand-painted furniture, pottery, and handmade clothing.

On Tuesday and Sunday in July and August, **Nauset Painters** (*Tues.* ✉*Depot Sq. at Old Colony Way Sun.* ✉*Sandwich Cooperative Bank, 51 Main St.*) presents outdoor juried art shows.

The **Orleans Art Association** (✉*137 Main St.*) holds outdoor art shows from 10 to 5 each Thursday and Friday in July and August on the grounds of the American Legion Hall.

At various times in June, July, and August, the **Orleans Professional Arts and Crafts Association** (✉*Rte. 28*) sponsors a giant outdoor show on the grounds of the Nauset Middle School featuring the works of more than 100 artists and craftspeople. For specific dates and times, check the free town guide published by the Chamber of Commerce.

The **Rowley Gallery & Doug Johnson Gallery** (✉*76 Rte. 6A* ☎*508/240–7827 and 508/255–3690*) includes an unusual mix of contemporary art and tribal artifacts.

★ **Tree's Place** (✉*Rte. 6A at Rte. 28* ☎*508/255–1330 or 888/255–1330*), one of the Cape's best and most original shops, has a collection of handcrafted kaleidoscopes, as well as art glass, hand-painted porcelain and pottery, handblown stemware, jewelry, imported ceramic tiles, and fine art. Tree's displays the work of New England artists, including Robert Vickery, Don Stone, and Elizabeth Mumford (whose popular folk art is bordered in mottos and poetic phrases). Champagne openings are held on Saturday night in summer.

## EASTHAM

*3 mi north of Orleans, 6 mi south of Wellfleet.*

Often overlooked on the speedy drive up toward Provincetown on U.S. 6, Eastham is a town full of hidden treasures. Unlike other towns on the Cape, it has no official town center or Main Street; the highway bisects Eastham, and the town is spread out on both Cape Cod Bay and the Atlantic. Amid the gas stations, convenience stores, restaurants, and large motel complexes, Eastham's wealth of natural beauty takes a little exploring to find.

One such gem is the National Seashore, which officially begins here and comprises thousands of acres of wooded areas, salt marshes, and wild, open-ocean beaches. The Salt Pond Visitor Center just off U.S. 6 is one of Cape Cod National Seashore's main centers, host to numerous nature and history programs and lectures; it also maintains a paved bike path. Nearby is the much-beloved Nauset Light, the red-and-white-stripe lighthouse saved from imminent destruction when it was moved from its perilous perch atop eroding cliffs. The Fort Hill area is another pretty spot, with lots of walking trails and a stately old mansion called the Penniman House.

It was here in 1620 that an exploring band of *Mayflower* passengers met the Nauset tribe on a bay-side beach, which they then named First Encounter Beach. The meeting was peaceful, but the Pilgrims moved on to Plymouth anyway. Nearly a quarter century later, they returned to settle the area, which they originally called by its Native American name, Nawsett. Eastham was incorporated as a town on June 7, 1651.

Like many other Cape towns, Eastham started as a farming community and later turned to the sea and to salt making for its livelihood; at one time there were more than 50 saltworks in town. A less typical industry that once flourished here was asparagus growing; from the late 1800s through the 1920s, Eastham was known as the asparagus capital of the United States. The runner-up crop, Eastham turnips, are still the pride of many a harvest table.

★ The road to the Cape Cod National Seashore's **Fort Hill Area** ( ⊠ *Fort Hill Rd., off U.S. 6*) winds past the **Captain Edward Penniman House,** ending at a parking area with a lovely view of old farmland traced with stone fences that rolls gently down to **Nauset Marsh** and a red-maple swamp. Appreciated by bird-watchers and nature photographers, the 1-mi **Red Maple Swamp Trail** begins outside the Penniman House and winds through the area, branching into two separate paths, one of which eventually turns into a boardwalk that meanders through wetlands. The other path leads directly to Skiff Hill, an overlook with benches and informative plaques that quote Samuel de Champlain's account of the area from when he moored off Nauset Marsh in 1605. Also on Skiff Hill is Indian Rock, a large boulder moved to the hill from the marsh below. Once used by the local Nauset tribe as a sharpening stone, the rock is cut with deep grooves and smoothed in circles where ax heads were whetted.

The French Second Empire–style **Captain Edward Penniman House** was built in 1868 for a whaling captain. The impressive exterior is notable for its mansard roof; its cupola, which once commanded a dramatic view of bay and sea; and its whale-jawbone entrance gate. The interior is open for guided tours or for browsing through changing exhibits. Call ahead to find out when tours are available. ⊠ *Fort Hill Rd., Fort Hill Area* ☎ *508/255–3421* ✉ *Free* ⊙ *Weekdays 1–4.*

The park at Samoset Road has as its centerpiece the **Eastham Windmill,** the oldest windmill on Cape Cod. A smock mill built in Plymouth in the early 1680s, it was moved to this site in 1793 and is the only Cape windmill still on the site where it was used commercially. The mill was restored by local shipwreck historian William Quinn and friends. The park often comes alive with town festivals and concerts, and occasionally demonstrations are given on the inner workings of the mill. Each September, just after Labor Day, Eastham celebrates its history and the change of the season with the annual Windmill Weekend, an event with a full roster of activities for all ages. ⊠ *U.S. 6 at Samoset Rd.* ☎ *Free* ☺ *July and Aug., Mon.–Sat. 10–5, Sun. 1–5.*

Frozen in time, the 1741 **Swift-Daley House** was once the home of Gustavus Swift, founder of the Swift meatpacking company. Inside the full Cape with bow roof you can find beautiful pumpkin-pine woodwork and wide-board floors, a ship's-cabin staircase that, like the bow roof, was built by ships' carpenters, and fireplaces in every downstairs room. The colonial-era furnishings include an old cannonball rope bed, tools, a melodeon (similar to an accordion), and a ceremonial quilt decorated with beads and coins. Among the antique clothing is a stunning 1850 wedding dress. Out back is a tool museum. ⊠ *U.S. 6, next to Eastham post office* ☎ *No phone* ⊕ *www.easthamhistorical.org* ☎ *Free; donations accepted* ☺ *July and Aug., weekdays 10–1; Sept., Sat. 10–1.*

A great spot for watching sunsets over the bay, **First Encounter Beach** (⊠ *End of Samoset Rd. off U.S. 6*) is rich in history. Near the parking lot, a bronze marker commemorates the first encounter between local Native Americans and passengers from the *Mayflower,* led by Captain Myles Standish, who explored the entire area for five weeks in November and December 1620 before moving on to Plymouth. The remains of a navy target ship retired after 25 years of battering now rest on a sandbar about 1 mi out.

☺ The Cape's most expansive national treasure, the **Cape Cod National**
Fodor'sChoice  **Seashore** was established in 1961 under the administration of Pres-
★  ident John F. Kennedy, for whom Cape Cod was home and haven. The 27,000-acre seashore, extending from Chatham to Provincetown, encompasses and protects 30 mi of superb ocean beaches; great rolling dunes; swamps, marshes, and wetlands; pitch-pine and scrub-oak forest; all kinds of wildlife; and a number of historic structures. Self-guided nature trails, as well as biking and horse trails, lace through these landscapes. Hiking trails lead to a red-maple swamp, **Nauset Marsh,** and to **Salt Pond,** in which breeding shellfish are suspended from floating "nurseries"; their offspring will later be used to seed the flats. Also in the seashore is the Buttonbush Trail, a nature path for people with vision impairments. A hike or bike ride to Coast Guard Beach leads to a turnout looking out over marsh and sea. A section of the cliff here was washed away in 1990, revealing the remains of a prehistoric dwelling.

**Salt Pond Visitor Center** is the first visitor center of the Cape Cod National Seashore that you encounter as you travel down-Cape toward the tip (the other, the **Province Lands Visitor Center,** is in Provincetown). The Salt Pond Visitor Center offers guided walks, tours, boat trips, demonstrations, and lectures from mid-April through Thanksgiving, as well as evening beach walks, campfire talks, and other programs in summer. The center includes a museum with displays on whaling and the old saltworks, as well as early Cape Cod artifacts including scrimshaw, the journal that Mrs. Penniman kept while on a whaling voyage with her husband, and some of the Pennimans' possessions, such as their tea service and the captain's top hat. A good bookstore and an air-conditioned auditorium showing films on geology, sea rescues, whaling, Henry David Thoreau, and Guglielmo Marconi are also here. Something's going on most summer evenings at the outdoor amphitheater, from slide-show talks to military-band concerts. ☒ *Doane Rd. off U.S. 6* ☎ *508/255–3421* ⊕ *www.nps.gov/caco* ☑ *Free* ⊙ *Daily 9–4:30 (hrs extended slightly in summer).*

Roads and bicycle trails lead to **Coast Guard and Nauset Light beaches** (☒ *Off Ocean View Dr.*), which begin an unbroken 30-mi stretch of barrier beach extending to Provincetown—the "Cape Cod Beach" of Thoreau's 1865 classic, *Cape Cod.* You can still walk its length, as Thoreau did, though the Atlantic continues to claim more of the Cape's eastern shore every year. The site of the famous beach cottage of Henry Beston's 1928 book, *The Outermost House,* is to the south, near the end of Nauset spit. Designated as a literary landmark in 1964, the cottage was, alas, destroyed in the Great Blizzard of February 1978.

Moved 350 feet back from its perch at cliff's edge in 1996, the much-photographed red-and-white **Nauset Light** (☒ *Ocean View Dr. and Cable Rd.* ☎ *508/240–2612* ⊕ *www.nausetlight.org*) still tops the bluff where the Three Sisters Lighthouses once stood; the Sisters themselves can be seen in a little landlocked park surrounded by trees, reached by paved walkways off Nauset Light Beach's parking lot. How the lighthouses got there is a long story. In 1838 three brick lighthouses were built 150 feet apart on the bluffs in Eastham overlooking a particularly dangerous area of shoals (shifting underwater sandbars). In 1892, after the eroding cliff dropped the towers into the ocean, they were replaced with three wooden towers. In 1918 two were moved away, as was the third in 1923. Eventually the National Park Service acquired the Three Sisters and brought them together in the inland park, where they would be safe, rather than returning them to the eroding coast. The Fresnel lens from the last working lighthouse is on display at the **Salt Pond Visitor Center.** Lectures on and guided walks to the lighthouses are conducted throughout the season, free of charge (donations accepted).

### WHERE TO EAT

$–$$$
SEAFOOD
✗**Arnold's Lobster & Clam Bar.** You can't miss this hot spot on the side of Route 6: look for the riot of colorful flowers lining the road and the patient folks waiting in long lines in the parking lot. That crowd is testament to the freshness and flavors that come out of this busy kitchen for lunch, dinner, and takeout, putting forth everything from grilled burgers to 3-pound lobsters. Unusual for a clam shack like this is the full bar, offering beer, wine, mixed drinks, and the house specialty, margaritas. There's ice cream for after dinner (or while you wait) and an artfully designed miniature-golf course to keep the kids happy. They're next to the bike trail. ☒ *3580 State Hwy. (U.S. 6), Eastham* ☎ *508/255–2575* ☐ *No credit cards* ⊙ *Closed Nov.–Apr.*

**$–$$**  ✕**Fairway Restaurant and Pizzeria.** The friendly family-run Fairway spe-
ITALIAN  cializes in Italian comfort food and pizzas. Attached to the Hole in
One Donut Shop (very popular among locals), the Fairway puts a jar
of crayons on every paper-covered table and sells its own brand of root
beer. Entrées come with salad and homemade rolls. Try the eggplant
Parmesan, fettuccine and meatballs, or a well-stuffed calzone. You
can order from the extensive breakfast menu from 6:30 to 11:30 AM.
✉*4295 U.S. 6* ☎*508/255–3893* ⚓*Reservations not accepted* ⊘*No
lunch* ▭*AE, D, DC, MC, V.*

**¢–$$**  ✕**The Friendly Fisherman.** Not just another roadside lobster shack with
SEAFOOD  buoys and nets for decoration, this place is serious about its fresh sea-
food. It's both a great place to pick up ingredients to cook at home—
there's a fish and produce market on-site—and a good bet for dining
out on such favorites as fish-and-chips, fried scallops, and lobster. The
market also sells homemade pies, breads, soups, stews, and pasta. ✉*U.
S. 6, North Eastham* ☎*508/255–6770 or 508/255–3009* ▭*AE, MC,
V* ⊘*Closed Nov.–Apr.*

## WHERE TO STAY

**$**  🏨**Cove Bluffs Motel.** This old-fashioned haven for nature lovers and
families is nestled among the trees and within walking distance of
Orleans Town Cove and several nature trails. Settle into a standard
motel room or choose a more self-sufficient getaway in studio or two-
bedroom housekeeping units with stoves, refrigerators, and micro-
waves. Grounds include basketball courts, shuffleboard, swing sets,
a playhouse, a sandbox, grills, and swinging hammocks in the shade.
**Pros:** peaceful setting near Town Cove; ideal for those traveling with
children; reasonable rates; good base from which to explore area.
**Cons:** not an in-town location; not for those looking for authentic his-
toric lodging. ✉*25 Seaview Rd. (U.S. 6), Box 297* ☎*508/240–1616*
⊕*www.covebluffs.com* ☞*5 rooms, 8 housekeeping units* ⚭*In-hotel:
pool, laundry facilities, no-smoking rooms, no elevator* ▭*MC, V*
⊘*Closed Nov.–late Apr.*

**$$$–$$$$**  🏨**Fort Hill Bed and Breakfast.** Gordon and Jean Avery run this enchant-
Fodor'sChoice  ing B&B in an 1864 Greek Revival farmhouse nestled in the tranquil
★  Fort Hill area. The location is perfect—minutes off busy Route 6, but
steps away from quiet, secluded trails that wind through cedar for-
ests, fields crisscrossed by old stone fences, and a red-maple swamp.
Two cozy suites in the main house, tastefully decorated with period
pieces and antiques, share a living room with fireplace. The crown
jewel, however, is the light and airy Nantucket Cottage, modeled after
a Truro barn. It's so homey—with stone floors, a gas fireplace, a clas-
sic white-and-blue Cape Cod bedroom loft, and a private garden—
that you'll want to move in. Breakfasts are superb, with offerings like
oven-poached pears in sweet cream, and buttermilk-currant scones;
the cheesy-chive egg soufflé is a masterpiece. **Pros:** serene, pastoral set-
ting; close to nature trails and superb views of National Seashore; pri-
vate and elegant lodging. **Cons:** not an in-town location. ✉*75 Fort
Hill Rd.* ☎*508/240–2870* ⊕*www.forthillbedandbreakfast.com* ☞*2
suites, 1 cottage* ⚭*In-room: no phones, kitchen (some), refrigerator,*

*DVD (some), VCR (some), Wi-Fi. In-hotel: no elevator* ⊟*No credit cards* ⊺◯⍁*BP.*

**$$–$$$$** ⛾**Four Points Sheraton.** This reliable if ordinary midrange chain hotel is within a mile of the entrance to the National Seashore. Rooms have views of the tropical indoor pool (with lush plants, pirate-theme bar, and resident live parrot), the parking lot, or the woods. Outside rooms are a little bigger and brighter and have mini-refrigerators. Several different themed packages are available. **Pros:** good location for exploring outer Cape area; great for those with kids (pools), full-service hotel. **Cons:** no water views or beachfront; standard chain-hotel fare rather than unique lodging. ✉*3800 U.S. 6* ☎*508/255–5000 or 800/533–3986* 📠*508/240–1870* ⊕*www.capecodfourpoints.com* ⟳*107 rooms, 2 suites* ⌖*In-room: refrigerator, Wi-Fi. In-hotel: restaurant, room service, bar, tennis courts, pools, gym, no elevator* ⊟*AE, D, DC, MC, V.*

**¢** ⛾**Hostelling International–Mid Cape.** On 3 wooded acres near the Cape Cod Rail Trail and a 15-minute walk from the bay, this hostel has cabins that sleep six to eight each; two can be used as family cabins. It has a common area and a kitchen, and there are a number of guest programs. Linens are provided (no sleeping bags); bring your own towels. Keep in mind that all guests must provide photo identification upon check-in (a valid driver's license or passport). **Pros:** perfect for those on limited budget; no-frills, family-style lodging; quiet location near bike trail and bay beaches; a step above camping. **Cons:** sharing lodging, bathrooms, and kitchens in dorm-style setting; not for those looking for privacy or luxury. ✉*75 Goody Hallet Dr.* ☎*508/255–2785* ⊕*www.usahostels. org* ⟳*8 cabins* ⌖*In-room: no a/c, kitchen, no TV, no elevator* ⊟*MC, V* ⊗*Closed mid-Sept.–mid-May.*

**$$–$$$$** ⛾**Inn at the Oaks.** If it weren't for this three-story inn's vivid-yellow paint job, it would be lost among the trees, even though it's right along U.S. 6. Both the Cape Cod Rail Trail and the Salt Pond Visitor Center are just across the road. Victorian touches at this 19th-century refuge include graceful high ceilings and intricate interior wood molding. Each room has antiques, brass beds, and soft down comforters, plus a few modern amenities such as DVD players; some have claw-foot tubs, which are great to slide into after a day at the beach. Whale-watching, biking, and "adventure" packages are available. **Pros:** very close to both Cape Cod Rail Trail and National Seashore; good bet for those traveling with kids who want to experience nonhotel lodging; can book on-site massage services. **Cons:** right off busy U.S. 6; not for those looking for quiet (away from kids) getaway. ✉*3085 County Rd. (U.S. 6)* ☎*508/255–1886* 📠*508/240–0345* ⊕*www.innattheoaks.com* ⟳*10 rooms, 4 suites* ⌖*In-room: DVD, Wi-Fi. In-hotel: some pets allowed (fee), no elevator* ⊟*AE, D, MC, V* ⊺◯⍁*BP.*

**$–$$** ⛾**Ocean Park Inn.** Rooms at this property, run by the same owners as the adjacent Four Points Sheraton, are clean, simple, and straightforward. There are larger family units available—one with a fireplace—but most rooms are for double occupancy, with full- or queen-size beds. You are welcome to use the amenities, including the pools and tennis courts, of the Four Points Sheraton. **Pros:** lots of special packages make for some good deals; good bet for those traveling with kids;

shares amenities with larger hotel next door; close to bike trail and area beaches. **Cons:** no water views or beachfront; just off busy Route 6. ⊠*3900 U.S. 6* ☎*508/255–1132 or 800/862–5550* 🖷*508/255–5250* ⊕*www.capecodopi.com* 📺*54 rooms, 1 suite* ⚷*In-room: refrigerator. In-hotel: laundry facilities, no elevator* ▭*AE, D, DC, MC, V* ⊗*Closed Nov.–Mar.*

$$–$$$$   ▥**Penny House Inn & Spa.** Tucked behind a wave of privet hedge,
★   this rambling gray-shingle inn's spacious rooms are furnished with antiques, collectibles, and wicker. The luxurious accommodations are cozy rather than stuffy; many are romantic, with whirlpool tubs, fireplaces, or both. Some rooms are larger, with sitting areas; suites have separate bedrooms and sitting rooms and can sleep up to five. Take a dip in the saltwater pool, or indulge in a massage, facial, or mud wrap in the on-site spa room. Common areas include a Great Room with lots of windows and a selection of videos, a combination sunroom-library, and a garden patio with umbrella tables. A full homemade breakfast starts the day, and afternoon tea is available. **Pros:** rooms are private and secluded; ideal for a romantic getaway; full range of luxury spa services to choose from; not far from National Seashore and area beaches. **Cons:** sits just off busy U.S. 6 (though set back a little); no water views or beachfront. ⊠*4885 County Rd. (U.S. 6)* ☎*508/255–6632 or 800/554–1751* 🖷*508/255–4893* ⊕*www.pennyhouseinn.com* 📺*10 rooms, 3 suites* ⚷*In-room: refrigerator (some), VCR (some) DVD (some), Wi-Fi. In-hotel: pool, spa, no kids under 8, no-smoking rooms, no elevator* ▭*AE, D, MC, V* �O|*BP.*

$$$–$$$$   ▥**Whalewalk Inn & Spa.** This 1830 whaling master's home is on 3 land-
Fodor's Choice   scaped acres. Wide-board pine floors, fireplaces, and 19th-century
★   country antiques provide historical appeal. Rooms in the main inn have four-poster twin, double, or queen-size beds; floral fabrics; and antique or reproduction furniture. Suites with fully equipped kitchens are in the converted barn and guesthouse. A secluded saltbox cottage has a fireplace, kitchen, and private patio. Deluxe rooms in the carriage house have fireplaces, hot tubs, and air-conditioning. The property also has an opulent state-of-the-art spa, complete with a small resistance pool and fitness center. Above the spa is the inn's most sumptuous suite, with vaulted ceilings, fireplace, entertainment center, and two-person hot tub. Breakfast is served in the cheerful sunroom or on the garden patio. **Pros:** beautiful grounds; elegantly appointed rooms with added benefit of decadent spa treatments. **Cons:** no water views or beachfront; not an in-town location. ⊠*220 Bridge Rd.* ☎*508/255–0617 or 800/440–1281* ⊕*www.whalewalkinn.com* 📺*11 rooms, 5 suites* ⚷*In-room: kitchen (some), refrigerator (some), DVD (some) VCR (some), Wi-Fi. In-hotel: pool, gym, spa, no-smoking rooms, no elevator* ▭*AE, D, MC, V* �O|*BP.*

⚠ **Atlantic Oaks Campground.** This campground in a pine-and-oak forest is less than 1 mi north of the Salt Pond Visitor Center and minutes from Cape Cod National Seashore. Primarily an RV camp (year-round hookups are available), it offers limited tenting as well. You can rent bikes, and there's direct access to the Cape Cod Rail Trail. Reservations are essential during peak season. ⚷*Flush toilets, full hookups,*

*drinking water, guest laundry, showers, fire grates, grills, picnic tables,
electricity, public telephone, general store, play area, swimming (pond
and ocean), public Wi-Fi ⤳99 RV sites, 12 tent sites ✉3700 U.S. 6
☎508/255–1437 or 800/332–2267 🖷508/247–8216 ⊕www.atlantic
oaks.com ▤D, MC, V ⊙Closed Nov.–Apr.*

### NIGHTLIFE & THE ARTS

The **Cape Cod National Seashore** ( ☎508/255–3421 *information*) sponsors summer-evening programs, such as slide shows, sunset beach walks,
concerts by local groups or military bands, and campfire sing-alongs.

The **Eastham Painters Guild** holds outdoor art shows every Thursday, Friday, and holiday weekends from 9 to 5, July through October, at the
Schoolhouse Museum. ✉*Next to Salt Pond Visitor Center, off U.S. 6.*

Monday and Wednesday evenings in July and August are filled with
the sounds of **Concerts on the Green**; local acts perform everything from
folk to reggae starting at 7 PM. ✉*Eastham Village Green, site of the
Eastham Windmill, off U.S. 6.*

**Sea Dog Restaurant & Saloon** ( ✉*4100 U.S. 6* ☎*508/255–2650*) serves
pub food and drinks in a lively atmosphere. Live acoustic music is
played year-round on varying nights; call for a schedule. There's also
free Wi-Fi on the premises.

### SPORTS & THE OUTDOORS

BEACHES   On the bay side of the Outer Cape, **First Encounter Beach** ( ✉*End of
Samoset Rd. off U.S. 6*) is open to the public and charges daily parking fees of $15 to nonresidents in season (weekly and season passes
are also available; call the town hall at ☎508/240–5972). Parking
fees or passes also apply to several other bay beaches and ponds, both
saltwater and freshwater.

★ **Coast Guard Beach** ( ✉*Off Ocean View Dr.*), part of the National Seashore, is a long beach backed by low grass and heathland. A handsome
former Coast Guard station is also here, though it's not open to the
public. The beach has no parking lot of its own, so park at the Salt
Pond Visitor Center or at the lot up Doane Road from the center and
take the free shuttle to the beach. At high tide the size of the beach
shrinks considerably, so watch your blanket. There are showers here,
and lifeguards are posted between June and August. A daily charge of
$15 for cars or a season pass (by far the best bargain) for $45 grants
admission to all six National Seashore swimming beaches.

Fodor'sChoice   **Nauset Light Beach** ( ✉*Off Ocean View Dr.*), adjacent to Coast Guard
★   Beach, continues the National Seashore landscape of long, sandy beach
backed by tall dunes, grass, and heathland. It has showers and lifeguards in summer, but as with other National Seashore beaches, there's
no food concession. Nauset charges $15 daily per car; a $45 season
pass admits you here and to the other five National Seashore swimming
beaches. Parking here fills up very quickly in the summer; plan to arrive
early (before 11 AM) or you may have to go elsewhere.

BICYCLING    The **Idle Times Bike Shop** ( ⊠*4550 U.S. 6 and Brackett Rd.* ☎*508/255–
8281*) provides bikes of all sizes and types and is right near the Cape
Cod Rail Trail.

The **Little Capistrano Bike Shop** ( ⊠*Salt Pond Rd. across from Salt Pond
Visitor Center* ☎*508/255–6515*) has plenty of bikes and trailers avail-
able for rent and is between the Cape Cod Rail Trail and the National
Seashore Bike Trail.

**Nauset Trail,** maintained by the Cape Cod National Seashore, stretches
1½ mi from Salt Pond Visitor Center through groves of apple and
locust trees to Coast Guard Beach.

HEALTH &    **Willy's Gym** ( ⊠*4730 U.S. 6, North Eastham* ☎*508/255–6370*
FITNESS CLUBS    ☎*508/255–6826*) is the astounding 100,000-square-foot branch of
the original Willy's in Orleans. Kids will love Play World, a massive
indoor playground. Other facilities include an Olympic-size, SaltSys-
tem indoor pool, a rock-climbing wall, an indoor NBA basketball
court, and indoor and outdoor tennis courts, along with a vast selection of exercise machines and studio classes. After your workout, relax
in the hot tub, steam room, or sauna—or book a massage or skin-care
treatment at Kembali Spa. You can also peruse the pro shop, or perhaps
grab a bite at the Tiger restaurant…and if you run out of things to
do, there's even free Wi-Fi access on-site. Willy's also hosts free movie
nights and other arts and community programs, which are open to the
public. You can buy a day, week, or month pass.

SURFING    Eastham's ocean beaches are great for surfing and trying out a new
sport that's gaining in popularity: kiteboarding. Basically a combination of surfing and windboarding, kiteboarding is a speedy sport that
will definitely get your blood pumping.

**Little Overhead Surf & Kiteboard** ( ⊠*4900 U.S. 6* ☎*508/240–1455* ⊕*www.
littleoverhead.com*) has a full stock of surfboards and kiteboards, as
well as all the necessary accoutrements; they even provide instruction.

# THE LOWER CAPE ESSENTIALS

*To research prices, get advice from other travelers, and book travel
arrangements, visit* ⊕*www.fodors.com.*

## TRANSPORTATION

### BY BOAT & FERRY

In season, the ferry from Harwich to Nantucket is a less hectic alternative to the Hyannis crowd. *For details,* ⇨*Boat & Ferry Travel in
Essentials in the back of this book.*

### BY BUS

A bus connecting Hyannis and Orleans serves the Lower Cape region.
*Year-round transport on the Flex service goes from Harwich to Prov-
incetown, serving the towns of Brewster, Orleans, Eastham, Wellfleet,*

*and Truro along the way. For details, ⇨ Bus Travel in Essentials in the back of this book.*

## BY TAXI

John's Taxi & Limousine picks up only in Dennis and Harwich but will take you anywhere on the Cape.

**Taxi Companies Eldredge Taxi** ( ✉ *Chatham* 📞 *508/945–0068*). **John's Taxi & Limousine** ( 📞 *508/394–3209*).

**Skip's Cabs** ( ✉ *Harwich* 📞 *508/432–0935*).

## CONTACTS & RESOURCES
## CONDO & HOUSE RENTALS

At the Cape Rentals lists vacation rentals in Brewster, Harwich, Chatham, Orleans, and Eastham. Cape Cod Rentals covers vacation homes in the Brewster community of Ocean Edge, as well as throughout the towns of Dennis, Harwich, Brewster, Chatham, Orleans, Eastham, Wellfleet, and Truro. Commonwealth Associates can assist in finding vacation rentals in the Harwiches, including waterfront properties. Great Locations Inc. specializes in vacation rentals in Brewster, Dennis, and Orleans.

**Local Agents At the Cape Rentals** ( ✉ *Orleans* 📞 *508/255–0136* ⊕ *www.atthecaperentals.com*). **Cape Cod Rentals** ( ✉ *Brewster* 📞 *508/896–4606* ⊕ *www.capecodrentals.com*). **Commonwealth Associates** ( ✉ *Harwich Port* 📞 *508/432–2618* ⊕ *www.commonwealthrealestate.com*). **Great Locations Inc.** ( ✉ *Brewster* 📞 *508/896–2090 or 800/626–9984* ⊕ *www.greatlocationsre.com*).

## VISITOR INFORMATION

Some local chambers of commerce are open only in season. The Brewster Chamber of Commerce is in the Brewster town offices building. The office includes a visitor center and the offices of the Brewster Chamber of Commerce and Board of Trade United.

**Tourist Information Brewster Chamber of Commerce** ( ✉ *2198 Main St. [Rte. 6A], Box 1241,* 📞 *508/896–3500* ⊕ *www.brewstercapecod.org*). **Chatham Chamber of Commerce** ( ✉ *Box 793, 02633* 📞 *508/945–5199 or 800/715–5567* ⊕ *www.chathaminfo.com Seasonal visitor center* ✉ *Rtes. 28 and 137, South Chatham Information booth* ✉ *533 Main St., Chatham*). **Eastham Chamber of Commerce** ( ✉ *U.S. 6 at Fort Hill Rd., Box 1329, 02642* 📞 *508/240–7211* ⊕ *www.easthamchamber.com*). **Harwich Chamber of Commerce** ( 📞 *508/432–1600 or 800/442–7942* ⊕ *www.harwichcc.com Seasonal visitor center* ✉ *One Schoolhouse Rd. and Rte. 28, Harwich Port*). **Orleans Chamber of Commerce** ( ✉ *Box 153, 02653 Information booth* ✉ *44 Main St.* 📞 *508/255–1386 or 800/856–1386* ⊕ *www.capecod-orleans.com*).

# The Outer Cape

5

**WORD OF MOUTH**

"If you go to P-town the choices are endless. Whale watch, Art's Dune Tours, Truro Vineyards (check my name for a post earlier today for links to those) . . . lots of bars and restaurants. Race Point in P-town is a beautiful beach, as far out into the Atlantic as you can get."

—gomiki

www.fodors.com/forums

By Andrew
Collins

**TECHNICALLY PART OF THE LOWER** Cape, the Outer Cape is nonethe-less its own entity, forming the wrist and fist of Cape Cod. There's a sense of abandon here, in the hedonistic summertime frenzy of Province-town and out on the windswept landscape of dunes and marshes. As you drive down here, the land flattens out, vegetation gets sparser and more coniferous, and the sea feels closer as the land narrows. Much of the region is undeveloped, protected by the Cape Cod National Sea-shore. Long, straight, dune-backed beaches appear to go on forever; inland, trails wind through wind-stunted forests of scrub pine, beech, and oak. Wellfleet is a quiet town, with art galleries, upscale shops, and a calm—but active—harbor. With an expanse of high dunes, estuaries, salt marshes, pine forests, rivers, and winding back roads, Truro is the least-populated, least-developed town on the entire Cape.

The promise of solitude has long drawn artists and writers out here. Provincetown has two faces—a quiet little fishing village in winter and a magnet for throngs of pleasure seekers (including a substan-tial gay and lesbian community) in summer, who come for the rugged beaches, photogenic streets lined with historic homes, zany nightlife, shops selling everything from antiques to zoot suits, and the galleries, readings, and art classes that carry on Provincetown's rich history as an art colony.

## EXPLORING THE OUTER CAPE

Making your way around narrow Outer Cape, you really have one key option for getting around: driving along U.S. 6. There are some less congested but slower and indirect roads between the area's two least-developed communities, Wellfleet and Truro. In Wellfleet, many businesses and attractions are strung along U.S. 6, but there's also a compact downtown with art galleries, cafés, and boutiques that's ideal for strolling. Truro has just the tiniest commercial district, and its few attractions are best reached by car, as they're somewhat far apart. In Provincetown, on the other hand, a car—especially in summer—can actually be a hindrance. This is a walkable town with two main thor-oughfares, Commercial and Bradford streets. You could easily spend a full day or two just walking around downtown and checking out the dozens and dozens of shops, galleries, and restaurants. Provincetown also has some excellent beaches, which are a short drive or bike ride from downtown.

## ABOUT THE RESTAURANTS

Dining on the Outer Cape means everything from humble fried-clam shacks to candlelit elegance. Many restaurants have withstood the tests of time and fashion and have developed loyal followings that keep their doors open year after year. Menus frequently highlight local sea-food. Wellfleet's restaurants, although not inexpensive, cater as much to families as to adult sophisticates and typically have menus offering a wide range of items, from less-expensive burgers and fried-seafood platters to creatively prepared steaks and fish grills. Truro has just a handful of restaurants spread out along the byways. Provincetown opens a world of great variation to the eager diner. There are a number of snazzy, hip restaurants in town, all aglow with candles, crystal, and fine linens, but you'll find an equal number of lively and boisterous cafés. Many have outdoor seating, providing good views of the town's constant action. Smoking is banned inside all of the town's bars and restaurants.

> **TOP 5**
>
> ■ Walking the ocean beaches on the Cape Cod National Seashore
>
> ■ Browsing Wellfleet's art galleries
>
> ■ Saying you saw Marconi Station
>
> ■ Strolling Commercial Street in Provincetown
>
> ■ Dune buggying Province Lands with Art's Dune Tours

In the height of the summer season, you may have to wait a while for a table—even if you have a reservation. To make matters worse, in the past few years Cape Cod has been experiencing a labor shortage; good help is at a premium, and this has caused some restaurants to shorten their season or reduce their hours.

## ABOUT THE HOTELS

Lodging options on the Outer Cape are diverse. Wellfleet has several cozy inns and bed-and-breakfasts in the center of town, with a few larger motels on busy U.S. 6. Despite the strict building codes, there are a surprising number of large (though not imposing) hotel complexes and cottage colonies spread out along Cape Cod Bay in North Truro. These places may be crowded, but they're also right on the sand, with commanding views of sunsets and the Provincetown skyline.

Provincetown's lodging scene has changed dramatically in recent years, as a number of old guesthouses and inns have been sold and converted to private homes. Those that remain have mostly transformed themselves from modest, affordable lodgings to sophisticated—and quite pricey—fine inns. With the shrinkage in available rooms, it's become even harder to find a room during the summer months. Minimum stays of at least three nights are often the norm during the peak season and holiday times, and sometimes there's a week minimum in July and August. That being said, more and more Provincetown properties have begun staying open for most or even all of the year—if you don't feel a need to visit during the busiest time of year, consider the quieter, yet still wonderfully atmospheric, off months. May, June, September, and October are especially nice, as most of the town's restaurants and shops are still open then, but hotel rates are lower and rooms easier to find.

# The Outer Cape

**ATLANTIC OCEAN**

CAPE COD NATIONAL SEASHORE

Nauset Beach

Nauset Harbor

Nauset Marsh

Coast Guard Beach

Nauset Light Beach

Nauset Light

Marconi Beach

Marconi Station

White Crest Beach

Cahoon Hollow Beach

LeCount Hollow Beach

Newcomb Hollow Beach

Great Pond

Gull Pond

Long Pond

South Wellfleet

Wellfleet

Indian Neck Beach

Massachusetts Audubon Wellfleet Bay Wildlife Sanctuary

Wellfleet Harbor

Mayo Beach

Chequessett Neck Rd.

Griffin Island Rd.

Great Island

Ballston Beach

Longnook Beach

Truro

Old Country Rd.

Pamet Harbor

Fisher Beach

Castle Rd.

Corn Hill

Ryder Beach

Duck Harbor Beach

Head of the Meadow Beach

Highland Light

North Truro

Great Hollow Beach

Corn Hill Beach

Pilgrim Heights Area

Pilgrim Lake

Provincetown Harbor

Province Lands Visitor Center

Race Point Beach

Race Point Light

Long Point Light

**Provincetown** see detail map

Herring Cove Beach

North Eastham

First Encounter Beach

Samoset Rd.

Rock Harbor

Eastham

Orleans

Skaket Beach

Beach Rd.

28

6

6

6A

Cape Cod Bay

TO BOSTON, PLYMOUTH, AND WHALE-WATCHING

0 — 2 miles

0 — 2 kilometers

## KEY

Cape Cod Rail Trail

Ferry

| WHAT IT COSTS | | | | | |
|---|---|---|---|---|---|
| | ¢ | $ | $$ | $$$ | $$$$ |
| Restaurants | under $10 | $10–$16 | $16–$22 | $22–$30 | over $30 |
| Hotels | under $90 | $90–$140 | $140–$200 | $200–$260 | over $260 |

Restaurant prices are per person for a main course at dinner. Hotel prices are for a standard double room, excluding 6% sales tax (more in some counties) and 1%–4% tourist tax.

## TIMING

Prime time on the Outer Cape—when everything is open—is from Memorial Day to around Columbus Day; July and August are by far the most crowded times. The shoulder seasons of late May and June, and after Labor Day, have become more and more popular with childless travelers who aren't locked into a school schedule. Rates are lower during these times, and restaurants and shops are still open. If the weather has been generous, swimming is still a pleasant possibility.

Wellfleet pretty much seals itself up after Columbus Day; most galleries and restaurants close, leaving just a handful of year-round businesses. But you'll have the entire outside world to explore, now free of thousands of others trying to do the same thing. Ocean climates keep winters milder than on the mainland. It's quiet—beautifully so—and distractions and pleasures take on a more basic flavor.

Provincetown clears out as well, but not as fully as Wellfleet. Various theme weekends throughout the year have boosted tourism in the off-season, and there are always readings, films, and places to eat. The off-season is truly a time to discover the essence of the place, see its changing natural beauty, and experience a more restful and relaxed pace.

## WELLFLEET & SOUTH WELLFLEET

*6 mi north of Eastham, 13 mi southeast of Provincetown.*

Still famous for its world-renowned and succulent namesake oysters and, with Truro, for having been a colonial whaling and cod-fishing port, Wellfleet is today a tranquil community; many artists and writers call it home. Less than 2 mi wide, it's one of the most attractively developed Cape resort towns, with a number of fine restaurants, historic houses, art galleries, and a good old Main Street in the village proper. The South Wellfleet section of town extends to the North Eastham border and has a wonderful Audubon sanctuary and a drive-in theater that doubles on weekends as a flea market. There's no village center here, just a handful of motels, restaurants, and businesses along busy U.S. 6.

The downtown center of Wellfleet is quite compact, so it's actually best to leave your car in one of the public parking areas and take off on foot. Historic buildings that once housed oyster and fish-drying shacks or stately residences now contain upscale art galleries, designer-clothing stores, and restaurants. Wellfleet's small-town nature still somehow accommodates the demands of a major tourist industry; the year-round population of around 2,800 residents explodes to more than 18,000 people in July and August.

Tourism isn't the only industry, though. Fishing boats still head out from the harbor daily in search of scallops, cod, and other fish. Shell-fishing accounts for a major portion of the town's economy. Whaling played a role in the 18th and 19th centuries; a raucous whaling tavern once thrived out on the now-sunken Billingsgate Island. Dozens of world-traveling sea captains found their way to Wellfleet as well, the effect evident in many of the grand old houses that line the narrow streets of town. The Wellfleet Historical Society is a fine stop for those who wish to see the town as it was in its early days. Natural splendor, as well as history and sophisticated artistic culture, accounts for Wellfleet's popularity. The beaches are spectacular, with their towering sand dunes, bracing surf, and miles of unfettered expanse. Seemingly endless wooded paths in the domain of the National Seashore make for terrific walking and hiking trails, and the sheltered waters of the tidal Herring River and Wellfleet Harbor are a favorite destination for canoeists, kayakers, windsurfers, and sailors.

★ **Marconi Station,** on the Atlantic side of the Cape's forearm, is the site of the first transatlantic wireless station erected on the U.S. mainland. Italian radio and wireless-telegraphy pioneer Guglielmo Marconi sent the first American wireless message from here to Europe—"most cordial greetings and good wishes" from President Theodore Roosevelt to King Edward VII of England—on January 18, 1903. The station broadcasted news for 15 years. An outdoor shelter contains a model of the original station, of which only fragments remain as a result of cliff erosion; parts of the tower bases are sometimes visible on the beach below, where they fell. The Cape Cod National Seashore's administrative headquarters is here, and though it is not an official visitor center, it can provide information at times when the centers are closed. Inside there's a mock-up of the spark-gap transmitter Marconi used. Off the parking lot, a 1½-mi trail and boardwalk lead through the **Atlantic White Cedar Swamp,** one of the most beautiful trails on the seashore; free maps and guides are available at the trailhead. **Marconi Beach,** south of the station on Marconi Beach Road, is another of the National Seashore's ocean beaches. ⊠ *Marconi Site Rd., South Wellfleet* ☎ *508/349–3785* ⊕ *www.nps.gov/caco* ☒ *Free* ☉ *Daily 8–4:30.*

For a **scenic loop** through a classic Cape landscape near Wellfleet's Atlantic beaches—with scrub and pines on the left, heathland meeting cliffs and ocean below on the right—take LeCount Hollow Road just north of the Marconi Station turnoff. All the beaches on this strip rest at the bottom of a tall grass-covered dune, which lends dramatic character to this outermost shore. The first of the four, **LeCount Hollow,** is restricted to residents or temporary residents in season, as is the last, **Newcomb Hollow,** with a scalloped shoreline of golden sand. In between, **White Crest** and **Cahoon Hollow** are town-managed public beaches. Cahoon has a hot restaurant and dancing spot, the Beachcomber. Backtrack to Cahoon Hollow Road and turn west for the southernmost entrance to the town of Wellfleet proper, across U.S. 6.

**NEED A BREAK?**

The **Blue Willow** ( ⊠ *South Wellfleet Post Office Sq., 1426 U.S. 6* ☎ *508/349–0900*) is tiny, but the food is grand, transcending what you'd find in other take-out places. Treats like crab cakes, crispy duck, tarragon chicken salad, and pasta dishes are made on the premises. For breakfast, there are daily frittata and quiche specials, as well as muffins, scones, and pastries. Outside is a mini–farmers' market with fresh vegetables and flowers. Right at the Cape Cod Rail Trail, it's a good spot to grab a snack or pick up the complete makings of a beach picnic or fine dinner. It's across from the chamber of commerce information booth and open daily year-round.

Wellfleet's **First Congregational Church** ( ⊠ *200 Main St., Downtown Wellfleet* ☎ *508/349–6877*), a courtly 1850 Greek Revival building, is said to have the only town clock in the world that strikes on ship's bells. The church's interior is lovely, with pale blue walls, a brass chandelier hanging from an enormous gilt ceiling rosette, subtly colored stained-glass windows, and pews curved to form an amphitheater facing the altar and the 738-pipe Hook and Hastings tracker-action organ, dating from 1873. To the right is a Tiffany-style window depicting a clipper ship. Concerts are given in July and August on Sunday at 8 PM.

For a glimpse into Wellfleet's past, the diminutive **Wellfleet Historical Society Museum** exhibits furniture, paintings, shipwreck salvage, needlework, navigation equipment, early photographs, Native American artifacts, and clothing. Short guided walks around the center of town are given Tuesday and Friday mornings at 10:15 in July and August for $3. ⊠ *266 Main St., Downtown Wellfleet* ☎ *508/349–9157* ⊕ *www.wellfleethistoricalsociety.com* ✉ *Free* ☉ *Late June–early Sept., Wed., Thurs., and Sat. 1–4, Tues. and Fri. 10–4.*

The **Wellfleet Public Library** ( ⊠ *55 W. Main St., Downtown Wellfleet* ☎ *508/349–0310* ⊕ *www.wellfleetlibrary.org*) reflects the literary life of Wellfleet with readings, lectures, and exhibits by noted writers and artists in the community, and the collection of books for adults and children is impressive. Also available are videos, books on tape, and Internet access. Among the writers who have spent time here are Mary McCarthy, Edmund Wilson, Annie Dillard, and Marge Piercy.

**Main Street** is a good place to start if you're in the mood for shopping.

**Commercial Street** has all the flavor of the fishing town that Wellfleet remains; galleries and shops occupy small weathered-shingle houses.

A good stroll around town would take in Commercial and Main streets, ending perhaps at **Uncle Tim's Bridge** ( ⊠ *Off E. Commercial St.,*

*Downtown Wellfleet*). The short walk across this arching landmark—with its beautiful, much-photographed view over marshland and a tidal creek—leads to a small wooded island.

NEED A
BREAK?

**Box Lunch** (⊠ *50 Briar La.* ☎ *508/349–2178* ⊕ *www.boxlunch.com*) is a popular Cape franchise that you may have seen elsewhere, but this is the original location. It serves hot and cold roll-up sandwiches, a style it claims to have invented and perfected. A wide variety of fillings are available for breakfast, lunch, or early dinner. This tiny place gets ferociously busy in the summer season—call your order in ahead of time if you can.

Commercial Street leads to the **Wellfleet Pier** (☎ *508/349–9818 for a fishing permit*), busy with fishing boats, sailboats, yachts, charters, and party boats. At the twice-daily low tides, you can dig on the tidal flats for oysters, clams, and quahogs.

Chequessett Neck Road makes for a pretty 2½-mi drive from the harbor to the bay past Sunset Hill—a great place to catch one. At the end, on the left, is a parking lot and wooded picnic area from which nature trails lead off to **Great Island** (⊠ *Off Chequessett Neck Rd., west of Downtown Wellfleet*), perfect for beachcombers and solitude seekers. The "island" is actually a peninsula connected by a sand spit built by tidal action. More than 7 mi of trails wind along the inner marshes and the water—these are the most difficult paths on the seashore because they're mostly in soft sand. In the 17th century, a tavern and shore whaling lookout towers stood here; residents pastured animals and engaged in oystering and cranberry harvesting. By 1800 the hardwood forest that had covered the island had been cut down for use in the building of ships and homes. The pitch pines and other growth you see here (and all over the Cape) today were introduced in the 1830s to keep the soil from washing into the sea. Cape Cod National Seashore offers occasional guided hikes on Great Island and, from February through April, seal walks. To the right of the Great Island lot, a road leads to **Griffin Island,** which has its own walking trail.

☾ A trip to the Outer Cape isn't complete without a visit to the **Massachusetts Audubon Wellfleet Bay Wildlife Sanctuary,** an 1,100-acre haven for more than 250 species of birds attracted by the varied habitats found here. The jewel of the Massachusetts Audubon Society, the sanctuary is a superb place for walking, birding, and watching the sun set over the salt marsh and bay. The **Esther Underwood Johnson Nature Center** contains two 700-gallon aquariums that offer an up-close look at marine life common to the Cape's tidal flats and marshlands. Other rotating exhibits illustrate different facets of the area's ecology and natural history. From the center you can hike five short nature trails, including a fascinating Boardwalk Trail that leads over a salt marsh to a small beach—or you can wander through the Butterfly Garden. Note that as of this writing the center was closed for repairs and reconstruction, and there's no timetable in place for when it will reopen—check first before going. The center's interpretive programs are still in place, however, and the sanctuary remains open for hiking.

Fodor'sChoice
★

The Audubon Society is host to naturalist-led wildlife tours around the Cape, including trips to the Monomoy Islands, year-round. There are bay cruises; bird, wildlife, and insect walks; hikes; snorkeling; winter seal cruises; and birding, canoe, and kayak trips. The sanctuary also has camps for children in July and August and weeklong field schools for adults. Phone reservations are required for some programs. ⊠*291 U.S. 6* ☎*508/349–2615* ⊕*www.massaudubon.org/wellfleetbay* ☜*$5* ⊙*Trails daily 8* AM*–dusk; nature center late May–mid-Oct., daily 8:30–5; mid-Oct.–late May, Tues.–Sun. 8:30–5.*

## WHERE TO EAT

$–$$
AMERICAN
✕**Bookstore and Restaurant.** This quirky place, with great views of Wellfleet Harbor and Great Island, serves consistently tasty—if predictable—fare. It's attached to a funky vintage bookstore close to the town docks, and there's ample outdoor seating. The kitchen serves American classics, from grilled filet mignon and vegetable penne primavera to fresh seafood (the shellfish comes right from Wellfleet Harbor), including a first-rate oyster stew. There's live music Thursday to Sunday in summer, and the adjoining Bombshelter sports bar is a diverting spot to watch a game on TV. ⊠*50 Kendrick Ave., across from Mayo Beach* ☎*508/349–3154* ⊕*www.wellfleetoyster.com* ⊟*AE, D, MC, V* ⊙*Closed mid-Dec.–mid-Feb.*

$$–$$$
Fodor'sChoice
★
AMERICAN
✕**Finely JP's.** Chef John Pontius consistently turns out wonderful, affordable food full of the best Mediterranean and local influences and ingredients at his beloved restaurant along U.S. 6. The unassuming roadhouse restaurant was redesigned and enlarged in 2006—it's an airy, handsome, Arts and Crafts–inspired structure. Appetizers are especially good, among them oysters *Bienville* (baked in a white wine–cream sauce topped with Parmesan cheese and bread crumbs), and jerk-spiced duck salad with a raspberry vinaigrette. The Wellfleet paella and the roast duck with cranberry-orange sauce draw rave reviews and a steady handful of locals, but the chef is not afraid to cook down-home barbecue pork ribs, either. Off-season hours vary, so call ahead—and be sure not to confuse this place with PJ's, down the road. ⊠*554 U.S. 6, South Wellfleet* ☎*508/349–7500* ⌔*Reservations not accepted* ⊟*D, MC, V* ⊙*Closed some nights during off-season. No lunch.*

¢–$
AMERICAN
✕**Flying Fish.** Set inside a handsome little Cape-style house with wood floors and a simple dining room, this downtown café serves a wide range of foods—spinach-feta pizzas, Greek salads, curried-chicken-salad sandwiches, hummus platters, ice cream, smoothies, and a full range of coffees and pastries. It's perfect for a full sit-down meal or a quick bite on the go. Don't forget to check out the selection of fresh-baked pastries. ⊠*28 Briar La.* ☎*508/349–7292* ⊟*MC, V* ⊙*Closed Oct.–Apr.*

$–$$
AMERICAN
✕**Lighthouse Restaurant.** A line snakes out the door of this simple wood-frame house on summer mornings for classic bacon-and-egg breakfasts and tasty blueberry pancakes. Try a plate of steamers and a beer for lunch and perhaps chowder, cod fritters, lemon-butter scallops, and another beer for dinner—but keep in mind that it's as much about the value and the people-watching here as the food itself. Mexican fare, margaritas, and Dos Equis beer are served on Thursday. There's a large

5

deck, and downstairs you can order coffees, gelato, and lighter fare from the Lighthouse To-Go-Shoppe. ✉ *Main St., Downtown Wellfleet* ☎ *508/349–3681* ⊕ *www.mainstreetlighthouse.com* ⚓ *Reservations not accepted* ▭ *D, MC, V.*

**¢–$$**
**★**
SEAFOOD
✕ **Mac's Seafood.** Right at Wellfleet Harbor, this ambitious little spot has some of the freshest seafood around. There's not a whole lot of seating here—some inside and some outside on picnic tables—but when you've got a succulent mouthful of raw oyster or fried scallop, who cares? You can always sit along the pier and soak up the great water views while you chow down. This place serves a vast variety of seafood, plus sushi, Mexican fare (grilled-scallop burritos), linguica sausage sandwiches, and raw-bar items. There's also a selection of smoked fish, pâtés, lobster, and fish you can take home to grill yourself. Mac's also has two take-out seafood markets (open year-round) in downtown Wellfleet and Truro, as well as **Mac's Shack** (91 Commercial St., 508/349–6333; closed Mon. and mid-Oct.–mid-May), a funky sit-down BYOB restaurant in a rambling mid-19th-century barn overlooking Duck Creek, with a lobster boat on the roof. ✉ *Wellfleet Town Pier, Wellfleet Harbor* ☎ *508/349–0404* ⊕ *www.macsseafood.com* ▭ *MC, V* ⊘ *Closed mid-Sept.–late May.*

**$–$$**
SEAFOOD
✕ **Moby Dick's.** A meal at this good-natured, rough-hewn fish shack with a hyper-nautical theme is an absolute Cape Cod tradition for some people. There's a giant blackboard menu (order up front, and food is brought to you); a big, breezy screened-in porch in which to eat; and red-checked tablecloths. Go for the Nantucket Bucket—a pound of whole-belly Monomoy steamers, a pound of native mussels, and corn on the cob served in a bucket. Also consider the rich and creamy lobster bisque or the complete lobster-in-the-rough dinner. Bring your own libations, and if you need to kill time, stop inside Moby's Cargo, the bustling gift shop next door, which has a great selection of toys, nautical crafts, and jewelry. ✉ *U.S. 6 near Truro border* ☎ *508/349–9795* ⊕ *www.mobydicksrestaurant.com* ⚓ *Reservations not accepted* ▭ *AE, MC, V* ⊘ *Closed mid-Oct.–Apr.* ⛴ *BYOB.*

**$–$$$**
SEAFOOD
✕ **PJ's Family Restaurant.** There's always a good-size but fast-moving line here, waiting for a heap of steamers or a creamy soft-serve cone. At PJ's you place your order and take a number. Food is served in utilitarian style: Styrofoam soup bowls, paper plates, plastic forks. The lobster-and-corn chowder doesn't have much lobster in it, so stick to the traditional clam chowder. Fried calamari and clam or oyster plates are generous and fresh. Try the dense, spicy stuffed clams and a pile of crispy onion rings. ✉ *U.S. 6 near Downtown Wellfleet exit* ☎ *508/349–2126* ⚓ *Reservations not accepted* ▭ *MC, V* ⊘ *Closed Nov.–mid-Apr.*

**$–$$**
SOUTHERN
✕ **Russ & Marie's Marconi Beach Restaurant.** The nondescript interior of this cavernous restaurant in South Wellfeet may not inspire you, but once you pull up and smell the enticing aroma of barbecue from the smoker in back, it's hard to resist the temptation to step inside for a meal. Drop in for a lighter dish, such as a pulled-pork sandwich or a few littlenecks and oysters from the raw bar, or savor a more substantial meal, perhaps a platter of smoked barbecue ribs, a grilled Porterhouse steak, or

fish-and-chips. It's all pretty tasty, but the barbecue stands out—you could order most of the other items on the menu at any nearby steak and seafood joint. ⊠ *545 U.S. 6* ☎ *508/349–6025* ⊕ *www.marconi beachrestaurant.net* ⊟ *MC, V* ☉ *Closed mid-Oct.–early Apr.*

$–$$$

SEAFOOD

✕ **Van Rensselaer's.** This cavernous, casual family seafood restaurant across from Marconi Station—not too far from the Eastham town line—stands out for its nice mix of traditional standbys (baked-stuffed lobster, prime rib) and more creative offerings. You might start with coconut tempura shrimp with an orange-ginger sauce or steamed little-neck clams with lemongrass-ginger-soy butter. Favorite main dishes include potato-crusted salmon with lobster-butter, and cranberry-orange duck with sweet-potato puree. Lighter and more affordable fare is available from a bistro menu. The restaurant also serves breakfast as well as an excellent Sunday brunch, where you might try smoked-salmon Benedict. The same family has run the place since 1968. ⊠ *U. S. 6* ☎ *508/349–2127* ⊕ *www.vanrensselaers.com* ⊟ *AE, D, DC, MC, V* ☉ *Closed Nov.–mid-Apr. No lunch.*

$$–$$$

Fodor's Choice

★

AMERICAN

✕ **Wicked Oyster.** In a rambling, gray clapboard house just off U.S. 6 on the main road into Wellfleet village, the Wicked Oyster serves up the most innovative fare in Wellfleet. Try the rosemary-and-scallion-crusted half rack of lamb over roasted-shallot-and-garlic potato salad, or the local mussels in tomato broth with smoky bacon, cilantro, jalapeño, and lime. Oyster stew and the Harry's Bar open-face burger (with cara-melized onions, fresh mozzarella, and Worcestershire mayonnaise) are among the top lunch dishes. Breakfast is a favorite here—try the smoked-salmon Benedict. There's also an outstanding wine list. Live music is offered many nights, and the bar keeps going until 1 AM. ⊠ *50 Main St. Wellfleet* ☎ *508/349–3455* ⊟ *AE, D, MC, V* ☉ *No dinner Wed.*

$$–$$$

★

SEAFOOD

✕ **Winslow's Tavern.** This 1805 Federal-style captain's house contains five dining rooms; try for a table on the porch overlooking the center of town. The kitchen specializes in bistro-inspired seafood, mostly with American and Italian preparations. Bacon-wrapped scallops with mango chutney, garlic-and-butter-grilled lobster with sweet-corn relish, and panfried ham-stuffed trout with roasted baby tomatoes rank among the better dishes. Head to the cozy lounge upstairs (it's open until 1 AM) for a drink—it's filled with plush sofas. The same owners run the popular Moby Dick's seafood restaurant. ⊠ *316 Main St., Downtown Wellfleet* ☎ *508/349–6450* ⊕ *www.winslowstavern.com* ⊟ *AE, DC, MC, V* ☉ *Closed mid-Oct.–mid-May.*

## WHERE TO STAY

$$–$$$

★

🏨 **Aunt Sukie's Bayside Bed & Breakfast.** Hosts Sue and Dan Hamar treat you like you're actual guests in their home, a part-contemporary, part-antique inn with three rooms and multiple decks. It's set on the marsh grass fronting Wellfleet Harbor and Cape Cod Bay, along a quiet residential stretch of road near Power's Landing. The birds, the water, and the stunning bay views will probably be enough to keep you content in the shade of trees with a pair of binoculars. Rooms are welcoming, with flowered quilts and private decks, and the two upstairs beds grant vistas of the water without a lift of the head. The room in the antique portion of the home has a gas fireplace, a brick patio, and a grand claw-foot tub.

The owners also have a full house for rent about a mile away; it comfortably accommodates two couples or a family of four and is rented weekly from May through October. **Pros:** property looks out at Cape Cod Bay; rooms are private and quiet; ample decks and pretty grounds. **Cons:** it's intimate (just two rooms); a little too far to walk to dining and shopping. ⊠ *525 Chequessett Neck Rd.* ☎ *508/349–2804 or 800/420–9999* ⊕ *www.auntsukies.com* ⊅ *2 rooms, 1 suite* ♿ *In-room: refrigerator, no TV, Wi-Fi. In-hotel: no elevator, beachfront, no kids under 10, no-smoking rooms* ▭ *MC, V* ♥ *Closed Nov.–mid-June* ⏹ *CP.*

$–$$    ⛺ **Even'tide.** Long a summer favorite, this motel is set back off the main road, surrounded by 5 acres of trees and lawns; it has direct access to the Cape Cod Rail Trail. A central attraction is the 60-foot indoor pool (although Wellfleet's beaches are also close by). Rooms have simple modern furnishings; choose from doubles, two-room family suites, and efficiencies with kitchens. Cottages speckled about the property are available for stays of a week or longer. The staff is friendly and enthusiastic. **Pros:** short drive or bike ride from beach; right by Cape Cod Rail Trail; two-room suites are a bargain for families. **Cons:** right on busy road; need a car to reach Wellfleet's charming downtown; motel-style rooms. ⊠ *650 U.S. 6, South Wellfleet* ☎ *508/349–3410 or 800/368–0007* 🖷 *508/349–7804* ⊕ *www.eventidemotel.com* ⊅ *31 units, 10 cottages* ♿ *In-room: kitchen (some), refrigerators, dial-up. In-hotel: pool, no elevator, laundry facilities, public Wi-Fi* ☞ *1- or 2-wk minimum for cottages in summer* ▭ *MC, V* ♥ *Closed Nov. and Dec.*

¢–$    ⛺ **Holden Inn.** If you're watching your budget and can deal with modest basics and rather drab furnishings, try this no-frills old-timey place on a tree-shaded street just outside the town center but within walking distance of several galleries and restaurants. Rooms are simply decorated with Grandma's house–type wallpapers, ruffled sheer or country-style curtains, and antiques such as brass-and-white-iron or spindle beds or marble-top tables. Private baths with old porcelain sinks are available in the adjacent 1840 and 1890 buildings. The lodge has shared baths, an outdoor shower, and a large screened-in porch with a lovely view of the bay and Great Island, far below. The main house has a common room and a screened front porch with rockers and a bay view through the trees. **Pros:** rock-bottom prices; walking distance to harbor and village shopping; pretty, tree-shaded grounds. **Cons:** rooms are bare-bones and very old-fashioned feeling; many units share a bath. ⊠ *140 Commercial St., Box 816, Wellfleet* ☎ *508/349–3450* ⊕ *www.theholdeninn. com* ⊅ *26 rooms, 10 with bath* ♿ *In-room: no phone, no TV. In-hotel: no elevator* ▭ *No credit cards* ♥ *Closed Nov.–Apr.*

¢–$    ⛺ **Inn at Duck Creeke.** Set on 5 wooded acres by a duck pond, a creek, and a salt marsh, this old inn consists of a circa-1815 main building and three other houses from the same era. Rooms in the main inn (except rustic 3rd-floor rooms) and in the Saltworks house have a simple charm but could use some upgrading. Typical furnishings include claw-foot tubs, country antiques, lace curtains, chenille spreads, and rag rugs on hardwood floors. The two-room Carriage House is cabin-like, with rough barn-board and plaster walls. There's full-service dining at Sweet Seasons or pub dining with live jazz at the Tavern Room.

**Pros:** very low rates; walking distance to downtown; good restaurant and pub on-site. **Cons:** some units share a bath; long walk to harbor or ocean. ⊠ *70 Main St., Box 364, Wellfleet* ☎ *508/349–9333* ⊕ *www. innatduckcreeke.com* ⇿ *26 rooms, 17 with bath* ♿ *In-room: no a/c (some), no phone, no TV. In-hotel: 2 restaurants, no elevator* ▭ *AE, MC, V* ⊗ *Closed Nov.–Apr.* †◯| *CP.*

**$–$$** ⟦⟧ **Southfleet Motor Inn.** Geared toward active families, this carefully maintained motor inn is directly across from the entrance to the National Seashore at Marconi Station for easy access to ocean beaches. Bring your bikes to cruise the 25-mi Cape Cod Rail Trail. Rooms, which have utilitarian furnishings and an assortment of beds, can sleep up to five people. Indoor and outdoor pools and game room (with a Ping-Pong table) keep the kids busy and happy. **Pros:** short drive or bike ride from beach; lots of on-site diversions for kids; reasonable rates. **Cons:** right on busy road, need a car to reach Wellfleet's charming downtown; motel-style rooms. ⊠ *U.S. 6, across from Marconi Station* ☎ *508/349–3580 or 800/334–3715* ⊕ *www.southfleetmotorinn. com* ⇿ *30 rooms* ♿ *In-room: refrigerator, Wi-Fi. In-hotel: 2 restaurants, bar, pools, bicycles, no elevator, laundry facilities* ▭ *AE, MC, V* ⊗ *Closed mid-Oct.–late Apr.*

**$$** ⟦⟧ **Stone Lion Inn.** B&Bs are meant to feel a bit like homes away from
**Fodor'sChoice** home—places to feel welcome, at ease, and taken care of. All of these
★ requirements are met at the Stone Lion Inn, a gracious mansard-roof Victorian just outside the town center and a short walk away from both the harbor and the village. Rooms have queen beds, ceiling fans to encourage the breezes, hardwood floors, and a mix of antiques and contemporary pieces that balance the house's 19th-century heritage with today's decorating sensibilities. Relax amid the gardens, in the outdoor shower, or in the pretty common room. New Yorkers may recognize the subtle Brooklyn theme—nostalgic, yet happily devoid of frenzy. **Pros:** short walk from harbor and shopping; stylish yet unpretentious decor; friendly and helpful owners. **Cons:** need a car to get to ocean; not appropriate for younger kids. ⊠ *130 Commercial St.* ☎ *508/349–9565* ⊕ *www.stonelioncapecod.com* ⇿ *3 rooms, 1 apartment, 1 cottage* ♿ *In-room: kitchen (some), refrigerators, no phone (some), no TV (some), Wi-Fi. In-hotel: no elevator, no kids under 10* ▭ *MC, V* †◯| *BP.*

**$$$–$$$$** ⟦⟧ **Surf Side Cottages.** Most of the units here are scattered on either
★ side of Ocean View Drive, and a few additional cottages are nearby. Accommodations range from units in a piney grove to well-equipped ocean-side cottages; all accommodate two or more guests (six can stay in the largest units). The cottages are a few minutes' walk from the Maguire's Landing town beach (LeCount Hollow), a beautiful wide strand of sand, dunes, and surf. Though most of the exteriors are retro-cool Floridian, with pastel shingles and flat roofs, cottage interiors are Cape-style, including knotty-pine paneling. All units have phones, wood-burning fireplaces, screened porches, kitchens, and grills. Some have roof decks with an ocean view and outdoor showers. Ocean-side cottages have dishwashers. **Pros:** you're steps from the ocean; ideal for longer holidays and cooking in your own unit; an architecturally

5

interesting compound. **Cons:** some of the decor and interiors in units could stand some updating; not within walking distance of shops or restaurants. ✉*Ocean View Dr.* 🏠*Box 937, South Wellfleet 02663* ☎*508/349–3959* 🖶*508/349–3959* ⊕*www.surfsidecottages.com* 🛏*25 cottages* 🔑*In-room: kitchen, no a/c, no TV. In-hotel: no elevator, some pets allowed (fee)* 🔄*1- to 2-wk minimum in summer* ▤*No credit cards* ⊗*Closed Nov.–Mar.*

$$ 🏨 **Wellfleet Motel & Lodge.** A mile from Marconi Beach, opposite the Audubon sanctuary, this clean and tasteful (although somewhat pricey) highway-side complex sits on 12 wooded acres. Rooms in the single-story motel aren't fancy but are renovated regularly; those in the two-story lodge are bright and spacious, with king- or queen-size beds and balconies or patios. The property offers direct access to the Cape Cod Rail Trail as well as indoor and outdoor pools; barbecue grills are available in a garden picnic area. **Pros:** short drive or bike ride from beach; right on Cape Cod Bike Trail; many units with balcony or patio. **Cons:** right on busy road; need a car to reach Wellfleet's charming downtown; motel-style rooms. ✉*146 U.S. 6* 🏠*Box 606, South Wellfleet 02663* ☎*508/349–3535 or 800/852–2900* 🖶*508/349–1192* ⊕*www.wellfleetmotel.com* 🛏*57 rooms, 8 suites* 🔑*In-room: Wi-Fi. In-hotel: restaurant, bar, pools, no elevator* ▤*AE, DC, MC, V* ⊗*Closed Dec.–Mar.*

## NIGHTLIFE & THE ARTS

THE ARTS During July and August the **First Congregational Church** (✉*200 Main St., Downtown Wellfleet* ☎*508/349–6877*) trades the serenity of worship for Sunday evening concerts. The music begins at 8 PM and could include opera, blues, jazz, or chamber music.

The drive-in movie is alive and well on Cape Cod at the **Wellfleet Drive-In Theater** (✉*51 U.S. 6, South Wellfleet* ☎*508/349–7176* ⊕*www. wellfleetcinemas.com*), which is right by the Eastham town line. Films start at dusk nightly in season (May through September), and there's also a standard indoor cinema with four screens, a miniature-golf course, and a dairy bar and grill.

Art galleries are open for cocktail receptions to celebrate show openings on Saturday evening in July and August during the **Wellfleet Gallery Nights.** You can walk from gallery to gallery, meeting the featured artists and checking out their works.

★ The well-regarded **Wellfleet Harbor Actors Theater (WHAT)** (✉*Kendrick St. past E. Commercial St., near Wellfleet Harbor* ☎*508/349–9428* ⊕*www.what.org*) opened a first-rate 200-seat theater, the Julie Harris Stage, in 2007. It complements the company's original 90-seat Harbor Stage, which is now used seasonally for more experimental works as well as serving as a venue for playwrights to produce new pieces. In the new theater, WHAT continues its tradition, since 1985, of showing provocative, often edgy, world premieres of American plays, satires, farces, and black comedies in its mid-May to late-November season.

NIGHTLIFE **Beachcomber** (✉*1120 Cahoon Hollow Rd., off Ocean View Dr.* ★ ☎*508/349–6055*) is big with the college crowd. It's right on the beach, with national touring acts most nights, weekend happy hours with live reggae, and dancing nightly in summer. You can order appetizers, salads, burgers, seafood, and barbecue indoors or at tables by the beachfront bar. There's also a raw bar. Beachcomber is closed October through April.

A number of organizations sponsor outdoor activities at night, including the **Massachusetts Audubon Wellfleet Bay Wildlife Sanctuary**'s night hikes and lecture series.

In the venerable Inn at Duck Creeke, the **Tavern Room** ( ⊠ *70 Main St., U.S. 6 exit to Downtown Wellfleet* ☎ *508/349–7369*), set in an 1800s building with a beam ceiling, a fireplace, and a bar covered in nautical charts, has live entertainment—anything from jazz and pop to country and Latin ensembles. Munchies are served alongside a menu of traditional and Latin/Caribbean-inspired dishes.

Kick up your heels and grab a twirling partner for a long-standing Wellfleet tradition, the **Wednesday Night Square Dance.** Down at the town pier in July and August, the music and live calling by master caller Irvin "Toots" Tousignant begins at 7 and lasts as long as *you* can.

## SPORTS & THE OUTDOORS

The state-of-the-art Skateboard Park down at **Baker's Field** ( ⊠ *Kendrick Ave. just past Wellfleet Town Pier, near Wellfleet Harbor*) was professionally designed for tricks and safety; it's manned by local teens.

BEACHES **Public Beaches.** Extensive storm-induced erosion has made the cliffs to most of Wellfleet's ocean beaches quite steep—so be prepared for a taxing trek up and down the dune slope.

**Cahoon Hollow Beach** ( ⊠ *Ocean View Dr.*) has lifeguards, restrooms, and a restaurant and music club on the sand. This beach tends to attract younger and slightly rowdier crowds; it's a big Sunday-afternoon party place. There are daily parking fees of $15 for nonresidents in season only; parking is free for those with beach stickers.

FodorsChoice **Marconi Beach** ( ⊠ *Off U.S. 6*), part of the Cape Cod National Seashore, ★ charges $15 for daily parking or $45 for a season pass that provides access to all six National Seashore swimming beaches. There are lifeguards, restrooms, and outdoor showers from late June through early September, which is the only period when admission fees are collected.

**Mayo Beach** ( ⊠ *Commercial St., adjacent to Wellfleet Pier*) is free, but swimming here is pleasant only around high tide—once the water recedes, it's all mud and sharp shells. You can park for free at the small lot by Great Island on the bay.

**White Crest Beach** ( ⊠ *Ocean View Dr.*) is a prime surfer hangout where the dudes often spend more time waiting for waves than actually riding them. Lifeguards are on duty daily 9 AM to 5 PM from July through Labor Day weekend. If you're up to the challenge, join one of the spontaneous volleyball games that frequently pop up. There are daily parking fees of $15 for nonresidents in season only; parking is free for those with beach stickers.

**Restricted Beaches.** Resident or temporary resident parking stickers are required for access to Wellfleet beaches in season only, from the last week of June through Labor Day. To get a three-day ($30), weekly ($60), or season ($200) pass, visit the Beach Sticker Booth on the town pier with your car registration in hand and a proof-of-stay form, available from rental agencies and hotels. For the rest of the year anyone can visit the beaches for free. Note that people arriving on foot or by bicycle can visit the beaches at any time; the sticker is for parking only. These parking restrictions apply to all beaches listed below.

For information about restricted beaches, call the **Wellfleet Beach Office** (☎ *508/349–9818*).

Ⓒ **Duck Harbor Beach** (⊠ *End of Chequessett Neck Rd.*) seems like it's nearly at the end of the world. Its shores are on the warm waters of Cape Cod Bay, and there's plenty of room to wander and find your own private space. You can look out to Provincetown across the bay, but the finest view by far is the nightly sunset.

**Indian Neck Beach** (⊠ *Pilgrim Spring Rd. off U.S. 6*) is on the bay side, fronting Wellfleet Harbor, and is thus affected by the tides. Low tide reveals plenty of beach but less water—you'll have to walk way out before your hips get wet. It's a good spot to watch the comings and goings of fishing boats from Wellfleet Pier. With its shallow and calm waters, warmer temperatures, and ample opportunity for treasure hunting at low tide, it's also a great beach for families.

★ **LeCount Hollow Beach** (⊠ *Ocean View Dr.*) is the beach closest to U.S. 6 in South Wellfleet, along the meandering Ocean View Drive. The dunes are steep here, so be prepared to carry all beach belongings down (and up) the sandy slope.

**Newcomb Hollow Beach** (⊠ *Ocean View Dr.*) is the northernmost beach on the Wellfleet strip, closest to Truro. If you keep your eyes on the horizon, it's not at all uncommon to see the distant spout of a passing whale. This beach is also a popular nighttime fishing spot.

The **Wellfleet Ponds,** nestled in the woods between U.S. 6 and the ocean, were formed by glaciers and are fed by underground springs. Mild temperatures and clear, clean waters make swimming here pleasant for the whole family, a refreshing change from the bracing salty surf of the Atlantic. The ponds are also perfect for canoeing, sailing, or kayaking (boats are available from Jack's Boat Rentals). A Wellfleet beach sticker is required to visit these fragile ecosystems in season (the sticker is only for cars, though—anyone can walk or ride a bike over to the ponds). Motorized boats are not allowed.

BICYCLING    The Cape Cod Rail Trail ends at the South Wellfleet post office. Other scenic routes for bicyclists include winding, tree-lined Old County Road, just outside Wellfleet center at the end of West Main Street. Ambitious riders can bike all the way to Truro on this often bumpy road, but be sure to watch for vehicular traffic around the tight curves. Ocean View Drive, on the ocean side, winds through miles of wooded areas; there are several ponds along the route that are perfect for taking a quick dip. The Wellfleet Chamber of Commerce publishes a pamphlet, "Bicycling in Wellfleet," with an annotated map.

**Cape Outback Adventures** (( ✉ *U.S. 6 and Lecount Hollow Rd.* ☎ *508/349–1617* ⊕ *www.capeoutback.com*) has friendly instructors and guided tours for kayakers, mountain bikers, and beginning surfers. Times and location are arranged by phone, and owner Richard Miller and his staff provide the equipment. Kayak trips explore areas in both Wellfleet and Truro, and off-road mountain-biking excursions take place in the vast wooded areas within the National Seashore. Surfing instruction is available by the hour. These trips are designed for all ages and skill levels.

**Idle Times Bike Shop, Inc.** ( ✉ *U.S. 6, just west of Cahoon Hollow Rd.* ☎ *508/349–9161* ⊕ *www.idletimesbikes.com*) opens Memorial Day and rents bikes, trailer bikes (a tandem bike with a backseat for children who are big enough to pedal), and trailer attachments for the smaller passengers. The shop also handles repairs and sells parts and assorted accessories. Depending on the crowds and weather, it usually remains open until Columbus Day, but there's a branch in Eastham open year-round.

BOATING **Jack's Boat Rental** ( ✉ *Gull Pond, south of U.S. 6* ☎ *508/349–9808 or 508/349–7553* ⊕ *www.jacksboatrental.com*) has canoes, kayaks, Sunfish, pedal boats, surfboards, Boogie boards, and sailboards. Guided kayak tours are also available.

**Wellfleet Marine Corp.** ( ✉ *25 Holbrook Ave., Wellfleet Harbor* ☎ *508/349–6417* ⊕ *www.wellfleetmarine.com*) rents sailboats and motorboats in various sizes by the hour or the day.

FISHING You can climb aboard the charter boat *Jac's Mate* ( ✉ *Wellfleet Town Pier, Wellfleet Harbor* ☎ *508/255–2978* ⊕ *home.comcast.net/~jacsmate*) for fishing expeditions in search of bass and blues.

The *Naviator* ( ✉ *Wellfleet Town Pier, Wellfleet Harbor* ☎ *508/349–6003* ⊕ *www.naviator.com*) operates fishing trips on a walk-on basis from spring through fall. Rods, reels, and bait are included.

GOLF & TENNIS Wellfleet maintains several tennis courts at **Baker's Field** near the town pier. Call the **Recreation Department** ( ☎ *508/349–0330*) for fees and reservations.

**Chequessett Yacht Country Club** ( ✉ *680 Chequessett Neck Rd., west of Downtown Wellfleet* ☎ *508/349–3704* ⊕ *www.cycc.net*) is a semiprivate club (public use on space-available basis) with a 9-hole golf course (there are two sets of tees, so you can play 18 holes by repeating the layout) and five hard-surface tennis courts by the bay. Lessons are available.

**Oliver's** ( ✉ *2183 U.S. 6, west of Downtown Wellfleet exit* ☎ *508/349–3330*), which has one Truflex and seven clay courts, offers tennis lessons and arranges matches.

SURFING  Atlantic-coast **Marconi** and **White Crest** beaches are the best for surfing. Surfboard rentals can be arranged at Jack's Boat Rental.

## SHOPPING

ART GALLERIES  **Andre Pottery** ( ⊠*5 Commercial St., Downtown Wellfleet* ☎*508/349–2299* ⊕*www.andrepottery.com*) specializes in handmade bowls, vases, and pitchers, mostly in greens, blues, and grays, the shades of the sea and shore.

**Blue Heron Gallery** ( ⊠*20 Bank St., Downtown Wellfleet* ☎*508/349–6724* ⊕*www.blueheronfineart.com*) is one of the Cape's best galleries, with contemporary works—including Cape scenes, jewelry, sculpture, and pottery—by regional and nationally recognized artists, among them Steve Allrich and Del Filardi.

★ **Brophy's Fine Art** ( ⊠*313 Main St., Downtown Wellfleet* ☎*508/349–6479* ⊕*www.brophysfineart.com*), one of the few year-round shops in Wellfleet, carries a nice selection of pottery, jewelry, and landscape paintings by several prominent New England artists as well as the beautiful stained-glass works of owner Thomas Brophy.

**Cove Gallery** ( ⊠*15 Commercial St., Downtown Wellfleet* ☎*508/349–2530* ⊕*www.covegallery.com*) displays the works of John Grillo, Tomie dePaola, and Leonard Baskin, among others. The gallery hosts Saturday-night artist receptions in July and August.

★ **Kendall Art Gallery** ( ⊠*40 Main St., Downtown Wellfleet* ☎*508/349–2482* ⊕*www.kendallartgallery.com*) carries eclectic modern works, including Harry Marinsky's bronzes in the sculpture garden, photography by Walter Baron and Alan Hoelzle, watercolors by Walter Dorrell, and contemporary art by several prominent Chinese artists. Receptions are held on Saturday evenings.

**Left Bank Gallery** ( ⊠*25 Commercial St., Downtown Wellfleet* ☎*508/349–9451* ⊕*www.leftbankgallery.com*) has a branch here (the other is in Orleans). The gallery displays the larger works of local and national artists and sells fine crafts in the back room facing Duck Creek.

**Nicholas Harrison Gallery** ( ⊠*25 Bank St., Downtown Wellfleet* ☎*508/349–7799* ⊕*www.thenicholasharrisongallery.com*) has made a name for itself in the area of lovely and unusual American crafts, including beautiful lamps, resin-and-silver jewelry, and hand-painted cabinets. Owners Mark and Laura Evangelista are also accomplished potters, and you'll see their vibrant ceramic works here as well.

SPECIALTY
STORES  **Abiyoyo** ( ⊠*286 Main St., Downtown Wellfleet* ☎*508/349–3422*) has a full line of Wellfleet T-shirts and sweatshirts, along with shoes, children's clothing, and bath and beauty products.

**Chocolate Sparrow** ( ⊠*326 Main St., Downtown Wellfleet* ☎*508/349–1333*) makes nine types of fudge, luscious hand-dipped chocolates, and a wide array of decadent baked goods and sweets. This is a seasonal branch of the well-known shop that began in Eastham and also has a location in Orleans; it's open May through early September.

**Eccentricity** ( ✉354 *Main St., Downtown Wellfleet* ☎508/349–3634) keeps the corner of Main and Briar offbeat. One of the most interesting stores on the Cape, it sells gorgeous kimonos, ethnic-inspired cotton clothing, African carved-wood sculptures, barbershop paintings, odd Mexican items, and trinkets. The owners also run Off Center, a similarly lively shop across the street.

★ **Herridge Books** ( ✉140 *Main St. Downtown Wellfleet* ☎508/349–1323) is the perfect store for a town that has been host to so many writers. Its dignified literary fiction, art and architecture, literary biography and letters, mystery, Americana, sports, and other sections are full of used books in very nice condition. Herridge also carries new editions on the Cape and its history.

**Jules Besch Stationers** ( ✉15 *Bank St., Downtown Wellfleet* ☎508/349–1231) has extraordinary cards, fine stationery, journals, papers, and pens. Proprietor Michael Tuck's warm and welcoming nature is as beautiful as his products are; he also offers full calligraphy services.

**Karol Richardson** ( ✉11 *W. Main St., Downtown Wellfleet* ☎508/349–6378 ⊕*www.karolrichardson.com*) fashions women's wear in luxurious fabrics and sells interesting shoes, hats, and jewelry.

**Kite Gallery** ( ✉75 *Commercial St., Downtown Wellfleet* ☎508/349–7387) overlooks a salt marsh and stocks kites and all kinds of colorful beach toys, windsocks, flags, and garden goodies.

**Pickle and Puppy** ( ✉355 *Main St., Downtown Wellfleet* ☎508/349–0606) has a bit of everything: housewares, T-shirts, fanciful foodstuffs, ceramics, and luxury bath and beauty-parlor items, plus a selection of unusual children's toys, games, and puzzles.

**Secret Garden** ( ✉*Main St., Downtown Wellfleet* ☎508/349–1444) doesn't waste any precious space—the walls are covered from floor to ceiling with whimsical folk-art pieces, handbags, clothing, and decorative accessories. They also have good buys on sterling silver jewelry.

**Wellfleet Marketplace** ( ✉295 *Main St., Downtown Wellfleet* ☎508/349–3156) is *the* place to pick up gourmet foods in town. In addition to a branch of Mac's Seafood, you'll also find great deli treats, organic produce, and other tasty foods.

FLEA MARKET     The giant **Wellfleet Flea Market** ( ✉51 *U.S. 6, South Wellfleet* ☎508/349–
Fodor's Choice     *0541* ⊕*www.wellfleetcinemas.com/flea_market.htm*) sets up shop in
★     the parking lot of the Wellfleet Drive-In Theater mid-April through June and September and October, weekends and Monday holidays 8 to 4; July and August, Monday holidays, Wednesday and Thursday, and weekends 8 to 4. You'll find antiques, sweat socks, old advertising posters, books, Beanie Babies, Guatemalan sweaters, plants, trinkets, and plenty more among the 300 vendors. On Monday and Tuesday in July and August the vendors make way for large arts-and-crafts shows. A snack bar and playground keep fatigue at bay.

If you're in the mood for a quiet, lovely ride winding through what the Cape might have looked like before Europeans arrived, follow **Old County Road** from Wellfleet to Truro on the bay side. It's bumpy and beautiful, with a stream or two along the way. So cycle on it, or drive slowly, or just stop and walk to take in the nature around you.

## TRURO

*2 mi north of Wellfleet, 7 mi southeast of Provincetown.*

Settled in 1697, Truro has had several names. It was originally called Pamet after the local Native Americans, but in 1705 the name was changed to Dangerfield in response to all the sailing mishaps off its shores. "Truroe" was the final choice, named for a Cornish town that homesick settlers thought it resembled; the final "e" was eventually dropped. The town relied on the sea for its income—whaling, shipbuilding, and cod fishing were the main industries.

Today Truro is a town of high dunes, estuaries, and rivers fringed by grasses, rolling moors, and houses sheltered in tiny valleys. It's a popular retreat for artists, writers, politicos, and numerous vacationing psychoanalysts. Edward Hopper summered here from 1930 to 1967, finding the Cape light ideal for his austere brand of realism. One of the largest towns on the Cape in terms of land area—almost 43 square mi—it's also the smallest in population, with about 1,400 year-round residents. Truro is also the Cape's narrowest town, and from a high perch you can see the Atlantic Ocean on one side and Cape Cod Bay on the other.

If you thought neighboring Wellfleet's downtown was small, wait until you see—or don't see—Truro's. It consists of a post office, a town hall, and a shop or two—you'll know it by the sign that says DOWNTOWN TRURO at a little plaza entrance. Truro also has a library, a firehouse, and a police station, but that's about all. The North Truro section contains most of the town's restaurants and accommodations, most either along U.S. 6 or fronting the bay along Route 6A (Shore Road), just south of the Provincetown border. Many who live or vacation in Truro choose it for its easygoing, quiet personality and lack of development—and its proximity to the excitement and commerce of Provincetown.

For a few hours of exploring, take the children to **Pamet Harbor** (⊠*Depot Rd.*). At low tide you can walk out on the flats and discover the creatures of the salt marsh. A nearby plaque identifies plants and animals and describes the area's ecological importance.

On **Corn Hill** (⊠*Off Corn Hill Rd.*), near the beach area of the same name, a tablet commemorates the finding of a buried cache of corn by Myles Standish and the *Mayflower* crew. They took it to Plymouth and used it as seed, returning later to pay the Native Americans for what they'd taken.

The **Truro Center for the Arts at Castle Hill,** in a converted 19th-century barn, has summer arts-and-crafts workshops for children, as well

CLOSE UP

## Truro's Edward Hopper

The Outer Cape has inspired thousands of acclaimed artists, but perhaps none is more closely associated with its serene yet romantic landscape than Edward Hopper, the esteemed realist painter who lived in Truro for most of the last four decades of his life. Quiet Truro, with its peaceful, sandy lanes, suited the introspective Hopper perfectly.

Hopper, born in Nyack, New York, in 1882, enjoyed little commercial or critical success before middle age. Early in his career, he worked as a commercial illustrator to support himself while living in New York City's Greenwich Village. At age 43 he married Josephine Nivison. It was during the 1920s, after his marriage, that Hopper achieved marked success as both an oil painter and watercolorist and became known for his starkly realistic scenes, often depicting public places filled with people, such as his most iconic work, *Nighthawks*.

Edward and Josephine first summered in Truro in 1930, and a few years later they designed their own Truro home. Much of Hopper's work conveyed the emptiness and alienation of big-city life, and although his Cape paintings were similar in their simplicity, they nevertheless offered a slightly more hopeful vision, if for no other reason than their tendency to focus more on the region's sensuous luminosity than strictly on lonely or bored people.

Most famously, his Truro work captured the undulating auburn hills along Pamet Road in *Corn Hill Truro Cape Cod.* Other notable paintings that portray the Outer Cape include *Cape Cod Evening* (1939), *Route 6 Eastham* (1941), *Martha McKeen of Wellfleet* (1944), and *Cape Cod Morning* (1950).

—by Andrew Collins

5

as courses and single classes in art, crafts, photography, and writing for adults. Teachers have included notable New York– and Provincetown-based artists. ⊠*10 Meetinghouse Rd.* ☎*508/349–7511* ⊕*www.castlehill.org.*

NEED A BREAK? **Jams (** ⊠*14 Truro Center Rd., off U.S. 6 in Truro Center* ☎*508/349–1616***)** **has fixings for a great picnic lunch: sandwiches, fresh produce, a bottle of wine or Evian, or a sweet treat. Unless you like getting your knees knocked, don't bother sitting at the bench outside—besides, the best part of the Cape awaits just outside the door.**

Built in 1907 as a summer hotel, the **Highland House Museum,** operated by the Truro Historical Society, has 17th-century firearms, mementos of shipwrecks, early fishing and whaling gear, ship models, a pirate's chest, and scrimshaw. One room exhibits wood carvings, paintings, blown glass, and ship models by Courtney Allen, artist and founder of Truro's historical society. The museum also holds local art and artifact shows each year. ⊠*6 Lighthouse Rd., off S. Highland Rd., North Truro* ☎*508/487–3397* ⊕*www.trurohistorical.org* ☎*$4; $6 for combo admission with Highland Light* ☉*Late May–Sept., Mon.– Sat. 10–4:30, Sun. 1–4:30.*

Truly a breathtaking sight, **Highland Light,** also called Cape Cod Light, is the Cape's oldest lighthouse. It was the last to become automated, in 1986. The first light on this site, powered by 24 whale-oil lamps, began warning ships of Truro's treacherous sandbars in 1797—the dreaded Peaked Hills Bars alone, to the north, claimed hundreds of ships. The current light, a white-painted 66-foot tower built in 1857, is powered by two 1,000-watt bulbs reflected by a huge Fresnel lens; its beacon is visible for more than 20 mi.

One of four active lighthouses on the Outer Cape, Highland Light has the distinction of being listed in the National Register of Historic Places. Henry David Thoreau used it as a stopover in his travels across the Cape's backside (as the Atlantic side of the Outer Cape is called). Erosion threatened to cut this lighthouse from the 117-foot cliff on which it stood and drop it into the sea; thanks to a concerted effort by local residents and lighthouse lovers, the necessary funds were raised, and the lighthouse was moved back 450 feet to safety (while remaining surrounded by the Highland Links golf course). Twenty-five-minute tours of the lighthouse are given daily in summer. Children must be at least 51 inches tall to climb the tower. ⊠ *Off S. Highland Rd.* ☎ *508/487-3397* ⊕ *www.trurohistorical.org* ☜ *$4; $6 for combo admission with Highland House Museum* ☉ *Mid-May–mid-Oct., daily 10–5:30.*

The gardens of **A Touch of Heaven** are beautiful—and, unlike most gardens, are meant to be picked. The lawns are set with benches and birdbaths, and the flowers are so abundant that you won't feel guilty about gathering a bunch to take home. ⊠ *Pond Village Heights, North Truro* ☎ *No phone* ☜ *Free* ☉ *Daily dawn–dusk.*

★ Worth a stop as much for its verdant grounds and tranquil setting inside a rambling 1830s farmhouse as for its enjoyable wines, **Truro Vineyards of Cape Cod Winery** produces a number of excellent wines. The new owners, who bought the winery in 2007, have greatly stepped up production, and have begun experimenting with some new vintages. At the moment, the vineyard makes a commendable Cabernet Franc, Chardonnay, sauvignon blanc, vignoles, blush, and several notable blends. They also make a red table wine that's flavored with cranberries and known for its unusual bottle, shaped like a lighthouse (along with two other "lighthouse" varieties)—it's a fun souvenir. Free daily tours are given in summer at 1 and 3. ⊠ *Rte. 6A, North Truro* ☎ *508/487-6200* ⊕ *www.trurovineyardsofcapecod.com* ☉ *Apr. and Dec., Fri. and Sat. 11–5, Sun. noon–5; May–Nov., Mon.–Sat. 11–5, Sun. noon–5* ☜ *Free.*

At the **Pilgrim Heights Area** ( ⊠ *Off U.S. 6*) of the Cape Cod National Seashore, a short trail leads to the spring where members of a Pilgrim exploring party stopped to refill their casks, tasting their first New England water in the process. Walking through this still-wild area of oak, pitch pine, bayberry, blueberry, beach plum, and azalea gives you a taste of what it was like for these voyagers in search of a new home. "Being thus passed the vast ocean..." William Bradford wrote in *Of*

*Plimoth Plantation,* "they had no friends to welcome them, no inns to entertain them or refresh their weather-beaten bodies; no houses, or much less towns to repair to, to seek for succour."

From an overlook you can see the bluffs of High Head, where glaciers pushed a mass of earth before melting and receding. Another path leads to a swamp, and a bike trail leads to Head of the Meadow Beach, often a less crowded alternative to others in the area.

## WHERE TO EAT

**$–$$$**
**AMERICAN**

✕**Adrian's.** Adrian Cyr's restaurant crowns a high bluff overlooking Pilgrim Lake and all of Provincetown; his cooking also hits great heights. Cayenne-crusted salmon with maple-mustard sauce is just one of the well-prepared dishes here. Tuscan salad is also a hit, with tomatoes, olives, fresh basil, plenty of garlic, and balsamic vinegar. Pizzas, too, are standouts, especially one made with cornmeal dough and topped with shrimp and artichokes. The outdoor deck overflows at the popular breakfasts and brunches, served every day in season and weekends in spring and fall—try the cranberry pancakes with orange butter. ⊠ *Outer Reach Hotel, 535 U.S. 6, North Truro* ☎ *508/487–4360* ⊕ *www.adriansrestaurant.com* ☐ *AE, MC, V* ⊗ *Closed mid-Oct.–mid-May and Mon.–Wed. spring and fall. No lunch.*

**$$**
**MEDITERRANEAN**

✕ **Babe's Mediterranean Bistro.** It looks like a modest roadhouse from the outside, but this rambling, casual space in North Truro serves quite authentic and sophisticated Middle Eastern, North African, and Spanish fare. Opened in 2006, the eatery is run by chef-owner Peter Thrasher, who whips up such memorable dishes as Istanbul-style far-falle pasta with slow-braised lamb and garlic yogurt, and Aegean-style meatballs studded with figs, pistachios, and bell peppers, tossed with a spicy tomato-yogurt sauce; Moroccan tagines are another specialty. Be sure to start your meal with the meze sampler. ⊠ *69 Shore Rd. (Rte. 6A), North Truro* ☎ *508/487–9955* ☐ *MC, V* ⊗ *Closed mid-Oct.–mid-May. No lunch.*

**$$–$$$**
★
**AMERICAN**

✕**Blackfish.** Opened by talented chef Eric Jansen (originally behind Wellfleet's celebrated Wicked Oyster), this favorite local spot sits inside a rambling old blacksmith shop. Fans of fresh and creative food convene here to sample rustic Italian fare using local ingredients. Consider the rare-tuna Bolognese-style, or a savory rabbit ragout over pappardelle pasta. The intimate, old-fashioned space is cozy and romantic—but it can get a little hot on summer nights. ⊠ *17 Truro Center Rd., Truro Center* ☎ *508/349–3399* ☐ *AE, MC, V* ⊗ *Closed late Oct.–mid-May. No lunch.*

**$$–$$$**
**Fodor's**Choice
★
**ECLECTIC**

✕**Terra Luna.** An insider's favorite for fresh and inventive bistro fare with an Italian slant, Terra Luna has an intimate art-filled dining room with lace curtains, beam ceilings, and simple wooden tables. The food is stylish, with sophisticated sauces for both fish and meat dishes. The littleneck clams with sausage, fennel, garlic, and tomatoes is a house favorite, and seared duck breast with rhubarb-fennel compote and Sardinian-style couscous is an excellent alternative to the usual fish. For dessert, don't miss the unusual blackberry polenta custard, or a more traditional chocolate-silk cake with caramel sauce. ⊠ *104 Shore*

5

*Rd. (Rte. 6A), North Truro* ☎*508/487–1019* ⊕*www.theterraluna.com* ▭*AE, MC, V* ⊘*Closed Nov.–early May. No lunch.*

**$$–$$$$**  ✕**Whitman House.** What began as a modest pancake house has been
**AMERICAN**  transformed by the Rice family into a vast—if touristy—restaurant, but pewter plates, candlelight, and rustic wood accents make the place feel comfortably tavernlike. Predictable seafood, steaks, and surf-and-turf combos (consider the crabmeat casserole with petite filet mignon) keep the menu uncomplicated and the portions ample. Lunch and lighter dinner fare are served daily in the Bass Tavern. If you have to wait for a table, browse in the adjacent Amish quilt shop. ⊠*Off U.S. 6, at Great Hollow Rd.* ☎*508/487–1740* ⊕*www.whitmanhouse.com* ▭*AE, D, DC, MC, V* ⊘*Closed Jan.–Mar.*

## WHERE TO STAY

**$–$$**  🏠**Cape View Motel.** The true appeal of this tan-clapboard roadside motel is its noble perch on a westward bluff, looking out over Cape Cod Bay sunsets and the distant lights of Provincetown. Deluxe rooms have private balconies, as well as fully equipped kitchenettes and a king bed or two doubles. The style inside can't compete with the vistas outside, but the rooms are clean, simple, reasonably priced, and a 10-minute drive from Provincetown. Free coffee and doughnuts are provided in the morning. **Pros:** inexpensive rooms; nice harbor views from the bluff-top location; some units have kitchenettes. **Cons:** simple but prosaic room decor; few restaurants or shops within walking distance; feels a bit dated. ⊠*Junction of U.S. 6 and Rte. 6A, Box 114* ☎*508/487–0363 or 800/224–3232* ⊕*www.capeviewmotel.com* ⇘*32 rooms* ⌂*In-room: kitchen (some), refrigerator, dial-up. In-hotel: pool, beachfront, no elevator* ▭*AE, MC, V* ⊘*Closed mid-Oct.–mid-Apr.*

**$$**  🏠**Crow's Nest Resort.** Amid the mostly run-of-the-mill motels and
**Fodor'sChoice**  cottage compounds along Route 6A in North Truro, this beautifully
★  modernized all-suites beachfront property stands head and shoulders above the rest. It's been around since the mid-1960s, but the rooms are refreshingly contemporary with tile-and-oak floors, modern kitchen appliances, light-wood furniture, and country quilts. Ground-floor units front an attractive wooden deck overlooking the bay, and upstairs units have private balconies with similar views. You can choose from studio, two-bedroom, and three-bedroom units, and all have full kitchens, fireplaces, Jacuzzi tubs, and washers and dryers, making them perfect for longer stays. The resort also rents three attractive beachfront bungalows, called Crown's Nest Cottages, about a ½ mi away. Given the prime location, friendly service, and top-notch facilities and furnishings, this is one of the Outer Cape's best values for families and friends traveling together. **Pros:** furnishings are tasteful and contemporary; rooms have fantastic water views; all units have decks or balconies. **Cons:** a long walk to Provincetown dining and shopping; no pool; along a busy strip of motels and cottages. ⊠*496 Rte. 6A, Box 177* ☎*508/487–9031 or 800/499–9799* ⊕*www.caperesort.com* ⇘*21 suites* ⌂*In-room: kitchen, DVD, Wi-Fi. In-hotel: beachfront, no elevator* ▭*AE, MC, V* ⊘*Closed late Nov.–early Apr.*

**$–$$**  🏠**Horizons Beach Resort.** You'll discover a wide range of accommodations at this nicely-cared-for compound fronting a stunning 480-foot stretch of beach, including spacious waterfront efficiencies, dune-facing studios (some of them set inside a distinctive pagoda-inspired building), and private bungalows with separate sitting areas, kitchenettes, and—in some cases—fireplaces. Rates vary greatly according to view and proximity to the water, but you're also relatively close to the beach as well as the resort's swimming pool. A professional, thoughtful staff, spotless rooms, and casual, contemporary furnishings make this a highly popular getaway among the several properties on North Truro's Route 6A. **Pros:** rooms are near or even face the beach and harbor; nice variety of accommodation styles and configurations; beautifully maintained. **Cons:** a long walk to Provincetown dining and shopping; pricey if you want a water-view unit, no Wi-Fi. ⊠ *190 Rte. 6A* ⌂ *Box 146, North Truro 02652* ☎ *508/487–0042 or 800/782–0742* ⊕ *www. horizonsbeach.com* ↩ *77 rooms, 3 bungalows* ⌂ *In-room: kitchen (some), refrigerator, VCR, dial-up. In-hotel: pool, beachfront, no elevator* ☰ *MC, V* ⊗ *Closed mid-Oct.–mid-May.*

¢ ⭐ ▥ **Hostelling International–Truro.** In a former Coast Guard station right on the dunes, this handsome, well-placed, and nicely maintained hostel has kitchen facilities, a common area, and naturalist-led programs—not to mention panoramic views of the ocean and dunes. It's also right by the ½-mi-long Cranberry Bog Trail, which takes you by a refurbished cranberry bog and an old bog house. The dorm rooms are single-sex, and there are no curfews or lockouts—just come and go as you like. Guided kayak tours are available. **Pros:** cheapest rooms on Outer Cape; fantastic beachside location; guided kayak tours and naturalist walks provide plenty of diversions. **Cons:** mostly dorm-style with several people per room; you share common bathrooms. ⊠ *N. Pamet Rd., Box 402, Truro* ☎ *508/349–3889 or 888/901–2086* ⊕ *www.capecodhostels.org* ↩ *42 beds, 2 private rooms* ☰ *MC, V* ⊗ *Closed early Sept.–late June.*

$–$$ ▥ **Sea Gull Motel.** This motel's location, right along 160 feet of private beach and close to the Provincetown border, is its real draw. It's been family run for decades, so you may feel like you're spending time in someone's summer house. Most rooms have splendid water views; lodging is in standard motel rooms, motel studios, and beach apartments—the latter two are rented weekly, but you can rent rooms by the night. **Pros:** reasonable rates; beachfront location; very family-friendly. **Cons:** rooms aren't especially fancy; a long walk to Provincetown dining and shopping; along a busy strip of motels and cottages. ⊠ *Rte. 6A* ⌂ *Box 126, North Truro 02652* ☎ *508/487–9070* ⊕ *www.capecodtravel.com/seagullmotel* ↩ *26 rooms* ⌂ *In-room: kitchen (some), refrigerator, dial-up. In-hotel: beachfront, no elevator* ☰ *AE, D, MC, V* ⊗ *Closed mid-Oct.–mid-May.*

$–$$ ⭐ ▥ **Top Mast Resort.** This North Truro beach motel complex, which sits on 52 acres across U.S. 6 from Cape Cod National Seashore, had seen better days before its owners purchased two adjacent buildings and began an extensive refurbishment and expansion, completed in 2008. Improvements include new kitchen appliances and cabinets, tile flooring and new carpeting, and attractive furnishings. The resort also has added a new office, a restaurant serving traditional American fare, a pool, tennis courts, a playground, a gym, an indoor pool, and a Jacuzzi. Most rooms are along the beach, but there are also some significantly less expensive units in a building across the road, facing the swimming pool and landscaped gardens. Two cottages are available on a weekly basis. **Pros:** has recently undergone a huge renovation; right on the harbor with great views; lots of on-site diversions for kids. **Cons:** a long walk to Provincetown dining and shopping; along a busy strip of motels and cottages; a rather large compound: not ideal if you're seeking intimacy and seclusion. ✉*209 Rte. 6A* 📮*Box 44, North Truro 02652* ☎*508/487–1189 or 800/917–0024* ⊕*www.topmasresort.com* 🛏*72 rooms, 2 cottages* 🛎*In-room: kitchen (some), refrigerator, Wi-Fi. In-hotel: restaurant, tennis courts, pool, gym, beachfront, public Wi-Fi, no elevator* 🖃*MC, V* 🕙*Closed late Oct.–early May.*

### THE ARTS

★ From mid-June through late September, the **Payomet Performing Arts Center of Truro** ( ✉*29 Old Dewline Rd., North Truro* ☎*508/487–5400,* ⊕*www.ppactruro.org*) presents a wide range of concerts, plays, films, and music inside a big tent at Cape Cod National Seashore. Past performers have included the Cape Cod Opera, Patty Larkin, and the Shakespeare on the Cape troupe. There's also a kids' summer stage, featuring children's entertainment.

### SPORTS & THE OUTDOORS

BEACHES Parking at a number of Truro's **town beaches** is reserved for residents and renters in season, although anyone can walk or bicycle in. Ask at the **beach office** ( ☎*508/487–6983*) about obtaining a seasonal sticker.

**Corn Hill Beach** ( ✉*Corn Hill Rd.*), on the bay, has beautiful views of Provincetown. The waters are generally calm and warm, typical of bay beaches. There are restrooms on-site. Parking requires a Truro beach sticker or a $10 daily fee.

Truro has several other accessible beaches stretched along Cape Cod Bay. All are beautiful and ideal for long, lazy days of watching boats go by and taking in views of Provincetown in the distance.

**Cold Storage Beach** ( ✉*Pond Rd. off Rte. 6A [Shore Rd.]*) is just as popular with anglers looking for passing blues and stripers as it is with sun-seekers and swimmers. A Truro beach sticker is required for parking.

Just off one of Truro's backcountry roads, **Fisher Road Beach** ( ✉*Fisher Rd.*) has a smaller parking area, so it's usually quiet. A Truro beach sticker is required for parking.

To get to **Great Hollow Beach** ( ✉*Great Hollow Rd. off U.S. 6*) you must be ready to scale some moderate stairs from the parking lot to the sands below. A Truro beach sticker is required for parking.

**Ryder Beach** ( ✉*Ryder Beach Rd. off Old County Rd.*) rests just below a rise in the small dunes. A Truro beach sticker is required for parking.

On the ocean side, three spectacular beaches are marked by massive dunes and bracing surf.

**Ballston Beach** ( ⊠ *Pamet Rd.*) lies at the end of the winding, residential Pamet Road, backed by the golden hills that artist Edward Hopper made famous in his Truro paintings. Parking is reserved for residents and renters in season, although anyone can walk or bicycle in.

Fodor'sChoice **Coast Guard Beach** ( ⊠ *Coast Guard Rd.*) sits just down the road from
★ Highland Light. Parking is for residents and renters with stickers only, although anyone can walk or bicycle in to enjoy this pristine swath of golden sand that stretches for miles in either direction and sees relatively few crowds—even in the heart of summer. Keep in mind that the parking area is small and tends to fill quickly.

**Head of the Meadow Beach** ( ⊠ *Head of the Meadow Rd. off U.S. 6*) in North Truro, part of the Cape Cod National Seashore, is often less crowded than other beaches in the area. There are basic restroom facilities available in summer and no showers. The daily parking fee is $10 in season (late June–early Sept.); you can also purchase a season pass ($45) that is good for all National Seashore locations.

A not-so-secret favorite of nude sunbathers, **Longnook Beach** ( ⊠ *Long Nook Rd.*) shares the senses of wildness and isolation synonymous with Truro's outer reaches. Truro beach stickers are required for parking.

The **Head of the Meadow Trail** provides 2 mi of easy cycling between dunes and salt marshes from High Head Road, off Route 6A in North Truro, to the Head of the Meadow Beach parking lot.

GOLF    The **Highland Golf Links** ( ⊠ *Lighthouse Rd., North Truro* ☎ *508/487–*
★ *9201* ⊕ *www.truro-ma.gov/html_pages/facilities/golf*), a 9-hole, par-35 course on a cliff overlooking the Atlantic and Highland Light, is unique for its resemblance to Scottish links.

SURFING    **Longnook Beach** ( ⊠ *End of Long Nook Rd., off U.S. 6*) is good for surfing.

### SHOPPING
**Atlantic Spice Co.** ( ⊠ *U.S. 6 at Rte. 6A, North Truro* ☎ *508/487–6100* ⊕ *www.atlanticspice.com*) has spices, teas, and potpourris, as well as herbs, dried flowers, soaps, sauces, and kitchenware items.

**Whitman House Quilt Shop** ( ⊠ *County Rd. just off U.S. 6, North Truro* ☎ *508/487–3204* ⊕ *www.whitmanhousequilts.com*) sells Amish quilts and other country items.

## PROVINCETOWN

*7 mi northwest of Truro, 27 mi north of Orleans, 62 mi from Sagamore Bridge.*

The Cape's smallest town in area and its second smallest in year-round population, Provincetown is a place of liberating creativity, startling originality, and substantial diversity. Like so much of Cape Cod, it's also a town that's become progressively—and rather dramatically—more upscale and sophisticated in recent years. A number of the casual—if cheesy—T-shirt and souvenir shops that once lined the town's main drag, Commercial Street, have given way to first-rate art galleries and upscale boutiques. Many of the town's funky B&Bs and inns, which once felt more like glorified boardinghouses than proper accommodations, have been sold as private homes or transformed into fabulous, upscale hideaways with fine antiques, flat-screen TVs and DVD players, and cushy amenities.

With the change has come at least a mild concern that Provincetown may become too upscale and cosmopolitan for its own good—but so far there's little evidence that this lovably eccentric, individualistic place will ever become any less free-spirited. A strong sense of community spirit and civic pride remains. In the busy downtown, Portuguese-American fishermen mix with painters, poets, writers, whale-watching families, cruise-ship passengers on brief stopovers, and gay and lesbian residents and visitors. In summer Commercial Street is packed with sightseers and shoppers hunting for treasures in the overwhelming number of galleries and crafts shops. At night raucous music and people spill out of bars, drag shows, and sing-along lounges galore. It's a fun, crazy place, with the extra dimension of the fishing fleet unloading their catch at MacMillan Wharf, in the center of the action.

The town's 8 square mi are also rich in history. The fist at the very tip of the Cape, Provincetown has shores that curve protectively around a natural harbor, perfect for sailors from any epoch to anchor. Historical records suggest that Thorvald, brother of Viking Leif Erikson, came ashore here in AD 1004 to repair the keel of his boat and consequently named the area Kjalarness, or Cape of the Keel. Bartholomew Gosnold came to Provincetown in 1602 and named the area Cape Cod after the abundant codfish he found in the local waters.

The Pilgrims remain Provincetown's most famous visitors. On Monday, November 21, 1620, the *Mayflower* dropped anchor in Provincetown Harbor after a difficult 63-day voyage from England. While in the harbor the passengers signed the Mayflower Compact, the first document to declare a democratic form of government in America. One of the first things the ever-practical Pilgrims did was come ashore to wash their clothes, thus beginning the ages-old New England tradition of Monday wash day. They lingered for five weeks before moving on to Plymouth. Plaques and parks throughout town commemorate the landing.

Incorporated as a town in 1727, Provincetown was for many decades a bustling seaport, with fishing and whaling as its major industries. In the late 19th century, groups of Portuguese fishermen and whalers began to settle here, lending their expertise and culture to an already cosmopolitan town. Fishing is still an important source of income for many Provincetown locals, but now the town ranks among the world's leading whale-watching—rather than whale-hunting—outposts.

Artists began coming here in the late 1890s to take advantage of the unusual Cape Cod light—in fact, Provincetown is the nation's oldest continuous art colony. Poets, writers, and actors have also been part of the art scene. Eugene O'Neill's first plays were written and produced

# Provincetown

TO RACE POINT BEACH, PROVINCE LANDS VISITOR CENTER & BEECH FOREST PICNIC AREA

TO ROUTE 6A

EAST END

Provincetown Harbor

MacMillan Wharf

Duck Pond

Shank Painter Pond

WEST END

TO RACE POINT LIGHT

TO LONG POINT LIGHT

Province Lands Rd.

Race Point Rd.

Howland
Harry Kemp Way
Bradford St.
Priscilla Alden
Brewster
Pearl
Law
Conwell
Arch
Center
Johnson
Cemetery
Standish
Alden
Jerome Rd.
Winslow
Ryder
Gosnold
Masonic
Prince
Carver
Court
Winthrop
Central
Shank Painter Rd.
Pleasant
Franklin
Nickerson
Creek Rd.
Blueberry
W. Vine
Tremont St.
Soper
Commercial St.

0   10 miles
0   10 kilometers

5

Fine Arts Work Center .....**5**
MacMillan Wharf .........**2**
Mayflower Compact Plaque ........**7**
Octagonal house ......**8**
Pilgrim Monument ......**1**
Pilgrim Plaque ........**10**

Provincetown Art Association and Museum .......**3**
Provincetown Inn .....**11**
Provincetown Public Library ........**4**
Seth Nickerson House ....**9**
Town hall ........**6**

here, and the Fine Arts Work Center continues to have in its ranks some of the most important writers working today.

During the early 1900s, Provincetown became known as Greenwich Village North. Artists from New York and Europe discovered the town's unspoiled beauty, special light, lively community, and colorful Portuguese flavor. By 1916, with five art schools flourishing here, painters' easels were nearly as common as shells on the beach. This bohemian community, along with the availability of inexpensive summer lodgings, attracted young rebels and writers as well, including John Reed (*Ten Days That Shook the World*) and Mary Heaton Vorse (*Footnote to Folly*), who in 1915 began the Cape's first significant theater group, the Provincetown Players. The young, then unknown Eugene O'Neill joined them in 1916, when his *Bound East for Cardiff* premiered in a tiny wharf-side East End fish house. After 1916 the Players moved on to New York. Their theater, at present-day 571 Commercial Street, is long gone, but a model of it and the old Lewis Wharf on which it stood is on display at the Pilgrim Monument museum.

Near the Provincetown border, **massive dunes** actually meet the road in places, turning U.S. 6 into a sand-swept highway. Scattered among the dunes are primitive cottages called dune shacks, built from flotsam and other found materials, that have provided atmospheric as well as cheap lodgings to a number of famous artists and writers over the years—among them poet Harry Kemp, Eugene O'Neill, e. e. cummings, Jack Kerouac, and Norman Mailer. The few surviving shacks are privately leased from the Cape Cod National Seashore, whose proposal to demolish the shacks was halted by their inclusion on the National Register of Historic Places in 1988. The dunes are fragile and should not be walked on, but paths lead through them to the ocean. You can see some of the shacks by van on Art's Dune Tours.

The **Province Lands** begin at High Head in Truro and stretch to the tip of Provincetown. The area is scattered with ponds, cranberry bogs, and scrub; unfortunately, this terrain provides optimal conditions for the deer tick, which can cause Lyme disease, so use extra caution. More than 7 mi of bike and walking trails lace through forests of stunted pines, beech, and oak and across desertlike expanses of rolling dunes. Protected against development, the Province Lands are the "wilds" of the Cape.

A beautiful spot to stop for lunch before biking to the beach, the **Beech Forest picnic area** (⊠*Race Point Rd., east of U.S. 6*) in the National Seashore borders a small pond covered with water lilies. The adjacent bike trails lead to Herring Cove and Race Point beaches, which are both part of the National Seashore.

Inside the **Province Lands Visitor Center** in the Cape Cod National Seashore, you'll find literature and nature-related gifts, frequent short films on local geology, and exhibits on the life of the dunes and the shore. You can also pick up information on guided walks, birding trips, lectures, bonfires, and other current programs throughout the seashore, as well as on the Province Lands' pristine beaches, Race Point and Herring

Cove, and walking, biking, and horse trails. Don't miss the awe-inspiring panoramic view of the dunes and the surrounding ocean from the observation deck. ✉*Race Point Rd., east of U.S. 6* ☎*508/487–1256* ⊕*www.nps.gov/caco* ✉*Free* ☉*Early May–late Oct., daily 9–5.*

Not far from the present Coast Guard station is the **Old Harbor Station,** a U.S. Life Saving Service building rescued from an eroding beach and towed here by barge from Chatham in 1977. It's reached by a boardwalk across the sand, and plaques along the way tell about the lifesaving service and the whales seen offshore. Inside are displays of such equipment as Lyle guns, which shot rescue lines out to ships in distress when seas were too violent to launch a surfboat, and breeches buoys, in which passengers were hauled across those lines to safety. There are reenactments of this old-fashioned lifesaving procedure at 6:30 on Thursday night in summer. ✉*Race Point Beach, end of Race Point Rd.* ☎*508/487–1256* ✉*Donations accepted; Thurs. night $3* ☉*July and Aug., daily 3–5 (also 6–8 on Thurs.).*

★ Provincetown's main downtown thoroughfare, **Commercial Street,** is 3 mi from end to end. In season, driving from one end to the other could take forever, so wear comfortable shoes and get ready to walk (although going on foot will take awhile, too, because of the crowds). You'll see signs for parking lots as you head into town. Take a casual stroll and check out the many architectural styles (Greek Revival, Victorian, Second Empire, and Gothic, to name a few) used in the design of the impressive houses for wealthy sea captains and merchants. Be on the lookout for blue plaques fastened to housefronts explaining their historical significance—practically the entire town has been designated part of the Provincetown Historic District. The Historical Society puts out a series of walking-tour pamphlets—available for about $1 each at many shops in town as well as at the chamber of commerce visitor center—with maps and information on the history of many buildings and the (more or less) famous folk who have occupied them. You may also want to pick up a free Provincetown gallery guide.

The center of town is where the crowds and most of the touristy shops are. The quiet East End is mostly residential, with an increasing number of nationally renowned galleries; the similarly quiet West End has a number of small inns with neat lawns and elaborate gardens.

**NEED A BREAK?** The **Aquarium Shops Food Court** ( ✉*205–209 Commercial St.*) contains a handful of excellent little fast-food spots. Grab outstanding Mexican fare at **Big Daddy's Burritos;** Asian snacks at **Fortune Cookie;** and silky smooth Italian ice cream, hot cocoa, and smoothies at **I Dream of Gelato.** The **Provincetown Fudge Factory** ( ✉*210 Commercial St., Downtown Center* ☎*508/487–2850* ⊕*www.ptownfudge.com*), across from the post office, makes silky peanut-butter cups, chocolates, saltwater taffy, yard-long licorice whips, custom-flavor frozen yogurt, and the creamiest fudge on the Cape—and will ship sweet goodies to you, too.

**1** The first thing you'll see in Provincetown is the **Pilgrim Monument.** This
★ grandiose edifice, which seems somewhat out of proportion to the rest
of the low-rise town, commemorates the Pilgrims' first landing in the
New World and their signing of the Mayflower Compact (the first colo-
nial-American rules of self-governance) before they set off from Provincetown Harbor to explore the mainland. Climb the 116 steps and 60
short ramps of the 252-foot-high tower for a panoramic view—dunes
on one side, harbor on the other, and the entire bay side of Cape Cod
beyond. On an exceptionally clear day you can see the Boston skyline.
At the tower's base is a museum of Lower Cape and Provincetown history, with exhibits on whaling, shipwrecks, and scrimshaw; a diorama
of the *Mayflower;* and another of a glass factory.

The tower was erected of granite shipped from Maine, according to a
design modeled on a tower in Siena, Italy. President Theodore Roosevelt laid the cornerstone in 1907, and President Howard Taft attended
the 1910 dedication. On Thanksgiving Eve, in a ceremony that includes
a museum tour and open house, 5,000 white and gold lights that drape
the tower are illuminated—a display that can be seen from as far away
as the Cape Cod Canal. They are lighted nightly into the New Year.
⊠*High Pole Hill Rd.* ☎*508/487–1310* ⊕*www.pilgrim-monument.
org* ⊠*$7* ⊘*Early Apr.–June and Sept.–Oct., daily 9–5; July and Aug.,
daily 9–7; Nov., weekends 9–5.*

**2** **MacMillan Wharf,** with its large municipal parking facility, is a sensible
place to start a tour of town. It's one of five remaining wharves of the
original 54 that once jutted into the bay. The wharf serves as the base
for P-town whale-watch boats, fishing charters, high-speed ferries, and
party boats. The **Chamber of Commerce** is also here, with all kinds
of information and events schedules. Kiosks at the wharf have restroom and parking-lot locations, bus schedules, and other information
for visitors.

The former Provincetown Marina building, on MacMillan Wharf,
holds the **Expedition** *Whydah* **Sea Lab and Learning Center,** a home for
artifacts recovered from the pirate ship *Whydah,* which sank off the
coast of Wellfleet in 1717. The *Whydah* is the only pirate shipwreck
ever authenticated anywhere in the world, and the museum, though
tiny, is entertaining and educational, with one display on the restoration and conservation processes and another on the untold story of the
18th-century pirating life. The curators hope to eventually collect all
the recovered pieces; some are on loan to other museums across the
country. ⊠*16 MacMillan Wharf, Downtown Center* ☎*508/487–8899
or 800/949–3241* ⊕*www.whydah.com* ⊠*$8* ⊘*June–early Sept., daily
10–8; Apr., May, and early Sept.–Oct., daily 10–5; Nov. and Dec.,
weekends 10–4.*

**3** Founded in 1914 to collect and show the works of artists with Provinc-
Fodor'sChoice etown connections, the **Provincetown Art Association and Museum** *(PAAM)*
★ has a 1,650-piece permanent collection, displayed in changing exhibits
that mix up-and-comers with established 20th-century figures, including Milton Avery, Philip Evergood, William Gropper, Charles Haw-

thorne, Robert Motherwell, Claes Oldenburg, Man Ray, John Singer Sargent, Andy Warhol, and Agnes Weinrich. Some of the work hung in the four bright galleries is for sale. The museum store carries books of local interest, including works by or about area artists and authors, as well as posters, crafts, cards, and gift items. PAAM-sponsored year-round courses (one day and longer) offer the opportunity to study under such talents as Hilda Neily, Franny Golden, and Doug Ritter. A stunning, contemporary wing was added in 2005, greatly expanding the exhibit space. ✉*460 Commercial St., East End* ☎*508/487–1750* ⊕*www.paam.org* ✉*$5* 🕑*Late May–Sept., Mon.–Thurs. 11–8, Fri. 11–10, weekends 11–5; Oct.–May, Thurs.–Sun. noon–5.*

❹★ The **Provincetown Public Library** occupies the beautifully restored and redesigned Center Methodist Church, a towering 1860 beauty in the East End whose steeple you can see from the harbor and much of town. On rainy days, this is a wonderful place to read, work, or check your e-mail on one of the several public computers. You can also check out *The Rose Dorothea*, a half-scale replica of an early 1900s fishing schooner that was built by some 15 Provincetown fishermen and woodworkers as a tribute to the town's rich nautical heritage. The 62-foot-long boat has ingeniously been built into the library's 2nd floor. Architecturally, this is one of the town's most striking and distinctive buildings, but it's also a great cultural resource, hosting children's storytelling on Wednesday and Saturday mornings, educational workshops, and other community events. There's also a children's room with computers, books, and educational resources. The building's lower level contains a gallery space showing rotating local exhibits. ✉*356 Commercial St., East End* ☎*508/487–7094* ⊕*www.ptownlib. com* ✉*Free* 🕑*Mon. and Fri. 10–5, Tues. and Thurs. noon–8, Wed. 10–8, Sat. 10–2, Sun. 1–5.*

**NEED A BREAK?**

**Wired Puppy** ( ✉*379 Commercial St., East End* ☎*508/487–0017*) is a slick but comfy Internet café with hardwood floors and mod seating. They serve outstanding organic coffees and teas—the knowledgeable staff can help you choose just the right beverage—plus a nice variety of cookies, brownies, and treats. There's free Wi-Fi if you bring your own laptop, or you can borrow a laptop here.

Nearby, the **Purple Feather Dessert Cafe** ( ✉*334 Commercial St., East End* ☎*508/487–9100*) comes in handy when you're craving superb handmade chocolates, decadent cakes, and house-made gelato and sorbets.

❺ To see or hear the work of up-and-coming artists, visit the gallery or attend a reading at the **Fine Arts Work Center** *(FAWC)*. A nonprofit organization founded in 1968, the FAWC sponsors 10 writers and 10 artists from October through May each year, providing them with a place to live and work, a stipend, and access to artists and teachers. A summer program has open-enrollment workshops in both writing and the visual arts. The buildings in the complex around the center, which it owns, were formerly part of Day's Lumber Yard Studios, built above a lumberyard by a patron of the arts to provide poor artists with cheap

5

accommodations. Robert Motherwell, Hans Hoffmann, and Helen Frankenthaler have been among the studios' roster of residents over the years. ⊠*24 Pearl St., East End* ☎*508/487–9960* ⊕*www.fawc. org* ☞*Free, $5 for events and readings* ⊙*Weekdays 9–5; events are usually held in evening.*

**6** The **town hall** was used by the Provincetown Art Association as its first exhibit space. Paintings donated to the town over the years—including Provincetown scenes by Charles Hawthorne and WPA–era murals by Ross Moffett—are still displayed here. ⊠*260 Commercial St., Downtown Center* ☎*508/487–7000* ⊙*Weekdays 8–5.*

**7** In a little park behind the town hall is the **Mayflower Compact Plaque** (⊠*Bradford St., Downtown Center*), carved in bas-relief by sculptor Cyrus Dalin and depicting the historic signing.

**8** An **octagonal house** (⊠*74 Commercial St., West End*) built in 1850 is an interesting piece of Provincetown architecture in the West End. The house is not open to the public.

**9** The oldest building in town, dating from 1746, is the small Cape-style **Seth Nickerson House** (⊠*72 Commercial St., West End*), which is still a private home. It was built by a ship's carpenter, with massive pegged, hand-hewn oak beams and wide-board floors. Modern renovations have somewhat obscured the glimpse into centuries past that it once provided, but it's still impressive.

**10** The bronze **Pilgrim Plaque** (⊠ *West end of Commercial St., Downtown Center*), set into a boulder at the center of a little park, commemorates the first footfall of the Pilgrims onto Cape soil—Provincetown's humble equivalent to Plymouth Rock.

**11** In the **Provincetown Inn** (⊠*1 Commercial St., West End* ☎*508/487–9500*) you can see a series of 19 murals, painted in the 1930s from old postcards, depicting life in the 19th-century town. The inn still operates as a hotel; the murals are in the lobby and hallways.

## WHERE TO EAT

**$–$$$**  ✕ **Bayside Betsy's.** Named for the feisty chef and co-owner, this campy,
AMERICAN   infectiously fun bar-and-grill serves a mix of homespun American favorites and slightly more contemporary dishes, such as lobster tortellini, seafood wontons with orange-horseradish sauce, and classic steamed mussels in white wine with garlic, shallots, and tomatoes. Nightly specials often reflect the luck of local fishermen. You might try pan-seared scallops with chorizo tossed with fettuccine. You can expect reliable food for breakfast (try the banana-walnut pancakes), lunch, and dinner year-round, but the real draws are the colorful people-watching, good-natured attitude, and nice views of Provincetown Harbor. ⊠*177 Commercial St.* ☎*508/487–6566* ⊕*www.baysidebetsys.com* ▤*AE, D, MC, V* ⊙*Closed Mon.–Wed. Nov.–May.*

**$$$–$$$$**  ✕ **Bistro at Crowne Pointe.** Set inside the snazzy Crowne Pointe Inn, this
Fodor'sChoice   intimate, casually handsome restaurant occupies the parlor and sunroom
★   of a grand sea captain's mansion. The kitchen serves finely crafted, healthful, modern American food, such as wakame-crusted tuna sashimi with a
AMERICAN

spicy blood orange–mango-wasabi drizzle, followed by smoky-seared duck breast with sauteed-carrot coulis and Asian vegetables, and prosciutto-wrapped pork tenderloin with a thyme-caramelized onion-wild mushroom sauce. A lighter menu offers veggie burgers, lobster rolls, and similarly casual fare for a fraction of the price. ✉82 Bradford St. ☎508/487-2365 ⊕www.provincetown-restaurant.com ⌨Reservations essential ▭AE, D, MC, V. ☾No lunch

---

**GHOST SHIP**

During the American Revolution, Provincetown Harbor was controlled by the British, who used it as a port from which to sail to Boston and launch attacks on colonial and French vessels. In November 1778, the 64-gun British frigate *Somerset* ran aground and was wrecked off Provincetown's Race Point. Every 60 years or so, the shifting sands uncover its remains.

---

**$–$$$**
**SEAFOOD**

✕**Bubala's by the Bay.** Look for the bright yellow building adorned on top with campy carved birds. The kitchen rarely stops, serving breakfast, lunch, and dinner; it's known for seafood bought directly off local boats, although the food here is less impressive than the views and the festive setting, with outdoor seats overlooking Commercial Street and indoor seating facing the bay. Lobster salad, seafood cassoulet with white beans and chorizo, and grilled venison rack with currant, sage, and shiitake demi-glace are reliable options. The wine list is priced practically at retail, and the U-shape bar picks up into the evening. It's one of the few Commercial Street restaurants with off-street parking. ✉183 Commercial St. ☎508/487-0773 ⊕www.bubalas.com ▭AE, D, MC, V ☾Closed late Oct.–late Apr.

**$$$–$$$$**
**★**
**AMERICAN**

✕**Cafe Edwige.** A longtime East End restaurant set rather discreetly up a flight of stairs, Cafe Edwige consists of an intimate dining room with varnished-wood floors and dim lighting, and a casual side patio with tile tables and billowing drapes. Start things off at the bar with one of their signature white-ginger cosmos, and perhaps the tuna-avocado tartare appetizer with sweet-chili vinaigrette and wasabi cream, which has long been a staple here. Popular entrées from the contemporary menu include the Brazilian seafood *moqueca* (halibut, shrimp, scallops, coconut milk, and palm oil simmered with basmati rice); and the grilled New Zealand rack of lamb with a feta-risotto-spinach cake, haricot vert, and a lamb demi-glace. For breakfast, consider the omelet with portobello mushrooms and Brie. ✉333 Commercial St. ☎508/487-4020 ▭MC, V ☾Closed Oct.–Apr., Mon.–Thurs. May–mid-June, and Wed.

**¢–$**
**CARIBBEAN**

✕**Caribbean Corner Café.** A simply, family-run spot in the heart of the Commercial Street retail and dining action, this cheerful café produces a staggering variety of Caribbean as well as Latin American treats. Prices are reasonable, the service is wonderfully friendly, and the crowd is a good mix of visitors and locals. The kitchen uses mostly natural and organic ingredients—start with *bollitos* (steamed cornmeal rolls with a homemade tomato-pepper-herb sauce) or a Venezuelan salad topped with fresh tuna. Popular mains include boneless pork stew with a rich and a slightly spicy Caribbean sauce and plantains, or curried chicken. The *quesillo* rum flan makes for a great ending. ✉206–208 Commercial St. ☎508/487-2023 ⊕www.caluvesu.com ▭MC, V.

$$ ✕**Central House Bar and Grille.** The dining component at the action-
AMERICAN  packed Crown & Anchor gay resort, Central House serves commend-
able contemporary American fare, such as pomegranate-honey-glazed
chicken with grilled pineapple relish; and pan-roasted scallops with
grits, buttered baby carrots, and snap-pea salad. Several lighter options
are offered, too, including three kinds of mac-and-cheese. For break-
fast, you might try the lobster Benedict or French toast topped with
Vermont syrup, sweet butter, and powdered sugar. Apart from the good
food, this is one of the best venues in town for socializing and observing
the assorted merry-makers who frequent the resort's many bars. Diners
get preferred seating at the resort's cabaret shows. ⊠247 Commercial
St. ☎508/487–1430 ⊕www.onlyatthecrown.com ▤AE, D, MC, V
⊘Closed Wed. and Thurs. off-season.

¢–$ ✕**Chach.** A cute, airy, and contemporary clapboard restaurant out on
CAFE  Shank Painter Road toward the beach, Chach is a big hit with locals.
It's a sweet little place serving creative omelets (try one with green chili,
cheddar, and sour cream), vanilla custard French toast with Vermont
maple syrup, fried chicken salad with buttermilk dressing, and falafel
sandwiches with cucumber-mint sauce. Fresh ingredients and artful
presentation make this a winner. Closing time is 3 PM. ⊠73 Shank
Painter Rd. ☎508/487–1530 ▤MC, V ⊘No dinner.

$$–$$$$ ✕**Ciro & Sal's.** Tucked inside a cozy house down an alley behind Com-
ITALIAN  mercial Street, this longtime local favorite offers a low-key, romantic
alternative to some of the town's busier restaurants. The most memorable tables are inside a cozy brick wine cellar. The rest fill a pair of art-
filled dining rooms; one is warmed by a huge fireplace. You can also relax
with a cocktail on the garden patio. The restaurant is justly known for its
fresh pastas and bountiful antipasto selections. Favorite entrées include
calamari sautéed with anchovies, lemon, garlic, and cream; and chicken
livers sautéed with prosciutto, marsala wine, and sage. Hours vary during the off-season—call ahead. ⊠4 Kiley Ct. ☎508/487–6444 ⊕www.
ciroandsals.com ▤AE, D, MC, V ⊘Closed Jan. and Wed. No lunch.

¢–$$ ✕**Clem & Ursie's.** It's worth the short drive or long walk from downtown
Fodor'sChoice  to sample the tantalizing seafood prepared at this colorful café, grocery
★  market, cocktail bar, and bakery. The mammoth menu touches on just
SEAFOOD  about every kind of food from the ocean: tuna steaks, crab claws, squid
stew, Japanese baby octopus salad, hot lobster rolls, lobster scampi.
The Buffalo shrimp are addictive, and be sure to try the Portuguese
clam pie. A nice range of nonfishy items is offered, too, from pulled-
pork barbecue to bacon cheeseburgers—plus great desserts like pista-
chio cake and stuffed ice-cream sandwiches dipped in chocolate. You
order and pay at the counter and grab a seat inside the decidedly casual
dining room; they bring your chow out to you. The market has the best
selection of cheeses in town plus countless seafood items, oils and vin-
egars, and gourmet goods. ⊠85 Shank Painter Rd. ☎508/487–2333
▤MC, V ⊘Closed mid-Nov.–mid-Apr.

$$–$$$$ ✕**Devon's.** This unassuming, tiny white cottage—with a dining room
Fodor'sChoice  that seats just 42 lucky patrons—serves some of the best food in town.
★  Specialties from the oft-changing menu include pan-seared halibut with
AMERICAN  caramelized orange glaze, black rice, and sautéed beet greens; and free-

# Where to Eat in Provincetown

EAST END

TO
ROUTE 6A →

Provincetown
◆ Art Association
and Museum

Provincetown Harbor

| | 10 miles |
| 0 | 10 kilometers |

Howland

Harry Kemp Way

Priscilla Alden

Brewster

Bradford St.

Pearl

Law

Cemetery

Conwell

Race Point Rd.

TO
RACE POINT
BEACH

Public
Library

Center

Johnson

◆ Pilgrim
Monument

Standish

Alden

MacMillan
Wharf

Duck
Pond

Jerome Rd.

Winslow

Ryder

Town
Hall

Gosnold

Masonic

Prince

Carver

Court

Winthrop

Central

Pleasant

Shank Painter Rd.

Shank
Painter Pond

Franklin

Nickerson

Creek Rd.

Blueberry

Tremont St.

W. Vine

Soper

Seth Nickerson
House

◆ Octagonal
House

Commercial St.

WEST
END

Commercial St.

TO
RACE POINT
LIGHT

TO
LONG POINT
LIGHT

Province Lands Rd.

range seared duck with a Syrah reduction, red-onion marmalade, and couscous primavera. Another plus is their great little wine list. Be sure to save some room for knockout dessert selections like blackberry mousse over ginger-lemon polenta cake with wildberry coulis. Devon's also serves up a terrific breakfast each day until 1 PM, where you might sample truffle cheese–and–baby spinach omelets with rosemary home fries. Hours are limited in May and October; it's best to phone ahead. ⊠ *401½ Commercial St.* ☎ *508/487–4773* ⊕ *www.devons.org* ⚓ *Reservations essential* ▤ *MC, V* ⊗ *Closed Wed. and Nov.–Apr.*

**$–$$$**
**★**
ECLECTIC

✗ **Fanizzi's by the Sea.** A dependable, year-round East Ender that sits directly over the bay and offers fine water views, Fanizzi's presents a varied menu strong on well-prepared comfort food (including a memorable chicken potpie and juicy burgers), but often with a few creative twists. The baked cod is served with a tangy coating of almonds and mustard, and the hearty roasted half chicken is glazed with fresh garlic, lemon juice, rosemary, and thyme. You can order burgers and substantive dinner salads, including a fine salmon Caesar. The dining room, lined with large windows, is softly lighted and casual. Sunday brunch is a favorite with locals. ⊠ *539 Commercial St.* ☎ *508/487–1964* ⊕ *www.fanizzisrestaurant.com* ▤ *AE, D, DC, MC, V.*

**¢–$$**
**★**
ECLECTIC

✗ **Frappo 66.** Adjoining the Provincetown Art House Theatre and Theatre Cinema Café, this eatery presents fresh and imaginative contemporary American fare in a low-cost, no-hassle setting—you can explore the prepared foods on display at the counter or order à la carte from a menu, mixing and matching main courses and sides as you wish, and then choose your own seat in the sunny dining room or on the patio overlooking Commercial Street (or order to go). Service is quick, and prices are low. The menu changes daily but might feature pork vindaloo, tomato-and-mint couscous, tuna-avocado tartare, fried oysters over baby spinach, sweet-pea-falafel sandwiches, warm flourless chocolate torte—the menu is seemingly endless. ⊠ *214 Commercial St.* ☎ *508/487–9066* ⊕ *www.frappo66.com* ▤ *MC, V.*

**$$$–$$$$**
**★**
MEDITERRANEAN

✗ **Front Street.** Front Street is very good and quite romantic, if not as revered by locals as it used to be (in part because several noteworthy competitors have opened in recent years). Here classic Italian cooking is linked to offerings from Greece, southern France, and even North Africa. There's a nightly char-grilled fish special: match salmon, halibut, or tuna with a Latin, Berber, or Cajun spice rub; lemon-caper butter; or a ginger-soy-wasabi glaze. Other stellar dishes include sage-and-butternut risotto with crisped baby spinach, and truffled wild-mushroom bisque. The wine list is also a winner. Finish things off with coffee-toffee pie. ⊠ *230 Commercial St.* ☎ *508/487–9715* ⊕ *www.frontstreetrestaurant. com* ⚓ *Reservations essential* ▤ *AE, D, MC, V* ⊗ *Closed Jan.–mid-May and Mon. and Tues. No lunch.*

**$–$$$**
SEAFOOD

✗ **Lobster Pot.** Provincetown's Lobster Pot is fit to do battle with all the lobster shanties anywhere (and everywhere) else on the Cape—it's often jammed with tourists, but that's truly a reflection of the generally high quality. The hardworking kitchen turns out classic New England cooking: lobsters, generous and filling seafood platters (try the seafood Pico with a half lobster, shrimp, littlenecks, mussels, calamari, and fish over pasta with tomatoes, rose wine, onions, and garlic), and some of the best chowder around. The Asian bouillabaisse is another favorite. The upstairs deck overlooks the comings and goings of the harbor and is a great spot for lunch. There's also a take-out lobster market and bakery on the premises. You'll have to wait in line, but you'll be in the center of town—an ideal place for people-watching. ⊠ *321 Commercial St.* ☎ *508/487–0842* ⊕ *www.ptownlobsterpot.com* ⌕ *Reservations not accepted* ▤ *AE, D, DC, MC, V* ⊘ *Closed Jan.*

$$–$$$
★
LATIN-
AMERICAN

✕ **Lorraine's.** In a cozy cottage toward the West End, Lorraine's has an intimate feel, but the nouvelle Latin American–inspired menu is as good as ever. An appetizer of blackened seafood tostadas with black bean–and-corn relish packs a punch, and the tender, slow-cooked pork carnitas are a revelation. Also wonderful is a mesquite-grilled rack of lamb with roasted-garlic chipotle demi-glace. The bar draws a loyal, lively crowd and is famous for its long list of premium tequilas. A tantalizing brunch is served in summer—consider the chorizo with scrambled eggs, tortillas, and beans. ⊠ *133 Commercial St.* ☎ *508/487–6074* ▤ *MC, V* ⊘ *Closed Mon.–Wed. Nov.–Mar. No lunch.*

$$–$$$
Fodor's Choice
★
AMERICAN

✕ **The Mews.** This perennial favorite with magnificent harbor views focuses on seafood and grilled meats with a cross-cultural flair. Some popular entrées include roasted vegetable and polenta lasagna with a tomato-olive sauce, and Vietnamese shaking beef wok sautéed with scallions and red onions and a lime–black pepper dipping sauce. A piano bar upstairs serves lunch (weekdays in summer) and dinner from a light, less expensive café menu (burgers, lobster dumplings in miso). The view of the bay from the bar is nearly perfect, and the gentle lighting makes this a romantic spot to have a drink. Brunch is also served daily in season. The restaurant claims its vodka bar is New England's largest, with some 230 varieties. ⊠ *429 Commercial St.* ☎ *508/487–1500* ⊕ *www.mews.com* ▤ *AE, D, DC, MC, V* ⊘ *Closed Jan. No lunch weekdays off-season or Sat. mid-Oct.–late May.*

$$–$$$
ECLECTIC

✕ **Napi's.** A steady favorite for its lively ambience and dependable Mediterranean fare, Napi's presents a long and varied menu. The food and the interior share a penchant for unusual, striking juxtapositions—a classical sculpture in front of an abstract canvas, for instance. On the gustatory front, look for sharp combinations such as Thai chicken and shrimp, cod amandine, and steak tenderloin topped with Brie. Asparagus ravioli is just one of several very nice vegetarian dishes. ⊠ *7 Freeman St.* ☎ *508/487–1145* ⊕ *www.napis-restaurant.com* ▤ *AE, D, DC, MC, V* ⊘ *No lunch May–Sept.*

¢
CAFE

✕ **The Outer Crepe.** In the same cute spot that held the much-loved Tofu-A-Go-Go, this festive, playfully named creperie has fast earned kudos for its delicious and affordable savory and sweet creations, which are served from 9 to 8 daily. Morning highlights include the fried-egg-and-cheddar breakfast sandwiches. Later you might consider the Frenchie crepe (with black-forest ham, Gruyère, and Dijon mustard), or the sweet Strawlala crepe, packed with fresh strawberries and rich Nutella spread. There's a casual dining area upstairs and more seating out on a front deck with great views of passersby along Commercial Street. ⊠ *336 Commercial St.* ☎ *508/487–6237* ⊕ *www.theoutercrepe.com* ▤ *No credit cards.* ⊘ *No dinner.*

5

**$–$$$**
AMERICAN

✗**Patio American Grill.** One of Provincetown's favorite see-and-be-seen spots for colorful cocktails (guava mojitos, mixed-berry caipirinhas), this hip restaurant in the center of town comprises a huge shaded patio overlooking Commercial Street, plus a more intimate indoor lounge and dining area. Although the drinks pack plenty of punch, don't overlook chef Todd Schiller's top-notch seafood-intensive cuisine, such as yellow-fin tartar with a lime vinaigrette, ginger-sesame lobster stir-fried with fresh veggies over jasmine rice, or the jalapeño-marinated hanger steak. A late-night bar menu is offered on weekends, and the Patio serves a popular weekend brunch. ⊠*328 Commercial St.* ☎*508/487–4003* ⊕*www.ptownpatio.com* ⊟*AE, MC, V.*

**$–$$$**
AMERICAN

✗**Post Office Cafe.** A dapper yet casual bistro beneath Provincetown's favorite cabaret bar, the Post Office serves food most nights until 1 AM, making it one of the area's best options for late-night snacking. The kitchen turns out a mix of substantial but straightforward American entrées, such as scallops Alfredo, along with lighter pub favorites. Sandwiches are a specialty; consider the grilled yellowfin tuna and greens on focaccia, or the grilled portobello mushroom with artichokes, sun-dried tomatoes, roasted red peppers, feta cheese, and mixed greens on a pita. The place becomes increasingly festive—even a little raucous—the later it gets. ⊠*303 Commercial St.* ☎*508/487–3892* ⊟*AE, D, MC, V.*

**¢–$**
PORTUGUESE

✗**Provincetown Portuguese Bakery.** This town standby makes fresh Portuguese breads and pastries and serves breakfast and lunch all day from March to October. Although it may be difficult to choose among the sweet splendor, favorite pastries include *malassadas*, a sweet fried dough, lemon custard, and the more unusual *trutas*, with rich, sweet potato filling. It's open until 11 PM in summer. ⊠*299 Commercial St.* ☎*508/487–1803* ⊟*No credit cards* ⊘*Closed Nov.–Feb. No dinner.*

**$$$–$$$$**
AMERICAN

✗**Red Inn.** Inside the striking red house on P'town's West End that's also an enchanting B&B, the Red Inn is perhaps even better known as one of the Outer Cape's most romantic dining destinations—the views are simply stunning. The remarkable setting aside, the inventive contemporary fare as well as the service can be hit-or-miss, especially given the lofty prices. You might start off with the Kobe beef mini-burgers seared rare with rémoulade sauce before moving on to chili-rubbed pork chops with a tomatillo salsa. Breakfast and lunch are also served. ⊠*15 Commercial St.* ☎*508/487–7334* ⊕*www.the-redinn.com* ⊟*AE, MC, V.*

**$$–$$$$**
★
AMERICAN

✗**Ross' Grill.** Likening itself to a French bistro with American tastes, the kitchen here is modest but busy, preparing everything from scratch, including its signature hand-cut, double-dipped french fries. Local fish and shellfish dominate the menu; a favorite is the sautéed local sea scallops with leeks, garlic, and pear tomatoes over linguine. Portions are generous—you'll get eight meaty racks of baby New Zealand lamb with an herb crust—and prices are reasonable. Choose from 75 wines by the glass. The location is grand: up on the 2nd floor of the Whaler's Wharf complex, views of Provincetown Harbor are unlimited. It's a popular place, so expect a wait. ⊠*237 Commercial St.* ☎*508/487–8878* ⊕*www.rossgrilltown.com* ⊟*AE, MC, V* ⊘ *No lunch Mon. and Thurs. Closed Tues., Wed., and Jan.–mid-Apr.*

¢ ✕**Spiritus.** The local bars close at 1 AM, at which point this pizza joint–
PIZZA coffee stand becomes the town's epicenter. It's the ultimate place to see
and be seen, pizza slice in hand and witty banter at the ready. In the
morning, the same counter serves restorative coffee and croissants as well
as Häagen-Dazs ice cream. ✉*190 Commercial St.* ☎*508/487–2808*
⊕*www.spirituspizza.com* ▤*No credit cards* ⊘*Closed Nov.–Apr.*

¢–$$ ✕**Thai Aroi Restaurant.** Bringing a much-needed dose of Asian cook-
THAI ing to the Outer Cape, this cozy eatery inside the shaggy Gifford
House Inn serves reasonably authentic, well-seasoned fare. You might
start with a salad of spicy minced chicken with fresh ginger, lime,
and roasted peanuts, or the fried crab rolls. Excellent main dishes
include sweet-and-sour squid with stir-fried pineapple and veggies,
basil fried rice with tofu and vegetables, salmon pad thai, and boneless
duck with tamarind sauce. There's also sushi available. ✉*9 Carver St.*
☎*508/487–0889* ▤*MC, V.*

$ ✕**Victor's.** This modern, light-filled restaurant on the western end of
AMERICAN Bradford Street became an instant hit during its first season in 2008,
thanks to chef Mike Fennelly's affordable, well-prepared small plates
and a slew of colorful cocktails (consider the Bellini fling, with cham-
pagne, strawberry puree, and strawberry schnapps). Among the deftly
prepared nibbles, be sure to try the baked oysters with pancetta and
Korean barbecue sauce, the seafood cakes with corn salsa and guaca-
mole, and the braised short ribs with quinoa, tomatoes, and a sweet
but savory port sauce. Although lunch isn't served in the main din-
ing room (except for brunch on weekends), throughout the day you
can pick up panini sandwiches, ice cream, and other light fare from a
"to go" window. ✉*175 Bradford St. Ext.* ☎*508/487–1777* ⊕*www.
victorsptown.com* ▤*AE, MC, V.* ⊘*No lunch.*

**WHERE TO STAY**

$–$$ ⌂**Ampersand Guesthouse.** Helpful, low-key owners Robert Vetrick and
Ken Janson (the latter an architect) run this peaceful West End inn that
feels far from the din of Commercial Street but is actually just a short
walk away. This natty mid-19th-century Greek Revival guesthouse contains nine eclectically furnished rooms, many with high-pitched ceilings,
fireplaces, and tall windows—furnishings tend toward simple, understated, and elegant. For more seclusion, book the studio apartment in
the neighboring carriage house, which also has a kitchen. Guests relax
in the leafy yard with pretty gardens, or out on the sundeck on the 2nd
floor, with views of the harbor a couple of blocks away. Robert bakes
fresh muffins each morning as part of the continental breakfast, which
is served before a fireplace on cooler days. **Pros:** peaceful and charming
West End location; stylish and well-chosen decor; great value. **Cons:** have
to walk a bit to reach East End businesses; some rooms smallish. ✉*6
Cottage St., West End* ☎*508/487–0959* ⊕*www.ampersandguesthouse.
com* ↩*9 rooms, 1 apartment* ⌂*In-room: kitchen (some), refrigerator
(some), DVD. In-hotel: no elevator* ▤*AE, MC, V* ⚏*CP.*

$$–$$$$ ⌂**Anchor Inn.** Run by the same talented team that operates the West
★ End's Red Inn, this regal, turreted beach house in the heart of Provinc-
etown enjoys a wonderful location just steps from bars, shops, and res-
taurants as well as unobstructed water views from most rooms (rooms

without water views cost a fraction of the price). White-picket porches and balconies envelope the inn's dapper shingle exterior. You won't find frill and excess here—the airy rooms are done in a palette of whites and tans, with tasteful wicker furniture and, in many cases, four-poster beds and fireplaces. Four cottage units have private entrances, and the three most romantic accommodations occupy the turret. With a spacious lobby and professional staff, the Anchor feels more like a small luxury hotel than a typical Provincetown guesthouse, but an air of informality keeps the vibe relaxed and fun. There's a substantial continental-breakfast buffet in the morning. **Pros:** unobstructed water views from most rooms; right in center of P'town action; rooms have sleek and luxurious style. **Cons:** among the highest rates in town; significant minimum-stay requirements in summer; busy location. ⊠*175 Commercial St., west of Downtown Center* ☎*508/487–0432 or 800/858–2657* ⊕*www.anchorinnbeachhouse.com* ➘*25 rooms* ♿*In-room: refrigerator, VCR. In-hotel: no elevator* ▭*MC, V* ⧉*CP.*

$$$–$$$$    🏨**Benchmark Inn & Central.** Made up of two separate buildings on a quiet, narrow street just a block from downtown, this is an inn of simple, refined luxury. Rooms are painted in soothing neutral tones, floors are bare wood, and fresh flowers are placed atop every stainless-steel wet bar; the bathrooms have marble tile and hair dryers. Most rooms have private entrances and fireplaces; some have skylights and private balconies with rooftop and water views. When you're ready to turn in, indulge in the nightly turndown service. There are also three very large and cushy penthouse suites. The management is environmentally conscious, using mostly "green" products and practices. **Pros:** large and in some cases huge rooms; immaculate and luxurious; an environmentally conscious property. **Cons:** among the highest rates in town; water views are limited or nonexistent from many rooms; significant minimum-stay requirements in summer. ⊠*6 and 8 Dyer St.* ☎*508/487–7440 or 888/487–7440* 🖷*508/487–3446* ⊕*www.benchmarkinn.com* ➘*11 rooms, 3 suites* ♿*In-room: refrigerator, DVD, Wi-Fi. In-hotel: pool, concierge, no elevator, laundry service, airport shuttle* ▭*AE, MC, V* ☾*Closed Jan.–late Feb.*

$$$–$$$$    🏨**Brass Key.** One of the Cape's most luxurious small resorts, this
Fodor's Choice    meticulously kept year-round getaway was purchased by the talented
★    owners of the Crowne Pointe Inn in 2008 and has undergone extensive improvements, including the addition of spa treatment rooms, an elegant outdoor (covered) wedding space, and a hip martini bar. The resort comprises a beautifully restored main house—originally an 1828 sea captain's home—and several other carefully groomed buildings and cottages. Rooms mix antiques with such modern amenities as Bose stereos and TV–DVDs (loaner laptops and iPod docks are also available). Deluxe rooms come with gas fireplaces and whirlpool baths or French doors opening onto wrought-iron balconies. A widow's-walk sundeck has a panoramic view of Cape Cod Bay. Complimentary cocktails are served in the courtyard; in winter, wine is served before a roaring fire in the common room. As is true of many of Provincetown's smaller hotels, the Brass Key draws a largely gay clientele, especially in summer, but the owners and staff make everyone feel welcome and pampered. **Pros:**

ultraposh rooms; beautiful and secluded grounds; pool on-site. **Cons:** among the highest rates in town; rooms close to Bradford Street can get a bit of noise; significant minimum-stay requirements in summer. ⊠67 *Bradford St.* ☎508/487–9005 *or 800/842–9858* 📠508/487–9020 ⊕*www.brasskey.com* ➥42 rooms ♻In-room: safe, DVD, Wi-Fi. In-hotel: pool, no elevator, no kids under 16 ⊟AE, D, MC, V ⭕CP.

**$–$$** ⬚**Christopher's by the Bay.** The rooms in this elegant but reasonably
**Fodor's Choice** priced art-inspired inn are named after the greats—Rembrandt,
★ Picasso, Monet, Van Gogh—and are warmly appointed with brass beds and rich fabrics. Several of these tall-windowed rooms have partial views of the bay, and all receive plenty of light. The building is a graceful old Victorian surrounded by carefully maintained gardens and brick patios. Rooms on the upper floors are compact and share bathrooms, but they're also very low-priced. Set back from the bustle, it's just a quick walk from the center of town. Helpful owners Jim Rizzo and Dave McGlothlin often throw guest barbecues on Sunday. **Pros:** excellent value; steps from East End shopping and dining; service is extremely friendly and professional. **Cons:** least expensive rooms share a bath; some units are very cozy; 3rd-floor rooms are a climb. ⊠8 *Johnson St., east of Downtown Center* ☎508/487–9263 ☎877/487–9263 ⊕*www.christophersbythebay.com* ➥10 rooms, 5 *with bath* ♻In-room: Wi-Fi, refrigerator, VCR. In-hotel: no elevator, some pets allowed (fee) ⊟AE, MC, V ⭕BP.

**$$$–$$$$** ⬚**Crown & Anchor.** If you're looking to eat, sleep, and live amid the pulsing entertainment center of Provincetown, this is the place. Upstairs from the daily clamor of drag shows and discos are 18 rooms handsomely adorned with Oriental rugs and deep cranberry hues. Deluxe rooms have two-person whirlpool tubs, fireplaces, and private balconies facing Provincetown Harbor; all rooms have the choice of a king or two full-size beds. In addition, two rooms are fully ADA compliant. One drawback, however, is that you can hear the din and vibration of music and conversation downstairs in the bars and discos until about midnight or 1 AM on many evenings. Complimentary continental breakfast is served, but why not take advantage of the choice room service and simply stay in bed? There's a dependable restaurant, Central House, as well. A highly professional staff with a great attitude holds everything together. **Pros:** many bars and dining options on-site; in heart of central P'town retail and entertainment district; some rooms have harbor views. **Cons:** noise from bars and clubs carries to many rooms; not a good choice if you have kids; contemporary vibe lacks historic quaintness of some older properties. ⊠247 *Commercial St.* ☎508/487–1430 📠508/487–3237 ⊕*www.onlyatthecrown.com* ➥18 rooms ♻In-room: refrigerator, kitchen (some), VCR (some), Wi-Fi. In-hotel: restaurants, bars, pool, beachfront, no elevator ⊟AE, D, MC, V ⭕CP.

**$$$–$$$$** ⬚**Crowne Pointe Historic Inn and Spa.** Created meticulously from six dif-
**Fodor's Choice** ferent buildings, this inn has not left a single detail unattended. Own-
★ ers Tom Walter and David Sanford skillfully mix luxury and comfort. Period furniture and antiques fill the common areas and rooms; a queen-size bed is the smallest you'll find, dressed in 300-thread-count

5

linens, with treats on the pillow for nightly turndown service. Many rooms have fireplaces: in one room, you can view the flames from your bed or the whirlpool tub. Penthouse suites have two floors of living space with a full kitchen, and many rooms have private balconies with water or town views. The grounds are accented with brick pathways, flowers, and trees. Start the day with a full, hot breakfast, then graze on freshly baked treats and wine and cheese in the afternoon—there's also an excellent restaurant, the Bistro at Crowne Pointe. In the handsome, full-service Shui Spa, you might opt for such soothing treatments as Shiatsu massage, craniosacral therapy, or the honey-almond body polish. **Pros:** great on-site amenities such as spa and restaurant; posh and luxurious room decor; professional and well-trained staff. **Cons:** among the highest rates in town; significant minimum-stay requirements in summer; contemporary vibe lacks historic quaintness of some older properties. ⊠*82 Bradford St.* ☎*508/487–6767 or 877/276–9631* ⊟*508/487–5554* ⊕*www.crownepointe.com* ⟳*37 rooms, 3 suites* ⚷*In-room: kitchen (some), refrigerator, DVD, Ethernet, Wi-Fi (some). In-hotel: pool, spa, concierge, no elevator, laundry service, public Wi-Fi, airport shuttle* ⊟*AE, D, MC, V* ⏏*BP.*

**$$–$$$**
★    ▦ **1807 House.** This weathered, craggy old house that dates to 1783 (it was moved to this spot in 1807, hence the name) doesn't look like much more than a cottage from the quiet stretch of Commercial Street it faces, but behind the facade you'll find a beautifully kept inn with cozy, low-ceilinged rooms. Several tastefully furnished and very private apartments and studios are in back. The dramatic Red Room, overlooking Provincetown Bay, contains a hulking four-poster mahogany bed, and the Artist's Studio, perhaps the most romantic unit, occupies a 2nd-floor perch with a balcony affording water views; French doors lead into this light-flooded room with a high cathedral ceiling. This is one of the West End's little treasures—and a good value to boot. **Pros:** charming West End location; feels secluded and private; elegantly furnished. **Cons:** long walk from East End businesses; sleepy vibe not ideal for social butterflies; kitchens only in some units. ⊠*54 Commercial St., West End* ☎*508/487–2173 or 888/522–1807* ⊕*www.1807house.com* ⟳*3 rooms, 1 suite, 4 apartments* ⚷*In-room: kitchen (some), refrigerator, VCR, Wi-Fi. In-hotel: no elevator* ⊟*AE, MC, V* ⏏*CP.*

**$–$$$**    ▦ **Fairbanks Inn.** This meticulously restored colonial inn a block from Commercial Street includes the 1776 main house and auxiliary buildings. Guest rooms have four-poster or canopy beds, Oriental rugs on wide-board floors, and antique furnishings; some have fireplaces or kitchens. Many original touches remain here, from the 18th-century wallpaper to artifacts from the inn's first residents. The baths are on the small side, but they help preserve the colonial integrity of the home. The garden and the wicker-filled sunporch are good places for afternoon cocktails or breakfast—which you can also enjoy inside before the warm glow of the fireplace on cold days. **Pros:** central location steps from shops and restaurants; nice variety of room sizes and configurations, rich with historic character. **Cons:** rooms close to Bradford Street can get a bit of noise. ⊠*90 Bradford St.* ☎*508/487–0386 or 800/324–7265* ⊕*www.fairbanksinn.com* ⟳*13 rooms, 1 efficiency* ⚷*In-room:*

# Where to Stay in Provincetown

| | |
|---|---|
| Ampersand Guesthouse | **17** |
| Anchor Inn | **14** |
| Benchmark Inn & Central | **4** |
| Brass Key | **13** |
| Christopher's by the Bay | **8** |

| | |
|---|---|
| Crown & Anchor | **10** |
| Crowne Pointe Historic Inn and Spa | **12** |
| 1807 House | **18** |
| Fairbanks Inn | **11** |
| Inn at Cook Street | **2** |
| Moffett House | **9** |

| | |
|---|---|
| Officer's Quarters | **15** |
| Oxford House | **16** |
| Race Point Lighthouse | **20** |
| Red Inn | **19** |
| Seasons | **5** |
| Snug Cottage | **3** |

| | |
|---|---|
| Somerset House Inn | **6** |
| Watermark Inn | **1** |
| White Porch Inn | **7** |

5

*kitchen (some), refrigerator (some), DVD, Wi-Fi. In-hotel: parking (no fee), no elevator* ☰*AE, MC, V* ⦿*CP.*

**$$$** 🛏 **Inn at Cook Street.** In winter 2006, this attractive East End inn just
★ off Bradford Street was sold to a developer who planned to convert it into condos, but Connecticut transplants Lisa Feistel and Doreen Birdsell quickly stepped in, snapped it up, and turned it back into a terrific place to stay. The enthusiastic innkeepers have done an admirable job decorating the 1836 Greek Revival where author Michael Cunningham penned *Home at the End of the World* one winter. The sophisticated rooms have high-thread-count linens, flat-screen TVs, and well-placed reading lights; two have decks, three have fireplaces, and three have private entrances. Continental breakfast includes organic cappuccino, herbal teas, fruit and breads, and a hot entrée such as pancakes or omelets. Guests can relax in a hammock out back amid the fragrant gardens or walk a block to the galleries along Commercial Street. **Pros:** top-notch staff and service; steps from East End shopping and dining; elegant yet unfussy furnishings. **Cons:** rooms close to Bradford Street can get a bit of noise; a bit of a walk from West End businesses; no water views. ⊠*7 Cook St.* ☎*508/487–3894 or 888/266–5655* ⊕*www.innatcookstreet.com* ⮑*5 rooms, 2 suites, 2 cottages* ♿*In-room: kitchen (some), refrigerator, DVD, Wi-Fi. In-hotel: no elevator, no kids under 16* ☰*MC, V* ⦿*BP.*

**¢–$** 🛏 **Moffett House.** This simple, affordable, handsomely refurbished Cape-style B&B lies down a charming, narrow alley that runs between Commercial and Bradford streets. There are 10 cheerfully furnished rooms, most of them with shared baths (some of these have unbelievably low rates), and all have top-notch linens and country quilts, and 20-inch flat-screen TVs; some rooms have pitched ceilings with rustic beams. You are free to use the common kitchen and a computer in the lobby, and may also borrow the inn's Trek mountain bikes at no charge. It's a friendly option that's ideal for budget travelers. **Pros:** great value; right in center of business district yet set back from street; free mountain bikes. **Cons:** most rooms have shared bath; minimal grounds; no optimal views. ⊠*296A Commercial St.* ☎*508/487–6615 or 800/990–8865* ⊕*www.moffetthouse.com* ⮑*10 rooms, 3 with bath* ♿*In-room: refrigerator, DVD, Wi-Fi. In-hotel: bicycles, no elevator* ☰*MC, V* ⦿*CP.*

**$$–$$$** 🛏 **Officer's Quarters.** Built in 1887 for a sea captain, this stately, white, mansard-roof Victorian is only a short walk from the center of town and is across the street from Provincetown Bay. The owners have done a wonderful job adding their own touches while maintaining this B&B's outstanding reputation. Room 3, done in vibrant reds, has a four-poster bed, a gas fireplace, and private access to the garden. Most rooms have water views; some have private decks. **Pros:** handsome 1880s sea captain's home; some pets allowed; great central location. **Cons:** right in center of action; rather intimate with just six rooms so not ideal if you're seeking anonymity; significant minimum-stay requirements in summer. ⊠*164 Commercial St.* ☎*508/487–1850 or 800/400–2278* ⊕*www.princealbertguesthouse.com* ⮑*6 rooms* ♿*In-room: refrigerator, DVD (some), Wi-Fi. In-hotel: no elevator, some pets allowed (fee)* ☰*AE, D, MC, V* ⦿*CP.*

**$$–$$$** ⚏**Oxford House.** Run by the former owners of the outstanding Beacon-
★ light Guesthouse, the Oxford sits in the heart of the West End along
a quiet lane and is decorated in the spirit of a British country house.
Rooms come with linen robes, CD player/radios, phones with voice
mail, and beds that have 480-thread-count linens and fluffy duvets—
rooms on the ground floor have wood-burning fireplaces. You can save
a bundle by booking either the Merton or Hertford rooms, which share
a bath; the Worcester Room has its own private entrance. The evening
wine hour is a great time to mingle with fellow guests. All phone calls
within the continental United States are free. **Pros:** highly professional
and friendly service; peaceful and charming West End setting; beautifully furnished. **Cons:** some rooms share a bath; it's a relatively long
walk to East End businesses; quiet locale may not work if you want to
be in center of action. ⊠ *8 Cottage St.* ☎ *508/487–9103 or 888/456–
9103* ⊕ *www.oxfordguesthouse.com* ⟋ *5 rooms, 3 with bath, 1 suite*
⚲ *In-room: refrigerator, VCR, Wi-Fi. In-hotel: no elevator* ☰ *AE, D,
MC, V* ¦⊙¦ *CP.*

**$$** ⚏**Race Point Lighthouse.** One of the most unusual lodging opportunities
on the Cape, the restored 1840 keeper's house at the stunning Race
Point Lighthouse has three sparsely furnished guest rooms with lace
curtains, braided rugs, and simple wooden chests and tables—pillows
and blankets are provided, but you'll need to bring your own linens,
towels, drinking water, and food. The house does have solar-powered
electricity and central heating. You don't stay here because it's cushy,
but rather to enjoy the seclusion and romance of staying at an authen-
tic, working lighthouse with a pristine beach just outside the window.
Opportunities to see whales, dolphins, and migratory birds abound,
both from the grounds and from the house itself. A gift shop on prem-
ises sells scrimshaw, sweatshirts, ball caps, and other keepsakes. The
maximum stay is four nights. If you're not able to spend the night, keep
in mind that the lighthouse itself is open for tours a few Saturdays per
month from mid-May through mid-October. **Pros:** one of the most
distinctive lodging experiences on Cape Cod; truly secluded setting;
might just see a whale or dolphin swimming outside your window.
**Cons:** very limited amenities; books up fast; extremely isolated. ⊠ *Off
Race Point Rd. at Cape Cod National Seashore* ⚲ *Box 570, North
Truro 02652* ☎ *508/487–9930* ⊕ *www.racepointlighthouse.net* ⟋ *3
rooms* ⚲ *In-room: no phone, refrigerator, no TV* ☰ *No credit cards*
⊘ *Closed mid-Oct.–Apr.*

**$$$–$$$$** ⚏**Red Inn.** A rambling red 1915 house that once was host to Franklin
and Eleanor Roosevelt, this small, luxurious inn has been completely
refurbished after several years of neglect. Most of the airy rooms afford
bay views, and all are fitted with big plush beds with high-thread-count
linens, goose-down comforters, and pillow-top mattresses. Other luxe
amenities include radio–CD players, phones with voice mail, and high-
speed Internet. The Cape Light Room contains a decorative fireplace
with an ornate hand-painted fresco, and the secluded Chauffer's Cot-
tage has a living room with a soaring vaulted ceiling and a sundeck
with far-reaching water views. The restaurant offers some of the best
bay views in town. **Pros:** charmed and peaceful West End setting, closer

5

to national seashore than most P'town accommodations; ultra-posh rooms. **Cons:** among the highest rates in town; far West End location is a long walk from most dining and nightlife; not geared to children. ⊠*15 Commercial St.* ☎*508/487–7334 or 866/473–3466* 🖷*508/487– 5115* ⊕*www.theredinn.com* 🖎*4 rooms, 2 suites, 2 cottages* ♿*In-room: refrigerator, VCR, Ethernet. In-hotel: restaurant, room service, no elevator, parking (no fee), no kids under 18* ☰*AE, MC, V* �†⊙*CP.*

$$ 🖼 **Seasons.** This petite 1860s cream-color Victorian with a Dutch-style gambrel roof is an outstanding value. Owners John Mirthes and Rick Reynolds run a relaxed ship, freely offering guests advice on local restaurants and lending out chairs, towels, and cooler bags for the beach. Rick is a professional chef and prepares exceptional breakfasts replete with filling hot entrées, such as pumpkin pancakes with maple-poached pears, which can render lunch unnecessary. Rooms contain mostly classic Victorian pieces, wallpapers, and fabrics—it's a little old-fashioned, especially compared with all the flashier and more social guesthouses in town, and that's a big reason many guests here come back year after year. Save a hello for sweet old Buddy, the house cat. **Pros:** excellent value; friendly and first-rate staff; easy walk to numerous shops and restaurants. **Cons:** rooms close to Bradford Street can get a bit of noise; a tad frilly. ⊠*160 Bradford St., east of Downtown Center* ☎*508/487– 2283 or 800/563–0113* ⊕*www.provincetownseasons.com* 🖎*5 rooms* ♿*In-room: no phone, refrigerator (some), DVD, Wi-Fi. In-hotel: no elevator* ☰*MC, V* �†⊙*BP.*

$$ 🖼 **Snug Cottage.** Noted for its extensive floral gardens and enviable perch atop one of the larger bluffs in town, this convivial Arts and Crafts–style inn dates to 1825 and is decked in smashing English country antiques and fabrics. The oversize accommodations have distinctly British names (Victoria Suite, Royal Scot); most are full suites with sitting areas, and many have wood-burning fireplaces and private outdoor entrances. The Churchill Suite has 10 big windows overlooking the flowers and bushes outside, and the York Suite has a partial view of Cape Cod Bay. All rooms have phones with voice mail and high-speed Internet, plus clock radios with CD players. Nightly turndown service and plush robes in each room lend a touch of elegance. **Pros:** steps from East End dining and shopping; stunning grounds and gardens; most units are extremely spacious. **Cons:** rooms close to Bradford Street can get a bit of noise; a bit of a walk from West End businesses; the top suites don't come cheaply. ⊠*178 Bradford St., east of Downtown Center* ☎*508/487–1616 or 800/432–2334* 🖷*508/487–5123* ⊕*www.snugcottage.com* 🖎*3 rooms, 5 suites* ♿*In-room: kitchen (some), DVD, Wi-Fi. In-hotel: no elevator, no-smoking rooms* ☰*AE, D, MC, V* �†⊙*BP.*

$$–$$$$ 🖼 **Somerset House Inn.** Competent and helpful owners run this cheer-★ ful property known for its hip, whimsical decor and superb personal service. From the outside, the inn looks like a classic 1830s Provincetown house, but inside it's a cozy den of mod sofas and cool colors. A communal computer is equipped with high-speed wireless, and you'll find reams of magazines throughout the common areas. The sleekly furnished rooms are compact but charming. Some have eclectic

themes—safari, Asia, modern—and all have updated amenities, such as flat-screen TVs, DVD players, and L'Occitaine toiletries. The 3rd-floor units, with pitched ceilings, are especially romantic; some have fireplaces. Somerset House serves one of the better breakfasts in town and also has an extensive afternoon wine-and-cheese social. **Pros:** top-notch service; steps from East End shopping and dining; lots of on-site amenities and perks. **Cons:** the creative room themes may not suit every taste; some units quite small; 3rd-floor rooms require some stair climbing. ⊠ *378 Commercial St., east of Downtown Center* ☏ *508/487–0383 or 800/575–1850* ⊟ *508/487–4237* ⊕ *www.somersethouseinn.com* ⤴ *12 rooms* ☖ *In-room: refrigerator, DVD, Wi-Fi. In-hotel: no elevator* ⊟ *AE, MC, V* ⊙ *BP.*

$$$–$$$$ ⊞ **Watermark Inn.** A modern all-suites inn facing the bay at the very east end of Commercial Street, the Watermark has enormous accommodations with separate living-dining rooms, making it a favorite for longer stays (weekly or daily rates are available in summer; rates are daily the rest of the year). Although these airy suites with tall windows feel more like rental condos than hotel rooms, they do come with fine linens and daily maid service. It's a very private setup, and guests enjoy plenty of independence. Four suites on the top level have private sundecks and panoramic water views; two less expensive ground-floor units overlook a courtyard. **Pros:** close to East End shopping and dining; spacious accommodations are nice for longer stays; great water views. **Cons:** feels more like a condo than a hotel; far East End location is a 10-to-15-minute walk from many businesses; least expensive rooms have no water view. ⊠ *603 Commercial St.* ☏ *508/487–0165* ⊟ *508/487–2383* ⊕ *www.watermark-inn.com* ⤴ *10 suites* ☖ *In-room: kitchen. In-hotel: no elevator* ⊟ *MC, V.*

$$–$$$ ⊞ **White Porch Inn.** Innkeepers Tom Bantle and Tom Shirk took what
★ had been a decrepit, almost dodgy, old-school Provincetown guesthouse and have transformed it into a sterling, light-filled B&B. Seven of the nine rooms, all of which are named for Cape Cod lighthouses, have gas fireplaces, and three have Jacuzzi tubs. White, tan, and chocolate color schemes, bead-board walls, and pedestal stinks in the bathrooms (some of these have radiant-floor heating) impart a crisp, clean modern-beach-house flair; large closets and drawers built in to the bottoms of custom-made beds are welcome amenities. Opt for one of the carriage-house rooms for more seclusion—you can always mingle with your fellow guests and gracious hosts on the inn's eponymous white porch while enjoying selections from the bounteous breakfast buffet. **Pros:** brand new and immaculate; steps from East End shopping and dining; enthusiastic and friendly staff. **Cons:** most rooms without much of a water view; somewhat long walk to West End shopping and businesses; limited grounds. ⊠ *7 Johnson St.* ☏ *508/364–2549 or 866/922–0333* ⊕ *www.whiteporchinn.com* ⤴ *9 rooms* ☖ *In-room: refrigerator (some), DVD, Wi-Fi. In-hotel: no elevator, airport shuttle* ⊟ *MC, V* ⊙ *CP.*

## NIGHTLIFE & THE ARTS

THE ARTS   The annual **Provincetown International Film Festival** ( ☎ *508/487–3456* ⊕ *www.ptownfilmfest.com*) has become so popular that most of the screenings sell out. Aside from a full schedule of independent films, there are guest appearances by such notables as director John Waters, Lily Tomlin, and Christine Vachon. The festival hits town in mid-June.

Established in 2005 as a merger of the Provincetown Repertory Theatre and the Provincetown Theatre Company, the **New Provincetown Players** ( ✉ *Provincetown Theatre, 238 Bradford St., Downtown Center* ☎ *508/487–9793* ⊕ *www.newprovincetownplayers.org*) hosts a wide variety of performances throughout the year, especially during the summer high season, including classic and modern drama as well as works by local authors.

**Whaler's Wharf** ( ✉ *237–241 Commercial St., Downtown Center* ☎ *508/487–4269*) resembles an old European marketplace, with a brick pathway that leads straight to the beach and a rotunda theater alive with street performers and entertainment. The 1st floor of the building holds shops; upstairs are artists' studios and a museum dedicated to the town's history. Across the street at the **Provincetown Art House Theatre** ( ✉ *214 Commercial St., Downtown Center* ☎ *508/487–9222* ⊕ *www.ptownarthouse.com*) moviegoers can view the latest in independent films, classics, and movies you won't find in the usual megaplex. The building, which was completely renovated in 2007, comprises two stages, improved seating, a terrific restaurant (Frappo 66), and a wall with changing art exhibits. Presentations by the local Theatre Go Round ( ⊕ www.theatregoround.com) including campy cabaret shows and generally humorous plays, are held here also.

NIGHTLIFE   **Atlantic House** ( ✉ *4 Masonic Pl., Downtown Center* ☎ *508/487–3821*),
★   the grandfather of the gay nightlife scene, is the only gay bar open year-round. It has several lounge areas and an outdoor patio.

**Boatslip Beach Club** ( ✉ *161 Commercial St., Downtown Center, toward West End* ☎ *508/487–1669*) holds a gay and lesbian late-afternoon tea dance daily in summer and on weekends in spring and fall on the outdoor pool deck. The club has indoor and outdoor dance floors. There's ballroom dancing here, in addition to two-stepping Thursday through Sunday nights.

The **Cape Cod National Seashore** schedules summer evening programs, such as slide shows, sunset beach walks, concerts (local groups, military bands), and sing-alongs, at its **Province Lands Visitor Center** ( ✉ *Race Point Rd., east of U.S. 6* ☎ *508/487–1256*); sunset campfire talks are also held on the beaches in Provincetown.

★   The gay-oriented **Crown & Anchor Complex** ( ✉ *247 Commercial St., Downtown Center* ☎ *508/487–1430*) has plenty of action—perhaps the most in town—with Wave video bar, the Vault leather bar, several stages, and a giant disco called Paramount. Seven nightly shows in summer range from cabaret to comedy.

## CLOSE UP

# Provincetown: America's Gay Summer Playground

America's original gay resort, Provincetown developed as an artists' colony at the turn of the 20th century. In 1899 a young artist and entrepreneur named Charles Hawthorne founded the Cape Cod School of Art. Within 20 years, a half-dozen art schools opened, the Provincetown Art Association staged its first exhibitions, and the Provincetown Players, a small band of modernist theater folk, began to produce plays on a small wharf in the town's East End.

After a year in Provincetown the Players moved to New York City's Greenwich Village, where gay culture was already thriving. This kinship helped spur Provincetown's early flourishing as a gay community. Tourism became a significant revenue source, and local homes began letting rooms to the hundreds of writers, painters, and other creative spirits drawn to the town's thriving arts community.

Over the next few decades, many innovative writers and artists spent time in Provincetown, including several openly gay luminaries such as Truman Capote and Tennessee Williams. The town became identified increasingly for its willingness to flout convention, and it was by the 1960s a haven for anyone whose artistic leaning, political platform, or sexual persuasion was subject to persecution elsewhere in America. This hotbed of counterculture naturally nurtured one of the country's most significant gay communities.

Today Provincetown is as appealing to artists as it is to gay and lesbian—as well as straight—tourists. The awareness brought by the AIDS crisis and, most recently, Massachusetts's becoming the first state to legalize same-sex marriage has turned the town into the most visibly gay vacation community in America.

–by Andrew Collins

**Governor Bradford Restaurant** ( ⊠*312 Commercial St., Downtown Center* ☎*508/487–9618*) is perhaps better known as a sometimes-rowdy pool and dance hall. In the afternoon you can play chess or backgammon at the tables by the window. After 8 PM, the place revs up with live music or a DJ spinning everything from hip-hop to disco.

**Pied Bar** ( ⊠*193A Commercial St., Downtown Center, toward West End* ☎*508/487–1527*) draws hordes of gay men to its post–tea dance gathering at 6:30 every evening in July and August and weekends during the shoulder seasons. Later in the evening, the crowd is mostly (though not exclusively) women. The club has a deck overlooking the harbor, a small dance floor with a good sound system, and two bars.

The **Post Office Cabaret** ( ⊠*303 Commercial St., Downtown Center* ☎*508/487–0006*) has long been a dishy and lively spot for piano cabaret, musical comedy, and drag performances. The upstairs lounge draws some of the top talents in the region, and downstairs an excellent restaurant serves dependable American bistro fare until 1 AM most nights.

The **Squealing Pig** ( ⊠*335 Commercial St., Downtown Center, toward East End* ☎*508/487–5804*) has DJs presenting rock, hip-hop, reggae, and house; they also show late-night movies on Monday. There's never a cover charge, and the kitchen turns out super-tasty bar chow, from burgers to fish-and-chips.

**Vixen** (✉ *336 Commercial St., Downtown Center* ☎ *508/487–6424*), a lively women's club, gets packed with dancers. On most nights, before the dance crowd sets in, there are both national and local women entertainers. Look for live music and comedy. There are also a couple of pool tables in the front room.

### SPORTS & THE OUTDOORS

BEACHES The entire stretch of Commercial Street is backed by the waters of Provincetown Harbor, and most hotels have private beaches. Farther into town there are plenty of places to settle on the sand and take a refreshing dip—just be mindful of the busy boat traffic.

**Herring Cove Beach** is relatively calm and warm for a National Seashore beach, but it's not as pretty as some because its parking lot isn't hidden behind dunes. However, the lot to the right of the bathhouse is a great place to watch the sunset. There's a hot-dog stand, as well as showers and restrooms. Lifeguards are on duty in season. From late June through early September, parking costs $15 per day, or $45 for a yearly pass to all National Seashore beaches.

For a day of fairly private beachcombing and great views, you can walk across the stone jetty at low tide to **Long Point,** a sand spit south of town with two lighthouses and two Civil War bunkers—called Fort Useless and Fort Ridiculous because they were hardly needed. It's a 2-mi walk across soft sand—beware of poison ivy and deer ticks if you stray from the path—or hire a boat at **Flyer's** ( ☎ *508/487–0898 or 800/750–0898* ⊕ *www.flyersrentals.com*) to drop you off and pick you up; the cost is $8 one-way, $12 round-trip.

FodorsChoice  **Race Point Beach** ( ✉ *Race Point Rd., east of U.S. 6*), one of the Cape
★ Cod National Seashore beaches in Provincetown, has a wide swath of sand stretching far off into the distance around the point and Coast Guard station. Behind the beach is pure duneland, and bike trails lead off the parking lot. Because of its position on a point facing north, the beach gets sun all day long (east coast beaches get fullest sun early in the day). Parking is available, there are showers and restrooms, and lifeguards are stationed in season. From late June through early September, parking costs $15 per day, or $45 for a yearly pass good at all National Seashore beaches.

BICYCLING The **Beech Forest bike trail** ( ✉ *Off Race Point Rd., east of U.S. 6*) in the National Seashore offers an especially nice ride through a shady forest to Bennett Pond.

**Gale Force Bikes** ( ✉ *144 Bradford St. Ext.* ☎ *508/487–4849* ⊕ *www. galeforcebikes.com*) stocks a wide variety of bikes for sale and for rent; it's also a good source for parts and repairs. There's also a deli on-site.

The **Province Lands Trail** is a 5¼-mi loop off the Beech Forest parking lot on Race Point Road, with spurs to Herring Cove and Race Point beaches and to Bennett Pond. The paths wind up and down hills amid dunes, marshes, woods, and ponds, affording spectacular views. More than 7 mi of bike trails lace through the dunes, cranberry bogs, and scrub pine of the National Seashore, with many access points, including Herring Cove and Race Point.

**P'town Bikes** ( ⌧ *42 Bradford St., east of Downtown Center* ☎ *508/487–8735* ⊕ *www.ptownbikes.com*) has Trek and Mongoose mountain bikes at good rates, and you can reserve online. The shop also provides free locks and maps.

BOATING &
KAYAKING

*Bay Lady II* **Excursion Schooner** ( ⌧ *MacMillan Wharf, Downtown Center* ☎ *508/487–9308* ⊕ *www.sailcapecod.com*), a beautiful 73-foot sailing vessel, heads out for two-hour cruises three times daily. You're welcome to bring your own spirits and snacks for this scenic and peaceful sail.

**Flyer's Boat Rental** ( ⌧ *131A Commercial St., West End* ☎ *508/487–0898 or 800/750–0898* ⊕ *www.flyersrentals.com*) has kayaks, surf bikes, Sunfish, Hobies, Force 5s, Lightnings, powerboats, and rowboats. Flyer's will also shuttle you to Long Point.

**Venture Athletics Kayak Shop** ( ⌧ *237 Commercial St., Unit 13A, Downtown Center* ☎ *508/487–9442* ⊕ *www.ventureathletics.com*) rents kayaks and equipment and offers guided kayak tours. The company also operates the nearby **Venture Athletics Outdoor Shop** ( ⌧ *306 Commercial St., Downtown Center* ☎ *508/487–2395*), which sells all kinds of sporting gear and clothing.

FISHING

You can go after fluke, bluefish, and striped bass on a walk-on basis from spring through fall with **Cee Jay Fishing Parties** ( ⌧ *MacMillan Wharf, Downtown Center* ☎ *508/487–4330*).

PARASAILING

**Provincetown Parasail** ( ⌧ *MacMillan Wharf* ☎ *508/487–8359* ⊕ *www.provincetownparasail.com*) offers high-flying parasailing adventures, which take you some 300 feet above town and Cape Cod Bay.

SPAS

**Jonathan Williams Salon & Spa** ( ⌧ *139A Bradford St.* ☎ *508/487–0422* ⊕ *www.jonathanwilliamssalonandspa.com*) offers a wide range of spa treatments, including skin treatments, hair care, pedicures, and aromatherapy. At the posh Crowne Pointe Historic Inn, the intimate and fabulous **Shui Spa** ( ⌧ *82 Bradford St.* ☎ *508/487–6767* ⊕ *www.crownepointe.com*) pampers guests with everything from hot stone massage to sweet-sugar body scrubs to grape wine–peel facials.

TENNIS

**Herring Cove Tennis Club** ( ⌧ *21 Bradford St. Ext., east of Downtown Center* ☎ *508/487–9512* ⊕ *www.herringcovetennis.com*) has five clay courts and offers lessons.

**Provincetown Tennis Club** ( ⌧ *288 Bradford St. Ext., east of Downtown Center* ☎ *508/487–9574,* ⊕ *www.provincetowntennis.com*) has five clay and two hard courts open to nonmembers; you can also take lessons with the resident tennis pro.

TOURS
Fodor'sChoice
★

**Art's Dune Tours** ( ✉ *Commercial and Standish Sts., Downtown Center* ☎ *508/487–1950* ⊕ *www.artsdunetours.com*) has been taking eager passengers into the dunes of Province Lands since 1946. Bumpy but controlled rides transport you through sometimes surreal sandy vistas peppered with beach grass and along shoreline patrolled by seagulls and sandpipers. Tours are filled with lively tales, including the fascinating history of the exclusive (and reclusive) dune shacks (18 still stand today). These one-hour tours are offered several times daily; especially intriguing are the sunset and moonlight tours. Rides coupled with clambakes or barbecues are popular; call for availability and pricing.

Harbor Tours on the *Viking Princess* ( ✉ *MacMillan Wharf, Downtown Center* ☎ *508/487–7323* ⊕ *www.capecodecotours.com*) are given in mornings throughout the summer. These narrated excursions tell stories of shipwrecks and pirate raids and pass by Civil War forts and the Long Point Lighthouse. There are also sunset cruises, "critter cruises" with onboard naturalists, and kids-oriented "pirate fun cruises."

★ **P-town Pedicab** ( ☎ *508/487–0660* ⊕ *www.ptownpedicabs.com*) provides highly enjoyable town tours in vehicles you won't find in too many places around the country. A guide pedals you and up to two more guests around town in an open-air three-wheel chariotlike cab, pointing out local sights and offering an unusual perspective on this already unusual town. The company also offers customized gallery-hopping, ghost-graveyard, shopping, and history tours. It's a memorable way to see the area.

**Provincetown Trolley** ( ☎ *508/487–9483* ⊕ *www.provincetowntrolley. com*) offers 40-minute narrated tours of Provincetown, which leave from outside town hall every 30 minutes daily 10 to 4, and every hour daily 5 to 7 PM. The ride takes you through downtown, out to the Pilgrim Monument, and by the beaches; the fare is $8.

WHALE-
WATCHING

One of the joys of Cape Cod is spotting whales swimming in and around the feeding grounds at Stellwagen Bank, about 6 mi off the tip of Provincetown. On a sunny day the boat ride out into open ocean is part of the pleasure, but the thrill, of course, is in seeing these great creatures. You might spot minke whales; humpbacks (who put on the best show when they breach); finbacks; or perhaps the most endangered great whale species, the right whale. Dolphins are a welcome sight as well; they play in the boat's bow waves. Many people also come aboard for birding, especially during spring and fall migration. You can see gannets, shearwaters, and storm petrels, among many others. Several boats take you out to sea (and bring you back) with morning, afternoon, or sunset trips lasting from three to four hours. All boats have food service, but remember to take sunscreen and a sweater or jacket—the breeze makes it chilly. Some boats stock seasickness pills, but if you're susceptible, come prepared.

The municipal parking area by the harbor in Provincetown fills up by noon in summer; consider taking a morning boat to avoid crowds and the hottest sun. Although April may be cold, it's one of the better months for spotting whales, who at that time have just migrated north

# Dune Shacks

Provincetown's rich artistic legacy continues to manifest itself in the dozens of galleries along Commercial Street and through countless resident writers and painters. But out along the seashore, along a 3-mi stretch of sand extending from about Race Point to High Head (in Truro), you can see a more unusual remnant of the town's artistic past—the dune shacks.

These small, austere structures were built by the Life Saving Service in the 19th century to house seamen. Sometime around the 1920s, long after the dune shacks ceased housing life-saving personnel, many of the community's creative or eccentric spirits began using them as retreats and hideaways. Probably the most famous of these was playwright Eugene O'Neill, who purchased one and spent many summers there with his wife, Agnes Boulton. O'Neill penned *Anna Christie* (1920) and *The Hairy Ape* (1921) while living in his shack, and in doing so gave the whole collection of dune shacks something of an arty cachet.

Other Provincetown artists soon followed O'Neill, including the self-proclaimed "poet of the dunes," Harry Kemp, who wrote many a verse about the seashore's stark, desolate splendor. Author Hazel Hawthorne-Werner wrote *The Salt House*, a memoir tracing her time amid the dunes, in 1929. It's said that this book helped get the shacks, along with the entire dunes district, onto the National Register of Historic Places, helping to preserve them for years to come. In later years, Jack Kerouac, e. e. cummings, Norman Mailer, and Jackson Pollack also lived in these primitive structures.

The dune shacks haven't been modernized much—none has electricity, running water, or toilets. You stay in them for a chance to be with nature and perhaps commune with the spirits of artists who have gone before you. The dune shacks are now all set along the part of the Cape Cod National Seashore that is known as the Province Lands. The park owns most of the Provincetown dune shacks, though a few are managed by nonprofit groups aimed at preserving them and their legacy. Some of these organizations, such as the Peaked Hills Bars Trust and the Provincetown Community Compact, allow visitors to stay in the dune shacks through a variety of arrangements. Both groups run an artist-in-residence program—artists can apply for short stays in some of the shacks during the summer season. Only a handful of applicants are admitted each year.

If you're not an artist, you can enter a lottery for the opportunity to lease one of the shacks for a week in spring or fall. If you're interested in applying to spend time in a dune shack or you'd like to join one of the nonprofit organizations that sponsors them, contact **Dune Shacks** (✉ *Box 1705, Provincetown 02657* ☎ *508/487-3635*).

If you're simply interested in exploring the terrain and seeing the shacks, you can either book a tour with **Art's Dune Tours** (☎ *508/487-1950 or 800/894-1951* ⊕ *www.artsdunetours. com*) or park behind the Cape Inn, on Snail Road just off U.S. 6, where a 3-mi trail winds through the dunes and past many of the dune shacks.

–by Andrew Collins

after mating and are very hungry. Good food is, after all, what brings the whales to this part of the Atlantic.

**Dolphin Fleet** tours are accompanied by scientists from the Center for Coastal Studies in Provincetown, who provide commentary while collecting data on the whale population they've been monitoring for years. They know many of the whales by name and will tell you about their habits and histories. Reservations are required. ⊠ *Ticket office: Chamber of Commerce building at MacMillan Wharf, Downtown Center* ☎ *508/240–3636 or 800/826–9300* ⊕ *www.whalewatch.com* ✉ *$37* ⊙ *Tours mid-Apr.–Oct.*

The *Portuguese Princess* sails with a naturalist on board to narrate. The snack bar sells Portuguese specialties. *Tickets* ⊠ *70 Shank Painter Rd., ticket office, east of Downtown Center* ⊠ *Whale Watchers General Store, 309 Commercial St., Downtown Center* ☎ *508/487–2651 or 800/442–3188* ⊕ *www.princesswhalewatch.com* ✉ *$37* ⊙ *Tours mid-May–Oct.*

## SHOPPING

ART GALLERIES  **Albert Merola Gallery** ( ⊠ *424 Commercial St., Downtown Center,*
★   *toward East End* ☎ *508/487–4424* ⊕ *www.universalfineobjects.com*) focuses on 20th-century and contemporary master prints and Picasso ceramics. The gallery showcases artists from in and around Provincetown, Boston, and New York, including James Balla, Richard Baker, and iconic gay filmmaker and arbiter of bad taste John Waters.

**Berta Walker Gallery** ( ⊠ *208 Bradford St., east of Downtown Center, toward East End* ☎ *508/487–6411* ⊕ *www.bertawalker.com*) specializes in Provincetown-affiliated artists, including Selina Trieff and Nancy Whorf, and such Provincetown legends as Ross Moffett, Charles Hawthorne, Hans Hofmann, and Karl Knaths.

**Charles-Baltivik Gallery** ( ⊠ *432 Commercial St., east of Downtown Center, toward East End* ☎ *508/487–3611* ⊕ *www.cbgallery.net*) features several leading contemporary artists and has a small sculpture garden.

The **DNA Gallery** ( ⊠ *288 Bradford St., east of Downtown Center, toward East End* ☎ *508/487–7700* ⊕ *www.dnagallery.com*) represents artists working in various mediums, including many emerging talents.

**Ernden Fine Art Gallery** ( ⊠ *397 Commercial St., Downtown Center, toward East End* ☎ *508/487–6700* ⊕ *www.erndengallery.com*) is one of the more recent additions to the emerging local art scene, showing works by an impressive range of both newer and established painters and photographers.

★  **Gallery Voyeur** ( ⊠ *444 Commercial St., east of Downtown Center, toward East End* ☎ *508/487–3678* ⊕ *www.voy-art.com*) shows artist-owner Johniene Papandreas's provocative, larger-than-life portraits, which are inspired by classical and Romantic artists of the past.

**Hilda Neily Art Gallery** ( ⊠ *432 Commercial St., Downtown Center, toward East End* ☎ *508/487–6300* ⊕ *www.hildaneilygallery.com*) is named for its featured artist, who was once a student of impressionist painter Henry Hensche.

Fodor's Choice
★ **Julie Heller Gallery** ( ⊠ *2 Gosnold St., Downtown Center* ☎ *508/487–2169* ⊕ *www.juliehellergallery.com*) has contemporary artists as well as some Provincetown icons. The gallery has works from the Sol Wilson and Milton Avery estates, as well as from such greats as Robert Motherwell, Agnes Weinrich, and Blanche Lazzell.

**Rice/Polak Gallery** ( ⊠ *430 Commercial St., Downtown Center, toward East End* ☎ *508/487–1052* ⊕ *www.ricepolakgallery.com*) stocks a remarkably comprehensive and eclectic variety of contemporary works, from paintings and pastels to photography and sculpture.

★ The **Schoolhouse Galleries** ( ⊠ *494 Commercial St., Downtown Center, toward East End* ☎ *508/487–4800* ⊕ *www.schoolhouseprovincetown. com*), in an 1844 former school, shows the works of more than 25 local and national artists and photographers.

**Simie Maryles Gallery** ( ⊠ *435 Commercial St., Downtown Center, toward East End* ☎ *508/487–7878* ⊕ *www.simiemaryles.com*) represents about 15 contemporary artists, most of whom work in traditional styles. Oil paintings, glasswork, ceramics, and metal sculpture are among the strong suits here.

The **William-Scott Gallery** ( ⊠ *439 Commercial St., Downtown Center, toward East End* ☎ *508/487–4040* ⊕ *www.williamscottgallery.com*) primarily shows contemporary works such as John Dowd's reflective, realistic Cape 'scapes.

SPECIALTY
STORES **Farland Provisions** ( ⊠ *150 Bradford St., Downtown Center* ☎ *508/487–0045*) proffers all kinds of fine foods and snacks, including excellent deli sandwiches.

**Forbidden Fruit** ( ⊠ *173 Commercial St., Downtown Center, toward West End* ☎ *508/487–9800*) is a one-stop shop for all irreverent and offbeat gifts, from strange costumes to erotic trinkets to Gothic tchotchkes.

**ID** ( ⊠ *220A Commercial St., Downtown Center, toward West End* ☎ *508/487–4300*) stocks a wonderful array of Mexican pottery, cool clocks, offbeat jewelry, and retro-hip greeting cards and stationery.

**Impulse** ( ⊠ *188 Commercial St., Downtown Center, toward West End* ☎ *508/487–1154*) has contemporary American crafts, including jewelry and an extraordinary kaleidoscope collection. The Autograph Gallery exhibits framed photographs, letters, and documents signed by celebrities.

**Kidstuff** ( ⊠ *381 Commercial St., Downtown Center, toward East End* ☎ *508/487–0714*) carries unusual, colorful children's wear.

**Lady'Z Vintage Clothing** ( ⊠ *389 Commercial St., Downtown Center, toward East End* ☎ *508/487–2251*) offers racks of sexy, campy, bold, and offbeat secondhand fashions. It's a favorite of drag queens, who especially favor the costume jewelry and boas, but there are all kinds of cool threads here.

**Little Gorgeous Things** ( ✉359 *Commercial St., Downtown Center, toward East End* ☎508/487–6171) has just the curious little tchotchke, collectible, vintage furnishing, painting, or objet d'art to complete your summer house. It carries the creations of more than 100 local craftspeople and artists.

**Marc Jacobs** ( ✉184 *Commercial St., Downtown Center, toward West End* ☎508/487–0723), the world-class designer, opened a Provincetown location in 2007. Drop in to peruse the fashion-forward threads.

★ **Marine Specialties, Inc.** ( ✉235 *Commercial St., Downtown Center* ☎508/487–1730) is full of treasures, knickknacks, and clothing. Here you can purchase some very reasonably priced casual- and military-style clothing, as well as seashells, marine supplies, stained-glass lamps, candles, rubber sharks (you get the idea), and prints of old advertisements.

**Moda Fina** ( ✉349 *Commercial St., Downtown Center* ☎508/487–6632) displays an eclectic selection of women's fashions, shoes, and jewelry—everything from flowing linen or silk eveningwear to funky and casual pieces. Unique Mexican crafts are also for sale.

**Now Voyager Bookstore** ( ✉357 *Commercial St., Downtown Center* ☎508/487–0848) is a first-rate independent bookstore with an emphasis on lesbian and gay titles; the store hosts prominent authors throughout the year (especially in summer) and has a small art gallery.

**Peter's Royal Navy** ( ✉120 *Commercial St., Downtown Center, toward West End* ☎508/487–7141), with its whimsical window displays, appeals to fans of all things British with a great selection of linens, authentic Royal Navy flatware, Bay Rhum toiletries, antique model ships, and fine nautical memorabilia.

**Provincetown Antique Market** ( ✉131 *Commercial St., Downtown Center, toward West End* ☎508/487–1115) has one of the town's better selections of vintage lighting, jewelry, Bakelite, costumes, toys, textiles, and furnishings.

**Remembrances of Things Past** ( ✉376 *Commercial St., Downtown Center, toward East End* ☎508/487–9443) deals with articles from the 1920s to the 1960s, including Bakelite and other jewelry, telephones, neon items, ephemera, and autographed celebrity photographs.

**Silk & Feathers** ( ✉377 *Commercial St., Downtown Center, toward East End* ☎508/487–2057) carries an assortment of fine lingerie, women's clothing, and jewelry.

**Tim's Used Books** ( ✉242 *Commercial St., Downtown Center* ☎508/487–0005) is packed with volumes of volumes—rooms of used-but-in-good-shape books, including some rare and out-of-print texts.

★ **Utilities** ( ✉393 *Commercial St., Downtown Center, toward East End* ☎508/487–6800) supplies customers with some of the coolest kitchen and bathroom gadgetry and decorative pieces around.

**Wa** (✉*220 Commercial St., Downtown Center, toward West End* ☎*508/487–6355*) is an oasis of peace and Zen-like tranquillity. Unusual- and Japanese-inspired items include fountains, home-accent pieces, and framed (and sometimes frightening) tropical insects.

**West End Antiques** (✉*146 Commercial St., Downtown Center, toward West End* ☎*508/487–6723*) sells everything from $4 postcards to a $3,000 model ship. Handmade dolls and high-quality glassware—Steuben, Orrefors, and Hawkes—are also available.

# THE OUTER CAPE ESSENTIALS

*To research prices, get advice from other travelers, and book travel arrangements, visit www.fodors.com.*

## TRANSPORTATION

### BY BOAT & FERRY

In season, ferries run from Provincetown to Boston and Plymouth. *For more information, see ⇨ Boat & Ferry Travel in Essentials in the back of this book.*

### BY BUS

Plymouth & Brockton Street Railway provides bus service to Provincetown from downtown Boston or Logan Airport, with stops en route. *For more information, see ⇨ Bus Travel in Essentials in the back of this book.*

The Shuttle, run by the Cape Cod Regional Transit Authority, provides a much-needed transportation boost. The route begins at Horton's Camping Resort in Truro and continues to Provincetown along Route 6A; it stops wherever a passenger or roadside flagger dictates. Once in Provincetown, the shuttle continues up Bradford Street, with alternating trips to Herring Cove Beach and Pilgrim Park as well as summertime service up to Provincetown Airport and Race Point Beach. It runs every 30 minutes and is outfitted to carry bicycles. The service is popular and reasonably priced ($2 for a single fare, $6 for a day pass), and the only trouble seems to be finding parking on the Truro end (plans are in the works to find alternative parking areas). The shuttle runs throughout the day from late May until mid-October, with more limited service during the off-season.

There are no bus stations or depots, per se, in the Outer Cape, though there are designated stops within each town: in Provincetown, in front of the Chamber of Commerce office on Commercial Street; in Truro, at Dutra's Market–Route 6A (Shore Road); in North Truro, at Depot Road, near the Truro Post Office and Jams store; in Wellfleet, at D& D market on U.S. 6 and in Wellfleet Village; and in South Wellfleet on Main Street in front of Town Hall.

**Bus Lines Plymouth & Brockton Street Railway** (☎*508/746–0378* ⊕*www. p-b.com*). **Shuttle** (☎*800/352–7155* ⊕*www.capecodtransit.org*).

### BY TAXI

The companies below provide cab service throughout the Outer Cape. Mercedes Cab Co. offers local and long-distance service in vintage Mercedes sedans.

Taxi Companies **Cape Cab** ( ✉ *Provincetown* ☎ *508/487–2222*). **Jody's Taxi** ( ✉ *Provincetown* ☎ *508/487–0265*). **Mercedes Cab** ( ✉ *Provincetown* ☎ *508/487–3333* ⊕ *www.mercedescab.com*). **Queen Cab** ( ✉ *Provincetown* ☎ *508/487–5500*).

## CONTACTS & RESOURCES

### VISITOR INFORMATION

The Provincetown Chamber of Commerce is open from March until New Year's Day and has the only staffed visitor center in town, just off Commercial Street near MacMillan Wharf. The Provincetown Business Guild specializes in gay tourism and is open year-round to offer answers over the phone or send out its directory—but it has no visitor center. The Truro Chamber of Commerce and Wellfleet Chamber are open daily from late May through early September, and on weekends from mid-April through late May and from early September through mid-October.

Tourist Information **Provincetown** ( ✉ *307 Commercial St., Box 1017* ☎ *508/487–3424* ⊕ *www.ptownchamber.com*). **Provincetown Business Guild (gay and lesbian)** ( ✉ *3 Freeman St., No. 2, Box 421–94* ☎ *508/487–2313 or 800/637–8696* ⊕ *www.ptown.org*). **Truro** ( ✉ *U.S. 6 at Head of the Meadow Rd.* ⬠ *Box 26, North Truro 02652* ☎ *508/487–1288* ⊕ *www.trurochamberofcommerce.com*). **Wellfleet** ( ⬠ *Box 571, 02667* ☎ *508/349–2510* ✉ *Information center off U.S. 6 in South Wellfleet* ⊕ *www.wellfleetchamber.com*).

# Martha's Vineyard

## WORD OF MOUTH

"...There is nothing like a Menemsha sunset, and the beach is full of people—and a lot of children—who set up for an early pre sunset dinner. Many get their dinner from the Bite for seafood, some of us pack what we want—we always bring appetizers and the cooler, chairs, etc and set up a huge picnic. The kids have a ball playing, we all watch sunset and head out—usually w/ kids falling asleep in the car on the ride back..."

—escargot

Updated
by Laura V.
Scheel

**FAR LESS DEVELOPED THAN CAPE COD**—thanks to a few local con-servation organizations—yet more cosmopolitan than neighboring Nantucket, Martha's Vineyard is an island with a double life. From Memorial Day through Labor Day the quieter, some might say real, Vineyard quickens into a vibrant, star-studded place. Edgartown floods with people who come to wander narrow streets flanked with elegant boutiques, stately whaling captains' homes, and charming inns. The busy main port, Vineyard Haven, welcomes day-trippers fresh off fer-ries and private yachts to browse in its own array of shops. Oak Bluffs, where pizza and ice-cream emporiums reign supreme, attracts diverse crowds with its boardwalk-town air and nightspots that cater to high-spirited, carefree youth.

Summer regulars have included a host of celebrities over the years, among them William Styron, Art Buchwald, Walter Cronkite, Beverly Sills, Patricia Neal, Spike Lee, and Diane Sawyer. Former president Bill Clinton and his wife, Senator Hillary Clinton, are frequent visitors. Concerts, theater, dance performances, and lecture series draw top tal-ent to the island; a county agricultural fair, weekly farmers' markets, and miles of walking trails provide earthier pleasures.

Most people know the Vineyard's summer persona, but in many ways its other self has even more appeal, for the off-season island is a place of peace and simple beauty. Drivers traversing country lanes through the agricultural center of the island find time to linger over pastoral and ocean vistas without being pushed along by a throng of other cars, bicycles, and mopeds. In nature reserves, the voices of summer are gone, leaving only the sounds of birdsong and the crackle of leaves underfoot. Private beaches open to the public, and the water sparkles under crisp, blue skies.

Locals are at their convivial best off-season. After the craziness of their short moneymaking months, they reestablish contact with friends and take up pastimes temporarily crowded out by work. The result for visitors—besides the extra dose of friendliness—is that cultural, edu-cational, and recreational events continue year-round.

## ABOUT THE RESTAURANTS

From fried fish at roadside stands to boiled lobster and foie gras at fancy French restaurants and a growing array of international influ-ences—Thai, Brazilian, Japanese, Mexican, to name just a few—the Vineyard serves an amazing variety of culinary choices.

The majority of eating establishments, both take-out and sit-down, are concentrated in the three Down-Island towns of Vineyard Haven, Oak Bluffs, and Edgartown. As you travel Up-Island—to West Tisbury, Chilmark, and Aquinnah—choices dwindle, especially when it comes to sit-down dinners. Sadly, Vineyard diners—all-American institutions where you can get an honest, no-frills meal at reasonable prices—are a dying breed. Luckily, you can pick up sandwiches, pastries, and other to-go specialties at a number of places around the island, and with good planning you can eat well on a modest budget and splurge for an elegant dinner.

Most restaurants are open on weekends starting in late spring, and by Memorial Day weekend most are serving daily. Although the season seems to stretch longer each year, most restaurants remain open full-time through Columbus Day weekend, then only on weekends through Thanksgiving (a small handful of die-hard restaurants remain open year-round). Dress, even for the upscale spots, is casual; a man in a sports jacket is a rare sight. Reservations are highly recommended in the summer months.

---

### TOP 5

- A ride on the enduring Flying Horses Carousel

- An outdoor candlelit meal at the Sweet Life Café

- The views at Aquinnah Cliffs

- Grazing at the West Tisbury Farmers' Market

- The fishing at Wasque Point on Chappaquiddick

---

## ABOUT THE HOTELS

6

The variety of lodging options on Martha's Vineyard ranges from historic whaling captains' mansions filled with antiques to sprawling modern oceanfront hotels to cozy cottages in the woods. When choosing your accommodations, keep in mind that each town has a different personality: Oak Bluffs tends to cater to a younger, active, nightlife-oriented crowd; Edgartown is more subdued and dignified. Chilmark has beautiful beaches and miles of conservation lands, but not much of a downtown shopping area. Vineyard Haven provides a nice balance of downtown bustle and rustic charm. Bear in mind that many of the island's bed-and-breakfasts, set in vintage homes filled with art and antiques, have age restrictions—call ahead if you're traveling with a family. And remember that in July and August, the height of the summer season, minimum stays of as many as four nights may be required. If you're planning to visit for a week or more, consider renting a house. *For more lodging information, including rental properties and B&Bs,* ⇨ *Accommodations in Essentials at the back of this book.*

| WHAT IT COSTS | | | | | |
|---|---|---|---|---|---|
| | ¢ | $ | $$ | $$$ | $$$$ |
| Restaurants | under $10 | $10–$16 | $16–$22 | $22–$30 | over $30 |
| Hotels | under $90 | $90–$140 | $140–$200 | $200–$260 | over $260 |

Restaurant prices are per person for a main course at dinner. Hotel prices are for a standard double room, excluding 6% sales tax (more in some counties) and 1%–4% tourist tax.

You should make reservations for summer stays as far in advance as possible; late winter is not too early. Rates in season are very high but can fall by as much as 50% in the off-season. The Martha's Vineyard Chamber of Commerce *(⇨ Visitor Information in Martha's Vineyard*

# Martha's
# Vineyard

**Up Island (see detail map)**

*Lake Tashmoo*

Lambert's Cove Rd.

Lambert's Cove Beach (restricted)

Stoney Hill Rd.

*Vineyard Sound*

Cedar Tree Neck Wildlife Sanctuary

Indian Hill Rd.

State Rd.

Old County Rd.

**Polly Hill Arboretum**

Waskosim's Rock Reservation

**West Tisbury**

Tea La.

North Rd.

Middle Rd.

South Rd.

**Sepiessa Point Reservation**

**Long Point**

*Tisbury Great Pond*

Menemsha Hills Reservation

*Menemsha Beach*

**Menemsha**

Long Point Beach

**Aquinnah Cliffs and Lighthouse**

Lobsterville Beach

**Aquinnah**

Beach parking

*Moshup Beach*

*Moshup Trail*

*Menemsha Pond*

**Chilmark**

Fulling Mill Brook Preserve

Beetlebung Corner

*Nashaquitsa Pond*

Lucy Vincent Beach (restricted)

State Rd.

Philbin Beach (restricted)

*Squibnocket Pond*

**Quitsa Pond Lookout**

Squibnocket Beach (restricted)

| 0 | | | | 4 miles |

| 0 | | | | 4 kilometers |

TO NEW
BEDFORD

TO WOODS
HOLE

TO
FALMOUTH

TO
WOODS
HOLE

TO
NEW
BEDFORD

TO HYANNIS

TO QUONSET POINT

*Nantucket Sound*

West Chop
Lighthouse

*Owen Park
Beach*

East Chop
Lighthouse

*Beach Rd.*

Oak Bluffs
see detail
map

TO
NANTUCKET

Vineyard Haven
(Tisbury)
see detail map

*Oak Bluffs
Beach*

*Lagoon
Pond*

*Edgartown–Vineyard Haven Rd.*

*County Rd.*

Felix Neck
Wildlife
Sanctuary

TO
FALMOUTH

*Cape
Poge*

*Sengekontacket Pond*

*Joseph A. Sylvia
State Beach*

Cape Poge
Wildlife Refuge
and Lighthouse

Island Alpaca
Company

Manuel F.
Correllus
State Forest

*Beach
Rd.*

*Edgartown
Harbor*

*Cape
Poge
Bay*

*East
Beach*

Airport Rd.

Airport

Edgartown
Lighthouse

Three Ponds
Preserve

Mytoi

Edgartown–West Tisbury Rd.

Edgartown
see detail
map

Chappaquiddick
Island

*Oyster
Pond*

*Edgartown
Great Pond*

Farm Institute

*Herring Creek Rd.*

*Katama Rd.*

Poucha Pond
Reservation

*Poucha
Pond*

Wasque
Reservation

*Katama
Bay*

South
Beach

Katama
(South Beach)

Wasque
Beach

Wasque
Point

*ATLANTIC OCEAN*

KEY

Bike Trail

Ferry

*Essentials at the end of this chapter)* maintains a listing of availability in the peak tourist season, from mid-June to mid-September.

## VINEYARD HAVEN (TISBURY)

*7 mi southeast of Woods Hole, 3½ mi west of Oak Bluffs, 8 mi northwest of Edgartown.*

Most people call this town Vineyard Haven because of the name of the port where ferries arrive, but its official name is Tisbury. Not as high-toned as Edgartown or as honky-tonk as Oak Bluffs, Vineyard Haven blends the past and the present with a touch of the bohemian. Visitors arriving here step off the ferry right into the bustle of the harbor, a block from the shops and restaurants of Main Street.

**NEED A BREAK?**
The delicious breads, pastries, and quick-lunch items at **Black Dog Bakery** ( ⊠ *11 Water St.* ☎ *508/693–4786*) are simply not to be missed—it's a popular stop for good reason.

The stately, neoclassic 1844 **Association Hall** houses the town hall and the Katharine Cornell Memorial Theatre, created in part with funds that Cornell (1898–1974)—one of America's foremost stage actresses in the 1920s, '30s, and '40s and a longtime summer resident—donated in her will. The walls of the theater on the 2nd floor are painted with murals depicting whaling expeditions and a Native American gathering, and the ceiling resembles a blue sky with seagulls overhead. Island artist Stan Murphy painted the murals on the occasion of the town's tercentenary in 1971. The theater occasionally holds performances of plays, concerts, and dances. ⊠ *51 Spring St.* ☎ *508/696–4200.*

One of two lighthouses that mark the opening to the harbor, the 52-foot white-and-black **West Chop Lighthouse** was built of brick in 1838 to replace an 1817 wood building. It's been moved back from the edge of the eroding bluff twice. ⊠ *W. Chop Rd. (Main St.).*

### WHERE TO STAY & EAT

¢–$
AMERICAN
✕ **ArtCliff Diner.** This vintage diner has been a year-round breakfast and lunch meeting place for locals since 1943. Owner-chef Gina Stanley, who was on call to make desserts for Blair House when she lived in Washington, D.C., serves anything but ordinary diner fare. She whips up pecan pancakes with real rum raisins for breakfast, and crepes with chèvre, arugula, or almost anything you ask for at lunch. There's a small porch with additional seating, but expect long waits (an hour or more in high summer) at breakfast. ⊠ *39 Beach Rd.* ☎ *508/693–1224* ▤ *MC, V* ☺ *Closed Wed. No dinner.*

¢
CAFE
✕ **Beetlebung Coffee House.** This cozy coffeehouse is within easy walking distance of the ferry terminal and downtown shops and restaurants. A hip crowd convenes here for the great sandwiches (try the Taos panini, with flame-roasted New Mexico green chilies, turkey, and cheddar), designer-coffee drinks, and delicious desserts. The breakfast "eggwich," with Black Forest ham, poached egg, and Vermont ched-

dar, is a treat. There's an attractive side patio that's perfect on a warm afternoon. ✉ *32 Beach St.* ☎ *508/696–7122* ▭ *MC, V.*

**$$–$$$$**
**AMERICAN**

✕ **Black Dog Tavern.** This island landmark—which is more popular with tourists than locals—lies just steps from the ferry terminal in Vineyard Haven. In July and August, the wait for breakfast (with an expansive omelet assortment) can be as much as an hour from 8 AM on. Why? Partly because the ambience inside—roaring fireplace, dark-wood walls, maritime memorabilia, and a grand view of the water—makes everyone feel so at home. The menu is heavy on local fish, chowders, and chops. Lighter fare is available until 7 PM in the Black Dog Bakery Cafe. ✉ *20 Beach St. Ext.* ☎ *508/693–9223* ⌖ *Reservations not accepted* ▭ *AE, D, MC, V* Ⓨ *BYOB.*

**$$$–$$$$**
**FRENCH**

✕ **Le Grenier.** Owner-chef Jean Dupon has been serving classic French food since the late 1970s above the M.V. Bagel Authority at the upper end of Vineyard Haven's downtown. All this time, he's been consistently loyal to the French standards: frogs' legs, sweetbreads, lobster flambéed with calvados, chicken livers Provençale, and tournedos are among the entrées. The decor is hardly stuffy in the French tradition; rather, it's almost backyard casual, with a string of lightbulbs and souvenir wine-bottle corks lining the walls. ✉ *Upper Main St.* ☎ *508/693–4906* ⊕ *www.legrenierrestaurant.com* ▭ *AE, MC, V* Ⓨ *BYOB* ⊘ *No lunch.*

**6**

**$–$$$$**
**MEDITERRANEAN**

✕ **Mediterranean.** Owned by well-regarded talented chefs and restaurateurs Leslie and Douglas Hewson, this sunny, informal eatery overlooking the harbor has become a favorite with locals for reliable, freshly prepared pan-Mediterranean food—ingredients and recipes reflect Moroccan, Spanish, French, and Italian influences. You might start with the savory artichoke Française sautéed in garlic, herbs, and lemon butter. Excellent main dishes include oven-roasted salt cod with crabmeat, and grilled sliced lamb with a rosemary reduction and a goat cheese–and–tomato tart. Pastry chef Leslie has earned a loyal following with her flaky baklava topped with lemon ice cream. ✉ *52 Beach Rd.* ☎ *508/693–1617 or 888/693–1617* ▭ *AE, D, MC, V* Ⓨ *BYOB* ⊘ *No lunch Sun.*

**¢–$$$**
**★**
**SEAFOOD**

✕ **Net Result.** It may not have quite the ambience of the fish markets in Menemsha, but this simple take-out market and restaurant in a shopping center just outside downtown Vineyard Haven serves some of the best food around, including superb sublime lobster bisque, hefty scallop and oyster platters, steamed lobsters, grilled swordfish sandwiches, and crab salad. There are always additional daily specials that reflect what's been caught that day, and Net Result also has a sushi counter: the Martha's Vineyard roll is a favorite, packed with tuna, salmon, yellowtail, and avocado and wrapped in seaweed. You can dine at picnic tables outside and view Vineyard Haven's harbor across the busy road. ✉ *Tisbury Marketplace, 79 Beach Rd.* ☎ *508/693–6071* ⊕ *www.mvseafood.com* ▭ *MC, V.*

**$–$$$**
**BRAZILIAN**

✕ **Tropical Restaurant.** The house specialty at this roadside restaurant is *rodizio*, a Brazilian style of barbecue where slow-roasted meats—in this case beef, chicken, sausage, pork, and lamb—are carved table-side and served continuously throughout your meal. Along with rice and beans, side dishes include collard greens and yucca. ⊠*Five Corners* ☎*508/696–0715* ▤*MC, V* ⛽*BYOB.*

**$$–$$$$** 🏠 **Crocker House Inn.** This 1924 farmhouse-style inn is tucked into a
★ quiet lane off Main Street, minutes from the ferries and Owen Park
Beach. The rooms are decorated casually with understated flair—pastel-painted walls, softly upholstered wing chairs, and white-wicker
nightstands. Each contains a small, wall-mounted "honor bar," with
a disposable camera, suntan lotion, and other useful sundries. Three
rooms have soothing whirlpool tubs, and two have fireplaces. No. 6,
with a small porch and a private entrance, has the best view of the
harbor. Breakfast is served at a large farmer's table inside the small
common room and kitchen area. Jeff and Jynell Kristal are the young,
friendly owners, and Jynell also creates whimsically painted glassware, which is available for sale. **Pros:** great owners; short walk from
town; easygoing vibe. **Cons:** you pay a premium for this location;
decor is more casual than posh; books up quickly in summer. ⊠*12
Crocker Ave., Box 1658* ☎*508/693–1151 or 800/772–0206* ⊕*www.
crockerhouseinn.com* ➟*8 rooms* ♿*In-room: DVD, Wi-Fi. In-hotel:
no elevator, no kids under 12* ▤*MC, V* ⫴❶*CP.*

**$$–$$$$** 🏠 **Greenwood House.** A low-key B&B on a quiet lane around the cor-
ner from Vineyard Haven's public library, the Greenwood House is

one of the better values in town. Affable innkeepers Kathy Stinson and Larry Gomez own this homey, three-story Arts and Crafts–style cottage with classic shingle siding and a shaded yard. The rooms are decorated with a mix of antiques and contemporary pieces, including brass and four-poster beds, island artwork, and functional but attractive nightstands and bureaus. It's a 10-to-15-minute walk from the ferry and even closer to many shops and restaurants. **Pros:** easy walk to shops and dining; good value; personal service. **Cons:** some rooms a bit small; no room phones. ⌧ *40 Greenwood Ave., Box 2734* ☎ *508/693–6150 or 866/693–6150* ⊕ *www.greenwoodhouse.com* ⇆ *4 rooms* ♿ *In-room: refrigerator, dial-up. In-hotel: no elevator* ▤ *AE, MC, V* ❢ *BP.*

> **BYOB**
>
> Part of how the Vineyard maintains its charm—and part of what makes it somewhat frustrating as well—is that alcoholic beverages have, until recently, been sold in retail stores and in restaurants in only three towns: Edgartown, Oak Bluffs, and Aquinnah. At restaurants in the so-called "dry" towns of Vineyard Haven, West Tisbury, and Chilmark you can BYOB, but expect to be charged up to $8 for corkage fees (this includes the opening of the bottle and the provision of glasses).

$$–$$$$  **Hanover House.** Set on ½ acre of landscaped lawn on a busy road—but within walking distance of the ferry—this three-property, children-friendly inn consists of a classic, home-style B&B, a country inn, and a carriage house. Rooms are decorated with a combination of antiques and reproduction furniture, mostly in the Victorian style, and each has individual flair: in one, an antique sewing machine serves as the TV stand. The three carriage-house suites have private decks or patios, two have kitchenettes, and one has a gas fireplace. **Pros:** Good value; 10-minute walk to shops and dining; kitchenettes in some units. **Cons:** off busy road; no water or beach views from most units; stall showers in a couple of units. ⌧ *28 Edgartown Rd., Box 2108* ☎ *508/693–1066 or 800/696–8633* ⊕ *www.hanoverhouseinn.com* ⇆ *12 rooms, 3 suites* ♿ *In-room: refrigerator (some), kitchen (some), Wi-Fi. In-hotel: no elevator* ▤ *AE, D, MC, V* ❢ *CP.*

$$$$  **Mansion House.** There has been a hostelry on this Main Street site just above Vineyard Haven Harbor since 1794 (though the building has burned to the ground twice since then). Today's Mansion House reopened in 2003. Apart from the cheerful, summery rooms—some with balconies, gas fireplaces, and soaking tubs—the cupola deck provides a pleasant spot for a respite. It affords sweeping views of the harbor, the town, and the lagoon that stretches between Vineyard Haven and Oak Bluffs. Afternoon cookies and lemonade are served there, or you can BYOB. The hotel's Zephrus Restaurant serves reliable American fare and is also a nice spot for cocktails. **Pros:** restaurant and spa on-site; steps from Vineyard Haven shopping and ferry; light-filled rooms. **Cons:** no grounds to speak of; center-of-it-all locale can be a little noisy; not historic. ⌧ *9 Main St., Box 428* ☎ *509/693–2200 or 800/332–4112* ⊕ *www.mvmansionhouse.com* ⇆ *32 rooms, 11 suites* ♿ *In-room: refrigerator, Wi-Fi (fee). In-hotel: restaurant, room service, pool, gym, spa* ▤ *AE, D, MC, V* ❢ *CP.*

**$$$$**  ⬛ **Thorncroft Inn.** On 2½ wooded acres about 1 mi from the ferry, this inn's main building, a 1918 Craftsman bungalow, combines fine colonial and richly carved Renaissance Revival antiques with tasteful reproductions to create a somewhat formal environment. Most rooms have working fireplaces and canopy beds; three rooms have two-person whirlpool baths, and two have private hot-tub spas. Rooms in the carriage house, set apart from the main house via a breezeway, are more secluded. **Pros:** short walk from town; antiques galore; carriage-house rooms have lots of privacy. **Cons:** a bit formal and fussy; antiques galore; some rooms are very small given the steep rates. ⌂*460 Main St., Box 1022* ☎*508/693–3333 or 800/332–1236* 🖷*508/693–5419* ⊕*www.thorncroft.com* ⥥*13 rooms, 1 cottage* ⚭*In-room: refrigerator (some), DVD/VCR, Ethernet, Wi-Fi. In-hotel: no kids under 16* ▭*AE, D, DC, MC, V* ⦿*BP.*

**¢–$$**  ⚠ **Martha's Vineyard Family Campground.** Wooded sites, a ball field,
★  a camp store, bicycle rentals, and electrical and water hookups are among the facilities at this 20-acre campsite a few miles from Vineyard Haven. A step up from tents are 21 rustic one- or two-room cabins, which come with electricity, refrigerators, gas grills, and combinations of double and bunk beds (but bring your own bedding). The campground also has hookups for trailers. This is the only campsite on the island, so book early; discounts are available for extended stays. No dogs or motorcycles are allowed. **Pros:** great value; secluded setting; has some private cabins. **Cons:** no dogs allowed; 1½-mi walk from town; books up fast. ⌂*569 Edgartown Rd., Box 1557* ☎*508/693–3772* 🖷*508/693–5767* ⊕*www.campmvfc.com* ⥥*130 tent sites, 50 RV sites, 21 cabins* ⚭*Refrigerator (some), bicycles, laundry facilities, play area* ▭*D, MC, V* ⊙*Closed mid-Oct.–mid-May.*

### NIGHTLIFE & THE ARTS

The **Vineyard Playhouse** ( ⌂*24 Church St.* ☎*508/696–6300* ⊕*www.vineyardplayhouse.org*) has a year-round schedule of professional productions. From mid-June through early September, a troupe performs drama, classics, and comedies on the air-conditioned main stage. Summer Shakespeare and other productions take place at the natural amphitheater at Tashmoo Overlook on State Road in Vineyard Haven—bring insect repellent and a blanket or lawn chair. Children's programs and a summer camp are also scheduled, and local art exhibitions are held throughout the year. The theater is wheelchair-accessible and provides hearing devices.

### SPORTS & THE OUTDOORS

**Lake Tashmoo Town Beach** ( ⌂*End of Herring Creek Rd.*) provides swimmers with access to the warm, relatively shallow, brackish lake—or cooler, gentler Vineyard Sound. **Owen Park Beach** ( ⌂*Off Main St.*), a small, sandy harbor beach, is just steps away from the ferry terminal in Vineyard Haven, making it a great spot to catch some last rays before heading home. **Tisbury Town Beach** ( ⌂*End of Owen Little Way off Main St.*) is a public beach next to the Vineyard Haven Yacht Club.

## SHOPPING

**The Belushi Pisano Gallery** (⊠*Kelly St., Edgartown* ☎*508/560–0706* ⊕*www.belushipisanogallery.com* ⊗*Open Memorial Day–Columbus Day*) is a contemporary fine-art gallery featuring works by local and nationally established artists. Mediums include original paintings, photography, mixed media, fine furniture, glasswork, and jewelry.

**Bowl & Board** (⊠*35 Main St.* ☎*508/693–9441*) is summer-home central. It carries everything you need to cozy up in a summer rental.

**Bramhall & Dunn** (⊠*23 Main St.* ☎*508/693–6437*) carries crafts, linens, hand-knit sweaters, and fine antique country-pine furniture.

**Bunch of Grapes Bookstore** (⊠*44 Main St.* ☎*508/693–2291*) had to start over from scratch after losing its entire inventory to a fire in the neighboring building in July 2007. This local stalwart sells new books and sponsors book signings.

**Midnight Farm** (⊠*18 Water-Cromwell La.* ☎*508/693–1997*) stocks furniture, clothes, shoes, jewelry, linens, dinnerware, books, soaps, candles, garden supplies, snack foods, and, of course, co-owner Carly Simon's books and CDs.

Fodor'sChoice ★ **Rainy Day** (⊠*66 Main St.* ☎*508/693–1830*), as the name suggests, carries gifts and amusements that are perfect for one of the island's gloomy rainy days, when you just need a warm, dry diversion. You'll find toys, crafts, cards, soaps, home accessories, gifts, and more.

**Tisbury Antiques & Interiors** (⊠*339 State Rd.* ☎*508/693–8333*) carries a vast selection of 18th- and 19th-century English, French, and Italian antiques, plus fine lighting fixtures, Cornishware, estate jewelry, and vintage books and postcards.

★ Nationally renowned for their distinctive, hand-sculpted metal weather vanes, **Tuck and Holand** (⊠*275 State Rd.* ☎*508/693–3914 or 888/693–3914*) has a studio gallery a 10-minute walk from downtown. Here you can examine Anthony Holand and the late Travis Tuck's otherworldly creations, including copper Martha's Vineyard wall maps, school-of-bluefish chandeliers, and the signature custom weather vanes.

**Wind's Up!** (⊠*199 Beach Rd.* ☎*508/693–4340*) sells swimwear, windsurfing and sailing equipment, Boogie boards, and other outdoor gear.

## OAK BLUFFS

*3½ mi east of Vineyard Haven.*

Circuit Avenue is the bustling center of the Oak Bluffs action, with most of the town's shops, bars, and restaurants. Colorful gingerbread-trimmed guesthouses and food and souvenir joints enliven Oak Bluffs Harbor, once the setting for several grand hotels (the 1879 Wesley Hotel on Lake Avenue is the last remaining one). This small town is more high spirited than haute, more fun than refined.

The **East Chop Lighthouse** was built out of cast iron in 1876 to replace an 1828 tower (used as part of a semaphore system of visual signaling between the island and Boston) that burned down. The 40-foot structure stands high atop a 79-foot bluff with spectacular views of Nantucket Sound. ⊠ *E. Chop Dr.* ☎ *508/627–4441* ✉*$5* ⊙ *Mid-June–mid-Sept., Sun. 1½ hrs before sunset–½ hr after sunset.*

**NEED A BREAK?**

The **Coop de Ville** ( ⊠ *Dockside Marketplace, Oak Bluffs Harbor* ☎ *508/693–3420*) teems with people eager to sample simple fried seafood and raw-bar delectables (the oysters are fantastic). Eat out on the patio deck overlooking the water to enjoy the view. It's open May to early November.

☼ A National Historic Landmark, the **Flying Horses Carousel** is the nation's oldest continuously operating carousel. Handcrafted in 1876 (the horses have real horsehair and glass eyes), the ride gives children a taste of entertainment from a TV-free era. ⊠ *Oak Bluffs Ave.* ☎ *508/693–9481* ✉*Rides $1.50, book of 8 tickets $10* ⊙ *Late May–early Sept., daily 10–10; Easter–late May, weekends 10–5; early Sept.–mid-Oct., weekdays 11–4:30, weekends 10–5.*

**Island Alpaca Company** is a great place to learn about alpacas and the superior wool they produce. There's a self-guided tour ($5) with informative markers along the way that lead to a special viewing area (it's not a petting zoo—alpacas are shy creatures) in an exquisite 200-year-old barn. The shop sells yarn and products made from the resident herd (numbering about 50), as well as knitting supplies. Look for classes on knitting all sorts of things, from hats to socks and even Christmas crafts. The farm is open daily in July and August, and mostly weekends in the spring and fall. The shop is open year-round. ⊠ *1 Head of the Pond Rd., off Edgartown/Vineyard Haven Rd. near the 4-way intersection* ☎*508/693–5554* ⊕*islandalpaca.com.*

★ Don't miss **Oak Bluffs Campground**, a 34-acre warren of streets tightly packed with more than 300 Carpenter Gothic Victorian cottages with wedding-cake trim, gaily painted in pastels. As you wander through this fairy-tale setting, imagine it on a balmy summer evening, lighted by the warm glow of hundreds of Japanese paper lanterns hung from every cottage porch. This describes the scene on Illumination Night at the end of the Camp Meeting season—which is attended these days by some fourth- and fifth-generation cottagers. Attendees mark the occasion as they have for more than a century, with lights, song, and open houses for families and friends. Note that because of overwhelming crowds of onlookers in seasons past, the date is not announced until the week before. Ninety-minute tours are conducted Tuesday and Thursday (meet at the Tabernacle), July and August, at 10 AM. ⊠ *Off Circuit Ave.* ☎ *508/693–0525* ⊕ *www.mvcma.org/* ✉*Tour $10.*

## WHERE TO STAY & EAT

$$–$$$
ITALIAN

✗**Jimmy Seas.** The irresistible fragrance of sautéed garlic wafting out these doors beckons lovers of the "stinking rose." Most dishes come in the pan they're cooked in and are among the biggest portions you'll find on the island. Classic red-sauce Italian dishes include *vongole*

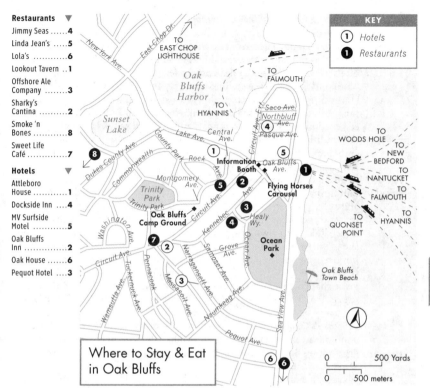

**Restaurants** ▼
Jimmy Seas ......**4**
Linda Jean's .....**5**
Lola's ...........**6**
Lookout Tavern ..**1**
Offshore Ale
Company ........**3**
Sharky's
Cantina .........**2**
Smoke 'n
Bones ...........**8**
Sweet Life
Café .............**7**

**Hotels** ▼
Attleboro
House ...........**1**
Dockside Inn ....**4**
MV Surfside
Motel ...........**5**
Oak Bluffs
Inn .............**2**
Oak House .......**6**
Pequot Hotel ....**3**

KEY
① Hotels
❶ Restaurants

**Where to Stay & Eat
in Oak Bluffs**

0        500 Yards
0      500 meters

(whole littleneck clams) marinara and linguine puttanesca. A brightly colored porch and painted ceilings add to the place's charm, although service can be a little uneven. ✉ *32 Kennebec Ave.* ☎ *508/696–8550* ⚲ *Reservations not accepted* ▤*MC, V.*

¢–$  ✕ **Linda Jean's.** This is a classic local hangout, a diner that serves food
★    the way a diner should: with hearty helpings and inexpensive prices.
AMERICAN  Want breakfast at 6 AM? No problem. Want breakfast at 11:30 AM? No problem. Tired of the gourmet world and want comfortable booths, friendly waitresses, and few frills? No problem. The only problem: you may have to wait—even at 6 AM. ✉ *34 Circuit Ave.* ☎ *508/693–4093* ⚲ *Reservations not accepted* ▤*AE, MC, V.*

$$–$$$$  ✕ **Lola's.** This festive spot draws a party crowd. On one side, a spirited
SOUTHERN  bar hosts live music; an enclosed patio for dining and a large separate dining room are on another side. Ribs as well as Southern and Louisiana standards such as crawfish étouffée and grilled swordfish with key lime–dill sauce fill the long menu; Sunday mornings are reserved for an all-you-can-eat buffet brunch, often with live gospel or jazz. This is more of a scene than a relaxing dining spot. However, the bar is big and welcoming, and the wall mural is full of familiar local faces. Lighter, less expensive fare, such as chicken jambalaya and fried catfish, is available from the pub menu. ✉*Beach Rd., about 1 mi from Oak*

*Bluffs* ☎*508/693–5007* ⊕*www.lolassouthernseafood.com* ▤*DC, MC, V* ☉*No lunch.*

¢–$$$ **✕Lookout Tavern.** There are two things about this easygoing Oak Bluffs
SEAFOOD seafood joint that make it stand out. First, its rustic dining room affords
direct views of the sea and incoming ferryboats—it's truly the perfect
"lookout" if you love watching boats ply the island's waters. Second, it
serves usual seafood platters plus first-rate sushi, from the salmon and
tuna rolls to more unusual treats, like the Inkwell Roll, with barbecued
eel, cucumber, avocado, crabmeat, and seaweed salad. Highlights from
the traditional menu include the grilled Cuban sandwich, the snow-
crab dinner, fish-and-chips, or the fried scallop plate. ⊠*8 Seaview Ave.
Ext.* ☎*508/696–9844* ▤*AE, D, DC, MC, V.*

$–$$$$ **✕Offshore Ale Company.** The island's first and only microbrewery res-
AMERICAN taurant has become quite popular. There are private wooden booths,
and there's dark wood throughout, a dartboard in the corner, and live
music throughout the year (Wednesday-night Irish-music jams are a
hoot). Take your own peanuts from a barrel by the door and drop the
shells on the floor; then order from a menu that includes steaks and
burgers, chicken, pasta, gumbo, and fish. However, to truly appreciate
the beer, try it with one of the wood-fired brick-oven pizzas. There's a
great shaded patio for outdoor dining in warmer weather. ⊠*30 Ken-
nebec Ave.* ☎*508/693–2626* ⊕*www.offshoreale.com* ⚑*Reservations
not accepted* ☉*No lunch Mon. and Tues. Oct.–May* ▤*AE, MC, V.*

¢–$$ **✕Sharky's Cantina.** Sharky's serves tasty—somewhat creative—Mexican
★ and Southwestern fare and great drinks, and you may wait awhile to
MEXICAN get a table. But once you're in, savor spicy tortilla soup, lobster quesadillas, steak burritos, chicken mole, and Gaucho-style skirt steak.
There's an extensive margarita list (they're strong here), and for dessert
try apple-pie empanadas drizzled with caramel sauce. Limited items
from the menu are served until around midnight during the summer
season. They have a second location in Edgartown. ⊠*31 Circuit Ave.*
☎*508/693–7501* ⊕*www.sharkyscantina.com* ⚑*Reservations not
accepted* ▤*AE, MC, V.*

$–$$$ **✕Smoke 'n Bones.** This is the island's only rib joint, with its own smoker
SOUTHERN out back and a cord of hickory, apple, oak, and mesquite wood stacked
up around the lot. Treats from the smoker include Asian-style dry-
rubbed ribs and North Carolina–style pulled pork. The homemade
onion rings are addictive. The place has a cookie-cutter, prefab feel-
ing, with all the appropriate touches—neon flames around the kitchen
and marble bones for doorknobs. If you're a true rib aficionado, this
may not satisfy you, but on the Vineyard it's an offbeat treat. A sec-
ond location, a bit smaller, is at 7 Circuit Ave. ⊠*20 Oakland Ave.*
☎*508/696–7427* ⊕*www.smokenbonesmv.com* ⚑*Reservations not
accepted* ☉*Closed Nov.–Mar.* ▤*MC, V.*

$$$$ **✕Sweet Life Café.** Housed in a charming Victorian house, this island
FodorsChoice favorite's warm tones, low lighting, and handsome antique furniture
★ will make you feel like you've entered someone's home—but the cook-
AMERICAN ing is more sophisticated than home-style. Dishes on the menu are
prepared in inventive ways (and change often with the seasons); duck
breast is roasted with a lavender-rosemary-honey glaze, and the gaz-

pacho is a white version with steamed clams, toasted almonds, sliced red grapes, and smoked-paprika oil. The desserts are superb; try the warm chocolate fondant (a sort of soufflé) with toasted-almond ice cream. There's outdoor dining by candlelight in a shrub-enclosed garden, with heaters for cold nights. ⊠ *Upper Circuit Ave. at far end of town* ☎ *508/696–0200* ⚄ *Reservations essential* ▤ *AE, D, MC, V* ⊙ *Closed Jan.–Mar.*

$  ▦ **Attleboro House.** This guesthouse, part of the Methodist Association Camp Grounds, is across the street from busy Oak Bluffs Harbor. The big 1874 gingerbread Victorian, an inn since its construction, has wraparound verandas on two floors and small, simple rooms with powder-blue walls, lacy white curtains, and a few antiques. Some rooms have sinks. Singles have three-quarter beds, and every room is provided linen exchange (but no chambermaid service) during a stay. The five shared baths are rustic and old but clean. **Pros:** super-affordable; steps from restaurants and shops; sinks in some rooms. **Cons:** shared bathrooms; zero frills; no Web site. ⊠ *42 Lake Ave., Box 1564* ☎ *508/693–4346* ⬳ *11 rooms with shared bath* ⚄ *In-room: no phone, no TV. In-hotel: no elevator* ▤ *AE, D, MC, V* ⊙ *Closed Oct.–May* ⦿ *CP.*

$$$–$$$$  ▦ **Dockside Inn.** This gingerbread Victorian-style inn built in the late '80s, decked with broad porches, sits right by the dock, steps from the ferry landing and downtown shops, restaurants, and bars. Kids are welcome, and they'll have plenty to do in town and at nearby beaches. Some rooms open onto building-length balconies. **Pros:** close to everything; very kid-friendly; big porches. **Cons:** front of inn right on street; busy location; lots of kids in summer. ⊠ *9 Circuit Ave., Box 1206* ☎ *508/693–2966 or 800/245–5979* ⊕ *www.vineyardinns.com* ⬳ *17 rooms, 5 suites, 2 apartments* ⚄ *In-room: kitchen (some), VCR, Wi-Fi. In-hotel: no elevator, Wi-Fi.* ▤ *AE, MC, V* ⊙ *Closed late Oct.–mid-May* ⦿ *CP.*

$$–$$$  ▦ **Martha's Vineyard Surfside Motel.** These two buildings stand right in the thick of things, steps from restaurants and nightlife, so they tend to get noisy in summer. Rooms are spacious and bright (especially corner units), smartly decorated with carpets, stylish wallpaper, tile floors, and fairly standard but attractive chain-style furnishings that include a table and chairs. Deluxe rooms have water views. Four suites have whirlpool baths, and two are wheelchair-accessible. The staff is helpful and courteous. **Pros:** affordable by MV standards; large rooms; close to dining and shopping. **Cons:** busy location; more functional than romantic; lots of kids. ⊠ *70 Oak Bluffs Ave., Box 2507* ☎ *508/693–2500 or 800/537–3007* ⬳ *508/693–7343* ⊕ *www.mvsurfside.com* ⬳ *37 rooms, 4 suites* ⚄ *In-room: refrigerator, Wi-Fi. In-hotel: restaurant, no elevator, some pets allowed (fee)* ▤ *AE, D, MC, V.*

$$$–$$$$  ▦ **Oak Bluffs Inn.** A tan octagonal viewing tower dominates this rosy-hue Victorian B&B with a veranda on Oak Bluffs' main street, a short stroll from the beach. Victorian and country pieces fill the high-ceilinged rooms, all of which have private baths and gauzy white curtains; one has a four-poster bed. One very large room in the carriage house can accommodate three adults or two adults and two kids. Way up on the 3rd floor is a newer two-bedroom apartment. **Pros:** steps from shops

and restaurants; handsome building; well-chosen antiques. **Cons:** in the thick of the commercial district; a tad frilly; location can be a little noisy. ⊠*64 Circuit Ave., at Pequot Ave., Box 2546* 📷*508/693–7171 or 800/955–6235* 📠*508/693–8787* ⊕*www.oakbluffsinn.com* ➹*10 rooms* ⚲*In-room: no telephone, no TV, Wi-Fi. In-hotel: no elevator* ▭*AE, MC, V* ⊗*Closed Nov.–late Apr.* ‖◯‖*CP.*

$$$–$$$$    🔲**Oak House.** The wraparound veranda of this courtly pastel-painted
★    1872 Victorian looks across a busy street to the beach and out across Nantucket Sound. Several rooms have private terraces or balconies; if you're bothered by noise, ask for a room in back. Ceilings, wall paneling, wainscoting, and furnishings are all in richly painted or polished oak, and all this well-preserved wood creates an appropriate setting for the choice antique furniture and nautical-theme accessories. An elegant afternoon tea with cakes and cookies is served in a glassed-in sunporch. **Pros:** stunning decor; romantic and adult-oriented; some rooms have water views. **Cons:** some rooms get street noise; old-fashioned vibe might turn off minimalists; busy location. ⊠*79 Seaview Ave., Box 299* 📷*508/693–4187 or 866/693–5805* ⊕*www.vineyardinns.com* ➹*8 rooms, 2 suites* ⚲*In-hotel: no kids under 10, no elevator, public Wi-Fi* ▭*AE, D, MC, V* ⊗*Closed mid-Oct.–mid-May* ‖◯‖*CP.*

$$–$$$    🔲**Pequot Hotel.** The bustle of downtown Oak Bluffs is a pleasant five-minute walk past Carpenter Gothic houses from this casual cedar-shingle inn on a tree-lined street. The furniture is quirky but comfortable; the old wing has the most atmosphere. In the main section of the building, the 1st floor has a wide porch with rocking chairs—perfect for enjoying coffee or tea with the cookies that are set out in the afternoon—and a small breakfast room where you help yourself to bagels, muffins, and cereal in the morning. The hotel is one block from the beaches that line Oak Bluffs–Edgartown Road. **Pros:** steps from shops and dining; reasonable rates; charmingly offbeat. **Cons:** dated decor; no room phones; some rooms are small. ⊠*19 Pequot Ave.* 📷*508/693–5087 or 800/947–8704* 📠*508/696–9413* ⊕*www.pequothotel.com* ➹*30 rooms, 1 3-bedroom apartment* ⚲*In-room: no phone. In-hotel: no elevator, public Wi-Fi* ▭*AE, D, MC, V* ⊗*Closed mid-Oct.–Apr.* ‖◯‖*CP.*

## NIGHTLIFE & THE ARTS

Dark and crowded, the **Island House** ( ⊠*11 Circuit Ave.* 📷*508/693–4516*) hosts a mixture of rock, blues, and reggae for younger crowds whose ears crave volume.

The **Lampost** ( ⊠*6 Circuit Ave.* 📷*508/696–9352*) is a good, old-fashioned neighborhood bar with a DJ and dancing. In addition to events such as an '80s night, a Brazilian night, and a Hawaiian night, there are also swing nights. The bar attracts a young crowd.

**Lola's** ( ⊠*Beach Rd.* 📷*508/693–5007*), a popular restaurant, has a lively bar that hosts local musicians. There's a great pub menu year-round, and you can also get regular restaurant cuisine at the bar.

The island's only family brewpub, **Offshore Ale** ( ⊠*Kennebec Ave.* 📷*508/693–2626*) hosts live Latin, folk, and blues year-round and serves its own beer and ales and a terrific pub menu. Cozy up to the fireplace with a pint on cool nights.

The **Ritz Café** ( ⊠*4 Circuit Ave.* ☎*508/693–9851*) is a popular year-round bar with a pool table that's removed in the summer to make way for dancing. There's an eclectic mix of live performances, including rock, blues, and reggae, from Monday through Saturday in summer and on weekends in the off-season.

## SPORTS & THE OUTDOORS

BEACH **Joseph A. Sylvia State Beach** ( ⊠*Between Oak Bluffs and Edgartown, off Beach Rd.*) is a 6-mi-long sandy beach with a view of Cape Cod across Nantucket Sound. Food vendors and calm, warm waters make this a popular spot for families.

FISHING **Dick's Bait & Tackle** ( ⊠*New York Ave.* ☎*508/693–7669*) rents gear, sells accessories and bait, and keeps a current copy of the fishing regulations.

GOLF **Farm Neck Golf Club** ( ⊠*1 Farm Neck Way, off County Rd.* ☎*508/693–3057*), a semiprivate club on marsh-rimmed Sengekontacket Pond, has a driving range and 18 holes in a championship layout. Reservations are required 48 hours in advance.

KAYAKING Carolyn "Chick" Dowd runs great kayaking tours and offers expert instruction through her company **Island Spirit Sea-Kayak Adventures** ( ☎*508/693–9727* ⊕*www.islandsspirit.com*). Tours range from day trips around Cape Pogue to evening sunset and champagne trips and full-moon paddles.

## SHOPPING

**Book Den East** ( ⊠*71 New York Ave.* ☎*508/693–3946*) stocks 20,000 out-of-print, antiquarian, and paperback books.

**B*tru** ( ⊠*40 Circuit Ave.* ☎*508/693–5222*) sells wonderfully stylish, offbeat, funky clothing and accessories.

If you're looking for out-of-the-ordinary, **Craftworks** ( ⊠*42 Circuit Ave.* ☎*508/693–7463*) carries outrageous painted furniture, ceramic figures, folk art, and home accessories—all handmade by American artists.

**Laughing Bear** ( ⊠*33 Circuit Ave.* ☎*508/693–9342*) carries women's clothing made of Balinese or Indian batiks plus jewelry and accessories from around the world.

The **Secret Garden** ( ⊠*41 Circuit Ave.* ☎*508/693–4759*), set in a yellow gingerbread cottage, has a complete line of Shelia collectibles—miniature wooden versions of Camp Ground houses and other island landmarks.

ART GALLERIES **Cousen Rose Gallery** ( ⊠*71 Circuit Ave.* ☎*508/693–6656*) displays works by many island artists, including Myrna Morris, John Breckenridge, Marietta Cleasby, Deborah Colter, Lynn Hoefs, Ray Prosser, and Renee Balter. During the summer months, be sure to inquire about children's art classes.

**Dragonfly Gallery** (⊠*Dukes County and Vineyard Aves.* ☎*508/693–8877*) changes shows weekly and holds artist receptions—featuring jazz pianist John Alaimo—every other Saturday during the summer from 4 to 7 PM. Check the local papers for a schedule of artists.

---

## EDGARTOWN

*6 mi southeast of Oak Bluffs.*

★ Stop at a complex of buildings and lawn exhibits that constitutes the **Martha's Vineyard Historical Society** to orient yourself historically before making your way around town. The opening hours and admission listed below apply to all the buildings and exhibits—including the Thomas Cooke House, the Francis Foster Museum, the Capt. Francis Pease House, and the Carriage Shed—and the Huntington Reference Library of Vineyard History, which contains archives of oral history, letters, and law documents. The museum sells an excellent Edgartown walking-tour booklet full of anecdotes and the history of the people who have lived in the town's houses over the past three centuries; you can purchase the booklet at the entrance gatehouse in summer or at the library in winter. ⊠*Cooke and School Sts.* ☎*508/627–4441* ⊕*www.marthasvineyardhistory.org* ⊠*$7* ⊙*Mid-Oct.–mid-June, Mon.–Sat. 10–4; mid-June–mid-Oct., Mon.–Sat. 10–5.*

Once a well-to-do whaling center, Edgartown remains the Vineyard's toniest town and has preserved parts of its elegant past. Sea captains' houses from the 18th and 19th centuries, ensconced in well-manicured gardens and lawns, line the streets.

The island's oldest dwelling is the 1672 **Vincent House Museum.** A tour of this weathered-shingle farmhouse takes you along a time line that starts with the sparse furnishings of the 1600s and ends in a Federal-style parlor of the 1800s. ⊠*Main St.* ☎*508/627–4440* ⊕*www.mvpreservation.org/tours.html* ⊠*Museum $5* ⊙*May–mid-Oct., Mon.–Sat. 10:30–3.*

The **Edgartown Lighthouse,** surrounded by a public beach, provides a great view (but seaweedy bathing). The white cast-iron tower was floated by barge from Ipswich, Massachusetts, in 1938, and is still an active navigational aid. Sunset tours are given on Thursday evenings; the lighthouse is open Thursday through Monday 11–5. Admission is $5. ⊠*Off N. Water St.*

**NEED A BREAK?**

If you need a pick-me-up, pop into **Espresso Love** (⊠*3 S. Water St.* ☎*508/627-9211*) for a cappuccino and a homemade raspberry scone or blueberry muffin. If you prefer something cold, the staff also makes fruit smoothies. Light lunch fare is served: bagel sandwiches, soups, and delicious pastries and cookies—all homemade, of course. It's by the Edgartown bus station.

☾ The 350-acre **Felix Neck Wildlife Sanctuary,** a Massachusetts Audubon Soci-
★ ety preserve 3 mi outside Edgartown toward Oak Bluffs and Vineyard

Haven, has 2 mi of hiking trails traversing marshland, fields, woods, seashore, and waterfowl and reptile ponds. Naturalist-led events include sunset hikes, stargazing, snake or bird walks, and canoeing. ⊠*Off Edgartown–Vineyard Haven Rd.* ☎*508/627–4850* 🔊*$4* ⊙*Center June–Aug., weekdays 8:30–4:30, Sat. 9:30–4:30, Sun. 10–3; Sept.–May, weekdays 9–4, Sat. 10–3, Sun. noon–3. Trails daily sunrise–dusk.*

A beautiful expanse of open fields and working barns, the **Farm Institute** is a teaching farm with a mission to educate adults and children about sustainable agriculture. There's plenty of produce and livestock to see while taking part in any of the numerous programs offered throughout the year, and visitors are welcome anytime for self-guided tours of the property. From June through September, stock up on the farm's bounty of produce, eggs, and meat (when available)—chances are, kids attending the summer program will be manning the farm stand. Try your luck at tackling the corn maze ($10 for adults, $5 for kids), open from about mid-July to early October. ⊠*14 Aero Ave., Katama* ☎*508/627–7007* ⊕*www.farminstitute.org.*

## WHERE TO STAY & EAT

$$$–$$$$
FRENCH

✕**Alchemy Bistro and Bar.** According to the menu, the dictionary meaning of *alchemy* is "a magic power having as its asserted aim the discovery of a panacea and the preparation of the elixir of longevity"—lofty goals for a French-style bistro. This high-class version has elegant gray wainscoting, classic paper-covered white tablecloths, old wooden floors, and an opening cut into the ceiling to reveal the 2nd-floor tables. The only things missing are the patina of age, experience, cigarette smoke—and French working folks' prices—but you can expect quality and imagination. One example is the fried cornmeal-dusted soft-shell crab with lemon risotto, sweet peas, and artichokes. The alcohol list, long and complete, includes cognacs, grappas, and beers. On balmy evenings, the half-dozen outdoor tables on the candlelit brick patio are highly coveted. ⊠*71 Main St.* ☎*508/627–9999* ⊟*AE, MC, V.*

$$$$
★
AMERICAN

✕**Atria.** One of the island's more urbane venues, Atria feels like a big-city bistro and cocktail lounge, with a swank dining room, glam crowd, and artful food presentations. Chef Christian Thornton uses eclectic, globally influenced ingredients to come up with such entrées as cracklin' pork shank with collard greens and sour cream–mustard sauce; and grilled lamb T-bones with Tuscan-style white beans, roasted tomatoes, grilled artichokes, and a red-wine reduction. Top starters include steak tartare with crisp shallots, capers, truffle oil, and aged balsamic vinegar; and braised-veal-cheek ravioli with stuffed squash blossoms, shaved Parmesan, and truffle oil. The chocolate-molten cake with cappuccino ice cream is a great finish. There's jazz certain evenings. ⊠*137 Main St.* ☎*508/627–5850* ⊕*www.atriamv.com* ⊟*AE, MC, V.*

$$$–$$$$
Fodor'sChoice
★
AMERICAN

✕**Detente.** A dark, intimate wine bar and restaurant with hardwood floors and rich banquette seating, Detente serves more than a dozen wines by the glass as well as numerous half bottles. Even if you're not much of an oenophile, it's worth a trip just for the innovative food, much of it from local farms and seafood purveyors. Try the complex starter of ahi-tuna tartare with toasted pine nuts, vanilla-pear puree, ginger, and arugula salad, followed by such choice entrées as roasted venison loin with thyme spaetzle, sautéed Swiss chard, blue cheese, roasted figs, and a port reduction; or lemon-honey-basted halibut with potato au gratin, truffled leek puree, roasted artichokes, and oven-dried tomatoes. ⊠*Nevin Sq., off Water St.* ☎*508/627–8810* ⊕*www.detentewinebar.com* ▤*AE, MC, V* ☾*Closed Tues. No lunch.*

¢    ✕**Edgartown Deli.** A no-frills place with a down-home, happy feeling, this deli has walls and a glass counter plastered with specials written
AMERICAN   on multicolored paper. Brightly lighted booths fill one side of the room, and customers line up at the counter for orders to go. Breakfast specials, served from 8 until 10:45, include egg, cheese, and *linguiça* (garlicky Portuguese sausage) on a roll. Lunch sandwiches include corned beef and Swiss, roast beef, turkey, pastrami, or steak and cheese. ⊠*52 Main St.* ☎*508/627–4789* ⋇*Reservations not accepted* ▤*No credit cards* ☾*Closed mid-Oct.–Apr. No dinner.*

$$$–$$$$   ✕**Lure.** The airy restaurant at Winnetu Oceanside Resort draws plenty
**Fodor's**Choice   of discerning diners, including plenty of nonhotel guests, to sample
★   some of the most exquisite and creatively prepared seafood on the
SEAFOOD   island. It's the only dining room with a south-facing water view, and it's a stunning one at that. The staff here is young, eager to please, and friendly, and chef Mark Goldberg, previously of Boston's famed Mistral restaurant, knows his way around a kitchen. You won't find a better lobster dish on the island than Lure's tender butter-poached version topped with roasted corn and fava beans and served alongside buttery corn bread. Locally caught fluke with littleneck clams, leeks, smoked bacon, and a rich chowder broth is another star. Finish off with the molten Valhrona chocolate cake with vanilla ice cream and raspberry coulis. If you've got children in tow, you'll appreciate the back dining area, complete with separate play area (you can actually have a relaxing and fine candlelit dinner with the little ones along—without the angry glares from your neighbors). ⊠*Katama Rd.* ☎*508/627–3663* ▤*AE, D, MC, V* ☾*No lunch.*

¢–$   ✕**Morning Glory Farm.** Fresh farm greens in the salads and vegetables in
★   the soups; homemade pies, breads, quiches, cookies, and cakes; and a
AMERICAN   picnic table and grass to enjoy them on make this an ideal place for a simple country lunch. ⊠*W. Tisbury Rd.* ☎*508/627–9003* ▤*MC, V* ☾*Closed late Dec.–Apr.*

$–$$$   ✕**Wharf Pub.** The name may sound generic, and the menu tends toward
AMERICAN   the predictable—shrimp scampi, prime rib, burgers, and steaks—but this lively bar and grill in the heart of Edgartown earns kudos for its well-prepared food, inviting dining room and pair of bars, and easygoing vibe. Standouts include the grilled flank steak with fries and a horseradish cream sauce, and the Cobb salad with ham and chicken. You can tune in to a game on the TV or mingle with locals. It's nothing fancy, but this year-round mainstay is consistently reliable and a great bet for singles, groups of friends, and—especially during the day—families. ⊠*Lower Main St.* ☎*508/627–9966* ▤*AE, D, MC, V.*

$$$$   ☐**Charlotte Inn.** From the moment you walk up to the dark-wood Scottish barrister's check-in desk at this regal 1864 inn, you'll be surrounded
**Fodor's**Choice   by the trappings and customs of a bygone era. Guests' names are hand-
★

written into the register by the dignified and attentive staff. Beautiful
antique furnishings, objets d'art, and paintings fill the property—the
book you pick up in your room might be an 18th-century edition of
Voltaire, and your bed could be a hand-carved four-poster. All rooms
have hair dryers and robes; rooms in the carriage house have fireplaces
and French doors that open into the brick courtyard as well as private
patios. The elegant atmosphere that pervades the property extends to
the inn's swank restaurant, the Catch. **Pros:** over-the-top lavish; quiet
yet convenient location; beautifully landscaped. **Cons:** restaurant has
changed a lot lately; can feel overly formal; intimidating if you don't
adore museum-quality antiques. ⊠*27 S. Summer St.* ☎*508/627–4751
or 800/735–2478* 🖷*508/627–4652* ⊕*www.charlotteinn.net* ➪*23
rooms, 2 suites* ⊘*In-room: Ethernet. In-hotel: restaurant, no elevator,
no kids under 14* ☐*AE, MC, V* ⃝*CP.*

$$–$$$  🏠**Edgartown Commons.** This condominium complex of seven buildings,
which includes an old house and motel rooms set around a busy pool,
is just a couple of blocks from town. Studios and one- or two-bedroom
condos all have full kitchens, and some are very spacious. Each has
been decorated by its individual owner, so the decor varies—some have
an older look, others are new and bright. Definitely family-oriented,
the place is abuzz with kids; rooms away from the pool are quieter.
**Pros:** nice big pool; full kitchens in units; great for families. **Cons:**

decor varies according to each unit's owner; lacks historical character; lots of kids. ✉*20 Pease's Point Way, Box 1293* ☎*508/627–4671 or 800/439–4671* 🖷*508/627–4271* ⊕*www.edgartowncommons.com* 🛏*35 units* ⌂*In-room: no phone, kitchen, some Wi-Fi. In-hotel: pool, laundry facilities, no elevator, public Wi-Fi* ▤*AE, MC, V* ⊙*Closed mid-Oct.–Mar.*

$–$$$$  🏨**Edgartown Inn.** The inside of the former home of whaling captain Thomas Worth still evokes its late-18th-century origins. In fact, its cozy parlor and antique-filled rooms look as if the captain still lives here. The inn was also the spot where Nathaniel Hawthorne wrote much of his *Twice Told Tales* during a stay. Many an Edgartonian joins inn guests in the paneled dining room or back garden for breakfast in summertime. Some rooms have harbor views. **Pros:** great value; main inn building is rich in history; close to Edgartown shopping and dining. **Cons:** no Internet access; doesn't accept credit cards; least expensive rooms have shared baths. ✉*56 N. Water St.* ☎*508/627–4794* 🖷*508/627–9420* ⊕*www.edgartowninn.com* 🛏*17 rooms, 2 with shared bath* ▤*No credit cards* ⊙*Closed Nov.–early Apr.*

$$$$  🏨**Harbor View Hotel & Resort.** The centerpiece of this historic hotel—
★  which continues to evolve during a multiyear, near $80 million overhaul—is a gray-shingle, 1891 Victorian building with wraparound veranda and a gazebo. Accommodations are also in a complex of nearby buildings in a residential neighborhood. The contemporary town houses have cathedral ceilings, decks, kitchens, and large living areas with sofa beds. Rooms in other buildings are laid out like upscale motor-lodge units but have the same fine decor and plush in-room amenities, from CD clock radios to L'Occitane bath products. A beach, good for walking, stretches ¾ mi from the hotel's dock, and the sheltered bay is a great place for kids to swim. Packages and theme weekends are available. The extensive children's program has a full roster of activities for kids ages 3–10, from Memorial Day to Labor Day. The hotel is also home to the Coach House restaurant, a worthy spot for a full meal that also has an excellent, lighter bar menu. **Pros:** great harbor views; not far from restaurants; recently renovated. **Cons:** close to but a few blocks from commercial district; less intimate than B&Bs; steep rates. ✉*131 N. Water St., Box 7* ☎*508/627–7000 or 800/225–6005* 🖷*508/742–1042* ⊕*www.harbor-view.com* 🛏*80 rooms, 30 suites* ⌂*In-room: kitchen (some), refrigerator, Wi-Fi. In-hotel: 3 restaurants, room service, tennis courts, pool, gym, concierge, laundry service* ▤*AE, DC, MC, V.*

$$$$  🏨**Harborside Inn.** Edgartown's only true waterfront accommodation, with boat docks at the end of its nicely landscaped lawn, this large inn provides a central town location, harbor-view decks, and plenty of amenities. Seven two- and three-story buildings sprawl around formal rose beds, brick walkways, a brick patio, and a heated pool. Rooms have colonial-style but modern furnishings, brass beds and lamps, and textured wallpapers. Some units have terraces facing Edgartown Harbor. **Pros:** steps from restaurants and shops; immaculate rooms; lovely gardens. **Cons:** in center of Edgartown action and crowds; it's run as condo/time-share; lots of kids in summer. ✉*3 S.*

*Water St., Box 67* ☎*508/627–4321 or 800/627–4009* 🖷*508/627–7566* ⊕*www.theharborsideinn.com* 🖙*85 rooms, 4 suites* ⚿*In-room: refrigerator, Wi-Fi. In-hotel: pool, no elevator* ▭*AE, MC, V* ⊘*Closed mid-Nov.–mid-Apr.*

$$$$  🖳**Hob Knob.** This 19th-century Gothic Revival eco-chic boutique hotel
★  blends the amenities and service of a luxury property with the ambience and charm of a small B&B. A short walk from the harbor, it's on the main road into town—but far enough out to avoid crowds. Rooms are gracious and quite large by island standards; the upper floors have dormer windows. Art and antiques help capture the island's rural, seaside charm, and many rooms overlook the spectacular gardens. The inn also runs fishing trips and charters on its 27-foot Boston Whaler. Full breakfast—organic and locally gathered—and lavish afternoon tea are included. **Pros:** spacious rooms; afternoon tea included; easy walk to harbor yet slightly removed from crowds. **Cons:** steep rates; near but not overlooking harbor. ✉*128 Main St.* ☎*508/627–9510 or 800/696–2723* 🖷*508/627–4560* ⊕*www.hobknob.com* 🖙*16 rooms, 1 suite* ⚿*In-room: DVD, Wi-Fi. In-hotel: gym, bicycles, spa, no elevator, no kids under 7* ▭*AE, MC, V* ⦿*BP.*

$$$$  🖳**Kelley House.** In the center of town, this sister property of the Harbor View combines services and amenities with a country-inn feel. The 1742 white clapboard main house and the adjacent Garden House are surrounded by pink roses. Large suites in the Chappaquiddick House and the two spacious town houses in the Wheel House have porches (most with harbor views) and living rooms. The Newes from America, a dark and cozy spot with original hand-hewn timbers and ballast-brick walls, serves typical pub victuals and microbrewed beers on tap. **Pros:** lots of historic charm; pretty gardens; some harbor views. **Cons:** on street with lots of pedestrian traffic; pricey; frequent wedding locale. ✉*23 Kelley St., Box 37* ☎*508/627–7900 or 800/225–6005* 🖷*508/627–8142* ⊕*www.kelley-house.com* 🖙*43 rooms, 11 suites* ⚿*In-room: kitchen (some), refrigerator, Wi-Fi. In-hotel: restaurant, bar, pool, laundry service* ▭*AE, DC, MC, V* ⦿*CP.*

$$$$  🖳**Mattakesett Properties.** This attractive resort complex, which is part of the nearby Winnetu Oceanside Resort, sits close to South Beach. Mattakesett differs from the Winnetu in that all of its units are owner-furnished town houses and condominiums with three to four bedrooms; guests at either property can use the amenities at both. All homes have fireplaces and decks. The children's programs are extensive, and the pool and barbecue grills make this a favorite for families. Bookings at Mattakesett are taken on a per-week basis only. A vintage fire truck and livery are used to shuttle you around the area. **Pros:** access to Winnetu facilities; pretty good value for large families; close to South Beach. **Cons:** some units more nicely decorated than others; not an in-town location; lots of kids in summer. ✉*Katama Rd., RFD 270* ☎*508/627–4747 or 978/443–1733* ⊕*www.winnetu.com* 🖙*92 units* ⚿*In-room: kitchen, Ethernet (some), Wi-Fi (some). In-hotel: tennis courts, pool, gym, children's programs (ages 3–12), laundry facilities, no elevator, some pets allowed (fee)* ▭*AE, MC, V* ⊘*Mattakesett closed mid-Oct.–mid-May.*

**6**

$$$–$$$$   🖼️**Victorian Inn.** White with the classic black shutters of the town's his-
★   toric homes and fronted by ornate columns, this appropriately named
inn sits a block from the downtown harbor; it was built as the home of
19th-century whaling captain Lafayette Rowley. Today the inn's three
floors are done in dark woods and bold floral wallpapers, with rugs over
wood floors. Several rooms hold handmade reproduction four-poster
beds. Breakfast, served in season in the brick-patio garden, includes
creative muffins and breads. **Pros:** staff is top-notch; super-romantic;
close to restaurants. **Cons:** you'd better love high-style Victoriana; not
geared toward families; lots of pedestrian traffic. ⊠*24 S. Water St.*
☎*508/627–4784* ⊕*www.thevic.com* ⇌*14 rooms* ⚙*In-room: Wi-Fi.
In-hotel: no elevator, no kids under 8* ⊟*MC, V* ⏆❘*BP.*

$$$$   🖼️**Winnetu Oceanside Resort.** A departure from most properties on the
Fodor's Choice   island, the contemporary Winnetu—styled after the grand multistory
★   resorts of the Gilded Age—both encourages families and provides a
contemporary seaside-resort experience for couples. This all-suites
property has units that can sleep up to 11 guests. All have kitchens
and decks or patios with views. Room decor is stylish and modern
but casual enough so that kids feel right at home. The resort arranges
bicycling and kayaking trips, lighthouse tours, and other island activi-
ties. A full slate of excellent children's programs is offered in July and
August. Complimentary shuttles run throughout the day to nearby
Edgartown, or take the scenic and lovely water taxi (small fee) for
an evening in town. The General Store carries snacks, and the superb
Lure restaurant, the only one on the island with a south-facing water
view, prepares tasty box lunches for the beach. (It's open to the public
and specializes in gourmet fish fare.) The staff will stock your kitchen
in advance of your arrival on request and can arrange a wide range of
island tours and activities, from bike trips to yoga classes. Clambakes
are held on the grounds on Wednesday evening. In summer, all stays
must be a minimum of three nights. Breakfast for two is included for
spring and fall stays. **Pros:** outstanding staff; tons of activities; fantas-
tic restaurant; private path to the beach. **Cons:** pricey; not an in-town
location; lots of kids in summer. ⊠*31 Dunes Rd.* ☎*508/627–4747 or
978/443–1733* ⊕*www.winnetu.com* ⇌*53 suites* ⚙*In-room: kitchen,
DVD, VCR, Ethernet (some), Wi-Fi (some). In-hotel: 2 restaurants,
tennis courts, pools, gym, concierge, children's programs (ages 3–12),
laundry facilities, room service, public Wi-Fi* ⊟*MC, V* ⏾*Closed late
Oct.–mid-Apr.*

## NIGHTLIFE & THE ARTS

NIGHTLIFE   Atria's **Brick Cellar Bar** ( ⊠*137 Main St.* ☎*508/627–5850*) is just out
of the central part of town, but that doesn't mean it's empty. It's a bit
like a swanky country club den, with leather chairs, a massive brass
bar, an extensive scotch collection, and a working fireplace. Enjoy one
of the clever drinks, including the Aunt Katherine Manhattan (Mak-
er's Mark and sweet vermouth, served neat), and the Espresso Martini
(Stoli vanilla vodka, Kahlúa, Tia Maria, and a shot of fresh espresso).
There's often live music during summer.

**Outerland** ( ✉ *Martha's Vineyard Airport, Edgartown–W. Tisbury Rd.* ☎ *508/693–1137*) books big-name acts such as Medeski, Martin and Wood, Ben Lee, Kate Taylor, and the Derek Trucks Band.

**The Wharf** ( ✉ *Lower Main St.* ☎ *508/627–9966*) is a great spot for tasty food and a terrific place for cocktails, people-watching, and listening to live rock and pop music.

## SPORTS & THE OUTDOORS

**Bend-in-the-Road Beach** ( ✉ *Beach Rd.*), the town's public beach, is backed by low, grassy dunes and wild roses. **Little Beach** ( ✉ *End of Fuller St.*) is a lesser-known beach that looks like a crooked pinkie pointing into Eel Pond; it's a great place for bird-watching (be careful of the fenced-off piping plover breeding grounds in the dunes).

**Coop's Bait and Tackle** ( ✉ *147 W. Tisbury Rd.* ☎ *508/627–3909*) sells accessories and bait, rents fishing gear, and books fishing charters from a roster of nearly two dozen outfits in the area. Choose from trips in search of bass, blues, and specialty off-shore shark and tuna ventures.

## SHOPPING

**Claudia** ( ✉ *51 Main St.* ☎ *508/627–8306*) brings you back to another era with its clever windows, antique display cases, and fabulous French fragrances. You'll find designer, vintage-looking, and fine gold and silver jewelry in a variety of price ranges.

David Le Breton, the owner of **Edgartown Books** ( ✉ *44 Main St.* ☎ *508/627–8463*), is a true bibliophile. He carries a large selection of current and island-related titles and will be happy to make a summer reading recommendation.

The **Edgartown Scrimshaw Gallery** ( ✉ *43 Main St.* ☎ *508/627–9439*) showcases a large collection of scrimshaw, including some antique pieces.

Pick up fine tea accoutrements, chocolates, and gourmet items at **English Butler** ( ✉ *22 Winter St.* ☎ *508/627–1013*), a dainty boutique that also serves high tea with all the proper accompaniments. You can arrange to have your own "scandal tea"—cheeky tea party (gossip is encouraged)—for a minimum of four people at your residence.

The **Old Sculpin Gallery** ( ✉ *58 Dock St.* ☎ *508/627–4881*) is the Martha's Vineyard Art Association's headquarters. Exhibits of the works of local juried artists change weekly; Sunday evenings are host to opening receptions beginning at 6 PM.

---

## PAGODA TREE

Extending ever up and outward over South Water Street is Edgartown's cherished pagoda tree. Brought home from China in a small flowerpot, this tree was planted by sea captain Thomas Milton in 1837. Believed to be the oldest one of its kind on the continent, the tree towers over the captain's home, braced with cables, its massive limbs reaching out in all directions.

6

## CHAPPAQUIDDICK ISLAND

*1 mi southeast of Edgartown.*

A sparsely populated area with many nature preserves, Chappaquiddick Island makes for a pleasant day trip or bike ride on a sunny day. The "island" is actually connected to the Vineyard by a long sand spit that begins in South Beach in Katama. It's a spectacular 2¾-mi walk, or you can take the ferry ($10 for car and driver and $3 for each additional passenger), which departs about every five minutes from 7 AM to midnight daily, June to mid-October, and less frequently from 7 AM to 11:15 PM mid-October to May.

The Land Bank's 226-acre **Three Ponds Preserve** ( ⊠ *Off Chappaquiddick Rd.*) is a popular, scenic picnicking spot. Mown grasses surround a serpentine pond with an island in its center and a woodland backdrop behind—a truly lovely setting. Across the road are fields, woods, and another pond.

Fodor'sChoice
★ The Trustees of Reservations' 14-acre **Mytoi** preserve is a serene, beautifully tended, Japanese-inspired garden with a creek-fed pool spanned by a bridge and rimmed with Japanese maples, azaleas, bamboo, and irises. A boardwalk runs through part of the grounds, where you're apt to see box turtles and hear the sounds of songbirds. There are few more enchanting spots on the island. The garden was created in 1958 by a private citizen. Restroom facilities are available. ⊠ *Dike Rd., .2 mi from intersection with Chappaquiddick Rd.* ☎ *508/627–7689* ⊠ *Free* ☺ *Daily sunrise–sunset.*

A conglomeration of habitats where you can swim, walk, fish, or just sit and enjoy the surroundings, the **Cape Poge Wildlife Refuge** ( ⊠ *East end of Dike Rd., 3 mi from Chappaquiddick ferry landing*), on the easternmost shore of Chappaquiddick Island, is more than 6 square mi of wilderness. Its dunes, woods, cedar thickets, moors, salt marshes, ponds, tidal flats, and barrier beach serve as an important migration stopover and nesting area for numerous sea- and shorebirds. The Trustees of Reservations leads some great tours of the refuge, including canoe and kayak trips, lighthouse, fishing, and natural-history tours. The best way to get to the refuge is as part of a naturalist-led **jeep drive** ( ☎ *508/627–3599* ⊕ *www.thetrustees.org*).

★ The 200-acre **Wasque Reservation** (pronounced *wayce*-kwee) is mostly a vast beach. Closing off the south end of Katama Bay, this is where Chappaquiddick connects to the mainland Vineyard. You can fish, sunbathe, take the trail by Swan Pond, walk to the island's southeasternmost tip at Wasque Point, or dip into the surf—use caution, as the currents are strong. Wasque Beach is accessed by a flat boardwalk with benches overlooking the west end of Swan Pond. It's a pretty walk skirting the pond, with ocean views on one side and poles for osprey nests on the other. Atop a bluff is a pine-shaded picnic grove with a spectacular, practically 180-degree panorama. ⊠ *At east end of Wasque Rd., 5 mi from Chappaquiddick ferry landing* ☎ *508/627–7260* ⊠ *Car and driver $12 round trip, plus $4 per adult; bike and rider $6* ☺ *Property 24 hrs. Gatehouse late May–mid-Oct., daily 9–5.*

## SPORTS & THE OUTDOORS

BEACHES    **East Beach,** one of the area's best beaches, is accessible by car from Dike Road. There is a $3 fee to enter the beach. **Wasque Beach,** at the Wasque Reservation, is an uncrowded ½-mi sandy beach with a parking lot and restrooms. The surf and currents are sometimes strong.

# WEST TISBURY

*8 mi west of Edgartown, 6½ mi south of Vineyard Haven.*

West Tisbury retains its rural appeal and maintains its agricultural tradition at several active horse and produce farms. The town center looks very much like a small New England village, complete with a white-steepled church.

★    A rich and expansive collection of flora and serene walking trails are the attractions of the **Polly Hill Arboretum.** Horticulturist and part-time Vineyard resident Polly Hill, now in her nineties, has over the years tended some 2,000 species of plants and developed nearly 100 species herself on her old sheep farm in West Tisbury. On-site are azaleas, tree peonies, dogwoods, hollies, lilacs, magnolias, and more. Hill raised them from seeds without the use of a greenhouse, and her patience is the inspiration of the arboretum. Now run as a nonprofit center, the arboretum also runs guided tours, a lecture series, and a visitor center and gift shop. ⊠*809 State Rd.* ☎*508/693–9426* ⊕*www.pollyhillarboretum. org* ⊠*$5* ⊙*Grounds daily sunrise–sunset. Visitor center late May–mid-Oct., daily 9:30–4; guided tours by appointment.*

NEED A
BREAK?

Step back in time with a visit to **Alley's General Store** (⊠*State Rd.* ☎*508/693–0088*), the heart of town since 1858. Alley's sells a truly general variety of goods: everything from hammers to housewares and dill pickles to sweet muffins as well as great things you find only in a country store. There's even a post office inside. Behind the parking lot, Garcia's at Back Alley's serves tasty sandwiches and pastries, pizza, hot soups, cakes, and pies, to go year-round.

**Long Point,** a 632-acre Trustees of Reservations preserve with an open area of grassland and heath, provides a lovely walk with the promise of a refreshing swim at its end. The area is bounded on the east by freshwater Homer's Pond, on the west by saltwater Tisbury Great Pond, and on the south by fantastic, mile-long South Beach on the Atlantic Ocean. Long Cove Pond, a sandy freshwater swimming pond, is an ideal spot for bird-watchers. ⊠*Mid-June–mid-Sept., turn left onto unmarked dirt road (Waldron's Bottom Rd., look for mailboxes) 3/10 mi west of airport on Edgartown–W. Tisbury Rd.; at end, follow signs to Long Point parking lot. Mid-Sept.–mid-June, follow unpaved Deep Bottom Rd. (1 mi west of airport) 2 mi to lot* ☎*508/693–7392* ⊕*www.thetrustees. org* ⊠*Mid-June–mid-Sept., $10 per vehicle plus $3 per adult; free rest of yr* ⊙*Daily 9–6.*

★    At the center of the island, the **Manuel F. Correllus State Forest** is a 5,000-acre pine and scrub-oak forest crisscrossed with hiking trails and circled

Where to Stay
& Eat Up-Island

by a paved but rough bike trail (mopeds are prohibited). You'll also find a 2-mi nature trail, a 2-mi par fitness course, and horse trails. The West Tisbury side of the state forest joins with an equally large Edgartown parcel to virtually surround the airport. ⊠*Headquarters on Barnes Rd. by airport* ☎*508/693–2540* ⚏*Free* ☉*Daily sunrise–sunset.*

A paradise for bird-watchers, **Sepiessa Point Reservation** consists of 164 acres on splendid Tisbury Great Pond, with expansive pond and ocean views, walking trails around coves and saltwater marshes, bird-watching, horse trails, swimming, and a boat launch. ⊠*New La., which becomes Tiah's Cove Rd., off W. Tisbury Rd.* ☎*508/627–7141* ⚏*Free* ☉*Daily sunrise–sunset.*

## WHERE TO STAY

$$$–$$$$

Fodor'sChoice

★

🛏 **Lambert's Cove Inn and Restaurant.** A narrow road winds through pine woods and beside creeper-covered stone walls to this posh, handsomely designed inn surrounded by gardens and old stone walls. In 2005, genial innkeepers Scott Jones and I. Kell Hicklin bought what had been a slightly fading 1790 farmhouse inn and gave it a clean, crisp makeover. The richly appointed rooms each have decorative schemes and antiques based on grand East Coast–resort towns, from Key West to Bar Harbor. Those in the outbuildings are airy and a bit more contemporary, some with decks and porches. Guests receive free passes to beautiful and private Lambert's

Cove beach. Fireplaces and hardwood floors lend warmth to the stellar contemporary restaurant ($$$; reservations essential), where you might dine on crab cakes with caper aioli and shaved-fennel salad, or a main course of braised veal cheeks with sweet corn–English pea risotto and a Madeira wine reduction. **Pros:** smart and contemporary decor; fantastic restaurant; serene and verdant grounds. **Cons:** need a car to explore island from here; not for budget travelers; total seclusion is a drawback if you love being in center of action. ⊠ *Off Lambert's Cove Rd.* ⌂ *R.R. 1, Box 422, Vineyard Haven 02568* ☎ *508/693–2298* 🖷 *508/693–7890* ⊕ *www.lambertscoveinn.com* ⟿ *15 rooms* ⌂ *In-room: DVD, Ethernet. In-hotel: restaurant, tennis court, pool, no elevator, public Wi-Fi* ⊟ *AE, MC, V* ꛫ *BP* ⊘ *Closed Jan.–Mar.*

¢ 🖬 **Martha's Vineyard International Hostel.** The only budget, roof-over-your-head alternative in season, this hostel is one of the country's best. The large, common kitchen is outfitted with multiple refrigerators and stoves (barbecue grills are available, too), the common room has a fireplace and plenty of books, and you'll catch wind of local events on the bulletin board. Morning chores are required in summer. The hostel runs summer programs on island history, as well as nature tours. It's near a bike path, and 2 mi from the airport and about 3 mi from the nearest beach. Buses stop out front. **Pros:** it's cheap; it's just off a bike path; it's a fun place to meet young and active backpackers. **Cons:** it's cheap; you need to rely on bus or bike to get to restaurants and towns; prepare to enjoy doing those morning chores during high season. ⊠ *Edgartown–W. Tisbury Rd., Box 158* ☎ *508/693–2665* ⊕ *www. usahostels.org* ⟿ *78 dorm-style beds* ⌂ *In-hotel: laundry facilities, no elevator* ⊟ *MC, V* ⊘ *Closed mid-Oct.–mid-Apr.*

### SPORTS & THE OUTDOORS

**Lambert's Cove Beach** ( ⊠ *Lambert's Cove Rd.*), one of the island's prettiest, has fine sand and clear water. The Vineyard Sound Beach has calm waters; it's good for children.

### SHOPPING

The **Granary Gallery at the Red Barn** ( ⊠ *Old County Rd.* ☎ *508/693–0455*) displays early-American furniture and exhibits artworks by island and international artists.

## CHILMARK

*5½ mi southwest of West Tisbury.*

Chilmark is a rural village where ocean-view roads, rustic woodlands, and lack of crowds have drawn chic summer visitors and resulted in stratospheric real-estate prices. Laced with rough roads and winding stone fences that once separated fields and pastures, Chilmark reminds people of what the Vineyard was like in an earlier time, before the developers came.

**NEED A BREAK?**

The **Chilmark Store** ( ⊠ *7 State Rd.* ☎ *508/645–3655*) serves pizza, burgers, salads, and deli sandwiches—it's a solid take-out lunch spot. If you've bicycled into town, the wooden rockers on the porch may be just the place to take a break—or find a picnic spot of your own nearby to enjoy a fish burger or a slice of the pizza of the day. It's open from May to mid-October.

## WHERE TO STAY

$$$–$$$$ 🏨 **Inn at Blueberry Hill.** Exclusive and secluded, this cedar-shingle retreat on 56 acres of former farmland puts you in the heart of the rural Vineyard. The restaurant, Theo's ($$$–$$$$), is relaxed and elegant, with fresh, health-conscious food that is thoughtfully prepared. You might dine on maple-spiced duck breast with sweet-potato gnocchi, or seared sea scallops with a basil-grapefruit-tarragon beurre blanc. A continental breakfast is included in the room rate (there's a full breakfast on weekends), and a box lunch is available for a picnic on the beach (the inn runs a guest shuttle to Lucy Vincent and Squibnocket beaches). Rooms are sparsely but tastefully decorated with simple island-made furniture; most have glass doors that open onto terraces or private decks. There is a large parlor-library with a fireplace, or you can relax with a scheduled massage. **Pros:** lots of privacy; many rooms have terraces with views; terrific restaurant. **Cons:** not on the water; a long drive from town centers; Wi-Fi in common room but not individual guest rooms. ✉ *74 North Rd.* ☎ *508/645–3322 or 800/356–3322* 📠 *508/645–3799* ⊕ *www.blueberryinn.com* 🛏 *20 rooms, 4 suites* ♿ *In-hotel: restaurant, tennis court, gym, airport shuttle, public Wi-Fi, some pets allowed (fee), no elevator* 🟰 *AE, MC, V* ⊙ *Closed mid-Oct.–mid-May* ⃝ *CP.*

## SPORTS & THE OUTDOORS

★ A dirt road leads off South Road to beautiful **Lucy Vincent Beach,** which in summer is open only to Chilmark residents and those staying in town.

**Squibnocket Beach** ( ✉ *Off South Rd.*), on the south shore, is a narrow stretch of boulder-strewn coastline that is part smooth rocks and pebbles, part fine sand. The area has good waves, and it's popular with surfers. During the season, this beach is restricted to residents and visitors with passes.

## SHOPPING

★ **Chilmark Chocolates** ( ✉ *State Rd.* ☎ *508/645–3013*) sells superior chocolates and what might just be the world's finest butter crunch, which you can sometimes watch being made in the back room.

★ **Martha's Vineyard Glassworks** ( ✉ *683 State Rd.* ☎ *508/693–6026*) makes a great stop not just to browse the colorful, stunningly crafted contemporary glass pieces but also to watch the artists at work in the glassblowing studio.

# MENEMSHA

★ *1½ mi northwest of Chilmark.*

Unspoiled by the "progress" of the past few decades, the working port of Menemsha is a jumble of weathered fishing shacks, fishing and pleasure boats, drying nets, and lobster pots. Several scenes from the movie *Jaws* were filmed here. The village is popular with cyclists who like to stop for ice cream or chowder.

CLOSE UP

## Martha's Vineyard Trivia

The year-round population of the island is about 15,000. On any given day in summer, the population increases five-fold, to an estimated 75,000.

Some four decades after the island was charted in 1602, Bay Colony businessman Thomas Mayhew struck a deal with the Crown and purchased Martha's Vineyard, as well as Nantucket and the Elizabeth Islands, for £40.

Jeanne and Hugh Taylor, the latter the brother of recording star James Taylor, operate the Outermost Inn, by the lighthouse in Aquinnah.

Total shoreline: 126 mi. Total land area: 100 square mi.

Martha's Vineyard was formed more than 20,000 years ago as great sheets of ice, as thick as 2 mi, descended from the frigid northern climes into what is now New England, pushing great chunks of earth and rock before them. When the glaciers melted and receded, the island, as well as Nantucket and Cape Cod, remained in their wake.

When residents say they are going "Up-Island," they mean they're heading to the western areas of Aquinnah, Chilmark, Menemsha, and West Tisbury. The designation is based on nautical terminology, where heading west means going "up" in longitude. "Down-Island" refers to Vineyard Haven, Oak Bluffs, and Edgartown.

During the height of the 19th-century whaling era, it was considered good luck to have an Aquinnah Wampanoag on board. The Wampanoags were renowned as sailors and harpooners. Town residents voted to change the name of Gay Head to Aquinnah in 1997, and the official change was signed into law on May 7, 1998.

The North American continent's last heath hen, an eastern prairie chicken, died in a forest fire on Martha's Vineyard in 1932. A monument to it stands in the State Forest just off the West Tisbury–Edgartown Road.

West Tisbury resident, farmer, and sailor Joshua Slocum became the first man to sail solo around the world. He set out in 1895 in his 36-foot sloop and returned three years later. Ten years later he was lost at sea.

Despite the fact that Great Harbour was renamed Edgartown after the young son of the Duke of York, the unfortunate three-year-old died one month before the name became official.

6

### WHERE TO STAY & EAT

¢–$

SEAFOOD

✕ **The Bite.** Fried everything—clams, fish-and-chips, you name it—is on the menu at this simple, roadside shack, where two outdoor picnic tables are the only seating options. Small, medium, and large are the three options: all of them are perfect if you're craving that classic seaside fried lunch. But don't come on a rainy day, unless you want to get wet—the lines here can be long. To beat the crowds, try arriving between traditional mealtimes. The best advice, however, is to be patient and don't arrive too hungry. The Bite is open 11 AM–3 PM in spring and fall and until 8:45 PM in summer. ⊠ *29 Basin Rd.* ☎ *509/645–9239* ⊕ *www.thebitemenemsha.com* ⊟ No *credit cards* ⊘ *Closed Oct.–late May.*

¢–$$

Fodor'sChoice

★

SEAFOOD

✕**Larsen's.** Basically a retail fish store, Larsen's has a raw take-out counter and will also boil lobsters for you. Dig into a plate of fresh littlenecks or cherrystones. Oysters are not a bad alternative. There's also seafood chowder and a variety of smoked fish and dips. Bring your own bottle of wine or beer, buy your dinner here, and then set up on the rocks, the docks, or the beach: there's no finer alfresco rustic dining on the island. Larsen's closes at 6 PM weekdays, 7 PM weekends. ⊠*Dutcher's Dock* ☎*508/645–2680* ☐*MC, V* 🍴*BYOB* ⊘*Closed mid-Oct.–mid-May.*

$$$$

★

🏠**Beach Plum Inn.** This mansard-roof inn, sister property of the nearby Menemsha Inn, is surrounded by 7 acres of lavish formal gardens and lush woodland; it sits on a bluff over Menemsha Harbor. The floral-theme rooms—five in the main house and six in cottages—have gorgeous furnishings, and some have whirlpool tubs; in the Daffodil Room, bathed in shades of yellow and blue, you'll find a hand-painted queen bed and a romantic balcony. A vaulted, beamed ceiling rises over the bedroom of the secluded Morning Glory Cottage. You are welcome to use the Menemsha Inn's tennis courts and gym, and passes to nearby Lucy Vincent and Squibnocket beaches are available. As romantic settings go, it's hard to beat the restaurant ($$$$) here, with its knockout harbor views, especially at sunset. For dinner, consider such memorable fare as pan-seared scallops with orange-mango-fennel salad, and the mixed grill of lamb chop with rhubarb compote, filet mignon, orange-infused duck, and chicken-apple sausage with truffle risotto. **Pros:** gardens will blow you away; short walk to adorable fishing village of Menemsha; superb restaurant. **Cons:** a bit of a drive from any major towns; public Wi-Fi but none in rooms; pricey. ⊠*North Rd.* ☎*508/645–9454* ⊕*www.beachpluminn.com* 🛏*11 rooms* ᕕ*In-room: refrigerator. In-hotel: concierge, public Wi-Fi, no elevator* ☐*AE, D, MC, V* ⊘*Closed late Oct.–mid-May* ❙⊘❙*BP.*

$$$–$$$$

🏠**Menemsha Inn and Cottages.** For 40 years the late *Life* photographer Alfred Eisenstaedt returned to his cottage on the hill here for the panoramic view of Vineyard Sound and Cuttyhunk beyond the trees below. These cottages, which are owned by the neighboring Beach Plum Inn, all have screened porches, fireplaces, and kitchens, tumble down a hillside behind the main house and vary in privacy and views. You can also stay in the 1989 inn building or the pleasant Carriage House. All rooms have private decks, most with sunset views. Suites include sitting areas, desks, and big tiled baths. A continental breakfast is served in a solarium-style breakfast room with a deck facing the ocean. Passes to both Squibnocket and Lucy Vincent Beaches are provided. Bicycles are available for rent. **Pros:** wonderfully secluded locale on 14 acres; short walk to adorable fishing village of Menemsha; sunset views from private decks. **Cons:** not for the budget-minded; need a car to explore island from here; public Wi-Fi but none in rooms. ⊠*North Rd., Box 38* ☎*508/645–2521* ⊕*www.menemshainn.com* 🛏*15 rooms, 11 cottages, 1 2-bedroom house* ᕕ*In-room: kitchen (some), refrigerator, VCR. In-hotel: tennis court, gym, public Wi-Fi, no elevator* ☐*MC, V* ⊘*Closed late Oct.–mid-May* ❙⊘❙*CP.*

## SPORTS & THE OUTDOORS

**Menemsha Hills Reservation** (⊠*North Rd. just north of Menemsha*) has 4 mi of some of the most challenging, steep, and breathtaking hiking trails on the island, including a stroll up to Martha's Vineyard's second-highest point and another ramble that descends down through the windswept valley to boulder-strewn Vineyard Sound Beach.

# AQUINNAH

*6½ mi west of Menemsha, 10 mi southwest of West Tisbury, 17 mi southwest of Vineyard Haven.*

Aquinnah, called Gay Head until the town voted to change its name in 1997, is an official Native American township. The Wampanoag tribe is the guardian of the 420 acres that constitute the Aquinnah Native American Reservation. Aquinnah (pronounced a-*kwih*-nah) is Wampanoag for "land under the hill." The town is best known for the red-hued Aquinnah Cliffs.

**Quitsa Pond Lookout** (⊠*State Rd.*) has a good view of the adjoining Menemsha and Nashaquitsa ponds, the woods, and the ocean beyond.

Fodor'sChoice ★ A National Historic Landmark, the spectacular **Aquinnah Cliffs** are part of the Wampanoag reservation land. These dramatically striated walls of red clay are the island's major attraction, as evidenced by the tour bus–filled parking lot. Native American crafts and food shops line the short approach to the overlook, from which you can see the Elizabeth Islands to the northeast across Vineyard Sound and Noman's Land Island—a wildlife preserve—3 mi off the Vineyard's southern coast. ⊠*State Rd.*

The brick **Aquinnah Lighthouse** is stationed precariously atop the rapidly eroding cliffs. It's open to the public on Friday, Saturday, and Sunday evenings at sunset, weather permitting. Across from the Aquinnah Lighthouse parking area, you'll see the historic Vanderhoop Homestead (www.vanderhoophomestead.org), a handsome 1880s house that's home to the **Aquinnah Cultural Center** (⊠*Lighthouse Rd.* ☎*508/645–7900* 🎟*$7*), a museum on Aquinnah's rich history. It's open Wednesday, Friday, and Saturday from 11 to 3; house tours are available, and there is an interesting lecture and craft series that covers topics such as beadwork, plant identification, religion, and more. ⊠*Lighthouse Rd.* ☎*508/645–2211* 🎟*$5.*

## WHERE TO STAY & EAT

$–$$$
AMERICAN ✕**The Aquinnah Restaurant.** At the far end of the row of fast-food takeout spots and souvenir shops at the Gay Head Cliffs is this restaurant owned and operated by members of the Vanderhoop and Madison families, native Wampanoags. The view is quite dramatic—especially from the outdoor deck, which is perched hundreds of feet above the open ocean. (Just watch out for bold seagulls, who are not at all afraid to relieve you of your calamari.) For breakfast try the Tomahawk Special, two homemade fish cakes covered with salsa on top of poached eggs with melted cheddar cheese. The lunch menu includes

sandwiches, burgers, and healthful-sounding salads. Dinner entrées include sautéed shrimp, scallops, and lobster with rotini in a chardonnay sauce, and striped bass in a mussel-and-saffron sauce. The home-baked pies (banana cream, pecan, or fruit) come wrapped in a moist and flaky crust. ⊠*State Rd.* ☎*508/645–3867* ☐*MC, V* ⊘*Closed mid-Oct.–mid-Apr.*

$–$$$$   ☷**Duck Inn.** The Duck Inn, originally an 18th-century home built by
★   Native American seafarer George Belain, sits on a bucolic 5-acre bluff overlooking the ocean, with the Aquinnah Lighthouse standing sentinel to the north. The eclectic, fun interior blends peach stucco walls, Native American rugs and wall hangings, and ducks. Three upstairs rooms come with balconies; a suite in the stone-wall lower level (cool in summer, warm in winter) has views of the rolling fields; and a small attached cabin (closed in winter) with separate bath is the least expensive room. The 1st floor's common room, with a working 1928 Glenwood stove, piano, and fireplace, is the heart of the inn. Massage therapies are available, and the healthful organic breakfast fare includes waffles with strawberries and omelets or chocolate crepes. This inn is very informal—kids and pets are welcome. You can hear the waves from the comfort of the outdoor hot tub. **Pros:** a good value on this part of the island; totally secluded; ocean views; within walking distance of the beach. **Cons:** a longish drive from any large town; a very informal operation with no Web site; peaceful setting isn't ideal if you like lots of bustle. ⊠*10 Duck Pond Way, off State Rd., Box 160* ☎*508/645–9018* ☐*508/645–2790* ✈*4 rooms, 1 suite* ⌂*In-hotel: no a/c, some pets allowed, public Wi-Fi* ☐*MC, V* ⦿*BP.*

$$$$   ☷**Outermost Inn.** This rambling, sun-filled inn by the Aquinnah Cliffs
★   stands alone on acres of moorland, a 10-minute walk from the beach. The house is wrapped in windows revealing views of sea and sky in three directions, and there are great views of the Aquinnah Lighthouse from the wide porch and patio. The inn is clean and contemporary, with white walls and polished light-wood floors. Each room has a phone, and one has a whirlpool tub. The restaurant, open to the public, serves dinner nightly in summer and is all prix-fixe at $65 (reservations are essential). **Pros:** spectacular setting high atop Gay Head Cliffs; wonderful food. **Cons:** Outermost location is far from bigger towns on island; steep rates; not suitable for young kids. ⊠*81 Lighthouse Rd., R.R. 1, Box 171* ☎*508/645–3511* ☐*508/645–3514* ⊕*www.outermostinn.com* ✈*7 rooms* ⌂*In-room: no a/c (some), Wi-Fi. In-hotel: restaurant, no elevator, no kids under 12* ☐*AE, D, MC, V* ⊘*Closed mid-Oct.–mid-May* ⦿*BP.*

# MARTHA'S VINEYARD ESSENTIALS

*To research prices, get advice from other travelers, and book travel arrangements, visit www.fodors.com.*

## TRANSPORTATION

### BY AIR
⇨*Air Travel in Essentials in the back of this book.*

**BY BIKE**

Martha's Vineyard offers superb terrain for biking—you can pick up a map that shows the island's many dedicated bike paths from the chamber of commerce. Several shops throughout the island rent bicycles, many of them close to the ferry terminals; some will even deliver your bike rental to your lodging establishment (R. W. Cutler has free delivery). Martha's Vineyard Strictly Bikes rents bike racks for your car.

Bike Rentals **Anderson's Bike Rental** ( ⊠ *Circuit Ave. Exit, Oak Bluffs* ☎ *508/693–9346*). **Edgartown Bicycles** ( ⊠ *Upper Main St., Edgartown* ☎ *508/627–9008*). **Martha's Bike Rentals** ( ⊠ *4 Lagoon Pond Rd., Vineyard Haven* ☎ *508/693–6593*). **R. W. Cutler Bike Rentals** ( ⊠ *1 Main St., Edgartown* ☎ *508/627–4052*).

**BY BOAT & FERRY**

⇨ *Boat & Ferry Travel in Smart Travel Trips in the back of this book.*

**BY BUS**

The big buses of the Martha's Vineyard Transit Authority (VTA) provide regular service to all six towns on the island, with frequent stops in peak season and very limited service in winter. The fare is $1 per town, including the town of departure. One-day ($6), three-day ($15), one-week ($25), and one-month ($40) passes are available at the Edgartown Visitors Center. The VTA also has two free in-town shuttle-bus routes, one in Edgartown and one in Vineyard Haven.

Bus Information **Martha's Vineyard Transit Authority** ( *VTA* ☎ *508/693–9940* ⊕ *www.vineyardtransit.com*).

**BY CAR**

Traffic can be a challenge on Martha's Vineyard, especially in season, but driving can be worth the hassle if you really want to see the whole island and travel freely between towns. Bringing a car over on the ferry in summer, however, requires reservations far in advance, costs almost double what it does in the off-season, and necessitates standing in long lines—it's sometimes easier and more economical to rent a car once you're on the island, and then only for the days when you plan to explore. Where you stay and what you plan on seeing can greatly influence your transportation plans; discuss the different options for getting around Martha's Vineyard with your innkeeper or hotel staff as soon as you've booked a room.

Note that certain equipment, permits, and fees are needed for driving on Katama Beach and Wasque Reservation. Contact the chamber of commerce or park rangers for details.

You can book rentals on Martha's Vineyard through the Woods Hole ferry terminal free phone. The agencies listed below have rental desks at the airport. Cost is $80 to $170 per day for a sedan; a four-wheel-drive vehicle costs around $150 per day (seasonal prices vary).

Martha's Vineyard Agencies **AAA Island** ( ☎ *508/627–6800 or 800/627–6333* ⊕ *www.mvautorental.com*). **Adventure Rentals** ( ⊠ *Beach Rd., Vineyard Haven* ☎ *508/693–1959*).

### BY TAXI

Taxis meet all scheduled ferries and flights, and there are taxi stands by the Flying Horses Carousel in Oak Bluffs, at the foot of Main Street in Edgartown, and by the steamship office in Vineyard Haven. Fares range from $6 within a town to $35 to $42 one-way from Vineyard Haven to Aquinnah.

Rates double between 1 AM and 7 AM. Note that limousine companies often provide service both on- and off-island.

**Martha's Vineyard Taxi Companies** **AdamCab** ( ☎ 508/627–4462 or 800/281–4462 ⊕ www.adamcab.com). **All Island Taxi** ( ☎ 508/693–2929 or 800/693–8294). **Atlantic Cab** ( ☎ 508/693–7110 or 877/477–8294). **Mario's** ( ☎ 508/693–8399).

## CONTACTS & RESOURCES

### TOURS

Liz Villard's Vineyard History Tours leads walking tours of Edgartown's "history, architecture, ghosts, and gossip," including a stop at the Vincent House. Tours are run from April through December; call for times. Liz and her guides also lead similar tours of Oak Bluffs and Vineyard Haven. Walks last a little more than an hour. Martha's Vineyard Sightseeing runs 2½-hour tours that cover the entire island.

**Contacts** **Martha's Vineyard Sightseeing Inc.** ( ☎ 508/627–8687). **Vineyard History Tours** ( ☎ 508/627–8619).

### VISITOR INFORMATION

The Martha's Vineyard Chamber of Commerce is two blocks from the Vineyard Haven ferry. The chamber information booth by the Vineyard Haven steamship terminal is open late May to the last weekend in June, Friday through Sunday 8 to 8; July through early September, daily 8 to 8; and early September through mid-October, Friday through Sunday 8:30 to 5:30. The chamber itself is open weekdays 9 to 5. There are also town information kiosks on Circuit Avenue in Oak Bluffs and on Church Street in Edgartown.

**Tourist Information** **Martha's Vineyard Chamber of Commerce** ( ⊠ Beach Rd. ☐ Box 1698, Vineyard Haven 02568 ☎ 508/693–4486 or 800/505–4815 ⊕ www.mvy.com).

# Nantucket

**WORD OF MOUTH**

"September is our favorite time to visit Nantucket. Gone are the summer folk, vacationers, and day trippers, for the most part. A few restaurants are closed after Labor Day, but the rest are all still open, along with nearly all the shops... The weather will still be pleasant (though not for sun bathing) with flowers still in bloom. Expect cool breezes (it's an island), however, and a significant drop in temps when the sun goes down."

—djkbooks

By Sandy
MacDonald

**FOR THE FIRST TIME SINCE** its golden age as a world-renowned whaling capital in the early 1800s, the tiny island of Nantucket is decidedly on a roll. Modest shingled cottages that might have gone begging for a buyer a few decades ago now fetch millions, economic downturn notwithstanding. The more than 800 pre-1840 structures that compose the core of Nantucket Town—a National Landmark Historic District—only rarely change hands, and then at exalted prices. As for the trophy houses—megamansions built in the hinterlands for rich arrivistes—they're consistently off the charts, setting new records only to break them.

Still, Nantucket's ascending chic isn't what attracts most people to the island in the first place, or keeps them coming back. Its allure has more to do with how, at the height of summer, a cooling fog will drift in across the multihued moors, or the way rambling wild roses, the gaudy pink Rosa rugosa, perfume a hidden path to the beach.

Essentially Nantucket is *all* beach—a boomerang-shape sand spit consisting of detritus left by a glacier that receded millennia ago. Off Cape Cod, some 26 mi out to sea, the island measures 3½ by 14 mi at its widest points while encompassing—such are the miracles of inlets and bays—about 80 mi of sandy shoreline, all of it open, as a matter of local pride, to absolutely everyone.

The small commercial area of Nantucket Town is the center of island activity, just as it has been since the early 1700s. It's only a few square blocks of mostly historic buildings, lovingly restored inns, and boutiques and galleries leading up from the pretty harbor and waterfront, where the ferries dock. Beyond it, quiet residential roads fan out to points around the island; Siasconset (known locally as 'Sconset) lies 8 mi to the east, Surfside 3 mi to the south, and Madaket 6 mi west of town. Thus far, the outlying areas appear relatively rural; however, increasing "infill" threatens the tranquillity.

Still, on a day when sun scintillates on sand and the thrumming waves hint at an eternal rhythm, it's hard to imagine that anything could ever go too terribly wrong here. As summer succeeds summer, children will continue to construct their fanciful if foredoomed sand castles and marvel over the odd treasures the tides drag in. Adults will gladly play along, if allowed, remembering their own seemingly endless days of summer and imagining more of the same for their children's children and so on and on.

## ABOUT THE RESTAURANTS

For such a tiny island, Nantucket is rife with great restaurants—"world class" would not be an exaggeration. Of course, with New York–level sophistication come New York–level prices. And whereas the titans of industry who flock here for a bit of high-rent R&R might not blink at the prospect of a $40 or even $50 entrée, the rest of us must sometimes suppress a nervous gulp. Is it worth it? Again and again, in venues that vie for the title of most recherché, the answer is yes.

Reservations can be hard to come by in high season, or during popular weekends such as December's Christmas Stroll and the Daffodil Festival in April, so plan and make dinner reservations well ahead. You may still be able to squeeze into a popular establishment at the last minute if you're willing to eat unfashionably early or decadently late. Restaurants tend to drop days from their schedules in the shoulder seasons, so call ahead to check the hours of operation in any month other than July or August.

### TOP 5

- Endless roaming along Nantucket's shoreline

- Unhilly bike paths that wind past moors, bogs, and forests

- The observation deck at the Whaling Museum

- Justifiably popular Surfside Beach

- A boat ride on *The Endeavor*, Slip 101, Straight Wharf

## ABOUT THE HOTELS

From small bed-and-breakfasts to the island's few surviving grand hotels, Nantucket knows the value of hospitality. A unique "product" plus good service—as busy as this little island gets—are the deciding factors that keep visitors coming back year after year. The majority of lodgings are in town, convenient to the shops and restaurants. Those seeking quiet might prefer the inns on the periphery of town, a 5-to-10-minute walk from Main Street. The most remote inns, in 'Sconset and Wauwinet, also tend to be among the most expensive. Families with children will probably want to consider the larger, less formal hotels, since many of the small, historic B&Bs are furnished with antiques.

Nantucket is notoriously expensive, so don't expect to find many bargains in terms of lodging, especially in summer. The best rates can be found in the off-season; however, the spring and fall shoulder seasons are also growing in popularity, and such special-event weekends as the Daffodil Festival in late April and Christmas Stroll in early December command peak-season rates. The only truly "budget" facility you'll find is the youth hostel, which is also the only option for roughing it, since camping is prohibited anywhere on-island.

| WHAT IT COSTS | | | | | |
|---|---|---|---|---|---|
| | ¢ | $ | $$ | $$$ | $$$$ |
| Restaurants | under $16 | $16–$23 | $24–$30 | $31–$40 | over $40 |
| Hotels | under $160 | $160–$230 | $231–$300 | $301–$400 | over $400 |

Restaurant prices are per person for a main course at dinner. Hotel prices are for a standard double room, excluding 9.7% sales tax.

# Nantucket

**Siasconset & Wauwinet (see detail map)**

**Nantucket Town** see detail map

TO HYANNIS

TO MARTHA'S VINEYARD (SUMMER ONLY)

ATLANTIC OCEAN

*Nantucket Sound*

*Nantucket Harbor*

*Coatue*

◆ Great Point Light

*Coskata Pond*

Wauwinet

Quidnet

*Sesachacha Pond*

Quidnet Rd.

Wauwinet Rd.

Polpis Rd.

Polpis

**Sankaty Head Lighthouse**

Polpis Rd.

**Windswept Cranberry Bog**

**Altar Rock**

**Milestone Bog**

Milestone Rd.

Siasconset

*Siasconset ("Sconset") Beach*

Tom Nevers Rd.

Polpis Rd.

Old South Rd.

**Nantucket Memorial Airport**

Surfside Rd.

*Surfside Beach*

**Brant Point Light**

*Children's Beach*

*Jetties Beach*

Cliff Rd.

*Dionis Beach*

Eel Point Rd.

Madaket Rd.

*Long Pond*

Madaket

*Eel Point*

*Madaket Beach*

**Sanford Farm / Ram Pasture**

Hummock Pond Rd.

Bartlett Farm Rd.

*Miacomet Pond*

*Miacomet Beach*

*Cisco Beach*

0    2 miles

0    2 kilometers

## KEY

🚲 Bike Trail

⛴ Ferry

---- Unpaved road

## NANTUCKET TOWN

*26 mi southeast of Hyannis, 107 mi southeast of Boston.*

At the height of its prosperity in the early 19th century, the little town of Nantucket was the foremost whaling port in the world. Shipowners and sea captains built elegant mansions, which today remain remarkably unchanged, thanks to a very strict building code initiated in the 1950s. The entire town of Nantucket is now an official National Historic District encompassing more than 800 pre-1840 structures within 1 square mi.

Given its compact nature, Nantucket definitely merits consideration as a day trip—a prospect made easier by the introduction of fast ferries (the crossing now takes an hour) from Hyannis. Day-trippers usually take in the architecture and historical sites and browse the pricey boutiques. After dining at one of the many delightful restaurants, you can hop a ferry back—or, if you're not in a hurry, stay the night at one of the town's luxurious historic inns.

Fodor'sChoice ★ The **Nantucket Historical Association (NHA)** (☎508/228–1894 ⊕*www. nha.org*) maintains an assortment of venerable properties in town, including the glorious Whaling Museum. An $18 pass gets you into all of the association's sites.

**❶ African Meeting House.** When the island abolished slavery in 1773, Nantucket became a destination for free blacks and escaping slaves. The African Meeting House was built in the 1820s as a schoolhouse, and it functioned as such until 1846, when the island's schools were integrated. A complete restoration has returned the site to its authentic 1880s appearance. ✉*29 York St.* ☎*508/228–9833* ⊕*www.afroam museum.org* ⊠*Free* ⊙*July and Aug., Tues.–Sat. 11–3, Sun. 1–3.*

**⓯ Brant Point Light.** The promontory where this 26-foot-tall, white-painted beauty stands offers views of the harbor and town. The point was once the site of the second-oldest lighthouse in the country (1746); the present, much-photographed light was built in 1902. ✉*End of Easton St., across footbridge.*

**⓭ First Congregational Church.** The tower of this church provides the best ★ view of Nantucket—for those willing to climb its 94 steps. Rising 120 feet, the tower is capped by a weather vane depicting a whale catch. Peek in at the church's 1852 trompe-l'oeil ceiling. ✉*62 Centre St.* ☎*508/228–0950* ⊕*www.nantucketfcc.org* ⊠*Tower tour $2.50* ⊙*Mid-June–mid-Oct., Mon.–Sat. 10–4; Daffodil and Memorial weekends, Fri. and Sat.; services Sun. 10 AM.*

**❼ Hadwen House.** The pair of magnificent white porticoed Greek Revival mansions on upper Main Street—commonly referred to as the Two Greeks—were built in 1845 and 1846 by wealthy factory owner William Hadwen. No. 94, built as a wedding gift for his adopted niece, was modeled on the Athenian Tower of the Winds, with Corinthian capitals on the entry columns, a domed-stair hall with statuary niches, and an oculus. The Hadwens' own domicile, at No. 96, is now a museum,

# Nantucket Town

TO
JETTIES
BEACH

Hulbert Ave.

E. Lincoln Ave.

N. Beach St.

Cliff Rd

Swain St.

Willard St.

Cornish Ave.

Walsh St.

**15**

*Nantucket Harbor*

**16** Sunset Hill

W. Chester St.

Wesco Place

Blackberry

Gull Island Ln.

Chester St.

N. Ave.

Easton St.

Mackay Way

Harbor View Way

Children's Beach

TO HYANNIS

*Lily Pond Park*

N. Liberty St.

Franklin St.

Grove La.

Woodbury La.

N. Liberty St.

Lily St.

Westminster

Step La.

Ash St.

Ash La.

Sea St.

Whalers La.

Steamboat Wharf

**13** Church Ct. Academy La.

Centre St.

Gay St.

Quince

Hussey St.

Broad St.

Chestnut St.

**14**

**7** (info)

Oak

S. Water St.

Easy St.

Old North Wharf

Straight Wharf

TO HYANNIS, MARTHA'S VINEYARD

Brooks Ct.

India St.

Liberty Ln.

Rose Ln.

Centre St.

Federal St.

**12**

♦ Post Office

Madison Ct.

Cambridge

Main St.

(info)

Liberty St.

**9** Pacific National Bank

♦ Murray's Toggery

**11**

(info)

Salem St.

New Whale St.

Old South Wharf

Gardner St.

Howard St.

Broom

Main St.

Pleasant St.

Winter St.

Walnut

Ray's Ct.

Stone Alley

Candle St.

Commercial St.

Commercial Wharf

**8**

**7** Hadwen House

Summer

Mooers La.

Lucretia Mott La.

Fair St.

Coffin St.

Washington St.

**10**

Town Pier

Main St.

Vestal St.

**6**

**5**

**4**

Green St.

New Dollar La.

Starbuck Ct.

School

Charter

Hiller

Martin's La.

Plumb

Union St.

Fayette

Meader

Quaker

Cooper La.

Milk St.

**3**

Mt. Vernon

Joy

New Mill St.

Prospect St.

N. Mill St.

Mill St.

S. Mill St.

High

Pine St.

Darling

Tattle Ct.

Farmer St.

Twin

Lyons

Flora

Mulberry

Francis

**2**

Candle House La.

Angola St.

Jefferson La.

Eagle La.

Silver St.

Weymouth St.

E. Dover

W. York

TO SURFSIDE BEACH

S. Mill St.

Pleasant St.

W. Dover

E. York

**1**

York St.

TO 'SCONSET

0    1/4 miles

0    1/4 kilometers

---

## KEY

*i* *Tourist information*

---

and its contents reflect how the wealthy of the period lived. Inside, on a guided tour, you'll see such architectural details as the grand circular staircase, fine plasterwork, and carved Italian-marble mantels. ⊠*96 Main St.* ☎*508/228–1894* ⊕*www.nha.org* ⊠*NHA Combination Pass or Historic Sites Pass only* ⊘ *Late May–mid-Oct., Mon.–Sat. 10–5, Sun. noon–5.*

**⑪ Main Street.** After the Great Fire of 1846 leveled all its wooden buildings, Main Street was widened to prevent future flames from hopping across the street. The cobblestone thoroughfare has a harmonious symmetry: the Pacific Club anchors its foot, and the Pacific National Bank, another redbrick building, squares off the head. The cobblestones were brought to the island as ballast in returning ships and laid to prevent the wheels of carts heavily laden with whale oil from sinking into the dirt. At the center of Lower Main is an old horse trough, today overflowing with flowers. From here the street gently rises; at the bank it narrows to its prefire width and leaves the commercial district for an area of mansions that escaped the blaze.

**NEED A BREAK?**

You can breakfast or lunch inexpensively at the lunch counter at **Nantucket Pharmacy** (⊠*45 Main St.* ☎*508/228–0180*). "The Strip," a hodgepodge of fun fast-food eateries on Broad Street near Steamboat Wharf, is another good option for a quick meal. Besides fresh-squeezed juices, the **Juice Bar** (⊠*12 Broad St.* ☎*508/228–5799*), open April through mid-October, serves homemade ice cream and frozen yogurt with waffle cones and toppings. Long lines signal that good things come to those who wait.

**Maria Mitchell Association (MMA).** Established in 1902 by Vassar students and astronomer Maria Mitchell's family, the association administers the

**⑥ Mitchell House** (⊠*1 Vestal St.* ☎*508/228–2896* ⊕*www.mmo.org* ⊠*$5 or MMA pass*), the

**⑤ Maria Mitchell Association Science Library** (⊠*2 Vestal St.* ☎*508/228–9219* ⊕*www.mmo.org* ⊠*Reserved for scholars, by appointment*), the

**③ Natural Science Museum at Hinchman House**(⊠*7 Milk St.* ☎*508/228–0898* ⊕*www.mmo.org* ⊠*$5 or MMA pass*), the

**⑩ MMA Aquarium & Museum Shop**(⊠*28 Washington St., near Commercial Wharf* ☎*508/228–5387* ⊕*www.mmo.org* ⊠*$6 or MMA pass*), the

**④ Vestal Street Observatory** (⊠*3 Vestal St.* ☎*508/228–9273* ⊕*www.mmo. org* ⊠*$5 or MMA pass*), and the

**② Loines Observatory** (⊠*59 Milk St. Ext.* ☎*508/228–9273* ⊕*www.mmo. org* ⊠*$10*). The MMA Museum Pass is a combination admission ticket to the Mitchell House, the Hinchman House, the Vestal Street Observatory, and the Aquarium; it's $10 for adults and $8 for children ages 3 to 17. In summer, the association conducts inexpensive classes for adults and children on astronomy, natural science, and Nantucket history. ⊠*4 Vestal St.* ☎*508/228–9198* ⊕*www.mmo.org.*

**⑫ ⟳ ★ Nantucket Atheneum.** Nantucket's town library is a great white Greek Revival building, with a windowless facade and fluted Ionic columns. Completed in 1847 to replace a structure lost to the 1846 fire, it's one of the oldest libraries in continuous service in the United States. Astronomer Maria Mitchell was its first librarian. Opening ceremonies included a dedication by Ralph Waldo Emerson, who—along with Daniel Webster, Henry David Thoreau, Frederick Douglass, Lucretia Mott, and John James Audubon—later delivered lectures in the library's 2nd-floor Great Hall. During the 19th century the hall was the center of island culture—a role it fulfills to this day. The adjoining Atheneum Park is a great place to relax for a while, and the spacious Weezie Library for Children hosts readings and activities—a welcome respite for a rainy day. ⊠ *1 India St.* ☎ *508/228–1110* ⊕ *www.nantucketatheneum.org* ⊗ *Late May–early Sept., Mon., Wed., Fri., and Sat. 9:30–5, Tues. and Thurs. 9:30–8; early Sept.–late May, Tues. and Thurs. 9:30–8, Wed., Fri., and Sat. 9:30–5.*

**⑯ Oldest House.** History and architecture buffs should be sure to get a look at this hilltop house, also called the Jethro Coffin House, built in 1686 as a wedding gift for Jethro and Mary Gardner Coffin. The most striking feature of the saltbox is the massive central brick chimney with a brick-horseshoe adornment said to ward away witches. Other highlights are the enormous hearths and diamond-pane leaded-glass windows. Cutaway panels show 17th-century construction techniques. An NHA interpreter will tell you about the home's history and the interior's sparse furnishings, including an antique loom. ⊠ *Sunset Hill (a 10-to15-min walk along Centre St. from Main St.)* ☎ *508/228–1894* ⊕ *www.nha.org* 🎫 *NHA Combination Pass or Historic Sites Pass* ⊗ *Mid-May–mid-Oct., Mon.–Sat. 10–5, Sun. noon–5.*

**⑨ Pacific National Bank.** Like the Pacific Club (a social club that counts whalers' descendants among its members) down the street, the bank, dating to 1818 and still in use today, is a monument to the far-flung voyages of the Nantucket whaling ships it financed. Inside, above old-style teller cages, are 1954 murals of scenes from the whaling days. Note the **Meridian Stone** on the south side of the building and to the left—it's about 3 feet high and pointed on top. Placed here in the 1830s by astronomers Maria Mitchell and her father, William, it marks the town's precise meridian—an important point to early navigators. ⊠ *61 Main St.*

**⑧ ★ "Three Bricks."** Many of the mansions of the golden age of whaling were built on Upper Main Street. These well-known identical red-brick homes, with columned Greek Revival porches at their front entrances, were built between 1836 and 1838 by whaling merchant Joseph Starbuck for his three sons. They are not open to the public. ⊠ *93–97 Main St.*

**⑭ ⟳** With exhibits that include a fully rigged whaleboat and a skeleton of a 46-foot sperm whale, the **Whaling Museum**—a complex that includes a restored 1846 spermaceti candle factory—is a must-see attraction that offers a crash course in the island's colorful history. The museum

Fodor's Choice ★

received a $14 million expansion and refurbishment in 2005. Items on view in the handsome galleries include harpoons and other whale-hunting implements; portraits of whaling captains and their wives (a few of whom went whaling as well); the South Seas curiosities they brought home; a large collection of sailors' crafts, a full-size try-works once used to process whale oil; and the original 16-foot-high 1850 lens from Sankaty Head Lighthouse. The Children's Discovery Room provides interactive-learning opportunities. Be sure to climb—or take the elevator—up to the observation deck for a view of the harbor. The museum is open until 8 on Wednesday in July and August. ⊠ *13–15 Broad St.* ☎ *508/228–1894* ⊟ *$15 or NHA Combination Pass* ⊙ *Late Dec.–early Jan., Sat.–Mon. 1–3; Feb.–mid-Apr., Sat. and Sun. 11–4; mid-Apr.–mid-May and Nov.–mid-Dec., Thurs.–Mon. 11–4; late May–mid-Oct., daily 10–5.*

> ### GREASY LUCK
>
> Nantucket's preeminence as the world's whaling capital (at least until the early 1800s, when New Bedford's deeper harbor took the lead) resulted from a fluke, when, in 1712, Captain Christopher Hussey's crew speared a sperm whale. The whale's waxy spermaceti, it was found, could be used for candles in place of lantern oil, produced by the messy, endless task of cooking down whale blubber. The captains made out like bandits—their grand houses still stand as proof—but the trade went into a downward spiral with the discovery of petroleum in 1836.

## WHERE TO EAT IN NANTUCKET TOWN

**$$$**
**Fodor's**Choice
★
AMERICAN

✕ **American Seasons.** Picture a farmhouse gone sexy: That's the mood—wholesome yet seductive—at this candlelit hideaway, where inspired young chef Michael LaScola marshals local bounty to concoct a culinary Trip-Tik that ranges across the countryside, from the Pacific Coast to New England, by way of the Wild West and Down South. From his signature foie gras–crème brûlée (served with a plum-ginger compote) to buttermilk-soaked guinea-hen breast with corn-bread-cheddar pudding, and onward to rarefied "s'mores," expect spectacular pan-regional pyrotechnics. ⊠ *80 Centre St.* ☎ *508/228–7111* ⊟ *AE, MC, V* ⊙ *Closed Jan.–mid-Apr. No lunch.*

**$$$**
AMERICAN

✕ **Arno's.** Arno's, a brick-walled storefront with a prime location right on Main Street, presents lush breakfasts (some featuring lobster), hearty lunches, and fairly ambitious dinners, all with generous portions. (Warning: the salads could constitute meals in themselves, and the 41-ounce rib eye could daunt even the most devoted of carnivores.) Owner Chris Morris is an oenophile: hence the growing California influence on the menu (e.g., grilled flatbread pizzas) and "the 41," a wine bar offering 41 options by the glass or flight. Expect some envious looks—from inside and outside—should you snag the window table, a perfect spot from which to observe the passing parade. ⊠ *41 Main St.* ☎ *508/228–7001* ⊕ *www.arnos.net* ⊟ *AE, D, MC, V* ⊙ *Closed Feb. and Mar.*

**$$**
★
AMERICAN

✕ **Black-Eyed Susan's.** From a passing glance, you'd never peg this seemingly humble storefront as one of Nantucket's chic eateries—but as the invariable lines attest, it is. The luncheonette setup is offset by improbably fancy glass chandeliers, and hard-core foodies lay claim to the stools to observe chef Jeff Worster's often pyromaniacal "open kitchen." (A note to the heat-averse: with no a/c, it can get toasty—you might want to request a patio table.) The dinner menu, which changes every few weeks, ventures boldly around the world: Wiener schnitzel, for instance, might star alongside chicken mole. The breakfasts (served until 1 PM) include such eye-openers as hearty Pennsylvania Dutch pancakes fortified with Jarlsberg cheese. ⊠ *10 India St.* ☎ *508/325–0308* ⊟ *No credit cards* 🍴 *BYOB* ⊙ *Closed Nov.–Mar. No dinner Sun. No lunch.*

**$$$**
MEDITERRANEAN
✕ **The Boarding House.** Beyond the throngs of twentysomethings noisily mingling at the bar, you'll encounter a vaulted semisubterranean space reminiscent of a private wine cellar, with leather banquettes circling antique-gold walls. Here, under the watchful eye of star chef-owner Seth Raynor, chef de cuisine Erin Zircher showcases her skill with Mediterranean market cuisine. Comfort is the universal watchword: it's implicit in the corn soup bejeweled with sea scallops crudo, grilled swordfish flanked by a fortress of tender chickpea panisses, and the signature dessert, warm dark-chocolate chocolate-chip cookies served with a pair of mini malted milk shakes. The only discomfort derives from the over-resonant noise level. In season, it's best to opt for the sidewalk café—provided you succeed in snagging a table. ⊠ *12 Federal St.* ☎ *508/228–9622* ⊕ *www.boardinghouse-pearl.com* ⊟ *AE, MC, V* ⊙ *Closed Jan.–Mar.*

**$$$–$$$$**
AMERICAN
✕ **Brant Point Grill.** With its beautiful broad lawn overlooking the harbor, the Brant Point Grill—in-house restaurant for the elegant White Elephant hotel—has ventured beyond its à la carte haute–steak house menu with some "Creativities," the best of which is a free-form lobster ravioli in a luscious pool of parsnip puree. Always appealing is the straightforward salmon grilled on a fire cone set up right outside, and the spritely salads, such as an exemplary white-anchovy Caesar. Desserts like the summery strawberry-rhubarb crepes with buttermilk ice cream are surefire resolution-destroyers, as is the Sunday brunch, featuring a make-your-own Bloody Mary station. ⊠ *50 Easton St.* ☎ *508/325–1320 or 800/445–6574* ⊕ *www.whiteelephanthotel.com* ⊟ *AE, D, DC, MC, V* ⊙ *Closed Jan.–Mar.*

**$$**
🐾
AMERICAN
✕ **The Brotherhood.** No, it's not really an 1840s whaling bar—though the atmospheric basement, which dates all the way back to 1972, presents a more convincing front than the open, family-friendly upper floors added in 2005. Upstairs or down, you can dive into the same juicy burgers and signature curly fries, and the entrées—such as braised lamb shank with cherry chipotle demi-glace—pack surprising sophistication. In summer, the lines trail down the block; in winter, it's a warm, inviting hideaway. ⊠ *23 Broad St.* ☎ *508/228–2551* ⊕ *www.brotherhoodofthieves.com* ⊟ *MC, V.*

**$$**
★
AMERICAN
✕ **Centre Street Bistro.** Tiny—there are 20 seats indoors, and as many out—and perfect, this gem of a bistro is a find that devoted locals almost wish they could keep to themselves. Chef-owners Tim and Ruth Pitts's sizzling cuisine is a match for the persimmon-orange color scheme of this cozy hideaway lined with cushioned banquettes. Portions—whether of the sesame-crusted shrimp atop red-curry rice

## Where to Eat in Nantucket Town

Hulbert Ave.

E. Lincoln Ave.

Swain St.

TO MADAKET, DIONIS BEACH

TO BRANT POINT LIGHTHOUSE

Willard St.

N. Beach St.

Cornish Ave.

Walsh St.

Cliff Rd.

North Ave.

Easton St.

Mackay Way

Harbor View Way

Chester St.

Centre St.

Step La.

N. Water St.

Sea St.

Beach St.

Children's Beach

Nantucket Harbor

TO HYANNIS

Academy La.

Church Ct.

Ash St.

Ash La.

Broad St.

Whalers La.

Whaling Museum

Steamboat Wharf

TO HYANNIS, MARTHA'S VINEYARD

First Congregational Church

Gay St.

Chestnut St.

Oak St.

Old North Wharf

Quince

Hussey St.

India St.

Centre St.

Federal St.

S. Water St.

Easy St.

Cambridge

Straight Wharf

Old South Wharf

Liberty Ln.

Rose La.

Main St.

Candle St.

Liberty St.

Main St.

Pacific National bank

Stone Alley

Salem St.

New Whale St.

Commercial St.

Commercial Wharf

Three Bricks

Ray's Ct.

Fair St.

Walnut

Water St.

Summer

Mooers La.

Lucretia Mott La.

School

Charter

Martin's La.

Plumb

Coffin St.

Washington St.

Maria Mitchell Aquarium

Town Pier

High

Hiller

Darling

Tattle Ct.

Farmer St.

Pine St.

Twin

Lyons

Orange St.

Union St.

Flora

Mulberry

Fayette

Meader

Francis

Candle House La.

Angola St.

S. Mill

Jefferson La.

Eagle La.

Silver St.

Weymouth St.

E. Dover

Washington St. Ext.

W. York

W. Dover

Pleasant St.

York St.

E. York

0 ————— 1/4 miles

0 ————— 1/4 kilometers

noodles, or the Angus-beef tenderloin with goat cheese and white-truffle oil—are so ample as to quell the heartiest of appetites. Desserts are as lavish (try the warm chocolate marquise wrapped in filo) as the prices are modest. ⊠*29 Centre St.* ☎*508/228–8470* ⊕*www.nantucketbistro.com* ▤*MC, V.*

**$$** ✕ **Cioppino's.** Tracy Root's elegant house-restaurant has been popular
AMERICAN since day one (in 1990). An appetizer of cool, deconstructed lobster with lemony hollandaise is the perfect answer to an overwarm evening, and awfully well priced. Beyond the signature dish—a San Franciscan seafood stew—the menu is ambitious, marrying classic technique and contemporary taste. Desserts—especially the tangy house-made key lime pie—have their own following. ⊠*20 Broad St.* ☎*508/228–4622* ⊕*www.cioppinos.com* ▤*AE, D, DC, MC, V* ☉*Closed Nov.–Apr.* ☉*No lunch.*

**$$$$** ✕ **The Club Car.** A longtime favorite among the moneyed set, this boxy
AMERICAN dining room—its adjoining piano bar is an actual railroad car from the dismantled 'Sconset narrow-gauge—took a while to shake off its continental origins, but now sings under chef Tom Proch. The "lobster ACK 'n cheese" (so named for Nantucket's airport code) is a lovely variation on an almost ubiquitous haute-comfort dish; a salad of paper-thin golden beets is beautifully bolstered by Roaring Forties Blue; and the rack of lamb gets a boost from minted Madeira sauce. While catering to a conservative clientele, Proch still manages to cut loose. ⊠ *1 Main St.* ☎*508/228–1101* ▤*AE, MC, V* ☉*Closed mid-Dec.–mid-May.*

**$$$** ✕ **Company of the Cauldron.** In this tiny dining room, a sconce-lighted
★ haven of architectural salvage, chef-owner All Kovalencik issues only
AMERICAN one menu per evening (Monday's, priced slightly higher, is lobster-centric). Fans gladly forgo multiple choice when the chef's choice is invariably so dead-on. Rundowns of the weekly roster are available over the phone or online, and a typically tantalizing lineup might span a fennel-jicama salad with preserved-lemon vinaigrette, "deconstructed" beef Wellington, and cheesecake with Grand Marnier crème anglaise. Having cherry-picked the menu, cognoscenti tend to book on a night when Mary Keller will be playing her celestial harp. ⊠*7 India St.* ☎*508/228–4016* ⊕*www.companyofthecauldron.com* ⚐*Reservations essential* ▤*MC, V* ☉*Closed Jan.–Mar. No lunch.*

**$$$** ✕ **DeMarco.** Northern Italian cuisine debuted on-island at this cored-
ITALIAN out clapboard house in 1980, slightly ahead of the wave. The delights endure: "badly cut" homemade pasta, for instance, in a sauce of wild mushrooms, prosciutto, and fresh sage, or luscious lobster cannelloni enrobed in a corn zabaglione. Beef short ribs come with a side of crispy goat cheese polenta, and the panna cotta gets a bit of added zip from a rhubarb compote. The prevailing aesthetic may be rustic, but the results read as rare delicacies in these parts. ⊠*9 India St.* ☎*508/228–1836* ⊕*www.demarcorestaurant.com* ▤*AE, MC, V* ☉*Closed Mid-Oct.-late May. No lunch.*

**$$** ✕ **Even Keel Cafe.** This former ice-cream parlor, with its tin ceilings
☺ and pretty backyard patio, is no mere restaurant—it's the very heart
AMERICAN of town, especially off-season, when, as a public service, patrons are treated to two-for-one entrées (price gouging is not in owner Marshall

Thompson's vocabulary). It's the first place to head for a fancy coffee or a creative meal. The grilled wild salmon salad with pomegranate vinaigrette makes for an ideal midday meal, and the bountiful lobster nachos invite a communal free-for-all. ⊠ *40 Main St.* ☎ *508/228–1979* ⊕ *www.evenkeelcafe.com* ⊟ *AE, MC, V.*

**$$$**
**AMERICAN**
✕ **Fifty-Six Union.** You can tell there's a playful spirit at work here, just from the overdressed mannequin propped up at a café table out front. Venture inside, though, and you'll find a city-sophisticated space, with a civilized grown-ups' bar. Inside or out (the lovely garden out back harbors a chef's table), Peter Jannelle's cuisine delivers global pizzazz. You'll want to make a habit of the truffle-asiago frites, not to mention the mussels in mild Thai curry broth, and the Javanese spicy fried rice. ⊠ *56 Union St.* ☎ *508/228–6135* ⊕ *www.fiftysixunion.com* ⊟ *AE, MC, V* ⊘ *No lunch.*

**$**
☾
**AMERICAN**
✕ **Fog Island Café.** Cherished year-round for its exceptional breakfasts (e.g., pesto scrambled eggs), Fog Island is just as fine a spot for lunch. The storefront space is cheerily decked out in a fresh country style (echoed in the friendly service), and chef-owners Mark and Anne Dawson—both Culinary Institute of America grads—seem determined to provide the best possible value to transients and natives alike. ⊠ *7 S. Water St.* ☎ *508/228–1818* ⊕ *www.fogisland.com* ⊟ *MC, V* ⊘ *No dinner.*

**$$$**
☾
**CHINESE**
✕ **Harbor Wok.** Islanders craving Chinese food used to have to fly it in from Hyannis—that is, until mogul Stephen Karp brought in Wellesley's Carol and Pui Chan. Juggling some of his Monopoly pieces, he has now installed them in the Jared Coffin House, where they prove a terrific fit. It was an easy transformation: just replace the dour sea-captain portraits with antique prints, throw in some potted plants, and presto, an elegant Asian restaurant that's also a good historic match (Nantucket was active in the China Trade). Patio seating is also an appealing option. The price range is the kindest you'll find downtown, and all the classic faves are well represented—especially crab Rangoon. ⊠ *29 Broad St.,* ☎ *508/325–1300* ⊟ *AE, D, DC, MV, V* ⊘ *Closed mid-Sept.–late May.*

**$$$–**
**★**
**FRENCH**
✕ **Languedoc Bistro.** While retaining its Gallic charm, this lovely auberge-style restaurant, founded in 1975, has long since gone native, which is to say eclectic, borrowing the best of a world of cuisines. A salade composée might consist of layers of whipped chèvre and pale-yellow Chioggia beets atop bed of fresh ground figs. A dazzling specialty, the oven-roasted lobster, arrives supine and desconstructed, the luscious chunks swimming in creamy polenta and festooned with parsnip "ribbons." Dining moods are divided into two modes: you can opt for the fairly formal upstairs rooms or the bistro-style conviviality of the cellar. In season, the patio is a lovely place to toy with a salad—or to tackle a decadent, over-generous dessert, such as the Sweet Inspirations butter crunch sundae. ⊠ *24 Broad St.* ☎ *508/228–2552* ⊕ *www.lelanguedoc. com* ⊟ *AE, MC, V* ⊘ *Closed Jan.–mid-Apr.*

**$$$**
**★**
**ECLECTIC**
✕ **Lo La 41.** Late in the evening, a hopping bar scene—Lo La 41 became *the* place to hang the minute it opened in '06—can impede the culinary experience here, but come early and you can enjoy a superb supper: lobster-avocado salad, say, or a more substantial "indulgent macaroni

**7**

& cheese," lavished with four artisanal North California varieties. Chef Robert Boslow has a deft hand with local catches, and desserts are killer, especially the tres leches cake soaked in sugar milk. ⊠*15 S. Beach St.* ☎*508/325–4001* ⊟*MC, V.*

**$$$**
**★**
AMERICAN
✗**Òran Mór.** In 2004 chef-owner Christopher Freeman abandoned the cushy confines of Topper's at the Wauwinet to strike out on his own at this tasteful little restaurant—a trio of butter-yellow rooms accessed via a copper-encased stairway. Though Freeman occasionally errs on the side of nouvelle-cuisine minginess (a Topper's carryover, perhaps), the innate generosity of a born chef shines through in exuberant dishes like braised rabbit ravioli with truffle butter, and Peking duck breast with quinoa and roast-plum chutney. Decades ago this space was a New American trendsetter known as the Second Story. Freeman does its legacy proud. ⊠*2 S. Beach St.* ☎*508/228–8655* ⊕*www.oranmorbistro.com* ⊟*AE, MC, V* ☾*Closed Dec.–mid-Apr. No lunch.*

**$$$**
**★**
ECLECTIC
✗**the pearl.** This ultracool space—a sophisticated upstairs cousin to the Boarding House—is seriously chic, with a white onyx bar lighted in a Curaçao blue and, behind an aquarium divider, cushy white-leather banquettes. These—plus the garden porch, where tasting dinners can be prearranged—are the power seats. However, everyone is well served by executive chef Seth Raynor's enthusiasm for the bold flavors of Asian cuisine, especially in its streetwise guise. You may have a tough time choosing between the beef barbecue with piquant Thai chili-lime sauce and the signature wok-fried lobster—so do yourself a favor and order both. Asian-themed restaurants often disappoint in the dessert round, but not so the pearl: pace yourself for dazzlers such as the mascarpone-and-chèvre-enriched cheesecake with cherry syrup and beet sorbet. ⊠*12 Federal St.* ☎*508/228–9701* ⊕*www.boardinghouse-pearl.com* ⊟*AE, MC, V* ☾*Closed Jan.–Apr. No lunch.*

**$$**
AMERICAN
✗**Queequeg's.** Tucked into a quiet side street behind the Atheneum, the restaurant proper—named for a forthright, upbeat Pacific islander in the novel Moby Dick—is a rather somber little space, resembling a ship's hull. (Little wonder most customers prefer to dine outside on the patio.) Either affords access to Henri Laaksonen's artful riffs on local provender: tiny bay scallops with goat-cheese mousse and beet risotto, halibut with preserved-lemon polenta. Such dishes could—and do—command much higher prices in the immediate vicinity, so the excellence to be found here tends to remain a closely guarded secret. The only dishes that don't measure up are the mass-produced desserts; Laaksonen deserves a pastry chef in his league. ⊠ *6 Oak St.* ☎*508/325–0992* ⊕ *www.queequegsnantucket.com* ⊟*MC, V* ☾*Closed Sun.*

**$$$**
AMERICAN
✗**Ships Inn.** Tucked beneath Captain Obed Starbuck's handsome 1831 mansion, this peach-tinted, candlelit restaurant is a light and lovely haven where French technique meets a California sensibility and both cultures are the richer for it. If you want to eat healthfully, you can—but why not sin a little and sample grilled Chatham sea scallops with black-truffle hollandaise, or a filet mignon with Roquefort crust? The grilled shrimp with Belgian endive (braised into sweet submission) is a guilt-free option—easily undone as you preorder the soufflé du jour.

⊠ *13 Fair St.* ☎ *508/228–0040* ⊕ *www.shipsinnnantucket.com* ▤ *AE, D, MC, V* ⊘ *Closed late Oct.–mid-Apr. No lunch.*

**$$$** ✕ **Slip 14.** With its picturesque setting at the end of a shell-lined lane
AMERICAN flanked by galleries, Slip 14 is an ideal spot to while away a summer noon or night: portions are large, prices are fair—and all is well with the world. Skip the dullish lobster cake (the delicate flavor gets subsumed) in favor of local fluke tacos or a creative salad. ⊠ *14 Old South Wharf* ☎ *508/228–2033* ⊕ *www.slip14.com* ▤ *AE, MC, V* ⊘ *Closed mid-Oct.–mid-May.*

**$$** ✕ **Starlight Café.** This tiny movie-theater anteroom and enclosed patio,
AMERICAN spiffed up with cinematic artifacts, offers a deceptively casual menu—mac-and-cheese, for instance, lavished with lobster. It's ideal for a pre- or post-flick feed, and yes, you're allowed to take your drinks into the theater. Also, with a dinner reservation you can get a movie reservation—a great way to leapfrog the line. ⊠ *1 N. Union St.* ☎ *508/228–4479* ⊕ *www.starlightnantucket.com* ▤ *AE, D, MC, V.*

**$$$** ✕ **Straight Wharf.** This loftlike restaurant with harborside deck has
Fodor'sChoice enjoyed legendary status since the mid-'70s, when chef Marion Morash
★ used to get a helping hand from culinary buddy Julia Child. The
AMERICAN young couple who took over in 2006—Gabriel Frasca and Amanda Lydon—were fast-rising stars on the Boston restaurant scene, but their approach here is the antithesis of flashy. If anything, they have lent this venerable institution a more barefoot air, appropriate to the place and season—hurricane lamps lend a soft glow to well-spaced tables lined with butcher paper; dish towels serve as napkins. Intense champions of local produce and catches, Frasca and Lydon concoct stellar dishes like lobster-stuffed zucchini flowers with saffron-tomato vinaigrette. Everything from cuisine to service enchants, and the price—for Nantucket—is right. If you'd like a preview, try the less costly café menu at the adjoining bar. ⊠ *6 Harbor Sq., Straight Wharf* ☎ *508/228–4499* ▤ *AE, MC, V* ⊘ *Closed mid-Oct.–mid-May.*

**$$$** ✕ **29 Fair Street.** Colorful silk pillows and cozy banquette seating have
AMERICAN softened the historic wood-paneled interior of this 1709 abode, now a satellite of 'Sconset's Summer House. The menu focuses on sunny Mediterranean staples, such as soupe à la pistou, along with welcome contemporary innovations like lobster wrapped in *kataif* (angel-hair filo). But fear not, fans of the beef Wellington and weekend-breakfast popovers for which the former Woodbox Inn was long famed: they remain on the menu, irresistible as ever. ⊠ *29 Fair St.* ☎ *508/228–7800* ▤ *AE, MC, V* ⊘ *Closed Mon. and Jan.–Apr. No lunch.*

**$$$$** ✕ **21 Federal.** An avatar of the New American culinary revolution since
★ 1985, 21 Federal retains its creative edge, thanks to the ever-avant
AMERICAN menus of chef Russell Jaehnig. Nothing is too outré, mind you, in this handsome 1847 Greek Revival house with sconce-lighted, dove-gray interiors—except perhaps the boisterous young crowd (the bar scene is quite popular). The cuisine, however, has a spark to match the spirited clientele: try the steamed local mussels with toasted-walnut pesto, or a tasteful surf-and-turf (short rib and half lobster) with white-truffle polenta. Desserts—like the roasted pineapple tart with basil ice cream—more than measure up. ⊠ *21 Federal St.* ☎ *508/228–*

7

2121 ⊕www.21federal.com ⊟AE, MC, V ⊗No lunch ⊗Closed mid-Oct.–Stroll Weekend and mid-Dec.–mid-May.

**$$**
**★**
AMERICAN

✕**Water Street.** Two stylish young couples initiated this chic eatery with cinnamon walls and handsome leather high-back chairs. The locally provisioned, all-organic cuisine calls on micro-diced taste explosions: it's purism without the penury. A sherry mignonette flecked with melon and scallion sparks the Island Creek oysters, and a warm white-bean salad with baby arugula and crushed pistachio nicely offsets the richness of grilled Niman Ranch lamb. The vanilla-laced Bartlett Farm corn soup, which packs a bonus chunk of crab, is nonpareil, and the closing Banana Chocolate Duo deeply satisfying. ⊠21 S. Water St. ☎508/228–0189 ⊕www.waterstreetnantucket.com ⊟AE, MC, V ⊗Closed Sun. and Jan.–Mar.

## WHERE TO EAT OUTSIDE NANTUCKET TOWN

⇨ Where to Stay & Eat Outside Nantucket Town map for these properties.

**$$$**
Fodor'sChoice
**★**
SPANISH

✕**Cinco.** With this eclectic tapas oasis, affable owner Michael Sturgis has made mid-island a true dining destination. The festive mood is irresistible: it starts with the setting (a candlelit patio leading to intimate rooms painted in dark, sexy colors) and culminates in a parade of thrilling "small plates" meant for sharing. Don't be surprised if you find yourself getting possessive over, say, the blue cornmeal–crusted soft-shell crab with sweet-corn emulsion, the grilled lamb chops with oregano-lime "mojo," or the pan-roasted bay scallops tossed with apple cider brown butter—just order more for the table. The big plates, such as crispy-skin striped bass with lemon and crème fraiche, are knockouts as well. Chef Jean-Luc Matecat tinkers with the menu daily, and keeps a bar menu going until 1 AM—ideal for those who like to observe a Spanish dinner hour. The wine list is 100% Español, and you'll have to resist the urge to toss your glass over your shoulder—the atmosphere is that exuberant. ⊠5 Amelia Dr. ☎508/325–5151 ⊕www.cinco5.com ⊟MC, V ⊗Closed Jan.–Mar. No lunch.

**¢**
**☺**
AMERICAN

✕**The Downyflake.** Locals flock here for bountiful breakfasts—featuring much-sought-after homemade doughnuts—and well-priced lunches, from codfish cakes to burgers. ⊠18 Sparks Ave. ☎508/228–4533 ⊟No credit cards ⊗Closed Jan.–Mar. No dinner.

**¢**
**☺**
LATIN-
AMERICAN

✕**El Rincon Salvadoreño.** Truly affordable restaurants are in very short supply—in fact, almost nonexistent—on-island. So everyone was overjoyed when Marcos and Angel Tejada (brothers with extensive Nantucket restaurant experience) turned a fancy failed steak house into a homey eatery specializing in their native Salvadoran cuisine. The prices at this "little corner" are low enough to make you feel outright guilty (puposas for $2, tamales for $3), and the platos tipicos—steak, chicken fish, etc., sided with heaps of rice, beans, and salad—are not only outright massive, but muy ricos. ⊠17 Old South Rd. ☎508/332–4749 ⊟No credit cards.

**$$$$**
AMERICAN

✕**Galley Beach.** A beloved institution since 1958, this cottage plunked right on the Cliffside Beach Club's swath of sand has managed to stay fresh and luxe thanks to three generations of congenial restaurateurs.

Though chef W. Scott Osif's menu encompasses all sorts of exotic ingredients (Honshimeji mushrooms accompany the poached lobster, chimichurri the Black Angus filet mignon), the results tend to be tastefully subdued to suit the crowd; it's rather like country-club cuisine, only with a more elaborate pedigree. (More adventurous palates might prefer the Galley Beach satellite, Lo La 41.) Still, the romance-to-price ratio is right—especially if you reserve a table right on the beach, where you can burrow your toes in cool sand. And go on the early side, pre-sunset: the restaurant, with its gay blue-and-white awning ringed with red geraniums, is perfectly oriented to capture what photographers call "the golden moment." ⊠ *54 Jefferson Ave.* 🕾 *508/228–9641* ▤ *AE, MC, V* ☾ *Closed mid-Oct.–mid-May.*

$$ ✕ **SeaGrille.** Though it may lack the flashy profile of other top island
AMERICAN restaurants, this mid-island eatery deserves its popularity. The lobster bisque alone, even without the bonus of a dill-flecked pastry bonnet, warrants a following, as does the free-form seafood ravioli. Chef-owner E. J. Harvey is happy to dash off classic fried seafood (hard to find, in this rarefied clime) but is also capable of coming up with creative stunners like a rock crab salad topped with sweet corn sorbet, or a pesto-slathered slab of swordfish. Off-season, the dining room is a peaceful haven. When summer arrives, so do the faithful hordes. ⊠ *45 Sparks Ave.* 🕾 *508/325–5700* ⊕ *www.theseagrille.com* ▤ *AE, MC, V.*

$$ ✕ **Sfoglia.** Culinary Institute of America grads Ron and Colleen Suha-
AMERICAN nosky appointed their celery-tinted trattoria with mismatched tables (including some enamel-top honeys from the '40s), chairs, crockery— even silverware. You'll feast on home-style Italian dishes such as gnocchi with sweet sausage and marinated peaches, or chicken "al mattone" (cooked under a brick). Desserts—Colleen's province—include rustic seasonal tarts and seductive semifreddos. (Sfoglia's New York branch on the Upper East Side has likewise earned solid foodie kudos.) ⊠ *130 Pleasant St.* 🕾 *508/325–4500* ⊕ *www.sfogliarestaurant.com* ▤ *AE, MC, V* ☾ *Closed early–late Nov. Closed Sun.*

## WHERE TO STAY IN NANTUCKET TOWN

Nantucket has a low profile, so none of the inns or hotels listed has an elevator. Some of the more recently renovated inns do have rooms compliant with the Americans with Disabilities Act; inquire ahead. Also, none of the properties listed permit smoking: Nantucket learned its lesson with the Great Fire of 1846.

$$$–$$$$ ⌂ **The Beachside at Nantucket.** Nantucket has only one "motel" in the
☾ classic rooms-around-a-pool configuration, and it's a honey—not at all out of place amid its tony neighbors. Located between the town and Jetties Beach (both are within an easy 10-minute walk), the complex ascends to two stories. Rooms—decor is of the cheery wicker-and-florals school—have little terraces separated by whitewashed latticework. Families naturally flock here, but business travelers are equally well served. **Pros:** kids have company; near the beach; pretty rooms. **Cons:** kids rule; sounds carry from the pool; location not actually beachside. ⊠ *30 N. Beach St.* 🕾 *508/228–2241 or 800/322–4433* 🖷 *508/228–8901* ⊕ *www.thebeachside.com* ➥ *90 rooms, 3 suites* ♿ *In-room:*

*refrigerator, Wi-Fi. In-hotel: pool, some pets allowed, no-smoking rooms* ⊟*AE, D, DC, MC, V* ⊘*Closed mid-Oct.–mid-Apr.* ⏺CP.

$–$$   ▦**Brant Point Inn & Atlantic Mainstay.** You can't beat the edge-of-town location (Jetties Beach is a 10-minute walk), especially given the modest rates that prevail at this pair of handsome post-and-beam guesthouses. Innkeeper Thea Kaizer grew up in a Nantucket inn; her husband, Peter, leads fishing charters, and should you catch something, he'll expedite it to the restaurant of your choice. **Pros:** friendly native owners; comfy/casual; near town and beaches. **Cons:** lack of air-conditioning (though unneeded); overly casual for some tastes; on busy road. ⊠*6 N. Beach St.* ☎*508/228–5442* 🖷*508/228–8498* ⊕*www.brantpointinn.com* 📞*17 rooms, 2 suites* ⚲*In-room: no a/c, refrigerator. In-hotel: no-smoking rooms* ⊟*AE, MC, V* ⏺CP.

$$$$   ▦**The Cottages at the Boat Basin.** These weathered-shingle cottages and ♻ lofts sit on South Wharf, amid the yachts—you could reserve a mooring and bring your own boat. Accommodations range from studios to three bedrooms, and each has attractive modern decor with a nautical flavor: white walls, navy-blue rugs, and polished-pine floors and furniture. All have water views, though they're not always equal—some cottages have picture windows plus a little garden terrace. **Pros:** right on the water; marina access; center of town. **Cons:** tourist central; attendant noise; occasional foghorns. ⊠*New Whale St., Box 1139* ☎*508/325–1499 or 866/838–9253* 🖷*508/228–7639* ⊕*www.thecottagesnantucket.com* 📞*23 cottages, 5 lofts* ⚲*In-room: kitchen, DVD, Wi-Fi. In-hotel: concierge, some pets allowed, no-smoking rooms* ⊟*AE, D, DC, MC, V* ⊘*Closed early Dec.–mid-May* ⏺BP.

$$$   ▦**Jared Coffin House.** The largest house in town when it was built in 1845, this three-story brick manse is still plenty impressive. The antiques-filled parlors are a study in timeless good taste, and diners have an improbably affordable option in Harbor Wok (open in season), where owner Stephen Karp has installed his favorite Chinese chefs. Rooms vary greatly in terms of size and grandeur (the inn even has some very affordable singles), and all are decorated in a low-key, traditional style. **Pros:** elegant parlors; knowledgeable concierge; old-money aura. **Cons:** a bit fusty; some tiny rooms; street noise for those in front. ⊠*29 Broad St., Box 1580* ☎*508/228–2400 or 800/248–2405* ⊕*www.jaredcoffinhouse.com* 📞*52 rooms* ⚲*In-room: no a/c (some), Wi-Fi. In-hotel: restaurant, concierge, no-smoking rooms* ⊟*AE, D, DC, MC, V*

$$$$   ▦**Nantucket Whaler.** Let's not mince words: the suites carved out of ★ this 1850 Greek Revival house and a Step Lane neighbor are gorgeous. Neither Calliope Ligelis nor Randi Ott, the New Yorkers who rescued the place in 1999, had any design experience, but they approached the project as if preparing to welcome friends. Each suite has a private entrance and a kitchen. The spacious bedrooms are lavished with flowers, well-chosen antiques, and fine linens, including plush robes. Couples who have come to explore not so much the island as each other will scarcely have to come up for air. **Pros:** pretty rooms; well kitted out; romantic. **Cons:** minimal reception area; lacks a common room; the usual in-town noise. ⊠*8 N. Water St., Box 1337* ☎*508/228–6597 or*

# Where to Stay in Nantucket Town

## Navigating the Rental Market

CLOSE UP

If you're going to be staying for a week or more, you might want to consider renting a cottage or house—an arrangement that gives you a chance to settle in and get a real taste of island living. Many visitors, especially those with children, find renting more relaxing than staying in a hotel or an inn. With your own kitchen, you'll save money by eating in; plus you can enjoy such homey summer pleasures as barbecues. Though decor can vary from chichi to weatherworn, most cottages come equipped with all you'll need to ensure a comfortable stay. Steer clear of a house without linens; it's a sign of bad things to come. The better houses come fully accoutered, not just with basics but with luxury touches like cable or satellite TV, a CD player, gourmet kitchen implements, beach chairs, and bikes.

Finding a great cottage or house can be tough, however, especially because so many are rented a year or more in advance by returning guests. The time to start your search is a summer ahead, though you can occasionally find a property as late as spring. A good way to shop is to stop in and

visit Realtors when you happen to be in town. Be prepared for a bit of sticker shock, though. Prices are generally about twice what you'd have to pay on Cape Cod or even the Vineyard. In summer, very rustic (read shabby) rentals start at about $1,500 a week and can run to many times that ($4,000 to $40,000) for multibed-room properties, with waterfront locations commanding a premium.

Information **Country Village Rentals** (✉10 Straight Wharf ☎508/228—8840 or 800/599-7368 ⊕www.cvrandr.com) knows its clientele, who like to flit to sweet spots like Stowe and St. Bart's. **Lucille Jordan Real Estate** (✉8 Federal St. ☎508/228–4449 ⊕www.jordanre. com) has a broad rental inventory; check the photos lining the storefront windows. The **Maury People** (✉35–37 Main St. ☎508/228–1881 🖷508/228–1481 ⊕www.maury people.com), associated with Sotheby's, has more than 1,000 private homes in its rental inventory, including historic and beach homes; service is not only knowledgeable but personal.

---

888/808–6597 🖷508/228–6291 ⊕*www.nantucketwhaler.com* 💬*12 suites* ☄*In-room: DVD, Wi-Fi. In-hotel: no kids under 12, no-smoking rooms* ☐*AE, MC, V* ☉*Closed Jan. and Feb.*

**$** 🏨**Nesbitt Inn.** The last real deal left in town, this homey Victorian has been in the same family since 1914. Fourth-generation proprietors Joanne and Steve Marcoux are so nice, and the rates so reasonable, that you're willing to overlook the shared baths and gently worn furnishings. Here you'll find the authentic, pre-glitz Nantucket. **Pros:** friendly native owners; no pretense; true island spirit. **Cons:** busy street; small rooms; shabby (but clean). ✉*21 Broad St., Box 1019* ☎*508/228–0156* 🖷*508/228–2446* 💬*13 rooms share 3 baths, 1 room with private bath, 2 cottages* ☄ *In-hotel: No-smoking rooms* ☐*MC, V* 🍽*CP.*

**$$** 🏨**The Periwinkle.** Sara Shlosser-O'Reilly's B&B (which extends to another house and a Brant Point cottage) has panache. Rooms range from affordable singles to nice-size quarters with canopied king-size beds and harbor views. In one especially pretty setting, the blue-ribbon pattern of the wallpaper matches the cushions and canopy: it's like living in a nicely wrapped gift. **Pros:** central location; heavenly baking aromas; garden for lounging. **Cons:** usual town noises; Children's the only nearby beach; tiny breakfast room (opt for the garden). ⊠*7–9 N. Water St., Box 1816* ☎*508/228–9267 or 800/837–2921* 🖷*508/228– 0245* ⊕*www.theperiwinkle.com* 🛏*16 rooms, 1 cottage* 👍*In-room: refrigerators, DVD (some), VCR (some), Wi-Fi. In-hotel: no-smoking rooms* 🖃*D, MC, V* ⍟*CP.*

**$$–$$$**   ⊡ **Pineapple Inn.** No expense was spared in retrofitting this 1838 Greek
★   Revival captain's house for its new role as pamperer. It's decorated with impeccable taste, with down quilts and marble-finished baths. Breakfast is served in a formal dining room or beside the garden fountain. Whaling captains displayed a pineapple on their stoops upon completion of a successful journey, signaling the neighbors to come celebrate; here that spirit prevails daily—as it does at three sister properties (The Summer House–Fair Street; The Summer House–India Street, and the 29 Fair Street Inn), comprising 48 in-town rooms all told, operated under the auspices of the splendid Summer House out in 'Sconset. **Pros:** true Nantucket elegance; quiet location; cushy quarters. **Cons:** some small rooms (Web site warns); no nearby beach; communal breakfast setup (not everyone's cup of cappuccino). ⊠*10 Hussey St.* ☎*508/228–9992* 🖷*508/325–6051* ⊕*www.pineappleinn.com* 🛏*12 rooms* 👍*In-room: Wi-Fi. In-hotel: concierge, no-smoking rooms* 🖃*AE, MC, V* ⊙*Closed mid-Dec.–late Apr.* ⍟*CP.*

**$$**   ⊡ **Safe Harbor.** The name is apt: children *and* pets are welcome at this
☺   homey B&B with an enviable location mere steps from Children's Beach. Some of the rooms harboring American and Oriental antiques have water views; some have private decks. Everyone's welcome to sit on the wide front porch and enjoy the ocean breezes. **Pros:** family-friendly; laid-back; well cared for. **Cons:** noise can carry from Children's Beach; boat-launch traffic; occasional foghorns. ⊠*2 Harborview Way* ☎🖷*508/228–3222 or 800/651–9262* ⊕*www.beesknees.net/safeharbor* 🛏*5 rooms* 👍*In-room: Wi-Fi. In-hotel: some pets allowed, no-smoking rooms* 🖃*AE, MC, V* ⍟*CP.*

**$$–$$$**   ⊡ **Seven Sea Street.** If this red-oak post-and-beam B&B looks awfully well preserved, that's because it was custom-built in 1987. Decked out in Early American style (decorative stenciling, fishnet-canopy beds, braided rugs), it offers the ambience of antiquity without all the creaky drawbacks. The Deluxe Suite, with its cathedral ceiling, full kitchen, gas fireplace, and harbor view, warrants a leisurely stay. Two satellite buildings up your odds of booking a room. **Pros:** quiet side street; central location; handsome decor. **Cons:** some rooms smallish; some darkish; Children's the only nearby beach. ⊠*7 Sea St.* ☎*508/228–3577 or 800/651–9262* 🖷*508/228–3578* ⊕*www. sevenseastreetinn.com* 🛏*13 rooms, 2 suites* 👍*In-room: refrigerator, DVD, VCR, Wi-Fi. In-hotel: some pets allowed, no kids under 5, no-smoking rooms* 🖃*AE, D, MC, V* ⍟*CP.*

**$$–$$$**   ⊡ **Ships Inn.** This 1831 home exudes history: it was built for whaling
★   captain Obed Starbuck on the site of the birthplace of abolitionist Lucretia Mott. Guest rooms, named for the ships Starbuck commanded, are

furnished with period antiques and pretty wallpapers. In the basement is a restaurant of the same name (delighted murmurings waft up), which generates a wonderful continental breakfast and afternoon tea. **Pros:** large rooms; handsome decor; fine in-house restaurant. **Cons:** front rooms face street; exuberant exiting diners; uphill from ferries. ⊠*13 Fair St.* ☎*508/228–0040 or 888/872–4052* ⊕*www.shipsinnnantucket. com* ⇱*13 rooms, 11 with bath* ⚷*In-room: refrigerator. In-hotel: restaurant, no kids under 8, no-smoking rooms* ⊟*AE, D, MC, V* ⊗*Closed Nov.–Apr.* ⏏⏐*CP.*

**$$$$**

**Fodor'sChoice**

★

**Union Street Inn.** Ken Withrow worked in the hotel business, Deborah Withrow in high-end retail display, and guests get the best of both worlds. This 1770 house, a stone's throw from the bustle of Main Street, has been respectfully yet lavishly restored. Guests are treated to afternoon treats, Frette linens, plump duvets, and lush robes (the better to lounge around in, my dear), as well as a full gourmet breakfast served on the tree-shaded garden patio—or in bed. Some rooms have that ultimate accessory for rekindling romance: a wood-burning fireplace. **Pros:** pampering by pros; sensual pleasures; pervasive good taste. **Cons:** no nearby beach; bustle of town; some small rooms (disclosed on Web site). ⊠*7 Union St.* ☎*508/228–9222 or 800/225–5116* 🖷*508/325–0848* ⊕*www.unioninn.com* ⇱*12 rooms* ⚷*In-room: Wi-Fi. In-hotel: concierge, no kids under 12, no-smoking rooms* ⊟*AE, MC, V* ⏏⏐*BP.*

**$$$**

★

**The Veranda House.** A fixture since the early 1880s, the former Overlook, whose tiers of balconies take in a sweeping harbor vista, has been treated to a trendy "retro-chic" overhaul. The exterior may look unchanged, but the rooms got a makeover that introduced Frette linens, Simon Pearce lamps, Italian-tile rainfall showers, and the like. The buffet breakfasts are equally lush, featuring fresh-baked pastries and artisanal cheeses, and conviviality is encouraged via afternoon tea and biweekly wine-and-cheese receptions. A thoughtful "beach concierge" service means you don't have to tote your own towels, chairs, and umbrellas. A trio of less aggressively stylish cottages is available for families with children in tow. **Pros:** central but quiet location; harbor views; impeccable condition. **Cons:** children's is the only close beach; inn decor a bit austere; pricey (though not for Nantucket). ⊠*3 Step La., Box 1112* ☎*508/228–0695* ⊕*www.theverandahouse.com* ⇱*14 rooms, 4 suites* ⚷*In-room: DVD, Wi-Fi. In-hotel: concierge, no kids under 10 in inn rooms, no-smoking rooms* ⊟*AE, D, MC, V* ⊗*Closed late Oct. to mid-May* ⏏⏐*BP.*

**$$$$**

**VNH–Vanessa Noel Hotel and Hotel Green.** Opened in 2002 by native New Yorker and island-summerer shoe designer Vanessa Noel, VNH is a living catalog of trendy decor: each of the eight rooms (some admittedly as small as shoe boxes) boasts Armani Casa bedside tables, Philippe Starck bathroom fixtures, Mascioni linens, and Bulgari toiletries. Though the concept might seem a bit at odds with the island aesthetic, you'd be hard pressed to name a hotel with these touches outside a metropolis. Organo-purists will want to check out Noel's 2006 addition a few doors down: the 10-room Hotel Green—distinguished by its grass window boxes—has milk-painted walls, hemp shower curtains (the water is dechlorinated), and Ayurvedic body products. Rooms in the latter are slightly less pricey. Both inns share an outdoor breakfast café, and VNH harbors the seasonal Cafe V Bar, serving light bites (caviar, champagne). **Pros:** centrally located; trendy; glamour quotient. **Cons:** street noise; size of rooms; preciousness factor. ⊠*5 Chestnut St., at Centre St.* ☎*508/228–5300* ⊕*www.vanessanoelhotel.com* ⤏*18 rooms* ⌂*In-hotel: bar, no kids, no-smoking rooms* ▤*AE, D, MC, V.*

$$$$ 🛏**White Elephant.** The White Elephant, a 1920s behemoth right on Nantucket Harbor, seems determined to keep raising the bar in service and style. The complex—a main building plus a cluster of cottages with breezy country-chic decor—hugs the harbor, leaving just enough room for a sweep of emerald lawn and the veranda of the hotel's in-house restaurant, the Brant Point Grill, where jazz combos entertain in season. Prices are lofty but, for the echelon it attracts, not all that extreme. The afternoon port-and-cheese reception offers a chance to hobnob. **Pros:** right on harbor; ferry shuttle; elegant; built-in entertainment. **Cons:** can be snooty; Children's the only nearby beach; expensive. ⊠*Easton St., Box 1139* ☎*508/228–2500 or 800/445–6574* ▤*508/325–1195* ⊕*www.whiteelephanthotel.com* ⤏*22 rooms, 31 suites, 11 cottages* ⌂*In-room: safe, refrigerator, DVD, Wi-Fi. In-hotel: restaurant, room service, bar, gym, spa, laundry service, concierge, no-smoking rooms* ▤*AE, D, DC, MC, V* ⊗*Closed mid-Dec.–mid-Apr.* ⦿*BP.*

## WHERE TO STAY OUTSIDE NANTUCKET TOWN

⇨*Where to Stay & Eat Outside Nantucket Town map for these properties.*

$$$$ 🛏**Cliffside Beach Club.** Which way to the beach? You're on it: this snaz-
☾ zily updated 1920s beach club stakes its claim with a flotilla of colorful
★ umbrellas—somewhat miffing natives, who consider sand rights anathema. Local politics aside, this is one prime chunk of gentle bay beach, and the complex makes the most of its site, with a gorgeous cathedral-ceiling lobby decorated with hanging quilts, and rooms of every size and shape enhanced by island-made modern furnishings. Best of all, the fine restaurant Galley Beach serves as de facto concession stand. **Pros:** right on beach; two pools; good restaurant. **Cons:** questionable private-beach karma; over-entitled guests; high prices. ⊠*46 Jefferson Ave., Box 449* ☎*508/228–0618 or 800/932–9645* ⊕*www.cliffside-beach.com* ⤏*21 rooms, 4 suites, 1 apartment, 1 cottage* ⌂*In-room: safe, kitchen (some), refrigerator, DVD and VCR on request, Wi-Fi. In-hotel: restaurant, pools, gym, beachfront, no-smoking rooms* ▤*AE* ⊗*Closed Nov.–May* ⦿*CP.*

$ 🛏**Robert B. Johnson Memorial Hostel.** One of the country's most pictur-esque hostels, this 49-bed Hostelling International facility occupies a former 1873 lifesaving station—known as "The Star of the Sea"—right on Surfside Beach, a 3½-mi ride from town on the bike path (or via shuttle). Dorm rooms come in male, female, and coed configurations; the five-bed private room, which is wheelchair-accessible, tends to book quickly. Common areas include a kitchen, where a complimentary breakfast is offered. There's no lockout (customary at many urban hostels) and—huzzah—no curfew. Reservations are always a good idea, and essential come summer. **Pros:** super-cheap; right on island's best beach; good company. **Cons:** little privacy; no frills; a long haul from town. ✉ *31 Western Ave.* ☎ *508/228–0433 or 888/901–2084* ⊕ *www. usahostels.org/cape/hint/index.shtml* ⇄ *44 dorm-style beds, 1 room* ⚐ *In room: no a/c, no phone, no TV. In-hotel: public Wi-Fi, no-smoking rooms* ☰ *MC, V* ⊙ *Closed Oct.–mid-May.*

## NIGHTLIFE & THE ARTS
Other than in-season charity galas and impromptu community fund-raisers that are held year-round (islanders look out for their own), the phrase "Nantucket nightlife" verges on an oxymoron. If it's glitz and nonstop action you're after, better stick to the mainland. On the other hand, if you like live music, you will rarely go wanting—at least in season.

For listings of events, see the *Inquirer and Mirror* (⊕ *www.ack.net*), the *Nantucket Independent* (⊕ *www.nantucketindependent.com*), and (in season) *Yesterday's Island* (⊕ *www.yesterdaysisland.com*); the latter two are distributed free. Posters around town announce coming attractions: check the board outside the Hub, a newsstand at the corner of Federal and Main streets.

FILM   The **Nantucket Film Festival** (☎ *508/325–6274 or 212/642–6339* ⊕ *www. nantucketfilmfestival.org*), held each June, emphasizes the importance of strong scripts. The final playlist—about two dozen short and feature-length films—always includes a few world premieres, and many selections have gone on to considerable commercial success. Shows tend to sell out, so it's best to buy online, well ahead. Informal daily coffee-klatch discussions with directors provide the inside scoop.

The **Starlight Theatre** (✉ *1 N. Union St.* ☎ *508/228–4435* ⊕ *www. starlightnantucket.com*) is a small screening room appended to a café of the same name. It presents two shows nightly in season, plus sporadic (mostly rainy-day) matinees.

FINE ARTS & CRAFTS   The **Artists Association of Nantucket** (✉ *Gardner Perry La.* ☎ *508/228–0722* ⊕ *www.nantucketarts.org*), founded in 1945, leads classes year-round in various mediums, often presented by some of the island's most noteworthy artists. The association's **gallery** (✉ *19 Washington St.* ☎ *508/228–0294*) hosts juried shows.

The **Nantucket Island School of Design and the Arts** (✉ *23 Wauwinet Rd.* ☎ *508/228–9248* ⊕ *www.nisda.org*), affiliated with the Massachusetts College of Art in Boston, teaches fine-art classes in many mediums; it also hosts shows, lectures, and events.

**Nantucket Lightship Basket Museum** (✉ *49 Union St.* ☎ *508/228–1177*) mounts demos Friday and Saturday in summer.

MUSIC   The **Boston Pops** puts on a blow-out concert on Jetties Beach in mid-August to benefit Nantucket Cottage Hospital (☎ *508/825–8250* ⊕ *www.nantuckethospital.org*).

The **Nantucket Arts Council** (✉ *Box 554, 02554* ☎ *508/228–8588* ⊕ *www.nantucketartscouncil.org*) sponsors a music series (jazz, country, classical) September to June, plus a summertime Shakespeare Festival and a fall Arts Festival.

The **Nantucket School of Music** (✉*11 Centre St.* ☎*508/228–3352* ⊕*www.ackmusic.com*) arranges year-round choral and instrumental instruction and puts on concerts featuring domestic and imported talent; choristers are always welcome.

**Nantucket Musical Arts Society** (☎*508/228–1287*) mounts concerts by internationally acclaimed musicians Tuesday evening at 8:30 July through August. The concerts are mostly classical but sometimes venture into jazz.

The **Nantucket Park & Recreation Commission** (✉*Children's Beach bandstand, off Harbor View Way* ☎*508/228–7213*) hosts free jazz/pop/classical concerts (and the occasional theater production) from July 4 to Labor Day. Programs begin at 6 PM. Bring blankets, chairs, and bug repellent.

The **Noonday Concert Series** (✉*Unitarian Universalist Church, 11 Orange St.* ☎*508/228–5466*), Thursday at noon in July and August, brings in visiting performers and also showcases outstanding local musicians. Concerts range from bluegrass to classical.

BARS & CLUBS The **Chicken Box** (*The Box* ✉*14 Dave St., off Lower Orange St.* ☎*508/228–9717*) rocks! Live music—including some big-name bands—plays six nights a week in season, and weekends throughout the year. On the off nights, you can always play pool, foosball, or darts.

The **Club Car Lounge** (✉*1 Main St.* ☎*508/228–1101*) is an actual club car, salvaged from the narrow-gauge railroad that once served 'Sconset. These days it makes a convivial piano bar, where requests and sing-alongs are encouraged.

At **Galley Beach** (✉*54 Jefferson Ave., at Cliffside Beach* ☎*508/228–9641*) you can sip mojitos among a moneyed throng as piano riffs mix with the rhythm of gentle surf.

**Lo La 41** (✉*15 Beach St., at Cliffside Beach* ☎*508/325–4001*) is Cougar Central, but maybe those gorgeously maintained socialites are just there to socialize over sake and sushi.

The **Muse** (✉*44 Surfside Rd.* ☎*508/228–6873*) hosts bands (including the occasional big-name act) year-round. DJs spin between sets and on nights when there's no live performance. The crowd (the barnlike space can accommodate nearly 400) has been known to get wild; tamer options include playing pool or Ping-Pong or scarfing pies produced on-site at **Muse Pizza** (☎*508/228–1471*).

At the White Elephant's **Brant Point Grill** (✉*50 Easton St.* ☎*508/325–1320 or 800/445–6574* ⊕*www.brantpointgrill.com*), the setting is country-elegant—Windsor chairs, varnished woodwork with hunter-green trim—and the patrons are patently moneyed, since many are hotel guests. A jazz-standards soloist or combo provides atmosphere (and takes requests).

You don't have to be fabulous to fit in at **the pearl** (✉*12 Federal St.* ☎*508/228–9701*), but it wouldn't hurt. Patrons tend to be as chic as the white onyx bar itself, whose blue lighting lends a mysterious glow to all assembled.

Cineastes and sociable sorts claim the bar stools and patio tables at the **Starlight Café** (✉*1 N. Union St.* ☎*508/228–4479*), which adjoins the Starlight Theatre; musicians serenade in season.

READINGS & TALKS

The **Nantucket Atheneum** (✉*1 India St.* ☎*508/228–1110* ⊕*www.nantucketatheneum.org*) hosts a dazzling roster of writers and speakers year-round. Except for a few big-name fund-raisers in summer, all events are free.

> ## MICHELANGELO ON THE BEACH
>
> Buddhas, dragons, mermaids, and, of course, whales invade Jetties Beach during the annual Sandcastle & Sculpture Day in mid-August. Creative concoctions such as porpoises, submarines, spaceships, flowers, and the famous light-ship baskets—creatively crafted out of sand, shells, seaweed, and even beach litter—contend for prizes. Anyone can stake out a patch of sand, though registration is required if you're digging to win: forms are available at the Nantucket Chamber of Commerce office, at Zero Main Street.

The **Nantucket Historical Association** (✉*15 Broad St.* ☎*508/228–1894* ⊕*www.nha.org*) hosts evening talks on a variety of topics touching on local history.

The **Nantucket Island School of Design and the Arts** (✉*23 Wauwinet Rd.* ☎*508/228–9248* ⊕*www./nisda.org*) hosts a cultural-arts lecture series, ranging from artistic to environmental topics, Wednesday nights in July and August.

THEATER

**Theatre Workshop of Nantucket** (✉*Methodist Church, 2 Centre St.* ☎*508/228–4305* ⊕*www.theatreworkshop.com*), a community theater founded in 1956, stages plays, musicals, and readings year-round.

### SPORTS & THE OUTDOORS

BEACHES

A calm area by the harbor, **Children's Beach** (✉*Off Harbor View Way*) is an easy walk north from the center of town and a perfect spot for small children. The beach has a grassy park with benches, a playground, lifeguards, a café, picnic tables, showers, and restrooms. The Nantucket Park & Recreation Commission puts on free Thursday and Sunday evening concerts and offers tie-dyeing classes Fridays at noon mid-July through August.

**Cisco** (✉*Hummock Pond Rd., South Shore*) has heavy surf and lifeguards, but no food or restrooms. It's not easy to get to or from Nantucket Town: it's 4 mi from town and there are no bike trails, so you'll have to ride in the road, walk, drive, or take a taxi. Also, the dunes are severely eroded, so getting down onto the beach can be difficult. Still, the waves make it a popular spot for board- and bodysurfers.

**Dionis Beach** (✉*Eel Point Rd.*) is, at its entrance, a narrow strip of sand that turns into a wider, more private strand with high dunes and fewer children. The beach has a rocky bottom and calm, rolling waters; there are lifeguards on duty and restrooms with showers. Take the Madaket Bike Path to Eel Point Road, about 3 mi west of town.

★ A short bike- or shuttle-bus ride from town, **Jetties Beach** ( ⊠ *Bathing Beach Rd., 1½ mi northwest of Straight Wharf*) is a popular family beach because of its calm surf, lifeguards, bathhouse, restrooms, and snack bar. It's a good place to try out water toys: kayaks, sailboards, and Day Sailers are rented in summer. On shore it's a lively scene, with playground and volleyball nets on the beach and adjacent tennis courts. There is a boardwalk to the beach (special wheelchairs are available). You'll have a good view of passing ferries—and an even better one if you clamber out on the jetty itself (careful, it's slippery).

**Madaket Beach** ( ⊠ *Off Madaket Rd., Madaket*) can be reached by shuttle bus from Nantucket Town or the Madaket Bike Path (5 mi from Upper Main Street); it has lifeguards and restrooms, and there's a market nearby. It's known for challenging surf (beware of the riptides: should you get swept away, swim parallel to shore until the current's force abates) and unbeatable sunsets.

Fodor'sChoice **Surfside Beach** ( ⊠ *Surfside Rd., South Shore*), accessible via the Surfside
★ Bike Path (3 mi) or shuttle bus, is the island's most popular surf beach, with lifeguards, restrooms, a snack bar, and a wide strand of sand. It draws teens and young adults as well as families and is great for kite flying and surf casting.

BIKING The best way to tour Nantucket is by bicycle. Some 25 mi of paved bike paths wind through all types of terrain from one end of the island to the other: for details, consult the maps posted by Wheels, Heels, and Pedals ( ⊕ *www.wheelsheelsandpedals.com*), which supports alternative modes of transportation. It is possible to bike around the entire island in a day—should you tire, you and your bike are welcome aboard the in-season Nantucket Regional Transit Authority (NRTA) buses. Most paths start within ½ mi of town, and all are well marked. Several lead to beaches. And if you're without your wheels, it's easy enough to rent some. The paths are also perfect for runners and bladers—but not mopeds, which must remain on the road (to the frustration of impatient drivers). Note that Nantucket now requires all bike riders—including adults—to wear a helmet.

The easy 3-mi **Surfside Bike Path** leads to Surfside, the island's premier ocean beach. A drinking fountain and rest stop are placed at about the halfway point.

The **Milestone Bike Path**, a straight shot linking Nantucket Town and 'Sconset, is probably the most monotonous of the paths but can still be quite pleasant. It's about 7 mi; paired with the scenic Polpis Path, it becomes a 16-mi island loop.

At 1.2 mi, the **Cliff Road Path**, on the north shore, is one of the easiest bike paths, but it's still quite scenic, with gentle hills. It intersects with the Eel Point and Madaket paths.

7

The **Eel Point/Dionis Beach Path** starts at the junction of Eel Point Road and Madaket Road and links the Cliff Road and Madaket bike paths to Dionis Beach. It's less than a mile long.

The **Madaket Path** starts at the intersection of Quaker and Upper Main Street and follows Madaket Road out to Madaket Beach on the island's west end, about 6 mi from the edge of Nantucket Town. About one-third of the way, you could turn off onto Cliff Road Path or the Eel Point/Dionis Beach Path.

**Island Bike & Sport** ( ⊠ *25 Old South Rd.* ☎ *508/228–4070* ⊕ *www. islandbike.com*), though located mid-island, offers free delivery.

**Nantucket Bike Shop** ( ⊠ *4 Broad St., Steamboat Wharf* ⊠ *Straight Wharf* ☎ *508/228–1999, 800/838–5311 for both* ⊕ *www.nantucketbikeshop. com*), open April through October, rents bicycles and mopeds (anathema to locals, so don't be surprised if you get some dirty looks). Ask about free delivery and pickup.

**Young's Bicycle Shop** ( ⊠ *6 Broad St., Steamboat Wharf* ☎ *508/228–1151* ⊕ *www.youngsbicycleshop.com*), established in 1931, rents bicycles, including tandems and children's equipment; weekly rates are available. The knowledgeable third-generation Young family and staff will send you off with everything you need—an excellent touring map, a helmet, and a quaint little Portuguese basket for your handlebars.

BIRD-
WATCHING

Hundreds of species flock to the island's moors, meadows, and marshes in the course of a year. Birds that are rare in other parts of New England thrive here, because of the lack of predators and the abundance of wide-open, undeveloped space (currently about 60 percent of the island). Almost anywhere outside of town you're sure to see interesting birdlife, not just in migratory season but year-round. Set up your spotting scope near the salt marsh at Eel Point any time of year and you're bound to see shorebirds feeding—low tide is the best time. Endangered piping plovers and least terns nest on the ocean side in spring. Folger's Marsh about 3 mi east of town and the Harbor Flats at the end of Washington Street on the eastern edge of town are also good shorebird-watching sites. Inland, a walk through Sanford Farm from Madaket Road to the south shore, traversing upland, forest, heath, and shore habitats, will bring you in range of Savannah sparrows, yellow warblers, osprey, and red-tailed hawks, the island's most common raptor. Be on the lookout for the protected Northern harrier. For woodland species, check out the trails through Windswept Cranberry Bog or the Masquetuck Reservation near Polpis Harbor.

**Eco Guides: Strong Wings** ( ⊠ *9 Nobadeer Farm Rd.* ☎ *508/228–1769* ⊕ *www.strongwings.org*) customizes environmentally savvy birding tours based on interest and group size; depending on your preferred degree of difficulty, the outing might include a hike, a bike ride, or a casual stroll.

The **Maria Mitchell Association** (*MMA* ⊠ *4 Vestal St.* ☎ *508/228–0898* ⊕ *www.mmo.org*) leads marine-ecology field trips and nature and bird walks weekly in spring and early summer and three times a week from June through Labor Day.

BOATING  During July and August, Nantucket is *the* place to study, close-up, some of the world's most splendid yachts—and the well-to-do people who own and sail them. Don't be surprised if you see yachts with piggyback motor launches, automobiles, and helicopters. Some spend only a few days here, perhaps en route from the Mediterranean via the Caribbean. If you don't happen to own a floating palace, you can still hit the water—Nantucket has plenty of boat charters, rentals, and scenic cruises.

**Nantucket Community Sailing** ( ✉ *4 Winter St.* ☎ *508/228–6600* ⊕ *www.nantucketcommunitysailing.org*) rents Sunfish sailboats, sailboards, and kayaks at Jetties Beach (Memorial Day to Labor Day); it also has youth and adult instructional sailing programs, as well as adaptive water-sport clinics for disabled athletes. NCS's Outrigger Canoe Club—a Polynesian tradition—heads out several evenings a week (depending on interest) in season.

**Sea Nantucket** ( ✉ *Washington St. Ext., ¼ mi southeast of Commercial Wharf* ☎ *508/228–7499*) rents kayaks and small sailboats by the hour or half day at the vest-pocket Francis Street Beach.

☾  The *Endeavor* ( ✉ *Slip 1015, Straight Wharf* ☎ *508/228–5585* ⊕ *www.*
★  *endeavorsailing.com*), a charter replica Friendship sloop, makes four 1½-hour trips into the sound daily in-season (including a sunset cruise); there's also a shorter (one-hour) midday excursion. Private charters and special theme trips for children—"Pirate Adventure" and "Songs and Stories of the Sea"—can be arranged.

**Shearwater Excursions** ( ☎ *508/228–7037* ⊕ *www.explorenantucket.com*) mounts various seaborne ecotours aboard a 50-foot power catamaran. One year-round option is a two-hour trip to view Muskeget Island's 3,000 resident gray seals. Whale watches head out thrice weekly in-season: Captain Blair Perkins guarantees a sighting, which means that if no mammals show up, you can go again for free. The *Shearwater* is also available for one-hour Ice Cream Cruises through the harbor (featuring the Juice Bar's nonpareil products) and private evening charters.

FISHING  Surf fishing is very popular on Nantucket, especially in the late spring when bluefish are running (the best place to go after them is Great Point). Freshwater fishing is also an option at many area ponds.

Many of the fishing charters will gladly make detours to spot whales.

Captain Peter Kaizer, a former commercial fisherman (and off-duty innkeeper), guarantees a good catch aboard the *Althea K* ( ☎ *508/228–3471* ⊕ *www.altheaksportfishing.com*); he also offers whale-watching and charter cruises.

**Captain Tom's Charters** ( ✉ *Public Landing, Madaket* ☎ *508/228–4225* ⊕ *www.captaintomscharters.com*) win consistent "best of" awards for Tom Mleczko's hands-on expertise. Choose among rips, bars, surf, open water, and flats (the latter for the added challenge of sight fishing with fly rods).

A permit is required for **shellfishing,** specifically foraging for littleneck and cherrystone clams, quahogs, scallops, oysters, steamers, and mussels. You can pick one up—along with tips on where and how to get the best catch—at the **Marine and Coastal Resources Department** ( ⊠ *34 Washington St.* ☎ *508/228–7261*).

FITNESS CLUBS  **The Nantucket Health Club** ( ⊠ *10 Young's Way* ☎ *508/228–4750* ⊕ *www. nantuckethealthclub.com*) has StairMasters, Lifecycles, treadmills, rowers, Airdyne bikes, New Generation Nautilus, and free weights; aerobics, spinning, and yoga classes; and personal trainers. You can get a short-term pass that covers the machines plus fitness classes (with the exception of Spinning).

HIKING  Nantucket supports approximately 1,200 species of vegetation: that's a greater variety than is found in any other area of equivalent size in the United States. It has 82 mi of beaches, and though almost 97% of the shoreline is privately owned, it's a point of pride that nearly all of it is open for public use. Distinctive ecosystems on the island include hardwood forests, salt marshes, cranberry bogs, squam swamps, freshwater ponds, and coastal heathlands, and, with Martha's Vineyard and nearby Tuckernuck Island, the island holds more than 90% of the acreage of sandplain grassland *worldwide*. The island is home to a huge number of deer; significant colonies of harbor seals, gray seals, and harbor porpoises; and turtles, frogs, rabbits, voles, and other reptiles and small field mammals. A lack of land-bound predators such as skunks and raccoons allows bird populations to thrive, and hundreds of species either live on the island or pass through on their annual migrations.

Nearly all of the 8,900 acres maintained by the **Nantucket Conservation Foundation** ( ⊠ *118 Cliff Rd.* ☎ *508/228–2884* ⊕ *www.nantucket conservation.com*) are open to the public; though only a few trails are marked, you can feel free to wander knowing that you can't get lost—if you keep going in one direction, you're bound to hit a road or a beach eventually. The foundation, open weekdays 8 AM to 5 PM, puts out maps and informative brochures on the most popular hiking spots. Remember that these conservation areas are set aside to preserve and protect Nantucket's fragile ecosystems—tread carefully—and also be aware that ticks are a serious problem here. Dress accordingly and carry plenty of repellent.

A 5-to-10-minute bike ride from Nantucket Town on the way to Madaket, the **Sanford Farm, Ram Pasture, and the Woods** ( ⊠ *Madaket Rd., between Milford and Cliff Rds.*) comprises 300 acres that were saved from developers by the Nantucket Conservation Foundation in 1971. The southern edge of the property borders the ocean.

The **Tupancy Links** ( ⊠ *165 Cliff Rd., 1¼ mi west of town*) runs between the Cliff Road bike path and Nantucket Sound. It's a smaller property that passes mainly through grassland populated by plants like false

## PETTICOAT ROW

During the whaling era—a time when women were generally considered better seen than heard—a circumstance developed in Nantucket Town that was perhaps unique in the country: a large portion of Centre Street shops near Main Street were almost completely run by female merchants. The area is known to this day as Petticoat Row. Women have always played a strong role in Nantucket's history, partly because of the Quaker philosophy of sexual equality and partly because on whaling expeditions men could be gone for years at a time—and it was up to women to keep the town going. They became leaders in every arena, from religion to business.

heather, oxeye daisy, and Queen Anne's lace, and it provides wonderful views once you reach the overlook at the water's edge. The cliff is only 42 feet above sea level, but from it you can see great stretches of the island's north shore.

SURFING  The relatively mild breakers at Cisco Beach make picking up the sport easier than it might be in, say, Maui. **Nantucket Island Surf School** (☎508/560–1020 ⊕*www.surfack.com*) owner Gary Kohner and his crew can tell you everything you need to know to get up and cruising, from surfing etiquette to ocean safety. Group and private lessons and equipment and wet-suit rental are available.

TENNIS  **The Jetties Beach Tennis Courts** (☎*508/325–5334*), six contiguous asphalt courts overseen by the Park & Recreation department, charge a nominal fee 8 AM to 6 PM in season and are much in demand, so call to reserve early in the day. Early- and latecomers play free, and off-season, you're golden: they leave the nets up year-round.

**Great Harbor Tennis Center**(⊠*23 Nobadeer Farm Rd., near airport* ☎*508/228–3700* ⊕*www.ghyc.com* ☉*Late May–Sept., daily 7* AM– *9:30* PM), part of the private Great Harbor Yacht Club, makes its eight fast-dry clay courts, five lighted courts, and pro shop available to the public. Lessons, rentals, clinics, and round-robins can be arranged.

### SHOPPING

The historic center of town doubles as the commercial district: shops are concentrated primarily in the grid formed by Main, Centre, Broad, and Easy streets, with a few shops trailing off along the periphery. The former boathouses of Straight Wharf and Old South Wharf, retrofitted as shops and galleries, attract well-heeled browsers as well. The necessities of island life—hardware, office supplies, etc.—tend to be clustered mid-island, where new stores offering nonessentials are gradually making inroads as well.

Most of Nantucket's shops are seasonal, opening in time for the Daffodil Festival in late April and closing soon after Christmas Stroll in early December; a hardy few stay open year-round and often offer rather astounding bargains off-season. On summer weekends, many shops stay open late (until 9 or 10). Most galleries hold their openings on Friday evening.

ANTIQUES **G. K. S. Bush** (⊠*13 Old South Rd.* ☎*508/325–0300*) carries ultrahigh-end American antique furniture, paintings, and decorative arts (winter headquarters are on New York's Upper East Side).

In business since 1974, **Lynda Willauer Antiques** (⊠*2 India St.* ☎*508/228–3631* ⊕*www.lyndawillauerantiques.com*) has amassed a stellar cache of American and English furniture, plus fine collectibles, including Chinese export porcelain and majolica; the shop winters in Greenwich, Connecticut.

★ **Nantucket Country** (⊠*38 Centre St.* ☎*508/228–8868* ⊕*www.nantucket countryantiques.com*) has an especially rich inventory of quilts and flags; another specialty—in addition to maritime and "Nantucketiana"—is antique children's toys.

**Nantucket House Antiques** (⊠*2 S. Beach St.* ☎*508/228–4604* ⊕*www. nantuckethouse.com*) displays a wealth of well-chosen artifacts, in inspired aggregations; the owners are interior decorators.

**Nina Hellman Marine Antiques & Americana** (⊠*48 Centre St.* ☎*508/228–4677* ⊕*www.nauticalnantucket.com*) carries scrimshaw, whaling artifacts, ship models, instruments, and other marine antiques, plus folk art and Nantucket memorabilia. Charles Manghis, a contemporary scrimshaw artist, demonstrates and exhibits his craft here.

Fodor's Choice **Rafael Osona Auctions** (⊠*American Legion Hall, 21 Washington St.* ★ ☎*508/228–3942* ⊕*www.rafaelosonaauction.com*) holds auctions of fine antiques most Saturday mornings from Memorial Day weekend to early December; the items—furniture, decorative accessories, art, jewelry, and more—are previewable two days in advance.

Established in 1927, **Sylvia Antiques** (⊠*167 Orange St.* ☎*508/228–0960* ⊕*www.sylviaantiques.com*) retains the richest stash of island-related antiquities.

ART GALLERIES The **Artists' Association of Nantucket** (⊠*19 Washington St.* ☎*508/228–0772* ⊕*www.nantucketarts.org*) is the best place to get an overview of the work being done on-island; many members have galleries of their own.

**Cavalier Galleries** (⊠*34 Main St.* ☎*508/325–4405* ⊕*www.cavalier galleries.com*) (also in Greenwich, Connecticut) offers a blend of traditionalist and trendy.

The **Gallery at Four India** (⊠*4 India St.* ☎*508/228–8509* ⊕*www. galleryatfourindia.com*) is a quiet, spacious refuge, with highly sought-after American and marine paintings dating from the 1850s to 1940s, plus a small sampling of contemporary realism.

## Nantucket Reds

Bermuda has its shorts, Fiji its sarongs. Nantucket's totemic clothing items are made of cotton dyed red so as to fade to a dull salmon shade. The reds were something of a secret code until they were singled out by *The Official Preppy Handbook* in 1980: "By their pink shirts ye shall know them" might be the watchwords for Nantucketers among the worldwide sailing community. Now reds are as site-specific as Martha's Vineyard's Black Dog line (attempting to com-

pete, of late, with a satellite shop on Straight Wharf).

The principal purveyor of Nantucket reds is Murray's Toggery Shop on Main Street, which has catered to conservative dressers since the early 1900s. (Roland Macy worked here at his father's shop in the early 1800s before setting off to rewrite retailing history.) From baby togs to tote bags, you'll find everything you could want here in the way of reds. But for that weathered look that sets them off so well, you'll have to get out on the water.

**Hoorn-Ashby Gallery** (⊠*10 Federal St.* ☎*508/228–9314*) favors realism, ranging from the whimsical to the highly polished.

**Paul La Paglia Gallery** (⊠*38 Centre St.* ☎*508/228–8760*) offers a range of vintage artworks (mostly with maritime, botanical, or regional themes) and beautiful custom framing.

**Quidley & Comopany** (⊠*26 Main St.* ☎*508/228–4300* ⊕*www.quidley andco.com*) specializes in high-end marine art.

**Robert Wilson Galleries** (⊠*51 Main St.* ☎*508/228–2096* ⊕*www.robert wilsongalleries.com*) carries contemporary American marine, impressionist, and other art.

★ The **South Wharf Gallery** (⊠*3 India St.* ☎*508/228–0406* ⊕*www.south wharfgallery.com*) has been showing top local work since 1978.

BOOKS Check the Nantucket Room at the back of **Mitchell's Book Corner** (⊠*54 Main St.* ☎*508/228–1080* ⊕*www.mitchellsbookcorner.com*) for regional titles. The front is filled with an astute sampling covering a broad range of categories. Author signings are held on summer Saturdays.

**Nantucket Bookworks** (⊠*25 Broad St.* ☎*508/228–4000* ⊕*www. nantucketbookworks.com*) carries an extensive inventory, with an emphasis on literary works and Nantucket-specific titles, as well as children's books and gift items.

CLOTHING **Current Vintage**(⊠*4 Easy St.* ☎*508/228–5073* ⊕*www.currentvintage*
★ *nantucket.com*)offers an unusual (perhaps unique) blend of inventory: vintage designer clothing *and* wine. Consider it one-stop shopping for the well-dressed oenophile.

**Eye of the Needle and Eye of the Needle Girls** (⊠*14–14A Federal St.* ☎*508/228–1923*) is a microcosm of urban fashion trends, playfully leavened.

The splashy resort wear so popular in the '60s is enshrined at the **Lilly Pulitzer Shop** ( ⊠*5 S. Water St.* ☏*508/228–0569* ⊕ *www.lillypulitzer.com*).

**Murray's Toggery Shop** ( ⊠*62 Main St.* ☏*508/228–0437* ⊕*www. nantucketreds.com*) can claim credit for introducing the signature "Nantucket reds"—now available in a range of styles for men, women, and children.

**Murray's Warehouse** ( ⊠*7 New St.* ☏*508/228–3584* ⊕*www.nantucket reds.com*) offers discounts of up to 75% on surplus stock from Murray's Toggery Shop.

Something about the Nantucket lifestyle prompts hat hunger. **Peter Beaton** ( ⊠*16½ Federal St.* ☏*508/228–8456* ⊕*www.peterbeaton. com*) shows an international array of beauties, all customizable with special trim.

**Vanessa Noel** ( ⊠*5 Chestnut St., at Centre St.* ☏*508/228–5300* ⊕*www. vanessanoel.com*) creates ultraglam shoes—they're expensive, to be sure, but fans gladly toe the line.

Island loyalties might be tested, but the **Vineyard Vines** ( ⊠*2 Harbor Sq.* ☏*800/892–4982* ⊕*www.vineyardvines.com*) line—from flip-flops to bathing trunks, not to mention the ties that started it all—is just so irresistibly preppy, resistance is futile.

Fodor'sChoice ★   The inviting windows of **Vis-a-Vis** ( ⊠*34 Main St.* ☏*508/228–5527* ⊕*www.visavisnantucket.com*) display relaxed-luxe women's fashions amid antique home furnishings, some of which, including hooked rugs, quilts, and collectibles, are also for sale.

CRAFTS   **Claire Murray** ( ⊠*11 S. Water St.* ☏*508/228–1913 or 800/252–4733* ⊕*www.clairemurray.com*) carries the designer's Nantucket-theme and other hand-hooked rugs and rug kits, quilts, and knitting and needlework kits; this little shop is where the empire got started.

**Erica Wilson Needle Works** ( ⊠*25 Main St.* ☏*508/228–9881*) embodies the enthusiasms of the famous British-born designer, an island resident since 1958. In addition to her own embroidery and needlepoint kits, the store carries winning clothing and accessories for women (look for Heidi Weddendorf's Nantucket knot jewelry), baby gifts, and appealing elements of home decor.

The **Four Winds Craft Guild** ( ⊠*15 Main St.* ☏*508/228–9623* ⊕*www. sylviaantiques.com*) has showcased local folk arts, including scrimshaw and lightship baskets (old and new), ship models, and duck decoys, since 1927; the guild also offers a kit for making your own lightship basket.

★   **Nantucket Looms** ( ⊠*16 Federal St.* ☏*508/228–1908* ⊕*www. nantucketlooms.com*) stocks luscious woven-on-the-premises textiles and chunky Susan Lister Locke jewelry, among other adornments for self and home.

WINE    Leslie Chumsae, former sommelier for the Chanticleer, stocks **The Cellar** ( ⊠*1 Windy Way* ☎*508/228–9123* ⊕*www.thecellarnantucket.com*) with personal picks priced modestly and on up—way up. You can sample the wares at free Saturday afternoon tastings.

The miniconglomerate of **Cisco Brewers, Nantucket Vineyard, and Triple Eight Distillery** ( ⊠*5 Bartlett Farm Rd.* ☎*508/325–5929* ⊕*www.cisco brewers.com*) makes boutique beers, wine, and vodka on-site.

**Tutto Sfoglia** ( ⊠*49A Pleasant St.* ☎*508/825–9900* ⊕*www.shoptutto sfoglia.com*) carries Italian-only wines and comestibles, some of them house-made by Sfoglia restaurant.

MARKETS    **Annye's Whole Foods** ( ⊠*14 Amelia Dr.* ☎*508/228–4554* ⊕*www.annyes wholefoods.com*) has organic staples, including fresh produce and prepared meals to go.

★

**Bartlett's Ocean View Farm** ( ⊠*Bartlett Farm Rd.* ☎*508/228–9403* ⊕*www.bartlettsoceanviewfarm.com*) encompasses 100 acres overseen by eighth-generation Bartletts. Healthy, tasty prepared foods—within a mini-supermarket—add incentive to visit. If you're not up for the trek, a produce truck is parked on Main Street through the summer.

**'Sconset Market** ( ⊠*4 Main St.* ☎*508/228–9915* 📠*508/228–4321*), though strictly seasonal, is well stocked with basics and gourmet comestibles alike.

Karen Fisher's **Coastal** ( ⊠*12 Oak St.* ☎*508/228–4662*) redefines seaside decor with beautifully spare antique and contemporary pieces.

GIFT SHOPS    **Diane Johnston** ( ⊠*35 Centre St.* ☎*508/228–4688*) blends select clothing (hand-knit sweaters, needlepoint slippers) with antique quilts, lush rugs (from kilims to contemporary creations), and whatever else strikes the owner's fancy; the mix is magical

In addition to fresh blooms, **Flowers on Chestnut** ( ⊠*1 Chestnut St.* ☎*508/228–6007* ⊕*www.flowersonchestnut.com*) carries appealing gifts, including books, baby presents, lamps, and picture frames.

**Leslie Linsley Nantucket** ( ⊠*37½ Union St.* ☎*508/325–4900* ⊕*www. leslielinsley.com*), the project of a widely published crafts aficionado, carries supplies, tasteful souvenirs, and other decorative touches.

The **Lion's Paw** ( ⊠*0 Main St.* ☎*508/228–3837*) is full of the sort of furnishings Nantucketers favor—fancy cottage-style.

An outreach program of the Nantucket Historical Association, the **Museum Shop** ( ⊠*11 Broad St., next to the Whaling Museum* ☎*508/228–5785* ⊕*www.nha.org*) sells island-related books, reproduction furniture and accessories, and toys.

**Vanessa @ Seven Seas** ( ⊠*46 Centre St.* ☎*508/228–8010* ⊕*www.vanessa noel.com*) gathers everything from handbags and jewelry to antique maps and furniture.

JEWELRY    **Diana Kim England, Goldsmiths** ( ⊠*56 Main St.* ☎*508/228–3766 or 800/343–1468* ⊕*www.dianakimengland.com*) has created an elegant contemporary line featuring unusual gems such as tourmaline, chalcedony, and tanzanite.

The **Golden Basket** ( ✉ *44 Main St.* ☎ *508/228–4344 or 877/453-2758* ⊕ *www.thegoldenbasket.com*) was founded in 1977 by designer Glenaan M. Elliott, who fashioned the first miniature lightship basket. Other popular motifs include starfish and shells.

**Jola Jewelry Designs** ( ✉ *29 Centre St.* ☎ *508/325–6999*) is a jewel box—the tiny, lovely atelier of Polish-born goldsmith Jolanta Gutnik, who creates "passionate statements" using unusual stones and rare pearls.

**Trianon/Seaman Schepps**( ✉ *47 Main St.* ☎ *508/325–5806* ⊕ *www.seamanschepps.com*) carries contemporary work—including some pieces incorporating Nantucket shells and sand—as well as the mostly nature-motif Seaman Schepps line, established in 1904.

PHARMACIES   With its much-beloved lunch counter, **Nantucket Pharmacy** ( ✉ *45 Main St.* ☎ *508/228–0180* ⊕ *www.nantucketpharmacy.com*) looks lifted from the '50s.

TOYS   Carrying plenty of its namesake items in various sizes and shapes, the **Toy Boat** ( ✉ *41 Straight Wharf* ☎ *508/228–4552* ⊕ *www.thetoyboat.com*) also sells other high-quality toys for youngsters, including Nantucket mermaids, and children's books based on local themes (look for Joan Aiken's classic *Nightbirds on Nantucket*).

## SIASCONSET & WAUWINET

★ *7 mi east of Nantucket Town.*

First a fishing outpost and then an artists' colony (Broadway actors favored it in the late 19th century), Siasconset—or 'Sconset, in the local vernacular—is a charming cluster of rose-covered cottages linked by driveways of crushed clamshells; at the edges of town, the former fishing shacks give way to magnificent sea-view mansions. The small town center consists of a market, post office, café, lunchroom, and liquor store–cum–lending library.

The tiny settlement of Wauwinet, a few miles north, is in a haulover—a spit of land so narrow, boats can be dragged across it—leading to the immense curving sandbar of Coskata, Great Point, and Coatue.

**Altar Rock.** Altar Rock Road, a dirt track about 3 mi west of the Milestone Road Rotary on Polpis Road, leads to the island's highest point, Altar Rock, from which the view is spectacular. The hill overlooks open moor and bog land—technically called lowland heath—which is very rare in the United States. The entire area is laced with paths leading in every direction. Don't forget to keep track of the trails you travel to find your way back.

**Nantucket Shipwreck & Lifesaving Museum.** After a $3.1 million renovation in 2008, this replica 1874 Life Saving Service (the Surfside Beach original is a hostel) is much better equipped to showcase the island's maritime history—including the hundreds of lives saved by the service

# Siasconset & Wauwinet

**Siasconset**

Sankaty Head Golf Club
Burnell St.
Coffin St.
King St.
W. Sankaty Rd.
New St.
TO NANTUCKET TOWN ←
New St.
Milestone Rd.
Main St.
Shell St.
Broadway
Front St.
Park Ln.
Codfish Park Ln.
Baxter Rd.
Sankaty Rd.
↑ TO SANKATY HEAD LIGHTHOUSE

**The Chanticleer**

**Siasconset Casino**
Post Office Square

*Siasconset ('Sconset) Beach*

**Sconset Union Chapel**

Lily St.
Cottage Ave.
Evelyn St.
Magnolia Ave.
Everett St.
Pochick St.
McKinley Av.
Morey St.
Ocean Av.

**The Summer House**

*Nantucket Sound*

*Coskata*

## KEY
🚲 *Bike Trail*
🚢 *Ferry*
- - - *Unpaved road*

Harbor
Coatue
Nantucket Harbor
Polpis Rd.
Wauwinet Rd.

**Wauwinet**

**Quidnet**
Quidnet Rd.

**Sesachacha Pond**

TO HYANNIS ◄

Polpis

**Brant Point Light**

*Children's Beach*

**Nantucket Shipwreck & Lifesaving Museum**

**Windswept Cranberry Bog**

**Sankaty Head Lighthouse**

Polpis Rd.

**Nantucket Town**

**Altar Rock**

**Milestone Bog**

Milestone Rd.

Old South Rd.

Surfside Rd.

**Siasconset**
see inset above

Tom Nevers Rd.

*Siaconset ('Sconset) Beach*

✈ **Nantucket Memorial Airport**

*Surfside Beach*

0 — 2 miles
0 — 2 kilometers

at a tim. when a foundering ship nearly always meant certain death. The collection includes original rescue equipment and boats, artifacts recover^d from the *Andrea Doria* wreck, and photos and accounts of daring ~e cues. ⊠*158 Polpis Rd.* ☎*508/228–1885* ⊕*www.nantucket lifesavingmuseum.com* ⊠*$5* ⊙*Mid-June–mid-Oct., daily 10–4.*

**Sankaty Head Lighthouse.** The red-and-white-striped beacon overlooking the sea on one side and the Scottish-looking links of the private Sankaty Head Golf Club on the other is one of New England's many endangered lighthouses. It's not open to the public, but you can approach it, via a seashell gravel road. ⊠*Baxter Rd..*

**NEED A BREAK?**

For a great picnic in 'Sconset, stop at **Claudette's** ( ⊠*Post Office Sq.* ☎*508/257–6622*) for a box lunch to go, or dig right in on the shady patio. It's open mid-May through mid-October.

**Sesachacha Pond.** This kettle pond (pronounced *Sah*-kah-cha) off Polpis Road is a good spot for bird-watching. It's circled by a walking path that leads to an Audubon wildlife area and is separated from the ocean by a narrow strand on its east side. It provides a good view of Sankaty Head Lighthouse.

**Siasconset Casino.** Despite its name, this property dating to 1899 has never been used for gambling—the meaning of casino was broader back when it was built—but was instead used from the beginning as a theater venue, particularly during the actors'-colony heyday, and as a gathering place. Some theater can still be seen here, but it's primarily a tennis club and informal cinema. ⊠*New St.* ☎*508/257–6661.*

**Wauwinet.** Now it's a hamlet of beach houses on the northeastern end of Nantucket. But early European settlers found the neck of sand above it to be the easiest way to get to the ocean for fishing. Instead of rowing around Great Point, fishermen would go to the head of the harbor and haul their dories over the narrow strip of sand and beach grass separating Nantucket Harbor from the ocean. Hence the name for that strip: the haulover.

**Windswept Cranberry Bog.** Throughout the year, the 105-acre conservation area off Polpis Road is a beautiful tapestry of greens, reds, and golds—and a popular hangout for many bird species. The bog is especially vibrant in mid-October, when the cranberries are harvested amid a festival with hayrides, bog tours, and cranberry product samples.

A map is available from the **Nantucket Conservation Foundation** ( ⊠*118 Cliff Rd.* ☎*508/228–2884* ⊕*www.nantucketconservation.com*).

## WHERE TO STAY & EAT

**$$$$**
**AMERICAN**

✕ **The Chanticleer.** Over the decades, 'Sconset's landmark restaurant had grown a bit ossified: it needed Susan Handy and chef Jeff Worster of Black-Eyed Susan's to freshen up the menu and atmosphere alike. It's still elegant—more so, really, without the attendant fussiness. Handy knows how to extend a warm (i.e., non-Gallic) welcome, and Worster continues to riff on the "brasserie moderne" theme (at admittedly non-brasserie prices). Not every combo works (trout almandine with a cold potato salad?), but some sing, like the Thai-spiced Maine lobster salad, and the must-have dessert, black Mission fig and mascarpone tart. The all-French wine cellar is as "deep" as ever, and the porch overlooking the herb garden remains the most coveted perch. ✉️*9 New St., Siasconset* ☎️*508/257–4499* ⊕*www.thechanticleer.net* 🗐*AE, MC, V* 🕙*Closed mid-Oct.–early May; no lunch Mon.*

$$$–$$$$ ⨉**The Summer House Restaurant.** An integral element of the rose-cano-
★ pied complex of shingled shacks that epitomizes 'Sconset, the Summer
AMERICAN House's main dining room is abloom with lavish floral displays set against a background of pastel linen and white wicker. Marc Orfaly, of Boston's Pigalle and Marco, is the master chef that this lovely setting has long awaited: sure-handed Mediterranean delights, like *arancini* (fried rice balls) with duck confit, foie gras, and white truffle aioli, or grilled swordfish with ratatouille and tapenade—celebrate the joys of summer. Brady Duhame (ex-Bouley and Picholine) tends to the Beach-side Bistro alongside the pool down below, where snacks—like the $22 Black Angus beef burger—tend to the splurgy. ✉️*17 Ocean Ave., Siasconset* ☎️*508/257–9976* ⊕*www.thesummerhouse.com* 🍴*Reservations essential* 🗐*MC, V* 🕙*Closed mid-Oct.–mid-May.*

$$$$ ⨉**Topper's.** The Wauwinet—a lavishly restored 19th-century inn on
★ Nantucket's northeastern shore—is where islanders and visitors alike
AMERICAN go to experience utmost luxury. Many take advantage of the complimentary launch, the *Wauwinet Lady* out of Straight Wharf, which frames the journey with a scenic harbor tour. Having traipsed past the croquet lawn, one enters a creamy-white dining room awash with lush linens and glorious flowers. David Daniel's cuisine sustains the fantasy with a menu of intentional "simplicity"—if that's how you would describe, say, Peking-style duckling with farrow confit risotto and cara-melized endive. The price scheme might seem almost reasonable, were it not for portions that tend to tapas scale (the "truffled rigatoni" with Gruyere, Gouda, and Pouligny fondue, though delectable, consists of about five bites). But you can always fill up on the luscious brown bread (the sticky, molasses-infused kind so rarely encountered these days), and follow up with an exquisite, if minuscule, dessert. ✉️*120 Wauwinet Rd., Wauwinet* ☎️*508/228–8768* ⊕*www.wauwinet.com* 🍴*Reservations essential* 🗐*AE, D, DC, MC, V* 🕙*Closed Nov.–Apr.*

$$$$ 🏨 **The Summer House–'Sconset.** Perched on a bluff overlooking 'Sconset Beach, this cluster of rose-covered cottages—cobbled from salvage in the 1840s—epitomizes Nantucket's enduring allure. The rooms, though small, are intensely romantic, with lace coverlets and pale pine armoires; most have marble baths with whirlpool tubs, and one has a fireplace. Contemplative sorts can claim an Adirondack chair on the lawn. Others may want to race down to the beach, perhaps enjoying lunch beside the heated pool en route. **Pros:** romantic setting; beautiful on-site restaurants; pool right on the beach. **Cons:** 20 minutes from town; cottages snug; sounds of restaurant revelry. ✉️*17 Ocean Ave.* ☎️*508/257–4577* 🖷*508/257–4590* ⊕*www.thesummerhouse.com* 🛏️*10 rooms* ♿*In-room: Wi-Fi. In-hotel: 2 restaurants, bars, pool, concierge, no-smoking rooms* 🗐*AE, MC, V* 🕙*Closed Nov.–late Apr.* 🍽️*CP.*

7

# Where to Stay & Eat Outside Nantucket Town

## KEY

- **①** Hotels
- **❶** Restaurants
- 🚲 Bike Trail
- ⛴ Ferry
- - - - Unpaved road

TO MARTHA'S VINEYARD
(SUMMER ONLY)

TO HYANNIS

Nantucket Sound

Coatue

Nantucket Harbor

ATLANTIC OCEAN

See "Where to Eat in
Nantucket Town" &
"Where to Stay in
Nantucket Town" maps

Eel Point
Dionis Beach
Jetties Beach
Brant Point Light
Nantucket Town
Madaket Beach
Madaket
Long Pond
Hummock Pond
Cisco Beach
Miacomet Beach
Miacomet Pond
Surfside Beach
Surfside Rd.
Nantucket Memorial Airport
Old South Rd.
Milestone Rd.
Altar Rock
Milestone Bog
Windswept Cranberry Bog
Polpis Rd.
Polpis
Quidnet
Sesachacha Pond
Wauwinet
Sankaty Head Lighthouse
Siasconset ("Sconset") Beach
Siasconset
Tom Nevers Rd.

Eel Point Rd.
Madaket Rd.
Cliff Rd.
Bartlett Farm Rd.
Wauwinet Rd.
Quidnet Rd.
Polpis Rd.

0   2 miles
0   2 kilometers

## Restaurants
The Chanticleer ............ **7**
Cinco ........................ **5**
The Downyflake ............ **4**
El Rincon Salvadoreño .... **6**
Galley Beach ............... **1**
The SeaGrille ............... **2**
Sfoglia ....................... **3**
The Summer House Restaurant ........ **8**
Topper's ..................... **9**

## Hotels
Cliffside Beach Club ....... **1**
Robert B. Johnson Memorial Hostel ....... **2**
The Summer House ........ **3**
Wade Cottages ............. **4**
Wauwinet ................... **5**

$$$ ⌂**Wade Cottages.** This 'Sconset complex of apartments, and cottages couldn't be better situated for beach aficionados. The buildings, in the same family since the 1920s, are arranged around a central lawn with a great ocean view. Furnishings tend to be of the somewhat worn beach-house school, but you'll be too busy—and happy—to waste a moment critiquing. **Pros:** old-style Nantucket; dazzling view; great for families. **Cons:** WASPily shabby (a plus in some eyes); not romantically inclined; very family-centric. ⊠*Shell St., Siasconset* ☎*508/257–6308 or 212/989-6423* ⊕*www.wadecottages.com* ⇘*5 apartments; 1 cottage* ⚭*In-hotel: laundry facilities, no-smoking rooms* ▭*AE, MC, V* ⊗*Closed mid-Oct.–mid-May* �|⊙|*CP.*

$$$$ ⌂**Wauwinet.** This resplendently updated 1850 resort straddles a
Fodor'sChoice "haulover" poised between ocean and bay—which means beaches
★ on both sides. Head out by complimentary van or launch to partake of utmost pampering (the staff-to-guest ratio exceeds one-on-one). Optional activities include sailing, water-taxiing to a private beach along Coatue, and touring the Great Point nature preserve by Land Rover. Of course, it's tempting just to stay put, what with the cushy country-chic rooms (lavished with Pratesi linens) and a splendid restaurant, Topper's. **Pros:** solicitous staff; dual beaches; peaceful setting. **Cons:** distance from town; overly chichi; 3rd-floor rooms are tiny. ⊠*120 Wauwinet Rd., Wauwinet* ⌂*Box 2580, Nantucket 02584* ☎*508/228–0145 or 800/426–8718* ⊟*508/228–7135* ⊕*www. wauwinet.com* ⇘*25 rooms, 5 cottages* ⚭*In-room: safe, DVD, Wi-Fi. In-hotel: restaurant, room service, bar, tennis courts, spa, beachfront, water sports, bicycles, concierge, no kids under 12, no-smoking rooms* ▭*AE, DC, MC, V* ⊗*Closed Nov.–Apr.* �|⊙|*BP.*

### NIGHTLIFE

BARS   The bar at the **Summer House Restaurant** ( ⊠*17 Ocean Ave.* ☎*508/257–9976*) is hands down the most romantic spot for a cocktail on-island. A pianist entertains devotees, who cluster around the bar or claim comfortable armchairs.

FILM   The **Siasconset Casino** ( ⊠*New St., Siasconset* ☎*508/257–6661*) shows first-run movies, auditorium-style, Tuesday, Thursday, and Sunday evenings at 8:30, June through Labor Day. Old hands know to bring pillows.

### SPORTS & THE OUTDOORS

BEACHES   **Siasconset Beach** ( ⊠*End of Milestone Rd.*) has a lifeguard (the surf runs moderate to heavy) but no facilities; restaurants and restrooms are in the nearby village.

BICYCLING   The 6½-mi **'Sconset Bike Path** starts at the rotary east of Nantucket Town and parallels Milestone Road, ending in 'Sconset. It is mostly level, with some gentle hills.

TENNIS   **Siasconset Casino** ( ⊠*10 New St., Siasconset* ☎*508/257–6585*) is a private club with 11 outdoor courts. Nonmember court time may be available, especially in the shoulder seasons; call ahead for information.

7

# NANTUCKET ESSENTIALS

*To research prices, get advice from other travelers, and book travel arrangements, visit www.fodors.com.*

## TRANSPORTATION

### BY BOAT & FERRY

*See ⇨ Boat & Ferry Travel in Essentials in the back of this book.* Nantucket has first-class marina and mooring amenities for yacht and boat owners.

Marina Contacts **Madaket Marine** (☎ 508/228-1163 ⊕ www.madaketmarine. com). **Nantucket Boat Basin** (☎ 508/325-1333 or 800/626-2628 ⊞ 508/228-8941 ⊕ www.nantucketboatbasin.com). **Nantucket Moorings** (☎ 508/228-4472 ⊞ 508/228-7441 ⊕ www.nantucketmoorings.com).

### BY BUS

The Nantucket Regional Transit Authority (NRTA) runs shuttle buses in town and to Madaket, to mid-island areas (including the airport and Surfside Beach), and to 'Sconset. Service is available late May to early October. Each of the routes has its own schedule (you can pick one up at the chamber of commerce, Visitor Services, the NRTA office, or at most any bus stop); service generally begins at 7 AM and ends at 11:30 PM. All shuttle buses have bike racks and lifts. Fares are $1 in town or mid-island; $2 to Madaket, Surfside, the airport, or 'Sconset; seniors pay half fare and children under seven—and pets—ride free. Passes run $7 for 1 day, $12 for 3, $20 for 7, $50 for 30, and $80 for the season, with attendant discounts available. Passes for up to a week can be bought on board; longer-term passes can be purchased at the NRTA office.

Bus Information **Nantucket Regional Transit Authority (NRTA)** ( ⊠ 3 E. Chestnut St., Nantucket ☎ 508/228-7025 ⊕ www.shuttlenantucket.com).

### BY CAR

The chamber of commerce strongly discourages bringing cars to Nantucket. They're really not needed—unless you're planning to stay a week or more, and renting far out of town, off the bus routes. The town itself is entirely walkable, and keeping a car there is not practical; the longest you're allowed to park is ½ to 1½ hours at a time ("summer specials"—supplemental police personnel—are right on it, keeping tabs by PDA). The entire island is easily accessible by bike, taxi, or public transportation.

If you're still determined to rent a car while on Nantucket, book early—and expect to spend at least $85 a day during high season.

Nantucket Agencies **Nantucket Island Rent A Car** ( ⊠ Nantucket Memorial Airport ☎ 508/228–9989 or 800/508-9972 ⊕ www.nantucketislandrentacar. com). **Nantucket Windmill Auto Rental** ( ⊠ Nantucket Memorial Airport ☎ 508/228-1227 or 800/228-1227 ⊕ www.nantucketautorental.com). **Young's Bicycle Shop** ( ⊠ 6 Broad St. ☎ 508/228-1151 ⊞ 508/228-3038 ⊕ www. youngsbicycleshop.com).

### BY TAXI

Taxis usually wait outside the airport, on Steamboat Wharf, and at the foot of Main Street. Rates are flat fees, based on one person with two bags, 6 AM to 1 AM (another rider adds $2 to the price, and late-night rides incur a $5 surcharge), $7 within town (1½-mi radius), and, from town, $12 to the airport, $21 to 'Sconset, and $23 to Wauwinet. Dogs and bikes cost a little extra.

**Nantucket Taxi Companies A1 Taxi** (☎ 508/325-3330). **All Point Taxi** (☎ 508/228-5779). **Val's Cab Service** (☎ 508/228-9410).

## CONTACTS & RESOURCES

### EMERGENCIES

There is no 24-hour pharmacy on the island. Call the **Nantucket Cottage Hospital** (✉ *57 Prospect St.* ☎ *508/825–8100* ⊕ *www.nantucket hospital.org*) in case of an emergency.

**For police, fire department, or emergency medical technicians dial 911.**

### INTERNET, MAIL & SHIPPING

The main post office is right in the center of town; if lines are daunting, try the mid-island annex on Pleasant Street or the quaint seasonal branch in 'Sconset. There's a UPS Store off Surfside Road. You'll find a FedEx box (pickup is early: 4 PM) at the Steamship office, and another near the airport. The Atheneum offers free Internet access, including Wi-Fi (sit on the steps if the library is closed), and Nantucket.net maintains an Internet café offering public access for a nominal fee.

**Internet Access Nantucket Atheneum** (✉ *1 India St.* ☎ *508/228-1110* ⊕ *www. nantucketatheneum.org*).**Natntucket.Net Public Access Room** (✉ *2 Union St.* ☎ *508/228-6777* ⊕ *www.nantucket.net*).

**Mail & Shipping FedEx** (☎ *800/238-5355* ⊕ *www.fedex.com*). **The UPS Store** (✉ *2 Windy Way* ☎ *508/325-8884*) ⊕ *www.ups.com.* **U.S. Post Office** (✉ *5 Federal St.* ☎ *508/228-4477 or 800/275-8777* ✉ *Annex, 144 Pleasant St.* ☎ *508/325-5682 or 800/274-8777*) ✉ *'Sconset, 6 Main St.* ☎ *800/274-8777*).

### MONEY MATTERS

ATMS ATMs are ubiquitous—you'll find them at the airport, ferry terminals, and supermarkets. The following are accessible 24 hours.

**24-Hour ATM Locations Bank of America**( ✉ *Pacific National, 15 Sparks Ave.* ✉ *Pacific Club, 15 Main St.*). **Nantucket Bank** ( ✉ *2 Orange St.* ✉ *104 Pleasant St.* ✉ *1 Amelia Dr.*).

### TOUR OPTIONS

ADVENTURE
TOURS No matter what you want to do around Nantucket, be it kayaking, mountain biking, climbing, birding, hiking, snorkeling, or scuba diving, Eco Guides: Strong Wings can customize a small-group tour.

**Tour Operator Eco Guides: Strong Wings** ( ✉ *9 Nobadeer Farm Rd.* ☎ *508/228-1769* ⊕ *www.strongwings.org*).

VAN TOURS Sixth-generation Nantucketer Gail Johnson of Gail's Tours narrates a lively 1½-hour van tour of the island's highlights: the moors, the cranberry bogs, and the lighthouses, in addition to Nantucket Town. The 13-passenger cranberry-red van heads out at 10, 1, and 3 in season; pickups at in-town inns can be arranged.

Contacts **Gail's Tours** ( ☎ *508/257–6557* ⊕ *www.nantucket.net/tours/gails*).

WALKING
TOURS
The Nantucket Historical Association's 90-minute Historic Nantucket Walking Tours, offered twice daily in season ($10 for adults, $4 for children 6–17), provide an overview of the island's history and encompass such sites as Petticoat Row, upper Main Street, and the wharves, churches, and library. The self-guided Black Heritage Trail tour covers nine sites in and around town, including the African Meeting House, the Whaling Museum, and the Atheneum. The trail guide is free from the Friends of the African Meeting House on Nantucket, which also leads a "Walk the Black Heritage Trail" tour by appointment in season.

Tour Operators **Friends of the African Meeting House on Nantucket** ( ⊠ *York and Pleasant Sts.* ☎ *508/228–9833* ⊕ *www.afroammuseum.org/afmnantucket. htm*). **Historic Nantucket Walking Tours** ( ⊠ *Whaling Museum, 15 Broad St.* ☎ *508/325–1894* ⊕ *www.nha.org*).

## VISITOR INFORMATION

You can stop by the Nantucket Visitor Services and Information Bureau, open weekdays 9 to 6 year-round, to get your bearings, as well as maps, brochures, island information, and advice. The bureau is also a great resource if you need a room at the last minute—they track cancellations daily and might be able to refer you to an inn with newly available rooms. It's in the center of town, within a couple of blocks of both ferry landings, each of which also has an NVS booth in season. The chamber of commerce is another great place to get maps and island information; it's open weekdays 9 to 5, year-round.

Tourist Information **Nantucket Chamber of Commerce** ( ⊠ *Zero Main St.* ☎ *508/228–1700* ⊕ *www.nantucketchamber.org*).**Nantucket Visitor Services and Information Bureau** ( ⊠ *25 Federal St.,* ☎ *508/228–0925* ⊕ *www.nantucket. net/town/departments/visitor.html*).

# Cape Cod, Nantucket & Martha's Vineyard Essentials

## PLANNING TOOLS, EXPERT INSIGHT, GREAT CONTACTS

There are planners and there are those who, excuse the pun, fly by the seat of their pants. We happily place ourselves among the planners. Our writers and editors try to anticipate all the issues you may face before and during any journey, and then they do their research. This section is the product of their efforts. Use it to get excited about your trip to Cape Cod, Nantucket & Martha's Vineyard, to inform your travel planning, or to guide you on the road should the seat of your pants start to feel threadbare.

# GETTING STARTED

We're really proud of our Web site: Fodors.com is a great place to begin any journey. Scan "Travel Wire" for suggested itineraries, travel deals, restaurant and hotel openings, and other up-to-the-minute info. Check out "Booking" to research prices and book plane tickets, hotel rooms, rental cars, and vacation packages. Head to "Talk" for on-the-ground pointers from travelers who frequent our message boards. You can also link to loads of other travel-related resources.

## ▌ RESOURCES

### ONLINE TRAVEL TOOLS

For general information, visit the Cape Cod Chamber of Commerce online at ⊕*www.capecodchamber.org*. Other resources include the Cape Cod Information Center (⊕*www.allcapecod.com*) and Cape Cod Online, the Web site of the *Cape Cod Times*, (⊕*www.capecodonline.com*).

### TRANSPORTATION

Smart Traveler (⊕*www.smartraveler.com*) provides real-time updates on traffic conditions on Cape Cod (just click on the link for Boston, and you'll find a further link to Cape Cod). You can look at live Web-cam pictures of the Bourne and Sagamore bridges at the Cape Cod USA site (⊕*www.capecodlivecam.com*), as well as Web-cam pictures of Commercial Street in Provincetown, the harbor in Hyannis, and the beach at Wellfleet.

For Cape Cod bus and trolley schedules, check with the Cape Cod Regional Transit Authority (⊕*www.capecodtransit.org*). The transportation information site of the Cape Cod Commission (⊕*www.gocapecod.org*) has links to transportation providers, updates on transportation-related construction projects, and information on bicycling and walking, including updates on the Cape Cod Rail Trail. The Massachusetts Bicycle Coalition (⊕*www.mass*

*bike.org*) has information for bicyclists. Rails-to-Trails Conservancy (⊕*www.railtrails.org*) provides general information about rail trails, such as the Cape Cod Rail Trail.

Island ferry information and schedules are available online from the Steamship Authority (⊕*www.islandferry.com*) and from Hy-Line (⊕*www.hy-linecruises.com*). For information on the Boston to Provincetown ferries, visit the site of Bay State Cruise Company (⊕*www.baystatecruise company.com*) or Boston Harbor Cruises (⊕*www.bostonharborcruises.com*).

### DISABILITY ACCESS

The Directory of Accessible Facilities lists accessible recreational facilities in Massachusetts (⊕*www.mass.gov/dcr/universal_access/index.htm*). Cape Cod Disability Access Directory (⊕*www.capecoddisability.org*) has useful information about facilities on Cape Cod.

### VISITOR INFORMATION

Before you go, contact the state's office of tourism and the area's chambers of commerce for general information, seasonal events, and brochures. For specific information on Cape Cod's state forests and parks, the area's farmers' markets and fairs, or wildlife, contact the special-interest government offices below. You can also check Web sites on the Internet (⇨ *Web Sites*). When you arrive, stop by the local chamber of commerce for additional information—each chamber is stocked with local brochures and produces a comprehensive annual guidebook on each town.

The Army Corps of Engineers has a 24-hour recreation hotline for canal-area events, weather, and tidal and fishing information.

**General Cape Contacts Cape Cod Chamber of Commerce** (✉U.S. 6 and 132, Hyannis ☎508/862–0700 or 888/332–2732 📠508/862–0727 ⊕www.capecodchamber.org). **Cape Cod National Seashore** (☎508/349–3785 ⊕www.nps.gov/caco).

**General Islands Contacts Martha's Vineyard Chamber of Commerce** (✉Beach Rd., Box 1698, Vineyard Haven ☎508/693–4486 or 800/505–4815 ⊕www.mvy.com). **Nantucket Chamber of Commerce** (✉48 Main St., 2nd fl., ☎508/228–1700 ⊕www.nantucketchamber.org).

**Massachusetts Contacts Department of Agricultural Resources** (☎617/626–1700 ⊕www.state.ma.us/dfa). **Department of Conservation and Recreation** (☎617/626–1250 ⊕www.mass.gov/dcr). **Department of Fish and Game** (☎508/626–1500 ⊕www.state.ma.us/dfwele).**Massachusetts Office of Travel & Tourism** (✉10 Park Plaza, Suite 4510, Boston ☎800/227–6277, 800/447–6277 brochures ⊕www.massvacation.com).

# ∎ THINGS TO CONSIDER

### GEAR

Only a few Cape Cod and island restaurants require a jacket and tie, as do some dinner cruises; the area prides itself on informality. Do **pack a sweater or jacket, even in summer,** for nights can be cool. *For suggested clothing to minimize bites from deer ticks and to prevent Lyme disease, see ⇨Health.* Perhaps most important of all, **don't forget a swimsuit** (or two).

### TRIP INSURANCE

What kind of coverage do you honestly need? Do you even need trip insurance at all? Take a deep breath and read on.

We believe that comprehensive trip insurance is especially valuable if you're booking a very expensive or complicated trip (particularly to an isolated region) or if you're booking far in advance. Who knows what could happen six months down the road? But whether or not you get insurance has more to do with how comfortable you are assuming all that risk yourself.

Comprehensive travel policies typically cover trip cancellation and interruption, letting you cancel or cut your trip short because of a personal emergency, illness, or, in some cases, acts of terrorism in your destination. Such policies also cover evacuation and medical care. Some also cover you for trip delays because of bad weather or mechanical problems as well as for lost or delayed baggage. Another type of coverage to look for is financial default—that is, when your trip is disrupted because a tour operator, airline, or cruise line goes out of business. Generally you must buy this when you book your trip or shortly thereafter, and it's available to you only if your operator isn't on a list of excluded companies.

Expect comprehensive travel-insurance policies to cost about 4% to 7% or 8% of the total price of your trip (it's more like 8% to 12% if you're over age 70). A medical-only policy may or may not be cheaper than a comprehensive policy. Always read the fine print of your policy to make sure that you are covered for the risks that are of most concern to you. Compare several policies to make sure you're getting the best price and range of coverage available.

# Trip-Insurance Resources

| INSURANCE-COMPARISON SITES | | |
|---|---|---|
| Insure My Trip.com | 800/487–4722 | www.insuremytrip.com |
| Square Mouth.com | 800/240–0369 or 727/490–5803 | www.squaremouth.com |
| COMPREHENSIVE TRAVEL INSURERS | | |
| Access America | 800/729–6021 | www.accessamerica.com |
| CSA Travel Protection | 800/873–9855 | www.csatravelprotection.com |
| HTH Worldwide | 610/254–8700 or 888/243–2358 | www.hthworldwide.com |
| Travelex Insurance | 800/228–9792 | www.travelex-insurance.com |
| Travel Guard International | 715/345–0505 or 800/826–4919 | www.travelguard.com |
| Travel Insured International | 800/243–3174 | www.travelinsured.com |
| MEDICAL-ONLY INSURERS | | |
| International Medical Group | 800/628–4664 | www.imglobal.com |
| International SOS | | www.internationalsos.com |
| Wallach & Company | 800/237–6615 or 540/687–3166 | www.wallach.com |

# BOOKING YOUR TRIP

Unless your cousin is a travel agent, you're probably among the millions of people who make most of their travel arrangements online.

But have you ever wondered just what the differences are between an online travel agent (a Web site through which you make reservations instead of going directly to the airline, hotel, or car-rental company), a discounter (a firm that does a high volume of business with a hotel chain or airline and accordingly gets good prices), a wholesaler (one that makes cheap reservations in bulk and then re-sells them to people like you), and an aggregator (one that compares all the offerings so you don't have to)?

Is it truly better to book directly on an airline or hotel Web site? And when does a real live travel agent come in handy?

## ■ ONLINE

You really have to shop around. A travel wholesaler such as Hotels.com or Hotel-Club.net can be a source of good rates, as can discounters such as Hotwire or Priceline, particularly if you can bid for your hotel room or airfare. Indeed, such sites sometimes have deals that are unavailable elsewhere. They do, however, tend to work only with hotel chains (which makes them just plain useless for getting hotel reservations outside of major cities) or big airlines (so that often leaves out upstarts like jetBlue and some foreign carriers like Air India).

Also, with discounters and wholesalers you must generally prepay, and everything is nonrefundable. And before you fork over the dough, be sure to check the terms and conditions, so you know what a given company will do for you if there's a problem and what you'll have to deal with on your own.

■TIP➜ To be absolutely sure everything was processed correctly, confirm reservations made through online travel agents, discounters, and wholesalers directly with your hotel before leaving home.

Booking engines like Expedia, Travelocity, and Orbitz are actually travel agents, albeit high-volume, online ones. And airline travel packagers like American Airlines Vacations and Virgin Vacations—well, they're travel agents, too. But they may still not work with all the world's hotels.

An aggregator site will search many sites and pull the best prices for airfares, hotels, and rental cars from them. Most aggregators compare the major travel-booking sites such as Expedia, Travelocity, and Orbitz; some also look at airline Web sites, though rarely the sites of smaller budget airlines. Some aggregators also compare other travel products, including complex packages—a good thing, as you can sometimes get the best overall deal by booking an air-and-hotel package.

## ■ WITH A TRAVEL AGENT

If you use an agent—brick-and-mortar or virtual—you'll pay a fee for the service. And know that the service you get from some online agents isn't comprehensive. That said, some agents (online or not) *do* have access to fares that are difficult to find otherwise, and the savings can more than make up for any surcharge.

A knowledgeable brick-and-mortar travel agent can be a godsend if you're booking a cruise, a package trip that's not available to you directly, an air pass, or a complicated itinerary including several overseas flights. What's more, travel agents that specialize in a destination may have exclusive access to certain deals and insider information on things such as charter flights. Agents who specialize in types of travelers (senior citizens, gays and lesbians, naturists) or types of trips (cruises, luxury travel, safaris) can also be invaluable.

■ TIP→ Remember that Expedia, Travelocity, and Orbitz are travel agents, not just booking engines. To resolve any problems with a reservation made through these companies, contact them first.

A top-notch agent planning your trip to Russia will make sure you get the correct visa application and complete it on time; the one booking your cruise may get you a cabin upgrade or arrange to have bottle of champagne chilling in your cabin when you embark. And complain about the surcharges all you like, but when things don't work out the way you'd hoped, it's nice to have an agent to put things right.

Agent Resources **American Society of Travel Agents** (☎703/739–2782 ⊕www.travelsense.org).

# ▌ACCOMMODATIONS

Accommodations on the Cape and islands range from campsites to bed-and-breakfasts to luxurious self-contained resorts offering all kinds of sporting facilities, restaurants, entertainment, services (including business services and children's programs), and all the assistance you'll ever need in making vacation arrangements.

Because real-estate prices have skyrocketed throughout the region in the past few years, many motels and hotels have been developed into more lucrative condominiums, and quite a few B&Bs have been sold and converted back to private homes. The effect is that the Cape has fewer lodging options than it has had in years, and lodging rates have risen a bit, too. That said, there are still plenty of overnight options.

Single-night lodgings for those just passing through can be found at countless tacky but cheap and conveniently located little roadside motels, as well as at others that are spotless and cheery yet still inexpensive, or at chain hotels at all price levels; these places often have a pool, TVs, or other amenities to keep children entertained in the evening. Bear in mind that many Cape accommodations, even simple motels, have two-, three-, and even four-night minimum stays on weekends in high season, generally from around Memorial Day through Labor Day. It's still worth checking with a property to see if you can stay for fewer days, especially if you're planning to come out for a last-minute visit, but be warned that finding a single-night accommodation on a June, July, or August weekend can prove extremely challenging.

Because of extremely high demand for accommodations on the islands, it's best to reserve especially well in advance when planning a stay on Nantucket or Martha's Vineyard, especially from June through early September. If you're looking to visit during the summer months or over a popular weekend, such as the Nantucket Daffodil Festival or Christmas Stroll, it's not a bad idea to book a full year in advance. Most inns on the islands require prepayment or nonrefundable deposits as well as three-night (or more) minimums in summer. And rates can be very high, averaging $250 a night or more on Nantucket and only slightly less on Martha's Vineyard.

Families may want to **consider condominiums, cottages, and efficiencies,** which offer more space; living areas; kitchens; and sometimes laundry facilities, children's play areas, or children's programs. Especially as single-night lodging options on the Cape diminish in number, this is an increasingly popular option, although many condo and cottage rentals have one-week minimum stays, especially in summer.

The lodgings we list are the cream of the crop in each price category. We always list the facilities that are available—but

# Online-Booking Resources

| AGGREGATORS | | |
|---|---|---|
| Kayak | www.kayak.com | looks at cruises and vacation packages. |
| Mobissimo | www.mobissimo.com | examines airfare, hotels, cars, and tons of activities. |
| Qixo | www.qixo.com | compares cruises, vacation packages, and even travel insurance. |
| Sidestep | www.sidestep.com | compares vacation packages and lists travel deals and some activities. |
| Travelgrove | www.travelgrove.com | compares cruises and vacation packages and lets you search by themes. |

| BOOKING ENGINES | | |
|---|---|---|
| Cheap Tickets | www.cheaptickets.com | discounter. |
| Expedia | www.expedia.com | large online agency that charges a booking fee for airline tickets. |
| Hotwire | www.hotwire.com | discounter. |
| lastminute.com | www.lastminute.com | specializes in last-minute travel; the main site is for the U.K., but it has a link to a U.S. site. |
| Luxury Link | www.luxurylink.com | has auctions (surprisingly good deals) as well as offers on the high-end side of travel. |
| Onetravel.com | www.onetravel.com | discounter for hotels, car rentals, airfares, and packages. |
| Orbitz | www.orbitz.com | charges a booking fee for airline tickets, but gives a clear breakdown of fees and taxes before you book. |
| Priceline.com | www.priceline.com | discounter that also allows bidding. |
| Travel.com | www.travel.com | allows you to compare its rates with those of other booking engines. |
| Travelocity | www.travelocity.com | charges a booking fee for airline tickets, but promises good problem resolution. |

| ONLINE ACCOMMODATIONS | | |
|---|---|---|
| Hotelbook.com | www.hotelbook.com | focuses on independent hotels worldwide. |
| Hotel Club | www.hotelclub.net | good for major cities and some resort areas. |
| Hotels.com | www.hotels.com | big Expedia-owned wholesaler that offers rooms in hotels all over the world. |
| Quikbook | www.quikbook.com | offers "pay when you stay" reservations that allow you to settle your bill when you check out, not when you book; best for trips to U.S. and Canadian cities. |

| OTHER RESOURCES | | |
|---|---|---|
| Bidding For Travel | www.biddingfortravel.com | good place to figure out what you can get and for how much before you start bidding on, say, Priceline. |

we don't specify whether they cost extra: when pricing accommodations, always ask what's included and what costs extra. Properties indicated by a ✕🏠are lodging establishments whose restaurant warrants a special trip even if you are not staying at that establishment.

Most hotels and other lodgings require you to give your credit-card details before they will confirm your reservation. If you don't feel comfortable e-mailing this information, ask if you can fax it (some places even prefer faxes). However you book, get confirmation in writing and have a copy of it handy when you check in.

Be sure you understand the hotel's cancellation policy. Some places allow you to cancel without any kind of penalty— even if you prepaid to secure a discounted rate—if you cancel at least 24 hours in advance. Others require you to cancel a week in advance or penalize you the cost of one night. Small inns and B&Bs are most likely to require you to cancel far in advance. Most hotels allow children under a certain age to stay in their parents' room at no extra charge, but others charge for them as extra adults; find out the cutoff age for discounts.

■TIP➜Assume that hotels operate on the European Plan (EP, no meals) unless we specify that they use the Breakfast Plan (BP, with full breakfast), Continental Plan (CP, continental breakfast), Full American Plan (FAP, all meals), Modified American Plan (MAP, breakfast and dinner), or are all-inclusive (AI, all meals and most activities).

### APARTMENT & HOUSE RENTALS
Many travelers to the Cape and the islands rent a house if they're going to stay for a week or longer rather than stay at a B&B or hotel. These can save you money; however, some rentals are luxury properties, economical only when your party is large. Many local real-estate agencies deal with rentals, and most specialize in a specific area; see the end of

each chapter for information on agents in your area.

If you do decide to rent, be sure to book a property well in advance of your trip, as many properties are rented out to the same families or groups year after year. Rental choices are often more abundant in the smaller, quieter towns, such as Yarmouth, Chatham, Wellfleet, and Truro, or Up-Island on Martha's Vineyard.

### BED & BREAKFASTS
Bed-and-breakfast inns have long been very popular on Cape Cod and the islands. Many of them occupy stately old sea captains' homes and other 17th-, 18th-, and 19th-century buildings; others are in newer homes.

In many cases, B&Bs are not appropriate for families—noise travels easily, rooms are often small, and the furnishings are often fragile—so be sure to ask. Many B&Bs do not provide phones or TVs in guest rooms, some are not air-conditioned, and all prohibit smoking indoors (some allow smoking on the grounds).

In summer you should reserve lodgings as far in advance as possible—several months for the most popular inns. Assistance with last-minute reservations is available at the Cape Cod Chamber of Commerce information booths and through the chamber of commerce's Web site (➪ *Web Sites*). Off-season, rates are much reduced, and you may find that it's easier to get to know your innkeeper.

Numerous B&B reservation agencies can aid you in choosing an inn.

**Reservation Services Bed & Breakfast.com** (☎512/322–2710 or 800/462–2632 ⊕www. bedandbreakfast.com) also sends out an online newsletter. **Bed & Breakfast Inns Online** (☎615/868–1946 or 800/215–7365 ⊕www. bbonline.com). **BnB Finder.com** (☎212/432–7693 or 888/547–8226 ⊕www.bnbfinder. com). **Classic Historic Inns of Cape Cod Bay** (⊕www.historiccapecodbay.com) offers a listing of distinctive and lovely inns along the

# Online-Booking Resources

| CONTACTS | | |
|---|---|---|
| Forgetaway | | www.forgetaway.weather.com |
| Home Away | 512/493-0382 | www.homeaway.com |
| Interhome | 954/791-8282 or 800/882-6864 | www.interhomeusa.com |
| Vacation Home Rentals Worldwide | 201/767-9393 or 800/633-3284 | www.vhrww.com |
| Villas International | 415/499-9490 or 800/221-2260 | www.villasintl.com |

Cape Cod Bay side of the Cape; many are carefully restored historic properties. One event of note sponsored by the inns is the annual Halloween murder mystery weekend.

**Reservation Services on the Cape Bed and Breakfast Cape Cod** (☎508/255-3824 or 800/541-6226 ⊕www.bedandbreakfastcape cod.com). **DestINNations** (☎207/563-2506 or 800/333-4667 ⊕www.destinnations.com).

**Reservation Services on the Islands Martha's Vineyard and Nantucket Reservations** (☎508/693-7200 ⊕www.mvreservations.com). **Nantucket Accommodations** (☎508/228-9559 ⊕www.nantucketaccommodation.com). **Nantucket Concierge** (☎508/228-8400 ⊕www.nantucketconcierge.com).

## CAMPING
There are many private and state-park camping areas on Cape Cod. For additional details on camping in specific areas, look for the 🛆 icon in that area's Dining and Lodging section.

## HOME EXCHANGES
With a direct home exchange you stay in someone else's home while they stay in yours. Some outfits also deal with vacation homes, so you're not actually staying in someone's full-time residence, just their vacant weekend place.

**Exchange Clubs Home Exchange.com** (☎800/877-8723 ⊕www.homeexchange. com); $99.95 for a 1-year online listing. **HomeLink International** (☎800/638-3841 ⊕www.homelink.org); $110 yearly for Web-only membership; $170 includes Web access

and two catalogs. **Intervac U.S.** (☎800/756-4663 ⊕www.intervacus.com); $78.88 for Web-only membership; $126 includes Web access and a catalog.

## HOSTELS
Hostels offer bare-bones lodging at low, low prices—often in shared dorm rooms with shared baths—to people of all ages, though the primary market is young travelers, especially students. Most hostels serve breakfast; dinner and/or shared cooking facilities may also be available. In some hostels you aren't allowed to be in your room during the day, and there may be a curfew at night. Nevertheless, hostels provide a sense of community, with public rooms where travelers often gather to share stories. Many hostels are affiliated with Hostelling International (HI), an umbrella group of hostel associations with some 4,000 member properties in more than 60 countries. Other hostels

## WORD OF MOUTH

Did the resort look as good in real life as it did in the photos? Did you sleep like a baby, or were the walls paper thin? Did you get your money's worth? Rate hotels and write your own reviews in "Travel Ratings" or start a discussion about your favorite places in "Travel Talk" on www. fodors.com. Your comments might even appear in our books. Yes, you, too, can be a correspondent!

are completely independent and may be nothing more than a really cheap hotel.

Membership in any HI association, open to travelers of all ages, allows you to stay in HI-affiliated hostels at member rates. One-year membership is about $28 for adults. Rates in dorm-style rooms run about $15 to $25 per bed per night; private rooms are more, but are still generally well under $100 a night. Members have priority if the hostel is full; they're also eligible for discounts around the world, even on rail and bus travel in some countries.

Cape Cod has some excellent hostels. In season, when all other rates are jacked up beyond belief, hostels are often the only budget-accommodation option, but you must plan ahead to reserve space. The hostel in Eastham has eight cabins that each sleep six to eight; two can be used as family cabins. In the Truro hostel, accommodations are dormitory-style. You may luck out on last-minute cancellations, but it would be unwise to rely on them. *See the lodging listings in the appropriate chapters for specifics.*

**Information Hostelling International—USA** ( ☎301/495–1240 ⊕www.hiusa.org).

## ▌AIRLINE TICKETS

Most domestic airline tickets are electronic; international tickets may be either electronic or paper. With an e-ticket the only thing you receive is an e-mailed receipt citing your itinerary and reservation and ticket numbers.

The greatest advantage of an e-ticket is that if you lose your receipt, you can simply print out another copy or ask the airline to do it for you at check-in. You usually pay a surcharge (up to $50) to get a paper ticket, if you can get one at all.

The sole advantage of a paper ticket is that it may be easier to endorse over to another airline if your flight is canceled and the airline with which you booked can't accommodate you on another flight.

■TIP➡ Discount air passes that let you travel economically in a country or region must often be purchased before you leave home. In some cases you can get them only through a travel agent.

## ▌RENTAL CARS

When you reserve a car, ask about cancellation penalties, taxes, drop-off charges (if you're planning to pick up the car in one city and leave it in another), and surcharges (for being under or over a certain age, for additional drivers, or for driving across state or country borders or beyond a specific distance from your point of rental). All these things can add substantially to your costs. Request car seats and extras such as GPS when you book.

Rates are sometimes—but not always—better if you book in advance or reserve through a rental agency's Web site. There are other reasons to book ahead, though: for popular destinations, during busy times of the year, or to ensure that you get certain types of cars (vans, SUVs, exotic sports cars).

■TIP➡ Make sure that a confirmed reservation guarantees you a car. Agencies sometimes overbook, particularly for busy weekends and holiday periods.

In Massachusetts you must be 21 to rent a car, and rates may be higher if you're under 25. When picking up a car, non–U.S. residents will need a reservation voucher (for prepaid reservations made in the traveler's home country), a passport, a driver's license, and a travel policy that covers each driver.

Base rates in Boston begin at $25 to $40 a day and $170 to $250 a week for an economy car with air-conditioning, automatic transmission, and unlimited mileage; rates tend to be slightly lower out of Providence and slightly higher out of Hyannis, but much depends on availability, which changes regularly. Keep in mind that taxes and a variety of surcharges typically add 30% to 40% to your total bill.

You can book car rentals on Martha's Vineyard through the Woods Hole ferry terminal free phone. A handful of local agencies, listed below, have rental desks at the airport. The cost is $100 to $150 per day for a sedan. Renting a four-wheel-drive vehicle costs around $160 per day (seasonal prices fluctuate widely).

If you're determined to rent a car while on Nantucket, be sure to book early. Expect to spend about $100 a day during high season.

### CAR-RENTAL INSURANCE

Everyone who rents a car wonders whether the insurance that the rental companies offer is worth the expense. No one—including us—has a simple answer. It all depends on how much regular insurance you have, how comfortable you are with risk, and whether or not money is an issue.

If you own a car and carry comprehensive car insurance for both collision and liability, your personal auto insurance will probably cover a rental, but read your policy's fine print to be sure. If you don't have auto insurance, then you should probably buy the collision- or loss-damage waiver (CDW or LDW) from the rental company. This eliminates your liability for damage to the car.

Some credit cards offer CDW coverage, but it's usually supplemental to your own insurance and rarely covers SUVs, minivans, luxury models, and the like. If your coverage is secondary, you may still be liable for loss-of-use costs from the car-rental company (again, read the fine print). But no credit-card insurance is valid unless you use that card for *all* transactions, from reserving to paying the final bill.

■TIP→Diners Club offers primary CDW coverage on all rentals reserved and paid for with the card. This means that Diners Club's company—not your own car insurance—pays in case of an accident. It *doesn't* mean that your car-insurance company won't raise your rates once it discovers you had an accident.

You may also be offered supplemental liability coverage; the car-rental company is required to carry a minimal level of liability coverage insuring all renters, but it's rarely enough to cover claims in a really serious accident if you're at fault. Your own auto-insurance policy will protect you if you own a car; if you don't, you have to decide whether you are willing to take the risk.

U.S. rental companies sell CDWs and LDWs for about $15 to $25 a day; supplemental liability is usually more than $10 a day. The car-rental company may offer you all sorts of other policies, but they're rarely worth the cost. Personal accident insurance, which is basic hospitalization coverage, is an especially egregious rip-off if you already have health insurance.

■TIP→ You can decline the insurance from the rental company and purchase it through a third-party provider such as Travel Guard (www.travelguard.com)—$9 per day for $35,000 of coverage. That's sometimes just under half the price of the CDW offered by some car-rental companies.

## ■ VACATION PACKAGES

Packages *are not* guided excursions. Packages combine airfare, accommodations, and perhaps a rental car or other extras (theater tickets, guided excursions, boat trips, reserved entry to popular museums, transit passes), but they let you do your own thing. During busy periods packages may be your only option, as flights and rooms may be sold out otherwise.

Packages will definitely save you time. They can also save you money, particularly in peak seasons, but—and this is a really big "but"—you should price each part of the package separately to be sure. And be aware that prices advertised on Web sites and in newspapers rarely include service charges or taxes, which can up your costs by hundreds of dollars.

■TIP➜ Some packages and cruises are sold only through travel agents. Don't always assume that you can get the best deal by booking everything yourself.

Each year consumers are stranded or lose their money when packagers—even large ones with excellent reputations—go out of business. How can you protect yourself?

First, always pay with a credit card; if you have a problem, your credit-card company may help you resolve it. Second, buy trip insurance that covers default.

Third, choose a company that belongs to the United States Tour Operators Association, whose members must set aside funds to cover defaults. Finally, choose a company that also participates in the Tour Operator Program of the American Society of Travel Agents (ASTA), which will act as mediator in any disputes.

You can also check on the tour operator's reputation among travelers by posting an inquiry on one of the Fodors.com forums.

**Organizations American Society of Travel Agents** (ASTA ☎703/739-2782 or 800/965-2782 ⊕www.astanet.com). **United States Tour Operators Association** (USTOA ☎212/599-6599 ⊕www.ustoa.com).

■TIP➜ Local tourism boards can provide information about lesser-known and small-niche operators that sell packages to only a few destinations.

# TRANSPORTATION

## ▌ BY AIR

Most long-distance travelers visiting Cape Cod head to a major gateway, such as Boston or Providence, Rhode Island, and then rent a car to explore the region. Flying time to Boston or Providence is 1 hour from New York, 2½ hours from Chicago, 6 hours from Los Angeles, and 3½ hours from Dallas.

Boston's Logan Airport is one of the nation's most important domestic and international airports, with direct flights from all over North America and Europe (as well as other continents). Providence's efficient T. F. Green Airport receives very few international flights (mostly from Canada) but offers a wide range of direct domestic flights to East Coast and Midwest destinations; it serves the western United States to a lesser extent. Discount carrier Southwest also flies out of Providence, which helps keep fares down.

Another option is connecting from a major airport to one of the two airports on the Cape, the most popular being Barnstable Municipal Airport in Hyannis, which has direct service to Boston, Providence, and New York (La Guardia), as well as to Martha's Vineyard and Nantucket. The other, Provincetown Airport, has direct flights to Boston. Flying to either of these smaller airports can be costly, especially during busy times in summer, but it can also save you plenty of time when compared with driving to the Mid, Lower, or Upper Cape from Boston or New York City. There are also numerous flights to Nantucket and Martha's Vineyard from Hyannis, Boston, New Bedford, and Providence, and you can fly between Nantucket and Martha's Vineyard as well.

■TIP➜ If you travel frequently, look into the TSA's Registered Traveler program. The program, which is still being tested in several U.S. airports, is designed to cut down on gridlock at security checkpoints by allowing prescreened travelers to pass quickly through kiosks that scan an iris and/or a fingerprint. How sci-fi is that?

**Airlines & Airports** Airline and Airport Links.com ( ⊕ www.airlineandairportlinks.com) has links to many of the world's airlines and airports.

**Airline-Security Issues** Transportation Security Administration ( ⊕ www.tsa.gov) has answers for almost every question that might come up.

### AIRPORTS

The major gateways to Cape Cod are Boston's Logan International Airport (BOS) and Providence's T. F. Green Airport (PVD). Smaller airports include the Barnstable (HYA), Martha's Vineyard (MVY), Nantucket (ACK), New Bedford (EWB), and Provincetown (PVC) municipal airports.

■TIP➜ Long layovers don't have to be only about sitting around or shopping. These days they can be about burning off vacation calories. Check out www.airportgyms.com for lists of health clubs that are in or near many U.S. and Canadian airports.

**Airport Information** Airline and Airport Links.com ( ⊕ www.airlineandairportlinks. com) has links to many of the world's airlines and airports. Boston: **Logan International Airport** ( ☎ 617/561–1806 or 800/235–6426 ⊕ www.massport.com/logan). Hyannis: **Barnstable Municipal Airport** ( ☎ 508/775–2020 ⊕ www.town.barnstable.ma.us). Martha's Vineyard: **Martha's Vineyard Airport** ( ☎ 508/693–7022 ⊕ www.mvyairport.com). Nantucket: **Nantucket Memorial Airport** ( ☎ 508/325–5300 ⊕ www.nantucketairport. com). New Bedford: **New Bedford Regional Airport** ( ☎ 508/991–6161 ⊕ www.ci.new-bedford.ma.us). Providence: **T. F. Green Airport** ( ☎ 401/737–8222 or 888/268–7222 ⊕ www.pvdairport.com). Provincetown: **Provincetown Airport** ( ☎ 508/487–0241).

## TRANSFERS BETWEEN AIRPORTS

Cape Destinations, Escort Coach, and King's Coach provide chartered limo service from Boston and Providence to the Cape; call ahead for reservations. Rates vary greatly, depending on your Cape destination, which airport you're flying into, and what kind of car or van you book.

**Limousine Agencies** **Cape Destinations** (☎866/760–2555 ⊕www.capedestinations.com). **Cape Cod White Tie Limousine** (☎508/548–8116 or 800/564–8116 ⊕www.whitetielimo.com). **King's Coach** (☎508/771–1000 or 800/546–6786 ⊕www.capecodlimo.com).

## FLIGHTS

All of the nation's major airlines—as well as many international airlines—serve Boston's Logan Airport, and all major national carriers serve Providence. Hyannis's Barnstable Municipal Airport is serviced by US Airways Express (with service to Boston and NYC's La Guardia), Nantucket Airlines (with service to Nantucket), Island Airlines (with service to Nantucket), and Cape Air (with service to Boston, Providence, Nantucket, and Martha's Vineyard); Provincetown Airport is serviced by Cape Air (with service to Boston).

**Smaller Airlines** **Cape Air** (☎508/771–6944 or 800/352–0714 ⊕www.flycapeair.com). **Island Airlines** (☎508/228–7575 or 800/248–7779 ⊕www.islandair.net). **Nantucket Airlines** (☎508/228–6234 or 800/635–8787 ⊕www.nantucketairlines.com). **US Airways Express** (☎800/428–4322 ⊕www.usair.com).

# ▌ BY BOAT & FERRY

In season, ferries connect Boston and Plymouth with Provincetown.

Ferries to Martha's Vineyard leave Woods Hole year-round. In summer you can also catch Vineyard ferries in Falmouth and Hyannis. All provide parking lots where you can leave your car overnight ($10 to $15 per night). A number of parking lots in Falmouth hold the overflow of cars when the Woods Hole lot is filled, and free shuttle buses take passengers to the ferry, about 15 minutes away. Signs along Route 28 heading south from the Bourne Bridge direct you to open parking lots, as does AM radio station 1610, which you can pick up within 5 mi of Falmouth.

Ferries to Nantucket leave Hyannis year-round. In season, a passenger ferry connects Nantucket with Martha's Vineyard, and a cruise from Hyannis makes a day trip with stops at both islands. From New Bedford you can take a ferry to Martha's Vineyard from mid-May to mid-October and to Cuttyhunk Island year-round (although between mid-October and mid-April, the schedule is very limited).

## FERRIES TO PROVINCETOWN

Bay State Cruise Company offers both standard and high-speed ferry service between Commonwealth Pier in Boston and MacMillan Wharf in Provincetown. High-speed service runs a few times daily from mid-May through September (with a few additional weekend runs through mid-October) and costs $71 round-trip; the ride takes 90 minutes. Standard service runs weekends from late June through early September and costs $33 round-trip; the ride takes three hours. On either ferry, the round-trip charge for bikes is $12.

Boston Harbor Cruises also offers high-speed service several times daily from mid-June to early September, with more limited service mid-May to mid-June and early September to mid-October. Rates are $71 round-trip and $10 for bikes.

Capt. John Boats runs a seasonal ferry between Plymouth and Provincetown, with daily service from late June through early September and weekend service from mid-June. The boat departs from State Pier (near the *Mayflower II*) in Plymouth and docks at MacMillan Wharf in Provincetown. The trip takes approximately 90 minutes. A round-trip ticket costs $37, the one-way fare is $22 (no one-way in July and August), and bikes cost $5 each way.

With recent rising fuel costs, many carriers have instituted additional fees; expect to pay an extra $3–$5 (each way) over the cost of the actual ticket. (In most cases, seniors and children are charged lower fares.)

**Boat & Ferry Lines Bay State Cruise Company** (☎617/748–1428 ⊕www.baystate cruisecompany.com). **Boston Harbor Cruises** (☎617/227–4321 or 877/733–9425 ⊕www. bostonharborcruises.com). **Capt. John Boats** (☎508/747–2400 or 800/225–4000 ⊕www. provincetownferry.com).

## FERRIES TO CUTTYHUNK ISLAND

The 149-passenger M/V *Cuttyhunk* runs ferries between New Bedford and Cuttyhunk Island, daily late May through September, several times a week from mid-April to late May and from early October to mid-October, and twice a week the rest of the year. Same-day round-trip fare is $40, one-way $25, bicycles $5 each way. The ride takes about an hour.

**Boat & Ferry Information** M/V Cuttyhunk (✉State Pier, New Bedford ☎508/992–0200 ⊕www.cuttyhunkferryco.com).

## FERRIES TO MARTHA'S VINEYARD

The Steamship Authority runs the only car ferries, which make the 45-minute trip from Woods Hole to Vineyard Haven year-round and to Oak Bluffs from late May through mid-October. There are several runs per day, but fewer during the off-season. In summer and on autumn weekends, you *must* have a reservation if you want to bring your car (passenger reservations are never necessary). You should **make car reservations as far ahead as possible;** in season the reservations office is open daily 8 AM to 5 PM, with extended phone hours in summer and during busy times from 7 AM to 9 PM. You can also make car reservations online at the Steamship Authority's Web

site. In season, standby car reservations are not available. One-way passenger fare year-round is $7.50; bicycles are $3. The cost for a car traveling one-way in season (April–October) is $67.50 (not including passengers); off-season, cars cost $42.50.

The *Island Queen* makes the 35-minute trip from Falmouth Harbor to Oak Bluffs from late May through early October. Ferries run multiple times a day from mid-June through early September, with less frequent (but still daily) service in the spring and fall; call for schedules. Round-trip fare is $16; bikes are $6. Only cash and traveler's checks are accepted for payment.

Begun in 2007, the Vineyard Fast Ferry offers high-speed passenger service from North Kingstown, Rhode Island (just a half hour south of Providence and a half hour northwest of Newport) to Martha's Vineyard. The ride takes 90 minutes, making this a great option for those flying in to T. F. Green Airport, just south of Providence. Service is from late May through early October and costs $52 each way ($6 for bikes).

Hy-Line offers both high-speed and conventional ferry service from Hyannis. The conventional ferries offer a 95-minute run from Hyannis to Oak Bluffs early May to late October. One-way fare is $19.50; bicycles cost $6. The high-speed runs from late May through late November, takes 55 minutes, and costs $34 (one-way); it costs $6 for bikes. The parking lot fills up in summer, so **call to reserve a parking space** in high season. From June to mid-September, Hy-Line's Around the Sound cruise makes a one-day round-trip from Hyannis with stops at Nantucket and Martha's Vineyard ($79.50).

The New England Fast Ferry Company makes the hour-long trip by high-speed catamaran from New Bedford to Oak Bluffs and Vineyard Haven from mid-

May to mid-October several times daily. One-way is $36, and bicycles are $6.

With recent rising fuel costs, many carriers have instituted additional fees; expect to pay an extra $3–$5 (each way) over the cost of the actual ticket. (In most cases, seniors and children are charged lower fares.)

**Boat & Ferry Information Hy-Line** (⊠Ocean St. dock ☎508/778–2600 or 800/492–8082 ⊕www.hy-linecruises.com). **Island Queen** (⊠Falmouth Harbor ☎508/548–4800 ⊕www.islandqueen). **New England Fast Ferry** (⊠State Pier Ferry Terminal ☎866/683–3779 ⊕www.nefastferry.com). **Steamship Authority** (☎508/477–8600 information and car reservations, 508/693–9130 on the Vineyard ⊕www.steamship authority.com).**Vineyard Fast Ferry** (⊠Quonset Point, North Kingstown, RI ☎401/295–4040 ⊕www.vineyardfastferry.com).

## FERRIES TO NANTUCKET

The Steamship Authority runs car-and-passenger ferries from Hyannis to Nantucket year-round, a 2¼-hour trip. There's also high-speed passenger ferry service, which takes only an hour, from late March through late December. Note that there are no standby car reservations on ferries to Nantucket. One-way passenger fare is $16.50, and bicycles are $6. Cost for a car traveling one-way April through October is $190, November through April, $130. One-way high-speed passenger ferry fare is $32.50, with bicycles $6.

Hy-Line's high-end, high-speed *Grey Lady* ferries run between Hyannis and Nantucket year-round in an hour. Such speed has its downside in rough seas—lots of bucking and rolling that some find literally nauseating. Seating ranges from benches on the upper deck to airline-like seats in side rows of the cabin to café-style tables and chairs in the cabin front. Make reservations in advance, particularly during the summer months or for holiday travel. One-way fare is $39, and bicycles are $6.

Hy-Line's slower ferry makes the roughly two-hour trip from Hyannis between early May and late October. The M/V *Great Point* offers a first-class section ($26 one-way) with a private lounge, restrooms, upholstered seats, carpeting, complimentary continental breakfast or afternoon cheese and crackers, a bar, and a snack bar. Standard one-way fare is $19.50, and bicycles are $6.

From Harwich Port, the Freedom Cruise Line runs express high-speed 75-minute ferries to Nantucket between late May and early October, allowing you to explore the rose-covered isle without having to brave the crowds of Hyannis. (Another plus is that for day trips to Nantucket, parking is free; it's $15 nightly, otherwise.) Round-trip fare is $64 ($39 one-way), $12 for bikes. Sightseeing and seal cruises are also offered daily.

With recent rising fuel costs, many carriers have instituted additional fees; expect to pay an extra $3–$5 (each way) over the cost of the actual ticket. (In most cases, seniors and children are charged lower fares.)

**Boat & Ferry Information Freedom Cruise Line** (⊠Saquatucket Harbor, Harwich Port ☎508/432–8999 ⊕www.nantucketislandferry. com). **Hy-Line** (⊠Ocean St. dock ☎508/778–2600 or 800/492–8082 ⊕www.hy-linecruises. com). **Steamship Authority** (⊠South St. dock ☎508/477–8600, 508/495–3278 on Nantucket for reservations ⊕www.steamship authority.com).

# ∎ BY BUS

The Cape Cod Regional Transit Authority operates several bus services that link Cape towns. All buses are wheelchair-accessible and equipped with bike racks. The SeaLine runs along Route 28 Monday through Saturday between Hyannis and Woods Hole (one-way fare $3.50

from Hyannis to Woods Hole; shorter trips cost less), with stops including Mashpee Commons, Falmouth, and the Woods Hole Steamship Authority docks. The SeaLine connects in Hyannis with the Plymouth & Brockton line as well as the Barnstable Villager, another bus line that runs along Route 132 between Hyannis and Barnstable Harbor, stopping at the Cape Cod Mall. It also connects with the Hyannis Villager, which runs through Hyannis. The driver will stop when signaled along the route.

The H2O Line offers daily regularly scheduled service year-round between Hyannis and Orleans along Route 28. The Hyannis–Orleans fare is $3.50; shorter trips are less. Buses connect in Hyannis with the SeaLine, the Barnstable Villager, and Plymouth & Brockton lines.

The b-bus is composed of a fleet of minivans that will transport passengers door to door between any towns on the Cape. You must register in advance to use the b-bus service (you pay in advance by a prepaid account system); phone the Cape Cod Regional Transit Authority 11 AM to 5 PM on weekdays to sign up. You must also make advance reservations when you want to ride the b-bus. After you are enrolled, call for reservations from 8 to 5 on weekdays; reservations may be made up to a week in advance. Service runs seven days a week, year-round. The cost is $3 per ride plus 10¢ per mi.

The Flex bus runs between Harwichport Chamber of Commerce and Shore and Highlands roads in Truro (from which free transfers are available to Provincetown, late May through mid-October), with stops in Brewster, Orleans, Eastham, and Wellfleet. Riders can also schedule additional off-route stops by calling the Cape Cod Regional Transit Authority. All one-way fares are $2, and buses run Monday to Saturday year-round.

The Cape Cod Regional Transit Authority also runs the seasonal trolleys in Fal-

mouth, Mashpee, Hyannis, Yarmouth, and Dennis. Fares and times vary; call for more information.

On the Outer Cape, Cape Cod Regional Transit Authority's Provincetown Shuttle serves North Truro and Provincetown daily from late May through mid-October, with more-limited service during the late fall and early spring, and no service in winter. The route begins at Dutra's Market in Truro and continues to Provincetown along Route 6A; it stops wherever a passenger or roadside flagger dictates. Once in Provincetown, the shuttle continues up Bradford Street, with alternating trips to Herring Cove Beach and Pilgrim Park as well as summertime service up to Provincetown Airport and Race Point Beach. It runs every 20 minutes and is outfitted to carry bicycles. The service is popular and reasonably priced ($2 for a single fare, $6 for a day pass).

The big buses of the Martha's Vineyard Transit Authority (VTA) provide regular service to all six towns on the island, with frequent stops in peak season and quite limited service in winter. The fare is $1 per town, including the town of departure. One-day ($6), three-day ($15), and one-week ($25) passes can be purchased on the bus and at Steamship Authority terminals.

The Nantucket Regional Transit Authority (NRTA) runs shuttle buses in town and to Madaket, mid-island areas (including the airport, 'Sconset, Surfside Beach, and Jetties Beach). Service is available late May to early September. Fares are $1 to $2, depending on the route. Passes cost $7 for one-day, $12 for three days, and $20 for one week.

**Bus Information** **Cape Cod Regional Transit Authority** (☎508/790–2613 or 800/352–7155 ⊕www.capecodtransit.org). **Martha's Vineyard Transit Authority** (VTA ☎508/693–9940 ⊕www.vineyardtransit.com). **Nantucket Regional Transit Authority (NRTA)** (✉22 Federal St., Nantucket ☎508/228–7025

⊕www.shuttlenantucket.com). **Plymouth &**
**Brockton Street Railway** (☎508/746–0378
⊕www.p-b.com).

### BUS TRAVEL TO & FROM CAPE COD

Greyhound serves Boston and Providence
from all over the United States; from there
you can connect to Greyhound's affiliate,
Peter Pan Bus Lines, which serves Barnstable, Bourne, Falmouth, Hyannis, Otis
Air Base (in Sandwich), Sagamore Circle,
and Woods Hole on the Cape, plus nearby
Fall River, New Bedford, and Plymouth.
The Plymouth & Brockton Street Railway buses travel all the way to Provincetown from Boston and Logan Airport,
with stops en route at a number of towns
throughout the Cape, including Plymouth, Sagamore, Barnstable, Hyannis,
Orleans, Eastham, Wellfleet, and Truro.

Bus Information **Greyhound** (☎800/231–
2222 ⊕www.greyhound.com).**Peter Pan Bus**
**Lines** (☎508/548–7588 or 888/751–8800
⊕www.peterpanbus.com).**Plymouth &**
**Brockton Street Railway** (☎508/746–0378
⊕www.p-b.com).

## ▌BY CAR

To reach Cape Cod from Boston (60 mi),
take Route Interstate 93 south, then Route
3 south, and cross the Sagamore Bridge,
which puts you onto U.S. 6, the Cape's
main artery, leading toward Hyannis and
Provincetown. From western Massachusetts, northern Connecticut, and upstate
New York, take Interstate 84 east to
the Massachusetts Turnpike (Interstate
90) and take Interstate 495 south to the
Bourne Bridge. From New York City and
southern Connecticut and Rhode Island,
take Interstate 95 north toward Providence, where you pick up Interstate 195
east (toward Fall River–New Bedford) to
Route 25 east to the Bourne Bridge. From
the Bourne Bridge you can take Route
28 south to Falmouth and Woods Hole
(about 15 mi), or—as you approach the
Bourne Bridge—follow signs to U.S. 6 if
you're headed elsewhere on the Cape.

Driving times can vary widely, depending
on traffic. In good driving conditions you
can reach the Sagamore Bridge from Boston in about 1½ hours, the Bourne Bridge
from New York City in about 5 hours.

On summer weekends, when more than
100,000 cars a day cross each bridge,
**make every effort to avoid arriving in late
afternoon,** especially on holidays. And be
sure to give yourself extra time if you're
driving to any of the ferry terminals to
Nantucket and Martha's Vineyard. U.S.
6 and Route 28 are heavily congested
eastbound on Friday evening, westbound
on Sunday afternoon, and in both directions on Saturday (when rental homes
change hands). On the north shore, the
Old King's Highway—Route 6A—paral-
lels U.S. 6 and is a scenic country road
passing through occasional towns.

When you're in no hurry, use back roads—
you won't get there any faster, but they're
less frustrating and much more rewarding.
Heading from the Bourne Bridge toward
Falmouth, County Road and Route 28A
are prettier alternatives to Route 28, and
Sippewisset Road meanders near Buzzards
Bay between West Falmouth and Woods
Hole. Just remember that some of these
roads travel through residential areas, so
keep your speed down.

Driving to Provincetown from other
points on the Cape is mostly a scenic
adventure. The wooded surrounds of
Truro break into a breathtaking expanse
of open water and sand dunes, with the
skyline of Provincetown beyond. The
busiest time is early morning—especially on days when the sun is reluctant
to shine—when it seems that everyone
on Cape Cod is determined to make it to
Provincetown. Traffic is heaviest around
Wellfleet, and because the road is just two
lanes until North Truro, it can be slow
going. Except during the traffic-heavy
season, you'll find the drive from Wellfleet to Provincetown beautiful and only
25 minutes in duration.

Traffic delays often result from congestion at the Sagamore and Bourne bridges, but in 2007 a "flyover" road was built connecting the Sagamore Bridge directly to Route 3 and thus greatly reducing the traffic jams that used to result from the much-despised and now-replaced traffic rotary on the mainland side of the bridge. This development has cut travel time onto the Cape by as much as 20 minutes on busy days.

Traffic can be a challenge on the islands, especially in season. Nantucket is small enough that you can easily get around on foot or by public transportation, but on Martha's Vineyard, it can be handy to have a car if you really want to see the whole island and travel freely among the different towns. Bringing a car over on the ferry in summer requires reservations far in advance, costs almost double what it does off-season, and necessitates standing in long lines—it's sometimes easier and more economical to rent a car once you're on the island, and then only for the days you plan on exploring. And consider public transportation and taxis if you're only making a few trips to different parts of the island, which has very good bus service that can get you to just about every major sight, village, and beach. Where you stay and what you plan on seeing can greatly influence your transportation plans. As soon as you've booked a room, discuss the different options for getting around Martha's Vineyard with your innkeeper or hotel staff.

## PARKING

Parking, in general, is a great challenge across much of Cape Cod and the islands from mid-June through early September, although many towns have metered lots and street parking or flat-fee or hourly pay lots. Popular and congested downtowns such as Falmouth, Provincetown, Hyannis, Oak Bluffs, Nantucket Town, and Chatham tend to prove especially tough. A number of smaller communities even have free street parking and municipal lots. In general, however, anytime you can walk, bike, or cab it somewhere, or you're able to travel in one car instead of two or more, do so. Off-season, parking is rarely a problem anywhere on the Cape or islands.

## RULES OF THE ROAD

In Massachusetts, highway speed limits are 55 mph near urban areas, 60 or 65 mph elsewhere. Speed limits on U.S. 6 on the Cape vary as it changes from four lanes to two lanes. Radar detectors are legal in Massachusetts.

Massachusetts permits a right turn on a red light (*after* a full stop) unless a sign says otherwise. Also, when you approach one of the Cape's numerous rotaries (traffic circles), note that the vehicles already in the rotary have the right of way and that those vehicles entering the rotary must yield. Be careful: some drivers forget (or ignore) this principle.

Massachusetts law requires that drivers **strap children under age five (or under 40 pounds) into approved child-safety seats.** Kids ages 5 to 12 must wear seat belts. Drivers (but not other passengers over age 12) are legally required to wear seat belts, but they can be ticketed for not wearing them only if they're pulled over for some other reason.

# ON THE GROUND

## ▌BEACHES

In season, you must pay to park at public beaches. Parking at "restricted" beaches is available only to residents and to visitors with permits. If you're renting a house, you can purchase a weekly beach permit; contact the local town hall for details. Walkers and cyclists do not need permits to use restricted beaches. The official season generally begins the last weekend in June and ends on Labor Day. Note that the lots are often open to all early in the morning (before 8) and late in the afternoon (after 4 or 5), even at resident beaches in season.

## ▌BIKE TRAVEL

Biking is very popular on Cape Cod and the islands, which have an abundance of excellent bike trails, some of them as busy as the region's roads in summer. Note that Massachusetts law requires children under 13 to wear protective helmets while riding a bike, even as a passenger. *For information on trails, maps, and rentals, see listings for specific towns.*

**Bike Maps Rubel Bike Maps** ( ⊠ Box 401035, Cambridge, MA ⊕ www.bikemaps.com).

## ▌BUSINESS HOURS

Hours on the Cape and the islands can sometimes differ from those elsewhere in New England, as many businesses and attractions are open only seasonally or have limited hours during the quieter months, from mid-fall to mid-spring. Within the region, shops and other businesses in the towns near the Cape as well as on the Upper Cape and even as far out as Barnstable and Hyannis tend to be less seasonal, catering to the larger year-round populations in those areas. The farther out you go, toward the Lower Cape and Outer Cape and on the islands, the more likely you are to encounter businesses that close or keep shorter hours off-season.

## ▌DAY TOURS & GUIDES

### BOAT TOURS

Cape Cod Canal Cruises (two or three hours, narrated) leave from Onset, just northwest of the Bourne Bridge. A Sunday jazz cruise, sunset cocktail cruises, and Friday and Saturday dance cruises are also available. Children 12 and under cruise free on Family Discount Cruises, Monday through Saturday at 4. Cruises cost between $11 and $18.

Patriot Boats has two-hour day and sunset cruises from Falmouth Harbor on the 74-foot schooner *Liberté II* in July and August. Another sunset cruise, which operates on Friday and Saturday evenings, passes six lighthouses in the Falmouth area. Fishing charters are also available.

Hy-Line runs one-hour narrated boat tours of Hyannis Harbor, including a view of the Kennedy compound. On Sunday, you can embark on a Ben & Jerry's make-your-own-sundae "ice-cream float" through Lewis Bay; ticket prices for all tours range between $14 and $15.

The gaff-rigged schooner *Bay Lady II* makes two-hour sails, including a sunset cruise, across Provincetown Harbor into Cape Cod Bay; fares are $18 to $24. Private charters are also available.

**Fees & Schedules** Bay Lady II ( ⊠ MacMillan Wharf, Provincetown ☎ 508/487–9308 ⊕ www.sailcapecod.com). **Cape Cod Canal Cruises** ( ⊠ Onset Bay Town Pier, Onset ☎ 508/295–3883 ⊕ www.hy-linecruises.com). **Hy-Line** ( ⊠ Ocean St. dock, Pier 1, Hyannis ☎ 508/778–2600 or 800/492–8082 ⊕ www. hy-linecruises.com). **Patriot Boats** ( ⊠ 227 Clinton Ave., Falmouth ☎ 508/548–2626 or 800/734–0088 ⊕ www.theliberte.com).

### TRAIN & TROLLEY TOURS

The Cape Cod Central Railroad offers two-hour, 42-mi narrated rail tours from Hyannis to the Cape Cod Canal (fare $18) from late May through October; trains generally run daily, but call for a schedule. You can have your fill of cranberry bogs, marshes, and woodlands, as well as such unusual sights as the Barnstable House of Corrections, where you'll spot inmates farming in the fields. From Hyannis, sit on the right side of the train for the best views. The second hour and its narration are a bit subdued, as you're traveling back the way you came, but the scenery and loud whistle blasts ought to keep you alert and engaged. You can also opt for the rail-sail option, which combines this trip with a Hy-Line Cruises *(see above)* harbor tour; the cost is $25 per person. There's also a three-hour, adults-only dinner train where you can settle back and watch the scenery as you nosh; it runs Thursday through Saturday in summer and less frequently spring and fall. The cost is $65.95 per person. Another dinner train, geared toward families, with a kids' menu and activities, runs on Monday through Wednesday evening and costs $39.95 for adults and $25.95 for kids under 12. A lunch train operates midweek from June through October and costs $39.95 per person. The Sunday Brunch train costs $39.95 per adult. Regularly scheduled "Mystery Train" rides include dinner and a who-done-it mystery show (all passengers are involved); the price is $85.95, adults only.

The Provincetown Trolley offers 40-minute narrated tours of Provincetown, leaving from outside town hall every 30 minutes daily 10 to 4, and every hour daily 5 to 7 PM. The ride takes you through downtown, out to the Provincetown Monument, and by the beaches. The fare is $10.

**Fees & Schedules Cape Cod Central Railroad** ( ✉ Hyannis Train Depot, 252 Main St., Hyannis ☎ 508/771–3800 or 888/797–7245 ⊕ www.capetrain.com). **Provincetown Trolley** ( ☎ 508/487–9483 ⊕ www.provincetown trolley.com).

### WALKING TOURS

Liz Villard's Vineyard History Tours leads walking tours of Edgartown's "history, architecture, ghosts, and gossip," including a stop at the Vincent House. Tours are run from April through December; call for times. Liz and her guides also lead similar tours of Oak Bluffs and Vineyard Haven. Walks last a little over an hour. Sixth-generation Nantucketer Gail Johnson of Gail's Tours narrates a lively 1½-hour van tour of the island's highlights.

**Fees & Schedules Gail's Tours** ( ☎ 508/257–6557 ⊕ www.nantucket.net/tours/gails). **Vineyard History Tours** ( ☎ 508/627–8619 ⊕ www.mvpreservation.org/tours.html).

## ∎ EATING OUT

The restaurants we list are the cream of the crop in each price category. Note that ordering a lobster dinner, which can be far more expensive than other menu items, may push your meal into a higher price category than the restaurant's price range shows. Properties indicated by a ✗▣ are lodgings with exceptional restaurants.

### CUTTING COSTS

Even the best of the region's restaurants offer slightly scaled-down portions of pricier dinner menus during lunchtime. Any time of day, you can indulge in fresh local seafood and clambakes at **seat-your-self shanties** for a much lower price than their fine-dining counterparts. Often the tackier the decor (plastic fish on the walls), the better the seafood. These laid-back local haunts usually operate a fish market on the premises and are in every town on the Cape.

Bear in mind that Cape Cod waters are occasionally plagued by red tide, an insidious algae that infests shellfish; 2005 saw a particular bad strain, which led to skyrocketing prices for fried whole-belly clams, but area waters have been largely back to normal ever since. During periods of red tide, you can still usually find most shellfish on menus, as it's easily brought in from other parts of the country, but whole-belly clams are expensive when shipped in from elsewhere, and menu prices reflect this.

### WINES, BEER & SPIRITS

Massachusetts is not a major wine-growing area, but Westport Rivers Winery in Westport and the Cape Cod Winery in East Falmouth produce respectable vintages. The family that owns Westport Rivers also runs the local Buzzards Bay Brewing Co. Wines from Truro Vineyards of Cape Cod are local favorites.

In Massachusetts, you can generally buy alcoholic beverages (wine, beer, and spirits) in liquor stores, known locally as package stores. A few exceptions allow some grocery stores to sell wine and beer. All of the towns on Martha's Vineyard except Oak Bluffs and Edgartown are "dry" and don't sell alcohol. Restaurants in these dry towns encourage diners to bring their own wine or beer; a corkage fee is usually charged for each bottle.

## ▌ EMERGENCIES

Cape Cod Hospital has a 24-hour emergency room. For rescues at sea, call the Coast Guard. Boaters should use Channel 16 on their radios.

**Emergency Services Ambulance, fire, police** (☎911 or dial township station). **Coast Guard** (☎508/888–0335 in Sandwich and Cape Cod Canal, 508/945–0164 in Chatham ⊕www.uscg.mil).

**Hospitals Cape Cod Hospital** (⊠27 Park St., Hyannis ☎508/771–1800 or 877/227–3263 ⊕www.capecodhealth.org). **Falmouth Hospital** (⊠100 Ter Heun Dr., Falmouth ☎508/548–5300 or 877/227–3263 ⊕www. capecodhealth.org). **Jordan Hospital** (⊠275 Sandwich St., Plymouth ☎508/746–2000 ⊕www.jordanhospital.org). **Martha's Vine-**

**yard Hospital** (⊠Linton La., Oak Bluffs ☎508/693–0410 ⊕www.marthasvineyard hospital.com). **Nantucket Cottage Hospital** (⊠57 Prospect St., Nantucket ☎508/825–8100 ⊕www.nantuckethospital.org).

**24-Hour Pharmacies CVS Falmouth** (⊠105 Rte. 28, Falmouth ☎508/540–4307). **CVS Hyannis** (⊠176 North St., Hyannis ☎508/775–8462). **Late-Night Pharmacy Leslie's Drug Store** (⊠65 Main St., Vineyard Haven ☎508/693–1010).

## ▌ GAY & LESBIAN TRAVEL

Provincetown, at the tip of the Cape, is one of the East Coast's leading lesbian and gay seaside destinations, and it also has a large year-round lesbian and gay community. Dozens of P-town establishments, from B&Bs to bars, cater specifically to lesbian and gay visitors, and all of the town's restaurants are gay-friendly; many are gay-owned and -operated. Hyannis has Cape Cod's sole gay bar outside P-town, but attitudes throughout Cape Cod tend to be extremely accepting and tolerant toward gays and lesbians. Martha's Vineyard, although lacking any gay-specific nightlife, has a number of gay-friendly businesses and accommodations and has become increasingly popular as a gay vacation spot in recent years. Nantucket is also quite tolerant but has less of a gay following than the Vineyard.

### Gay- & Lesbian-Friendly Travel Agencies

**Different Roads Travel** (☎760/325–6964, 800/429–8747 Ext. 14 ✉lgernert@tzell. com). **Kennedy Travel** (✉130 W. 42nd St., Suite 401, New York, NY ☎800/237–7433 or 212/840–8659 🖷212/730–2269 ⊕www. kennedytravel.com). **Now, Voyager** (✉4406 18th St., San Francisco, CA ☎415/626–1169 or 800/255–6951 🖷415/626–8626 ⊕www. nowvoyager.com). **Skylink Travel and Tour/ Flying Dutchmen Travel** (☎707/546–9888 or 800/225–5759) serving lesbian travelers.

# ∎ HEALTH

## LYME DISEASE

Lyme disease, so named for its having been first reported in the town of Lyme, Connecticut, is a potentially debilitating disease carried by deer ticks, which thrive in dry, brush-covered areas, especially on Cape Cod. Always **use insect repellent**; it's imperative that you protect yourself from ticks from early spring through summer. To prevent bites, **wear light-colored clothing and tuck pant legs into socks.** Look for black ticks about the size of a pinhead around hairlines and the warmest parts of the body. If you have been bitten, **consult a physician, especially if you see the telltale bull's-eye bite pattern.** Influenza-like symptoms often accompany a Lyme infection. Early treatment is imperative.

## PESTS & OTHER HAZARDS

Cape Cod's greatest insect pest is mosquitoes, which are at their worst after snowy winters and wet springs. The best protection is **repellent containing DEET.** A particular pest of coastal areas, especially salt marshes, is the greenhead fly. Their bite is nasty, and they are best repelled by a liberal application of Avon Skin So Soft.

Poison ivy is a pervasive vinelike plant, recognizable by its leaf pattern: three shiny green leaves together. In spring new poison-ivy leaves are red; likewise, they can take on a reddish tint as fall approaches. The oil from these leaves produces an itchy skin rash that spreads with scratching. If you think you may

have touched some leaves, **wash as soon as you can** with soap and cool water.

## SHELLFISHING

Cape Cod attracts seafood lovers who enjoy harvesting their own clams, mussels, and even lobsters; permits are required, and casual harvesting of lobsters is strictly forbidden. Amateur clammers should be aware that New England shellfish beds are periodically visited by red tides, during which microorganisms can render shellfish (excluding lobsters, scallops, and all fin fish) poisonous. To keep abreast of the situation, inquire when you apply for a license (usually at town halls or police stations) and pay attention to red-tide postings as you travel.

Lyme Disease Info **Massachusetts Department of Public Health** (☎508/947–1231, 866/627–7968 public health hotline ⊕www. state.ma.us/dph). **National Centers for Disease Control and Prevention** (☎888/232–3228 general information, 877/394–8747 travelers' health line, 800/311–3435 public inquiries 🖷888/232–3299 ⊕www.cdc.gov).

# ∎ TAXES

The state hotel tax varies from town to town but never exceeds 9.7%.

## SALES TAX

Massachusetts state sales tax is 5%.

# INDEX

**Photo Credits:** 9 (left), *Strauss/Curtis/age fotostock.* 9 (right) and 11 (left), *Raymond Forbes/age fotostock.* 11 (right), *Joe Viesti/viestiphoto.com.* 14, *Raymond Forbes/age fotostock.*15, *Walter Bibikow/ viestiphoto.com.*16, *Strauss/Curtis/age fotostock.* 17, *Walter Bibikow/viestiphoto.com.*18, *Susan Rosenberg.*19, *Jeff Greenberg/age fotostock.* 20, *Joe Viesti/viestiphoto.com.* 21, *Raymond Forbes/age fotostock.* 22, *Craig Lovell/viestiphoto.com.* 23, *Susan Rosenberg.* 24, *Joe Viesti/viestiphoto.com.*

# NOTES

# NOTES

# NOTES

# NOTES

# ABOUT OUR WRITERS

Former Fodor's staff editor and long-time Cape Cod contributor **Andrew Collins** updated the Outer Cape chapter for this edition and helped write the Experience chapter. Andrew grew up in New England and has visited Cape Cod for many years, writing about it for *Fodor's Gay Guide to the USA*, several other Fodor's titles related to New England, and a number of newspapers and magazines. He has contributed to *Fodor's New Mexico*, *Fodor's Essential USA*, *Travel & Leisure*, *Out Traveler*, *Sunset*, and *New Mexico Magazine*, and teaches a course on travel writing for New York City's Gotham Writers' Workshop.

Living up to her turn-of-the-millennium resolution, freelancer **Susan MacCallum-Whitcomb** jettisoned her professorial robes and traded university teaching for full-time travel writing in 2000. In the years since, she has spent an inordinate amount of time zipping around the globe from her home base in Halifax, Nova Scotia—and the results can be read in *Fodor's* guidebooks (she's contributed to seven thus far) as well as Fodors.com and a host of leading Canadian magazines and newspapers. Susan co-wrote the Experience Cape Cod chapter for this year's guide.

Nantucket resident **Sandy MacDonald** is a seasoned travel writer who has written several New England guidebooks and contributed to others. She has also written about the island for publications such as *Boston Magazine* and *New England Travel & Life*. For this book, she covered Nantucket's good life—including dining, lodging, nightlife, the arts, and shopping.

**Laura V. Scheel** updated the Upper Cape, Mid Cape, Lower Cape, and Martha's Vineyard chapters of this edition. She has written frequently for Fodor's, contributing to titles such as *Fodor's Maine Coast* and *Fodor's The Thirteen Colonies*. When not writing about travel, history, and the arts, she raises oysters in Wellfleet on the Outer Cape.